The Almoravid and Almohad Empires

THE EDINBURGH HISTORY OF THE ISLAMIC EMPIRES
Series Editor: Ian Richard Netton

Available or forthcoming titles

The Umayyad Empire
Andrew Marsham

The Abbasid Empire
Matthew Gordon

The Almoravid and Almohad Empires
Amira K. Bennison

The Seljuk Empire of Anatolia
Sara Yur Yildiz

The Great Seljuk Empire
A. C. S. Peacock

The Fatimid Empire
Michael Brett

The Mamluk Empire
Jo van Steenbergen and Patrick Wing

The Ayyubid Empire
Gerald Hawting

The Mongol Empire
Timothy May

The Ottoman Empire
Gokhan Çetinsaya

edinburghuniversitypress.com/series/ehie

The Almoravid and Almohad Empires

Amira K. Bennison

EDINBURGH
University Press

Edinburgh University Press is one of the leading university presses in the UK. We publish academic books and journals in our selected subject areas across the humanities and social sciences, combining cutting-edge scholarship with high editorial and production values to produce academic works of lasting importance. For more information visit our website: edinburghuniversitypress.com

Edinburgh University Press Ltd
The Tun – Holyrood Road
12 (2f) Jackson's Entry
Edinburgh EH8 8PJ

Typeset in 11/13pt Adobe Garamond Pro by
Servis Filmsetting Ltd, Stockport, Cheshire

A CIP record for this book is available from the British Library

ISBN 978 0 7486 4681 4 (hardback)
ISBN 978 0 7486 4680 7 (paperback)
ISBN 978 0 7486 4682 1 (webready PDF)
ISBN 978 0 7486 9498 3 (epub)

Published with the support of the Edinburgh University Scholarly Publishing Initiatives Fund

Contents

List of Box Text vi
List of Illustrations vii
Acknowledgements ix
Abbreviations and Note on Transliteration xi

1 Introduction 1
2 The Almoravids: Striving in the Path of God 24
3 The Almohads: Revelation, Revolution and Empire 62
4 Society in the Almoravid and Almohad Eras, 1050–1250 118
5 Economy and Trade Within and Beyond Imperial Frontiers, 1050–1250 177
6 Malikism, Mahdism and Mysticism: Religion and Learning, 1050–1250 227
7 'The most wondrous artifice': The Art and Architecture of the Berber Empires 276
8 Conclusion 329

Chronological Outline 336
List of Place Names with Latin and Arabic Designations 347
Glossary of Arabic Terms 350
Bibliography 356
Index 370

Box Text

Chapter 4

Slavery in Islam 138

The Maghribi Tribes 140

Sanhaja Matrilineal Succession 157

The *Dhimma* 165

Chapter 5

Islamic Taxation 210

Land Grants 212

Chapter 6

Kharijism and Religious 'Others' 232

Jihad 240

The Sufi Path 268

Illustrations

(Author photographs except where indicated)

1.1	Map: the Maghrib and al-Andalus, 1050–1250	xiv
1.2	The genealogies of the Berber tribes according to Ibn Khaldun	13
2.1	Map: the distribution of the Berber peoples, *c.* 1050	25
2.2	Map: the Almoravid empire	48
2.3	Genealogical table of the Almoravid Banu Targut	51
3.1	Map: the Almohad empire	91
3.2	Genealogical table of the Almohad rulers and important Mu'minid *sayyids*	110
5.1	The ruins of Sijilmasa	201
5.2	Map: the Maghribi and trans-Saharan trade routes, *c.* 1050	202
5.3	An Almoravid gold *dīnār* minted in Córdoba (Fitzwilliam Museum, Cambridge, Accession No. CM.PG.7805-2006 © Fitzwilliam Museum)	217
5.4	An Almohad square silver *dirham* minted in Málaga (Fitzwilliam Museum, Cambridge, Accession No. CM.IS.279-R © Fitzwilliam Museum)	218
5.5	The Menara gardens, originally an Almohad *buḥayra*, Marrakesh (the pavilion dates to the nineteenth century)	220
7.1	Aghlabid minaret, Great Mosque of Qayrawan	279
7.2	Reception hall, Madinat al-Zahra'	282
7.3	Umayyad-style minaret, Qarawiyyin Mosque, Fes	287
7.4	The Almoravid Qubbat al-Ba'diyyin, Marrakesh	293
7.5	Interior ceiling, Qubbat al-Ba'diyyin, Marrakesh	295
7.6	Brick piers, Almoravid great mosque, Algiers	297
7.7	Great mosque, Tinmall (photograph Mariam Rosser-Owen)	310
7.8	*Miḥrāb*, great mosque, Tinmall (photograph Mariam Rosser-Owen)	311
7.9	Kutubiyya minaret, Marrakesh	313

7.10 Giralda minaret, Seville 317
7.11 Tour Hassan minaret, Rabat 323
7.12 Detail, Almohad gateway, Qasaba of the Udaya, Rabat 325
7.13 Torre del Oro, Seville 326

Acknowledgements

The writing of any book is a long and sometimes arduous process in which the encouragement and assistance of many come to bear. A volume of this kind, which covers a large swathe of history, can only ever be the product of research, reading and conversations that have accumulated over many years. I am grateful to the numerous scholars, young and old, with whom I have had the pleasure of interacting during that time, and the many students who have discussed the Berber dynasties with me, and obliged me to provide a coherent narrative of this complex era. Particular thanks are due to Michael Brett for his ongoing support and interest in my work; to Maribel Fierro for her always stimulating, challenging and erudite perspectives on the Almohads; to Camilo Gómez-Rivas, Allen J. Fromherz and Mariam Rosser-Owen, younger scholars who have opened fresh vistas on the Almoravids and Almohads, respectively; and to Shady Hekmat Nasser who read and commented on the draft and provided numerous edifying snippets of information on religious scholars and many other topics.

I am also grateful to the Leverhulme Trust for a two-year research grant to explore political legitimacy in the Maghrib assisted by a post-doctoral fellow, James A. O. C. Brown, and to the Department of Middle Eastern Studies, University of Cambridge, and Magdalene College for granting me a year's sabbatical from teaching and administrative duties to complete the writing of this book. Thanks are also due to Professor Ian Netton with whom I first discussed the idea of adding a volume on the western Islamic dynasties to the Edinburgh series, and to the editorial staff at Edinburgh University Press, particularly Nicola Ramsey and Ellie Bush, who have been unfailingly courteous, despite the time it has taken me to fulfil my side of the bargain. I should also like to thank Dr Adrian Popescu and the Fitzwilliam Museum for supplying and allowing the reproduction of images from the coin collections, and Mariam Rosser-Owen for kindly sharing her photographs of Tinmall with me.

I am painfully aware that a whirlwind tour through two hundred years of history naturally leads to a process of selectivity, with which not everyone will agree, and many unacknowledged intellectual debts, all such errors and *lacunae* are my own responsibility and I hope that readers may forgive me for them.

Abbreviations and Note on Transliteration

EI2 *Encyclopedia of Islam*, 2nd edition, ed. P. Bearman, Th. Bianquis, C. E. Bosworth, E. van Donzel and W. P. Heinrichs (Leiden: Brill, referenceworks.brillonline.com).

EI3 *Encyclopedia of Islam*, 3rd edition, ed. Kate Fleet, Gudrun Krämer, Denis Matringe, John Nawas and Everett Rowson (Leiden: Brill, referenceworks.brillonline.com).

This book follows the current British system of Arabic–English transliteration, used by the *Encyclopedia of Islam 3*, for the majority of technical Arabic terms and Berber terms in Arabic. In accordance with Edinburgh University Press guidelines, place names and personal names are rendered with markers for hamza (') and 'ayn (') but no other diacritics, except in the Index where they are fully vocalised. Similarly, names of authors and book titles transliterated from Arabic are fully vocalised in the Bibliography. Words that are now common in English and can be found in English dictionaries, such as amir, imam and jihad, are not vocalised or italicised. Place names present a particular problem in the Maghrib in that many now have common French, Spanish or English forms. In the case of Iberia, the Arabic place names of the past, sometimes themselves transliterated from Latin or Romance, now often have common Spanish forms. It has therefore proved impossible to be entirely consistent. Where a common English form of a name exists, such as Tangier or Algiers, I have used that in preference to transliteration or other European forms of the name. Where the Spanish or French form is widely used, I have adopted that, Córdoba and Tlemcen, for instance. In the case of less well-known destinations in the Maghrib, those whose names are quite different in Arabic and European languages, or have changed over time, I have transliterated the names from Arabic, for example, Qasr al-Majaz rather than Ksar es-Seghir, Ribat al-Fath rather than Rabat, Bijaya rather than Bougie. I have provided a list of place names giving both their common European and vocalised Arabic forms as an appendix which readers may consult if they wish.

For Tshiami

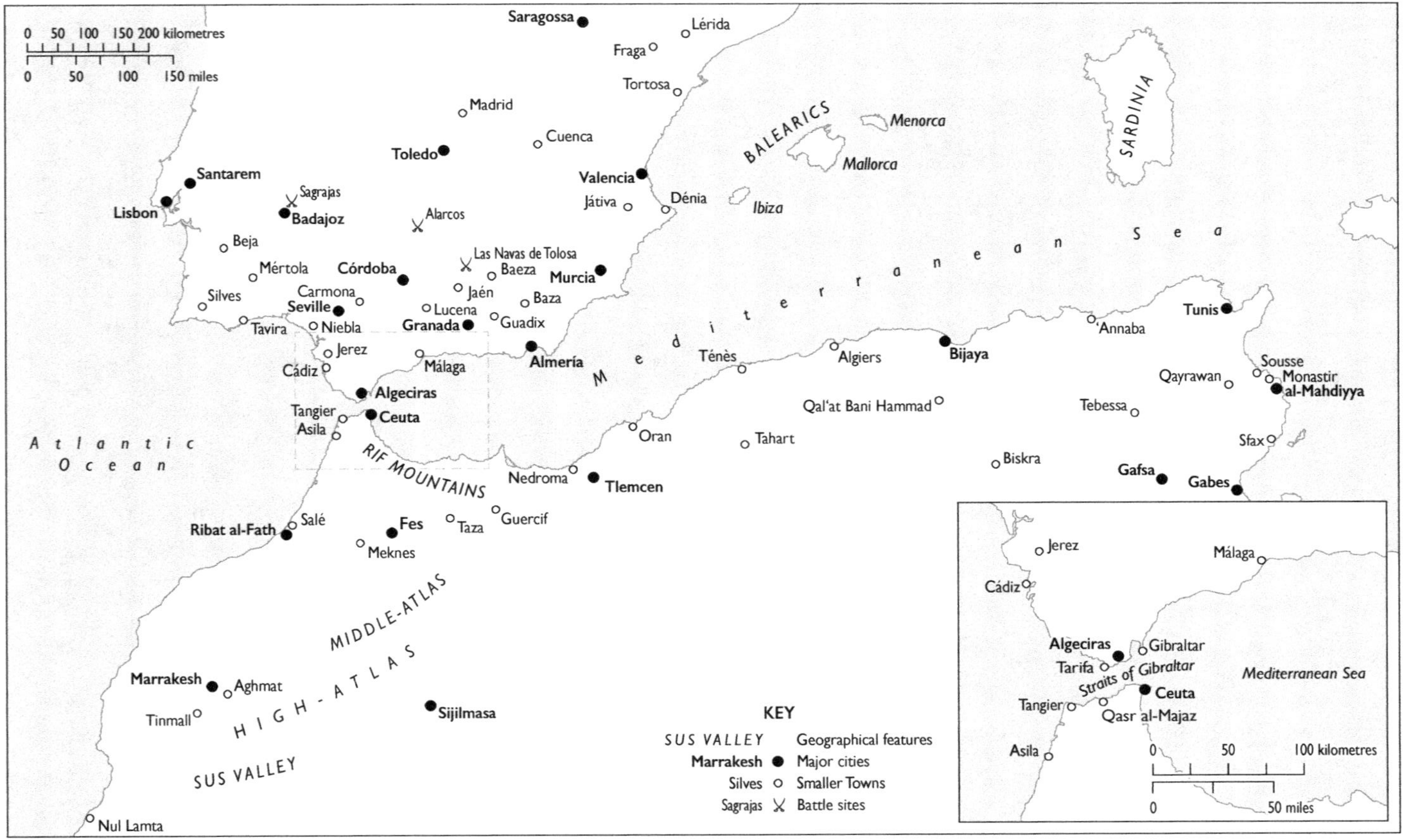

Figure 1.1 The Maghrib and al-Andalus, 1050–1250

1

Introduction

This volume provides an introduction to the history of the Almoravids and the Almohads, two of the most important empires of the medieval Islamic west, an area defined here as al-Andalus (southern Spain and Portugal), the Maghrib and Ifriqiya (modern Morocco, Algeria, Tunisia and western Libya). The Almoravid and Almohad empires were the second and third of three great empires which ruled substantial parts of the Islamic west between the tenth and mid-thirteenth centuries CE. The first empire, that of the Fatimids, is relatively well known due to their origins in the Middle East and the transfer of the dynasty from Ifriqiya (Tunisia) to Egypt in 972 CE, a move that brought them into the full light of Middle Eastern Islamic history. Their successors, however, who remained in the Maghrib and expanded north into the Iberian peninsula remain relatively unfamiliar outside the spheres of Andalusi and Maghribi history, both of which have traditionally been the preserve of French and Spanish rather than Anglophone scholarship,[1] despite their integral place in the wider Islamic historical panorama as powerful contemporaries of the Fatimids, Seljuks, Zangids and Ayyubids; as participants in the Muslim response to the Crusades in their Iberian and North African manifestations; and as the dominant powers in the western Mediterranean for two centuries.

The founders of these empires were two different Berber tribal peoples, the Sanhaja of the western Sahara and the Masmuda of the High Atlas mountains and the Sus valley in modern Morocco, who emerged from their respective homelands to conquer extensive territories in the name of their

[1] The standard histories of the Almoravid and Almohad empires are J. Bosch Vilá, *Los Almorávides*, republished with a new foreword by Emilio Molina López, and A. Huici Miranda, *Historia política del imperio almohade*. More recently, the two empires have been dealt with extensively in the *Historia de España, vol. 8: El retroceso territorial de Al-Andalus: Almoravides y Almohades siglos XI al XIII*, ed. María Jesús Viguera Molins. See also Vincent Lagardère, *Les Almoravides I* and *Les Almoravides: le djihâd andalou*, and Maribel Fierro's numerous publications on the Almohads, some of which are collected in *The Almohad Revolution: Politics and Religion in the Islamic West during the Twelfth–Thirteenth Centuries*.

interpretations of Islam. The Almoravids emerged from the western Sahara in the 1050s to impose their control over the politically and religiously disunited western Maghrib, where Islam, in one form or another, was still often the religion of city rather than mountain or plain. They then crossed the Straits of Gibraltar into al-Andalus, which had previously been ruled by the Umayyads of Córdoba, but was a troubled and politically divided region in the eleventh and twelfth centuries. The fragmentation of the Muslim political scene was in contrast to the slow consolidation of the Christian powers in the north, Castile-León, Aragon and later Portugal, all of whom proved eager to expand their territories at the expense of each other and the small Muslim kingdoms to the south, and it was this threat that led to the Almoravid intervention in al-Andalus. The Almoravid conquest took many decades, however, and shortly after their empire had reached its fullest extent in the 1110s, their control began to be challenged in the Maghrib by the nascent Almohad movement.

The Almohads emerged from the High Atlas mountains during the 1130s, and by the time they conquered Marrakesh in 1147 they controlled most of the Almoravids' erstwhile territories in the Maghrib and had begun to consolidate their control of al-Andalus too. They then went on to conquer the rest of the Maghrib as far east as modern Tunisia, creating the largest Berber empire to have ever existed. Their power began to falter in the 1220s, however, as a result of external challenges and internal political and logistical problems and, by the 1250s, a series of smaller Islamic monarchies or sultanates had emerged across the region from Granada to Tunis and the Almohads controlled little more than Marrakesh, which they finally lost to the Zanata Berber Marinids in 1269.

The heartlands of both these empires were situated in what is now Morocco and centred upon the fertile Atlantic plains that stretch inland from the coast to the eastern circle of the Middle Atlas, High Atlas and Anti-Atlas mountain ranges. Both Fes and Marrakesh are located in this extended lowland region, whose agriculture has always been a vital source of tax revenue along with the fruits of long-distance trade. Indeed, it was the arteries of trade which dictated the direction of expansion for these two empires. Over the course of two centuries, the Almoravids and Almohads established impressive administrative and judicial systems to rule their domains and contributed to the slow but steady Islamisation and Arabisation of the Maghrib, whilst also bringing the Berbers into the fractious family of great Islamic peoples. By the end of the Almohad era, the vast majority of the Maghribi population were Muslim and the sectarianism of earlier centuries was fading in favour of Maliki Sunnism, and a fertile synthesis of the cultures on each side of the Straits of Gibraltar had occurred. Each regime also made significant and sometimes spectacular contributions to intellectual, artistic and architectural life during the centuries of their dominance, in the Islamic west itself and in the wider Mediterranean, African and Middle Eastern spheres too.

Their achievements can be justly compared with those of contemporary eastern Islamic dynasties of Turkic origin, such as the Ghaznavids and the Seljuks, or the Kurdish Zangids and Ayyubids. As Michael Brett has delineated in several places, developments on the northeastern Turkic and southwestern Berber fringes of the Islamic world share many features, despite their specificities. Both the Turks and the Berbers were tribal peoples whose rise to imperial status was predicated on their opposition to the Fatimid caliphate and its Isma'ili offshoots, and support for the Sunni response, personified by the 'Abbasid caliph in Baghdad whom the Ghaznavids, Seljuks and Almoravids acknowledged as the caliph of Islam. The Almohads, meanwhile, in a unique display of self-confidence, appropriated the idea of the Shi'i imam and *mahdī* for themselves and proclaimed themselves Islam's true caliphs and the Berbers as central rather than peripheral to the Islamic project.[2] The Almohads' independence in this respect demonstrated the growing confidence of Maghribi Berbers in enunciating their own superior understanding of the truth.

However, from the Iberian perspective, which has been dominated by Spanish and Portuguese nationalist concerns, the North African Almoravids and Almohads were 'fanatical' in their approach to Islam and imperialist in their attitude towards al-Andalus. Both have often been vilified as responsible for the passing of the diverse and glittering cultural life previously apparent in al-Andalus and the introduction of a dour and oppressive religious and cultural atmosphere, which compromised the sophisticated but delicate balance of elements achieved within Andalusi society under the Umayyads of Córdoba (757–1031).[3] To put it crudely, 'African barbarians' destroyed the tolerant and essentially 'European' interaction of Muslims, Christians and Jews known as *convivencia* which characterised the centuries before their arrival.

Both have also been criticised for their ultimate failure to prevent the Christians of northern Iberia from advancing into al-Andalus and reducing Muslim territory to the small kingdom of Granada by 1250, in contrast to the successful Levantine campaigns of the Zangids, Ayyubids and Mamluks against the Crusaders in the Levant. Certainly, the Almoravids and Almohads each entered al-Andalus with a self-proclaimed mission to unify

[2] See Brett, *Rise of the Fatimids*, pp. 430–2; Brett, "Abbasids, Fatimids and Seljuks', pp. 689–98.

[3] Menocal, *Ornament of the World*, pp. 43, 45.

the Muslim population, hold the frontier and ideally to regain territory lost to the Christian powers, and the insurmountable challenge of holding the frontier eventually contributed to the escalation of opposition to them and their demise. However, the fact that Portugal, León-Castile and Aragon had ended Muslim rule in the majority of the peninsula by the 1250s should not obscure the fact that the Almoravid and Almohad presence slowed down and complicated that advance for generations.

This volume starts from three premises: the first is that these empires of the Maghrib deserve to be ranked with the Islamic empires of the Mashriq as major contributors to the story of Islamic civilisation, and the Berbers placed with the Arabs, Persians and Turks as a major Islamic people. My second premise is that the Almoravids and Almohads were quite different from each other and thus need to be contrasted as well as considered together as Berber empires. The third premise is that the modern conceptual division between the African south and the European north of the Straits of Gibraltar obscures the complexities of the relationship between these Berber peoples, other indigenous Berber and Arab inhabitants of the Maghrib, and the population of al-Andalus. The story of these empires is not a tale of 'European' Andalusis faced by 'African' invaders but, as recent scholarship shows, a series of negotiations and conflicts among different tribes, rural communities, and urban constituencies in the Maghrib and al-Andalus to secure their own best interests in which the Almoravids and Almohads could be both winners and losers. Telling this story in a single volume is undoubtedly an over-ambitious undertaking and there are inevitably simplifications and elisions within the narrative, but, nonetheless, it provides a starting point for the student or scholar and a springboard for those wishing to delve deeper into the history of this fascinating time and place within the broader span of Islamic history.

Given my second premise that the Almoravids and Almohads were very different, their inclusion in a single volume requires some justification, particularly as they have traditionally been considered together in studies of al-Andalus on the negative grounds that they were both 'uncivilised' if not 'fanatical' Berber regimes from North Africa. To place them together thus appears to perpetuate this wholly negative approach and to obscure the fact that, although lumped together under the rubric 'Berber', the Almoravids and Almohads drew their support from opposed and linguistically distinct groups of tribes in North Africa, and that the latter overthrew the former. That being said, there are also ways in which the two can be seen as comparable, if not similar, and in many instances the Almohads built on Almoravid foundations. Moreover, both provided some of the key data upon which the fourteenth-century thinker and politician Ibn Khaldun based his famous cyclical theory of empire formation and collapse.

In a modern dialogue with Ibn Khaldun, Brett sees in the Fatimids, Almoravids and Almohads a series of imperial adventures which had the stated aim of Islamic revolution or reform, but actually entailed the Islamisation of the tribal hinterland of the Maghrib, large sections of which had been left virtually untouched by the Islamic conquests of the late seventh and early eighth centuries.[4] While the Fatimids undertook this endeavour among the Kutama tribes of Ifriqiya, the Almoravid and Almohad missions to the Sanhaja and Masmuda, respectively, arose in geographically contiguous areas, the western Sahara and the High Atlas mountains. Moreover, both regimes aspired to rule similar areas and integrate them into centralising administrative systems, which manifestly changed the geopolitical map of the Maghrib. They also both faced the challenge of ruling al-Andalus and dealing with the aggressive advance of Christian powers into territory held by Muslims for several centuries, and both of them funded their imperial endeavours by means of the trans-Saharan trade and its Mediterranean offshoots in addition to rural taxation.

A further point in favour of considering the Almoravids and Almohads together is actually the intense rivalry between them in search of a common goal: integration into the 'Islamic world' writ large as represented by al-Andalus, Ifriqiya and the Mashriq. While they adopted different religio-political ideologies, they fought for the same stakes: control of the Maghrib under the banner of normative Islam, however defined. The gradual amalgamation of these trends fostered the emergence of the Islamic society that endured, in Morocco especially, until the early twentieth century, making the Almoravid and Almohad eras a crucial phase in the region. Focus on these dynasties as key contributors to the maturing of an Islamic society in the Maghrib avoids seeing them as either African invaders of Spain or Berber nationalists, and puts them in their proper context: medieval Mediterranean and Islamic history. At the same time, it does not ignore the massive contributions made by al-Andalus and, indeed, Ifriqiya to the evolution of society in the Islamic west between the late eleventh and the mid-thirteenth centuries, and the rise of the west as an equal, if not dominant, part of the Dar al-Islam.

The Berber Empires in Khaldunian Thought

As we have already seen above, the Berber empires have been interpreted from many different perspectives in modern scholarship which have often been inflected with concerns alien to the medieval era, particularly nationalism and

4 See Brett, *Ibn Khaldun*, esp. chs I and VI.

the Europe versus Africa binary, which is a variation on the civilised Occident versus decadent Orient theme. It is therefore instructive to turn to the indigenous, although equally subjective, interpretation of the Berber empires to be found in the writings of ʿAbd al-Rahman b. Khaldun, the famous fourteenth-century thinker, politician and courtier, renowned for the introduction (*muqaddima*) to his voluminous history of the Arabs and Berbers, the *Kitab al-ʿIbar*.[5] Although Ibn Khaldun's theories are perhaps cited too freely, the advantage of using them as a frame here is that he perceived the Almoravid and Almohad ventures as similar from a paradigmatic point of view and he is one of the main medieval historical authorities on their empires.

Moreover, the fact that western scholars of the Maghrib have so persistently referred to him over the last century makes engagement with his theories unavoidable. French colonial historians of Morocco, in particular, adopted his view that both empires were indigenous Berber state-building experiments, but added the interpretative twist that the demise of each empire was a cumulative Berber political failure that ultimately allowed 'foreign' Arab dynasties to impose themselves over a restive Berber population, a situation not resolved or rectified until the imposition of French colonial control. From a different standpoint, many modern anthropologists and historians have used Ibn Khaldun's theories as their starting place and have analysed the great man's life and *œuvre* as exceptional contributions to Islamic history, philosophy and even sociology.[6]

The *Muqaddima* to Ibn Khaldun's history of the Arabs and Berbers presents his detailed analysis of human society and covers much more than the rise and fall of empires. He was, nonetheless, especially fascinated by the relationship between government and society and the role of tribes in the interplay between the two, a recurrent issue in the Maghrib of his day. Ibn Khaldun's underlying premise, shared by many other Muslim thinkers, was that government preserved humankind from rampant savagery and was thus essential to the smooth functioning of society and the emergence of

5 Ibn Khaldun, ʿAbd al-Rahman, *Kitab al-ʿIbar wa-Diwan al-Mubtada' wa'l-Khabar fi Ayyam al-ʿArab wa'l-ʿAjam wa'l-Barbar* (henceforth *Kitab al-ʿIbar*). The sections on North Africa were translated into French by W. MacGuckin de Slane as *Histoire des Berbères* (henceforth *Histoire des Berbères*).

6 It is not possible to give a full account of the copious literature on Ibn Khaldun. Classic works on him include: Muhsin Mahdi, *Ibn Khaldun's Philosophy of History*; Walter Fischel, *Ibn Khaldun in Egypt*; Yves Lacoste, *Ibn Khaldun: The Birth of History and the Past of the Third World*; Aziz Al-Azmeh, *Ibn Khaldun, An Essay in Reinterpretation*. Recent studies of his life and work include Abdesselam Cheddadi, *Ibn Khaldûn: l'homme et le théoreticien de la civilisation*; Gabriel Martinez-Gros, *Ibn Khaldoun et les sept vies de l'Islam*; Fromherz, *Ibn Khaldun, Life and Times*.

civilised urban life (*'umrān*). However, civilisation had its own downside in that it fostered an effete, decadent and morally questionable lifestyle in comparison with the simple, virtuous and hardy ways of the tribes, who also enjoyed the military capacity to capture cities. One key distinction Ibn Khaldun perceived between tribesmen (*badw*) and urbanites and peasants (*ḥaḍar*) was that the former had a much stronger sense of solidarity. Ibn Khaldun described the bonds uniting groups of tribesmen as *'aṣabiyya*, which has been translated variously as group or tribal solidarity, kinship or blood ties. This defined insiders and outsiders, thereby creating a metaphorical wall around a particular tribe or group. He believed that it was this quality, combined with their martial skills, that empowered tribesmen such as the early Arabs, the Almoravid Sanhaja and the Almohad Masmuda to move from arid or mountainous regions to conquer stable agrarian areas and urban centres and found great empires when galvanised by a religious message of some kind. Conversely, a charismatic leader in an urban context was likely to remain a demagogue or a rebel due to his limited military capacity.

The acquisition of cities and the encounter with *'umrān* had an ambivalent transformative impact on tribal conquerors that included the decline of their *'aṣabiyya* and their virile fighting capacity, the swapping of the 'first among equals' ethos of tribal leadership for a more hierarchical dynastic model, and a consequent rise in tension between the dynasty and its tribal following. This pattern of 'corruption' meant that most tribal empires could only endure for three generations before they were swept away by fresh tribal conquerors with whom the cycle restarted. The only way to delay the inevitable turning of the wheel of fortune was for a dynasty to slow its decline by recruiting new military resources – slaves, mercenaries or tribal auxiliaries – to bolster their power and compensate for the decreasing loyalty and strength of their own tribal contingents.

From the Khaldunian perspective, then, the formation of the Almoravid and Almohad empires demonstrated how two different tribal peoples could surmount their internal differences and feuds and create a large political entity (*dawla*) when their sense of *'aṣabiyya* was amplified by a charismatic leader with a particular religious message. The prime example of the phenomenon, however, was the rise of the Arabs themselves under the banner of Islam, with the Seljuk Turks in the east also providing grist for his theoretical mill. In Ibn Khaldun's view, the importance of tribal peoples to state formation was not, therefore, a purely Maghribi phenomenon, but a broader characteristic of Islamic, if not global, history in which the rise of the Turks and later the Mongols figured alongside the achievements of the Arabs and the Berbers. He too, therefore, considered the Berbers as only one in a series of Muslim tribal peoples who played the same game and as the western counterparts of the Arabs and Turks.

It is helpful at this point to consider what the term 'tribe' actually means since many of the modern debates around Ibn Khaldun's theory relate to the definition of a tribe, the role of kinship within tribal society, and the relationship between tribalism and nomadism. There are myriad ways of defining tribes, but some key elements are, first, the belief that all the members of the group are joined by kinship, whether real or fictive; secondly, a keen interest in genealogical ancestry to determine social and political relationships; and, thirdly, reliance on a form of political organisation often described by anthropologists as 'segmentarity', a theoretically egalitarian type of organisation in which several family 'segments' form one clan, several clan 'segments' form one tribe, several tribal 'segments' form a larger tribal people or confederation. Although 'segments' at each level may have disputes with each other, they unite in the face of a threat from outside or, in Ibn Khaldun's theory, when inspired by a religious ideology. It is important to note that Maghribi tribesmen followed a wide range of lifestyles from sedentary agriculture to transhumance and full nomadism depending on the terrain in which they lived. In other words, the terms tribesman and nomad were not synonymous and tribesmen were often villagers in the Maghrib.

One of the problems that arises in connection with Ibn Khaldun's theory is the real role of tribes and kinship in empire building. Lapidus, for instance, argues that it was not tribes based on kinship, but chieftaincies based on religious or warrior credentials that actually expanded to become empires and, although tribesmen provided essential military support, it can be argued that most movements sought to surmount tribal divisions and also integrated a motley assortment of groups into their ruling elites, including townsmen and additional tribes with no kinship bonds to the dominant group.[7] Moreover, *'aṣabiyya* and religion interacted with other factors, such as control of trade and other types of wealth in successful empire formation. Others have argued that the decline of *'aṣabiyya* and the incorporation of other elements into the ruling elite was not a problem but a necessity as empires transitioned from the conquest phase into a stable period of governance, and should not therefore be seen as a factor in the relative brevity of empires.[8] Others again point out that Ibn Khaldun's analysis, albeit brilliant, is not as universal as he thought but relevant only to particular types of society.[9] Despite these caveats, Ibn Khaldun's theory remains a powerful and provocative tool in the analysis

[7] See Lapidus, 'Tribes and state formation', pp. 25–47.

[8] See Messier, 'Rethinking the Almoravids', pp. 59–80.

[9] See Gellner, *Muslim Society*, pp. 88–9.

of relations between tribes and state formation. Even if one can and should question the precise roles of tribes, *'aṣabiyya* and religion in Islamic empire formation, all three were undeniably present in the rise of the Almoravids and Almohads. Understanding the formation of the Berber empires, however, requires not only an understanding of the historiographical landscape, but also some background knowledge of the history of the Berbers and of the regions they came to rule. It is to this background that we now turn.

The Maghrib and Ifriqiya before the Era of the Berber Empires

The indigenous inhabitants of northwest Africa are collectively known in Arabic writing as the Berbers, a term derived from the Latin *barbarus* that indicated someone whose language was beyond the pale of Graeco-Roman civilisation. Berber had a similar connotation in Arabic to the term *'Ajam* used for the Persians and other non-Arabic speakers in the Middle East. The so-called 'Berbers' did not, however, consider themselves to be one people but several, all speaking their own related but distinct languages which shared characteristics with Ethiopic and other languages of the neo-Hamitic family. In ancient times some Berbers used a script described as Old Libyan or Numidian, which became known as Tifinagh in a later form and is the basis of the modern Amazigh script.[10] However, Berber languages were not for the most part written and so we have to depend on external sources to elucidate the world of the Berbers, and the picture we draw may be partial or biased at times. The Berbers are assumed to have been tribal peoples since earliest times, but it should be remembered that we see them through the lenses of the Classical writers of Antiquity and medieval Arab (or Arabised) authors and little is actually known about their social and political organisation.

Given the vast sweep of territory inhabited by the Berber-speaking peoples from the western oases of Egypt to the Atlantic coast, it is hardly surprising that they had very varied modes of subsistence, which we shall explore in more detail in Chapter 5. Suffice to say here that on the fertile coastal plains Berbers lived in village communities and cultivated the land. Similar village communities could be found in many of the mountain ranges cutting across northwest Africa. Where the land was less fertile, tribes supplemented their cultivation with herding sheep and goats between summer pastures up in the hills and mountains and winter pastures at lower altitudes. Some tribes travelled in great annual circuits in search of pastures for their flocks. In the most arid parts of North Africa adjacent to the Sahara desert, tribes resorted to full nomadism, ranging over vast areas and living off the meat and milk

[10] Smith, 'What happened to the ancient Libyans?', p. 463, n. 8.

of their animals with occasional supplements of dates and wheat bartered or bought from sedentary communities.

Both the Phoenician Carthaginians and Romans left their mark on North Africa and encouraged the urbanisation of large sections of the Mediterranean littoral and the cultivation of wheat and oil for export to Rome. The Romans identified the 'barbarians' of North Africa as Libyans, Numidians, Garamantes and Mauritanians and sought to draw their chiefs into the Roman elite, a process that bore fruit with the appointment of the Roman-educated Juba II as client king of Mauritania. In time, Christianity spread into North Africa and gained a firm foothold in the area from eastern Algeria to Libya, Roman Africa, which produced St Augustine and a new sedentary Latin Christian community of mixed Berber and migrant parentage, later called Afariqa (Africans) by the Arabs.[11]

As the Roman Empire contracted, the Vandals swept down through Iberia and crossed the Straits of Gibraltar to the Maghrib, moving swiftly eastwards to what is now Tunisia and Libya where they established a Vandal kingdom that perpetuated late Roman culture during the fifth and sixth centuries, after which the Byzantine general Belisarius restored direct eastern 'Roman' rule over the hinterland of Carthage and a string of coastal enclaves, including Ceuta. Other parts of the Maghrib reverted to indigenous Berber control, provincial Roman towns such as Volubilis near modern Meknes in Morocco shrank in size, and many attenuated urban communities retreated from vulnerable locations to easily defensible hilltops. Although the silence of the sources has encouraged many to assume that the Berbers were divided into numerous small, tribal chieftaincies during these centuries, two huge stepped pyramid tombs near Tiaret in Algeria hint that a substantial post-Roman kingdom existed in the western Maghrib.[12] The idea that the people who built the tombs may have been from the Sahara where similar tombs have also been found provides an intriguing parallel with the later northward movement of the Almoravids.

When the Arabs pushed west in the late seventh century CE after their conquest of Byzantine Egypt in 642, the society they encountered in what is now Libya and Tunisia, an area they called Ifriqiya (after Roman Africa), was one of tribal peoples akin to their own organised in smaller or larger chieftaincies and kingdoms interspersed with sedentary Latinate Christian townsmen and villagers, the Afariqa.[13] The relationship that developed between the incoming Arab tribesmen and the Berber tribes is an interesting one.

[11] Amara, 'L'Islamisation du Maghreb centrale', pp. 113–14.

[12] Brett and Fentress, *The Berbers*, pp. 77–9.

[13] Prevost, 'Les dernières communautés chrétiennes', pp. 469–70.

The Berbers put up stiff resistance and many tribes had to be defeated in battle several times before they capitulated to the new order and, as a result, they came to be stereotyped as rebellious and awkward in Arabic literature. The other side of the coin, however, was that the processes of war – alliance, defeat, captivity, enslavement and liberation through conversion – tied the Arabs and Berbers closely together.[14] Many Berber men entered the Islamic armies as clients of Arab masters, and many Berber women ended up in the harems of the Middle East where they became mothers to important figures such as the first Umayyad amir of al-Andalus, 'Abd al-Rahman I, whose mother was a Nafza Berber.[15]

As the Islamic armies moved west through North Africa, they thus became more and more Berber in their composition. By the time they reached what is now Morocco and cast their gaze across the Straits of Gibraltar to Visigothic Spain, not only was the rank and file of the army predominantly Berber, there were also Berber clients in positions of command, the most famous being the conqueror of Visigothic Spain, Tariq b. Ziyad, client of the Arab general Musa b. Nusayr. Although these new Berber recruits were nominally Muslim, the majority did not speak Arabic.[16] The Andalusi historian Ibn al-Qutiyya recounts that when 'Abd al-Rahman I was trying to drum up support in al-Andalus in the 750s, he sent Berbers to speak to their kinsmen in the Berber tongue (*kalām al-Barbar*) to persuade them to join him.[17] In contrast to the Middle East and al-Andalus where Arabisation occurred more speedily than conversion to Islam, in North Africa linguistic Arabisation continued to lag behind conversion for centuries in the countryside. It was only in the Almohad era that more thorough-going rural Arabisation began to occur as a result of the Almohads' westward transfer of the Arab Banu Hilal and Banu Sulaym tribes, who had previously migrated from Egypt into Ifriqiya, to serve as auxiliary troops. The Berber languages were gradually pushed back into the mountains, but did not die out: in Morocco today Berber languages remain the mother tongue of 40–60 per cent of the population.

Despite the absorption of numerous Berbers into the army, the Muslim conquest was initially limited to a series of towns and their hinterlands, while most rural areas remained fairly untouched. The most important of these Islamic urban communities was that of Qayrawan in Ifriqiya, a new

14 See Norris, *The Berbers in Arabic Literature.*

15 Ruggles Fairchild, 'Mothers of a hybrid dynasty', p. 70.

16 Some of those from Ifriqiya may have spoken Latin as well as a Berber vernacular. Wasserstein, 'The language situation in al-Andalus', p. 4, cited in Gallego, 'Languages of medieval Iberia', p. 119, n. 30.

17 Ibn al-Qutiyya, *Ta'rikh*, p. 53; James, *Early Islamic Spain*, p. 72.

garrison town on the land route west from Egypt across North Africa that soon attracted migrants from Arabia and other parts of the Middle East, and developed into the cultural and religious as well as political capital of Ifriqiya and a vital hub connecting the Maghrib and the Mashriq, a role it played until the eleventh century. Small Muslim garrisons could also be found in many captured pre-Islamic towns along the coastal littoral to Tangier, and it was from these nodes that the transformation of the Berber interior began as the result of the Kharijite rebellion that erupted in 739–40.

The Kharijites were a group of Arab Muslims who objected to the way issues of succession and leadership in the Islamic community were handled by the fourth caliph, ʿAli, and his rival for power, Muʿawiya. As a result, they left (*kharaja*) the rest of the Muslim community and spread the message that the caliph should be selected for his qualities as a Muslim and a leader rather than because of his ancestry. This message was very appealing to Berber troops who resented their inferior status to the Arabs and willingly joined the Kharijite rebellion when it started in Tangier in 739. As a consequence of the revolt, several new Kharijite Muslim states emerged in the interior, and indigenous and eastern Islamic missionaries initiated the conversion of the Berbers to Islam by example, persuasion and trade rather than by warfare. One such Kharijite missionary was Ibn Rustam, whose father was a Persian soldier in Qayrawan, while another ideological refugee to establish a new polity backed by Berber tribes was the ʿAlid Idris b. ʿAbd Allah who migrated west from Egypt and founded Fes.

These small states had a major social impact. Not only did they act as bulwarks for rural Berber Islamisation, they also functioned as motors for urbanisation in areas where it had previously been very limited and encouraged the migration of Arabs, Persians and also non-Muslim traders, especially Jews, into the interior. While the Idrisids founded Fes, the Rustamids founded Tahart (modern Tiaret in Algeria) and the Miknasa Berber Midrarids founded Sijilmasa, the great caravan city that lured the Almoravids from the desert. Conversely, Berbers from these towns began to travel to Córdoba, Qayrawan and the Middle East for trade, religious education and to perform the pilgrimage to Mecca, giving them knowledge and experience of the wider Islamic world which they brought back to the most remote corners of the Maghrib. The involvement of Berbers in such peregrinations was instrumental in generating both the Almoravid and Almohad movements.

In the centuries following the conquest, Arabic writers evolved a full genealogical ancestry for the Berbers, which divided them into two main groups descended from eponymous ancestors, the supposedly nomadic Butr and the predominantly sedentary Baranis, each of which contained numerous tribes and peoples such as the Nafusa, Nafzawa and Miknasa (Butr), and the

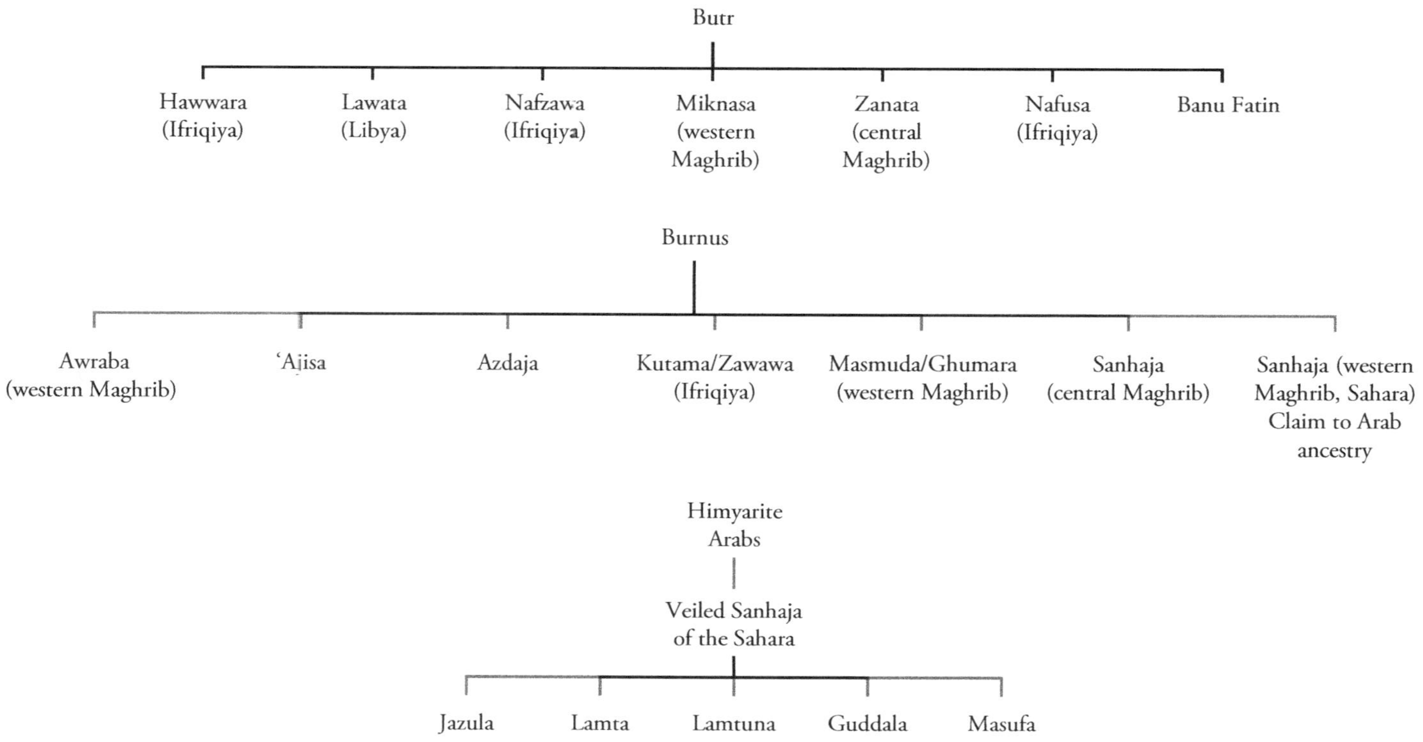

Figure 1.2 The genealogies of the Berber tribes according to Ibn Khaldun

Awraba, 'Ajisa, Azdaja, Masmuda, Kutama, Hawwara and Sanhaja (Baranis).[18] From early on, the dominant Arab-Islamic paradigm of history depicted the Berbers as erring and ignorant, but as Berbers learnt to express themselves in Arabic they were able to depict their own world in their new language, creating works such as the 'Boasts of the Berbers' (*Mafakhir al-Barbar*) which gave them an honourable place in the civilisation of which they were becoming part and inserted them within its Semitic foundation myths.[19] One important aspect of this was the development of legends of origin that connected the Berbers to Middle Eastern Semites, either as migrants in Biblical times or as Yemeni Arabs who migrated west prior to the rise of Islam and gradually adopted the language and mores of the peoples around them. This desire to create a connection with the scripturally endorsed genealogical past of the Semitic peoples of the Middle East and classical Islamic civilisation manifested itself in the foundation myths and genealogies of both the Almoravids and Almohads, who gave the Berbers a more politically dominant role than ever before.

Al-Andalus before the Era of the Berber Empires

Like coastal North Africa, the Iberian peninsula was part of the Roman Empire and many of its cities, including Córdoba, Mérida and Tarragona, had served as Roman provincial capitals. After Constantine made Christianity the religion of the Roman Empire, most of the urban inhabitants of Iberia converted to the new religion, although many rural communities, especially in the isolated mountainous northwest, retained older pre-Christian beliefs and practices for centuries. During the fifth and sixth centuries, the Visigoths entered Iberia and gradually established a post-Roman monarchy comparable to the kingdom of the Vandals in Ifriqiya but of longer duration. At first there were deep tensions between the Visigothic warrior aristocracy, who professed Arianism, and the Catholic Iberian churchmen. However, during the sixth century many Visigoths converted to Catholicism and parallel Arian and Catholic episcopal hierarchies emerged, paving the way for the official conversion of the kingdom itself to Catholicism at the Third Church Council in Toledo in 589 and the development of a mutually supportive relationship between the king and clergy.[20]

During this era, Iberian society consisted of the Visigothic warrior

[18] For the problems in using literary sources to classify the peoples of North Africa, see Smith, 'What happened to the ancient Libyans?'.

[19] See Shatzmiller, *The Berbers and the Islamic State*, pp. 5–39; Sánchez, 'Ethnic disaffection', pp. 181–4.

[20] Collins, *Visigothic Spain*, p. 67.

aristocracy, the Romano-Iberian churchmen, Iberian townsfolk, a small Jewish minority and a large rural peasantry. Although urban life continued in Córdoba and the foremost Visigothic towns of Toledo and Seville, Roman towns decreased in size and, in more vulnerable and isolated locations, the population often moved to defensible hill-top locations as in North Africa. Across the countryside, the great slave-worked latifundias of the Roman era seem to have been replaced by hamlets and villages inhabited by free peasants who paid tribute rather than being subjected to serfdom.[21] The Visigoths and the Church certainly held large tracts of land, but the way they were administered and the status of those who worked on them is unknown despite controversial speculations about proto-feudalism.[22]

Post-conquest anecdotes in the history written by a Muslim of Visigothic ancestry, Ibn al-Qutiyya, suggest the extent of such landed estates and their maintenance into the Islamic era. The sons of Witiza, the penultimate Visigothic king, supposedly agreed to ally with the Muslim invaders in return for keeping their 3,000 estates, and decades later 'Abd al-Rahman I became quite jealous of one son, Artabas, due to the constant arrival of supplies from his numerous estates outside his tent when they were travelling together. 'Abd al-Rahman confiscated the estates, but later returned twenty of them to avert the complete impoverishment of Artabas.[23] Another anecdote depicts Artabas generously giving a Muslim ascetic an estate with which to support himself and then being implored for similar gifts by Muslim notables, to which he graciously responded by doling out 100 more estates![24]

The agricultural abundance of southern Iberia and its settled village-based society made it an appealing destination for Berber raids from North Africa. In 711, however, this pattern of raids turned into the crossing of a large well-organised Muslim army led by Tariq b. Ziyad, probably with the collusion of the lord of Ceuta, Julian, and other partisans of the recently deceased King Witiza, including his sons, who opposed the accession of Roderic.[25] The Muslims defeated Roderic's army in battle near Medina Sidonia and initiated the Islamic conquest of Iberia, a development that Roderic's opponents probably had not foreseen.[26] This was a very different conquest to that

[21] Collins, *Visigothic Spain*, pp. 205–9.

[22] Ibid., pp. 4–5.

[23] Ibn al-Qutiyya, *Ta'rikh*, pp. 30, 57–8.

[24] Ibid., pp. 58–9.

[25] While it is likely that the Muslims had the assistance of whoever was in control of Ceuta and its fleet, much of the information about Julian, such as the rape of his daughter by Roderic, is mythic rather than factual.

[26] Hitchcock, *Muslim Spain Reconsidered*, pp. 14–21.

of North Africa for several reasons. First, the Iberian population were not, for the most part, trained combatants. They expected the Visigothic army to fulfil their defensive needs, and when it was defeated communities were ill-prepared to defend themselves, unlike the tribes of North Africa, and were therefore willing to negotiate. Secondly, since Iberia was populated by Christians, at least in the towns, the Muslim conquerors offered them protection and freedom to practice their religion in return for payment of the poll tax (*jizya*) in keeping with practices in conquered Byzantine and Sasanian lands in the east. In effect, the conquest replaced one military aristocracy, the Visigoths, with another, the Muslims, and while churchmen lamented the defeat of a Christian power by followers of the strange new religion or heresy of Islam, the population at large were reassured by the continuity of daily life.

Furthermore, the Arabs clustered in the main towns and river valleys and initially made little mark on more remote country areas, while the mountainous, rainy regions of Galicia, Asturias and the Basque country were not conquered at all. Even in conquered regions, many Visigothic lords such as Theodemir in Murcia continued to hold their estates and lands and paid the Muslims an agreed tribute. Berbers, the bulk of the conquest force, probably settled more widely in the countryside, especially in the Guadiana and Tajo valleys, although the absence of incontrovertible evidence has stimulated considerable debate on the point.[27] From the longer-term perspective, however, the important thing is the phenomenon of Berber migration into Iberia. While significant Arab migration ceased after the arrival of Arab contingents from Syria in the 740s, following the Kharijite rebellion in North Africa, the sporadic movement of Berbers, usually as military recruits, became a major feature of the relationship between the two sides of the Straits of Gibraltar and culminated in the Almoravid and Almohad absorption of al-Andalus into their respective empires.

Naturally, Iberian society was not static between the Muslim conquest and the arrival of the Almoravids nearly four hundred years later. Social change began in the towns in or near which Arab military contingents (*junds*) settled such as Córdoba, which soon became the capital of Muslim al-Andalus, Seville, Elvira (Granada), Jaén and Tudmir (Murcia). In this new urban and sedentary environment, the old tribal genealogies of the Arabs came to function as indicators of aristocratic lineage for individual families rather than as a mode of organisation or military mobilisation and, over the centuries, many non-Arabs acquired such genealogies as markers of status. The Muslim presence also impacted upon indigenous Christian Iberians as

[27] Hitchcock, *Muslim Spain Reconsidered*, pp. 24–9; Kennedy, *Muslim Spain and Portugal*, pp. 16–18.

Arabic and Islam became dominant across the south, gradually reducing the Latin Christian majority to an Arabised Christian minority known in scholarship as the Mozarabs, although recently scholars have become wary of this denomination and favour Andalusi Christians instead.[28] Arabisation also affected the predominantly urban Jewish minority, but conversion to Islam was uncommon and the Jewish community probably expanded rather than diminished. It was also invigorated by the opportunity Muslim rule presented to Jews to form new commercial and intellectual connections with co-religionists across the Islamic world.

In charting social change, we are best informed about Córdoba, which became a centre for the dissemination of Arabic, Islamic learning and, by the tenth century, literary and artistic culture. Migrants from the east contributed to these developments as did Arabised Berbers and indigenous Iberian converts to Islam, creating a society in which Arabic was dominant but Romance-Arabic bilingualism common.[29] In most Andalusi towns and cities, Arabisation led slowly but surely to the conversion of a substantial proportion of the Christian population to Islam with a surge of conversion probably occurring in the mid-ninth century at the time of the Córdoban martyr movement, led by the monk Eulogius who whipped a significant section of the Christian population into resistance to rampant Arabisation and Islamisation. His adherents, many of whom came from families of mixed religious affiliation, made repeated public denunciations of the Prophet Muhammad, an act punishable by death in Islamic law, and were ultimately executed after refusing to recant.[30] Arabisation and conversion also occurred in the countryside, albeit more slowly and in a manner that de Epalza describes as 'default conversion', that is, the drift of the population from one religion to the other as the rural Christian infrastructure contracted and disappeared.[31] The sparse evidence for the rural situation, however, has led to stark differences of interpretation between those who believe that the countryside remained Christian and Romance speaking and those who uphold widespread Arabisation and conversion to Islam.

From the late ninth to early tenth centuries, conversion triggered immense social tensions between the different Muslim communities in al-Andalus – the Arabs, the Berbers and Iberian converts known as Muwalladun – manifested in revolts and bids for provincial autonomy from Umayyad Córdoba in which the Muwalladun fought for parity with those claiming superior aristocratic

[28] Hitchcock, *Muslim Spain Reconsidered*, p. 59.
[29] Gallego, 'Languages of medieval Iberia', pp. 119–37.
[30] See Coope, *The Martyrs of Córdoba*.
[31] de Epalza, 'Mozarabs', pp. 149–70.

status based on their purported Arab ancestry. The irony of this was that the racial or ethnic distinctions between groups were often minimal because the social construction of identity was predicated, in most cases, solely on patrilineality, that is, one's father's identity. The Umayyad ruling family provide an illustrative case: the mothers of several Umayyad amirs were northern Christian concubines, often of Basque or Navarrese extraction, and many amirs were blond and blue-eyed.[32] However, no one considered them other than a pure Meccan Arab lineage based on their paternal line. While those of Arab ancestry carefully recorded and vaunted their genealogies, conversion, intermarriage and concubinage gradually produced a social reality of Arabic-speaking Andalusi Muslims of varied origins with close relationships to the Arabised Christian and Jewish minorities who shared their language and culture.

During the tenth century newcomers – fresh waves of Berber tribal migrants from North Africa and 'Slavs' (*ṣaqāliba*)[33] imported from the north to serve in the Umayyad army – came to be conceptualised as the 'outsiders' in contrast to the Andalusi Muslim majority of townsmen and peasants and their non-Muslim neighbours. Most of these newcomers were fighters who entered the politico-military ruling group and several of their chiefs and commanders became rulers of Ta'ifa principalities, such as the 'Slav' Mujahid who became lord of Dénia and the Sanhaja Berber Zirids of Granada. These 'new' Berbers were considered to be distinct from the 'old' Berbers who had settled in al-Andalus during the conquest era, and their arrival prefigured that of the Almoravids a century later.

The overall impression given of al-Andalus in the eleventh century is a relatively densely populated, fertile land in which village communities, professing Islam or Christianity, tilled the soil and tended their gardens, orchards and flocks. The ruling class consisted of Andalusis but also the Berber or Slavic newcomers mentioned in the previous paragraph, all of whom sought to exploit the wealth of the countryside through direct taxation or land grants. Al-Andalus was more urbanised than most of the Maghrib and sustained a thriving urban culture characterised by a sophisticated industrial sector, interest and investment in Arabic literature, and a self-confident religious class. The protected religious minorities were prominent and, in the Christian case, quite numerous with churches and monasteries as well as mosques within urban and suburban zones.

[32] Ruggles Fairchild, 'Mothers of a hybrid dynasty', p. 69.

[33] The *ṣaqāliba* were slaves from the central and eastern reaches of Europe, although some were Slavic, others were Frankish and Germanic and a handful came from the Mediterranean.

A more militarised society pertained in the areas closest to the Christian-ruled north where raiding into the northern principalities and defence against their raiding in the opposite direction was a regular occurrence. Despite the formal enmity exhibited in religio-political rhetoric, this pattern had engendered familiarity and contact across the marches (*thughūr*) for centuries and one must be wary of seeing this as religious warfare rather than territorial aggrandizement prior to the era of the Crusades and Maghribi jihad. However, as the Christian kingdoms began to exert both military and financial pressure on the Ta'ifa rulers, the old equilibrium began to falter, leading to repeated Andalusi appeals for Almoravid help to halt the Castilian advance beyond Toledo, which fell in 1085. Yusuf b. Tashfin responded to their pleas in 1086 thus setting in train the Almoravid conquest of the Ta'ifa kingdoms, the incorporation of al-Andalus and the Maghrib into a single empire, and the rise of a new jihad-based political paradigm shared by the Almoravids and the Almohads.

*

The following chapters utilise Arabic primary sources and the copious scholarship on these dynasties, both classic studies and more recent reappraisals, to present an *aperçu* into the political formation of these empires and their position within the longer span of Islamic and western Mediterranean history, while also considering the society and economy over which they ruled and the kinds of religious and material culture they supported. Chapters 2 and 3 provide a chronological and political narrative of each regime. Although such narratives are sometimes considered rather dry, it is impossible to understand the Almoravid and Almohad eras without establishing the chronological framework and the geopolitical context within which these dynasties functioned. Moreover, dynastic chroniclers considered the succession of rulers and military campaigns to be of paramount importance, therefore these chapters also reflect the preoccupations and biases of some genres of Islamic historiography. For many medieval Muslim writers, for instance, a vital dimension of the history of this period was resistance to the Christian advance in Iberia, often understood as jihad just as Christians frequently understood their actions as crusade or the 'reconquest' (*reconquista*) of Christian land.

Chapter 2 charts the rise of the Almoravid movement among the Sanhaja tribes of the northwestern Sahara, their use of jihad ideology to combat rivals of other sects and ethno-linguistic groups, and their creation of a territorial domain centred on their new capital of Marrakesh. This gave the Almoravids a new 'Moroccan' geopolitical focus which drew them north and led on to their intervention in Iberia, creating an important commercial, political and cultural corridor from West Africa to central Iberia. The chapter will then explore how the Almoravid jihad gained a new dimension in the form of military campaigns to hold the Muslim frontier against growing pressure from the nascent kingdoms of the Christian north, signalled by the fall of Toledo to Alfonso VI of Castile in 1085. Holding the Iberian frontier soon entailed incorporating the fractious Andalusi Muslim Ta'ifa kingdoms into the Almoravid empire, a development that transformed al-Andalus from the western Islamic metropole it had been for centuries into a province of empires whose heartlands were in North Africa. The chapter will conclude with the contraction of the Almoravid empire from the 1120s and its replacement by a new Maghribi power, the Almoravid's greatest rivals, the Almohads.

Chapter 3 turns to the Almohads of the High Atlas mountains and the Sus valley, beginning with the mission of its founder Ibn Tumart, the development of the Almohad movement, and then its transformation into an empire-building project. It will go on to survey the new geopolitical axis created by the Almohads who exerted no control over the Sahara, but moved to dominate the entire fertile coastal strip of North Africa as far as Ifriqiya (Tunisia) and the southern part of the Iberian peninsula. The chapter will explore the revolutionary conquest phase of the Almohad movement and their jihad against the Normans and Iberians, their slow creation of a stable, centralised empire, and the factors that led to the collapse of the empire and the emergence of a series of Almohad successor states in the early thirteenth century.

Chapter 4 will move on to consider the social configurations of the period, beginning with some general comments on Muslim theorisations of society and regional society prior to the rise of the Almoravids. It will then look at the social composition of the Almoravid and Almohad ruling elites, starting with the nomadic Almoravid Sanhaja and their tribal solidarity, which, to a large degree, defined the ruling cohort, then moving on to additional elements that became more or less integrated into the elite. The chapter will then explore the social background of the Almohads, whose support was recruited predominantly, but not exclusively, among the Masmuda of the High Atlas, and the subsequent diversification of the elite through the formation of a new scholarly cohort of mixed background, the recruitment of other Berber tribes, and the transfer of numerous Arab tribes from Ifriqiya to Morocco.

After reviewing the social structure of the Almoravid and Almohad elites, the chapter will turn to wider society, rural and urban, tribal and non-tribal. Gender roles and relations with other Muslims, Christians and Jews will also form part of the discussion. A feature of Almoravid society was the relative freedom of Sanhaja women that appeared to others to be at variance with 'Islamic' norms. The Almohads repeatedly criticised the Almoravids for their inversion of gender roles, indicating that the status of women was a live issue at the time. Below the level of the elite, however, the reality of life for most women was probably fairly constant over the Almoravid and Almohad centuries and determined by a range of local customs and attitudes which we shall try to glimpse through the scattered references to women in the sources.

Although both eras have been seen as negative for the status and position of religious minorities, the Almoravids and Almohads diverged significantly in their treatment of them. The Almoravids adopted a strict legalistic approach which entailed firm application of the Shariʿa rules related to the position of protected minorities, in cities at least, while the Almohads are reported to have denied the existence of the *dhimma*, or pact of protection, historically accorded to monotheistic religious minorities. This section will show that the actual experience of minority communities, however, depended as much on political and strategic exigencies as on religious dogma, and it had begun to deteriorate in al-Andalus prior to the arrival of the Almoravids as the pressure from the northern Christian kingdoms increased. On the other hand, both regimes ultimately bowed to military and economic pressures and recruited Christian soldiers and permitted Christian merchants to ply their trade in their lands.

Chapter 5 will look at the economic underpinnings of the Almoravid and Almohad empires, which involved direct and indirect agricultural exploitation and promotion of the trans-Saharan and Mediterranean trades. Right from the outset, the Almoravids sought to control the trans-Saharan trade and this was one of their motivations for expanding across the Sahara and capturing the 'port' cities of Sijilmasa and Awdaghust on either side of the desert. Secure access to salt, gold and slaves was a major factor in their success and Almoravid gold dinars became the most valued currency in the Mediterranean at the time. The Almohads were similarly keen to benefit from trade and, despite their supposed intolerance towards non-Muslims in their domains, they allowed non-Muslim traders to reside in several coastal and inland entrepôts to keep trade buoyant. This chapter will consider the workings of the economy and commerce, and suggest how ordinary people made a living by reference to geographical accounts of the agriculture, markets and manufactures of the Maghrib and al-Andalus at this time. It will also explore how each regime interacted with the economy through taxation, the granting of estates and investment in agricultural development.

In Chapter 6, we will move on to investigate the types of faith, religious practice and knowledge that existed in al-Andalus and the Maghrib from the mid-eleventh to the mid-thirteenth centuries, beginning with an overview of the prior development of Islamic law (Shariʿa) and its methodology (*fiqh*), theology (*kalām*) and mysticism (Sufism) in the Islamic west. The chapter will then return to the imperial religious ideologies of the Almoravids and

Almohads themselves which defined the dominant 'state' form of religion and played a major role in shaping the subsequent religious landscape of the Maghrib. The Almoravids adopted Maliki Sunnism as an imperial legal framework which they then implanted from Córdoba to West Africa, creating an unprecedented level of religio-legal homogeneity in the region. While not as sophisticated as the famous Ottoman integration of *qānūn* (in this case, customary law) with the Shari'a, the Almoravids had a similar end in mind by requiring that legal decisions made in Marrakesh on the Berber periphery concurred with opinions from the existing centres of Maliki law – Córdoba and Qayrawan. Almohadism contributed in a different way by promoting a more sophisticated approach to religion which integrated scholastic theology, philosophy, law and Sufism. Although Malikism remained the dominant *madhhab* of the Maghrib, it was leavened by the Almohad theological contribution.

The chapter will also explore the complex relationship between religious and non-religious sciences, exemplified by the Almohads' perceived religious dogmatism and simultaneous patronage of Aristotelian philosophy, and look at issues of grassroots conversion and alternative sites of religious authority. On a popular level, the conversion of the majority of the rural population to Islam and the diffusion of Sufism across the region encouraged the spread of new forms of religiosity which were person- rather than text-centred. Several of the founding fathers of Andalusi and Maghribi mysticism lived at this time and while the population in general may not have understood the intricacies of the mystical path, they responded wholeheartedly to those of a pious, ascetic and mystical bent who settled among them. As we shall see, relations between Sufis and the state were ambivalent because of their growing popularity among the masses which appeared to rulers to have potential political ramifications, regardless of whether Sufis themselves were politically inclined.

Chapter 7 will turn to material culture as one of the most striking aspects of this period is the flourishing of art and architecture in the far west of North Africa and the emergence of a regional style that stretched from al-Andalus across to Ifriqiya. There is little to suggest that the earlier towns founded in the area that is now Morocco had truly monumental buildings. The most important city was almost certainly Sijilmasa which had a large great mosque by the tenth century, while Fes was made up of two warring townships, neither of which boasted particularly splendid great mosques. The Almoravids changed this with the foundation of Marrakesh *c.* 1070, which became an imperial centre embellished with fine palaces, mosques and markets within one to two generations. The Almoravids also transformed Fes into a single entity and built large great mosques across their domains, as well as numerous smaller ones. In doing so, they created a new Maghribi architectural style that blended Andalusi, Saharan and eastern Islamic elements in a new synthesis carried forward by the Almohads.

Although the Almohads were deeply hostile to the Almoravids, and in some cases demolished their mosques on the grounds that they were not correctly aligned towards Mecca, they fully understood the power of imperial art and architecture and quickly moved to produce a series of strident, militant Almohad monuments, including mosques, fortified citadels, looming gateways and city walls. Their hallmark was the square tower minaret of such huge proportions that each one they built dominated the skyline of its host city, but, as fragments of their palace in Seville show, they did not completely eschew luxurious and delicate decoration. They also began to use the faience mosaics and tiles that came to be a quintessential feature of both Andalusi and Maghribi art from the thirteenth century onwards, alongside the carved stucco already used by the Almoravids before them. Together these dynasties established the artistic and architectural canon which we now perceive as characteristic of much of the Maghrib.

Chapter 8 will conclude the volume by enumerating the achievements of the Almoravids and Almohads in Islamising the Maghrib and trying to hold the Muslim frontier against the Christian kingdoms in al-Andalus. It will flag up their contribution to the future shape of the Maghrib and also the areas in which both regimes faltered. It will then compare their track records with developments across the Islamic world at the same time to locate them in the broader span of Islamic history and place them alongside their rivals and peers in the Mashriq.

2

The Almoravids: Striving in the Path of God

This chapter and Chapter 3 explore the political contours of the Almoravid and Almohad states as a prelude to investigating the society and culture over which they presided. In both empires, politics and military activity were deeply entwined and therefore military campaigns are the uppermost strand in the chronicles, and rulers appear first and foremost as commanders in chief, recruiting, mobilising and leading their armies. However, political life also involved the formation of a judicial system, administrative structures to gather taxes and maintain correspondence, and the nurturing of the religious and intellectual environment. Medieval Islamic government was minimal in comparison with modern government, so for the majority of the population in both al-Andalus and the Maghrib, 'good' government meant a regime capable of maintaining law and order, and one that gathered taxes permitted by the Shari'a (Islamic law) in a fair manner. The limited range of Shari'a taxes, however, meant that rulers usually had to collect non-canonical taxes, risking unpopularity and even rebellion.

In the religious sphere, rulers were expected to be personally pious and devout and to defend the faith. This took two main forms in the eleventh to thirteenth centuries. First, rulers had to defend Islam by force of arms, a task usually described as jihad, which might entail warfare against Muslims of other 'heretical' sects or action against rebels as well as fighting against the Christian powers of Iberia and the northern Mediterranean. Secondly, rulers also had to show respect and deference to religious professionals, collectively known in this region as the *'ulamā'* (scholars) or *fuqahā'* (jurists), and contribute to the religious infrastructure by building or augmenting mosques and other religious facilities. The creation of a form of imperial government that responded to these established Islamic religio-political conventions entailed a very steep learning curve for the Almoravids and the Almohads, given their origins beyond Islamic state control in the deserts and mountains of the south.

The first of the two, the Almoravid movement, drew its support from a small cohort of Sanhaja Berber tribes who resided in the Sahara, the Guddala,

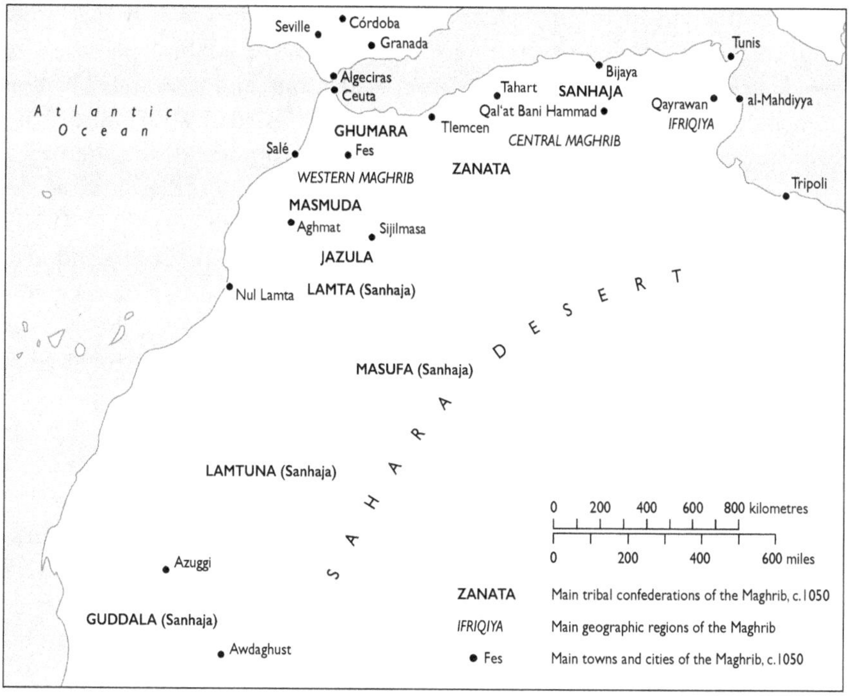

Figure 2.1 The distribution of the Berber peoples, *c.* 1050

the Lamtuna and the Masufa. They were pastoralists who roamed the desert, moving from well to well with their flocks and felt tents. Living far beyond the area of the early Islamic conquests, they were almost certainly introduced to Islam between the ninth and eleventh centuries by Kharijite Muslim Berber traders participating in the trans-Saharan trade who needed their protection and assistance.[1] We know very little about the pre-Islamic history of the Sanhaja, but later quasi-historical accounts claimed that they were descendants of the ancient Himyaritic kings of Yemen.

> There is no relationship between the Lamtuna and the Berbers, except on the maternal side. The Sanhaja trace their lineage to Himyar. They left the Yemen and travelled to the Sahara which became their home in the Maghrib.[2]

This was a mythical genealogy claimed by many Berber tribes to give them a place within the Arab-Islamic scheme of history. The details of the

[1] See Lewicki, 'Les origines de l'Islam dans les tribus berbères du Sahara occidental'.
[2] *al-Hulal al-Mawshiyya*, pp. 17–18.

Almoravid myth of origin, which will be reviewed in Chapter 4, further claimed that the Sanhaja were forced to flee from the Arabian peninsula to avoid persecution for their monotheistic inclinations, and were thus Muslims even before the revelation of Islam. It also addressed the very distinctive Sanhaja practice of male veiling which gained the Almoravids the alternative name of 'The Veiled Ones' (*al-mulaththamūn*). One of our earliest sources, the geographical work of al-Bakri dating to the mid-eleventh century (*c.* 1068), simply describes how proudly Sanhaja men wore the veil (*lithām*) and how shameful they considered it if a man's lower face was revealed, without giving the practice an Islamic justification.[3] However, in later sources, the face veil became a commemoration of the Sanhaja escape from Yemen disguised as women and, therefore, another mark of their devotion to Islam.

The development of the Almoravid movement among the Sanhaja tribes of the western pre-Sahara is similarly shrouded in myth. In the absence of verifiable facts, we can only present the story as it appears in Arabic sources and endeavour to tease out the implications embedded within it and sometimes its discrepancies. The story generally begins with a pilgrimage to Mecca undertaken by Yahya b. Ibrahim, chief of the Guddala tribe, probably in the company of men regarded as religious experts by the Sanhaja, including an individual called Jawhar b. Sakkum. Although often dated to 1048–9, a date repeated in many medieval Arabic sources, current scholarship prefers an earlier date between 1035 and 1038 based on al-Bakri's statement that the movement was well underway by 1048–9 and the death of Abu 'Imran al-Fasi, whom the pilgrims purportedly met in Qayrawan, in 1038–9.[4] This dating discrepancy of around a decade persists through the first forty years of the movement.

The Islamic world that Yahya and his companions encountered with its burgeoning cities and rival Muslim sects was very different to his sparsely populated Saharan homeland. The dominant power in much of the Maghrib was the Isma'ili Fatimid caliphate which ruled Ifriqiya and Egypt, but there were also numerous Kharijite principalities, and strong support for Malikism, one of the Sunni legal schools, in the cities of Ifriqiya. Scholars with different perspectives and views gathered in the great mosques of the cities, exchanging legal and theological views at a level completely unfamiliar to the Sanhaja pilgrims, who probably sought to acquire knowledge from these teachers based in the cities on their route, as pilgrims commonly did.

As a result, Yahya came to feel that his fellow tribesmen were in desperate

[3] al-Bakri, *Description de l'Afrique*, Arabic text, p. 170; French text, pp. 320–1.

[4] Bosch Vilá, *Los Almorávides*, pp. 49–50; Norris, 'New evidence', p. 259; Lagardère, *Almoravides I*, p. 45; Messier, *Almoravids*, p. 192; Ibn 'Idhari, *al-Bayan*, vol. 4, p. 7, n. 3.

need of education in their professed religion. On his return from Mecca he stopped in Qayrawan, the main city of Ifriqiya, and asked Abu 'Imran al-Fasi, a Maliki scholar that he encountered, if he could send someone to instruct the Guddala. According to an amusing but plausible anecdote, none of Abu 'Imran's students in Qayrawan were prepared to leave their city comforts to go off to the Sahara, so he gave Yahya b. Ibrahim a letter for Wajjaj or Waggag b. Zalwi who was the head of a religious settlement (*ribāṭ*) in the Sus valley below the High Atlas mountains, relatively close to Sanhaja lands.[5] Waggag in his turn appointed one of his students, 'Abd Allah b. Yasin of the Jazula or Gazula, a tribe often considered part of the Sanhaja confederation, to instruct the Guddala about Islamic ritual and law. One source, the *Kitab al-Madarik* written by Qadi 'Iyad of Ceuta, makes no mention of either Yahya or Abu 'Imran reporting instead that the jurist Jawhar b. Sakkum asked Waggag directly for someone to educate his fellows.[6] This omission may reflect Qadi 'Iyad's particular interest in scholars or the later elaboration of a myth to connect the Almoravids with the hugely influential Abu 'Imran and personalise their attachment to Malikism, just as the later myth of Ibn Tumart's meeting with al-Ghazali performed the same function for the Almohads.

Ibn Yasin's mission to the Guddala is another aspect of early Almoravid history that is riddled with contradictions and *lacunae*. He was a man of the desert himself, whose mother Tin Izamaren lived in Tamamanawt, a village al-Bakri describes as located on the edge of the 'Sahara of the city of Ghana'.[7] As a young man, he made the arduous journey to study in Córdoba and returned to the Maghrib keen to 'reform' Islam and relieve the Sanhaja tribes of their subjugation by the Barghawata and Zanata, leading Lagardère to ask whether he was first and foremost a jurist or a political agitator.[8] When he arrived among the Guddala as the guest of Yahya b. Ibrahim, Ibn Yasin received a warm welcome and set about forcing them to adhere to Maliki law in their ritual and social behaviour. He recruited a number of disciples and, according to al-Bakri, founded a town called Aratnanna,[9] which may have been a teaching centre similar to Waggag's *ribāṭ* in the Sus from which he had come.[10] However, the geographical location of Ibn Yasin's *ribāṭ* or town

[5] al-Bakri, *Description de l'Afrique*, Arabic text, pp. 164–5; French text, p. 312. Although this phrase is taken to mean the northern side of the desert (Bosch Vilá, *Los Almorávides*, p. 51), the reference to Ghana implies its southern side.

[6] Norris, 'New evidence', pp. 255–6, 259–60.

[7] al-Bakri, *Description de l'Afrique*, Arabic text, p. 165; French text, p. 312.

[8] Lagardère, *Almoravides I*, p. 47.

[9] al-Bakri *Description de l'Afrique*, Arabic text, p. 165; French text, p. 313.

[10] Bosch Vilá distinguished between Ibn Yasin's *ribāṭ* and Aratnanna, which he located opposite Awdaghust; *Los Almorávides*, p. 70.

is unknown and most of the locations adduced in later sources, such as the estuary of the Senegal river, near Nouakchott, or Arguin island, seem to be folkloric tropes rather than factual reports.[11]

At some point relations between Ibn Yasin and the Guddala soured. This may have been triggered by the harsh punishments he meted out for even rather minor religious infractions, or his sometimes idiosyncratic interpretations of Islamic law. Al-Bakri reports that Jawhar b. Sakkum and two Guddala chiefs questioned his religious knowledge and interpretations, thereby inciting the Guddala to reject his religious leadership, pillage his home and chase him from their midst.[12] However, the accounts also imply other reasons for the decline in Guddala support for Ibn Yasin related to changes in the leadership of the tribe triggered by the death of his patron, Yahya b. Ibrahim. Norris argues that while many Guddala notables wished for a patrilineal succession to keep the chieftainship within the Guddala, the affiliated Lamtuna tribe supported the succession of one of their chiefs, Yahya b. 'Umar, whose mother Safiyya was from the Guddala and probably the sister of Yahya b. Ibrahim. Although the idea that the son of a deceased man's sister should inherit might seem unusual, it was, in fact, a common matrilineal inheritance pattern among the Sanhaja and it seems to have won the day, with Ibn Yasin's approval.[13] Yahya b. 'Umar emerged as chief and as Ibn Yasin's patron and foremost aristocratic disciple, support which Ibn Yasin could not do without, despite his talents as a religious preacher.

By the early 1050s, a triumvirate of Ibn Yasin, Yahya b. 'Umar and his brother Abu Bakr b. 'Umar had emerged and the movement was dominated by the Lamtuna rather than the Guddala. Moreover, the perspective had shifted from educating the Sanhaja tribes who accepted Ibn Yasin's religious leadership to forcibly correcting the religious deficiencies of neighbouring tribes and communities by means of jihad. The first victims of Lamtuna assertiveness were other Sanhaja tribes – the now hostile Guddala, the Masufa and the Lamta. This was a Lamtuna bid for hegemony over the Sanhaja as a whole, understood and legitimised as a religious mission to impose 'correct' Maliki Islam on religious deviants and, although the Guddala continued to resist for many years, the Masufa and Lamta soon joined the Lamtuna, creating a large Sanhaja military federation, known as the Murabitun (Almoravids). The newly recruited devotees then turned against the non-Muslim tribes of the Dar'a valley south of the High Atlas in an expansive wave in which Sanhaja

[11] Norris, 'al-Murābiṭīn'.

[12] al-Bakri, *Description de l'Afrique*, Arabic text, pp. 165–6; French text, p. 313. For more detail on Ibn Yasin's doctrine, see below, pp. 238–40.

[13] Norris, 'New evidence', pp. 261–2.

'aṣabiyya gained mass through their adherence to Maliki Islam and their desire to propagate it through jihad.

When the Almoravid jihad entailed warfare against other Muslims rather than non-Muslims, however, it was inspired not simply by notions of correct versus deviant interpretations of Islam or Sanhaja chauvinism, but also by the often deeply held conviction that Muslims should form one political and religious community obedient to one caliph. From this perspective, jihad was an important integrative mechanism and a process of religio-political unification. Ibn 'Idhari, who witnessed the last dark days of the Almohad empire and the fall of many Andalusi cities to the Christians, expresses this view very clearly when he presents Ibn Yasin's mission as the unification of Muslims to follow Islam's way or law (*sharī'at al-Islām*) under a single imam in place of the fissiparous partisan politics of both al-Andalus and the Maghrib where each tribe or community had its own chief or leader (*amīr*) and only followed the rulings (*ḥukm*) of its own tribe or sect.[14] In contrast, the Almoravid amir was the commander of Truth (*amīr al-ḥaqq*), in the sense of true religion, a figure whose virtue lay in making the Muslim *umma* one.[15]

This use of religion to unite and focus a group of tribes, previously given to raiding and competing for resources amongst themselves, was one of the examples upon which Ibn Khaldun based his theory of the complementary roles of *'aṣabiyya* and religion in tribal state-building. Those Sanhaja who joined the movement found a new identity as Almoravids that enabled them to harness their martial abilities and use them to expand their power rather than dissipating them in internal feuds. As Ibn 'Idhari suggests, however, their appeal was also potentially wider than to the Sanhaja alone, and their rivals description of them as Lamtuna or Mulaththamun was a slur to diminish the religious component of their movement, encapsulated in the title al-Murabitun/Almoravids. It is a point of speculation, however, when and why the Sanhaja affiliates of Ibn Yasin came to be known as Almoravids.[16] Possibly, it had the sense of 'Men of the *ribāṭ*' of Ibn Yasin or his master Waggag. Conversely, it may have had a more spiritual or metaphorical meaning, in the sense of 'men bound to God' from the Arabic root r-b-ṭ meaning 'to tie'. Writing in the thirteenth century, Ibn 'Idhari says that Ibn Yasin gave them the name to indicate their fortitude and devotion to their cause after they lost half their fighters in a battle around 1054 against non-Muslim tribes in the Dar'a valley.[17] This may well be a later rationalisation of the term, but

[14] Ibn 'Idhari, *al-Bayan*, vol. 4, pp. 9–10.
[15] Ibid., vol. 4, p. 11.
[16] Bosch Vilá, *Los Almorávides*, pp. 55–6; Lagardère, *Almoravides I*, pp. 58–60.
[17] Ibn 'Idhari, *al-Bayan*, vol. 4, p. 11.

it is also an explanation that closely linked *ribāṭ* to jihad in the sense of a physical and spiritual girding of the loins for battle. This militancy was a key feature of the movement.

It was not solely religious fervour or *'aṣabiyya* that underpinned the Lamtuna desire for Saharan dominance. Life in the Sahara desert was extremely hard and the competition for scant resources was fierce at all times, rising to critical levels if the population rose or drought struck, factors that may well have contributed to the rise of the Almoravids.[18] Although something of an exaggeration, al-Bakri describes the Sanhaja as living solely on strips of dried meat and milk in a land where few animals beyond wild gazelles and foxes could sustain themselves.[19] In this harsh environment, survival depended on possession of as many water sources as possible and control of the routes taken by the trans-Saharan caravans carrying salt, grain, gold and slaves, whose caravaneers paid good money to be led safely through the desert, and swapped their grain for pastoral products. As in many pre-modern contexts, the combination of religious, political and economic motives driving the Sanhaja does not mean that the Almoravids were insincere. Like the early Muslims and their Almohad successors, they associated military victory and political power with divine favour and saw the material benefits they gained as a reward from God that proved they were on the right path.

Truly profitable exploitation of the trans-Saharan trade required possession of Sijilmasa and Awdaghust, the great northern and southern desert-edge cities, dominated by the Zanata and the Soninke, respectively. It is therefore hardly coincidental that these were the first cities targeted by the Almoravids after they had consolidated their control over the desert itself. After moving into the Dar'a valley to wage war against the non-Muslim tribes they found there, the Almoravids advanced east towards Sijilmasa in 1054–5. According to al-Bakri, they offered its Zanata Maghrawa lord, Mas'ud b. Wanudin, and the city notables a deal, presumably the chance to submit and accept Maliki Sunnism in place of Kharijism, but they attacked the city after their approach was rejected.[20] Later chronicles embellish the story by adding that disgruntled elements within the population called upon the Almoravids to help them against their 'tyrannical' Zanata Berber rulers.[21] Framed in this way, the Almoravid attack constituted a jihad to restore justice and transform a city that was a hotbed of Kharijism, Fatimid Shi'ism and lax morality into a bastion of Maliki orthodoxy, as well as an attempt to dislodge the Zanata.

[18] McDougall, 'The Sahara reconsidered', p. 268.
[19] al-Bakri, *Description de l'Afrique*, Arabic text, pp. 164, 170–1; French text, pp. 310, 322.
[20] Ibid., Arabic text, p. 167; French text, p. 315.
[21] Ibn Abi Zar', *Rawd al-Qirtas*, p. 161.

Stories of the Almoravids abolishing non-Qur'anic taxation, breaking musical instruments and burning down wine shops served to confirm this narrative. Although the Almoravids took the city fairly easily, when the majority of their warriors returned to the desert to raid Awdaghust to the south and capture it from the pagan Soninke ruler of Ghana, the Maghrawa returned and slaughtered the small Almoravid garrison as they prayed or sought refuge in the great mosque.[22]

Ibn Yasin responded to this reverse by summoning the Almoravids for a second attack on the Maghrawa to regain Sijilmasa, but the Guddala refused and returned to their desert homelands bordering the Atlantic. This was an important moment for the Almoravids. Reading between the lines, there appears to have been tension between Ibn Yasin and those Sanhaja who saw their future beyond the desert and others, such as the Guddala, who did not wish to become embroiled in conflict with the powerful Zanata tribes or venture too far beyond their familiar desert lands. Yahya b. 'Umar was obliged to campaign against the recalcitrant Guddala and died fighting them in either 1055 or 1056.[23] The desertic south and the fertile lands to the north continued to pull the Almoravids in two ways for many years. It must also have become obvious after the Sijilmasa insurgency that while cities might be easy to conquer, they were not so simple to govern and hold, and that the cooperation of at least some of the urban elite was essential. This provided the rationale for the consistent Almoravid recruitment of Maliki jurists of urban background to complement the military capabilities of the Sanhaja as their empire expanded.

After the death of Yahya b. 'Umar and the reconquest of Sijilmasa, Ibn Yasin and Abu Bakr b. 'Umar consolidated Almoravid control over the caravan route from Sijilmasa westwards through the Sus valley to Nul Lamta at the expense of the Zanata, some of whom were adherents of the mysterious Shi'i Bajaliyya sect.[24] Then they cast their eyes north towards the snow-covered peaks of the High Atlas mountains and the rich trading town of Aghmat, another Zanata stronghold, beyond. Ibn Yasin had crossed the mountains on his journeys to and from Córdoba, and he took to the high passes once again to persuade the Masmuda tribes to make common cause with the Almoravids against the Zanata. Although they were familiar with the rigours of the desert, the mountains were unfamiliar and dangerous territory for the Almoravids and their animals, and they would have found the crossing

[22] al-Bakri, *Description de l'Afrique*, Arabic text, p. 168; French text, p. 315. For more detail, see Bosch Vilá, *Los Almorávides*, pp. 73–4.

[23] Bosch Vilá, *Los Almorávides*, p. 76.

[24] Ibid., pp. 83–5; Lagardère, *Almoravides I*, p. 66.

almost impossible without Masmuda support. Indeed, they found mountain engagements perilous for the duration of their rule and lost control of the Atlas when the Masmuda turned against them in the early twelfth century.

In 1058, however, the alliance held and the Almoravids crossed the High Atlas, possibly via the westernmost pass, the Tizi Mashu, which would have brought them down the Shishawa valley, after which they travelled east to Aghmat and laid siege to it.[25] Like Sijilmasa, Aghmat was a prosperous commercial town embedded in the trade networks that stretched eastwards to Qayrawan and northwards across the Straits of Gibraltar to Córdoba, with sufficient economic and cultural weight to have attracted migrants from al-Andalus and Ifriqiya and a sizable coterie of Jewish traders. It was a double town made up of Aghmat-Warika and Aghmat-Ilan (Ar. Haylana), named after the Masmuda Berber tribes that inhabited each settlement, controlled by a Zanata Berber warlord, Laqqut b. Yusuf, who had connections with the Zanata Banu Ifran lords of Salé further north. The Almoravids took it after a short siege accompanied by negotiations with local notables, while Laqqut b. Yusuf escaped and sought refuge with the Zanata of the Tadla region only to be killed in battle with the Almoravids later.[26]

After they had expelled the Zanata from Aghmat, the Almoravids renewed their northward mission against the Barghawata tribes of the Atlantic littoral who had long been considered heretical due to their belief that Muhammad and the Qur'an were the prophet and the book of the Arabs while one of their own chiefs, Salih, was the prophet of the Berbers and had given them their own book. Ibn Yasin took the initiative as he had with the Masmuda of the High Atlas and travelled among the Barghawata tribes calling them to Malikism, but he was over-confident: his advances were rejected and he was killed in 1059, an event much embellished in the *Rawd al-Qirtas*.[27] Sulayman b. 'Addu, another pupil of Waggag, succeeded Ibn Yasin as religious leader of the movement, but he was less charismatic and he died soon after fighting the Barghawata as the Almoravids sought revenge for Ibn Yasin's death. After that, effective leadership of the movement passed to the Lamtuna chief Abu Bakr b. 'Umar and his cousin Yusuf b. Tashfin, who had already begun an offensive against the Zanata tribes north and east of Sijilmasa which steadily took the Almoravids towards the more northerly towns of Salé, Meknes, Fes and Tlemcen.

The Almoravid experience in the first years after their traversal of the High

[25] Bosch Vilá, *Los Almorávides*, p. 85.

[26] Ibn Khaldun, *Kitab al-'Ibar*, vol. 8, p. 376; Bosch Vilá, *Los Almorávides*, pp. 87, 90; Lagardére, *Almoravides I*, pp. 69–70.

[27] Ibn Abi Zar', *Rawd al-Qirtas*, p. 167; Lagardère, *Almoravides I*, p. 71.

Atlas is encapsulated in two stories. The first revolves around the enigmatic figure of Zaynab daughter of Ishaq al-Hawwari or al-Nafzawi who has the distinction of being one of the few women in Maghribi historical writing to enjoy a public profile. Her father was an Ifriqiyan merchant from Qayrawan who had migrated to Aghmat. Although chroniclers differ as to whether he was of Nafzawa (Ibn 'Idhari and Ibn Khaldun) or Hawwara (Ibn Abi Zar') origin,[28] both these Berber tribes subscribed to Kharijite Islam, primarily in its Ibadi form, confirming that Aghmat was a town heavily influenced by Kharijism like Sijilmasa south of the High Atlas.[29]

Zaynab herself is variously described as the wife of the Maghrawa chief Laqqut b. Yusuf and thus the 'queen' of Aghmat, or the concubine of a previous chief, Yusuf b. 'Ali.[30] More fancifully, she was said to have refused to marry anyone but the ruler of the Maghrib and was reputed to be a soothsayer or sorceress in contact with the jinn and the keeper of an immense secret treasure.[31] After Laqqut was killed in the course of the Almoravid campaigns in the Tadla region, Zaynab was a widow of substance and around 1067–8 she became the wife of Abu Bakr, thereby putting her wealth and experience at the disposal of the new masters of the area. While not challenging the historicity of Zaynab, fantastical legends about her extraordinary beauty and her secret riches symbolise the wealth that the Atlantic plains offered the newcomers, while her marriage and cooperation with Abu Bakr indicate the Almoravids' need for local interlocutors and collaborators, and the fact that their empire was not founded exclusively by violent military conquests but also by alliances and negotiation.

The second set of stories relate to the foundation of the city of Marrakesh. Initially the Almoravids took up residence in Aghmat-Warika, sometimes described as the residence of the town's notables, but this put considerable stress on the existing infrastructure and led to overcrowding and complaints from the population. After some years, the chiefs of the local Masmuda tribes, the Warika and the Haylana, went to Abu Bakr and asked him to establish a new garrison town (*miṣr*) away from Aghmat. After a period of

[28] Ibn Abi Zar', *Rawd al-Qirtas*, p. 170; Ibn 'Idhari, *al-Bayan*, vol. 4, p. 16; Ibn Khaldun, *Kitab al-'Ibar*, vol. 8, p. 376; Ibn Khaldun, *Histoire des Berbères*, vol. 2, p. 71.

[29] Pellat, 'Nafzāwa'.

[30] The names of the Maghrawa chief, Laqqut b. Yusuf b. 'Ali, and his predecessor Yusuf b. 'Ali, suggest that we may be dealing with a father and son, or the same person. Messier sees the two names as belonging to one person (*Almoravids*, p. 40), while Bosch Vilá follows Ibn Khaldun (*Kitab al-'Ibar*, vol. 8, p. 376) in seeing them as two different amirs, one of whom married Zaynab and one of whom previously possessed her as a concubine (*Los Almorávides*, p. 90). Lagardère notes her relationships, but prefers the myth that she had refused to marry until she met the man who would rule the Maghrib (*Almoravides I*, p. 72).

[31] Ibn 'Idhari, *al-Bayan*, vol. 4, p. 16.

disagreement over the site, they offered the Almoravids a plot of land that straddled the territories of the two tribes, described as empty of all but a few ostriches and colocynth plants and therefore suitable for desert nomads.[32] While overcrowding in Aghmat-Warika and tribal competition to have the Almoravids on 'their patch' may have been reasons for the foundation and siting of Marrakesh, the shift from more temporary residential arrangements signified the Almoravids' commitment to remaining north of the High Atlas, to expanding their control over the rich, well-watered Atlantic plains, and to dominating the Maghribi trade routes north and east.

Ibn 'Idhari dates the foundation of Marrakesh to May 1070,[33] and depicts the direct involvement of Abu Bakr and the Almoravid elite alongside ordinary labourers in the construction process, a role chroniclers frequently attributed to Islamic monarchs for whom the foundation of a city marked a watershed moment in the evolution of a new polity, and harked back to the Prophet's paradigmatic transformation of pagan Yathrib into Islamic Medina.[34] However, Abu Bakr was not destined to enjoy the full benefit of the northern expansion of the Almoravid empire due to the division of its leadership between the Saharan and Maghribi theatres of engagement in the 1070s, triggered by yet another rebellion in the Almoravids' Saharan homeland. The rebellion threatened Almoravid control of the desert trade routes and could not be ignored, therefore Abu Bakr left Marrakesh in 1071 to return to the Sahara and quell the insurrection.[35] Shortly before his departure, he appointed his cousin Yusuf b. Tashfin as his deputy in the Maghrib and made the decision to divorce Zaynab on the condition that Yusuf b. Tashfin marry her after her legal waiting period was over.[36] The fourteenth-century chronicler Ibn Abi Zar' describes Abu Bakr as making this decision on the chivalric grounds that Zaynab was too delicate and cultured for desert life:

> You are a tender woman, the desert is no place for you so I divorce you. When your waiting period is completed, marry my cousin Yusuf b. Tashfin.[37]

32 There are some discrepancies over the two tribes to whom the land belonged, with not only the Warika and Haylana mentioned but also the Hazmira and Haskura. Ibn 'Idhari, *al-Bayan*, vol. 4, pp. 16–17, 301; *al-Hulal al-Mawshiyya*, pp. 15–16; Lagardère, *Almoravides I*, pp. 74–6; Messier, *Almoravids*, pp. 41–2.

33 Taken together, Arabic chronicles give a variety of dates between 1062 and 1072 (Lagardère, *Almoravides I*, p. 75, n. 25) and some attribute the foundation to Yusuf b. Tashfin (Bosch Vilá, *Los Almorávides*, pp. 104–5)

34 See O'Meara, 'The foundation legend of Fez'.

35 Bosch Vilá dates Abu Bakr's return to the desert a decade earlier; *Los Almorávides*, p. 96.

36 Ibn 'Idhari, *al-Bayan*, vol. 4, p. 18.

37 Ibn Abi Zar', *Rawd al-Qirtas*, p. 170.

However, it is more likely that Zaynab, a mature and independent woman who had been married at least once before, asked for a divorce and refused to accompany him and was perhaps already allied with Yusuf to achieve this outcome: Ibn 'Idhari reports, 'It is said that [Zaynab] herself asked him to divorce her and he complied with her wishes.'[38] Zaynab went on to not only marry Yusuf, but also to act as his foremost adviser and political partner in ruling the Almoravids' Maghribi domains. Since most medieval Arabic sources barely mention women except as the mothers of princes, these references to Zaynab's active political role alongside Yusuf b. Tashfin stand out and resemble early Islamic narratives about Khadija, the first wife of the Prophet Muhammad, as well as reports of the prominence of some Turkish women in the Seljuk empire.

At this point in his account, Ibn 'Idhari describes Yusuf b. Tashfin as giving the Almoravid empire the governmental structures associated with an Islamic polity. He says that he set up administrative offices (*dawāwīn*) and formalised the organisation of the army and diversified it by the purchase of 2,000 slaves from sub-Saharan Africa and 240 Christian horsemen from al-Andalus, thereby creating a diversified army of a 'royal' type.[39] His growing power and prestige also encouraged many additional Sanhaja warriors to enter his service, slowing leaching manpower away from Abu Bakr in the Sahara. While it is not clear how formal the structure of Almoravid government actually was at this point and where or from whom Yusuf b. Tashfin might have acquired knowledge of the usual workings of an Islamic polity, he was evidently creating for himself an independent power base centred on Marrakesh from which he dispatched his generals north towards Salé, Meknes and Fes supported by the flow of manpower from the desert.

In late 1072, Abu Bakr returned from the Sahara and set up camp near Aghmat with the intention of resuming control of his capital and governing the Maghribi as well as the Saharan parts of the Almoravid empire. According to the sources, his return threw Yusuf into a state of panic because he had no desire to betray his cousin but equally no intention of relinquishing to him the wealth and power he had accrued 'after he had tasted its sweetness'.[40] Zaynab advised him not to respond to Abu Bakr's summons, which would imply subservience, but to send him a substantial present, which would signal goodwill but also their new political parity, on the assumption that Abu Bakr was too moral a man to fight his cousin for material gain. Meanwhile,

[38] Ibn 'Idhari, *al-Bayan*, vol. 4, p. 19.

[39] Ibid., vol. 4, p. 20. Lagardère sees the army as modelled on that of the Umayyads of Córdoba, *Almoravides I*, pp. 81–2.

[40] Ibn 'Idhari, *al-Bayan*, vol. 4, p. 20.

large numbers of Sanhaja warriors left Abu Bakr's camp and flocked to see the sights of Marrakesh where Yusuf showered them with gifts and honours, thereby encouraging them to join his entourage.

Abu Bakr appears to have quickly grasped the reality of the situation and he decided to voluntary confirm his cousin's position rather than risk a battle for control of Marrakesh. The chronicles inject a strong sense of political theatre into the meeting of the two men that ensued on neutral ground between Marrakesh and Aghmat. Yusuf b. Tashfin approached his cousin surrounded by his warriors and slaves and greeted him while still mounted on his horse to indicate that he was no longer of lower rank. He then dismounted and sat with Abu Bakr on a cloak laid out for that purpose. In the course of their discussion, Abu Bakr offered Yusuf control over the Maghrib on the pretext that he was still required in the Almoravids' Saharan domains. This left him as nominal head of the Almoravids and Yusuf as *de facto* ruler of the Maghrib. The Lamtuna chiefs then gathered to formalise the arrangement, along with legal witnesses (*'udūl*) and the shaykhs of other tribes. For his part, Yusuf followed Zaynab's advice and ameliorated relations with his cousin by sending a substantial gift of richly caparisoned horses, weapons, textiles, slaves and foodstuffs to his camp. Abu Bakr accepted the gift and returned to the Sahara, thereby preserving the honour of both chiefs.[41]

Although this was a coup d'état of sorts, it is difficult to know how the Almoravids themselves perceived the situation. Clan leadership rather than autocratic rule was common in tribal societies and can be seen in the perpetual subdivision of the domains of the contemporary Seljuk sultanate in the Middle East as well as in the Almoravid empire. Yusuf acknowledged Abu Bakr as chief Almoravid amir on coinage until the latter's death *c.* 1087 and the two men are never described as enemies.[42] Rivalry is evident, however, between Yusuf and Ibrahim, one of Abu Bakr's sons, recognised as amir of Sijilmasa on coinage from at least 1071 to 1076, who marched to Aghmat to claim his father's patrimony around 1076.[43] He was, however, persuaded to leave for the desert to join his father rather than dragging the Almoravids into a civil war by the prominent Almoravid amir Mazdali, who was related to both men.[44] From a historiographical as well as a historical perspective,

41 Ibn 'Idhari, *al-Bayan*, vol. 4, p. 21–2. Bosch Vilá, *Los Almorávides*, pp. 97–8; Lagardère, *Almoravides I*, p. 83; Messier, *Almoravids*, pp. 57–8.

42 Messier, *Almoravids*, p. 59.

43 Some sources therefore date Abu Bakr's death to 1076 (469 AH). This perpetuates the persistent dating discrepancy of a decade in different accounts of the early Almoravid movement.

44 Ibn 'Idhari, *al-Bayan*, vol. 4, pp. 25–6.

the political division of the Almoravid empire into Saharan and Maghribi flanks had major consequences by producing a bifurcation between the study of their Saharan domains, which are a topic of interest to Africanists, and their Maghribi and later Andalusi domains, which fall within the purview of Islamic Maghribi studies.

The Almoravids in the Sahara and Sahel

The history of the Saharan flank of the Almoravid movement is particularly vague and contradictory in the medieval Arabic sources, and it is often left out of histories of the Maghrib despite the importance of control of the Saharan trade routes to the Almoravid empire as a whole. In the absence of textual sources, archaeology sheds some light on the southern Almoravids, but their impact is highly contested among Africanists and also marked by concerns that are not evident in the study of the northern Almoravid empire. The Arabic narrative, such as it is, posits that Abu Bakr b. ʿUmar returned to the Almoravids' southern base or capital at Azuggi in modern Mauritania with a handful of Maliki jurists, including Abu Bakr Muhammad al-Muradi from Qayrawan,[45] to orchestrate the Almoravid advance south against the Soninke kingdom of Ghana, which was successfully conquered around 1076–7 and subsequently collapsed. Abu Bakr, aided by his sons, continued raiding against the non-Muslims of the desert and Sahel and was killed by an arrow *c.* 1087.[46]

The subsequent history of the Almoravids in the south is almost a complete void and even the 'conquest' of Ghana raises questions that may never be fully answered. In a famous article titled 'The conquest that never was', Conrad and Fisher reviewed and rejected the evidence for a northern 'white' Almoravid conquest of ancient Ghana in the form of an offensive against the sedentary 'black' inhabitants of the Sahel, in favour of a more collaborative venture between the 'white' Almoravids and the 'black' inhabitants of Ghana who became Muslim around the same time, with the latter rather than the former as the dominant partner.[47] However, the counter-argument is that authors writing in Arabic were unfamiliar with the Sahel and not interested in it and, therefore, sparse or contradictory textual evidence does not mean that a conquest did not take place or that the Saharan Almoravid empire did not exist. Moreover, the basic idea of a dichotomy between 'white' Almoravids and 'black' Sahelian Africans is very problematic given the high levels of marriage, concubinage and cooperation between the Sanhaja Berber tribes and

[45] Lagardère, *Le djihâd andalou*, pp. 165–6.
[46] Bosch Vilá, *Los Almorávides*, pp. 99–102.
[47] Conrad and Fisher, 'The conquest that never was'.

the non-tribal peoples of the Sahel.[48] Yusuf b. Tashfin, for instance, is often described as having 'black' features.[49] The most recent summation of the debate traces the European imperial lineage of a conquest thesis based on the 'white' domination of 'black' peoples and reiterates the lack of hard evidence for an Almoravid conquest of Ghana.[50]

The nature of the Almoravid encounter with Ghana – conquest or partnership – and the ethnic and religious origins of those involved is impossible to determine in the absence of new sources. However, the Almoravids clearly achieved control of the salt trade and the gold flow north, their primary economic objective, and Islam did take root among the population of Ghana, their religious objective. Abu Bakr maintained Almoravid control of the Sahara at least in the vicinity of Azuggi, and the expansion of the Sanhaja eastwards appears to have been led by the Almoravid Masufa, a group with strong marriage and maternal connections to the Lamtuna, who migrated into the vast zone between Sijilmasa and Waraqlan, led quite possibly by Abu Bakr's son, Yahya, known as al-Masufi due to his maternal lineage.[51] Cultural ties also existed between the Sahel and the Almoravid north. For instance, archaeological evidence from Gao-Sané, conquered or converted seven years after Ghana according to al-Zuhri, in the form of luxurious tomb *stelae* made of carved marble from an atelier in Almería, show that these kings were certainly influenced by the Almoravids, if not actually adherents of the Almoravid movement or Berbers themselves.[52]

The Almoravids in the Maghrib and al-Andalus

While Abu Bakr and his sons consolidated Almoravid control over the Sahel and the trans-Saharan trade, Yusuf b. Tashfin and other members of his clan continued to extend Almoravid control over the fertile lands north of the High Atlas. This involved further campaigns against the Masmuda Berber Barghawata of the Tamesna region and the Zanata Berber principalities that stretched across the Maghrib from the Atlantic plains into modern Algeria. These principalities were incorporated into the Almoravid empire by a combination of tactics including negotiations as well as violent conquest. The pattern presented by Ibn 'Idhari, calqued on the Prophet's practice, was for the Almoravid army, usually commanded by one of Yusuf b. Tashfin's kinsmen,

[48] Burkhalter, 'Listening for silences in Almoravid history'.

[49] Lagardère, *Almoravides I*, pp. 79–80; Messier, *Almoravids*, p. 55.

[50] Masonen and Fisher, 'The Almoravid conquest of Ghana'.

[51] Burkhalter, 'Listening for silences in Almoravid history', pp. 108–9.

[52] See de Moraes Farias, *Arabic Medieval Inscriptions from the Republic of Mali*; Hunwick, 'Gao and the Almoravids'; Lange, 'Les rois de Gao-Sané et les Almoravides'.

to advance on a town, set up camp, and then to send messengers with letters containing the terms of submission to the Zanata amir who controlled the area. In the case of a surrender, the amir would be dispatched to Marrakesh to be honourably received by Yusuf b. Tashfin, and allowed to remain in possession of the town, or at least in residence, under the supervision of an Almoravid garrison and military governor. If the town's amir refused to accept terms, the town was besieged and taken by violent means.

The precise chronology of the Almoravid advance is unclear and oscillates between the 1060s and the 1070s thanks to Ibn Abi Zar''s colourful but contradictory account penned 300 years later.[53] In earlier sources, the main Almoravid thrust north is dated to 1073–4 when Yusuf b. Tashfin's paternal cousin, Mazdali, took an army to reduce Salé on the Atlantic coast and Yati b. Isma'il marched against Meknes, which was controlled by the Zanata amir Khayr b. Khazar.[54] The Almoravid commander sent the requisite messengers to Khayr b. Khazar who consulted with the other Zanata chiefs in Meknes, who finally agreed to submit if they could go to Marrakesh and negotiate their own terms with Yusuf b. Tashfin. Yati accepted this, appointed an Almoravid governor to Meknes, and returned to Marrakesh with Khayr b. Khazar and his fellow amirs who were well received by Yusuf. Ibn 'Idhari reports that Khayr then returned and 'continued to live just outside Meknes until he died'.[55]

According to Ibn 'Idhari it was at this point that Yusuf b. Tashfin took the title Commander of the Muslims (*amīr al-muslimīn*) and publicly associated the Almoravid movement with the 'Abbasid caliphs in Baghdad.[56] The following year one of Yusuf's numerous cousins, Yahya b. Wasinu, led the advance on the northern city of Fes which was controlled by two Zanata Maghrawa brothers, Futuh and Dunas b. Hamama.[57] They refused to submit and the Lamtuna are said to have launched a bloody seven-day assault during which they killed the Maghrawa and their fellow Zanata of the Banu Ifran tribe 'in the mosques and streets' of the city.[58] Eventually, Futuh and Dunas

53 Lagardère, *Almoravides I*, pp. 92–3.

54 Ibn 'Idhari, *al-Bayan*, vol. 4, pp. 22–3.

55 Ibid., vol. 4, p. 23.

56 Ibid.

57 Ibid., vol. 4, p. 24. According to Ibn Abi Zar', the brothers were called Futuh and 'Ajisa b. Dunas b. Tamim; *Rawd al-Qirtas*, p. 141.

58 According to the account of the Fasi chronicler, Ibn Abi Zar', which bears a suspicious resemblance to the story of the conquest of Sijilmasa, the Almoravids first besieged Fes in 1065 (457 AH) and, when the Zanata fled, they made a truce with the inhabitants before moving further north. The Zanata, led by Tamim, the son of Futuh's cousin Mu'ansar, returned and recaptured the city, killing the entire Almoravid garrison in the process. This

sued for a safe conduct (*amān*) and were allowed to leave the city. Fes was to become an important Almoravid provincial capital, and it was the Almoravids who finally united its two pre-existing townships into a single city encircled by one wall.[59] From Fes, the Almoravids moved eastwards along the Taza corridor towards the Muluwiya valley and Tlemcen, which was invested by Mazdali and his son Yahya in 1075–6. The Zanata chief, al-'Abbas b. Yahya, decided to negotiate a settlement and journeyed to Marrakesh to be honourably received by Yusuf b. Tashfin before returning to Tlemcen as an Almoravid client ruler under the oversight of Yahya b. Mazdali, who had become the town's military governor. A new Almoravid citadel called Tagrart was built alongside old Tlemcen (Agadir) to house Yahya and an Almoravid garrison.[60]

Following the trade routes as ever, the Almoravid advance now turned in two separate directions. One line of advance took them east from Tlemcen into the central Maghrib to Ténès, Oran and, finally, Algiers in the early 1080s.[61] The other line traversed the Muluwiya valley west through the Rif mountains towards the Mediterranean coast, the Ghumara and Gharb regions and, finally, the Straits ports of Tangier and Ceuta, which were controlled by Saqqut al-Barghawati, previously a governor for the Hammadids, who had become independent ruler of a Maghribi principality similar to the Ta'ifa kingdoms in al-Andalus. Saqqut died in the Almoravid conquest of Tangier in 1077–8 after which his son, Diya' al-Dawla, fell back on Ceuta until that too fell to the Almoravids in 1083–4. This was the culmination of the Almoravid project to break the hegemony of the Zanata and Barghawata over the Maghrib.[62] Yusuf b. Tashfin largely managed the conquests from his capital, Marrakesh, and as each area was conquered he gave it a new administrative structure that transformed tribal lands and urban principalities into Almoravid provinces controlled from major towns by garrisons of Almoravid warriors, councils of Maliki jurists and offices of Arabised scribes.

The Almoravid Crossing into al-Andalus

Yusuf b. Tashfin had no initial strategy to cross the Straits of Gibraltar and incorporate al-Andalus into his growing empire, given that his interests and those of the Almoravids lay in the conquest of the Sahara and the Maghrib.

triggered the second Almoravid siege of the city and its eventual capture around 1070; *Rawd al-Qirtas*, p. 141.

59 Bosch Vilá, *Los Almorávides*, p. 115.

60 Ibn 'Idhari, *al-Bayan*, vol. 4, p. 25.

61 Bosch Vilá, *Los Almorávides*, p. 125.

62 Lagardère, *Almoravides I*, p. 97.

However, as Almoravid control over the Maghrib stabilised during the 1080s, Yusuf b. Tashfin became increasingly aware of the precarious Muslim political position in al-Andalus, visible across the glittering waters of the Straits of Gibraltar. Messages from the Andalusi Muslim community pleaded with the Almoravid amir to take on another jihad, the defence of al-Andalus from the advance of the Christian powers of northern Iberia who had begun to exploit the political fragmentation that had resulted from the slow demise of the Umayyad caliphate of Córdoba, abolished in 1031.

As the power of the Umayyads had diminished, political power had passed to an assortment of local notables, ex-Umayyad governors and military commanders based in the many cities of al-Andalus, who are collectively known as the Ta'ifa kings (Ar. *mulūk al-ṭawā'if*, Sp. Taifas Reyes), which is often rendered in English as 'Party Kings'. Although 'party' here carries the sense of a political group or faction, ironically, many Ta'ifa rulers were reputed to greatly enjoy wine, women and song. Although this is something of a caricature, there was a stark contrast between the rather opulent lifestyle of the Andalusi ruling elite and the more austere mores of the Almoravids still fresh from the desert, which fed into a perception that the Ta'ifa rulers were degenerate Muslims in contrast to the simple, pious Almoravids.[63]

This perception was strengthened by the fact that the Ta'ifa kings generally avoided battle with the Christian enemy by making large tribute payments (*parias*) to the kings of Castile or Aragon, who thereby seemed to be the Ta'ifa kings' masters in the eyes of the Muslim population. These tribute payments could be funded only through the imposition of heavy uncanonical taxes and they did not necessarily prevent devastating Christian raids, which further exacerbated popular resentment against the Ta'ifa rulers as well as undermining the tax base. In reality, this policy of appeasement reflected the fact that the size of most Ta'ifa principalities made it difficult for them to field large armies, while political divisions and rivalries among them prevented the formation of an effective Muslim coalition against the Christian kingdoms. Moreover, relations of marriage, kinship and friendship blurred the boundaries between Christian and Muslim among the ruling elites on either side of the frontier. Alfonso VI, the most dangerous enemy of the Ta'ifa kings, had spend time as the guest of the Dhu'l-Nunids of Toledo and one of his concubines was an aristocratic Muslim woman, known in Spanish as *la mora Zaida*.[64]

[63] See Wasserstein, *The Rise and Fall of the Party Kings*.

[64] Barton, *Conquerors, Brides and Concubines*, pp. 123–7.

Despite these ties, growing Castilian pressure upon the Ta'ifa kingdoms pushed al-Mu'tamid b. 'Abbad, the ruler of Seville, to appeal to Yusuf b. Tashfin and the Almoravids to protect the Muslims of al-Andalus from the Christian advance. The immediate cause of his plea seems to have been a rupture in the treaty between León-Castile and Seville occasioned by al-Mu'tamid's late payment of his annual tribute, although the legend that he refused Alfonso VI's request that his pregnant wife be allowed to come to either the great mosque of Córdoba or Madinat al-Zahra' to give birth points to the close almost familial relations between Christian and Muslim monarchs.[65] Al-Mu'tamid added insult to injury by intemperately assassinating Alfonso VI's ambassador, an Andalusi Jew called Ibn Shalib whom the Ta'ifa king saw as a presumptuous traitor. Alfonso reacted with a retributive raid in spring 1083 during which he pillaged and plundered the countryside all the way to Tarifa on the Straits. The geographer al-Himyari gives an epic account of the rising tensions between the kings enlivened with fanciful literary vignettes, such as when he depicts Alfonso arriving outside Seville during the course of his campaign and sending a message to al-Mu'tamid, demanding a fan to cool himself and brush away the flies that plagued him. His 'vassal' replied provocatively, 'I see fans of *lamṭiyya* leather in the hands of the Almoravid armies for you and they will relieve [me] of you rather than offer you relief!'[66] Here, 'fans' of *lamṭiyya* leather signified the famous Almoravid shields made with the leather of the desert gazelle (*lamṭ*), which were light but very difficult to penetrate.[67]

Yusuf b. Tashfin was more reluctant to enter al-Andalus than al-Mu'tamid's ebullient response to Alfonso VI suggested: the sources describe him expressing his commitment to wage jihad against the enemies of the Muslims, but regretfully pointing out that he could do nothing in al-Andalus unless he gained control of Ceuta, the most important Maghribi port on the Straits of Gibraltar. At this point the Almoravids had no fleet and no naval experience and it is possible that Yusuf b. Tashfin regarded al-Mu'tamid's approach as a useful way of securing naval assistance to capture Ceuta, which was virtually impregnable by land. Certainly, the conquest of Ceuta soon after was facilitated by the Almoravids' use of a large ship belonging to al-Mu'tamid to strengthen their naval blockade of the port.

In the meantime, the situation in al-Andalus steadily worsened and the Andalusis dispatched letter after letter to a still hesitant Yusuf b. Tashfin

[65] al-Himyari, *Rawd al-Mi'tar*, p. 84. Huici Miranda considered this story absurd; *Las grandes batallas*, pp. 21–5.

[66] al-Himyari, *Rawd al-Mi'tar*, p. 85.

[67] al-Idrisi, *Opus Geographicum*, fasc. 1–4, p. 224.

begging for assistance. The eventual trigger for the Almoravids to enter the Andalusi arena was the capture of Toledo by Alfonso VI of León-Castile in 1085. This was the first major Muslim city to fall into Christian hands and its loss sent shock waves through the Andalusi Muslim community, who feared that it was just the start. ʿAbd Allah b. Buluggin, Ta'ifa king of Granada, describes Alfonso VI's subsequent policy as, 'to exact tribute from a city year after year and to harass it with various forms of aggressions until it weakened and succumbed, as Toledo had done'.[68] Al-Muʿtamid and the other Ta'ifa kings argued over the best course of action and reluctantly decided that help from the Almoravids was probably the least bad option in the circumstances. This was the context for al-Muʿtamid's famous quip, 'Better a camel keeper than a swineherd', meaning that it was preferable to serve the Muslim Yusuf b. Tashfin than be subjugated by the Christian Alfonso.[69]

The Ta'ifa kings, therefore, sent an embassy of eminent jurists across the Straits of Gibraltar to meet Yusuf b. Tashfin in person between Tangier and Ceuta and to plead for assistance.[70] Al-Muʿtamid offered the Almoravid amir Algeciras as a base for his troops and promised to evacuate it in thirty days. Yusuf b. Tashfin, perhaps already wary of the good faith of the Ta'ifa kings, mobilised his Almoravid warriors and sailed immediately across the Straits to occupy Algeciras, the first Andalusi possession of the Almoravids, where 'they permitted the fighters (*ghuzāt*) to enter . . . and the mosques and public squares filled up with humble volunteers'.[71] Meanwhile, the Zirid rulers of Granada, Sanhaja Berbers themselves, celebrated the coming of the Almoravids with drumming and public festivities heartened by the 'widespread reports of their good deeds, their zeal for the hereafter and their justice'.[72]

Yusuf b. Tashfin then moved to rendezvous with al-Muʿtamid and the Ta'ifa kings of Granada and Badajoz for an offensive against Alfonso VI of León-Castile, who advanced to meet the Muslims sure that he would win after years of successful raiding in Muslim territory. Although the Muslim sources exaggerate the size of his army and depict a vast Christian coalition, it seems that Alfonso VI's over-confidence persuaded him to advance with a relatively small army. The two sides met at the Battle of Zallaqa (Sagrajas) on Friday, 23 October 1086, near Badajoz in western al-Andalus and, although it was a hard fought battle, victory went to the Muslim coalition amongst

68 Tibi, *The Tibyan*, p. 113.
69 al-Himyari, *Rawd al-Miʿtar*, p. 85.
70 Bosch Vilá, *Los Almorávides*, pp. 132–3.
71 al-Himyari, *Rawd al-Miʿtar*, p. 87.
72 Tibi, *The Tibyan*, p. 115.

whom the Sevillans and the Almoravids distinguished themselves.[73] Although the scale of the Muslim victory at the Battle of Zallaqa is inflated in Arabic sources, it did mark a halt in the Castilian offensive. Yusuf b. Tashfin did not pursue the victory, however, and returned to the Maghrib soon afterwards without regaining Toledo for the Muslims, despite al-Muʿtamid's desire that they push their advantage home.[74] This sudden withdrawal, attributed to the death of his son Sir or to unspecified matters related to a fleet in the Straits, showed the limits of his ambition in al-Andalus at this point. With the benefit of hindsight, ʿAbd Allah b. Buluggin of Granada gives another reason for Yusuf b. Tashfin's precipitous departure for the Maghrib, saying:

> The Amir of the Muslims made for home once he had heard and seen for himself such disagreement among us that he could visualise no prospect of our survival in the peninsula.[75]

In fact, it was the toxic combination of Ta'ifa disunity and Christian raiding that persistently pulled the Almoravids into the complicated Andalusi political and military arena. While the Maghrib remained stable, Yusuf b. Tashfin was drawn back to al-Andalus four more times by the faction fighting among the Ta'ifa kings that allowed the Christians to raid, pillage and capture Muslim territory. From the perspective of the Arab-Islamic chronicle tradition, the last decades of Yusuf's reign were first and foremost a series of crossings to al-Andalus for a jihad that rapidly mutated from warfare against Christian aggressors into the Almoravid conquest of the Ta'ifa principalities to achieve the Muslim unity and common purpose necessary to hold the frontier of the Dar al-Islam. It is worth remembering that the Muslim world had not sustained any major territorial losses prior to this era and that the Christian advance in Iberia and the Levantine Crusades that began in 1096 were traumatic and unexpected reversals of what Muslims had assumed was God's plan. From this perspective, the Almoravids appeared as military saviours in contrast to the Ta'ifa kings whose manoeuvres struck even their own subjects as betrayals of Islam.

Yusuf b. Tashfin's second expedition took place in 1088 in response to appeals from al-Muʿtamid and Muslim notables from eastern al-Andalus, threatened by the roving Christian nobleman Rodrigo Díaz de Vivar, who served Alfonso VI or the Ta'ifa kings of Saragossa, depending on the winds of political fortune, and another nobleman, García Jiménez, who had possession of the fortress of Aledo from which he could raid Muslim land between

[73] See Huici Miranda, *Las grandes batallas*, pp. 44–77; Lagardère, *Le vendredi de Zallaqa*.
[74] al-Himyari, *Rawd al-Miʿtar*, p. 93.
[75] Tibi, *The Tibyan*, p. 118.

Murcia and Lorca.[76] The Almoravids joined the Ta'ifa kings to recapture Aledo, but the siege that followed was a complete failure partly due to the persistent rivalries between the Ta'ifa kings, several of whom canvassed and lobbied Yusuf to support them against other Ta'ifa kings rather than focusing on the campaign.[77] They compounded their errors in his eyes by reverting to negotiations with Alfonso VI and agreeing once again to pay him annual tribute. In 1090, Yusuf b. Tashfin crossed to Algeciras once more, but this time he had a plan,

> to put an end to the reigns of these Andalusi lords who neglected the affairs of their governments, lacked any spirit of solidarity or courage to oppose the [Christian] reconquest, and indulged in pleasures and a dissolute lifestyle, while burdening their subjects with illegal taxes and levies.[78]

While he did not arrive in response to further pleas from the Ta'ifa kings for military assistance, he did have support and encouragement from many members of the Maliki juridical establishment in al-Andalus.[79] The *qāḍī* of Granada, for one, had been in communication with Yusuf b. Tashfin for some time asserting that the Zirids had lost their right to rule, a stance that the Zirid king, 'Abd Allah b. Buluggin, considered a betrayal. Granadan territories lay close to the Almoravid bridgehead at Algeciras and Yusuf quickly travelled to Granada and forced 'Abd Allah to abdicate before returning to Málaga and ousting his brother Tamim. 'Abd Allah vainly tried to preserve a modicum of his wealth and possessions as Yusuf's men went through his inventories appropriating cash, jewellery, clothing and slaves, while threatening him with banishment to the Sahara if he withheld anything.[80] He and his brother were then dispatched to the Maghrib with their families, while Yusuf appointed his nephew Sir b. Abi Bakr as governor of the new province and returned to Marrakesh.

The acquisition of Zirid Granada gave the Almoravids a significant presence in southern al-Andalus from which to prosecute the jihad against both Christian and Ta'ifa kings, and the new Almoravid governor of Granada soon moved against 'Abbadid Seville. Almoravid contingents fanned out to invest al-Mu'tamid's main towns – Tarifa, Córdoba and Seville – while another contingent marched east to besiege Almería, the seat of al-Mu'tasim b. Sumadih. Al-Mu'tamid called on his previous enemy

[76] Lagardère, *Almoravides I*, pp. 122–3; Barton and Fletcher, *The World of El Cid*, pp. 114–15.
[77] Bosch Vilá, *Los Almorávides*, pp. 138–43.
[78] Lagardère, *Almoravides I*, p. 126.
[79] Bosch Vilá, *Los Almorávides*, p. 145.
[80] Tibi, *The Tibyan*, p. 158.

Alfonso VI for aid, but, even with the help of the Castilian nobleman Alvar Fañez, his possessions fell one by one culminating with Seville itself in September 1091. A few years later in 1094, Sir b. Abi Bakr moved against al-Mutawakkil of Badajoz for consorting with Alfonso VI. Meanwhile, Muhammad b. 'A'isha, one of Yusuf b. Tashfin's sons, extended Almoravid control eastwards to Murcia.

Slightly further north up the coast, Valencia remained in the hands of its Ta'ifa ruler, al-Qadir, the ousted Dhu'l-Nunid ruler of Toledo who held Valencia as a Christian fief, bolstered not by Muslim forces but by an aristocratic Castilian mercenary, Rodrigo Díaz de Vivar, 'El Campeador', later immortalised in legend, song and even film as 'El Cid', either from the Arabic *al-sayyid* (the nobleman) or *al-sīd* (the lion), a more suitable epithet for a fighter.[81] In reality, Rodrigo Díaz was not an uncomplicated champion of the Castilian Catholic cause, like so many other actors in this drama, he operated strategically to secure his own interests, serving Muslim masters while in exile from Castile and then usurping power from them to regain favour with the monarchs of León-Castile and Aragon. The population of Valencia deeply resented the *de facto* rule of Rodrigo and his knights on behalf of al-Qadir and the harsh taxes they were forced to pay, and in 1092, emboldened by Rodrigo Díaz's temporary absence from the city, the city's *qāḍī*, Abu Ahmad Ja'far b. Jahhaf, called on the Almoravids in Murcia, commanded by Muhammad b. 'A'isha, for aid. Al-Qadir realised the danger he was in and tried to remove his family and treasure from the city and escape, but he was captured and put to death by the slave of a man he had previously killed.[82]

An Almoravid garrison arrived soon after only to find itself embroiled in the conflictual politics of the city. Despite his popular mandate, Ibn Jahhaf's assumption of the autocratic manner of a Ta'ifa king soon lost him support and when Rodrigo returned to besiege Valencia, Ibn Jahhaf ended up making a treaty with him and ousting the Almoravid garrison. Many Valencians resisted Rodrigo Díaz's return to the city, but after a bitter siege of over a year and a half waiting for help from the Almoravids that never came, starvation forced them to open the gates to him in 1094. On his re-entry to the city, Rodrigo had Ibn Jahhaf publicly burnt to death, ostensibly in revenge for his role in the death of al-Qadir but also for his vacillations between Rodrigo and the Almoravids.[83] The latter were not prepared to relinquish Valencia,

[81] Hitchcock, *Muslim Spain Reconsidered*, pp. 130–1; Rodrigo Díaz de Vivar was related to Alvar Fañez, mentioned above, who had helped al-Mu'tamid to resist the Almoravid advance.

[82] Ibn 'Idhari, *al-Bayan*, vol. 4, pp. 27–8.

[83] Ibid., vol. 4, p. 33.

however, and Yusuf b. Tashfin ordered a series of generals to march against Rodrigo.

When they made no headway, the elderly Yusuf b. Tashfin prepared to cross to al-Andalus once again in 1097 to personally direct an Almoravid offensive. Although his Sanhaja warriors, heartened by his presence, defeated Christian contingents at Consuegra, Cuenca and Alcira, they did not manage to dislodge Rodrigo from Valencia.[84] That end was achieved only after Yusuf b. Tashfin's return to the Maghrib and Rodrigo's death in 1099, which left Valencia in the hands of his wife, Jimena, who evacuated the city at the behest of Alfonso VI in 1102. The veteran Almoravid amir Mazdali, ensconced nearby, led his men in to the city to find the population decimated and buildings ravaged by fires lit by the departing Christians.[85]

The Ta'ifa kings' gamble had not paid off: although they had halted the Christian advance with Almoravid help, the latter proved to be an even greater threat to their existence than Castile. They felt they had little option but to seek assistance from their erstwhile enemy Alfonso VI and Christian mercenaries such as El Cid, but such strategic choices laid them open to sharp, religiously grounded criticism from their subjects, voiced most effectively by Maliki *fuqahā'*. At each stage of the Almoravid military advance, Yusuf b. Tashfin's actions were legitimised by a plethora of legal opinions from such jurists denouncing the Ta'ifa kings and lauding the righteousness of the Almoravid jihad. He even received positive legal opinions from such eastern luminaries as al-Ghazali.[86] Beaten by this combination of polemic and power, successive Ta'ifa rulers, including 'Abd Allah b. Buluggin of Granada and al-Mu'tamid of Seville, had to pack their bags and make the long journey south to Aghmat where they spent the rest of their days in exile. Others, such as al-Mutawakkil b. al-Aftas of Badajoz and al-Qadir of Valencia, were killed by the Almoravids or their own irate subjects for treachery.

The same year that Valencia was retaken, Yusuf b. Tashfin held ceremonies in Marrakesh and then Granada attended by an array of Almoravid amirs and other notables to publicly acknowledge his son 'Ali as his heir over his Maghribi and Andalusi domains.[87] During 'Ali's reign (r. 1106–43) the remaining Ta'ifa kingdom of Saragossa near the Pyrenees (1110) and the Balearic Islands (1115) were conquered and absorbed into the empire, transforming the Almoravids from the distant exotic Saharan movement described by al-Bakri working at his desk in Almería in the 1060s to an important

[84] Bosch Vilá, *Los Almorávides*, pp. 160–2.

[85] Barton and Fletcher, *World of El Cid*, p. 147; Ibn 'Idhari, *al-Bayan*, vol. 4, pp. 36–7.

[86] Bosch Vilá, *Los Almorávides*, pp. 149–50.

[87] Ibn 'Idhari, *al-Bayan*, vol. 4, p. 37.

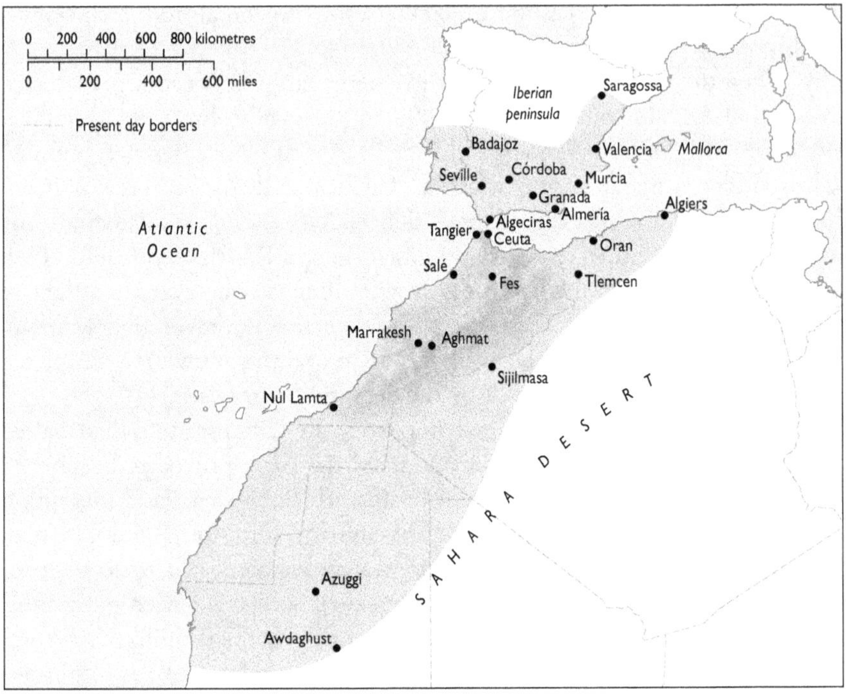

Figure 2.2 The Almoravid empire

western Mediterranean power, ruling from Ghana in the south to the lands of the Franks in the north. In the course of their conquests, the Almoravids had moved further and further from their Saharan homeland and become masters of a diverse collection of tribes, towns and rural communities. At the outset, they had little experience of government and even less of administering an empire, therefore, it was a major challenge for them to create an effective bureaucracy stretching from the Sahara to Saragossa. However, the structures put in place at the start of the movement by Ibn Yasin and Yahya b. 'Umar – the military power and clan loyalties of the Sanhaja directed by the religio-legal framework of Malikism – provided the basis upon which the Almoravids could fit themselves into wider Islamic paradigms of power and authority and construct a legitimate government.

Almoravid Government

By the eleventh century, there were two forms of legitimate Islamic rule. First, the caliphate, a form of universal religio-political rule either as a 'successor' (*khalīfa*, caliph) of the Prophet or as God's deputy (*khalīfa*) on earth which was a theoretically universal position held by the 'Abbasids of Baghdad until their line was extinguished by the Mongols in 1258, although they faced earlier challenges for the position from the Fatimids and the Umayyads of Córdoba. Prior to the demise of the 'Abbasid caliphate in the mid-thirteenth century, Muslim theorists saw the existence of legitimate Muslim rule as essential to validate the religious life of the entire community, so when the 'Abbasid caliphs lost real power to the Buyids and the Seljuks in the tenth and eleventh centuries, some scholars felt constrained to legitimise the *de facto* rule of these warlords.

A generally accepted precondition for a claim to the caliphate was Qurashi Arab ancestry, therefore it was unthinkable to elevate these warlords to that esteemed role. The result was the articulation of a second institution of rule, the sultanate, whose holder, a sultan, was more likely to be a politico-military figure who based his legitimacy upon appointment by the caliph or defence of the faith rather than on his own religio-political authority. The sultanate was not inherently universal and soon became a plural form of rule, enabling the Almoravids to insert themselves into a legitimate framework of rule by taking on the role of 'Abbasid lieutenants in the Islamic west, expressed through their use of the title 'Commander of the Muslims' (*amīr al-muslimīn*), which mirrored the caliphal title 'Commander of the Faithful' (*amīr al-mu'minīn*). A Lamtuna chief was thus transformed into a sultan in the service of the 'Abbasids who were themselves connected back in time to the Prophet himself.

Ibn 'Idhari attributes the moment at which Yusuf b. Tashfin took the title 'Commander of the Muslims' to 1073–4 and connects it to Yusuf's public recognition of the 'Abbasid caliph as his symbolic overlord, an apparent mark of humility that nonetheless enabled the Almoravids to tap into the huge reservoir of Islamic legitimacy inherent in the caliphate without taking the risk of attempting to claim it for themselves.

> The shaykhs of the tribes gathered before the amir Abu Ya'qub Yusuf b. Tashfin and said to him, 'You are the caliph of God (*khalīfat Allāh*) in the Maghrib and your status is too high for you to be called other than Commander of the Faithful (*amīr al-mu'minīn*).' He replied, 'God forbid that I should be called by this title, for the caliphs are known by this title and I am the servant of the 'Abbasid caliph and the champion of his cause in the west.' They said, 'You must have a title to distinguish yourself.' He replied to them, 'It will be Commander of the Muslims.'[88]

Although some accept this dating, Lévi-Provençal believed that Yusuf b. Tashfin took this title somewhat later when his rule was more

[88] Ibn 'Idhari, *al-Bayan*, vol. 4, p. 23.

firmly established and the conquest of the Ta'ifa kingdoms was underway.[89] Whatever the exact chronology, the combination of the title *amīr al-muslimīn* and recognition of the 'Abbasid caliph appears to have been in place by the 1090s. Between 1096 and 1098, the young jurist Abu Bakr b. al-'Arabi and his father secured formal recognition of Yusuf b. Tashfin's status by the 'Abbasid caliph al-Mustazhir when they were in the Islamic east, a trip that some see as an official Almoravid embassy and others as a more serendipitous move on the part of Ibn al-'Arabi's father to improve his prospects of a post with the Almoravids when he returned west.[90] According to the case they made to the 'Abbasid caliph, it was already normal practice for the Friday prayer in Yusuf b. Tashfin's domains be given in the name of the 'Abbasid caliph as well as his own. The recognition that Yusuf received from the 'Abbasid caliph and eastern jurists like al-Ghazali therefore helped to strengthen a legitimating construct already in place.

Use of the title *amīr al-muslimīn* with its connotations of 'Abbasid investiture passed from Yusuf b. Tashfin to his direct lineal descendants, as the Saharan practice of transferring power to the most senior male in the clan gradually shifted towards dynastic rule and the succession of the son named as heir during his father's lifetime. Regardless of their elevation above the other Sanhaja amirs and recognition by the 'Abbasids, however, the Almoravid rulers were still considered to be *primus inter pares* rather than autocrats, and they cultivated the accessibility also characteristic of the early Umayyads and the Seljuks. As we shall see, Ibn Tumart, the founder of the Almohad movement, was able to address 'Ali b. Yusuf directly in the great mosque of Marrakesh, unhindered by body guards or a royal enclosure.

In contrast to some Seljuk sultans, however, who rarely entered Baghdad, their capital, Yusuf b. Tashfin swapped the nomadic pattern of his forebears for a more sedentary lifestyle in Marrakesh, which he developed into the permanent centre, *ḥaḍra*, of the empire and the heart of the administration, a policy continued by his son 'Ali. Although Almoravid rulers did travel through their Maghribi domains and cross over to al-Andalus, they spent a noticeable amount of their time in Marrakesh, maintaining oversight over their territories by use of a network of messengers who carried letters backwards and forwards to the provinces in which Almoravid rule took the form of urban-based military governors and garrisons, often housed in newly constructed enclaves or citadels.

These provincial governors had overarching responsibility for the

[89] Lévi-Provençal, 'Le titre souverain des Almoravides', pp. 268–70.

[90] Lagardère, *Almoravides I*, pp. 165–6; Bennison, 'The necklace of al-Shifā'', pp. 269–72.

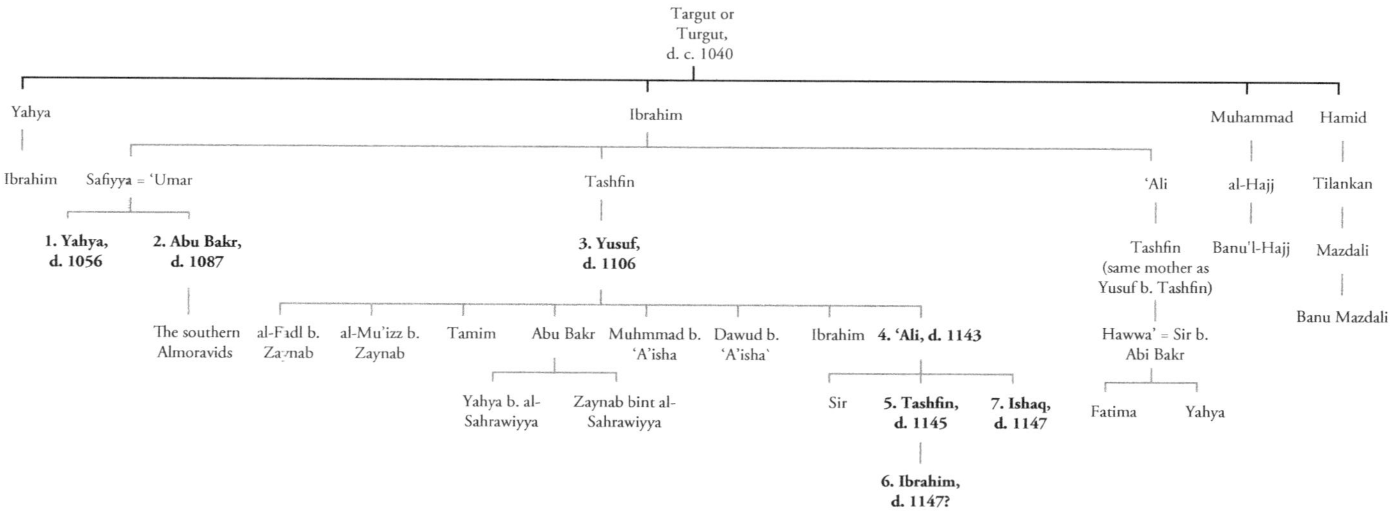

Figure 2.3 Genealogical table of the Almoravid Banu Targut

collection of taxes, the mobilisation of military contingents and the direction of campaigns, when commanded by the amir. Although the social composition of the Almoravid ruling elite will be considered in more detail in Chapter 4, it is worth noting here that provincial military governorships rotated among a relatively small pool of men drawn from Yusuf b. Tashfin's clan, the Banu Targut or Turgut of the Lamtuna, and clans related to them by marriage and kinship. His many sons held governorships and military commands, as did his numerous cousins and nephews. These posts were not generally held for life, but were rotated fairly regularly at the command of the amir.

The rank and file of the Almoravid army was originally drawn from the Sanhaja tribes, some of whom remained in their homelands while others were resettled in garrisons or granted conquered lands (*inzālāt*) to support themselves and their animals. In the early days of the Almoravid movement, their remuneration took the form of a share of the booty captured during campaigns, but Yusuf b. Tashfin introduced salaries funded by taxation paid out to those registered in the military registers (*dīwān al-jund*).[91] Although the number of combatants mobilised for different campaigns is often inflated in the sources, the overall impression given is that the Almoravid military presence across the empire was quite sparse and highly dependent upon the cooperation of local communities as they moved further from the Sahara. As in the early Islamic conquests where relatively small numbers of Arabs ruled a large area, the number of Sanhaja warriors remained low and smaller towns and tribes remained largely self-governing as long as their representatives offered the Almoravids their allegiance, paid taxes and contributed men to military campaigns. As the empire developed, the army became more diversified: Yusuf b. Tashfin recruited a corps of black slaves and in the later Almoravid empire, Christians, both slaves and mercenaries, were a vital military resource, although they were deployed only in the Maghrib where they would not be required to fight co-religionists.

Military governors were assisted in the religious, legal and civilian aspects of government by Maliki judges and officials drawn for the most part from Arabic-literate urban populations. Some were appointed to serve in their own communities, but high judicial personnel were often circulated and posted to other cities to avoid their loyalties being divided between their community and the Almoravids. Moreover, it was not uncommon for Maghribi jurists to serve in al-Andalus and vice-versa, giving them broad experience of the empire as a whole.[92] As in most medieval Islamic government, law

[91] Lagardère, *Almoravides I*, pp. 194–6.
[92] See El Hour, 'El Cadiazgo en Granada bajo los Almorávides'.

encompassed both the Shari'a administered by the *qāḍī* and the 'justice' meted out by the ruler or his representative which could take arbitrary forms, particularly in cases related to rebellion, public disorder and other politically loaded forms of criminality.

The replacement of local customs by a standardised Islamic Maliki legal framework was central to the Almoravid project and, as we have seen, many Maliki jurists enthusiastically endorsed it. Although the Almohads later mocked and criticised the Almoravid amirs for their inability to take religious and political decisions without the assistance of a jurist, the initial impression given by their reliance on the *fuqahā'* was more positive. It is easy to forget that there was very little uniformity in legal and administrative praxis in the Maghrib prior to the rise of the Almoravids. In the same way that the Ottomans relied on the Hanafi jurist, Ebu's-Su'ud to synthesise varied customary laws (*qānūn*) with the Shari'a to create a rational empire-wide legal system in the sixteenth century, so the Almoravid amirs recruited Maliki jurists to create a legal system for their empire over and above the myriad versions of customary law (*'urf*) followed by the tribes. This was the process alluded to by Ibn 'Idhari when he contrasted the pre-Almoravid situation where every tribe followed its own amir's rulings (*ḥukm*) to the Almoravid jihad to propagate the Shari'a and the Truth.[93]

The Almoravids also recruited secretaries (*kuttāb*) and other civilian administrators who possessed the requisite Arabic language skills to staff their offices of government. Many of these individuals came from al-Andalus but migrated to serve the Almoravids in Marrakesh which became a conduit for the spread of Arab-Islamic culture in the southern Maghrib. The Almoravid resort to an established bureaucratic class fitted a common pattern of conquering warrior tribesmen utilising the scribal and literary talents of their new subjects, and both the Seljuks and the Mongols similarly relied upon the Persian bureaucrats of Iraq and Iran. When the Almoravid amir wished to transmit instructions or information, he would inform one of his chief secretaries of the required content and the latter would compose a missive in the correct kind of literary Arabic, usually *saj'* (rhyming prose). If multiple copies were required for dispatch to provincial governors, a team of scribes would prepare the additional copies.

Other civilian officials with numerical as well as literary skills ran the fiscal administration. Although the Almoravid ruler determined what taxes should be collected in consultation with the jurists (*fuqahā'*), their actual collection and jurisdiction over the treasury (*bayt al-māl*) was often managed

[93] Ibn 'Idhari, *al-Bayan*, vol. 4, pp. 9–10.

by local civilian bureaucrats overseen by a civilian financial administrator, the *mushrif* or *'āmil*, who was responsible to the Sanhaja military governor. This could give civilians considerable leverage over the Sanhaja. Towards the end of the Almoravid era, for instance, the military governor of Fes, Yahya b. al-Sahrawiyya, a grandson of Yusuf b. Tashfin, is described as virtually begging al-Jayyani, the *mushrif* of Fes, for money to celebrate his wedding![94] Shortly afterwards, this same *mushrif* betrayed the Almoravids and admitted the Almohads to Fes.

Although the Almoravids are often seen as being very exclusive and only allowing certain Sanhaja Lamtuna clans to enjoy the fruits of conquest, their reliance on Maliki jurists and Andalusi bureaucrats provided an *entrée* into their ranks for at least a section of the urban Arab(ised) elites of the Maghrib and al-Andalus. Scholars disagree, however, as to whether such bureaucrats and jurists can be considered 'Almoravids' or not. On the one hand, Messier sees a stark difference between the veiled Sanhaja politico-military elite and those who served them out of mere opportunism.[95] On the other hand, over time intermarriage could blur those lines: for instance, Zaynab, Yusuf b. Tashfin's granddaughter, married Ahmad b. 'Atiyya, a scribe of Andalusi origin born in Marrakesh who worked for the Almoravids as his father had done before him.[96] Regardless of whether we see civilian jurists and scribes as Almoravids or not, their incorporation into government was a tactical move that provided the religio-legal and administrative expertise that the Sanhaja lacked, and added considerable legitimacy to the Almoravid enterprise by giving it a normative Islamic character.

The Reigns of 'Ali b. Yusuf (1106–43) and Tashfin b. 'Ali (1143–5)

Yusuf b. Tashfin died at an advanced age, although probably not the 100 lunar years claimed by Ibn Abi Zar', in September 1106, and he was succeeded by one of his younger sons, 'Ali, who had been born in Ceuta to a Christian concubine and educated in the Andalusi Arabic tradition.[97] 'Ali had formally received the oath of allegiance as heir in Marrakesh and Granada in 1102 and his succession was publicly supported by his brother, Abu'l-Tahir Tamim who led him out by the hand to receive the oath of allegiance after their father's death. He then travelled with him on a tour through the Maghrib and

[94] Ibn al-Abbar, *al-Hulla al-Siyara'*, vol. 2, p. 236; Ibn 'Idhari, *al-Bayan*, vol. 4, p. 102.

[95] Messier, 'Rethinking the Almoravids', pp. 74–5.

[96] See Bennison, 'The salutory tale of Ibn 'Aṭiyya'.

[97] Ibn Abi Zar', *Rawd al-Qirtas*, p. 174; Following Bosch Vilá (*Los Almorávides*, p. 167), Lagardère suggests that Yusuf b. Tashfin was born between 1010 and 1020; *Almoravides I*, p. 149.

across the Straits of Gibraltar to al-Andalus to calm the inevitable fears generated by the death of Yusuf b. Tashfin and the fizzling opposition to his succession from some other members of the clan. His nephew Yahya b. Abi Bakr, governor of Fes, fled to Tlemcen as the new amir approached, but was persuaded to reconcile with his uncle by the veteran amir Mazdali after which he went on pilgrimage, an honourable way to let the dust settle.[98] In al-Andalus the recalcitrant governors of Granada and Córdoba were replaced and Abu'l-Tahir Tamim, the amir's trusted brother, took charge.

'Ali b. Yusuf is often seen as a pale reflection of his father and accounts of his thirty-seven-year reign (1106–43) are frequently reduced to its disastrous second half, but its first decade witnessed the culmination of the Almoravid conquests in al-Andalus and the central Maghrib led by 'Ali and his most trusted Sanhaja generals. Moreover, Marrakesh, 'Ali's main residence throughout his reign, became a flourishing centre of Islamic culture and commerce due in part to his investment in major building programmes that attracted a constant flow of skilled migrants and merchants. The fact that more gold currency came out of the mints during his reign than ever before confirms the wealth of the Almoravids in the first decades of the twelfth century.

The second half of 'Ali b. Yusuf's reign, however, was dominated by problems on the northern frontier of the Almoravid empire in al-Andalus and rising opposition in the vicinity of its capital, Marrakesh. This developed into nearly constant pressure to wage war on two fronts which proved impossible for the Almoravids to sustain. The steady accrual of territories that had characterised Yusuf b. Tashfin's reign and the start of 'Ali b. Yusuf's reign reversed around 1118 and the remainder of 'Ali's reign and the brief reigns of his son Tashfin (r. 1143–5), his grandson Ibrahim (r. 1145–7) and/or his son Ishaq (r. 1145–7) witnessed the loss of Andalusi territories to the Christian kingdoms and a new generation of Muslim 'Ta'ifa' rulers, and the capture of Maghribi lands by the rival Almohads expanding out from the High Atlas mountain range.

After 'Ali b. Yusuf's rule had been accepted across the empire, he made preparations to visit his Andalusi domains and fulfil the responsibility of an Almoravid amir to wage jihad. By this time, Alfonso VI of León-Castile was an elderly man and Portugal was being ruled by a female regent. However, both the kingdom of Aragon and the county of Barcelona were ruled by energetic men, Alfonso I and Raymond Berenguer III, keen to expand their territories south into the neighbouring Muslim Ta'ifa kingdom of Saragossa. In 1108, 'Ali crossed the Straits to direct a campaign against the small fortress

[98] Bosch Vilá, *Los Almorávides*, pp. 175–6.

of Uclés, southeast of Madrid, which was successfully captured. This relatively small victory was transformed into a major blow for Castile when Alfonso VI's son and heir, Sancho, arrived with a relieving force and was killed in the ensuing battle against the Almoravids.[99] In the following year, the Almoravids launched another campaign, this time towards Talavera, southwest of Madrid, which was retaken in 1109, allowing the Almoravid forces to proceed east towards Toledo and ravage the countryside around it while the Castilians, preoccupied with the death and succession of Alfonso VI, were in no position to respond.

The death of al-Musta'in, the Ta'ifa king of Saragossa, the following year offered another opportunity for Almoravid expansion as a section of the population appealed to them to take control of the city. Once they controlled Saragossa, the Almoravids moved to absorb its Balearic dependencies, the islands of Mallorca and Menorca. An apocryphal account of the advice Yusuf b. Tashfin gave to 'Ali on his deathbed included a warning to leave Saragossa as a buffer between Almoravid and Christian territory and, with the benefit of hindsight, it certainly seemed as if the capture of Saragossa over-extended the Almoravids and engaged them in the defence of a city and territory that it was impossible for them to hold, but this was not obvious at the time.[100] Other changes during the years following the capture of Saragossa also had their impact, most notably the deaths of the loyal veterans Sir b. Abi Bakr, who had administered Seville for many years, in late 1113, and Mazdali, who had distinguished himself as governor of Tlemcen and Córdoba prior to his death in battle outside Córdoba, in early 1115.[101]

After a period in Marrakesh, where he initiated several irrigation and building projects, 'Ali b. Yusuf crossed to al-Andalus again in 1117 and presided over a campaign in the west that took him past Lisbon and Santarem, which Sir b. Abi Bakr had regained from the Portuguese, to Coimbra. The latter was only besieged for a short time before 'Ali abandoned the siege and returned to Seville, but raiding *en route* yielded enough booty and captives to give the campaign a veneer of success.[102] The tide began to turn the next year, however, when Alfonso I El Batallador of Aragon, in association with the renowned Crusader Gaston de Béarn, launched an offensive to capture Saragossa with papal backing and the military support of crusading contingents. Saragossa fell in 1118 and when one of 'Ali's brothers, Ibrahim b. Ta'ayasht, tried to push back and regain Saragossa two years later,

[99] Huici Miranda, *Las grandes batallas*, pp. 103–34.
[100] *al-Hulal al-Mawshiyya*, pp. 82–3.
[101] Ibn 'Idhari, *al-Bayan*, vol. 4, pp. 49, 53.
[102] Ibid., vol. 4, p. 56.

he was severely defeated at the Battle of Cutanda near Catalayud in July 1120 which decimated the Almoravid army. The Almoravids had enjoyed the political fruits of their victory at Zallaqa in 1086 for several decades. It had enabled them to remove the Muslim Ta'ifa kings and absorb their territories into the empire, but their legitimacy in al-Andalus was heavily contingent upon their ability to prevent Christian depredations in Muslim territory and this was fatally compromised by the fall of Saragossa and their defeat at Cutanda.

In 1121, a major rebellion against the Almoravids in Córdoba was sparked when an Almoravid 'servant' assaulted a woman. The seriousness of the situation forced 'Ali b. Yusuf to travel to the city himself to calm Córdoban antagonism towards the Sanhaja presence in their city and broker a peace between the population and their Almoravid governor. Popular disgruntlement towards the Almoravids was further exacerbated by Alfonso I El Batallador's leisurely rampage through Muslim territory in the hope of capturing Granada in 1125. Although the Aragonese king did not manage to take Granada, he laid waste to large swathes of Muslim land all the way to Tarifa on the Straits of Gibraltar, leading the Andalusis to wonder why they should put up with arrogant, strangely dressed, Sanhaja warriors in their midst and rising levels of taxation.

Taxation was an especially sore point, the original Almoravid mission was not only jihad against the Christian threat, but also the abolition of illicit taxation and the injustice it represented. As many scholars have noted, the Almoravids were popular, or at least tolerated, as long as they were perceived to be effective protectors against the Christian threat and they did not impose unwelcome extra taxes. Unfortunately, these two objectives were mutually exclusive as it was simply not possible to run an empire and maintain an effective army on the revenue from Qur'anic taxation alone, and 'Ali b. Yusuf was forced to reintroduce taxes considered illicit by many at the same time as Almoravid defence of the marches faltered.

Manpower posed an additional problem. The revitalisation of the Almoravid army with contingents from the Maghrib was becoming impossible due to a rebellion fomented among the Masmuda of the High Atlas by the Almohads. 'Ali b. Yusuf followed the lead of his father and recruited black slaves and Christian mercenaries, some of whom converted to Islam, into the army to supplement the overstretched Sanhaja tribesmen. The military use of slaves and other peripheral groups was a common resort of Islamic rulers, but the rising number of Christians in the Almoravid armies, whether they were converts to Islam or not, was another potential source of criticism.

Another reason given for the reversal of Almoravid military fortunes in al-Andalus is their fighting style. Although the original tactics of the Sanhaja, a combination of camel riders and foot soldiers with long lances, had been modified as they moved north with the substitution of horses for camels and the acquisition of new technologies and tactics from al-Andalus, it is often argued that, while they achieved many military successes on the field of battle where their swift cavalry could be used to good effect, they lacked the military technology or skills to maintain sustained sieges of heavily fortified towns and recapture key cities lost to the Christians. The key to sieges was often, however, a matter of manpower and patience – the ability to fully encircle a city and prevent communications and supplies reaching it and then wait until the starving population opened the gates. Rodrigo Díaz's siege of Valencia, for instance, did not succeed due to a successful assault but due to the complete exhaustion of the city's food supplies. The Almoravids tended to withdraw rather than maintain a siege and in those circumstances when they did recapture towns and fortresses such as Lisbon (1093), Santarem or Uclés (1108), they struggled to adequately garrison or fortify them, which suggests a dearth of manpower as much as tactical problems.

However, the stiffest and most ideologically sophisticated opposition to the Almoravids arose not in al-Andalus but in the Maghrib, a stone's throw from Marrakesh. It took the form of the Almohad movement, a new religio-political mission led by Muhammad b. Tumart, a Masmuda Berber preacher from the Sus valley south of the High Atlas mountains who travelled north to study in Almoravid Córdoba and the Islamic east before returning with the intention of overthrowing the Almoravids in favour of a new regime with sounder religious credentials. Ibn Tumart (d. *c.* 1130) did not live to see the movement he founded become an empire, that was the achievement of his successor (*khalīfa*, caliph), 'Abd al-Mu'min, who fought regular campaigns against the Almoravids for well over a decade before finally capturing their Maghribi cities and crossing the Straits of Gibraltar to claim their Andalusi possessions.

It was these constant campaigns more than any other events that marred the last decade or so of 'Ali b. Yusuf's reign. After his 1121 visit to restore order in Córdoba, 'Ali never visited al-Andalus again and delegated affairs there to his sons, most notably Tashfin, who proved to be an energetic and capable viceroy supported by his relative Yahya b. Ghaniya, governor of Valencia. Despite Tashfin's competent administration of al-Andalus, 'Ali felt obliged to recall him in 1138 in order to prosecute the offensive against 'Abd al-Mu'min and the Almohads who were steadily consolidating their power over the High and Middle Atlas ranges and the southern oasis valleys. Ibn 'Idhari adds the personal twist that Tashfin's brother Sir, the heir apparent, or Sir's mother, were jealous of his success in al-Andalus and therefore engineered his recall.[103]

[103] Ibn 'Idhari, *al-Bayan*, vol. 4, p. 83.

The costs of combatting the Almohads were huge. 'Ali was forced to invest in building a string of fortresses through the High Atlas, and the number of Almoravids killed in action against the Almohads made the renewal of the army virtually impossible. Slowly but surely the Almoravids lost control of the Atlas ranges as their tribes joined the Almohad movement and, in the 1140s, the final contest for the cities and the plains began.

'Ali b. Yusuf died in January 1143 and was succeeded by Tashfin who had become heir after the death of his brother some years earlier. The new amir continued the fight against the Almohads for control of what is now western Algeria with the aid of his loyal chief commander, Reverter, titular viscount of Barcelona, who headed the Almoravids' Christian militia. In 1144, Reverter died during the successful Almohad onslaught on Tlemcen. The Almohads then advanced on the amir Tashfin, who had retreated to the Almoravid fortress at Oran. Ibn 'Idhari gives a dramatic account of Tashfin's end, which is worth quoting in full for the way it captures the sense of the Almoravids as a brave but embattled group lacking the support of the local population and confronted by a powerful and motivated enemy:

> [The Almohad troops] returned to Oran and gathered that day on the mountain overlooking Oran and gave a mighty shout with one voice, 'The light has come, Praise be to God'. The Lamtuna did not shout this phrase so when the commanders of Tashfin's soldiers heard this a tremor ran through them but he ordered them not to advance, fearing an ambush. The Almohads stayed in their camp until noon and then set out to water their animals at the spring from which the people of Oran drank. They returned in a single thrust towards the tent of Tashfin which was pitched opposite the fortress he had built and threw themselves upon him and those with him, including Ibn Mazdali and Bashir al-Rumi. Many commanders died as they sought refuge behind the walls of Oran. The Almohads took the goods, the firewood and other things from Tashfin's camp and piled them at the gate of the fortress and set fire to them, thereby burning down the gates. Tashfin remained at the highest point of the fortress until darkness fell and the fire danced higher. As he watched it, Tashfin became certain of his own destruction and he sallied forth with Ibn Mazdali, the renegade Christian (*'ilj*) Bashir, and Sandal the eunuch. As for Bashir, his beard and the mane and tail of his horse were burnt. As for Sandal the eunuch, he fell into the fire and became a lump of charcoal. As for Ibn Mazdali, he rode between the dead around the fortress then slipped away secretly until he reached the walls of Oran, his mind stunned. He remained stupefied for three days and then died. Tashfin and the renegade Bashir headed to the mill on the river but the people at the mill stood against them, so they

> turned to the salt pans and rode. Bashir managed to escape but the leg of Tashfin's horse, Rayhana, buckled and she fell into a great ditch and her neck broke. So died the horse of Tashfin on the night of 17 Sha'ban . . . [Afterwards] they searched for Tashfin and found him dead. They exposed his corpse on a cross at his fortress and sent his head to Tinmall.[104]

The details of Tashfin's last stand have an embellished and fictive quality. The individuals with him seem to symbolise the groups that made up the Almoravid politico-military elite at this time: the Banu Targut kin-group represented by Ibn Mazdali, Christian mercenaries in the form of Bashir, and also slaves such as Sandal the eunuch.[105] There is also a certain grim humour in the account with Sandal, a name meaning Sandalwood, transformed by the fire into a lump of charcoal as he tried to escape! According to some sources, Tashfin's body was never found, leaving his fate open to popular myth transforming him into a hero who rode into the sea to return one day much like King Arthur.

Whatever the true circumstances of Tashfin b. 'Ali's death, his passing marked the effective end of the Almoravid era. Although his young son, Abu Ishaq Ibrahim, was the heir apparent, a child did not seem the best choice in the circumstances and a few months after he received the *bay'a* in Marrakesh he was replaced by his uncle, Ishaq b. 'Ali, who was himself only around sixteen.[106] The Lamtuna now had no experienced amir to lead them and some defected to the Almohad side, notably the Masufa amirs led by Yahya b. Ishaq and the naval commander 'Ali b. Isa b. Maymun. Many others fought hard to prevent the Almohad advance, but they seem to have done so in a piecemeal fashion. Tashfin's half-brother, Yahya b. al-Sahrawiyya, fell back from Tlemcen to Fes, which he tried to hold against a besieging Almohad force; Ibn Wuljit al-Lamtuni put up a spirited defence of Meknes; while the sixteen-year-old amir, Ishaq b. 'Ali, and his supporters held Marrakesh until 1147.[107] The siege lasted many months, but eventually the Almohads stormed the city walls with ladders. After several days of fighting, they began to get the upper hand, aided by the defection of the Almoravids' Christian corps, but they still had to fight hard to secure the Almoravid citadel at its heart which, according to al-Baydhaq, was defended

[104] Ibn 'Idhari, *al-Bayan*, vol. 4, p. 99.

[105] Mehdi Ghouirgate makes a similar point. Ghouirgate, *L'Ordre almohade*, pp. 46–7.

[106] *al-Hulal al-Mawshiyya*, p. 135; Bosch Vilá, *Los Almorávides*, pp. 269–70. Ibn 'Idhari's account moves directly from Tashfin to Ishaq b. 'Ali; *al-Bayan*, vol. 4, p. 102.

[107] Ibn 'Idhari, *al-Bayan*, vol. 4, pp. 104–6; al-Baydhaq says Ishaq b. Yintan, the governor of Marrakesh, directed affairs; *Akhbar*, p. 116. The author of the *Hulal al-Mawshiyya* says the amir was Abu Ishaq Ibrahim, p. 139.

doggedly by a virgin warrior, Fannu bint 'Umar, whose sex was only revealed after her death when her armour was removed.[108]

Although many resisted the Almohads for years to come, such as Yahya b. al-Sahrawiyya in the Maghrib and the Banu Ghaniya in the Balearics and later Ifriqiya, it was impossible for them to turn the tide and a new empire infused with a new religious ethos and dominated by a different Berber tribal group came to the fore. The beleaguered last years of the Almoravids should not, however, obscure their achievements. They united al-Andalus and the western Maghrib into a single empire for the first time and promoted an empire-wide Maliki judicial system. They also participated in the fuller Islamisation of the Sahara and, by founding Marrakesh, they nurtured urbanisation and cultural development in the south, stimulated by contact with al-Andalus. Although they did not permanently halt the advance of the Christian kingdoms in Iberia, they deterred it for many decades and on several occasions held the military advantage in the peninsula. They also presided over a period in which southern Andalusi towns such as Granada and Almería flourished and benefitted from their closer relationship with the Maghrib and access to the flow of gold from West Africa.

[108] al-Baydhaq, *Akhbar*, p. 117; Ibn 'Idhari, *al-Bayan*, vol. 4, pp. 106–7.

3

The Almohads: Revelation, Revolution and Empire

Ibn Khaldun saw a strong structural similarity between the Almoravid and Almohad empires in their charismatic religious founders, their mobilisation of a particular Berber tribal group by means of religious ideology, and their jihad against fellow Muslims to create an empire. However, emphasis on such undoubted structural similarities runs the risk of eliding the many differences in character and emphasis between the two movements. As we have already seen, the Almohad movement developed in opposition to the Almoravids, an opposition that was predicated both on Masmuda resentment towards Sanhaja domination and a starkly different interpretation of Islam. Although fellow Maghribis, the Almohads put up a more sustained and visceral resistance to the Almoravids than any Andalusi constituency and saw few commonalities with them.

The oft-recounted story of the Almohad movement begins with a young Masmuda Berber from the Hargha tribe resident in the Sus valley south of the High Atlas called Muhammad b. Tumart.[1] His biography, the *Kitab Akhbar al-Mahdi*, written by his disciple al-Baydhaq, is as much hagiography as history and presents Ibn Tumart as an ideal type. It is also a text designed to laud the achievements of Ibn Tumart's successor (caliph), 'Abd al-Mu'min, and depict his establishment of the Almohad caliphate as fore-ordained by Ibn Tumart rather than a straightforward account of the life of the latter. Nonetheless, al-Baydhaq was a disciple of Ibn Tumart and he provides an invaluable contemporary window into the events of the early twelfth century (sixth century AH), even if his text should be handled with caution. His account is supplemented by the *Nazm al-Juman* of the late Almohad scholar, Ibn al-Qattan, and synopses in other Arabic historical works.

According to these sources, Ibn Tumart came from a family known for religious learning, for which he showed an early propensity, spending long

[1] The most detailed account of the Almohad empire based on the Arabic sources is still Huici Miranda's *Historia política*, which provides additional information to that provided in this chapter.

nights in the mosque reading by the light of a candle.[2] Like other young men who showed such aptitude, he set out on an educational journey, a *ṭalab al-ʿilm* (search for knowledge), probably around 1106, which purportedly took him to Córdoba, Almería, Alexandria and Baghdad. Many sources recount his meeting in Baghdad with the famous Shafiʿi jurist and theologian al-Ghazali (d. 1111), who gave him a mission to overthrow the Almoravids, after he heard that the Almoravid judge in Córdoba, Ibn Hamdin, had ordered the burning of his famous work, the *Ihya' ʿUlum al-Din* (*The Revival of the Religious Sciences*).[3] However, the likelihood that Ibn Tumart met or studied with al-Ghazali was rejected by Ibn al-Athir, doubted by other Muslim writers, and dismissed by the majority of Orientalist and later western scholars from Goldziher onwards on the grounds of chronological infeasibility: al-Ghazali had retired to Tus before Ibn Tumart could have journeyed to Baghdad.[4] Griffel suggests that he visited the Nizamiyya Madrasa in Baghdad where al-Ghazali had taught and imbibed his teachings from the next generation of Shafiʿi scholars,[5] while García-Arenal points out that there is no conclusive evidence that he travelled either to al-Andalus or to the east.[6] Fletcher adds a twist to the debate by suggesting that al-Ghazali and Ibn Tumart may actually have met in Alexandria when the former was considering seeking employment with the Almoravids, but the details of both men's itineraries are too vague to support this and more chronological issues arise.[7]

Part of the problem lies in the fact that the first part of al-Baydhaq's *Kitab Akhbar al-Mahdi* is lost and the portion that we have begins with Ibn Tumart in Tunis on his lengthy journey home. The point of the story was, however, to legitimise Ibn Tumart's teachings as derived from the Ghazalian view of Islam and present his campaign against the Almoravids as a commission from the great eastern scholar. Al-Baydhaq contrasts Ibn Tumart's eloquent preaching and extensive (eastern) learning to the poor rhetorical skills and limited knowledge of his Maliki scholarly interlocutors. He also depicts Ibn Tumart as a zealous moralist and preacher, irritated by the ignorance of Muslims about their own faith, and he praises his brave and sometimes

2 Ibn Khaldun, *Kitab al-ʿIbar*, vol. 8, p. 465; Ibn Khaldun, *Histoire des Berbères*, vol. 2, p. 162.

3 Ibn al-Qattan, *Nazm al-Juman*, pp. 70–3; *al-Hulal al-Mawshiyya*, p. 104; Ibn Abi Zarʿ, *Rawd al-Qirtas*, pp. 218–19; Ibn Khaldun, *Kitab al-ʿIbar*, vol. 8, p. 466; Ibn Khaldun, *Histoire des Berbères*, vol. 2, p. 163.

4 Huici Miranda, *Historia política*, vol. 1, pp. 29–32; Griffel, 'Ibn Tumart's rational proof', pp. 753–6.

5 Griffel, 'Ibn Tumart's rational proof', pp. 756–7.

6 García-Arenal, *Messianism and Puritanical Reform*, p. 163.

7 See Fletcher, 'Ibn Tumart's teachers', p. 305.

violent insistence upon public adherence to Islamic values which built on al-Ghazali's notion of *ḥisba* (commanding right and prohibiting wrong).[8]

His activism, which much exceeded that prescribed by al-Ghazali, was often unwelcome and he was thrown out of Tunis and Bijaya in turn. He sought refuge with his growing corps of disciples in a village called Malala where he met a young Kumiya (or Gumiya) Berber from the Tlemcen area called 'Abd al-Mu'min b. 'Ali, who was on his way to Mecca to perform the *ḥajj*, or, according to Ibn al-Qattan, came to ask Ibn Tumart to replace one of his students, a teacher who had recently died at the *ribāṭ* of Tlemcen.[9] This meeting is surrounded by legend, but the bare bones of the story are that Ibn Tumart persuaded 'Abd al-Mu'min to abandon his pilgrimage, if that was his purpose, and recruited him to his band which soon headed west towards Almoravid territories, reforming local religious and judicial praxis along the way.[10] During his journey west, he was liable to take violent action against practices he deemed to be contrary to Islam, such as wine drinking, the mixing of men and women, and the performance of music, and he spoke out against juridical decisions he viewed as wrong.

Ibn Tumart's mission to reform Islamic praxis brought him into conflict not only with jurists and the general population, but also with the political authorities of his time, whom he publicly chastised for failing in their duty to uphold the Shari'a and thus neglecting the religious responsibilities that came with political power. From the Islamic perspective, the ultimate purpose of political life was not merely to maintain earthly justice and prosperity, but to prepare people for the afterlife and rulers had a heavy responsibility to put their subjects on the path leading to eternal salvation rather than damnation. When he reached Marrakesh, the charge that Ibn Tumart made against the Almoravids was precisely that they were too ignorant and dependent on Maliki jurists to provide adequate religious leadership for their subjects. The confrontation between Ibn Tumart and the Almoravids began in the great mosque of Marrakesh where he publicly criticised the Almoravid ruler 'Ali b. Yusuf for wearing the traditional male face veil (*lithām*) of the Sanhaja and for sitting on a rich silk cloak in the mosque.

> [Ibn Tumart] said to them: Where is the amir? I see only veiled slave girls. When 'Ali b. Yusuf heard this, he lifted the veil from his face and said to them: He speaks the truth. When the Infallible One saw him he said: The

[8] For a fuller account of Ibn Tumart's doctrine, see below, pp. 246–53.

[9] Ibn al-Qattan, *Nazm al-Juman*, p. 77.

[10] For the symbolism of this meeting, see Brett, 'The lamp of the Almohads', in *Ibn Khaldun and the Medieval Maghrib*.

> caliphate belongs to God not to you, 'Ali b. Yusuf. Then he said to him: Oh 'Ali, abandon these immoral things so that you may be a just ruler, and get up off that objectionable cloak (*ghifāra*).[11] He removed the cloak and returned it to its owner and asked: Why change it? [Ibn Tumart] said: Because it is [a form of] impurity (*najāsa*).[12]

While these criticisms may seem obscure to us, they were gauged to highlight Almoravid customs which other Muslims found strange and also suggest 'Ali's ignorance of Islamic religious norms. As we have seen in the previous chapter, in Almohad rhetoric, the wearing of the *lithām* became a mark of Almoravid inversion of gender norms, of men dressed as women, which correlated with the inappropriate freedom Almoravid women enjoyed. In a similar vein, Ibn Tumart is also reported to have harangued 'Ali b. Yusuf's sister for not wearing a veil as she rode through the streets of Marrakesh, scaring her horse so that it reared and she fell off.[13] Meanwhile, the reference to the *ghifāra* (or *ghuffāra*), generally understood as a luxurious, urban-style cloak of silk or wool, is slightly opaque in conjunction with the term 'impurity' where one might simply expect 'forbidden' (*ḥarām*), but it may be seen as a demonstration of Ibn Tumart's knowledge of the Shafi'i position on silk which forbade male use of silk furnishings as well as clothing.[14] The thrust of Ibn Tumart's comment was to show the amir's ignorance of legal rules concerning purity during prayer and possibly his corruption by urban luxuries in place of simpler robes.[15]

In the Almohad report of this encounter, 'Ali b. Yusuf is depicted as deferential to Ibn Tumart and ready to acknowledge his own ignorance and, rather than responding himself, he sought recourse with his religious advisers, the Maliki *fuqahā'*, and organised a debate between them and Ibn Tumart. The Almohad sources naturally depict Ibn Tumart as rendering his opponents speechless with his superior knowledge and dialectic skills in a contest between the sterile legalistic Malikism promoted by the Almoravids and the religious approaches that Ibn Tumart had learnt about in the east, a binary that exaggerated the gulf between the two sides as we shall see in Chapter 6.

11 Corriente and Ghouirgate give *ghifāra* as alternately 'cloak' or 'cap', Corriente, *Dictionary of Andalusi Arabic*, p. 380; Ghouirgate, *L'Ordre almohade*, pp. 209–11, while Dozy distinguishes between a cloak (*ghuffāra*) and a cap (*ghifāra*), Dozy, *Dictionnaire*, pp. 312–19.

12 al-Baydhaq, *Akhbar*, pp. 56–7.

13 Ibn Khaldun, *Kitab al-'Ibar*, vol. 8, p. 468; Ibn Khaldun, *Histoire des Berbères*, vol. 2, p. 167; Ibn al-Athir, *al-Kamil fi'l-Ta'rikh*, vol. 10, pp. 570–1.

14 al-Jaziri, *al-Fiqh 'ala al-Madhahib al-Arba'a*, vol. 1, pp. 412–13; al-Ghazali, *al-Wasit fi'l-Madhhab*, vol. 2, p. 321.

15 Ghouirgate, *L'Ordre almohade*, pp. 209–11.

Regardless of the intellectual capabilities and knowledge of Ibn Tumart and his opponents, however, he was a popular, charismatic preacher able to fire up a crowd, which made him more politically dangerous than most religious scholars. 'Ali b. Yusuf's chief religious adviser, Malik b. Wuhayb, recommended that Ibn Tumart be arrested and killed to avert the threat he posed, but a Sanhaja chief, Yintan b. 'Umar, aware of his popular support and perhaps personally awed by him, suggested exile instead.[16] This turned out to be a fatal mistake for the Almoravids.

Ibn Tumart defiantly made his way to a cemetery outside the walls of Marrakesh and set up a tent from which he continued to preach in what he described as the domain of God himself! When the situation became more tense he departed for nearby Aghmat where he converted one faction of the population to his interpretation of Islam whilst another resisted and complained to 'Ali b. Yusuf about the troublemaker. The Almoravid amir sent an army to apprehend Ibn Tumart, but he fled from Aghmat across the High Atlas to his natal region of the Sus where he soon built up a significant following among the Masmuda tribes who felt little affinity with the Almoravids. Safe among the Masmuda, Ibn Tumart exploited the tribal networks of the region, traditional Berber forms of alliance and his growing reputation for sanctity to consolidate his position.[17] As more tribesmen flocked to the *ribāṭ* he founded at Igilliz in the Sus, the possibility of a military offensive against the Almoravids must have become apparent to him and informed his transformation from a preacher to a religio-political leader.

Central to this shift was Ibn Tumart's recognition as the *mahdī*, a messianic figure sent to restore true Islam and an era of peace and justice for its adherents. It was a fortuitous moment to make such a claim due to the eschatological expectations generated by the passing of the Islamic year 500 in 1106–7. Ibn Tumart heightened these expectations by asserting that the Almoravids were the decadent people alluded to in Hadith who would appear at the end of days and show their deviance by allowing their women to appear unveiled and thus parade what should be hidden.[18] He also encouraged people to think that he might indeed be the *mahdī* by constantly alluding to Hadith about his own possession of the attributes of this messianic figure in conjunction with the 'signs' that his appearance was imminent. Sources such

[16] al-Baydhaq, *Akhbar*, p. 58.

[17] Fromherz, *The Almohads*, pp. 54–9.

[18] Ibn Hanbal, *al-Musnad*, vol. 6, pp. 490–2 (Hadith 7083: 'In the last days of my community (*umma*) there will be men of dubious manhood who ride upon their saddles and dismount at the mosque doors, their women cloaked but with heads bare like the humps of emaciated camels. They will curse [the women] and they will be cursed . . .').

as the *Rawd al-Qirtas* baldly dismiss all this as blandishments and deceit, but around 1121 (515 AH) Ibn Tumart was recognised by his inner circle of disciples and the Masmuda tribes as the *mahdī*.[19]

This was a crucial moment in the evolution of the Almohad movement since an essential characteristic of the *mahdī* is his active political and military role to implement the righteous order that he is destined to head. In this, he is the renewer and reviver of Muhammad's message, and the Almohad sources thus depict the ensuing stages in Ibn Tumart's career as calques on the life of the Prophet. Just as the Prophet moved from preacher to leader of a new community through his migration or exile (*hijra*) from pagan Mecca to Medina, so Ibn Tumart's exile from Marrakesh and Aghmat paved the way for his establishment of a new militant community in the High Atlas town of Tinmall (or Tinmalal), an easily defensible mountain settlement approached by a single causeway, which the Almohads occupied *c.* 1124. This became the Almohads' *dār al-hijra* (place of retreat), a term also used for Medina. Similarly, just as Muhammad purged Medina of Jewish tribes whom he considered lukewarm or duplicitous in their support for him, so Ibn Tumart went on to institute a bloody purge called the *tamyīz* to remove uncommitted tribesmen from Tinmall.[20] This was a controversial act, probably made palatable only by the evocation of the Prophet's example. Ibn 'Idhari reports that a jurist from Ifriqiya challenged Ibn Tumart by asking why he had done such a thing and in response Ibn Tumart had him killed and exposed on a cross for doubting his infallibility as the *mahdī*.[21]

It was key to the success of the movement that the tribesmen render unquestioning obedience to Ibn Tumart, just as the Almoravids had been obliged to submit to the dictates of Ibn Yasin. However, a distinctive feature of the Tinmall community was Ibn Tumart's attention to the religious education of his followers, a process that was as much Islamisation as reform given the rudimentary religious knowledge of many tribesmen. Several sources allude to his composition of books in the local Berber language as well as in Arabic, and his use of Berber to educate the tribesmen in their faith.[22] Ibn Abi Zar' says that all the Berber tribesmen had to memorise one of these works, the *Tawhid*, which 'had the status of the glorious Qur'an among the Masmuda tribes'.[23] He also dispatched members of his entourage conversant

[19] Ibn Abi Zar', *Rawd al-Qirtas*, pp. 226–7; *al-Hulal al-Mawshiyya*, p. 107; Huici Miranda, *Historia política*, vol. 1, pp. 61–4.

[20] al-Baydhaq, *Akhbar*, pp. 71–2; Huici Miranda, *Historia política*, vol. 1, pp. 71–3.

[21] Ibn 'Idhari, *al-Bayan*, vol. 4, p. 60.

[22] *al-Hulal al-Mawshiyya*, p. 109.

[23] Ibn Abi Zar', *Rawd al-Qirtas*, p. 227.

with Almohad beliefs to tribes who joined the movement to teach their fellows. Such strategies reflected Ibn Tumart's belief that each believer should personally know and understand their religion and created a contrast between his own engaged religio-political leadership and what he considered the ignorant and befuddled approach of the Almoravid amirs. Equally, however, it bound the Masmuda tribes together in the same way that identification with Maliki law had bound the Sanhaja together.

The growing cohorts of Almohads were ranked in the military and political hierarchy according to the chronology of their acceptance of Ibn Tumart's leadership, just as the early Muslims had been ranked according to their acceptance of Islam in a system that both used and modified tribal identity and organisation. Ibn Tumart's earliest and most loyal disciples were known as the Council of Ten, evoking the ten companions of the Prophet promised paradise. This council had members from a variety of tribes belonging to the Masmuda, the Zanata and the Sanhaja confederations, including 'Abd al-Mu'min al-Kumi (Zanata), the chronicler al-Baydhaq (Sanhaja) and the tribal chief Abu Hafs 'Umar al-Hintati (Masmuda). The members of Ibn Tumart's household, some of whom served in the various councils, were known as the *ahl al-dār* (people of the house) and, like the Council of Ten, their status derived primarily from their adherence to Almohadism and their proximity to Ibn Tumart rather than to their tribal origin. The chiefs or shaykhs of the Masmuda tribes that had joined the movement made up the Council of Fifty, an important consultative group whose status rested upon a combination of tribal and religious credentials. Some sources also talk about a Council of Seventy, but whether this was a separate tribal council or an enlarged Council of Fifty is not clear.[24]

Although the date when this hierarchy first emerged is not known, there is no reason to suppose that it did not exist in some form from early on. It had the advantage of both transcending tribal affiliations in favour of religious conviction and devotion to the *mahdī* while also exploiting them for organisational purposes. While the Masmuda tribesmen who joined the movement became Almohads (*al-muwaḥḥidūn*) united by their belief that Ibn Tumart was the *mahdī*, when they mobilised to militarily implement his will, the majority remained in their own tribal contingents either led by their own shaykhs or Ibn Tumart's close companions, as the early Muslim Arabs had been. A connection between tribal identity and the Almohad movement was made by placing each tribe in the Almohad marching order in accordance

24 See Hopkins, 'The Almohade hierarchy'. Primary source references include the *Kitab al-Ansab* in Lévi-Provençal, *Documents inédits d'histoire almohade*, pp. 18–49; Ibn al-Qattan, *Nazm al-Juman*, p. 82; al-Marrakushi, *al-Mu'jib*, pp. 420–6.

with the chronological order in which they had offered their allegiance. In time other contingents were added to the Almohad army, including black slaves, Arab tribesmen, Turks and Christians, but the so-called 'Almohads', the Masmuda tribes, remained its core.[25]

The objective of the Almohad army was to overthrow the Almoravids, perceived as akin to the pagans of Mecca, and institute the true Islamic order represented by Ibn Tumart's teachings. This was not a straightforward task: although the Almohads were able to easily repel Almoravid sorties into the High Atlas, as a result of their greater familiarity with the mountainous terrain for which Almoravid fighting tactics were completely unsuited, they did not fare so well on the plains. When the over-confident Almohads skirted around the line of hastily built Almoravid fortresses in the High Atlas foothills to attack the Almoravids on the plains around Marrakesh, many died in combat. Ibn Abi Zar', who is overtly hostile to Ibn Tumart, provides an anecdotal and probably fabricated account of the extreme tactics he used to galvanise his followers to fight on after a battle in which they sustained heavy losses.

> An example of [Ibn Tumart's] trickery and belittling of bloodshed was that he took a group of his followers and buried them alive [on the battlefield], making for each a breathing hole in his grave, saying to them, 'If you are greeted, say we have truly found the increased reward that our Lord promised for waging jihad against the Lamtuna and we have obtained the high rank accorded to martyrs, so strive on in your jihad against the enemy. The Imam-Mahdī, your master calls you to the Truth.'[26]

In return he promised that they would be dug out of their graves and accorded high status. The next morning, he led the tribesmen to the battlefield and the 'dead' called out to them as planned, after which their fervour for fighting the Almoravids was rekindled. Ibn Tumart, however, did not release the buried men but closed their breathing holes so that they would never talk about the trick to others.

This phase of fighting culminated in the siege of Marrakesh in the late 1120s. At first the Almohads successfully pushed back the small bands of Lamtuna warriors who emerged from the city to repel them, but when Almoravid contingents arrived from other areas they roundly defeated the Almohads at the Battle of the Buhayra in 1130 during which several important Almohad commanders were killed. Shortly afterwards Ibn Tumart himself died, creating a major crisis within the Almohad movement which could

[25] Fromherz, *The Almohads*, pp. 87–100.
[26] Ibn Abi Zar', *Rawd al-Qirtas*, p. 234.

easily have led to its demise and remembrance as no more than one of many religiously inspired rebellions. That it did not collapse appears to have been largely down to the genius of 'Abd al-Mu'min, Ibn Tumart's successor as leader of the movement, and the support he secured among Ibn Tumart's inner circle, perhaps aided by the death of his rivals at the Battle of the Buhayra.

It is almost impossible to ascertain exactly what happened as the source closest to the event, al-Baydhaq's *Kitab Akhbar al-Mahdi*, is manifestly hagiographical and presents 'Abd al-Mu'min's emergence as leader as a forgone conclusion. According to al-Baydhaq, Ibn Tumart fell ill and set off for Tinmall. On the way he passed a field of peas and told his companions to pick as many as they could, prophesying that they would grasp the world in the same way after his passing. When he arrived in Tinmall he gave a sermon, another calque from the Prophet Muhammad's biography, before entering his house. He emerged an hour later and told the gathered crowd that he was going on a journey. When they begged to join him, he told them, 'This is not a journey anyone can make with me, it is for me alone.'[27] He then disappeared into his house for ever, although his closest circle, including 'Abd al-Mu'min and his sister Zaynab, supposedly communed with him for a further three years before his death was announced. This period is described as a *ghayba*, a Shi'i term denoting the occultation from ordinary time of the last imam who is destined to return one day, pointing to the likelihood of Shi'i influences on Almohad thinking.

In his usual analytic way, Ibn Khaldun suggests that the reason behind this odd period of 'occultation' was that the Almohad leadership, which was of mixed tribal background, feared that the Masmuda majority would resent a leader who was not of their own people.[28] It was therefore impossible for 'Abd al-Mu'min, a Berber from the Zanata Kumiya tribe, to play his hand immediately after Ibn Tumart died. Instead, his 'occultation' provided a period in which 'Abd al-Mu'min was able to secure his position and persuade important Masmuda chiefs, particularly Abu Hafs 'Umar of the Hintata, of his status as Ibn Tumart's destined successor or caliph. An important factor in this process was 'Abd al-Mu'min's undoubted military and political abilities. He abandoned head-on attacks against the Almoravids in the vicinity of Marrakesh and focused instead upon the slow, steady conquest of the mountain ranges ringing the Atlantic plains, the High Atlas, the Middle Atlas and finally the Rif. Once the majority of the Atlas tribes had joined

[27] al-Baydhaq, *Akhbar*, p. 77.

[28] Ibn Khaldun, *Kitab al-'Ibar*, vol. 8, p. 472; Ibn Khaldun, *Histoire des Berbères*, vol. 2, p. 173.

the Almohads, the latter resumed their attacks on the lowlands: the Sus valley, the Gharb plain and the Muluwiya valley. 'Abd al-Mu'min's leadership was crucial to this process and eventually secured him the allegiance of the Masmuda tribes, although resentments remained.

In describing the decades of war between the Almoravids and the Almohads, the chronicles list a kaleidoscopic array of tribes rallying to each side, defecting and returning as the war went in favour of one side then the other. Although the relentless advance of the Almohads is presented as a forgone conclusion, the chronicles also record significant and sustained support for the Almoravids in some areas and ongoing Sanhaja opposition to the Almohads after their victory. The Almohads are depicted, however, as numerous, politically and religiously united, and brutal towards the Almoravids and those they considered to have collaborated with them. Many non-Almohad sources comment on the violence shown by the Almohads. The eastern historian al-Nuwayri says that although 'Abd al-Mu'min had many good qualities he was much given to spilling blood,[29] and Ibn Taymiyya also criticised the way the Almohads killed other Muslims.[30] Some instances of violence, however, probably indicated longstanding tribal rifts. For instance, it was a Zanata amir called Yaslatin to whom Ibn 'Idhari attributes the killing of a group of Tlemcen's notables who had the 'misfortune' (lit. 'God ruled against them') to encounter him when seeking pardon from 'Abd al-Mu'min, an incident that suggests an opportunistic strike rather than Almohad 'policy' given the enduring rivalry between the Zanata and Sanhaja in the area.[31]

As mentioned in the previous chapter, the Almoravid amir 'Ali b. Yusuf died in 1143 and his son, Tashfin, an able soldier who had shown his mettle as his father's representative in al-Andalus before returning to the Maghrib to lead the counter-offensive against the Almohads in 1138, became amir in his place. In 1144–5, however, the situation turned decisively in favour of the Almohads when the Zanata tribes of what is now western Algeria came over to them, encouraged by their sense of kinship with 'Abd al-Mu'min who came from the same area. Key Almoravid amirs of the Masufa tribe also defected to 'Abd al-Mu'min, enabling Almohad forces to capture Tlemcen and Oran, killing the Almoravid commander Reverter and then Tashfin b. 'Ali in the process.

Yusuf b. Tashfin's grandson, Yahya b. Abi Bakr known as Ibn al-Sahrawiyya, retreated west through the Taza corridor to Fes, pursued by the Almohads who besieged it in 1146. They also besieged Meknes and the

29 al-Nuwayri, *Nihayat al-Arab*, vol. 24, p. 175.
30 Shatzmiller, 'al-Muwaḥḥidūn'.
31 Ibn 'Idhari, *al-Bayan*, vol. 4, p. 100.

indefatigable 'Abd al-Mu'min travelled to and fro between the two camps monitoring the sieges. The Almohads eventually gained entry to Fes by cutting the city's water supply after which al-Jayyani, the town's financial administrator (*mushrif*) whom we encountered briefly in the last chapter, sent a secret message saying he would open the gates, becoming one of the many Andalusi officials serving the Almoravids to change sides.[32] Yahya b. al-Sahrawiyya narrowly escaped with his life, but many Almoravids were not so lucky and died at the hands of the Almohads before the latter marched south via Meknes and Salé to capture the jewel in the Almoravid crown, Marrakesh, the city they had founded some 70–80 years before.

This was a critical juncture, but Tashfin b. 'Ali's death had left the Almoravids without a seasoned amir to rally them. As we saw in the previous chapter, Tashfin's young son Ibrahim, held power for a short time before being replaced by his teenage uncle, Ishaq b. 'Ali, who found himself barricaded inside Marrakesh by the Almohads who finally took the city after a siege of several months. Many of the Almoravid elite, including the sixteen-year-old Ishaq, were captured and executed along with their supporters, while Almoravid women and children were enslaved and sold,[33] events that generate a certain tension in the chronicles concerning the normativity of such behaviour towards other Muslims. The Almohads, like the Almoravids before them, understood their mission as a jihad and such righteous warfare normally involved respectful treatment of non-combatants and Muslims. However, the Islam that the Almohads propounded was not Maliki Sunnism, but the teachings of Ibn Tumart, the *mahdī* and, in the Almohad view, those who rejected Ibn Tumart were not simply misguided Muslims, they were apostates whose blood was therefore licit. Ibn 'Idhari tried to ameliorate the impact of this report by claiming that although 'Abd al-Mu'min authorised what happened, he purchased the enslaved Almoravid women and children back from the Almohad warriors and released them in a show of magnanimity.[34]

In spring 1148, the year after 'Abd al-Mu'min had captured Marrakesh, the Almohads were faced with a serious religio-political challenge which threatened to unite their fragmented and leaderless opposition.[35] The instigator was an individual called Muhammad b. 'Abd Allah al-Massi, a man of

[32] al-Baydhaq, *Akhbar*, p. 113.

[33] Ibid., pp. 117–18, 120; Ibn 'Idhari, *al-Bayan*, vol. 4, p. 106.

[34] Ibn 'Idhari, *al-Bayan*, vol. 4, p. 106.

[35] The chronology of the rebellion is not clear with some authors talking of al-Massi's rebellion in 1147 and others 1148. Huici Miranda preferred the later date; *Historia política*, vol. 1, p. 149.

humble origin, disparagingly described by Ibn 'Idhari as a fuller from Salé whose father had been a market broker.[36] At the great *ribāṭ* of Massa on the coast of the Sus, an area close to the Sanhaja homelands, he declared himself *al-hādī* or 'the guide', a title from the same root as the word *mahdī* with similar connotations of divine inspiration and messianic leadership, reinforced by his possession of the same name as the prophet – Muhammad b. 'Abd Allah. Many tribes flocked to the banner of al-Massi, the counter-*mahdī* to Ibn Tumart and the Almohads, and the towns of Salé, Sijilmasa and Ceuta rebelled against their new Almohad governors. The famous Maliki jurist Qadi 'Iyad of Ceuta crossed to Algeciras and asked the chief Almoravid amir in al-Andalus, Yahya b. Ghaniya, to appoint an Almoravid governor for Ceuta. He nominated the fugitive Almoravid prince Yahya b. al-Sahrawiyya who returned from al-Andalus with Qadi 'Iyad to govern Ceuta.

The first Almohad force sent from Marrakesh against al-Massi was routed, but then the seasoned veteran Abu Hafs 'Umar al-Hintati took to the field with a force estimated at 6,000 cavalry and 6,000 foot soldiers and defeated and killed al-Massi. The Almohads made much of the victory, but it took many more months for Abu Hafs 'Umar to reduce the Haylana, Haskura and Barghawata tribes that had supported al-Massi, as well as the urban communities of Nafis, Sijilmasa, Salé and Ceuta. 'Abd al-Mu'min himself campaigned for six months to reduce and punish the Dukkala tribes on the plains north of Marrakesh. Once the Almohads had regained the upper hand, Ceuta and Salé renewed their allegiance, but the calm was superficial. Although al-Massi was subsequently demonised as a rebel and spreader of discord, there obviously remained a great deal of opposition to the Almohads and their interpretation of Islam in the Maghrib at this point. To make matters worse, the Almoravid prince Yahya b. al-Sahrawiyya remained at large and a potential focus for anti-Almohad sentiment.[37] Furthermore, his ability to move between Tangier, Ceuta and the Andalusi ports on the northern side of the Straits of Gibraltar brought home the vulnerability of the Almohads' Maghribi domains to attack by the Almoravids in al-Andalus. It thus became 'Abd al-Mu'min's next objective to fully extirpate the Almoravid regime in al-Andalus and absorb it into his empire.

[36] Ibn 'Idhari, *al-Bayan*, vol. 4, p. 109.

[37] Although Ibn 'Idhari mentions the capitulation of Yahya b. al-Sahrawiyya at this point (1147–8), al-Baydhaq gives a later date of 1154. Ibn 'Idhari, *al-Bayan*, vol. 4, p. 115; al-Baydhaq, *Akhbar*, p. 145.

Almohad Expansion into al-Andalus

Ibn ʿIdhari describes the Almohad mission (*daʿwa*) in al-Andalus as starting in 1145, around the same time that they captured Tlemcen and began their final campaign to take the Almoravids' last key cities, Fes and Marrakesh.[38] At this point Andalusi political life entered a new phase of disaggregation comparable to the eleventh-century Ta'ifa era and thus sometimes called the 'second Ta'ifas'. Although Yahya b. Ghaniya controlled Seville and Granada and his brother, Muhammad b. Ghaniya, retained the Balearics, many local Andalusi notables drawn from the judiciary or the military asserted their independence from the Almoravids, creating new 'Ta'ifa' principalities whose rulers manoeuvred as best they could between the Christian kingdoms of the north, the Almoravids and the rising Almohad power in the Maghrib.

In Córdoba, the Almoravid *qāḍī* Ibn Hamdin briefly asserted his independence in 1145 and usurped the titles of Yusuf b. Tashfin and his descendants, 'Commander of the Muslims' (*amīr al-muslimīn*) and 'Champion of Religion' (*nāṣir al-dīn*), the latter of which also evoked the glories of the Umayyad caliphate of Córdoba, thereby reclaiming the title for an Andalusi Córdoban regime. Although Yahya b. Ghaniya was able to quell Ibn Hamdin's bid for independence and regain Córdoba, he was not able to prevent the secession of eastern al-Andalus where Ibn Hud, an individual claiming descent from the previous eponymous Ta'ifa rulers of Saragossa, gained Castilian backing to establish himself in Valencia and Murcia. Although Ibn Hud's initiative was short-lived, he was ousted not by the Almoravids but by the Banu Mardanish, who similarly sought alliance with the Castilians to create a principality which lasted from 1146 until 1172. Further west, Ibn Qasi, a mystical preacher of Christian origin from Silves gathered a large following of disciples (*murīdīn*) and declared himself the *mahdī*, a development linked to the general spread of popular mystical and messianic sentiments that had inspired the Almohad movement itself. Ibn Qasi captured Mértola in 1144 and found local allies in the form of Yusuf b. Muhammad al-Bitruji, the lord of Niebla, and Sidray b. Wazir, lord of Beja.

As the above references to the alliances between Ibn Hud, Ibn Mardanish and León-Castile indicate, the Almohad destruction of the Almoravid empire in the Maghrib provided renewed opportunities for the Christian powers of the north to become involved in the politics of the Muslim south. In addition to entering into alliances with local Muslim lords, Alfonso VII of León-Castile (r. 1126–57) began to menace Córdoba. In a fairly rare moment

[38] Ibn ʿIdhari, *al-Bayan*, vol. 4, p. 112.

of Christian unity, he also formed a coalition with Aragon, Navarre and the Genoese fleet which enabled him occupy Almería in 1147 and hold it for a decade. Further north, the Aragonese consolidated their control over the lower Ebro valley, which had begun in 1118 with their capture of Saragossa, by capturing Tortosa, Lleida and Fraga in Catalonia. In the west, the ambitious count of Portugal, Enrique I, called Ibn al-Rink in Arabic sources, captured both Santarem and Lisbon in 1147 and used the expansion of his territory south, at Muslim expense, to transform his county into a kingdom.

As had been the case with the Almoravids sixty years before, Almohad involvement in the Iberian peninsula began with appeals from local Andalusi power brokers, several of whom rebelled against the Almoravids or defected from them and declared for the Almohads as a power more capable of resisting renewed Christian encroachments. One of the first to change sides was ʿAli b. ʿIsa b. Maymun, the Almoravid naval commander in al-Andalus who gave his allegiance to ʿAbd al-Muʾmin during the siege of Fes and then promptly took Cádiz for the Almohads in 1145. Although ʿAli b. ʿIsa proved to be a loyal recruit, others, including Ibn Qasi, offered their allegiance to the Almohads in a more tactical and contingent manner. Although initially very successful, Ibn Qasi's support in the southwest had begun to falter after his *murīdīn* were defeated by the Almoravid amir Yahya b. Ghaniya. In the face of threats by his former ally, Sidray b. Wazir, the lord of Beja, he went to ʿAli b. ʿIsa to declare his submission to the Almohads and then travelled across the Straits of Gibraltar to meet ʿAbd al-Muʾmin outside Fes in 1146 or 1147. Despite the obvious theological problem that Ibn Qasi and Ibn Tumart could not both be the *mahdī*, the two men cobbled an agreement together. Al-Marrakushi gives this a comic twist by reporting that ʿAbd al-Muʾmin interrogated Ibn Qasi, saying, 'I have heard that you claim to be the *mahdī*,' to which the latter replied, 'Are there not two dawns, one false and one true, I was the false dawn!,' causing the caliph to burst out laughing.[39] After this an Almohad force led by another Almoravid defector, Abu Ishaq Barraz al-Masufi, crossed over to al-Andalus with Ibn Qasi and initiated the conquest of the southwestern section of the peninsula, including Jerez, Niebla, Mértola, Silves and Beja.

The Almohads then turned towards Seville which they besieged in 1147. The Almoravids fled to Carmona, and Seville's elite, headed by the *qāḍī* Abu Bakr b. al-ʿArabi, proffered their submission to the Almohads. A delegation of notables then travelled to the newly conquered capital of Marrakesh to personally pledge their allegiance to ʿAbd al-Muʾmin and the Almohads.

[39] al-Marrakushi, *Muʿjib*, p. 309.

In addition to the *qāḍī* Ibn al-'Arabi, it included such luminaries as the historian Ibn Sahib al-Salat and the jurist Abu Bakr b. al-Jadd who delighted the members of the caliph's *majlis* with their elegant Arabic addresses. Ibn al-'Idhari reports, however, that during their trip it was whispered that Seville had defected and they were put under house arrest until the loyalty of their city had been confirmed.

> When this delegation reached Marrakesh and the tribes 'apostatised' (*irtadda*) because of the rise of al-Massi, someone falsely informed the caliph that Seville and its inhabitants had 'apostatised' too. The news spread but the delegation knew nothing of it and had no inkling until the Almohads surrounded the house that they were in with spears and swords. Some of them fainted, some were stunned and perceived their imminent death. Guards surrounded them day and night and they believed that their death was unavoidable. That continued for three days until a letter arrived from the shaykh Abu Ya'qub b. Sulayman in Seville with the truth.[40]

Ibn 'Idhari's conflation of rebellion and apostasy (*ridda*) reflects the highly charged atmosphere during what was essentially a revolution, but those who opposed the Almohad revolutionaries did not necessarily see things in the same light. Many saw the claim that Ibn Tumart was the *mahdī* as beyond the pale of Islam and suspected that a new Masmuda-dominated order would not be in their interests. The relationship between the suspected secession of Seville, the insurgence of al-Massi, and more or less contemporaneous reports of poor Almohad governance in Seville is not at all clear, but Kennedy suggests that news of the violent Almohad reaction to the rebellion of al-Massi may have persuaded Andalusi lords that the Almohads would not be lenient masters, leading many to retract their oaths of allegiance.[41] A more immediate cause for Sevillan unhappiness with prospective Almohad rule during 1147 and 1148 was the heavy-handedness of the city's new governors, Abu Ishaq Barraz al-Masufi and then Ibn Tumart's brothers, 'Abd al-'Aziz and 'Isa, and the destructive behaviour of the Almohad garrison billeted in the Jabbana quarter.[42]

Andalusi concerns about the nature of Almohad rule were compounded by suspicions that Ibn Tumart's brothers were plotting against al-Bitruji of Niebla despite his declaration for the Almohad cause and assistance to them, which may well have brought the fate of the Ta'ifa kings at the hands of the Almoravids to mind. Several Andalusi lords renounced their allegiance to the

40 Ibn 'Idhari, *al-Bayan*, vol. 4, pp. 111–12.
41 Kennedy, *Muslim Spain and Portugal*, p. 203.
42 Ibn 'Idhari, *al-Bayan*, vol. 4, p. 114.

Almohads allowing the Almoravid Yahya b. Ghaniya to retake the Straits port of Algeciras and besiege Seville, while Qadi ʿIyad and Yahya b. al-Sahrawiyya remained in control of Ceuta giving the Almoravids control of the Straits of Gibraltar. The Almohad response to Andalusi opposition was as quick as their response to al-Massi's Maghribi rebellion. Ibn ʿAzzun of Jerez, who had remained pro-Almohad, recaptured Algeciras from the Almoravids and ʿAbd al-Muʾmin appointed a new Almohad governor, the shaykh Abu Yaʿqub Sulayman, to Seville with instructions to initiate campaigns to restore Almohad control over the southwest and capture Córdoba and Carmona from Yahya b. Ghaniya. This stalwart Almoravid amir found himself caught between the Almohads and the Castilians and agreed to negotiate with the ex-Almoravid amir, Barraz b. Ishaq al-Masufi, who persuaded him to retire to Jaén and cede Córdoba and Carmona to the Almohads. Yahya b. Ghaniya died soon after in Granada leaving the Almoravid Lamtuna in mainland al-Andalus with no obvious leader and a choice between submission to the Almohads or flight to Yahya's brother, Muhammad b. Ghaniya, in Mallorca. By 1149, southwest and central al-Andalus acknowledged the Almohads and their form of Islam, superficially at least.

In 1150, ʿAbd al-Muʾmin took the opportunity to summon the Andalusi notables who had renewed their allegiance, described tartly as insurgents (*thuwwār*), to Salé where he was busy building the citadel of Ribat al-Fath (al-Mahdiyya) opposite Salé. The delegation, which included Sidray b. Wazir of Beja, al-Bitruji of Niebla, Ibn ʿAzzun of Jerez, Muhammad b. al-Hajjam of Badajoz, ʿAmir b. Muhib of Tavira among others, camped a few miles from Salé before they were allocated houses to stay in. They first met ʿAbd al-Muʾmin on 20 April 1151, the first day of the Muslim year 546. He used the occasion to intimidate as much as welcome them to indicate his displeasure at events in al-Andalus, playing the rough, gruff Berber with his *wazīr* Ibn ʿAtiyya, a man of Andalusi origin known for his command of literary Arabic, acting as an urbane foil.

Ibn ʿIdhari, relying on the eye witness testimony of Ibn Sahib al-Salat, says that ʿAbd al-Muʾmin met the group in the courtyard of the requisitioned palace of the Banu ʿAshara[43] sitting on a mat wearing a rich purple cloak and a turban of wool while Ibn ʿAtiyya presented the delegation to him. When they spoke, however, the caliph interjected by cursing Alfonso VII and then puffing and coughing in a harsh way that reduced them to silence.

[43] The Banu ʿAshara were an eminent learned family in Salé including jurists and *qāḍī*s who had become its *de facto* rulers. Ibn Tumart stayed with the *qāḍī* Hassun b. ʿAshara when he passed through Salé *en route* to Marrakesh and ʿAbd al-Muʾmin appropriated their palace after the Almohad conquest. al-Baydhaq, *Akhbar*, p. 55.

The jurist Abu Bakr b. al-Jadd saved the situation with an elegant address that stressed the virtues of the line of 'Abd al-Mu'min and the obligation of submission.[44] The following day the caliph's *majlis* reconvened so that the notables could formally surrender their lands and give their allegiance to the Almohads in return for confirmation of their positions and incorporation into the Almohad ruling class.

Despite 'Abd al-Mu'min's theatrical humbling of the notables of southwestern al-Andalus, the Almohads were actually in no position to carry out harsh reprisals because they needed Andalusi collaboration to control their peninsular territories. As in the Almoravid case, it was simply not possible for the Almohads to rule any of their territories without the assistance of local partners, including military leaders and religious scholars. Where they did not enjoy a modicum of local support, conquest was neither quick nor easy. Despite the truce made in 1148 with the Almoravids of Granada, the Almohads were unable to take direct control of the city until 1155. It took them a further two years to dislodge the Castilians from the vital port of Almería, while the Muslim lord of eastern al-Andalus, Ibn Mardanish, did not capitulate until 1172, often preferring alliance with the Castilians to surrender to the Almohads. Although the Almohads frequently denounced the Banu Mardanish as wine-swilling friends of the Christian infidel, 'Abd al-Mu'min's successor, Abu Ya'qub Yusuf, welcomed them to court with open arms when they finally surrendered and he confirmed the new cordiality of the relationship by marrying Ibn Mardanish's daughter because the Almohad position in al-Andalus was untenable without such allies.[45]

'Abd al-Mu'min's Expansion of the Empire East: the Campaigns against Bijaya and al-Mahdiyya

In contrast to Yusuf b. Tashfin who campaigned in al-Andalus several times, 'Abd al-Mu'min showed a marked reluctance to enter the peninsula and sent his sons to manage affairs there while he focused his energies on the consolidation of his government in the western Maghrib and the extension of his power eastwards across North Africa to Ifriqiya. This was in many ways a natural direction of expansion for the Almohad movement. From the ideological point of view, Ibn Tumart's claim to be the *mahdī*, the true guide and keeper of Islam, implicitly required the Almohads to restore the true faith throughout Islamic lands by means of their jihad. While the Almoravids had accrued legitimacy by proclaiming their devotion to the 'Abbasid caliphate in

[44] Ibn 'Idhari, *al-Bayan*, vol. 4, pp. 122–3.

[45] Ibn Sahib al-Salat, *al-Mann bi'l-Imama*, pp. 424–5; Ibn 'Idhari, *al-Bayan*, vol. 4, p. 208. See also pp. 136–7, below.

Baghdad, the Almohads rejected all caliphates but their own and considered the rampant sectarianism of eastern Islam to be a sign of decadence that was in contrast to the religious homogeneity and unity they were instilling in the Maghrib. From their perspective, the Berbers had a mission to restore the Dar al-Islam which the Arabs had failed to preserve.[46]

A further interrelated jihad incentive was provided by the broad sense of a Christian–Muslim Mediterranean confrontation engendered by the Crusades in the Levant, the loss of Fatimid Sicily to the Norman de Hauteville lineage, and the piecemeal advances of the Christians in Iberia. This was compounded in the late 1140s when the Normans took advantage of the changes wrought by the demise of the Zirid regime in Ifriqiya and the migrations of the Arab Banu Hilal and Sulaym tribes who had drifted west from Egypt over the previous century, to capture and occupy several Ifriqiyan ports, including the old Fatimid coastal capital of al-Mahdiyya in 1148–9. The ability of Christian powers to invade Muslim lands could easily be interpreted as one of the most telling signs of the internal 'corruption' against which the Almohads were fighting, as well as an infidel threat to the lands of Islam which a universalist jihad movement such as the Almohad mission could not ignore.

On the more pragmatic side, as a native of the Tlemcen area, 'Abd al-Mu'min had a sense of affinity with the Zanata there and he had strengthened his position by recruiting many of them into the Almohad army. He had also cultivated some links with the Sanhaja Banu Hammad of the central Maghrib, who had initially offered their support to their Almoravid fellows during the siege of Tlemcen but then transferred their allegiance to the Almohads. This had given 'Abd al-Mu'min nominal authority over the coastal town of Bijaya in the central Maghrib and drew the Almohad gaze eastwards to Ifriqiya where the power vacuum caused by the waning of the Zirid regime had been gravely exacerbated by the Norman occupation of the coast, enabling local lineages to take control of towns and tribes to dominate the hinterland unfettered by any central power. The Almohads therefore had both motive and opportunity to march eastwards.

'Abd al-Mu'min's first eastern campaign was designed to impose direct Almohad control over Bijaya and the domains of the Sanhaja Banu Hammad. This brought him into contact with the Arab Banu Hilal and Sulaym tribes who gathered against the Almohads only to be defeated at the Battle of Setif in 1153. From this point onwards, the Arab tribes of Ifriqiya began to play an important role in Almohad affairs.[47] Although many of them fiercely

[46] Sánchez, 'Ethnic disaffection', p. 177.
[47] Huici Miranda, *Historia política*, vol. 1, pp. 166–7.

resisted the Almohads, their skills as fighters attracted 'Abd al-Mu'min who 'persuaded' them to serve him by capturing and transferring their families to Marrakesh as hostages who would be released if their menfolk entered the Almohad army. He sweetened the pill with generous material incentives. Over time this led to the resettlement of Arab tribes such as the Riyah, the Khult and the Zughba in what is now Morocco and the commencement of the rural Arabisation of the western Maghrib. It also added a new element to the Almohad army alongside the Masmuda and Zanata tribes already serving 'Abd al-Mu'min. In contrast to the Berbers, however, 'Abd al-Mu'min seems not to have expected ideological commitment from the Arabs, and throughout the Almohad era they remained potentially disruptive if material compensation was not forthcoming.

'Abd al-Mu'min combined his campaigns to the east with the gradual consolidation of Almohad government and the elaboration of the simple hierarchy established by Ibn Tumart three decades before in Tinmall. By this time, several members of the original Councils of Ten and Fifty had died, and their sons, known as the 'sons of the Almohads' (*abnā' al-muwaḥḥidīn*) or the 'kin of the Fifty' (*ahl khamsīn*) were taking their place. The Masmuda shaykhs of the movement, including Ibn Tumart's brothers, 'Abd al-'Aziz and 'Isa, now shared power with 'Abd al-Mu'min's Zanata relatives and other new members of the elite such as Almoravid defectors, Andalusi lords and Arab tribal shaykhs.

As time passed, the ideological structure and coherence of the movement was preserved through the institutionalisation of two cohorts, the *ṭalaba* or elite Almohad scholars and the *ḥuffāẓ* or Almohad cadres. The *ṭalaba* seem to have coalesced out of the small group of disciples around Ibn Tumart. At the outset they were the group most conversant with Ibn Tumart's teachings and included men such as 'Abd al-Mu'min who were also fighters for the cause. As the empire developed, however, the *ṭalaba* became a more conventional scholarly group, the religious experts and jurists of the Almohad movement involved in teaching and disseminating the Almohad message. Al-Marrakushi, writing in the early thirteenth century, describes them as falling into two groups, the *ṭalabat al-ḥaḍar* and the *ṭalabat al-muwaḥḥidīn*:

> It was [the Almohads'] custom to write to the provinces requiring the dispatch of scholars of every subject (*fann*) to their capital (*ḥaḍra*) and especially experts in theological disputation (*'ilm al-naẓar*) whom they called *ṭalabat al-ḥaḍar*. They were sometimes many in number and sometimes few. There was another category of Masmuda whose occupation was religious science called the *ṭalabat al-muwaḥḥidīn*.[48]

[48] al-Marrakushi, *Mu'jib*, p. 484.

There is some scholarly disagreement about the meaning of these uniquely Almohad terms which were part of the wider lexical distinctiveness of the Almohads. Lévi-Provençal and the generation of scholars who followed him interpreted the *ṭalabat al-ḥaḍar* as provincial scholars and the *ṭalabat al-muwaḥḥidīn* as the core scholarly group around the caliph. More recently, however, Fricaud has argued that actually the reverse was true with *ḥaḍar* signifying not 'city folk' in this case but those gathered in the presence (*ḥaḍra*) of the caliph while the *ṭalabat al-muwaḥḥidīn* were stationed in the provinces.[49] The definition given by al-Marrakushi, however, actually contains both ideas, suggesting that the *ṭalabat al-ḥadar* were drawn from the provinces to serve in the caliph's entourage.

While the *ṭalaba* formed the Almohad intellectual elite, the Almohad rank and file were collectively known as the *ḥuffāẓ* (memorisers), a term used by the chronicler al-Baydhaq for the tribal fighters of the Almohad movement.[50] Although the term *ḥāfiẓ* (pl. *ḥuffāẓ*) usually denotes someone who has memorised the Qur'an, in the Almohad context it meant those who had been taught and had memorised the principal tenets of Almohadism in the centres of learning established by 'Abd al-Mu'min.[51] As previously mentioned, Ibn Tumart had put considerable stress on educating the early Almohad tribes and getting them to memorise the *Tawḥīd*, and religio-political indoctrination remained an important feature of the movement. In addition to religious education, however, the *ḥuffāẓ* also underwent military training and even, according to some sources, swimming lessons to prepare them for the crossing to al-Andalus![52] This process helped to transform tribesmen of varied backgrounds into more coherent cadres of Almohads. However, the *ḥuffāẓ* were predominantly Masmuda Berbers and there is no extant indication that the Arab Banu Hilal and Sulaym tribes who entered Almohad service from the Battle of Setif onwards were trained in the same way or considered to be Almohad *ḥuffāẓ*, underlining the ethnic as well as ideological ramifications of these terms.[53]

The Almohad fighting forces were a key institution of the state and recruiting, funding and managing the army formed an important, if not the paramount, task of the caliph and his government. The Almohad army continued to rely heavily on tribal structures for mobilisation purposes and tribal shaykhs were vitally important as the *de facto* military commanders

[49] Fricaud, 'Les *ṭalaba* dans la société almohade', pp. 348–9.
[50] al-Baydhaq, *Akhbar*, p. 124.
[51] Huici Miranda, *Historia política*, vol. 1, p. 174.
[52] *al-Hulal al-Mawshiyya*, p. 114.
[53] Bennison, 'The salutory tale of Ibn 'Aṭiyya', pp. 267–70.

of their men. As such, they were regular attendees at the caliph's *majlis*, particularly when he wished to consult them on matters of military policy. The most important Almohad shaykhs led military campaigns when 'Abd al-Mu'min could not personally do so and many were also appointed as military governors across the empire. Although the use of tribal shaykhs as military commanders and governors was similar to the Almoravids, the pool from which the Almohads drew their military personnel was much larger and more diverse than that of their predecessors and, in addition to the assorted Berber and Arab tribes, it came to include Andalusi units, black slaves, Turkish and Kurdish cavalry from the Middle East and Christian mercenaries.

The Almohad administration was staffed by urban Arabic-literate officials, many of whom had previously served the Almoravids, but with a much larger proportion of Maghribis to Andalusis due to the expansion of Maghribi cities under the Almoravids and the Almohad incorporation of the more densely urbanised eastern Maghrib into their empire. The control exercised by the central government in Marrakesh was closer than in Almoravid times, and officials, such as governors, could expect to be summoned to Marrakesh with their registers of taxation for audits. The caliph himself relied upon a circle of officials and advisers, headed by one or more ministers (*wazīr*, *wuzarā'*) who were selected on merit rather than background, and secretaries (*kuttāb*) who handled official correspondence.

Around 1154–5, after the Bijaya campaign and the absorption of the territories of the Banu Hammad into the Almohad empire, 'Abd al-Mu'min made a series of moves to preserve the rule of the Almohad empire in the hands of his lineal descendants, the Mu'minids who were known collectively as the *sayyids*, a term used in eastern Islamic lands for descendants of the Prophet but meaning princes of the blood in the Almohad context. First, 'Abd al-Mu'min appointed his son Muhammad as his heir in place of the veteran Almohad shaykh Abu Hafs 'Umar al-Hintati. Although Ibn 'Idhari describes the Almohad shaykhs as begging 'Abd al-Mu'min to take these steps, he had rallied the Arab shaykhs and his own kinsmen in support of this change, leaving the Masmuda with little choice but to acquiesce.[54]

The Almohad succession was actually a very contentious and potentially volatile issue, as it had been in early Islamic times. The succession to the Prophet Muhammad had not been hereditary until the fifth caliph, Mu'awiya of the Umayyad clan, designated his son Yazid as his heir, triggering a civil war between those who felt that if the caliphate was hereditary it should belong to the family of the Prophet and those who accepted the

[54] Ibn 'Idhari, *al-Bayan*, vol. 4, pp. 127–8; Huici Miranda, *Historia política*, vol. 1, pp. 169–70.

establishment of a hereditary Umayyad caliphate. It was similarly contentious for 'Abd al-Mu'min to make the succession to Ibn Tumart hereditary in his own line rather than in the line of Ibn Tumart, known as the Banu Amghar. Potentially, this not only excluded the *mahdī*'s own lineage from supreme rule, but also confirmed the meta-shift of power from the Masmuda to the Zanata Kumiya, whom al-Marrakushi described seventy years later as the most powerful tribe in the empire despite their origins as peasants, shepherds and market traders selling the humblest commodities![55]

'Abd al-Mu'min compounded the situation by following his successful extraction of oaths of allegiance to his son Muhammad with the announcement of the appointments of several of his other sons to major governorships across the empire in the place of Almohad shaykhs. Although all these appointments probably did not occur simultaneously, al-Baydhaq provides a list naming Abu Muhammad 'Abd Allah as governor of Bijaya, Abu Hafs 'Umar as governor of Tlemcen, Abu Ya'qub Yusuf to Seville, Abu Sa'id 'Uthman to Ceuta and then Granada, Abu'l-Hasan 'Ali as governor of Fes, Abu'l-Rabi' Sulayman as governor of Tadla in the Middle Atlas and Abu Zayd b. al-Lamtiyya to the Sus valley, although the latter was apparently too young to actually take up his post.[56] Including the caliph himself in Marrakesh, this placed a Mu'minid prince in authority in virtually every important town of the empire.

The overt transference of supreme power from the Almohad shaykhs was a blow that 'Abd al-Mu'min softened by dispatching one or more eminent Almohad shaykhs drawn from the Councils of Ten and Fifty and their descendants, the 'Sons of the Almohads' (*abnā' al-muwahhidīn*), with each *sayyid* to act as their advisers, deputies and military commanders. This was particularly important in the case of young or inexperienced *sayyids* and gave them the chance to learn the political and military ropes and, ideally, become effective members of the ruling elite, a training strategy also followed by the early Ottoman sultans. Almohad shaykhs also took up governorships when the *sayyids* were absent from their posts on campaign or on visits to Marrakesh. This ensured that the Almohad shaykhs remained an important part of the Mu'minid administration and it seems to have reconciled the majority to the ascendance of the Mu'minid *sayyids*.

For others, though, including 'Abd al-'Aziz and 'Isa, the half-brothers of Ibn Tumart, 'Abd al-Mu'min's usurpation of Ibn Tumart's patrimony by founding his own dynasty was the final straw. Relations between the Mu'minids and the Banu Amghar had been tense for many years. The

[55] al-Marrakushi, *Mu'jib*, p. 481.
[56] al-Baydhaq, *Akhbar*, p. 138.

generally pro-Mu'minid, and therefore not unbiased, sources depict Ibn Tumart's brothers as incompetent and corrupt, and by 1154 they had been deprived of the governorship of Seville and internally exiled to Fes for various misdemeanours inspired, according to Ibn 'Idhari, by their envy of 'Abd al-Mu'min.[57] Unsurprisingly, they responded to the further concentration of power in the hands of the Mu'minid clan by escaping from Fes and launching a rebellion supported by other disgruntled Masmuda shaykhs.

The uprising took place in the Almohad capital Marrakesh where the brothers exploited 'Abd al-Mu'min's absence in Ribat al-Fath-Salé to join up with other dissidents and kill the governor. A pitched battle between supporters and opponents of 'Abd al-Mu'min ensued with the victory eventually going to the former. Both Ibn Tumart's brothers were killed and 'Abd al-Mu'min took rapid and violent action against other Almohads implicated in the rebellion. Al-Baydhaq asserts that a saddlebag containing documents, including the names of conspirators, was discovered at the rebels' camp in the lakeside gardens outside Marrakesh. All those involved were then ceremoniously paraded between lines of loyal townsfolk, armed for the occasion, to the prison where they were killed by castration. If they protested, the paper bearing their name was solemnly waved in their face.[58]

After this shocking but decisive display of power, 'Abd al-Mu'min returned to Ribat al-Fath-Salé in order to monitor the situation in al-Andalus. He continued to leave the actual prosecution of Andalusi affairs, military and political, to his sons and the Almohad shaykhs with them, however, suspecting perhaps that if he left the Maghrib it might enable Masmuda Almohad dissenters to renew their opposition. It may have been the barely concealed rifts within the Almohad elite that encouraged 'Abd al-Mu'min to incorporate the Almoravid Lamtuna of Granada into his entourage when they negotiated their surrender and accepted Almohadism in 1156. The erstwhile dissident Almoravid prince, Yahya b. al-Sahrawiyya, who had finally surrendered around 1155 after supporting a rebellion by the Gazula and Lamta in 1153–4, became the leader of this group.[59]

The presence of a large group of ex-Almoravid Lamtuna in the elite of Marrakesh proved to be disruptive and triggered the fall in 1158 of 'Abd al-Mu'min's famous minister, Ahmad b. 'Atiyya, who happened to be married to Yahya b. al-Sahrawiyya's sister, Zaynab.[60] Although the social

[57] Ibn 'Idhari, *al-Bayan*, vol. 4, p. 126.

[58] al-Baydhaq, *Akhbar*, p. 145.

[59] Ibid., p. 145; al-Marrakushi, *Mu'jib*, pp. 291–2.

[60] This brother and sister were children of Abu Bakr, one of the sons of Yusuf b. Tashfin. Although their mother's name is not recorded, her Lamtuna origin is preserved in the

implications of this event will be considered in Chapter 4, the political aspects shed light on the nature of 'Abd al-Mu'min's government at this point. Ibn 'Atiyya, a native of Marrakesh whose father had migrated from al-Andalus, had served as an Almoravid scribe before gaining a position as 'Abd al-Mu'min's secretary (*kātib*) and then minister (*wazīr*) due to his excellent command of literary Arabic. This was a career path that many other Almoravid officials had followed, including 'Abd Allah b. Khiyar al-Jayyani, the *mushrif* of Fes. After his brother-in-law, Yahya b. al-Sahrawiyya, submitted to the Almohads, however, there were accusations that Ibn 'Atiyya was too close to the Almoravid 'enemy' within,[61] many of which came from others who had served the Almoravids and, ironically, gained an entrée to the Almohad ruling elite through the good offices of Ibn 'Atiyya.

The rumours about Ibn 'Atiyya's continued loyalty to the Almoravids seemed to be proved when Yahya b. al-Sahrawiyya made critical comments about 'Abd al-Mu'min and Ibn 'Atiyya warned him to flee to Almoravid Mallorca rather than remaining neutral in the matter and preserving the confidentiality of the caliphal *majlis*. For this breach of trust and display of hubris, Ibn 'Atiyya was arrested, publicly humiliated and taken to the shrine of Ibn Tumart in Tinmall, before being put to death, along with his younger brother, on the road back to Marrakesh.[62] A number of observations can be made about this. First, both Ibn 'Atiyya and his accusers were from urban Arabic-literate families who had become a vital part of Almohad government. This confirms the importance of the established bureaucratic class to both the Almoravids and the Almohads and the frequent transfer of their loyalties. Secondly, it is clear that the Almohads integrated a variety of individuals and groups into the ruling class to provide essential expertise and act as a counter-balance to the Masmuda shaykhs. Thirdly, the killing of Ibn 'Atiyya, like that of Masmuda dissidents, showed how critical loyalty was to 'Abd al-Mu'min as the glue that kept the Almohad elite together: betrayal, whether real or perceived, had to be brutally and decisively punished. One suspects that personal loyalty was more important to 'Abd al-Mu'min than the profession of Almohad Islam.

In fact, the religio-political ideology of 'Abd al-Mu'min and his successors was gradually modified to supplement its Almohad elements, first and foremost of which was the declaration that Ibn Tumart was the *mahdī*, with

description of her children as son and daughter of 'the Saharan woman' (*al-Ṣaḥrāwiyya*). al-Marrakushi, *Mu'jib*, p. 291.

61 Bennison, 'The salutory tale of Ibn 'Aṭiyya', pp. 261–5.

62 Ibid., p. 265.

more generic Islamic elements that enabled 'Abd al-Mu'min and his descendants to derive their legitimacy not only from being the caliphs or successors of Ibn Tumart but as Islamic monarchs in the tradition of the Umayyads of Córdoba, in other words caliphs in the usual Islamic, rather than the narrow Almohad, sense. This strategy of legitimation was quite different to that of the Almoravids who had legitimised themselves as lieutenants of the 'Abbasid caliphs not as caliphs themselves. As Fierro has demonstrated, 'Abd al-Mu'min cultivated an Arab genealogy which was a prerequisite for assuming the position of caliph in non-Almohad circles.[63] He also acquired a relic from Córdoba, the so-called Qur'an of 'Uthman, which was closely associated with the Umayyads and their ancestor, 'Uthman b. 'Affan, the third Rightly-Guided Caliph (r. 644–56). After his sons dispatched this artefact from Córdoba to Marrakesh, it became a central element in Almohad parades, creating a symbolic link between the Mu'minids and the Maliki Sunni Umayyads of al-Andalus, despite the radical difference in the theology of the two regimes.[64]

The other pillar of Mu'minid legitimacy was jihad. The Almohad jihad had begun as a mission to remove the Almoravids, which mushroomed into an ambitious undertaking to return the Muslim population of the Maghrib to a true understanding of Islam by means of conquest. This was broadly similar to the Almoravid jihad, but, rather than championing an existing religious position, the Almohads introduced their own brand of Islam. The incorporation of tribes and urban communities into the Almohad empire was a dual process that involved giving obedience (*ṭā'a*) and 'becoming Almohad' (*waḥḥada*), a verb that could simply mean acceptance of monotheism but in the Almohad conquest narrative clearly means accepting Almohad monotheism, including its chief tenet that Ibn Tumart was the *mahdī*. Jews and Christians in the empire were also pressurised into converting to 'true' monotheism by threats that they would be killed or exiled if they did not comply, a radical deviation from the normal Islamic position vis-à-vis the 'peoples of the book', which we shall explore further in Chapter 4.[65]

This jihad within the Dar al-Islam had greater validity when connected to defence of Muslim territory from Christian attacks and occupation, a form of fighting possessing incontrovertible religio-political legitimacy which justified internal jihad to unify the community as a precondition for successful jihad against the Christians. On both the Christian and Muslim sides

[63] See Fierro, 'Las genealogías de 'Abd al-Mu'min'.

[64] See Bennison, 'The Qur'ān of 'Uthmān'.

[65] For a range of views on the situation of religious minorities under the Almohads, see Bennison and Gallego (eds), *Religious Minorities under the Almohads*.

of the Mediterranean, the Crusades generated eschatological expectations which fed into militant narratives about the impending final struggle between Christianity and Islam. For ʿAbd al-Muʾmin, who captured Marrakesh a few short years after the Second Crusade in 1144, during which the Crusaders attempted to conquer Damascus, the advance of the Almohads through the Maghrib, al-Andalus and Ifriqiya was part of a single jihad to unite the Muslims and push back the Christian hordes who threatened them across the Mediterranean. Such ideas were generalised through the reading of victory notices in great mosques and the celebration of every victory against a Christian contingent, whether minor or major, with drum rolls, banner waving and feasting.[66]

The apogee of ʿAbd al-Muʾmin's reign in later Islamic historiography was therefore his celebrated jihad to liberate al-Mahdiyya from Norman occupation, a campaign actually designed to impose Almohad authority throughout Ifriqiya. The sources report that ʿAbd al-Muʾmin travelled to Ribat al-Fath in 1158 and commanded that preparations for a jihad campaign should be undertaken. The word was given out that he planned to campaign in al-Andalus, but he switched the destination to Ifriqiya, possibly in order not to alert the ever-restive tribes of the western Maghrib to the prospect of a long absence on his part. The army set out in March 1159 on a slow and stately journey across North Africa. ʿAbd al-Muʾmin was an excellent tactician and he was aware that religio-political theatre had as much impact as actual victory in battle. In Ibn al-Athir, al-Nuwayri and al-Tijani's accounts of the campaign derived from the Tunisian Ibn Shaddad, it is presented as a model of good practice and religious devotion with the army carefully marching between the crops so as not to damage them, well-diggers advancing ahead of the main army to ensure it had water, and the army gathering for communal prayer at which everyone had to be present.[67] Although deeply involved in the blood, sweat and tears of conquest, ʿAbd al-Muʾmin also established the ceremonial paradigm still in place in the early thirteenth century when al-Marrakushi, writing to impress an ʿAbbasid audience, similarly described the solemn, religiously inflected progress of Almohad troops punctuated by regular recitation of the Qurʾan and gatherings for ritual prayer.[68]

As in al-Andalus, the Almohads lacked sufficient military strength in the central Maghrib and Ifriqiya to reject local allies and they had to temper righteous violence with political realism as they advanced from their

[66] Ibn Sahib al-Salat, *al-Mann biʾl-Imama*, pp. 74–5, 209 ff.

[67] Ibn al-Athir, *al-Kamil fiʾl-Taʾrikh*, vol. 11, pp. 241–2; al-Nuwayri, *Nihayat al-Arab*, vol. 24, p. 171; al-Tijani, *Rihla*, p. 346.

[68] al-Marrakushi, *Muʿjib*, p. 485.

heartlands. The three main constituencies with whom the Almohads had to engage were Berber and Arab tribes and urban communities. Relations with Berbers pastoralists and sedentary villagers followed the patterns of alliance-making already established in the western Maghrib: Berber tribes who allied with the Almohads gained a *carte blanche* to pillage and subdue their rivals whose only protection lay in offering their own submission to the Almohads who then took on the role of mediators. The Almohads interacted with the nomadic Arab tribes they encountered as they had with those they met on the Bijaya campaign – military engagement, followed by the capture of Arab women and children, and their release in exchange for the integration of their menfolk into Almohad ranks.

In the case of urban communities, ʿAbd al-Mu'min made repeated offers of an *amān* (guarantee of security) in return for submission before attacking and he granted *amān*s to delegations that brought the submission of towns not yet invested by the Almohad armies. His response to communities that did not submit was harsher. When the Almohads approached Tunis, the city's ruling lineage, the Banu Khurasan, rejected the Almohad offer of an *amān* and the city was then subjected to a violent Almohad onslaught and a massive confiscation of wealth and property from its inhabitants. ʿAbd al-Mu'min's infamous decree that Christians and Jews should convert, go into exile or risk death was also issued at Tunis. The Almohad army moved on to the suburbs of al-Mahdiyya, which they besieged for several months until the Norman garrison negotiated its surrender and departed by ship for Sicily. The town was occupied and its mosque ceremoniously purified and re-dedicated as a Muslim place of worship. In triumphant letters to the western Almohad provinces, ʿAbd al-Mu'min announced the end of the Christian Norman occupation of Ifriqiya and the cleansing of its cities from the pollution of the infidels.[69]

ʿAbd al-Mu'min's absence in Ifriqiya could not be prolonged, however, and he set off almost immediately for the western Maghrib in response to pleas for assistance from his son, Abu Yaʿqub Yusuf, in Seville who was struggling to cope with the depredations of the Castilians and their Muslim ally, Ibn Mardanish.[70] Despite such problems, ʿAbd al-Mu'min was not to be cheated of his moment and, as he approached his natal region of Tlemcen, he sent messages to his son Abu Saʿid ʿUthman in Granada to construct a new Almohad palatine city at Gibraltar, now renamed Mountain of Victory (Jabal al-Fath), where the empire's elite could celebrate the expulsion of the

[69] Ibn Sahib al-Salat, *al-Mann bi'l-Imama*, pp.72–3.

[70] Ibid., pp.75–6.

Normans and the consolidation of Almohad power.[71] In 1160, the *sayyids*, the Almohad shaykhs and Andalusi lords gathered in the new, somewhat hastily, erected palace for a round of state festivities. This was an opportunity for Andalusi lords to meet with 'Abd al-Mu'min, experience his hospitality, and be reminded of the awe-inspiring power of the Almohads in a grander, more ceremonial manner than at the Ribat al-Fath-Salé gathering in 1151. It also functioned as an opportunity for the reinforcement of bonds among the Mu'minid princes (*sayyids*) and the Almohad shaykhs. The recitations of eulogistic poetry and feasting that ensued were a foretaste of the spectacular political theatre and imperial display favoured by 'Abd al-Mu'min's successors.[72]

Despite this show of wealth and power, al-Andalus was hardly pacified, but 'Abd al-Mu'min was now aging and he advanced no further into Iberia, preferring to return to Marrakesh in the company of his son, Abu Hafs 'Umar, who had become his right-hand man and chief minister. Although it is not explicitly stated, it is possible that 'Abd al-Mu'min, who had spent his life actively engaged in military and political life, took the uncharacteristic step of relinquished control to his son because he was ailing. He left prosecution of the Almohad cause in al-Andalus to the *sayyids*, Abu Sa'id 'Uthman in Granada and Abu Ya'qub Yusuf in Seville. They battled on in their efforts to constrain Ibn Mardanish, his father-in-law Ibn Hamushk, and their Christian allies in eastern al-Andalus. This struggle had an ideological colour which divided as well as united Muslims: while the Almohads depicted their actions as a jihad against the infidels and their depraved Muslim allies, Ibn Mardanish claimed to be waging a jihad against Almohad deviance on behalf of the distant 'Abbasids in Baghdad. The population of al-Andalus had mixed feelings about both these claims and about the relative merits of Almohad, Andalusi or Christian rule.

Communal fault lines emerge clearly in Granada where the city's 'Islamised' (*islāmiyyūn*) Jews, who had been obliged to convert by the Almohads, exploited Abu Sa'id 'Uthman's absence 'on a trip' in 1162 to enter into negotiations with Ibn Hamushk to secretly open the city gates to his forces.[73] As a result, the Almohads were besieged in the lower citadel (*qaṣaba*) while Ibn Hamushk occupied the upper 'red citadel' (*al-qaṣaba al-ḥamrā'*), site of the later Alhambra. Abu Sa'id 'Uthman and Abu Muhammad, son of the shaykh Abu Hafs 'Umar al-Hintati, mobilised an army to relieve the garrison, but Ibn Hamushk and his Christian allies defeated them and drove them

[71] Ibn Sahib al-Salat, *al-Mann bi'l-Imama*, p. 84.
[72] Ibid., pp. 92–110.
[73] Ibid., p. 124.

back stumbling into the streams criss-crossing the plain outside Granada. Ibn Hamushk was soon joined by Ibn Mardanish and his army, including a large Christian contingent, who together intensified the siege of the beleaguered Almohad garrison and, according to Ibn Sahib al-Salat, taunted them by torturing and killing their captive fellows before their very eyes.[74] Granada was retaken only when Abu Ya'qub Yusuf, Abu Sa'id 'Uthman and the veteran shaykh Abu Ya'qub Yusuf b. Sulayman returned with a large Almohad army and ambushed Ibn Hamushk's position from behind, forcing Ibn Mardanish to abandon his camp and retreat quickly to Murcia. When the relieving army entered the city, the Almohad garrison emerged and 'fought those of the inhabitants who had behaved treacherously', a comment that flags up again the ambiguous sentiments of the population, Muslim and non-Muslim, towards Almohad rule.[75]

During the winter of 1162–3, 'Abd al-Mu'min performed a pilgrimage to the shrine of Ibn Tumart in Tinmall and then travelled to Ribat al-Fath to preside over preparations for what would have been his first campaign in al-Andalus if he had made the crossing. Before he could leave, however, he was taken mortally ill and died on 21 May 1163 attended by the *sayyid* Abu Hafs 'Umar. His body was ceremoniously conveyed to Tinmall by another *sayyid*, Abu'l-Hasan 'Ali, and he was buried alongside Ibn Tumart in the grand complex he had built a decade before.[76] Over the course of 'Abd al-Mu'min's reign, the Almohads had gone from a small embattled community in the High Atlas mountains to the masters of the Maghrib and a fair part of al-Andalus. They had an effective army, a centralised administration and a reasonably coherent ruling class dominated by 'Abd al-Mu'min's sons, the *sayyids*, in alliance with a broad coterie of tribal shaykhs drawn from the Masmuda, the Zanata and the Arab Banu Hilal and Sulaym. Much of this was the achievement of 'Abd al-Mu'min himself, a Berber boy of humble background who had risen against the odds to become caliph of a vast Islamic empire, 'the most glorious and enduring' in the medieval Maghrib, and arguably larger than any other Islamic state of its time, in view of the *de facto* fragmentation of the Seljuk sultanate in the east.[77] It remained to be seen, however, whether his sons possessed the same political and military acumen and whether they would be able to build on their father's success.

[74] Ibn Sahib al-Salat, *al-Mann bi'l-Imama*, p. 126.
[75] Ibn 'Idhari, *al-Bayan*, vol. 4, pp. 152–5.
[76] Ibn Sahib al-Salat, *al-Mann bi'l-Imama*, pp. 154–5.
[77] Huici Miranda, *Historia política*, vol. 1, p. 209.

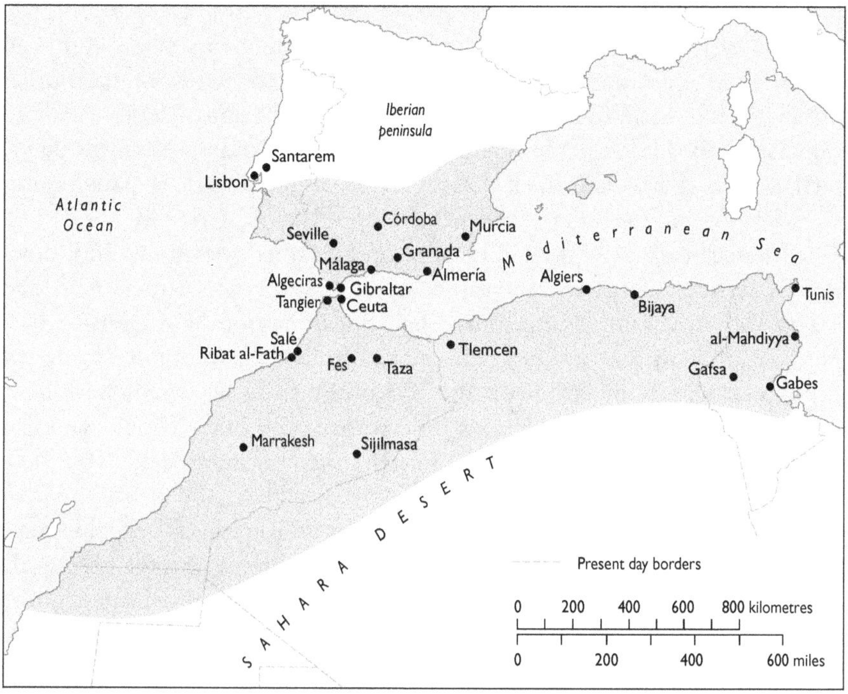

Figure 3.1 The Almohad empire

The Apogee of the Almohad Empire: the Reigns of Abu Yaʿqub Yusuf and Yaʿqub al-Mansur

The reigns of ʿAbd al-Mu'min's son Abu Yaʿqub Yusuf (r. 1163–84) and his grandson Abu Yusuf Yaʿqub, later known as al-Mansur (r. 1184–99), proved to be the high point of the Almohad era. While both rulers faced a normal degree of Berber and Arab tribal turbulence and had to engage in regular military campaigns to hold the frontier against the Christians and their Muslim allies in al-Andalus, they were fairly successful at maintaining Almohad control throughout the territories won by ʿAbd al-Mu'min. The main exception to this was Ifriqiya, where the incursions of the Almoravid Banu Ghaniya from the Balearics and their frequent alliances with Arab and Berber tribes regularly undermined the Almohad position from 1184.

Despite the marked preference for reporting military campaigns over every other kind of activity, the chronicles from this era do give brief insights into the Almohad caliphs' other endeavours, some of which had lasting effects upon western Islamic culture. Abu Yaʿqub and Abu Yusuf were patrons of the arts and intellectual life flourished during their reigns, producing such luminaries as the philosophers Ibn Tufayl and Ibn Rushd. In addition, they founded or augmented the main architectural monuments of the Almohad era, the great mosques of Seville, Rabat and Marrakesh, alongside many other urban projects, including gardens, palaces and fortifications. Under these two caliphs, Almohad pomp and ceremony also matured and the eloquent poetic recitations they hosted in their palaces and their grand military parades provided inspiration for many subsequent western Islamic dynasties.

The accession of Abu Ya'qub Yusuf on his father's death in 1163, however, was not a forgone conclusion as his half-brother Muhammad had been 'Abd al-Mu'min's undisputed heir apparent from 1155 until 1163. He was suddenly and unexpectedly ousted from the succession during the caliph's last illness in favour of Abu Ya'qub Yusuf in what may have been a coup orchestrated by the latter's full-brother, Abu Hafs 'Umar, who had been running the empire as chief minister (*wazīr*) from at least 1160.[78] To understand the situation, it is important to realise that 'Abd al-Mu'min had numerous wives and concubines, who had produced several capable male children who had close relations with their full siblings but not necessarily with their half-brothers. The *sayyid*s were, therefore, not a united group but a set of potential rivals for power, a situation that worsened as the number of *sayyid*s in each generation multiplied. According to the chronicle tradition, 'Abd al-Mu'min changed his mind on his deathbed in disgust at Muhammad's behaviour during the previous winter pilgrimage to Tinmall when he rode out drunk and vomiting in full view of his father and the other Almohads.[79]

This may be a *post facto* justification, however, for the sudden change of heir in favour of Abu Ya'qub Yusuf, a change recorded by none other than his powerful brother, Abu Hafs 'Umar, who had already taken over the day-to-day management of the caliphate from his father. Why did Abu Hafs 'Umar, the strongest contender, not seek the caliphate for himself? Perhaps, his usurpation of power would have been too obvious if he had persuaded his father to remove Muhammad in his own favour. By supporting the accession of his full brother, Abu Ya'qub Yusuf, the hero of the recapture of Granada from Ibn Hamushk, Abu Hafs 'Umar appeared to be acting for the good of the empire rather than making a personal grab for power. The sources are quite clear, however, that he used the affectionate relationship he had with his brother to remain in full charge of affairs. Abu Ya'qub Yusuf seems to have begun his reign so dependent on his brother that the chronicler Ibn Sahib

[78] Ibn Sahib al-Salat, *al-Mann bi'l-Imama*, p. 154.

[79] Ibid., p. 150.

al-Salat, who served the Almohads at this time, depicts him constantly deferring to Abu Hafs ʿUmar's judgement and describes the latter as the 'Most Exalted Prince' (*al-sayyid al-aʿlā*), while Abu Yaʿqub Yusuf is rather disparagingly termed 'Commander' (*amīr*) rather than 'Commander of the Faithful' (*amīr al-muʾminīn*), the full caliphal title of his father.[80]

The other *sayyids* responded in a variety of ways. Some accepted the *fait accompli* and offered their *bayʿa* or oath of allegiance to Abu Yaʿqub Yusuf with relatively little hesitation. Others were more reticent: Ibn Sahib al-Salat describes Abu'l-Hasan ʿAli, who took charge of his father's burial, as becoming ill with envy and rancour and dying soon afterwards![81] Abu Muhammad ʿAbd Allah, the governor of Bijaya, ignored requests to come and pay his respects and then died *en route* when he finally decided to make the trip to Marrakesh in 1165. The most important *sayyid* in al-Andalus, Abu Saʿid ʿUthman, remained in Córdoba and similarly refused to come to acknowledge his brother's accession. In the end, Abu Hafs ʿUmar forced his hand by bringing a massive Almohad army to Ceuta in spring 1165. Abu Saʿid ʿUthman mobilised his forces and his Andalusi allies at Jabal al-Fath (Gibraltar). His brother then crossed the Straits with his army, their banners waving and their drums beating to be received by Abu Saʿid and his army, similarly arrayed.[82] Although this is described as a joyous reunion accompanied by festivities and recitation of poetry, the tension is palpable. Abu Saʿid ʿUthman was obliged to accompany Abu Hafs ʿUmar back across the Straits to Marrakesh, where he was forced to endure a similar meeting with the caliph Abu Yaʿqub Yusuf and thereby tacitly recognise his accession.[83] He was only allowed to return to al-Andalus after two months in Marrakesh.

This seems to have marked the end of the resistance among the *sayyids* to the rule of the duumvirate of Abu Hafs ʿUmar and Abu Yaʿqub Yusuf. The brothers, whose mother, Zaynab, was the daughter of Musa al-Darir, a Masmuda shaykh from Tinmall, may also have had the backing of their maternal relatives who saw in their rule a timely restoration of Masmuda influence. For four years Abu Hafs ʿUmar took the political and military lead, travelling around the empire and heading military campaigns, while Abu Yaʿqub Yusuf remained mostly in Marrakesh, which seems to have been extremely prosperous and stable. As time passed, however, the diffident caliph slowly began to assert himself. In 1166–7, he took control of issuing his own correspondence and the year after he finally assumed the full caliphal

80 Ibn Sahib al-Salat, *al-Mann biʾl-Imama*, pp. 163, 165, 168, 169 ff.
81 Ibid., p. 170; Ibn ʿIdhari, *al-Bayan*, vol. 4, p. 162.
82 Ibn Sahib al-Salat, *al-Mann biʾl-Imama*, pp. 180–2.
83 Ibid., p. 187.

title, Commander of the Faithful (*amīr al-mu'minīn*), apparently prompted by his brother in eulogistic verses.

> Greetings, Oh heroic king, upon your circle who continue wishing you peace.
> May your days continue to be peaceful while boulders shower on your enemies.
> For you are the Imam of this people every one, and even if they pass away, the Imam remains.
> By your perspicacity, their cares are alleviated and the clouds slake the thirst of the earth.
> If it was not for the empire which you support neither the licit nor the illicit would be known.
> Nor would the morning rain water the earth or the pigeons coo in the branches.
> You spend the night awake seeking noble things, and the people arise with the good fortune of your rule.
> Time passes so slowly for me, indeed every day that passes without seeing you feels like a year.
> These nights bloom to reveal you like the buds bloom to show the calyx.[84]

While this poem may simply have expressed the sentiments expected of a courtier, Abu Ya'qub Yusuf and the circle around him chose to take it as an endorsement from the influential, if not all-powerful, Abu Hafs 'Umar and dispatched letters to the other Mu'minid princes in post, instructing them to ensure that everyone renewed their oath of allegiance and accepted Abu Ya'qub's caliphal status.[85]

There seems to have been a considerable difference in the characters of Abu Ya'qub Yusuf and Abu Hafs 'Umar which may help to explain the division of power between them. The latter was a man in his father's mould, an indefatigable soldier active against insurgents in the Maghrib and Muslim and Christian opponents of the Almohads in al-Andalus. Conversely, although Abu Ya'qub Yusuf was no stranger to military campaigns, he comes across as a cultured man who much preferred religious discussion with the Almohad *ṭalaba* and intellectual exchanges with the great minds of his day to the political and military aspects of government, which were by now well established enough to function without continual oversight. Ibn Sahib al-Salat, who was in his entourage, provides the following vignette:

[84] Ibn 'Idhari, *al-Bayan*, vol. 4, p. 174.
[85] Ibn Sahib al-Salat, *al-Mann bi'l-Imama*, pp. 258–9.

> The amir Abu Ya'qub Yusuf – may God be pleased with him – was full of virtue, just, and most pious. He knew the Qur'an, the Book of God Most High, by heart and he could explicate its abrogating and its abrogated [verses] and recite the text having memorised the pauses and points of inception.[86] He was also knowledgeable about the Hadith of the Messenger of God – May God's blessing be upon him – [and knew which] were sound, divergent, fair and unusual, and their chains of transmission. He excelled in the sciences of the Shari'a and the sources, foremost in knowledge of the imam-*mahdī* – may God be satisfied with him – and master of the areas of knowledge which [the *mahdī*] had dictated and which he had studied.[87]

This intellectual and bookish caliph also suffered from a long bout of illness which afflicted him for fourteen months from autumn 1169 and had his doctors, including Ibn Tufayl, prescribing all kinds of food and drink to restore him.[88] He could not, however, neglect his politico-military responsibilities indefinitely: to wage jihad was part of an Almohad caliph's obligations, and so, after nearly a decade of rule from Marrakesh, once his health had improved, Abu Ya'qub Yusuf finally mobilised a large army of Almohad and Arab tribal contingents over the winter of 1170–1 for a campaign in al-Andalus, which he had not visited since his years as a governor on behalf of his father. As in the Maghrib, the targets of Almohad jihad included Muslim opponents conceptualised as 'apostates' as well as non-Muslim enemies, and in this case the target was Ibn Mardanish who had been deserted in 1169 by Ibn Hamushk, whose daughter he had divorced, and besieged in his capital Murcia by the *sayyid* Abu Hafs 'Umar. The broader objective of the campaign was to show the Almohad caliph to his subjects and spread the cost of maintaining the army and his entourage across his domains. The Almohad army moved slowly in state and it was the caliph's obligation to settle the affairs of each major centre that he passed through, to re-establish justice and to correct abuses, all activities encompassed within the polysemic term 'jihad'.

The caliph left Marrakesh in March 1171 in a stately procession, preceded by the white caliphal banner and its infantry escort and followed by an array of other flags, guards and drums 'according to the customary marching arrangement'.[89] Immediately before him in the procession came two

86 This references to *nāsikh* (abrogating) and *mansūkh* (abrogated) verses indicates Abu Ya'qub's detailed knowledge of the Qur'an and methods of correctly extrapolating law from it.

87 Ibn Sahib al-Salat, *al-Mann bi'l-Imama*, p. 165.

88 Ibid., pp. 323–4.

89 Ibid., p. 350.

copies (*muṣḥaf*, *maṣāḥif*) of the Qur'an, the so-called Qur'an of 'Uthman b. 'Affan, transported from Córdoba at the end of 'Abd al-Mu'min's reign, and the Qur'an of Ibn Tumart. When the army approached al-Mahdiyya (Ribat al-Fath-Salé), it halted outside so that a similarly lavish procession could be organised for the caliph's entry to the town, although in this case the drums and banners preceded the caliph with the Qur'ans, an order that Ibn Sahib al-Salat notes was contrary to 'Abd al-Mu'min's custom but made the caliph's entry to al-Mahdiyya all the more splendid.[90] These ceremonial departures and entries to towns pointed to the maturing of Almohad ceremonial and the frequently mentioned role played within it by the abovementioned Qur'ans.[91]

The Mu'minid caliphs lavished particular attention on the Qur'an of 'Uthman: Ibn Sahib al-Salat says that it had 'a red cover to protect it' and its case was decorated with 'precious gems, rubies (*al-yāqūt al-aḥmar*), topaz (*al-yāqūt al-aṣfar*), rare green corundum (*al-yāqūt al-akhḍar al-gharīb*), and precious, wondrous green emeralds' which had been brought to 'Abd al-Mu'min and to Abu Ya'qub Yusuf himself, who decided to use them on the Qur'an case. According to one of the craftsmen, one of the jewels resembled a horse's hoof and had originally belonged to Khumarawayh b. Ahmad b. Tulun, 'Abbasid governor of Egypt in the ninth century.[92] When the Qur'an was prepared for Abu Ya'qub Yusuf's procession into al-Mahdiyya, he increased the effect by adding,

> four small flags on poles surmounted by gold globes which gleamed and sparkled in the light. The flags were coloured and made of red, yellow and white silk (*khuldī*) and they were placed at the corners of the *muṣḥaf*'s tabernacle.[93]

As we shall see below, the Qur'an of 'Uthman was particularly valued by the Mu'minid caliphs for its Sunni Umayyad associations, which helped them to appeal to those of their subjects who were not convinced by Almohad ideology, particularly the *mahdī*-hood of Ibn Tumart, and wished to see their rulers as part of the broader Islamic tradition.

From Ribat al-Fath-Salé, Abu Ya'qub Yusuf followed the usual route north to Qasr Masmuda on the Straits of Gibraltar before crossing to Algeciras and proceeding to Seville, which he reached in June 1171. He

90 Ibn Sahib al-Salat, *al-Mann bi'l-Imama*, p. 356.

91 On the Qur'an of 'Uthman, see Bennison, 'The Qur'ān of 'Uthmān'; Zadeh, 'From drops of blood'; Buresi, 'Une relique almohade'; Ghouirgate, *L'Ordre almohade*, pp. 337–50.

92 Ibn Sahib al-Salat, *al-Mann bi'l-Imama*, p. 351; Bennison, 'Qur'ān of 'Uthmān', p. 150.

93 Ibn Sahib al-Salat, *al-Mann bi'l-Imama*, pp. 355–6.

went to Córdoba to celebrate the festival of the sacrifice and then returned to overwinter in Seville, where he instigated the construction of the Buhayra estate and the new great mosque as well as making preparations for a military campaign against the Muslim and Christian opponents of the Almohads during the 1172 campaigning season. This was a propitious moment for a campaign in eastern al-Andalus as Ibn Mardanish had died, his family's opposition to the Almohads was wavering and his son Hilal had proffered his allegiance. Abu Ya'qub Yusuf, Abu Hafs 'Umar, several other *sayyids* and Almohad shaykhs therefore decided to proceed east to Murcia and attempt the recapture of the small town of Huete from the Castilians on the way.[94] This should have been fairly easy, but, after a promising start, the campaign began to falter when the Almohads hesitated to push their advantage and take the city, a situation Ibn Sahib al-Salat attributes to Abu Ya'qub Yusuf's preference for discussing theology with his religious scholars rather than providing decisive leadership on the field.[95] As the siege dragged on, the Almohad camp was damaged by repeated violent storms which provided the besieged Christians in Huete with much needed water and strengthened their resolve while undermining the morale of the Almohads. When news arrived that Alfonso VIII of León-Castile was approaching, the Almohad high command decided to burn their siege engines and leave Huete.[96]

After departing in some disorder, the lumbering Almohad campaign force came to Cuenca which had been under Christian siege for five months and scored a few small victories against Christian forces, but then disaster struck. During the next stages of the journey from Cuenca on to Valencia, Játiva and Murcia, the Almohad army lost its marching order and its contingents became separated, leaving many without supplies, tents or equipment. Numerous men and animals died from thirst and hunger in the sweltering summer heat as their units meandered across the countryside.[97] Shortly after they reached Murcia in August, the army was disbanded in response to the desperate pleas of the starving troops. Ibn Sahib al-Salat tried to make the best of the situation by talking of the rumbling Almohad drums striking fear into the heart of the enemy as they marched through the land and the celebrations at Játiva and Murcia on their arrival, but there were few real military gains.[98]

In the southwestern corner of the peninsula, what is now the Algarve, the

[94] Huici Miranda, *Historia política*, vol. 1, pp. 258–65.
[95] Ibn Sahib al-Salat, *al-Mann bi'l-Imama*, pp. 406–8.
[96] Ibid., pp. 410–13.
[97] Ibid., pp. 420–1.
[98] Ibid., pp. 414, 419, 423.

Almohads faced similar pressures from the colourful Portuguese adventurer, Giraldo Sem Pavor, and local Muslims who sometimes threw in their lot with the advancing Christians.[99] By the early 1170s, the Portuguese were well established in Santarem and Lisbon and had their eye on Beja, which they seized in 1172 with the collusion of some of its Muslim inhabitants. The Almohads regained the town in 1174 as the result of a truce, but the Portuguese remained as strong a potential threat to the security of the Muslim southwest as the Leónese, Castilians and Aragonese further east. Giraldo Sem Pavor, feeling betrayed by his king, did an about-turn and entered Almohad service with 350 of his knights and crossed to the Maghrib. He was initially stationed in the Sus, but, after correspondence between himself and the Portuguese king surfaced, he was transferred away from the Atlantic coast and subsequently executed by the governor of the Dar'a.[100]

Despite Giraldo's unfortunate end, his transfer of allegiance, the cooperation of the Muslims of Beja with the Portuguese and the Almohad–Portuguese truce remind us that we should not interpret the politics of this period as a clear-cut binary struggle between Muslims and Christians. While Muslim chroniclers speak of jihad and Christian sources construct a crusading narrative revolving around the 'reconquest' (*reconquista*) of Christian land from infidel hands, the reality was altogether more complex, as it had been a century earlier when El Cid served Christians and Muslims in turn. The kings of León and Castile, which were separate kingdoms between 1158 and 1230, Aragon and Portugal were often mutually antagonistic and keen to make treaties with the Almohads against their Christian rivals. For instance, it was a joint Almohad–Leónese offensive in 1169 that restored Badajoz to Almohad control, after its capture by Giraldo in 1165.[101] Moreover, the Christian kings were as liable as the Almohads to face challenges from internal opponents. It was not uncommon for Christian dissidents to seek refuge with the Almohad caliphs and, likewise, for Muslims to serve Christian kings. Both sides had mercenaries of the other religion and it was entirely possible to find allied Muslim and Christian forces fighting similarly mixed contingents. Although Muslims were ultimately expelled from the Iberian peninsula, this was neither a linear process nor a forgone conclusion.

After the Huete campaign, Abu Ya'qub Yusuf remained in Seville for another three years, during which time he presided over quite extensive investment in fortifications and the urban redevelopment projects he had

[99] For Giraldo Sem Pavor's campaigns, see Huici Miranda, *Historia política*, vol. 1, pp. 231–41.

[100] Huici Miranda, *Historia política*, vol. 1, pp. 271–2.

[101] Ibid., vol. 1, p. 236.

commenced before the campaign. Although he did not perhaps quite 'restore prosperity and civilisation in place of desolation', as Ibn Sahib al-Salat declares, he did add gardens, palaces and a new great mosque to the city.[102] After this long period away from the Maghrib, the caliph suddenly decided to return in spring 1176 leaving his entourage and Andalusi allies to follow hastily behind. This turned out to be unfortunate timing as Marrakesh was struck by plague a little over a month after Abu Ya'qub Yusuf's arrival. The epidemic lasted a year and decimated the ruling class as well as the general population with as many as 200 people dying per day at its height. The caliph and his brother Abu Hafs 'Umar fell ill for an extended period, and several other *sayyids*, scholars and shaykhs died, including the redoubtable Abu Hafs 'Umar al-Hintati, the last of the old guard.[103]

When the caliph had recovered, he marched against the rebellious Sanhaja of the south to renew his authority, and he made a round of governmental appointments to replace the dead and refresh the ruling elite. These included the appointment of his son Abu Yusuf Ya'qub as commander of the military in Marrakesh, with Abu 'Abd Allah b. Yusuf b. Wanudin as his shaykh, and the appointment of a new set of *sayyids* in al-Andalus. This phase of renewal and change in the ruling elite culminated in 1179 with the death of the caliph's powerful brother, Abu Hafs 'Umar. Soon afterwards, in 1180, Abu Ya'qub Yusuf decided to go on campaign to reinstall Almohad power over Gafsa in Ifriqiya and recruit the Arab tribes for jihad in al-Andalus, where the Portuguese and Castilians had reneged upon their truces and renewed their attacks on exposed Muslim settlements.[104] Like the caliph's earlier campaign to al-Andalus, this lengthy campaign across the Maghrib to Ifriqiya was also necessary to introduce him to his more easterly subjects, in particular those Arab tribes who had shrugged off Almohad rule. He settled first at Tlemcen to await the arrival of further Almohad contingents and then proceeded to Bijaya and Gafsa where the Arab shaykhs speedily gathered to ask him for pledges of safety (*amān*) despite their rebelliousness. After he had restored Almohad rule over Gafsa, he proceeded to Tunis and then returned slowly to Marrakesh, forging and renewing bonds of loyalty along the way.

During the caliph's absence, the situation in al-Andalus had worsened and delegates soon arrived begging him to relieve the straitened Almohad forces in the peninsula where Alfonso VIII of Castile was launching regular raids on the Guadalquivir valley and the Portuguese and Almohad fleets

[102] Ibn Sahib al-Salat, *al-Mann bi'l-Imama*, p. 167. See also Chapter 7, below.
[103] Ibn 'Idhari, *al-Bayan*, vol. 4, pp. 209–10.
[104] Ibid., vol. 4, pp. 213–15.

were battling for control of the southwestern seaboard. Instead, Abu Ya'qub Yusuf prioritised the reassertion of his authority closer to home and travelled south to the Sus valley where mining communities had been failing to deliver the caliph his share of the ore, most likely silver. Metal ore, and silver especially, was a natural resource that the caliph needed for currency, but, over and above that, the Sus and the High Atlas mountains were the cradle of the Almohad movement and could not be allowed to slip from their control. The caliph combined his trip with a pilgrimage to Tinmall and insisted that his Andalusi visitors in Marrakesh also ascend the mountain to pay their respects at the tombs of Ibn Tumart and 'Abd al-Mu'min.[105] On his return to Marrakesh and through 1182, Abu Ya'qub Yusuf concentrated on expanding the bustling city of Marrakesh to the south to accommodate its ever-growing population. Eventually, however, he felt impelled to travel once more to al-Andalus, where the situation in the southwest remained highly volatile, despite the vigorous campaigning of the Almohad shaykh Yusuf b. Wanudin.

The stages of the caliph's campaign are again described in great detail which reveal much about the character of the Almohad state at its height, including its imperial pomp and ceremony, its wealth, the role of the Mu'minid clan in government and the administrative as well as military functions of such campaigns. Preparations for the campaign began outside the imperial capital, Marrakesh, at the Buhayra or Lake estate, a feature of most major Almohad cities where facilities for travelling Almohad contingents and water for their animals were required. While at his Buhayra palace, Abu Ya'qub Yusuf reviewed the Almohad and Arab troops in residence tribe by tribe, a process that took around three weeks and he ordered the construction of ten mangonels, a type of war machine that reminds us that the Almohads were better prepared for sieges and more determined to maintain them than their Almoravid predecessors.[106]

The *sayyids*, a group that now included the caliph's sons as well as his brothers, had been summoned to Marrakesh, a regular occurrence in this very centralised empire, to receive new commissions and join the caliph. Once preparations at the Buhayra were complete, Abu Ya'qub Yusuf returned to the caliphal palace in Marrakesh in a procession with 'his sons proceeding on foot before him'.[107] He then announced the *sayyids*' new postings. Four of the caliph's sons received governorships in al-Andalus – Abu Ishaq was appointed to Seville, Abu Yahya to Córdoba, Abu Zayd al-Hardani to Granada and

[105] Ibn 'Idhari, *al-Bayan*, vol. 4, p. 220.
[106] Ibid., vol. 4, p. 228.
[107] Ibid.

Abu 'Abd Allah to Murcia – and left immediately (December 1183) with the Almohad troops allocated to them to prepare the ground in al-Andalus for the caliph's own arrival. The caliph also appointed a raft of new judges, including Ibn Rushd al-Hafid, who became *qāḍī* of Córdoba, following in the footsteps of his grandfather, Ibn Rushd al-Jadd, who had served Yusuf b. Tashfin and 'Ali b. Yusuf in the same capacity.

During Ramadan, preparations for the caliph's own departure continued, including the distribution of horses, weapons, tents and salaries. Although one needs to be cautious about the numbers and amounts cited in chronicles, they give the impression of considerable wealth in the western Maghrib. An additional financial incentive, described as a 'blessing' (*baraka*) was distributed to the troops and then the entire cavalcade set off for al-Mahdiyya (Ribat al-Fath) at the end of February 1184 in the customary manner designed to showcase the splendour of the empire and convey messages about its legitimacy.[108] The caliph commenced with a reading from the Qur'an and an exhortation to his gathered troops. He then set off preceded by his white banner and followed by the empire's most treasured artefacts, 'the Qur'an of 'Uthman b. 'Affan – may God be satisfied with him – inlaid with precious gems elevated upon a white camel covered by a red domed structure to protect it, followed by the Qur'an of the *mahdī* on a mule'.[109] As we have already seen, these tomes represented the two traditions of most importance to the Mu'minids, the Córdoban Umayyad tradition and that of Ibn Tumart. However, by this point, it is clear that the Umayyad heritage had become pre-eminent: not only was the Qur'an of 'Uthman encased in a jewel-encrusted box and protected by a red howdah, it was now mounted on a white camel, a much higher value beast than the mule that bore the more simply decorated Qur'an of Ibn Tumart.[110] That being said, the mule was the traditional mount of the Shi'i imam-*mahdī* and therefore had its own eschatological associations. After these splendid objects, came the *sayyid*s and an array of many coloured flags, followed by the tribes in their marching order. This was the Almohad empire on show.

The caliph arrived at al-Mahdiyya (Ribat al-Fath) two and a half weeks later and met up with Arab tribal contingents arriving from Ifriqiya who were showered with robes, salaries and other benefits, another display of the wealth of the empire. The *sayyid* Abu Hafs, one of the caliph's sons, was delegated to lead the Arab contingents north to cross into al-Andalus while the caliph proceeded inland to Meknes and then Fes to review their affairs, a

108 Ibn 'Idhari, *al-Bayan*, vol. 4, p. 229.

109 Ibid., vol. 4, p. 229. See also al-Marrakushi, *Mu'jib*, pp. 366–7; *al-Hulal al-Mawshiyya*, pp. 152–3.

110 Bennison, 'Qur'ān of 'Uthmān', p. 152; Ghouirgate, *L'Ordre almohade*, pp. 347–8.

reminder of the peripatetic administrative aspect of journeys of this kind. A number of financial officials (*'ummāl*), including the chief financial overseers (*mushrifūn*) of Meknes, Taza and Fes, and the latter's treasurers of coin and foodstuffs, were dismissed for embezzlement and their wealth reduced to a single residence each.[111]

Finally, in April 1184, the caliph himself proceeded to Ceuta where he rested for a month before crossing the Straits of Gibraltar to Jabal al-Fath from whence he travelled to Algeciras. From the Andalusi coast, the Almohad cavalcade moved north to Seville arriving towards the end of May 1184. The caliph's love of learning is symbolised by the anecdotal account of the renewal of his acquaintanceship with the eminent jurist Abu Bakr b. al-Jadd on his arrival in Seville:

> When [the caliph] caught sight of Ibn al-Jadd – may God have mercy on him – rushing on his way to greet him, he dismounted from his horse and the two men met. Ibn al-Jadd threw himself upon the commander of the faithful's hand and kissed it, and placed it upon his cheek, saying, 'Praise be to God who has brought us together, [you who are] so dear to me and the beloved of the people.' The caliph smiled at his words.[112]

Conversely, a disappointed Ibn Sahib al-Salat reports that he was unable to reach the caliph in the crush of well-wishers![113] The caliph established his camp at the Buhayra estate built during his last visit and awaited the arrival of the Andalusi contingents to join the Almohads and Arabs already gathered for his campaign. The ultimate objective of this jihad was the Almohad recapture of Santarem, lost nearly forty years before, from the Portuguese. The Almohad army set out from Seville on 8 June 1184 in splendour, with the troops bearing 'Indian swords and [Saharan] Lamta shields' and made its way slowly westwards to Santarem via Badajoz, picking up additional troops and volunteers along the way. Initially things went well: the Almohad army set up camp on a hill overlooking the walls of Santarem, destroyed an external suburb and assaulted the town, and after a week of hard fighting in which the Almohads destroyed two churches, they seemed poised to capture the city.

Then, for reasons that were opaque to even the most sympathetic Arabic chroniclers, Abu Ya'qub Yusuf ordered his troops to stop fighting and move camp, a decision that 'astonished everybody' and 'destroyed their hopes' of taking Santarem.[114] It is likely, however, that the strong resistance of the

[111] Ibn 'Idhari, *al-Bayan*, vol. 4, p. 230.
[112] Ibid., vol. 4, p. 231.
[113] Quoted by Ibn 'Idhari, *al-Bayan*, vol. 4, p. 231.
[114] Ibid., vol. 4, p. 234.

population of Santarem and the approach of Ferdinand II of León, occulted from the Arabic sources, contributed to the decision.[115] Unfortunately, the unexpected move was rather disorganised: the caliph and his tents were left isolated and the Portuguese attacked while he hastened to leave. They were held off by his son, Abu Yusuf Ya'qub, and the small band of Almohad and Andalusi notables with him, many of whom were killed. Once they were alerted to the Portuguese sortie, the bulk of the army drove the attackers back but the caliph was wounded. He continued to issue orders for the sack and devastation of the surrounding countryside from his horse, but he soon retreated to a covered conveyance and within days he was dead, despite the efforts of the physicians with him.[116] He was forty-seven years old.

Abu Ya'qub's Yusuf's sudden death had the potential to trigger a political and military crisis, so it was initially concealed by Abu Yusuf Ya'qub in the hope that he could get back to Seville and secure the caliphate for himself before any other contenders declared themselves. He was assisted in this by his cousin, Abu Zayd 'Abd al-Rahman, the son of Abu Hafs 'Umar who had played the role of kingmaker a generation before. Now Abu Zayd confirmed the solidarity between the fraternal lineages by ensuring that the caliphal tent and enclosure were erected as usual as the royal cortège moved across country. The dead caliph was carried in his sedan removed from view after a small group were allowed to view the shrouded corpse to secure their allegiance to Abu Yusuf Ya'qub and their support for him in Seville.[117] Things seem to have gone smoothly and Abu Yusuf Ya'qub received the oath of allegiance from the ruling Almohad elite and the various towns of al-Andalus in succession before travelling to Tarifa to cross to the Maghrib. Delegates from the northern Maghribi towns of Meknes and Fes offered him their oath of allegiance at Ribat al-Fath where his father's corpse was kept in the caliphal palace before being transferred to Tinmall in a casket to lie with the bodies of Ibn Tumart and 'Abd al-Mu'min.[118] Abu Yusuf Ya'qub then continued to Marrakesh to secure the allegiance of the Almohad shaykhs in the capital and performed a pilgrimage to Tinmall to pay his respects at the tombs of the *mahdī* and his ancestors to underline his commitment to the Almohad movement.

The new caliph, the son of a Christian concubine called Sahir, is described by al-Marrakushi as a dark-skinned, good-looking man of action.[119] His most famous achievement is probably his defeat of a Christian coalition at the

[115] Huici Miranda, *Historia política*, vol. 1, p. 305.
[116] Ibn 'Idhari, *al-Bayan*, vol. 4, p. 236.
[117] Ibid., vol. 4, p. 242. See also al-Marrakushi, *Mu'jib*, pp. 382–3.
[118] al-Marrakushi, *Mu'jib*, p. 377.
[119] Ibid., p. 378.

Battle of Alarcos (al-Arak) in 1195 from which he took his sobriquet 'al-Mansur' meaning 'The Victorious'. He was also celebrated for his attention to the conditions of his subjects, his personal meting out of justice, and his firm adherence to Shari'a norms in a manner compared with that of the *mahdī* Ibn Tumart. His approach seems to have been much more 'hands-on' than that of his father: he is described as personally hearing cases in the great mosque next to the Qasr al-Hajar in Marrakesh and he preferred to be with his men in battle. On the other hand, he was jealous of his royal prerogatives and roundly criticised the Almohad elite in Taza when they met him dressed in 'purple robes and musk-perfumed cloaks' of the type the caliph wore.[120] Like his predecessors, Ya'qub al-Mansur was also a great builder and it was during his reign that al-Mahdiyya (Ribat al-Fath) expanded from a coastal citadel south of Salé into a caliphal city. He also completed the Almohad redevelopment of Seville and added the royal annex, known as Tamurakusht or al-Saliha, to Marrakesh.[121]

Despite his eventual success at Alarcos four years before he died, Ya'qub al-Mansur's military credentials were tested to the full during his reign. In what had become a classic pattern over the previous century, he was frequently obliged to face threats on both Andalusi and Maghribi fronts and while the chronicles have a tendency to concentrate on the jihad in al-Andalus, the most serious challenge to his rule actually arose in the Maghrib. This was the somewhat unexpected landing of 'Ali b. Ishaq b. Ghaniya, Almoravid ruler of the Balearics on the coast of Ifriqiya in 1184 and his capture of Bijaya. As we saw in the last chapter, the Banu Ghaniya were an aristocratic Almoravid lineage who took charge of al-Andalus after the death of Tashfin b. 'Ali and established an independent principality in the Balearics when Almoravid rule in al-Andalus was extinguished. The founder of this principality was Yahya b. Ghaniya's brother, Muhammad, who was succeeded by his son, Ishaq, who agreed to a truce with the Almohads. Al-Marrakushi says that relations soured after the Almohads demanded the full submission of the Banu Ghaniya in 1182.[122] When Ishaq b. Ghaniya died the following year, a coup ensued in which his presumed heir Muhammad was ousted by his brother 'Ali, who used the Mallorcan fleet to take the war to the Almohads in the Maghrib.

'Ali b. Ghaniya's conquest of Bijaya in 1184 heralded half a century of disturbances in the central Maghrib and Ifriqiya during which 'Ali and then his brother Yahya formed alliances with a variety of Arab tribes, military adventurers from Ayyubid Egypt, and local Berber opponents of the Almohads

[120] Ibn 'Idhari, *al-Bayan*, vol. 4, p. 258.
[121] See pp. 320–1, below.
[122] al-Marrakushi, *Mu'jib*, p. 388.

and persistently attacked communities loyal to them. Marçais succinctly sums up their impact as 'sowing ruin' due to their inability to actually replace the Almohads while being able to repeatedly ravage their lands.[123] Huici Miranda similarly refers to their insatiable taste for rapine and cruelty which led to the destruction of land and cities.[124] While this is probably an exaggeration of the impact of the Banu Ghaniya incursions, such persistent political difficulties in Ifriqiya obliged the new caliph to follow the pattern established by his father of alternate peregrinations from Marrakesh to Ifriqiya and al-Andalus, which constantly strained the resources of the empire despite its wealth.

After Yaʿqub al-Mansur had established himself in Marrakesh and made his pilgrimage to Tinmall, he prepared to travel east, stopping *en route* at Fes and Taza to check for administrative abuses and put local affairs in order. In 1186, he arrived in Tunis and dispatched one of his many cousins, Abu Yusuf b. Abi Hafs, against ʿAli b. Ghaniya, but he was defeated the following year at the Battle of ʿUmra near Gafsa, a Banu Ghaniya stronghold, by a coalition of Arab tribes, the Mallorcan Almoravids and 'Turks' from Ayyubid Egypt sent by Salah al-Din. Yaʿqub al-Mansur responded by leading a large Almohad army forth to engage his opponents. He defeated them in October 1187 at the Battle of Hamma, which is described by Ibn ʿIdhari as such a convincing defeat of the enemy that the Almohad army were able to pray fully rather than shortening the prayer as they normally did in battle conditions, and the caliph was able to retire to his scarlet tent and emerge without armour despite being on campaign![125] The Almohad army proceeded to Gabes and toured through what is now southern Tunisia, capturing any Turks they came across. The caliph, however, did not punish these military adventurers but drafted them into the Almohad military as a new corps, just as ʿAbd al-Mu'min had previously done with the Arab tribes. The campaign culminated with Yaʿqub al-Mansur's siege and capture of Gafsa in December 1187 or January 1188, after which he returned to Tunis.[126] He then appointed his cousin, Abu Zayd ʿAbd al-Rahman, his staunchest family ally, as governor of Ifriqiya and set off for Marrakesh.

The caliph's absence in Ifriqiya and news of the defeat at al-ʿUmra had allowed the *sayyids*, 'jealous of his accession', in the west a free rein and reports began to arrive of disturbing developments in the governorates of Tlemcen, Tadla and Murcia. Yaʿqub al-Mansur acted with characteristic decisiveness.

[123] Marçais, 'Banū Ghāniya'. For a detailed history of the Banu Ghaniya in North Africa, see Baadj, *Saladin, the Almohads and the Banū Ghāniya.*

[124] Huici Miranda, *Historia política*, vol. 2, p. 413.

[125] Ibn ʿIdhari, *al-Bayan*, vol. 4, p. 262.

[126] Huici Miranda, *Historia política*, vol. 1, p. 338.

When he reached Tlemcen, he summoned the governor, his uncle Abu Ishaq b. ʿAbd al-Muʾmin, and publicly humiliated him by ʿordering him to stand up [after which] he was thrown out on his face and his riding animal taken away so he had to go on foot to his house with the common people trampling on his robes'.[127] Abu Ishaq died soon afterwards. The caliph then summoned his brother al-Rashid, governor of Murcia, who was accused of fraternising with Alfonso VIII of Castile and imposing excessive illegal taxes, and sent an army to apprehend his uncle Abu'l-Rabiʿ, governor of Tadla, whom he suspected of colluding with the local tribes against him. When they arrived in Marrakesh, he sent them both to al-Mahdiyya (Ribat al-Fath) in chains where they were kept under house arrest before being executed, supposedly with the concurrence of the Almohad shaykhs.[128] Their deaths seem to have been on the caliph's conscience, however, and on his deathbed he begged the womenfolk of the dead princes for forgiveness.[129]

Yaʿqub al-Mansur had now been in power for around five years and he had not returned to al-Andalus since his accession, although the advance of the Portuguese against Silves in the Algarve and Castilian raids in the Guadalquivir valley around Seville continued to threaten Almohad domains. His next task, therefore, was a campaign to the Iberian peninsula. He began by issuing a general summons for jihad volunteers 'in the southern mountains and the western lands', after which 'the peoples of the mountains and plains thronged [to Marrakesh] eager to volunteer' and 'many folk came from Ghana and the Sahara without delay and men of all colours (lit. the red and the black) and tongues gathered in the capital'.[130] Whether exaggerated or not, the depiction of this great gathering signalled the unity of the empire under Yaʿqub al-Mansur, despite the recent challenges to his rule from his relatives. At the start of 1190, the caliph travelled from Marrakesh to Ribat al-Fath, the usual mustering point for the Almohad and Arab contingents. He then made his way to Qasr al-Majaz on the Straits of Gibraltar and crossed to Tarifa in April. He finally arrived in Córdoba in June 1190.

During his stay in Córdoba he made his famous visit to the ruins of the Umayyad palatine city of Madinat al-Zahra' and removed the female statue, probably a Roman Venus, from its gate.[131] There has been much speculation as to why he did this. Was he collecting Umayyad *spolia* like his grandfather ʿAbd al-Muʾmin who had acquired the Qur'an of ʿUthman? Or was

[127] Ibn ʿIdhari, *al-Bayan*, vol. 4, p. 268.
[128] Ibid., vol. 4, pp. 269–70.
[129] Ibid., vol. 4, p. 305.
[130] Ibid., vol. 4, p. 271.
[131] Ibid., vol. 4, p. 275.

he removing a graven image distasteful to his Muslim sensibilities? While he was keen on enforcing the Shariʿa, he was also very interested in architecture, but since no further reference to the statue is made, we can only surmise his motives. From Córdoba, Yaʿqub al-Mansur travelled to Seville, the Almohad capital of al-Andalus, where he stayed for nearly a year directly administering affairs. As in Marrakesh, he followed Ibn Tumart's lead in 'commanding right and prohibiting wrong', and cracked down on the consumption of alcohol and other forms of 'dissipation'. He also received a visit from Salah al-Din's ambassador, Ibn Munqidh, who requested Almohad naval aid against the Crusaders in the Levant. It is not clear whether the caliph decided to help the Ayyubids or not, but the request again stresses the international importance of the Almohad empire at this time.[132]

During his extended stay in al-Andalus, Yaʿqub al-Mansur made a number of forays to the southwest against Portuguese-held towns and fortresses while the Almohad fleet prowled along the coasts. His 1190 tour was largely unsuccessful, but in spring 1191 he marched west again and successfully retrieved Silves from the Portuguese. He returned to Seville having proved himself in the jihad and left for Marrakesh in autumn 1191. After his return to the capital, he suffered a bout of serious illness and took the precaution of nominating his son, Abu ʿAbd Allah Muhammad, as heir apparent. The power brokers of the time – the *sayyids*, the Almohad shaykhs and now also the shaykhs of the Arab Riyah and Sulaym tribes who were fully integrated into the military – all offered their oaths of allegiance to the prince and letters were dispatched to the provinces requiring governors to also collect oaths of allegiance in their localities.

Soon news arrived of further trouble in Ifriqiya in the form of a rebellion in the Zab area led by a man nicknamed al-Ashall, meaning 'paralysed'. He masqueraded as a monarch, accepting oaths of allegiance from Arab tribesmen and the 'rabble', and holding court dressed in splendid robes and a green turban, hinting at descent from the Prophet, with a decorated sword placed in front of him. Ibn ʿIdhari says he could not enunciate his words properly, suggesting that he may have been the victim of a stroke. His followers probably saw his affliction as a mark of divine grace. The Almohad governor of Bijaya, Abu Zakariya', managed to put a stop to al-Ashall's movement only by kidnapping the children of his Arab supporters and refusing to release them

132 Ibn Khaldun states that the Almohad caliph refused but then relented and sent a fleet. *Kitab al-ʿIbar*, vol. 8, p. 514; Ibn Khaldun, *Histoire des Berbères*, vol. 2, p. 216; Ibn ʿIdhari mentions the visit but not the request for assistance; *al-Bayan*, vol. 4, pp. 279–80. Baadj sees the underlying purpose of the visit as a peace treaty after the *de facto* war between the Almohads and the Ayyubids in Ifriqiya; *Saladin, the Almohads and the Banū Ghāniya*, pp. 146–53.

unless they handed al-Ashall or his head over to him. At the insistence of their womenfolk, the Arabs captured al-Ashall and his minister and handed them over. They were both beheaded and al-Ashall's head was taken to Bijaya to be mounted on the city gate as a deterrent to other would-be agitators.[133]

This rebellion was quickly followed by news about further problems from Ibn Ghaniya and the Arab tribes, in response to which Ya'qub al-Mansur prepared to travel east to Ifriqiya again, but, when he reached Meknes, he decided to go north to al-Andalus instead to avert the threat presented by the lapse of the existing treaty with Castile and hostile movements from its king, Alfonso VIII. When he reached Seville he marched north and encountered the Castilians at Alarcos (al-Arak) in one of the relatively rare field battles of the period. The preparations are described in loving detail by Ibn 'Idhari, drawing on the histories of Ibn Sahib al-Salat and Yusuf b. 'Umar, from the mustering of the troops at the various lakeside estates outside Seville, to the caliph's appearance in the great mosque, the parades of the troops in dress uniform, and their gathering near Alarcos in July 1195.[134] The caliph and his functionaries gave a series of rousing addresses to the troops and then sent them onto the field against the Castilians. The initial clashes went against the Almohads, but then Ya'qub al-Mansur himself engaged, urging them on to a victory which 'the people compared to the Battle of Zallaqa', the great victory of Yusuf b. Tashfin in 1086, 'speaking of nothing else'.[135]

A triumphant Ya'qub al-Mansur returned to Seville for the winter, but launched a new campaign against the Castilians the following spring. He repeated this pattern the following year, but, after Alarcos, the Castilians preferred not to meet the Almohads in open, pitched battle so the Almohad army could not achieve much more than the capture of small settlements and the pillaging of the countryside. In the face of this stalemate, the two sides entered into negotiations and renewed their truce in 1197. In between campaigns, the caliph supervised his building projects, dealt with the persistent problem of 'corrupt' officials and took other steps to ameliorate relations with his Andalusi subjects, who were growing restive about heavy taxation in the absence of fresh victories against the Christians.

These steps included the rather unexpected internal exile of Ibn Rushd al-Hafid who had served the Almohads for many years as a judge. It is possible that the precarious nature of the truce with Castile and tense relations with the other Christian kingdoms provided the rationale for this puzzling incident in which Ya'qub al-Mansur bowed to pressure from a cohort of jurists who

133 Ibn 'Idhari, *al-Bayan*, vol. 4, p. 287.
134 Ibid., vol. 4, pp. 288–91.
135 Ibid., vol. 4, p. 291.

accused Ibn Rushd, a well-known philosopher as well as jurist, of harbouring un-Islamic beliefs deriving from his attachment to the knowledge of 'the Ancients', and sent him into temporary exile in the small town of Lucena.[136] A general decree against the study of philosophy followed. These steps may have been an attempt to bridge the gap between the Almohad ruling elite and the Maliki jurists of al-Andalus, whose position remained strong despite the official replacement of Malikism by Almohadism. Certainly, this stand against Ibn Rushd and philosophers in general seems to have gone against the caliph's personal predilections and, when he departed for the Maghrib in 1198, he took the opportunity to rehabilitate the elderly philosopher and jurist, whom he invited to join his entourage in Marrakesh.

The caliph died the following year in Marrakesh aged forty-eight after a relatively short reign of sixteen years. Like many of the events of his reign, Ya'qub al-Mansur's death is depicted by Ibn 'Idhari as a grand, staged public performance. After he fell ill, he summoned his relatives, his household and the Almohad elite to his sickbed and gave a speech of such eloquence that his audience was reduced to tears. The purpose of the gathering was to confirm the accession of his son, Abu 'Abd Allah Muhammad, and the positions of the most powerful *sayyids* and Almohad shaykhs through the force of his personality and his dying exhortations. In particular, he entrusted his cousins, the *sayyids* Abu'l-Hasan b. Abi Hafs and Abu Zayd b. Abi Hafs, with supporting and advising the young Muhammad until he reached maturity. The most contentious acts of his reign in the view of Ibn 'Idhari were his executions of his brother al-Rashid and his uncle Abu'l-Rabi' Sulayman, and he devotes considerable space to recording the caliph's last request for forgiveness from al-Rashid's mother and Abu'l-Rabi''s wife (or mother) as well as justifying the executions by providing a long list of Muslim rulers who executed male relatives! When Ya'qub al-Mansur died shortly afterwards, he was interred temporarily in the hall of his residence in Marrakesh and then taken to Tinmall for burial alongside his ancestors and Ibn Tumart.[137]

The Waning of the Almohad Empire

As he wished, Ya'qub al-Mansur was succeeded by his seventeen-year-old son, Abu 'Abd Allah Muhammad, who had been heir apparent since his childhood. His mother was a Christian concubine called Zahr and he was a light-skinned youth with dark blue eyes and a reddish beard.[138] He took the regnal title al-Nasir li-Din Allah ('Champion of God's Religion'), a title

[136] See Chapter 6, below, and Serrano Ruano, 'Explicit cruelty, implicit compassion'.
[137] Ibn 'Idhari, *al-Bayan*, vol. 4, pp. 302–6.
[138] al-Marrakushi, *Mu'jib*, p. 438.

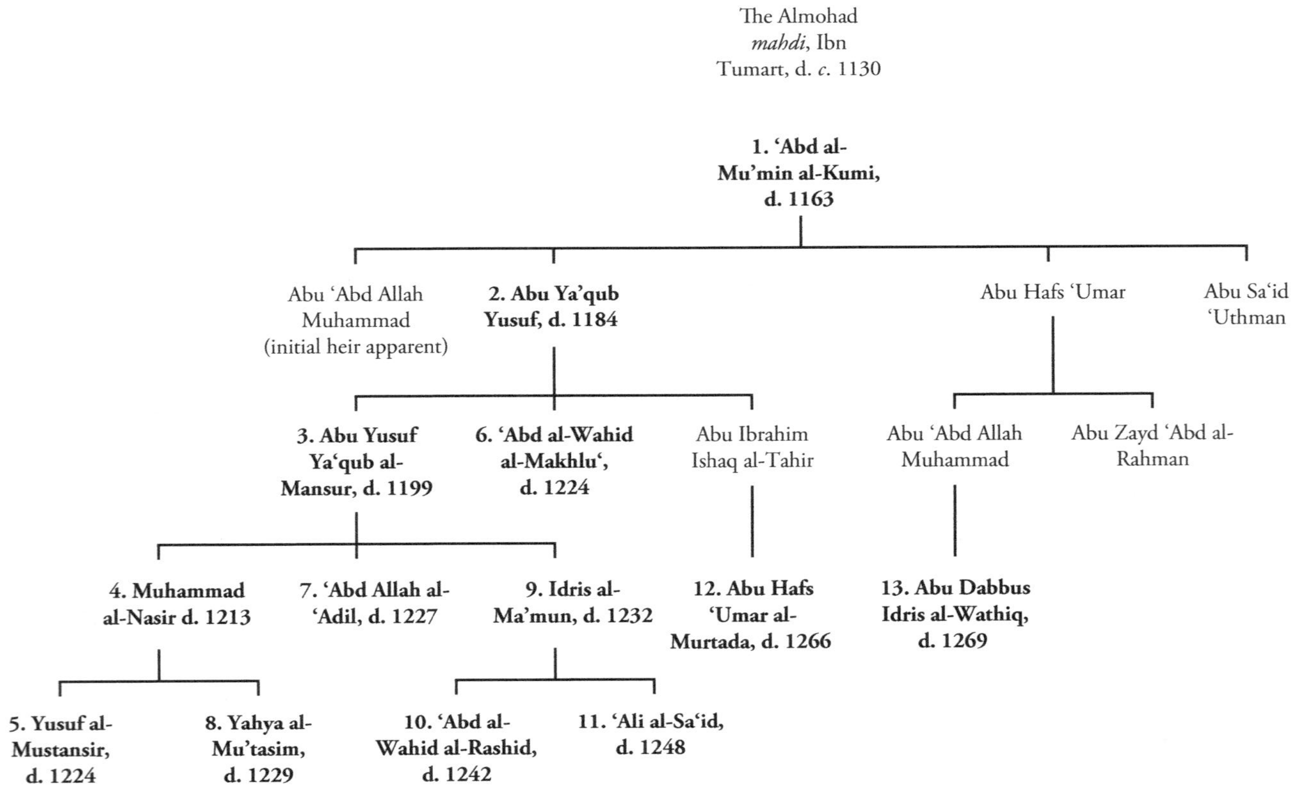

Figure 3.2 Genealogical table of the Almohad rulers and important Mu’minid *sayyid*s

previously adopted by Yusuf b. Tashfin and other Almoravid amirs due to its association with the Córdoban Umayyad caliph, 'Abd al-Rahman III. Like the title 'al-Mansur', this honorific evoked military victory and added a religious dimension to it, stressing the caliph's role as a champion of the jihad against the Christian kingdoms in Iberia. It is therefore ironic that the best-known event in the reign of al-Nasir li-Din Allah is the thorough defeat of the Almohad army by a Christian coalition at the Battle of Las Navas de Tolosa (al-'Uqab) in 1212. Regardless of the actual military impact of this battle, which was, after all, only one among many, it has gone down in history as the watershed that changed the fortunes of the Almohads and heralded the slow but inexorable collapse of their empire and the triumphant Christian expulsion of Muslims from the Iberian peninsula.

Both the medieval Christian and Islamic sources considered Las Navas de Tolosa a pivotal moment in the balance of power between the Almohads and the Christian kingdoms, and western scholarship has on balance taken the same view. However, current reassessments of the battle's impact show that it was as much the circumstances following Las Navas de Tolosa as the actual defeat itself that contributed to the problems faced by the Almohad empire in the following decades.[139] These problems included the premature death of al-Nasir a year after the battle, internecine struggles within the Almohad ruling clan, the accession of minors to the caliphate, the emergence of hereditary governorships, a loss of ideological coherence, and the drain on resources created by constant military campaigns in both al-Andalus and the Maghrib. Just as the Almoravids were brought down by the Almohads in the High Atlas rather than by Christian or Muslim challenges in al-Andalus, the Almohads found their own empire undermined by the Almoravid Banu Ghaniya and the Arab tribes in the Maghrib as much as by their Christian and Muslim opponents in the Iberian peninsula. Neither empire could sustain perpetual war on two fronts.

An over-concentration on Las Navas de Tolosa also obscures the fact that the first thirteen years of al-Nasir's reign were a continuation of that of his father and featured several military successes as well as defeats. After receiving the *bay'a*, al-Nasir, directed by his advisers, made a new series of appointments among which was the dispatch of his uncle, Abu'l-Hasan, son of the *sayyid* Abu Hafs 'Umar b. 'Abd al-Mu'min, to Bijaya to continue the struggle against the Banu Ghaniya and their Arab allies. He was rapidly defeated by an Arab army after which Abu Zayd b. Yujjan, an Almohad

[139] See the collection of essays reassessing the impact of Las Navas de Tolosa in the *Journal of Medieval Iberian Studies*, 4(1) (2012).

shaykh recently appointed as minister, led an army east to chastise the Arab tribes. However, the chronic instability in Ifriqiya persisted due to the ability of the Almohads' opponents to melt away into the countryside only to return after the Almohad armies had passed on. The tide turned slightly in favour of the Almohads when they finally conquered Mallorca from the Banu Ghaniya in 1203, and the following year the caliph himself went to Ifriqiya on a campaign to make his presence felt on the eastern outskirts of his empire. Ibn 'Idhari mentions a victory against the Arabs, but his vagueness suggests a rather inconclusive campaign and, after a stint in Marrakesh renewing appointments to the Almohad governorates of al-Andalus, al-Nasir set off once again for Ifriqiya in February 1205 on a major military expedition.[140]

This was a lavish affair of the now traditional Almohad kind. While the caliph advanced slowly visiting Ribat al-Fath, Fes and other Maghribi towns to settle their affairs *en route* to Ifriqiya, the Almohad fleet sailed from Ceuta to Tunis, which Yahya b. Ishaq b. al-Ghaniya, who had succeeded his brother 'Ali as head of the clan in 1188, had taken as his base. At the approach of the Almohad fleet, the Almoravid amir fled south while his supporters barricaded themselves into the fortress at al-Mahdiyya further down the coast. By the time al-Nasir arrived with the bulk of the army, Almohad control had been restored over Tunis and the Almohad fleet had blockaded al-Mahdiyya, the city recaptured from the Normans by his great-grandfather 'Abd al-Mu'min, which the caliph was determined to retrieve from rebel hands. He mobilised the Almohads' local allies for a siege while he restored Almohad control the length of the seaboard and Ibn Ghaniya retreated inland towards the Sahara. The defenders of al-Mahdiyya hurled down torches 'likes birds from the nest' which set the Almohads' wooden catapults alight, but the latter were not to be deterred.[141] They gathered more catapults, battering rams and ladders and built watchtowers overlooking al-Mahdiyya, while the fleet prevented the defenders receiving supplies by sea.

During the siege, the Almohad shaykh 'Abd al-Wahid b. Abi Hafs al-Hintati marched inland in an effort to defeat the elusive Ibn Ghaniya and his Arab allies in battle. He caught them near Gabes and returned victorious to al-Mahdiyya with a vast amount of booty and the rebels' black banner, a reference to their Almoravid and thus pro-'Abbasid proclivities, in his possession.[142] At this point, January 1206, the defenders of al-Mahdiyya surrendered and al-Nasir entered the city. Although opposition to Almohad rule continued to fizzle, the conquest of al-Mahdiyya was a major symbolic

[140] Ibn 'Idhari, *al-Bayan*, vol. 4, p. 313.
[141] Ibid., vol. 4, p. 315.
[142] The colour of the 'Abbasids was black in contrast to the white of the Almohads.

victory for the young caliph. After a short stay in al-Mahdiyya, he returned to Tunis, which was rapidly becoming the bustling Almohad capital of Ifriqiya, where he oversaw the region's affairs until spring 1207. On his departure for the Maghrib he appointed 'Abd al-Wahid b. Abi Hafs as governor of Ifriqiya, a decision that ultimately led to the establishment of his Hafsid descendants as independent rulers of the region from the mid-thirteenth until the fifteenth century.

Once al-Nasir reached Fes, he was besieged by people complaining about the behaviour of Almohad officials in Fes and Meknes during his absence. He dealt with the immediate problems and continued on to Marrakesh via Meknes and Ribat al-Fath. Back in the imperial capital, he seems to have instigated a major investigation of Almohad officials (*'ummāl*) in the Maghrib and al-Andalus. Head officials and their teams were summoned to Marrakesh to have their books audited, a process designed to rectify abuses and embezzlement of state funds, but that unfortunately allowed slanderers to accuse the innocent of misdemeanours. The Almohad bureaucrat and historian Yusuf b. 'Umar, for instance, was temporarily imprisoned as a result of slander before being exonerated of wrongdoing.[143]

Meanwhile, Ibn Ghaniya returned to disrupt the Almohad peace, this time in the area of Tlemcen where the Zanata tribes had rebelled. One Almohad governor resigned and his replacement was killed in battle with Ibn Ghaniya's forces. The area was not pacified until Ibn Yujjan, al-Nasir's minister, led an Almohad army to the area and Ibn Ghaniya retreated once again. Finally, in 1209–10, matters began to turn in favour of the Almohads when 'Abd al-Wahid b. Abi Hafs, governor of Ifriqiya, defeated Ibn Ghaniya in battle and his brother, Sir b. Ishaq b. Ghaniya, surrendered and travelled to Marrakesh to offer his submission to the Almohads.[144] The Almohad position seemed more secure than ever before when news arrived that several Sicilian towns were offering the *khuṭba* to the Almohads rather than the 'Abbasids.[145]

In Marrakesh, al-Nasir made another round of administrative reappointments, an annual or bi-annual custom at this point, and began to prepare for a trip to al-Andalus 'to wage jihad' in response to attacks on the province of Valencia from Barcelona. Although it may be a bias within the sources, al-Nasir seems to have paid particular attention to the imperial administration and regularly investigated administrators and rotated positions, so he was furious when he found that Almohad officials had not properly prepared for the supply and provisioning of the army on his route to the Straits of Gibraltar. He

[143] See p. 215, below.
[144] Ibn 'Idhari, *al-Bayan*, vol. 4, pp. 327–8.
[145] Ibid., vol. 4, p. 329.

had the chief administrators of Fes and Ceuta, 'Abd al-Haqq b. Abi Dawud and Muhammad b. al-Masufi, arrested and imprisoned along with their staff.[146]

Having seen to the administrative affairs of his Maghribi domains, al-Nasir crossed the Straits of Gibraltar and travelled up to Seville, arriving in spring 1211. In June, he began to mobilise the Almohad contingents in al-Andalus for a campaign against the fortress of Salvatierra, which was successfully recaptured from the Castilians in mid-September 1211.[147] Letters extolling the victory and announcing the restoration of Islam in Salvatierra were dispatched across the empire, triumphantly stating, 'God replaced the bell with the call to prayer and the church became a mosque once again'.[148] After over-wintering in Seville, al-Nasir sent orders to the Maghrib for the execution of the governors of Fes and Meknes who had been deemed guilty of financial improprieties and he mobilised once again for a campaign against the Christians. This campaign culminated in the fateful battle of Las Navas de Tolosa near Jaén in which the Almohads met a Christian army composed not only of Castilians, but also other Iberians and Crusaders from other parts of Latin Christendom.[149] Although al-Nasir fought bravely and remained 'facing the lances' of his enemy, Ibn 'Idhari says that the Almohads lacked conviction and unity as a result of their disquiet about the executions of officials ordered by the caliph, and they were defeated.[150]

Although the Christian victors did not immediately capitalise on their victory, it gained its place in later Christian annals as a decisive moment in the *reconquista*. The Arabic chronicles make less of the battle, but they do allude to it as a pivotal moment that led on to the ruin of al-Andalus.[151] It had both psychological and demographic consequences. From the psychological perspective, the Almohads' reputation as *mujāhidīn* was severely dented and those who had given them their allegiance on the unstated assumption that they would be protected began to reconsider their options. On the demographic side, the death toll at the battle is described as leading to widespread depopulation in the northwest Maghrib in the anonymous *al-Dhakhira al-Saniyya*, which charts the rise of the Banu Marin dynasty who replaced the Almohads in the western Maghrib.[152]

146 Ibn 'Idhari, *al-Bayan*, vol. 4, pp. 331–2.
147 Huici Miranda, *Las grandes batallas*, pp. 231–9.
148 Ibn 'Idhari, *al-Bayan*, vol. 4, p. 334.
149 See Huici Miranda, *Las grandes batallas*, pp. 253–72; García Fitz, *Las Navas de Tolosa*; O'Shea, *Sea of Faith*, pp. 205–30.
150 Ibn 'Idhari, *al-Bayan*, vol. 4, pp. 334–5.
151 García Fitz, 'Was Las Navas a decisive battle?', pp. 5–9.
152 *al-Dhakhira al-Saniyya*, p. 26.

If al-Nasir had lived longer, he might have been able to restore confidence in Almohad rule, but he returned to Marrakesh following his defeat and died in 1213. Some suspected that he had been poisoned at the behest of Almohad shaykhs who feared that he was going to continue his drive for administrative reform and dispossess or even kill them.[153] Al-Nasir's unexpected death at barely thirty and the accession of his ten-year-old son, Yusuf al-Mustansir, who reigned for a decade as the puppet of various relatives and eminent Almohad shaykhs, heralded a phase in which rivalries for power between different *sayyids* of the Mu'minid house and the sectors of the Almohad elite who backed them gradually escalated. According to the *Dhakhira al-Saniyya*, a hostile source which eulogises the Marinid successors of the Almohads,

> [Yusuf al-Mustansir] was an inexperienced youth who stayed in his palace indulging in frivolity and wine while he left governing to his uncles and relatives, and delegated matters to his ministers and [tribal] shaykhs. They were envious of each other's power and contradicted each other, leaving the chiefs and governors astonished and affairs fell apart. Low people took over their affairs, the *'ulamā'* distanced themselves and ignorant people drew close. Corruption tainted their rule and their religion became weak. Oppression appeared in their judgements and in their lands and their power decreased.[154]

The situation only got worse when Yusuf al-Mustansir died in 1224: a succession of eight caliphs came to power over the next forty-four years, with the majority ruling for less that three years and very few dying natural deaths. This loss of cohesion at the heart of government in Marrakesh triggered a new cycle of political fragmentation and the emergence of provincial lords of both Almohad and non-Almohad background across the empire. In Valencia, the descendants of Abu Hafs 'Umar b. 'Abd al-Mu'min, the brothers Abu Zayd, 'Abd Allah and Abu Dabbus b. Muhammad, refused to recognise the caliph 'Abd Allah al-'Adil, himself a rival to Yusuf al-Mustansir's elderly successor, 'Abd al-Wahid b. Yusuf, who had been ousted from the caliphate and killed within months of his accession in 1224. The situation rapidly spiralled out of control with Mu'minid lineages battling against each other backed by different elite factions. Some even looked to the Christian kingdoms for help. Most notorious of all was 'Abd Allah b. Muhammad who responded to al-'Adil's accession by holing himself up in Baeza, seeking the protection of Ferdinand III of Castile, and possibly converting to Christianity. With

[153] Ibn 'Idhari, *al-Bayan*, vol. 4, p. 337.
[154] *al-Dhakhira al-Saniyya*, p. 24.

his new liege lord's help he took control of Córdoba only to be killed by the incensed Muslim population.[155]

The collapse of the Almohad empire was speeded along by the emergence of a deep ideological rift. In 1229, a new caliph, Idris al-Ma'mun (r. 1226–32), one of al-Nasir's brothers and the son of Ibn Mardanish's daughter, rejected the key tenet of Almohad Islam, belief that Ibn Tumart was the *mahdī*, and removed references to him from coinage and other public statements. This may have been a gambit to appeal to an Andalusi constituency to support him against his rival, his nephew, Abu Zakariya' Yahya, who controlled Marrakesh, but it left the Almohads without an ideological platform and allowed the governors of Ifriqiya, the descendants of Ibn Tumart's companion Abu Hafs 'Umar al-Hintati, to declare their independence as the true Almohads. Henceforth, the eastern section of the Almohad empire became the independent Hafsid state.

Closer to home in what is now western Algeria, another line of Almohad governors, the Zanata Berber Zayyanids, gradually asserted their independence from the control of Marrakesh and made Tlemcen the capital of a second autonomous principality. Meanwhile, the Banu Marin, Zanata Berber pastoralists from the Zab or Figuig region, had begun to filter westwards through the Taza corridor into the Atlantic plains where they were able to exploit the apparently disastrous demographic consequences of al-Nasir's last Andalusi campaign to raid and pillage across what is now northern Morocco. The weak Almohad response to the Banu Marin incursions, emboldened the tribesmen to turn into state-builders themselves in the Khaldunian mould. During the 1230s and 1240s, they forced tribes across the area to submit to them and subjugated the towns of Fes and Meknes, reducing Almohad domains to an area between the Umm al-Rabi' River and the Sahara. The last Almohad caliphs, al-Sa'id (d. 1248), al-Murtada (d. 1266) and Abu Dabbus (d. 1269), battled in vain to unite the Almohads and push back against the Marinids, losing Ribat al-Fath-Salé, Sijilmasa and finally Marrakesh to them.[156]

On the northern fringes of the empire in al-Andalus, a new generation of Muslim lords asserted their autonomy along the eastern seaboard, including Muhammad b. Hud and Zayyan b. Mardanish. In 1228, Ibn Hud declared his independence from the Almohads, transferred his allegiance to the 'Abbasids, and established himself in Murcia. He rapidly expanded his power across the south at the expense of Ibn Mardanish and the Almohad

155 Kennedy, *Muslim Spain and Portugal*, pp. 262–4. Ramírez-del-Río, '*Al-Ḏajīra al-Saniyya*: una fuente relevante', pp. 28–31.

156 See Shatzmiller, *The Berbers and the Islamic State*, pp. 45–54; Kably, *Société, pouvoir et religion*, pp. 20–72; Bennison, 'Drums, banners and *baraka*', pp. 196–7.

governor, Abu Zayd, and gained recognition of his status from the 'Abbasid caliph in 1232.[157] However, the invigorated Christian kingdoms of Portugal, Castile and Aragon also took the opportunities presented by Almohad disarray to advance south. The victory at Las Navas de Tolosa two decades before had opened the way to the Guadalquivir valley and Ferdinand III of Castile took advantage of this to capture Córdoba in 1236 and Seville in 1248 while Jaime I of Aragon advanced into Valencia. The Almohad *sayyid* Abu Zayd tried to improve his position by alliances with Castile and then Aragon, which lost him popular Muslim support and led to his exile to Aragon and his conversion to Christianity.[158] By the mid-thirteenth century, the only significant territory in the peninsula to remain in Muslim hands was the small kingdom of Granada, founded by a Muslim adventurer called Muhammad b. Nasr b. al-Ahmar, who assisted Ferdinand at the siege of Seville in return for a truce to preserve his own southern kingdom.[159] The era of the Berber empires was finally over.

157 Krasner-Balbale, 'Jihād as a means of political legitimation', pp. 92–7.
158 See Fancy, 'The last Almohads'.
159 See Harvey, *Islamic Spain, 1250–1500*, pp. 20–40; Boloix Gallardo, *De la Taifa de Arjona al Reino Nazarí de Granada (1232–1246)*.

4

Society in the Almoravid and Almohad Eras, 1050–1250

In the mid-eleventh century when the Almoravid Sanhaja emerged from the Sahara, the societies of al-Andalus, the Maghrib and Ifriqiya were in many ways very distinct. Two hundred years later when the Christian kings expelled the Almohads from the Iberian peninsula and a series of Muslim successor states emerged from Granada to Tunis, North Africa and al-Andalus hosted much more fully Islamised societies with a great deal more in common than previously, in towns and cities at least. The social changes that had taken place were by no means solely achieved by the Almoravids and the Almohads themselves, who were elites perched at the top of society. However, their Islamisation of rural populations, their perpetual movement through their empires, their transfers of people across the Straits of Gibraltar and across North Africa, their foundation of new cities and expansion of others, and their generous patronage of religious scholars and thinkers certainly contributed to the slow integration of the 'wild western' Maghrib into the Islamic ecumene.

This chapter will look briefly at the way Muslims conceptualised society as a prelude to exploring its constituent parts in the age of the Berber empires from the ruler and the ruling elite, to wider rural and urban society. It will also consider the social status of women from the mid-eleventh to mid-thirteenth centuries and conclude with a section on the thorny issue of the status of Christian and Jewish religious minorities under the Almoravids and Almohads. However, there are several taxonomies that come into play when we consider society in this period, some helpful and others less so, of which we should be conscient before proceeding. Although we talk about the indigenous inhabitants of North Africa as 'Berbers' for convenience, there were great differences between the Almoravid and Almohad tribes and the social structure of the political elites they promoted, despite the fact that they were both 'Berber' dynasties. Conversely, if we follow the prevalent tendency to see Andalusi and Maghribi societies as completely distinct, we may elide the similarities that did exist between sectors of each society and the social diversity within them. For instance, the inhabitants of the Maghribi

Mediterranean port of Ceuta had much more in common with their counterparts across the water in Iberian Almería or Tarifa than with the Masmuda tribes of the High Atlas mountains.

Another set of categorisations relate to modes of social organisation and subsistence. Ibn Khaldun considered the distinction between sedentarists (*ḥaḍar*) and tribesmen (*badw, qabā'il*) a key social binary within North Africa, but this was not applicable to the same degree in Iberia where tribalism was much more limited in scope. Nonetheless, Muslim tribal groups, Arab and Berber, regularly crossed the Straits of Gibraltar from 711 onwards modifying Iberian urban and rural society in different ways, a process that culminated with the successive arrivals of the Almoravid Sanhaja and the Almohad Masmuda in the eleventh and twelfth centuries, respectively. The Islamic west was not unique in this respect, a feature of this period across the Islamic world was the creation of empires by tribesmen from the periphery who therefore formed not only a proportion of the rural population, but also the dominant component of the ruling elite. As we shall see, the social consequences of this tended to be the bifurcation of the ruling group into a politico-military section dominated by tribesmen and a civilian element drawn from the established literate, urban stratum, creating many gradations between the poles of *ḥaḍar* and *badw*.

In a comparable manner, dividing society into highly differentiated urban and rural sectors can conceal interdependencies and social connections. The towns and cities of the Islamic west were very varied in origin, but they all tended to differ from their hinterlands through the relative social diversity of their populations from the perspectives of language, religion, origin and profession. It was common for towns to harbour speakers of Arabic in monolingual Berber areas, Christian and Jewish minorities, merchants from far-flung corners of the Islamic world, and men and women working in many different professions, trades and crafts. However, the difference between a large village and a small town was rarely clear and they were often not the 'organismes étrangers' within the rural environment envisaged by Montagne.[1]

A final set of premises relate to the treatment of Christians and Jews, the protected non-Muslim minorities known collectively as the 'people of the covenant' (*ahl al-dhimma*) or the 'people of the book' (*ahl al-kitāb*). This issue is more highly charged and sometimes emotive than any other due to its entanglement with modern history, national identity, and contemporary notions of tolerance and civility between religious groups in western society. While Andalusi Muslims have come to be seen as tolerant proponents of

[1] Montagne, *Les Berbères et le Makhzen*, p. 37.

convivencia (living together), partly due to their 'European-ness', the Berber dynasties are often depicted as carriers of a fanatical extremist version of Islam rooted in Africa and the Middle East that persecuted the Christians and the Jews, a position that reflects contemporary anxieties as much as historical realities. Neither of these stances, however, captures the complexity of the situation or the marked differences between the Almoravid and Almohad strategies towards Christians and Jews in al-Andalus and the Maghrib. Moreover, stark divisions between 'tolerant' Andalusi and 'intolerant' Maghribi attitudes towards religious minorities are not really sustainable in view of the role of Andalusis in formulating 'governmental' policy.

Islamic Society in Theory

Although we tend to juxtapose state and society, many medieval thinkers considered society as inconceivable without its head, the ruler, who stood at the apex of a pyramid with groups of increasing size arrayed in tiers below him or disposed as the parts of a body to be moved at his will. The composition of the tiers (or body parts), however, varied from society to society as did the possibility of movement between them. In the case of Islamic societies, the early equality of believers soon came under the influence of older static Near Eastern models of society which placed a higher value on the maintenance of everyone in their correct social niche than on egalitarianism and social mobility.[2]

Even in the case of rulers, the qualifications for Islamic leadership and the route to it showed a tension between social credentials such as aristocratic Arab ancestry, which the caliphal dynasties possessed, and politico-military capabilities, which they often did not possess. This disjuncture between ancestry and aptitude reached a head with the Buyid and then the Seljuk usurpation of real power from the 'Abbasid caliphs in the tenth and eleventh centuries, respectively, leaving them as little more than religio-political figureheads. On the eve of the rise to power of the Almoravids, then, legitimate Islamic sovereignty had come to be understood not just as caliphal, but as delegated by the caliph to other 'powers' (*sulṭāns*). In contemporary 'Mirrors for Princes' literature, the ideal characteristics previously associated with the caliph were quickly transposed to sultans, eliding the difference between the two.

Such an Islamic prince, whether a caliph, a sultan or an amir, was the symbolic embodiment of the state without whom a complex society could not flourish, and he was expected to show justice and piety as well as political and military skills. In the words of Ibn 'Abdun of Seville, a jurist and servant of the Almoravid state:

[2] See Marlow, *Hierarchy and Egalitarianism in Islamic Thought*, pp. 1–10.

> [The prince] is the axis of the community and like the central point of a circumference which only forms a harmonious and perfect line without flaw if the centre is fixed and immovable. The prince is also like the intelligence in relation to a man: if it is firm, it brings understanding and opinions that are both beautiful and weighty. The good state of society is the product of the good qualities of the prince and the decadence of its organisation is a product of his faults.[3]

Although an Islamic ruler was theoretically absolute in his own territories as God's shadow or representative on Earth, in reality all rulers depended on some assortment of advisers, ministers and generals and, when they were sultans or amirs of tribal background who did not claim a religio-political role, their male kin and fellow tribesmen preferred to see them as *primus inter pares*. This powerful coterie, which formed a penumbra around each ruler, was a key component of the *khāṣṣa*, an Arabic term denoting those individuals in society meriting individual recognition for their power, position or status, and also those who received revenue and gifts rather than paying taxes. More specifically, the *khāṣṣa* consisted of the ruler's family or clan, his household, which included close advisers and also servants whose role could be humble but who accrued power through their access to the ruler, Men of the Sword – military commanders and the army – and Men of the Pen – scribes, civilian officials and men of religion, upon whom monarchs were dependent and who often held more real power than their masters. The ruling elite overlapped with other elite elements in society who also enjoyed *khāṣṣa* status, namely, urban notables with mercantile or religious backgrounds, and tribal chiefs or rural lords who might or might not serve the central dynastic power.

The bulk of the population were termed the *ʿāmma* (general population) or the subject flocks (*raʿāyā*), the mostly respectable, tax-paying majority who were governed as communities and groups through a number of intermediaries drawn from among local notables (*wujūh*, *aʿyān*) and religious leaders, including Muslim judges (*qāḍis*) and jurists (*fuqahā'*), bishops and rabbis. This numerically large group included Ibn Khaldun's *ḥaḍar*, sedentary townsmen and rural peasant populations, but not necessarily tribesmen, the *badw* or *qabā'il*, whose position within theoretical depictions of society was always problematised by their independence towards political authorities, and their ability to fight and to found states in the right circumstances. While not always a central factor in al-Andalus, tribes were a decisive element in all political equations in the Maghrib. At the bottom of the social

[3] Ibn ʿAbdun, *Séville Musulmane*, p. 5.

hierarchy were the poor, indigent and those involved in prostitution, banditry and other criminal activities who had no place in idealised depictions of society. Collectively called derogatory names such as the rabble (*awbāsh*), mob (*ghawghā'*) or dregs of society (*sifla*), this group could swell in times of hardship to include a sizeable proportion of the population, especially as *'āmma* opposition to rulers or their tax collectors could easily lead to their denunciation by the latter as part of the 'mob'. Similarly, the rural supporters of popular religious leaders were often dismissed as an uneducated 'rabble'.

The relationship between these broadly defined social groups was often conceptualised as a wheel called the circle of equity or justice according to which it was the ruler's responsibility to maintain Islamic justice in the form of the Shari'a supported by his Men of the Sword and the Pen, who were in their turn financially supported by the productive capacities of townsmen and above all the peasantry. The long-term productivity of the peasantry, however, depended upon the ruler maintaining justice in the form of security and equitable taxation and so on around the circle. This ancient Near Eastern view of society, derived from Greek and Persian sources, was popular in the medieval Islamic world and the Ottoman empire, and it received new life in twentieth-century Marxist scholarship which characterised the Islamic world as a series of tributary societies in which 'the state' directly exacted tribute from peasant proprietors to remunerate its Men of the Sword and Pen in the absence of a feudal nobility able to block the state's access to such resources.

However, these models fitted the circumstances of peasant societies from Iran to al-Andalus rather better than tribal environments in which tribesmen straddled the line between the Men of the Sword and the subject population, and could block the state's access to resources as effectively as feudal lords due to their tendency to evade taxation and their military propensities. Negotiations with the tribes, co-optation of some and punishment of others formed the default position of the Maghribi state in the hands of both the Almoravids and the Almohads. Although it is based on the analysis of later times, Gellner's comparison of the Moroccan tribes to wolves, some of whom were tamed to act as the ruler's sheep-dogs, captures the ambivalence of the triangular relationship between government, tribes and non-tribal subjects.[4]

The Almoravid Ruling Elite

The upper echelons of the Almoravid elite were drawn from a small number of Sanhaja tribes of western Saharan origin. The medieval Arabic term 'Sanhaja'

[4] Gellner, *Muslim Society*, pp. 30–1.

is a vague designation that seems to apply to an ethno-linguistic group, the speakers of Znaga Berber, and was more relevant to literary taxonomies of the Berbers than to the social reality of North Africa where Sanhaja, both sedentary and nomadic, could be found scattered across the region from Ifriqiya to the Sahara. The western Saharan Sanhaja were divided into a number of tribes of whom the most important were the Lamtuna, Guddala, Masufa and Lamta. However, the relevance of genealogically defined tribes and their relationship to social classes such as nobles or religious leaders is debated and there are references to various kings or chiefs who controlled large confederations in the centuries before the rise of the Almoravids.[5]

From a cultural perspective, the western Saharan Sanhaja were distinct from many other Berber tribes, including the Sanhaja of Ifriqiya, due to their nomadic lifestyle herding camels and smaller livestock and their matrilineal inheritance patterns which accorded women relatively high status. The most visually distinctive aspect of their culture was the face veil (*lithām*) worn by Saharan Sanhaja men, an item of clothing that was eminently practical to protect the lower face in harsh desert conditions, but gained symbolic meaning over time as a mark of male honour, which was severely compromised by its removal. As we have already seen in Chapter 2, the Almoravids are routinely called *mulaththamūn* (wearers of the *lithām*) by Arabic writers, a characteristic that is depicted in hostile sources as an inversion of Islamic gender norms and a mark of the religious ignorance and deviance of the Almoravids, which gave the lie to their religio-political self-identification as 'men of the *ribāṭ*' (*al-murābiṭūn*).

The *lithām* was important to the Almoravids, however, and it became entwined with their claim to southern Arabian ancestry in the myth that we touched on briefly in Chapter 2. Following the speculations of eastern Islamic historians about the Arabian or Near Eastern origins of the Berbers,[6] the Almoravids finessed a legend that the Sanhaja were not Berbers but Arabs of Himyaritic origin to embed themselves in the ancient history of Arabia and the Middle East and to explain and glorify their usage of the *lithām*. According to the legend, a religious scholar had told one of the ancient kings of southern Arabia about God's dispatch of scripture to his messengers, adding that he would send one who was the seal of the prophets to all the nations. The king believed him and went to the Yemen and called the people of his kingdom to believe too.

> The only ones to respond positively were a group of his people from Himyar. When he perished the people of unbelief overcame the people of faith and

[5] Smith, 'What happened to the ancient Libyans', p. 474.

[6] Shatzmiller, *The Berbers and the Islamic State*, pp. 19–21.

> all those who believed him and followed his religion were killed, exiled and hunted and they became fugitives. At that point they veiled themselves in the manner of their women at that time and fled for their lives. They were scattered in all directions. This was the cause of the departure of the ancestors of the Veiled Ones from Yemen, so it is said. They were the first to veil. They wandered from region to region and place to place until they reached the farthest Maghrib in the land of the Berbers. They made camp there and made it their home and the veil became a form of dress that God favoured them with, and by its means they were saved from their enemy. They therefore valued it and adhered to it and it became the dress of their descendants until today. Their language became Berber because of their proximity to them and their marriage relations with them.[7]

Most scholars regard this as simply a myth, although its ubiquity across North Africa may contain the memory of an early migration of peoples across the Red Sea from Arabia to Africa.[8] Such a myth of Arab origin was probably irrelevant to the majority of the Maghrib's Berber speakers, but it reveals a need felt by ruling elites such as the Almoravids – or their chroniclers – to appropriate Arab ancestry as a mark of nobility in the Islamic environment and to differentiate themselves from other Berbers.[9] The Almoravid version of the myth also connected the wearing of the *lithām* to Islam by presenting the veiled Sanhaja as 'Muslim' even before the revelation of Islam, and attributed their use of the *lithām* to this moment of sacrifice for Islam, a fact that they wished to commemorate in perpetuity. Instead of being an inversion of Islamic gender norms, the *lithām* was thus the sign of a unique, long-standing devotion to Islam and, in this sense, the story may transpose to ancient Arabia a custom the Muslim Sanhaja of the western Sahara adopted to differentiate themselves from the animists of West Africa.[10]

This narrative also identified the *lithām* as a marker of high social status and the veiled warrior tribes as the most socially elevated group within the Almoravid ruling elite, a situation that Almohad criticism of Almoravid men veiled as women sought to destroy. In this context, it is noteworthy that affiliates of the veiled Lamtuna and Masufa tried to wear the *lithām* too, as we shall see below, and, conversely, that some Almoravids later removed them as part of their submission to the Almohads in the 1140s. The veiled Almoravid

[7] *al-Hulal al-Mawshiyya*, pp. 18–19.

[8] Norris, 'Yemenis in the western Sahara', p. 321.

[9] Shatzmiller sees the myth of Arab origin as 'a frozen and sterile literary motif'; Shatzmiller, *The Berbers and the Islamic State*, p. 27.

[10] Ghouirgate, *L'Ordre almohade*, p. 48.

elite was dominated by the Lamtuna Banu Targut or Turgut, the clan of Abu Bakr b. ʿUmar, Yusuf b. Tashfin and his descendants. Male siblings, cousins and nephews from the Banu Targut played a major part in government as commanders and governors across the Almoravid empire. A small number of other Lamtuna and Masufa clans, some associated with the Banu Targut by marriage, also joined the highest echelons of the politico-military elite. A list compiled by Lagardère of the origins of Almoravid amirs and commanders mentioned in the chronicles shows the predominance of the Lamtuna who made up 61 per cent (thirty-seven) of the total in comparison with the Masufa at 8 per cent (five) and individuals of unspecified origin at 31 per cent (nineteen), of whom several could also have been members of the Lamtuna.[11]

Although Ibn Khaldun saw *ʿaṣabiyya* as a positive, and indeed necessary, force during the formative phase of an empire, subsequently the expectations formed by kinship could be a persistent problem with uncles, brothers, cousins, sons and nephews all hoping for a piece of the governmental pie. Neither primogeniture nor father–son succession could be assumed, and the dynastic kin group tended to increase exponentially over time due to polygamy and concubinage. Conflict resolution was therefore a crucial aspect of elite social relations. A powerful amir could contain conflict through his personality, military might and judicious distribution of material privileges, and if this was not sufficient then other clan members might use traditional forms of mediation to achieve a resolution. Abu Bakr was forced to accept Yusuf b. Tashfin's rule over the north through carefully calibrated gift-giving, while Abu Bakr's son, Ibrahim, was persuaded not to contest Yusuf b. Tashfin's rule by the mediation of Mazdali, a senior clan member who also acted on other occasions to settle intra-elite disputes. A different problem with *ʿaṣabiyya*-based ruling cliques was that excessive reliance on a narrow group of kinsmen could prevent the formation of a larger, more inclusive and thus more effective ruling class, an argument that Messier makes with regard to the Almoravids, whom he sees as losing power due to an excess of *ʿaṣabiyya* rather than the dilution that Ibn Khaldun posited as the root cause of the collapse of tribal empires.[12]

Other veiled Lamtuna and Masufa clans formed the core units of the Almoravid army. Some remained in the Sahara or in Marrakesh, the newly founded Almoravid capital just north of the High Atlas mountains, while others were stationed in garrisons located within or near major towns and cities. Although little is known of the social structure of urban Almoravid communities and garrisons, in early Marrakesh, and presumably their desert

[11] Lagardère, *Almoravides I*, pp. 190–1.
[12] See Messier, 'Rethinking the Almoravids'.

town of Azuggi, each extended family seem to have resided in separate walled forts or houses known as *quṣūr* (sing. *qaṣr*) with substantial Almoravid citadels added to the periphery of larger or strategically important cities such as Tlemcen and Fes.[13] Some of the best known Almoravids are those who resided in Seville due to extant legal rulings concerning tensions that arose between them and the local population, a not uncommon phenomenon when soldiers of foreign origin were stationed in cities in the Islamic world, but one that often revolved around the most distinctive Saharan Sanhaja feature, the male face veil, in the Almoravid case.

Disputes related to the *lithām* show, on the one hand, the separation of the Almoravids from their subjects, but, on the other hand, local attempts to appropriate the *lithām* as a mark of status and the practical imbrication of the lives of the Almoravids and their subjects. One source of disagreement was the fact that the proud Almoravid warriors insisted on retaining their face veils even in the mosque, a practice viewed askance by the Andalusi population, who felt this was against normative Islamic practice which requires the uncovering of both men and women's faces during prayer.[14] For the Almoravids, however, not only their honour but their elite status within the community stood to be compromised by removing the *lithām*, and therefore the famous Andalusi jurist, Ibn Rushd al-Jadd, who served as Almoravid *qāḍī* of Córdoba and legal adviser to the amirs, ruled that the practice was permitted.

The *lithām* proved to be a bone of contention in other ways too. In a small treatise on good government and the regulation of public life, the Sevillan *muḥtasib* (market inspector) Ibn 'Abdun complained that some non-Sanhaja troops and random individuals wore the *lithām* to inspire terror in the population and commit all kinds of abuses when only the Sanhaja, Lamtuna and Lamta should wear it. He suggested that, at the very least, different ranks of the army should wear different types of veil so that they could not pretend to be of a higher social rank than they were in order to claim immunity for misdemeanours, showing that the *lithām* was being widely adopted by other Almoravid recruits.[15]

In the same passage Ibn 'Abdun also asserted that troops should not be allowed to bear arms in the city because 'the Berbers are people who don't hesitate to kill or wound when they are angered', sentiments that are reminiscent of the resentment of the population of Baghdad towards the new Turkish soldiery in the early ninth century.[16] Although undoubtedly negative, this recommendation does point to the fact that the Almoravids and their followers

[13] See Chapter 7, below.
[14] Hopley, 'Nomadic populations and the challenge to legitimacy', pp. 235–7.
[15] Ibn 'Abdun, *Séville Musulmane*, pp. 61–2; Hopley, 'Nomadic populations', pp. 237–9.
[16] Ibn 'Abdun, *Séville Musulmane*, p. 62.

could be found throughout Seville and joined in with daily life. This proved to be a smouldering fuse that exploded into rebellion in Córdoba in 1120 when an Almoravid 'servant' made unwelcome advances to a woman during public celebrations for the feast of the sacrifice but the authorities failed to punish the culprit, showing both the communality of social life and the ways in which Almoravid exceptionalism might be exploited.[17] Although there were wider political reasons for this rebellion, mentioned in Chapter 2, social tensions between the Córdoban population and those of lower rank hoping to exploit the privileged status of the Saharan Sanhaja also played their part. Meanwhile, in the countryside, the Sanhaja disrupted the rural economy by cattle-rustling, a useful way of keeping cavalry skills honed in the desert and negotiating relations between Saharan tribes, but rather less welcome in al-Andalus.[18]

What emerges from these scattered cases is the socio-cultural separation that existed between the dominant Sanhaja elements in the Almoravid elite and their Andalusi subjects, a situation replicated in many Maghribi towns where they were no less foreign. However, social and cultural distance is not a stable or impermeable barrier and some individuals and groups in society drew closer to the Almoravids over time in more positive ways than wearing the *lithām* to bully locals or to commit crimes! In the domestic sphere, elite Sanhaja men quickly altered their traditional pattern of marrying free Saharan women by cohabiting with Christian concubines from al-Andalus and marrying members of the urban elite as well, immediately creating a maternal link with very different sectors of the population. Both 'Ali b. Yusuf and his son Sir were the children of Christian concubines, while Yusuf b. Tashfin's granddaughter married into the bureaucratic Banu 'Atiyya family.

In the military realm, as the above references to misuse of the *lithām* imply, the Almoravid army included a range of contingents in addition to Sanhaja tribesmen, including tribal auxiliaries from other Berber groups, Andalusi militias, black slaves purchased from sub-Saharan Africa, white Christian mercenaries and slaves from Iberia, some of whom converted to Islam, and volunteers for individual campaigns. In addition, the Almoravid navy, which enabled them to conquer the Balearic islands and become a western Mediterranean maritime power, was manned by sailors recruited from ports such as Ceuta, Almería, Dénia and Valencia. In his study of the reign of 'Ali b. Yusuf, Lagardère quotes Guichard's opinion that a highly critical letter sent by an Andalusi Almoravid scribe, Abu Marwan b. Abi'l-Khisal, to a Lamtuna contingent may have been as vitriolic in its denunciation of them

[17] Lagardère, *le djihâd andalou*, pp. 89–90

[18] Hopley, 'Nomadic populations', pp. 239–42.

as it was because the scribe did not realise that the Lamtuna were any more than one contingent among many in the army![19]

While such recruits were not seen as Almoravids in the sense of Sanhaja tribesmen, they were part of the larger Almoravid ruling elite, as were the many Andalusi and Maghribi jurists, scribes and bureaucrats who sought employment in the judicial and governmental administration. In fact, one of the distinguishing characteristics of the Almoravid movement was their strong reliance upon jurists from the Maliki school of law, predominantly of Andalusi origin, many of whom migrated to Marrakesh. By far the most famous of these jurists was Ibn Rushd al-Jadd, the grandfather of Ibn Rushd al-Hafid (Averroes), who personally advised ʿAli b. Yusuf and issued religio-legal opinions (*fatāwā*) on political and social matters, and Abu Bakr b. al-ʿArabi who brought the ʿAbbasid caliph's letter of recognition to Yusuf b. Tashfin. These Andalusi jurists were joined by Maghribis such as Qadi ʿIyad of Ceuta and Musa b. Hammad, one of the first Sanhaja tribesmen to become an eminent jurist and also chief judge of Marrakesh.[20]

The Almoravids' heavy reliance on Maliki jurists and bureaucrats has often been seen as an indication of their ignorance of Islamic law and social norms and, at the outset, their poor command of Arabic language and culture. The oft-quoted quip of the Ta'ifa king of Seville, al-Muʿtamid b. ʿAbbad, that it was marginally better to drive camels than herd pigs, encapsulates this position.[21] This trope of the uneducated and uncouth Sanhaja tribesman was the riposte to the tribesmen's own pride in their austere desert heritage and their perception that many Andalusis were decadent and corrupt Muslims. This did not, however, mean that the Almoravids rejected Arabic or harboured Berber 'nationalistic' sentiments. Although it is generally recognised that the first generation of Almoravids were not fully literate in Arabic, and Yusuf b. Tashfin is said to have used an interpreter, the Sanhaja claim to be descendants of the Arabs of Himyar who spoke Berber as a result of living among the Berbers and intermarrying with them expressed their aspiration to claim both cultural worlds as their own. As Lagardère points out, Yusuf's son and successor ʿAli was given the type of Arabic education enjoyed by generations of Andalusi princes.[22] He also actively recruited eminent Andalusi secretaries, and one of his female cousins, Hawwa' bint Tashfin, was a competent Arabic poet.[23]

[19] Lagardère, *Le djihâd andalou*, pp. 137–8.

[20] Gómez-Rivas, *Islamization of Morocco*, p. 57.

[21] al-Himyari, *Rawd al-Miʿtar*, p. 85.

[22] Lagardère, *Le djihâd andalou*, p. 14.

[23] al-Marrakushi, *Muʿjib*, p. 255. On Hawwa' bint Tashfin, see p. 159, below.

One can fruitfully compare the experience of the Sanhaja Almoravids with that of their contemporaries, the Seljuk Turks in Iraq and Iran. The Ghuzz Turks, from whose ranks the Seljuks emerged, were also newly and probably quite superficially Islamised when they filtered into Islamic lands. They were also tribal pastoralists whose fighting skills enabled them to seize power from other warrior elites, the Turkish Ghaznavids in Afghanistan and the Daylamite Buyids in Iraq and Iran, and finally assume the protectorship of the 'Abbasid caliphs in Baghdad. Like the Almoravids, the Seljuks relied heavily on the existing urban bureaucratic class, conversant in Arabic and Persian in the latter case, to determine the shape of their government while maintaining their customary Turkic practices and speaking Turkish. Although none of the Almoravids' servants achieved quite the fame of the Seljuk chief minister, Nizam al-Mulk, those bureaucrats and jurists who served the Almoravid regime could wield a great deal of power and they cannot be seen as external to Almoravid policymaking or completely excluded from Saharan Sanhaja society. When 'Ali b. Yusuf had to decide whether to transfer south populations of Andalusi Christians who had collaborated with Alfonso I El Batallador of Aragon during his 1125 campaign against Granada, he turned to Ibn Rushd al-Jadd for an opinion. Similarly, when Ibn Tumart arrived in Marrakesh and publicly criticised 'Ali b. Yusuf in the great mosque, the amir consulted not only his Sanhaja kinsmen but also the eminent jurist, Malik b. Wuhayb, on how to respond.

The Almoravid ruling elite was thus an amalgam of Sanhaja and non-Sanhaja constituencies bound together by their mutual adherence to the Maliki school of law and militarily supported not only by the veiled desert tribes, but also by Maghribi, Andalusi and Christian contingents who perceived their interests to lie with the regime. From a social rather than a political perspective, the disintegration of this elite occurred as a result of rising dissension within the Banu Targut that could not be mediated by elders, rifts between the Lamtuna and their Masufa allies, and the fact that the Maliki jurists only represented one group of interests in al-Andalus and the Maghrib and were perceived by many of the Almoravids' subjects to be exploiting their influence to acquire wealth and privilege rather than ensuring just and moral governance. As the Almoravid leadership fractured, many of the elite who were not killed in conflict transferred their loyalties to the rising Almohads, including Andalusi jurists and secretaries and, more unexpectedly, veiled warriors who, on occasion, cast off their veils to join the new social order.

> Yahya b. Ishaq al-Ingimar came to 'Abd al-Mu'min with a group of his Masufa kinsmen all wearing their veils which they cast off outside Fes to put

on Almohad dress (*wa-kulluhum mulaththamūn thumma azālūhu bi-ẓāhir Fās wa ṣārū fī ziyy al-muwaḥḥidīn*).[24]

The Almohad Ruling Elite

Although the Almohads were also supported by a particular tribal people, the Masmuda of the High Atlas and Sus, the early Almohad ruling class was more diverse than that of the Almoravids since membership was predicated on acceptance of Ibn Tumart as the *mahdī* over and above tribal *'aṣabiyya*. From the outset, the Almohad elite included Sanhaja and Zanata Berbers as well as the majority Masmuda, and the key group around Ibn Tumart, his companions (*ṣaḥāba*) who made up the Council of Ten, was not drawn from a single clan, tribe or Berber people. Nonetheless, the support of the Masmuda tribes was crucial to the success of the Almohad movement: they protected Ibn Tumart as a fellow Masmuda tribesman before accepting him as a religious leader, and their tribal chiefs, the Almohad shaykhs, remained the most important political chiefs and military commanders in the empire for a century or more, despite the incorporation of other military elements into the Almohad army, most notably Arab tribes from further east.

These core Almohad Masmuda tribes of the High Atlas mountains and the Sus valley were sedentary villagers with a very different culture to the Saharan nomads who dominated the Almoravid elite. When Ibn Tumart returned from his travels and was exiled for preaching against the religious deficiencies of the Almoravids, the Hargha tribe sheltered him out of dislike for the Sanhaja as well as commitment to his message. Almohadism then spread among the numerous Masmuda tribes through complex processes of education in the local Berber language, activation of tribal modes of alliance-making, and egregious violence against opponents, demonstrated most obviously in the capture of Tinmall and the bloody purge (*tamyīz*) of those who were not convinced by Ibn Tumart's claim to *mahdī*-hood.

As we saw in Chapter 3, Ibn Tumart or 'Abd al-Mu'min actively moulded a new hierarchy that both subsumed previous tribal identities by creating a new supra-tribal religious identity and used them by adapting the tribal council form into new Almohad councils and using tribal groups as military units. The Almohad writer Ibn al-Qattan describes the early Almohad hierarchy as a succession of groupings beginning with the Council of Ten made up of Ibn Tumart's closest disciples, his household, the Council of Fifty, the Council of Seventy, the *ṭalaba*, the *ḥuffāẓ*, the different tribes who adhered to the movement, and other military recruits such as black slave troops (*'abīd*) captured

[24] Ibn 'Idhari, *al-Bayan*, vol. 4, p. 102.

from the Almoravids.[25] Although this hierarchy modified Masmuda tribal structures, it also gave early Masmuda converts high status thereby winning Ibn Tumart their fierce support during the first decades of the movement.

In contrast to the Almoravid social elite, which undoubtedly relied on Berber but privileged Arabic in public discourse, the role of the 'western tongue' (*al-lisān al-gharbī*) was much more pronounced among the Almohad elite. From Ibn Tumart's efforts to compose books and teach in Berber to the presence of Berber sermon-givers in al-Andalus, the Almohad movement had a distinct and revolutionary Berber agenda that identified the Masmuda as a new chosen people.[26] In his list of the imams and sermon-givers (*khaṭībs*) of Fes, the fourteenth-century chronicler al-Jazna'i, himself of Berber extraction, mentioned that during the Almohad era, these religious functionaries had to know Ibn Tumart's book, the *Tawḥīd*, in Berber as well as in Arabic, presumably so that they could teach or give sermons in Berber.[27] From a socio-linguistic perspective this was a revolutionary experiment which inserted Berber into urban religious life as never before, but, like so much of the Almohad religious programme, this innovation did not endure and the Berber languages remained relegated to the rural and domestic domains rather than gaining parity with Arabic as a religious and public idiom.

The number of languages spoken within the Almohad elite – several Berber languages and Arabic – probably had some role to play in this, as did the social diversification that resulted from the succession of 'Abd al-Mu'min to the Almohad caliphate. As we have seen, 'Abd al-Mu'min was not a Masmuda Berber but a member of the Zanata Kumiya tribe, and therefore his accession to power and establishment of a dynastic caliphate had important repercussions for the social structure of the Almohad elite. In the first place, 'Abd al-Mu'min further modified the power of purely tribal *'aṣabiyya* in the ruling elite by inculcating an Almohad *esprit de corps* through the rigorous ideological and physical education of the descendants of the original tribal leaders of the movement to expand the *ḥuffāẓ* cadres and the scholarly elite, the *ṭalaba*, who actively instructed others in the tenets of Almohadism. Although the members of the early Council of Fifty and their descendants, the *ahl* or *ait khamsīn*, retained their status, references to gatherings of the Almohad tribal councils fade away.[28]

Secondly, because the heavily out-numbered Mu'minid rulers were keen

[25] Ibn al-Qattan, *Nazm al-Juman*, p. 82; Hopkins, 'The Almohade hierarchy'; Fromherz, *The Almohads*, p. 92.
[26] Ghouirgate, *L'Ordre almohade*, pp. 227–31.
[27] al-Jazna'i, *Zahrat al-As*, p. 56.
[28] Hopkins, 'The Almohade hierarchy', p. 95.

to find a counter-balance to the powerful Masmuda shaykhs, they recruited their Zanata kinsmen, as well as the Arab Banu Hilal and Banu Sulaym tribes from Ifriqiya, to the military, creating a much more diverse politico-military elite. An indication of the meteoric rise of the Kumiya was the appointment of 'Abd al-Salam b. Muhammad al-Kumi, 'Abd al-Mu'min's step-brother, as his chief minister in 1158. According to Ibn Sahib al-Salat, 'Abd al-Salam went on to abuse his position when he was appointed viceroy of the west during 'Abd al-Mu'min's campaign to recapture al-Mahdiyya in Ifriqiya by accusing the Mu'minid *sayyids* of drinking and not taking their posts seriously, while siphoning off wealth and allowing his Kumiya fellows to oppress the people. This led to a rallying of the *sayyids*, Masmuda shaykhs and the subject population against him, his arrest and his death.[29]

Ibn Sahib al-Salat's account of this episode is both symbolic and revelatory of social relations. In one version of the story, 'Abd al-Salam was killed by poison mixed into his daily bread ration in prison, an exchange that inverted the paternal relationship formed by the caliph's feeding of his servants that 'Abd al-Salam had compromised by his corruption. However, his fall also demonstrated social stresses in the elite, caused by rivalries between the *parvenu* Kumiya and the Masmuda shaykhs, two of whom – Tamim and 'Abd al-Haqq b. Wanudin al-Hintati – were such avid opponents of 'Abd al-Salam that they threatened their nephew, Muhammad b. Yusuf b. Wanudin, 'If you don't stop protecting him, we will kill you!'[30] On the other hand, Muhammad's friendship with 'Abd al-Salam reminds us that tribal enmities were not everything and bonds of friendship and patronage could link people across the elite.

The rise of the Arab tribes was of a different nature and had long-term effects for the Maghrib. The gradual migration of the Banu Hilal and Banu Sulaym tribes from Arabia into Egypt and on to Ifriqiya was an epic movement of peoples that has been variously considered cause or symptom of the reversion of land in Ifriqiya to pastoralism and the demise of the Zirid polity.[31] From the socio-cultural perspective, the most significant aspect of the Hilali migrations was the introduction of Arabic-speaking tribes into the rural environment and the rural Arabisation that ensued. This would not have affected what is now Morocco, however, had it not been for the Almohad recruitment of Arab tribes into the army and their transfer westwards to fight in the Maghrib and al-Andalus.[32] Ibn Sahib al-Salat frequently refers to the mobilisations of

[29] Ibn Sahib al-Salat, *al-Mann bi'l-Imama*, pp. 112–19.
[30] Ibid., p. 118.
[31] See Chapter 5, below.
[32] Ibn Sahib al-Salat, *al-Mann bi'l-Imama*, pp. 111–12.

large numbers of Arab tribesmen in Marrakesh and Ribat al-Fath from 1162 onwards, something that would have been a completely new phenomenon at this time.[33] By the later Almohad era, the Arabs were so embedded in the Almohad elite that they were partners in giving the *bay'a* to a new caliph, and by the mid-thirteenth century, they were intermarrying with Berber tribes such as the powerful Banu Marin, creating a new Arabo-Berber tribal elite.

This Arab tribal element was, however, totally distinct from the Arabised urban cadre that also found a place within the new Almohad order as it had during the Almoravid era. 'Abd al-Mu'min and his successors followed the time-honoured path of recruiting secretaries and bureaucrats from the existing Arabic-literate civilian elite, such as the Sevillans, Ibn Sahib al-Salat and Abu Bakr b. al-Jadd, and the Córdoban philosopher and jurist Ibn Rushd al-Hafid, ensuring a high level of governmental continuity between the Almoravid and Almohad eras in the chancery (*dīwān al-inshā'*). Andalusis and Maghribis who had served the Almoravids and then entered Almohad service included the famous secretary and poet, Ahmad b. 'Atiyya, the financial administrator (*mushrif*) of Almoravid Fes, 'Abd Allah b. Khiyar al-Jayyani, and an Almoravid judge of Valencia, Abu 'Abd al-Malik Marwan b. 'Abd Allah.[34] However, while the Almoravids by and large recruited administrators from al-Andalus, the Almohad bureaucratic cohort included men who were born in the Maghrib or were employed there by the Almoravids, even if they had Andalusi antecedents.

Abu Ja'far Ahmad b. Ja'far b. 'Atiyya, whose fall and execution we discussed in the previous chapter, is a good example of this phenomenon. His father came from the village of Cambrila in the province of Tortosa, south of Barcelona in the northeastern part of the Iberian peninsula. Ja'far entered Almoravid service as a scribe at some point and moved south to Dénia, followed by Marrakesh where Ahmad was born. The latter grew up in Marrakesh and served the amirs 'Ali b. Yusuf, Tashfin b. 'Ali and Ibrahim b. Tashfin as a scribe or secretary, and married Zaynab, a granddaughter of Yusuf b. Tashfin and sister of Yahya b. al-Sahrawiyya, the Almohads' most persistent Almoravid opponent in the Maghrib.[35] The Almohads killed Ibn 'Atiyya's father during their conquest of Fes, and, when they took Marrakesh soon after, Ibn 'Atiyya concealed his identity and entered Almohad military ranks as a humble archer to avoid also being killed as an Almoravid servant. His fortunes changed, however, when Abu Hafs 'Umar al-Hintati defeated al-Massi in the Sus in 1147. The doughty Masmuda general despaired of being able to inform 'Abd al-Mu'min of the victory in suitable Arabic epistolary

[33] Ibn Sahib al-Salat, *al-Mann bi'l-Imama*, p. 130 ff.
[34] See Bennison, 'The salutory tale of Ibn 'Aṭiyya', pp. 255, 257–60.
[35] See pp. 84–5, above.

style until he was directed to Ibn 'Atiyya, who could not resist showing off his fine Arabic writing skills despite fearing the consequences! When Abu Hafs 'Umar heard his draft missive,

> He was overcome with astonishment at it and praised [Ibn 'Atiyya] and lavished his care upon him because he believed that he was a treasure whom he could present to 'Abd al-Mu'min.[36]

The caliph felt the same and decided that Ibn 'Atiyya's command of Arabic was rare and precious enough to overlook his previous service to the Almoravids, and he rose to the position of chief minister before his fall, indicating that despite the space given to Berber in Almohad public contexts, Arabic was still a required language of government and religion. That being said, although it is nowhere stated, it is likely that Ibn 'Atiyya had some familiarity with Berber languages, given his childhood and youth in Marrakesh, and he should be viewed as a member of a new Maghribi urban class fully conversant with the Andalusi Arabic heritage but Maghribi by birth. His successors as secretaries were Abu Muhammad 'Ayyash b. 'Abd al-Malik from Córdoba, a traditional source of administrators, but also Abu'l-Qasim 'Abd al-Rahman al-Qalami from Bijaya in Ifriqiya, who was succeeded in the reign of Abu Ya'qub Yusuf by Abu'l-Fadl Ja'far b. Ahmad, known as Ibn Mahshuwwa, also from Bijaya, showing that the eastern provinces of the empire also provided bureaucratic manpower.[37] Even more interesting is the entry to the scribal class of men whose names indicate Berber origin, such as Abu 'Abd Allah Muhammad b. Yakhluftan b. Ahmad al-Fazzazi who served the caliph al-Nasir.[38]

The same phenomenon is evident in the composition of the judicial elite and the judges of Marrakesh, whom al-Marrakushi lists for the reign of each caliph, who include individuals from the Maghrib, Ifriqiya and al-Andalus. 'Abd al-Mu'min's judges were 'Abd Allah b. Jabal from Oran and 'Abd Allah b. 'Abd al-Rahman, 'the Malagan', who held the post into the reign of Abu Ya'qub Yusuf.[39] He was then replaced by 'Isa b. 'Umran al-Tazi, 'a booming orator, an eloquent speaker and a wonderful poet', from the Zanata Berber Tsul tribe of the hinterland of Taza. Al-Marrakushi knew this family personally and adds that all 'Isa b. 'Umran's sons also served as judges, including 'Ali who was judge of Bijaya then Tlemcen, Talha who also served as judge of Tlemcen, Yusuf who was judge of Fes, and Musa who was judge

[36] Bennison, 'The salutory tale of Ibn 'Aṭiyya', pp. 258–9.
[37] al-Marrakushi, *Mu'jib*, pp. 292–3.
[38] Ibid., p. 444.
[39] Ibid., p. 293.

of Marrakesh around 1217 when al-Marrakushi headed east.[40] Ya'qub al-Mansur's judges, Abu 'Abd Allah Muhammad b. Marwan and Abu'l-Qasim Ahmad b. Muhammad, came from Oran and Córdoba, and al-Nasir's judges included a man from Fes called Muhammad b. 'Abd Allah [b.] Tahir.[41]

Whether all these individuals should be considered Almohads or not is a debated point that has both ideological and ethno-linguistic dimensions. From the ideological perspective, did such servants of the regime subscribe to Almohad Islam and accept Ibn Tumart as the *mahdī* or did they simply work for it? Sometimes there seems to be a scholarly reluctance to acknowledge that the movement did have some appeal to Andalusi Muslims and was not just an alien ideology imposed by Berber 'fanatics', but our uncertainty also reflects obscurities about the corporate nature of the *ṭalaba* group. Did scholars, jurists and other religious personnel hold permanent or temporary membership of the *ṭalaba* corps and does the removal of specifically Almohad terms in post-Almohad texts, a process Fricaud has termed 'de-Almohadisation', conceal participation in it?[42] While high-ranking scholars and officials such as Ibn Rushd, who served as an Almohad judge and probably composed the 1183 version of the Almohad creed (*'aqīda*), and Ibn Sahib al-Salat, who studied for a period with the Almohad *ṭalaba* in Marrakesh, are likely to have been Almohads in a religio-political sense,[43] lower rank jurists and bureaucrats, many of Andalusi origin, who held more mundane judicial and administrative roles, may well have subscribed to Almohadism only superficially, if at all.

On the ethno-linguistic front, to what extent is 'Almohad' a synonym for the Berber tribes, Masmuda in particular, who supported the movement rather than a more general term indicating those who proffered loyalty to the regime and its version of Islam? The sources persistently distinguish between the 'Almohads' in the sense of Berber tribes, and other military contingents, such as the ex-Almoravid Lamtuna, Arab tribes or the Andalusi militias, giving the term an ethno-linguistic dimension. The situation was in some ways similar to that pertaining in early Islam when the categories of Arab and Muslim were conflated or differentiated depending on circumstances. What can be said is that, despite Ibn Tumart's desire that all Muslims should submit and recognise his interpretation of Islam as the authentic monotheistic message of Muhammad and the prophets who preceded him, the

[40] al-Marrakushi, *Mu'jib*, pp. 357–8.
[41] Ibid., pp. 382, 445.
[42] Fricaud, 'La place des *ṭalaba* dans la société almohade mu'minide', p. 526.
[43] Ibn Sahib al-Salat, *al-Mann bi'l-Imama*, p. 185; Fletcher, 'The doctrine of divine unity', p. 190.

term 'Almohad' tended to be an elite identifier that distinguished the ruling lineage and its Maghribi Berber military supporters from its Arab tribal auxiliaries and the subject population, many of whom continued to subscribe to the Maliki school of law and held aloof from Almohad mahdism.

This partly reflected the fact that there was as stark a socio-cultural difference between the Masmuda Berber mountaineers and their new urban subjects as there had been between the latter and the veiled Saharan Sanhaja. As we have seen, many Masmuda tribesmen did not speak or write Arabic and while they did not wear 'effeminate' garb such as the *lithām*, they could seem as alien and disruptive as their predecessors in the conquered cities of their empire. Ibn 'Idhari reports that when the Almohads acquired Seville, the first Almohad contingents were settled in the old 'Abbadid palace, where they were conveniently separated from the general population, but when further troops arrived they were billeted in the adjacent Jabbana quarter, where they quickly demonstrated their ignorant, uncouth and destructive nature by burning the houses' roofing for firewood, using the reception areas of the houses to corral their animals, and generally abusing the properties as well as stealing from the inhabitants of nearby areas who fled.[44]

On the other hand, during the conquest period, individuals and communities are described as 'converting to Almohad Islam' (*waḥḥada*), including prominent Almoravids such as Yahya b. al-Sahrawiyya, who thus technically became Almohads. Moreover, the Mu'minids continually forged links with other groups and broadened the social base of the ruling elite through war, negotiation, service recruitment and marriage. The eventual submission of the Andalusi Banu Mardanish of Murcia, recounted in Chapter 3, provides a case in point. As we have seen, when the Almohad armies first arrived Muhammad b. Sa'd b. Mardanish, lord of Murcia, and his father-in-law Ibn Hamushk fought bitterly against them and sought military assistance from the Castilians. As a result, the Almohads harshly denounced the Banu Mardanish, but when Ibn Mardanish died in March 1172 his son Hilal and his brothers and their paternal uncle Abu'l-Hajjaj Yusuf not only entered Almohad service but also became members of Abu Ya'qub Yusuf's council (*majlis*).

> [The caliph] indicated to them that they would not only be considered part of the Almohad cohort (*jumlat al-muwaḥḥidīn*) but among his kin and those of highest esteem. He ordered them to prepare to travel with him and all come to his capital [Marrakesh] . . . He settled the uncle, Abu'l-Hajjaj Yusuf b. Mardanish, in Valencia and gave him command over its districts.[45]

44 Ibn 'Idhari, *al-Bayan*, vol. 4, p. 114.
45 Ibn Sahib al-Salat, *al-Mann bi'l-Imama*, p. 425.

Ibn Mardanish's daughter subsequently became one of Abu Ya'qub Yusuf's wives, creating a genuine familial bond between the Banu Mardanish and the Mu'minids.[46] Her son was the infamous thirteenth-century Almohad caliph al-Ma'mun who formally rejected Almohadism in 1229, a decision sometimes attributed to his more Andalusi than Maghribi sensibilities, showing the distance that the Mu'minids had moved from their rural Maghribi origins.

Another group that found a place within the Almohad elite were the so-called Ghuzz or Aghzaz, a name derived from that of the Ghuzz Turks but used in the Maghrib in a looser way to denote military adventurers from Ayyubid lands of varied Turkish, Kurdish and Armenian origin who came west.[47] The best known of such men was Qaraqush, an Armenian Mamluk who led the band of men who allied with the Banu Ghaniya against the Almohads, but then accepted service with the Almohad caliph Ya'qub al-Mansur after he defeated them at the battle of Hamma in 1187.[48] These Ghuzz and their successors became a small but exotic component within the army which was subsequently absorbed into the Marinid army after the death of the Almohad caliph al-Sa'id in battle in 1248. Although the Ghuzz enhanced the international and imperial character of the Almohad army, their social impact was minimal. A more significant group in this respect were the large numbers of Christians who entered the late Almohad army, either as mercenaries or as enslaved prisoners of war. This was a practice shared with the Almoravids and also, in reverse form, with Christian Iberian rulers of the time who frequently used Muslim mercenaries, although such troops were not deployed against their own co-religionists.[49] There may have been as many as 12,000 Christian troops stationed in Marrakesh in the early thirteenth century during the caliphate of al-Ma'mun, which cannot have failed to have had an appreciable effect on the demographics of the capital.[50]

The fact that some of the Almohads' Christian troops were probably slaves, reminds us that both the Almoravids and Almohads possessed domestic and military slaves and freedmen, as did the majority of Islamic polities. Although direct references to slaves are few, it is clear that black and white slaves were part of the Almoravid and Almohad ruler's household: they were one of the items in the gift that Yusuf b. Tashfin gave his cousin Abu Bakr b. 'Umar and several rulers of this era had slave mothers from northern Christian territories, who will be discussed in the section on women later in this chapter.

[46] Ibn 'Idhari, *al-Bayan*, vol. 4, p. 208.

[47] al-Marrakushi, *Mu'jib*, pp. 412–14.

[48] Ibn 'Idhari, *al-Bayan*, vol. 4, pp. 262–3.

[49] See Fancy, 'Theologies of violence'.

[50] Fromherz, 'North Africa and the twelfth-century renaissance', pp. 49–50.

Many domestic servants were slaves or freedmen and women and a proportion of this group were eunuchs, although the identification of individuals as eunuchs is made more complicated by the tendency of the sources to use the word *khādim*, which may simply mean servant, as a euphemism for a eunuch (*khaṣī*). Eunuchs were favoured as men with no familial bonds who could thus be expected to be more loyal to their master than any other category of person.

Slavery in Islam

Although Islamic law prohibits the enslavement of Muslims, it condones slavery and the practice, inherited from Antiquity, was widespread in medieval Islamic lands. The wealthy used slaves as sexual partners, domestic servants and agricultural labourers, while rulers recruited large numbers of slaves for military purposes. Slaves, especially those in the army, could rise to very high positions, hold property and marry, making medieval Islamic slavery a complex institution very different to trans-Atlantic plantation slavery. Because Muslims could not be legally enslaved, slaves were brought from the peripheries of the Islamic world, including Turkic Central Asia, Byzantium, the Latin Christian and pagan north, Berber lands and sub-Saharan Africa.

Among the eunuchs in Almoravid and Almohad service were those who had served the Zirids of Granada and expected to be taken into Yusuf b. Tashfin's service,[51] Sandal the eunuch who stood alongside Tashfin b. ʿAli at his last stand,[52] and a number of Almohad *ḥujjāb* (sing. *ḥājib*), a term often translated as chamberlain which denoted the individual who granted others access to the caliph and thus enjoyed considerable power. Yaʿqub al-Mansur's *ḥājib* was a eunuch called Kafur (Camphor) and al-Nasir's two chamberlains, Rayhan (Thyme) and Mubashshir (Messenger), were also eunuchs.[53] In the military sphere, sub-Saharan Africans were often used as a royal bodyguard called the *ḥasham* or *ʿabīd al-makhzan*, and the chamberlain Kafur commanded the caliph's slave bodyguard (*ʿabīd al-khāṣṣa*) as part of his role.[54] Black units served alongside Christian prisoners of war like the Catalan Reverter.

This social diversification of the elite, and of the army especially, had a number of aspects to it. An army and household of many colours was a visible sign of imperial power: descriptions of the army of the Umayyad

[51] Tibi, *The Tibyan*, p. 153.
[52] See pp. 59–60, above.
[53] al-Marrakushi, *Muʿjib*, pp. 356, 443.
[54] Ibid., p. 348.

caliphs of Córdoba, for instance, highlighted the ability of the caliph to command men of all colours and races, and Almohad recruitment of sub-Saharan Africans, Maghribis, Andalusis, Ghuzz and northern Christians should be seen in the same symbolic light. Moreover, medieval Muslim regimes often diversified their armies to gain the tactical expertise of different groups, while the existence of ethnically distinct corps helped to preclude mutinies of the whole army. In terms of the Khaldunian cycle, the recruitment of deracinated groups without deep connections to local society, usually in the form of slave soldiers or mercenaries, what Gellner terms the 'Mamluk option', was a sure means of perpetuating a dynasty when the *ʿaṣabiyya* of the initial tribal coalition that had brought it to power had faded.[55]

In the Almohad case, of course, unifying *ʿaṣabiyya* was compromised from the start by the non-Masmuda Mu'minid seizure of power and, even if the recruitment of new, loyal troops could postpone the passing of a dynasty, Ibn Khaldun and his contemporaries regarded it as natural and inevitable in the end. From this perspective, it is no surprise that the Almohad ruling elite began to break down in the thirteenth century. Although it was not as small as the Almoravid Sanhaja elite, it faced some of the same problems, including contested successions and intra-lineal conflicts, exacerbated in the Almohad case by the large size of the ruling Mu'minid clan and its collateral branches, which grew rapidly due to the access of men to numerous wives and concubines and the resulting high number of children. Although rulers rarely faced the problem of not having eligible sons to succeed them, numerous competent and ambitious candidates was equally destabilising. While Mu'minid siblings and cousins fought amongst themselves for the spoils of power, other members of the elite established their own independent appanages, most notably the descendants of the Masmuda shaykh Abu Hafs 'Umar al-Hintati in Ifriqiya, and once again local power brokers, bureaucrats and religious scholars reconsidered their socio-political strategies.

The Rural *Ḥaḍar* and *Badw*

Although the machinations of the ruling elite dominate the pages of the Arabic chronicles, the majority of the inhabitants of the Maghrib and al-Andalus, the non-elite *ʿāmma* (general population) or *raʿāyā* (flocks), formed the vital tax-paying base of tribes, peasants and townsmen upon which each dynasty depended. Although a handful of tribes transformed their circumstances through empire-building, the majority remained subjects within the huge silent majority in the Maghrib and al-Andalus whose lifestyle and

55 Gellner, 'Tribalism and the state in the Middle East', pp. 113–16.

experiences we struggle to grasp. For the Maghrib we have to rely on a combination of descriptive geographical works, chronicles and legal materials, supplemented by the observations of French colonial and Anglophone post-colonial anthropologists such as Robert Montagne, Ernest Gellner, David Hart, Clifford Geertz and Lawrence Rosen. Despite their often fine observation and analysis, there is obviously a danger for historians in projecting their findings a millennium back in time. The situation is slightly better for al-Andalus where the records made by Christian conquerors seeking to establish seigneurial and fiscal relations with their new Muslim subjects, the *repartimientos*, provide additional insight into the rural landscape in the mid-thirteenth century. Although they are the most elusive group, we shall begin with the rural majority population of the Berber empires, the tribes of North Africa and the non-tribal peasantry in al-Andalus, while the following section will move on to the slightly better illuminated urban communities.

The Maghribi Tribes

Tribes are communities organised around the notion of kinship, which can be real or fictive, but, in either case, provides the rationale for mutual cooperation and defence. This type of social organisation flourished in areas that were either stateless or where the state had limited effective powers and people needed to band together for survival. Lineal solidarity was expressed through tribal epithets, which were usually composed of the name of an eponymous ancestor preceded by the Berber *ait* or the Arabic *banū* or *awlād*, all meaning 'sons of', in contrast to the word *ahl* or 'people of' commonly used for townsfolk. Tribes and clans were, however, mutable groupings that could absorb and assimilate other groups and create 'kinship' through ritual meals, shared breast-feeding to create milk-brothers and clientage. Actual kinship could rarely be demonstrated further back than three generations and oral genealogies were adapted to explain contemporary socio-political relations rather than remaining constant over time. The central point is, therefore, not that tribesmen and women were always blood relations, but that they understood and rationalised their social relations in terms of kinship and genealogy rather than other factors such as place of residence or occupation.

From the perspective of tribesmen, the main contrast between themselves and the rural non-tribal peasantry and city-dwellers (*ḥaḍar*) was the freedom they gained from their tribal solidarity, *'aṣabiyya* and military prowess. Both Arab and Berber tribesmen considered themselves free men (Ar. *aḥrār*, B. *imazighen*) because they could resist aggressors, including central state tax collectors, while the servile *ḥaḍar* had to pay taxes and seek protectors. Although Ibn Khaldun depicted Berber history as a struggle for Maghribi hegemony between the great Berber peoples, the Sanhaja, the Masmuda and the Zanata who had to share the landscape with the Banu Hilal and Banu Sulaym Arabs by the Almohad era, this was a somewhat artificial taxonomy imposed upon the tribal landscape and many tribesmen probably had no sense of this meta-narrative of great tribal peoples pitted against each other due to the enormously wide dispersal of Berber groups such as the Sanhaja and Zanata across North Africa, and the numerous subdivisions within them.

From the outside perspective, the main characteristic of the Maghribi tribes was the lack of a civilian–military divide in tribal society since every man, and many women, were trained from childhood to defend themselves and their kin group. In contemporary writing, the tribesmen of North Africa are characterised as warlike and militarily capable, while the non-tribal Andalusis are often seen as peaceable and averse to fighting. ʿAbd Allah b. Buluggin, the Sanhaja Zirid ruler of Granada in the Ta'ifa era, expressed this stereotype in his memoir, written in Aghmat to which Yusuf b. Tashfin had exiled him. In speaking of the Umayyad minister, Ibn Abi ʿAmir's recruitment of Berbers, he talks of their 'horsemanship and skill in the arts of war' in contrast to the 'peasantry of al-Andalus' who were 'unequal' to the task of repelling the Christians and 'not a warlike people'.[56] On the Andalusi side, this is problematic as the militarisation of a society was not dependent upon whether it was tribal or not. The Iberian Christians living in the frontier zone developed a highly effective warrior ethos, as did the Ottomans in Anatolia later, begging the question as to why Andalusi villagers did not. However, the warrior capabilities of the Berber and Arab tribes of North Africa cannot be doubted.

Daily life for tribesmen, however, did not revolve around warfare but more mundane affairs, including access to agricultural land, water and pastures, marriage, divorce and disputes, which were managed by groups of elders, generally called shaykhs (B. *amghār*) in our period, who gathered in councils (Ar. *jamāʿa*, B. *agraw*) to resolve communal issues. Such shaykhs achieved their position through experience and proven military and political abilities, although descent from an important shaykh helped to provide opportunities for younger men to show their talents. The management of affairs by such groups of shaykhs has led many anthropologists to describe

[56] Tibi, *The Tibyan*, p. 44.

tribal society as 'democratic' or 'oligarchic', and it certainly did have many participatory aspects, but it was also true that successful shaykhs could attempt to monopolise power and impose their authority, creating permanent tension between the theoretically egalitarian character of tribal life and actual inequalities in power and wealth.[57]

Another important figure was the *mizwār*, an elder chosen by his fellows to manage internal tensions over the use of tribal land for agriculture or pasture and other such disputes, due to his deep knowledge of tribal custom (*'urf*).[58] In later centuries, the *mizwār* might also be head of a rural religious lodge and, in that context, equivalent to the Arabic *muqaddam*. In some tribes, status was allocated by clan rather than individual, with some clans considered 'noble' by virtue of their warrior accomplishments, like the Lamtuna, and others seen as 'religious' through their monopoly over religious knowledge and/or literacy, or their claim to be descendants of the Prophet (*sharīf, shurafā'*). Both Ibn Tumart and 'Abd al-Mu'min attempted to claim descent from the Prophet, and one of the clans of the Banu Marin, the Banu 'Ali, are described in the thirteenth-century Marinid chronicle, the *Dhakhira al-Saniyya*, as sharifian.[59] These clans often played a similar mediating role to the *mizwār*, assisted by their claim to sharifian ancestry, which enhanced their sanctity and underlined their outsider status and thus neutrality in tribal disputes.

Other common institutions of tribal life included the blood feud and the confederacy or alliance group. The blood feud was a mechanism to regulate conflict by imposing harsh 'like for like' penalties for violent acts along the lines of the *lex talionis*. Unnecessary killing was not punished by arrest and imprisonment, but by the right of a murder victim's family to demand a life from the murderer's kin group or a large sum of blood money. Although the 'eye for an eye' approach to justice acted as a significant deterrent to killing, when a murder or killing did occur, it could trigger a negative spiral of killing and counter-killing that went on between groups for generations, a phenomenon that weakened the ability of the group to coalesce in the case of outside aggression or opportunity. The confederacy, known as a *laff* or *ṣaff*, operated as a more occasional form of tribal organisation or mobilisation. Twentieth-century anthropologists saw the tribal alliance group or confederation formed in opposition to other such confederations as typical to relations between tribes in the early modern Maghrib. If one tribe within a *laff* was attacked, all the tribes in the group would join the retaliatory attack, thereby providing

[57] Montagne, *Les Berbères et le Makhzen*, pp. vii–viii.

[58] Fromherz, *The Almohads*, pp. 108–9

[59] *al-Dhakhira al-Saniyya*, p. 21.

a deterrent to gratuitous attacks. In normal circumstances, the *laff* or *ṣaff* was probably the largest grouping of active concern to tribesmen rather than membership of a particular Berber 'people'. Traces of similar alliance patterns in the eleventh to thirteenth centuries occur in the way in which both the Almoravids and Almohads were able to recruit tribes from outside the Sanhaja and Masmuda, respectively, who then used their new affiliation to attack and raid tribes in rival confederations. Conversely, the existence of such 'fault lines' among tribes made the total pacification of the countryside virtually impossible.

One important question relating to tribal life in the eleventh to thirteenth centuries is the degree to which Berber tribes were Muslim and what they might have understood by that. The Fatimid, Almoravid and Almohad empire-building experiments were also movements to Islamise the Kutama, Saharan Sanhaja and Masmuda, respectively, and thus deepen Islam's penetration into rural North Africa. That is not to say that the tribes who subscribed to these movements did not already consider themselves to be Muslim, but they did not always have a very detailed knowledge of Islamic praxis or theology and admixed them with local customs and beliefs of a much older vintage, which we get a glimpse of via the geographers' reports of the strange sects of the Berber interior.

Pre-Islamic Berber beliefs attributed sacred significance to natural features such as wells, springs and trees, and tribes had religious figures whom we might call shamans. These figures could be male or female and, in the case of women, are described using the Arabic term *kāhina*, a soothsayer or priestess able to predict the future. During the Arab conquest, one of their most determined opponents was the Kahina, the queen-priestess of the Jarawa tribe of Ifriqiya, and in his description of the Ghumara region near Tetuan, al-Bakri recounts the story of a 'false prophet' called Ha-mim who instructed his followers to recite a prayer formula that expressed belief in his father and his paternal aunt, Tangit or Talit, who is described as a *kāhina*. Ha-mim's sister was also a *kāhina* whom the tribe relied upon to prophesy whether a raid would be successful.[60] It is worth noting in this respect that both Ibn Yasin and Ibn Tumart acted in ways that responded to this ancient paradigm of the shaman or *kāhin*. Ibn Yasin went to teach the Islamic orthopraxy of Qayrawan to the ill-informed Saharan Sanhaja, but indulged in non-Islamic rituals and punishments to do that. As Ibn Tumart travelled across North Africa towards Marrakesh, he repeatedly worked to assuage the

[60] al-Bakri, *Description de l'Afrique*, Arabic text, p. 100; French text, pp. 197–8. Ibn Abi Zar' gives the aunt's name as Talit; *Rawd al-Qirtas*, p. 122.

ignorance of country people about Islam but, at the same time, he exploited rural beliefs by acting as a soothsayer himself, making predictions and writing out amulets in his own hand (*khaṭṭ*) to bless those who hosted and fed him.[61]

The world of the peasantry in al-Andalus was very different to that of the tribes in North Africa due to the higher degree of outside political and fiscal control and the low incidence of nomadic or transhumant pastoralism, except in some areas of Arab or Berber tribal settlement. As mentioned in the introductory background, the Andalusi countryside was only slowly absorbed into the Arab-Islamic sphere and consisted of settled southern provinces (*kūra, kuwar*) and the marches (*thughūr*), with Christian lands that ran in a diagonal line up from the Lower March in the Algarve to the Upper March in the Ebro valley near the Pyrenees. One detailed study of all aspects of life in Muslim times is Guichard's painstaking reconstruction of life in the province of Valencia from the eleventh to the thirteenth centuries based on Arabic and Latin texts and archaeological evidence which gives an *aperçu* into the organisation of the countryside in eastern al-Andalus. His work suggests that each province was divided into *aʿmāl*, a word that probably indicates fiscal areas. The *aʿmāl* contained numerous villages and hamlets of varying size often called *qurā* (sing. *qarya*) in the Arabic sources. Another term that occurs frequently is *ḥiṣn* (pl. *ḥuṣūn*) indicating a fortification or a fortified settlement of a larger size than a village but smaller than a town.[62] The usage of these terms, however, was very elastic with some 'villages' possessing fortifications and the term *ḥiṣn* used for defensive points as well as settlements of an intermediate size. Rural areas also contained private estates (*ḍayʿa, ḍiyāʿ*) controlled by wealthy urbanites, amirs or the ruler himself particularly in the hinterlands of towns, which we shall consider more fully in the next chapter on the economy.

The basic unit of rural organisation, the village (*qarya*), was inhabited by a community (*jamāʿa*), rendered in post-conquest Christian documents as *aljama*, composed of tens of households inhabited by families with free private or communal control of their land.[63] In densely populated areas, clusters of hamlets were grouped around larger villages and the countryside seemed an endless succession of farms, fields and settlements. These village clusters were themselves grouped around a larger urban centre (*ḥiṣn* or *madīna*) where one could find a judge for more tricky legal issues, markets, military authorities and tax officials. In some areas, such as the hinterland of Córdoba, villages are

[61] al-Baydhaq, *Akhbar*, pp. 44, 45.

[62] Guichard, *Musulmans de Valence*, vol. 1, pp. 194–202.

[63] Ibid., vol. 1, p. 235.

described as having great mosques for the performance of the Friday prayer, but it is likely that small hamlets did not have such a mosque and their inhabitants might congregate for Friday prayer in the villages that did have one, creating important social and religious networks between them.[64] In addition to free proprietor farmers, village communities also included a handful of craftsmen and artisans, landless labourers, and at least one religious scholar (*faqīh*) who ministered to the spiritual needs of the population, providing a smattering of education, religious leadership and legal expertise. In some cases the *faqīh* may have acted as a local magistrate, although, as in tribal areas, custom played as important a role in the allocation of agricultural land, pasture and access to water as Islamic law.[65]

One enduring question relating to the social structure of the rural population of al-Andalus is the degree to which Islamic and Arabo-Berber tribal norms supplanted the pre-Islamic social organisation of the population. Naturally this varied extensively across al-Andalus. In the 1970s, Guichard put forward a working hypothesis that turned out to be highly controversial, which categorised social structures as either 'Oriental' or 'Occidental'. The 'Oriental' social structures that Guichard associated with Arabs and Berbers included strong patrilinearity, important relations with agnatic lineages, endogamous marriage between cousins, and weak social bonds between husband and wife reflected in easy divorce, polygamy and the use of concubines. In contrast, he identified bilinear recognition of both maternal and paternal ancestry, the strength of the married couple as a social unit, a preference for exogamous marriage and, as a consequence, weaker bilateral lineages, as 'Occidental' structures shared by Muwallad, Mozarab and northern Christian societies.[66]

In the case of eastern al-Andalus, he suggested that the prevalence of toponyms beginning with *banī* (sons of) meant that many such village communities contained extended agnatic groups of distant tribal ancestry descended from the large number of Berbers settled in the region. This led to the implantation of 'Oriental' and Maghribi social structures in eastern al-Andalus in contrast to the 'Occidental' structures that prevailed in central and western al Andalus where such settlement was more limited.[67] However, the extent to which tribal or clan structures survived in al-Andalus has been contested and in many cases places names including *banī*, or its Hispanised forms, indicate the Arab or Berber aristocratic lineage dominant in a locale

[64] Lagardère, *Campagnes*, p. 176.
[65] Guichard, *Musulmans de Valence*, vol. 2, pp. 353–6.
[66] See Guichard, *Structures sociales 'orientales' et 'occidentales'*.
[67] Guichard, *Musulmans de Valence*, vol. 1, pp. 227–30.

rather than an egalitarian tribal group.[68] In reality, it is impossible to be sure of the social impact of the arrival of Arab or Berber settlers on village life, particularly when Islamic and pre-Islamic social structures interacted with each other over time in completely unrecorded ways. Lagardère sees village life, in the sense of a mode of organisation for the agricultural exploitation of a piece of land, as essentially similar, regardless of the social structures in place.[69] In ordinary times, the primary concern of villagers was agricultural production, the management of water resources and the payment of tribute or taxes in cash, kind and labour services, which will be covered in the next chapter.

The Social Life of the City

The town or city (*madīna*) had huge socio-political and cultural importance for medieval Muslims who saw it as the site of religion, wealth and civilisation, consequently chroniclers, geographers and travel writers, and the authors of biographical dictionaries have much more to say about urban centres than villages or the countryside. Western scholars, however, have often drawn a negative comparison between a rather idealised vision of medieval Latin cities with institutionalised legal status and Islamic cities deemed to lack any such legal autonomy. From this perspective, the Islamic city is simply a concentration of people not a community able to administer itself and represent its own interests before rulers and, in the Latin Christian case, the church. The basis for this distinction is attributed to the replacement of Roman law in Islamic lands and the tendency for Muslim rulers, their representatives and the politico-military elite to live in towns rather than as a feudal aristocracy on the land. Comparative studies, however, show that perhaps the differences were not always so well defined: Latin towns could be under the thumb of rulers and Islamic cities could sometimes assert their autonomy.[70]

The towns and cities of North Africa and al-Andalus shared many characteristics with their counterparts across the Islamic world due to similarities of climate and culture, although the social composition of urban populations differed from region to region in terms of the precise mix of ethnicities, languages and religions. The degree of urbanisation also varied. The valleys and coasts of al-Andalus were densely packed with large and small towns, as was the coastal littoral of Ifriqiya, while the interior and western parts of the Maghrib were significantly less urbanised with few major cities and a sprinkling of market towns prior to the foundation of Marrakesh and Ribat

68 See Manzano Moreno, 'Quelques considérations sur les toponymes en Banū-', pp. 247–63.
69 Lagardère, *Campagnes*, pp. 177–8.
70 See Lantschner, 'Fragmented cities in the later Middle Ages'.

al-Fath and the expansion of Tlemcen and Fes.[71] Political powers were usually based in cities, but dynasties of rural tribal origin such as the Almoravids and Almohads were rarely able to rule without the cooperation and compliance of townsfolk, and, as we have seen, both elites included large cohorts of civilian bureaucrats, *literati* and scholars drawn from the urban notability.

Urban notables (*aʿyān, wujūh*) usually came from judicial, religious and mercantile backgrounds. The most eminent were often the religious scholars (*ʿulamāʾ, fuqahāʾ*) who specialised in jurisprudence (*fiqh*) and law, which gave them an indispensable social as well as religious role. This is certainly the impression given by the biographical dictionaries that are our main source of information about this group, although the cultural and social cachet of religious scholarship can mean that other facets of scholars' lives are elided from the record and the biographies for notables of other backgrounds are omitted. Nonetheless, religious personnel did genuinely have extensive influence in people's lives since they provided education, directed communal religious life, and also adjudicated civil cases relating to inheritance, marriage and divorce, and property rights. They also had fiscal responsibility for the inheritances of orphans and properties donated to the community as pious endowments, which provided them with opportunities to become very wealthy, sometimes by less than moral means. One such *cause célèbre* from a later era concerned the *khaṭīb* of the Qarawiyyin Mosque in Fes, Abu'l-Fadl al-Mazdaghi, who embezzled money, including orphans' inheritances, speculated in grain with it, and got caught out when he went bankrupt.[72]

The *fuqahāʾ* were also the group most likely to represent the population of a town before the ruler and his representatives or to take charge of affairs in the absence of a strong ruler or during an interregnum of some kind. Some of the Ta'ifa kings came from the ranks of the *fuqahāʾ*, most notably the ʿAbbadids of Seville who served as *qāḍī*s of the city before assuming rule over it. The *qāḍī* Ibn Jahhaf tried to replace al-Qadir of Valencia during the contest for the city between the Almoravids and El Cid, and the *qāḍī* Ibn Hamdin briefly held power in Córdoba as Almoravid power waned in the 1140s. Similar figures re-emerged from the urban elite during the decline of the Almohad empire, often entitled *raʾīs* (chief, head) in eastern al-Andalus.[73]

Such urban self-governance took multifarious forms. In some places, the assumption of power by local notables gave towns more autonomy than they had previously enjoyed. In Ceuta an oligarchic style of government based on a consultative group of jurists, the *shūrā*, enabled local social and

[71] See Chapter 7, below, for details on Almoravid and Almohad urbanisation projects.

[72] Shatzmiller, 'The fall of the Khaṭīb Abu'l-Faḍl al-Mazdaghī', pp. 71–81.

[73] Guichard, *Musulmans de Valence*, vol. 2, pp. 364–7.

economic interests to be placed ahead of those of distant and sometimes ineffectual dynasties during the confused years when the Almohads were trying to capture the city and again when the Almohad empire began to decline. In each phase, the *qāḍī*, Qadi 'Iyad and then Abu'l-Qasim al-'Azafi, headed the *shūrā* and managed the affairs of the city. On the other hand, some religious scholars acted in exactly the same way as rulers of other backgrounds once in control: al-Mu'tadid b. 'Abbad of Seville, for instance, was renowned for his capricious temper and cruelty, despite his family's urban juridical heritage. However, the ability of petty rulers, as opposed to imperial representatives, to behave in an autocratic way depended very much on whether their rule appeared to be beneficial to the town overall. The *qāḍī* of Granada complained to Yusuf b. Tashfin about the behaviour of the Zirid ruler, Ibn Buluggin, and facilitated the Almoravid conquest, and Ibn al-Aftas of Badajoz, who solicited Almoravid help against the Portuguese in the 1080s, was later ousted by his own subjects for impoverishing them.

Another role played by jurists (*fuqahā'*) was that of spokesmen for the community and its negotiators with power in times of difficulty. As we have seen in previous chapters, Andalusi jurists wrote to Yusuf b. Tashfin asking for Almoravid assistance against the Christians; jurists were prominent in the delegations that offered the submission of Andalusi and Ifriqiyan towns to 'Abd al-Mu'min; and jurists and scholars always formed the party of greeting for Almohad princes and caliphs as they approached a city. In the 1240s, when many Maghribi communities repeatedly switched their allegiance between the Almohads and their Marinid challengers, eminent jurists played an important role in interceding with rulers on behalf of communities that had changed their loyalties.

When the Almohad caliph al-Sa'id approached Meknes, 'the shaykh and jurist, the pious *khaṭīb* (sermon-giver) Abu 'Ali Mansur b. Harzuz' led the men, women and children of Meknes who 'raised copies of the Qur'an and Qur'an boards over their heads' as they begged al-Sa'id for pardon, which he duly granted.[74] When a delegation of 'jurists and shaykhs led by the pious shaykh 'Abd Allah b. Musa al-Fishtali' came out of Fes, however, they did not receive such a warm reception. Al-Sa'id refused to enter the city and when he left some weeks later, he is reported to have said, 'If God returns me to this village [Fes] with its iniquitous inhabitants, I shall kill their prophet,' meaning the jurist 'Abd Allah al-Fishtali. This was reported to al-Fishtali who said, 'He will not return,' a prophecy that became a malediction when al-Sa'id

[74] *al-Dhakhira al-Saniyya*, p. 71.

died in an ambush soon afterwards.[75] Whether the outcome was positive or not, all these incidents show the importance of jurists as representatives of urban communities.

Another important component of the urban notability was the representatives of the residential urban quarters of which each town and city was composed, often called 'shaykhs', a polysemous term utilised for urban leaders as well as tribal chiefs, and also for spiritual figures by the thirteenth century, making it difficult to know exactly what references to shaykhs signify in different contexts. When the term is qualified as *shaykh al-balad* or *shaykh al-madīna*, however, we can be more certain that the term has an administrative rather than a religious meaning. Urban shaykhs represented their quarters and, although our sources do not tell us what the criteria for being accepted as *shaykh al-balad* may have been, wealth and status derived from ancestry, scholarship or trade are likely to have played their part, alongside military credentials in some cases. To use Ceuta as an example again, it is clear that in Almoravid times, the captains of the vital Ceutan fleet were as important personages in the running of the city as the council (*shūrā*) of Maliki jurists headed by Qadi 'Iyad and the heads of each urban quarter. Collectively, the shaykhs provided continuity because even when a town was officially under the rule of a governor, that person was often a stranger to the city who only held his post for a limited time and was therefore dependent on local advisers.

Many other townsmen were involved in local government, even if they were not members of large important urban families such as the Banu Hamdin or Banu Rushd. Lower-level magistrates, deputy judges, market inspectors all came from within *fuqahā'* ranks. There were also large numbers of middle-ranking scribes and officials who worked for governors and financial administrators in all the major cities of the Berber empires and enjoyed a certain social status while not being notables. Master craftsmen formed another influential social group from which men of experience, knowledge and probity could be called to monitor the affairs of their fellow craftsmen on behalf of the market inspector (*muḥtasib*), whose activities will be described more fully in the next chapter.

The majority of urbanites were ordinary craftsmen and tradesmen whose range of professions will be explored in Chapter 5. They resided in the quarters or neighbourhoods of each town with their families in communities defined by occupation and religion as well as lineage or origin. Although there were no ghettos as such during this era, it was quite common for people to cluster near their relatives or co-religionists, creating concentrations of

[75] *al-Dhakhira al-Saniyya*, p. 71.

Muslims, Jews and Christians in different parts of a town. The quotidian social life of Muslim townsfolk revolved around the home and quarter, where one could find local amenities such as a communal oven, a neighbourhood mosque, small stalls and shops, and a public bath. In an age when the existence of God was taken for granted by the vast majority, the neighbourhood mosque played an important role as a daily meeting place for the men of an urban quarter and it was often the site of the local primary school (*kuttāb*), although Ibn 'Abdun frowned on this practice due to the tendency for children's clothes and shoes to be grubby and and so soil the mosque.[76] Churches and synagogues played a similar role in areas of dense Christian and Jewish settlement.

Although the inhabitants of a quarter were not necessarily all related, they did tend to know each other and view askance the penetration of strangers beyond the main thoroughfares of the city. They would also lock the gates of their quarter at night and sometimes young men would form a militia, or, from a less sympathetic perspective, a gang, able to defend their neighbourhood. These groups, which were very prominent in some eastern Islamic cities where they overlapped with the *futuwwa* or chivalric orders, are less evident in Maghribi and Andalusi sources. Ibn 'Abdun mentions young people carrying arms as one of many problems of public order, but does not explain whether they constituted organised groups.[77] In order to control the movement of strangers within these close-knit communities, travellers were required to stay overnight in inns or hostelries called *funduq*s rather than being allowed to roam through the city. These *funduq*s accommodated merchants and provided space for their pack animals and merchandise and thus played an important role in economic life, but they also had the important social function of protecting and monitoring strangers who were considered potentially disruptive of local society.[78] The other public spaces that could provide accommodation for those passing through were the mosques. Al-Baydhaq's biography of Ibn Tumart repeatedly alludes to his use of mosques for the lodging of his small group of disciples on his long journey back from Ifriqiya to Marrakesh, including the Rayhana Mosque in Bijaya, and several mosques in Fes: the Masjid Ibn al-Ghannam, Masjid Ibn al-Maljum and Masjid Taryana, the last of which had a room in its tower where Ibn Tumart slept and held classes.[79]

[76] Ibn 'Abdun, *Séville Musulmane*, p. 53.

[77] Ibid., p. 120.

[78] Olivia Constable gives a full history of *funduq*s and their Antique antecedents in *Housing the Stranger in the Mediterranean World.*

[79] al-Baydhaq, *Akhbar*, pp. 36, 51.

Beyond the quarters stood the main thoroughfares leading to the central, public parts of town, the great mosque, the market zone and industrial areas. In many ways, the great mosque functioned like the Roman forum since its courtyard (*ṣaḥn*) was often the largest open area inside the city walls apart from the parade grounds or plazas (*sharīʿa, raḥba, sāḥa*) outside royal or gubernatorial residences. It was also the place where the majority of the adult male population was expected to gather on a weekly basis for the Friday prayer not only to pray, but also to renew political allegiances and social bonds. Outside the times of prayer, religious scholars gathered to teach in the great mosque precincts and the judge gave his rulings in the shade of its arcades. The main markets were often close by and some vendors set up stalls in the mosque courtyard to serve those going to and fro, while on Fridays it was often the case that the congregation gathered for prayer spilled out into the market streets adjacent to the great mosque, creating a fluid boundary between sacred and profane space.

Although women could be found in the mosques and market areas, they were primarily public spaces for male sociability. In contrast, the cemetery or cemeteries built outside the city walls provided a space where women and children could socialise, enjoy the fresh air and picnic during visits to offer prayers at the graves of dead family members. This was very important for many women as it was one of the few 'respectable' reasons for leaving the home along with trips to the baths. However, the gathering of women in cemeteries was one of the many sources of concern for the perpetually disapproving Ibn ʿAbdun, who lamented that vendors often set up their stalls in the cemeteries to admire unveiled women praying at gravesides and young men loitered there during festivals to ogle the (female) visitors.[80]

Certain groups were excluded from respectable society due to their poverty or pursuit of professions considered morally dubious by the majority of the population. Indigents, prostitutes and petty criminals all fell into this category, along with wandering storytellers, magicians and tricksters who plied their trade in the markets and during festivals when people were out and about. The treatise of the Sevillan Ibn ʿAbdun gives some hints and insights about life at this level of society too. Despite the above-attested use of mosques to house travellers in the Maghrib, he states that no one should be allowed to sleep in the mosques of Seville at night, implying that they were a common refuge for beggars who had nowhere else to go, as well as for travellers.[81]

80 Ibn ʿAbdun, *Séville Musulmane*, p. 59.
81 Ibid., p. 49.

He also comments on professions that should be prohibited due to their connections to the criminal underworld, giving some delightful glimpses of street scams around 1100. Apparently, itinerant perfumers were a suspicious lot who enveloped passers-by with incense or fragrance from censers to allow the pick-pockets collaborating with them to strike while their victim was distracted by the perfumer's clouds of fragrance. Interestingly enough, prostitution was not prohibited but regulated because it was a source of tax revenue, and Ibn 'Abdun restricts his comments to stating that prostitutes should not tout their wares on the street by standing with their heads uncovered outside the brothel and, conversely, that 'respectable' women should not dress in such a way that they might be mistaken for prostitutes to avoid confusion between the two and the scandal of men propositioning 'decent' women.[82]

The close proximity of people in towns could, of course, lead to outbreaks of disease, and urban populations were regularly ravaged by epidemic diseases of various kinds including plague, cholera and typhoid. Ibn Sahib al-Salat mentions an epidemic that ravaged the Maghrib, arriving in Marrakesh in May 1176, where 100–190 or more people a day died making it impossible for those left to convey them to the great mosque for funerary prayers. The caliph therefore permitted the recitation of prayers in any mosque to ease the problem. The epidemic persisted for a year during which both rich and poor fell victim to it, including the caliph Abu Ya'qub Yusuf and his powerful brother, Abu Hafs 'Umar, who both recovered. At the epidemic's peak, as many as thirty palace servants and slaves died each day, leaving it virtually deserted.[83] Many other Almohad *sayyid*s and shaykhs across the Maghrib and Ifriqiya died, suggesting that the epidemic must have had a devastating effect on the urban population as a whole. In the mid-1180s, Bijaya faced a similar sweeping epidemic whose effects were compounded by the Banu Ghaniya insurrection and famine.

Many other anecdotal examples of the ravages of epidemic disease can be adduced, but without hard statistics it is impossible to assess the level of mortality or the long-term social and economic impact of disease upon urban populations. An Almohad innovation in the western Maghrib to alleviate the sufferings of the urban sick, including the mentally afflicted and lepers, was the hospital in Marrakesh founded by Ya'qub al-Mansur that al-Marrakushi describes as unparalleled in the world, a statement that perhaps reflects the barely submerged competition between Ya'qub al-Mansur and the Ayyubid sultan, Salah al-Din, who founded an equally splendid hospital in Cairo. Al-Marrakushi says:

[82] Ibn 'Abdun, *Séville Musulmane*, p. 113.

[83] Ibn 'Idhari, *al-Bayan*, vol. 4, pp. 209–10.

> [Ya'qub al-Mansur] allocated 30 *dīnār*s per day for food and expenses, not including remedies and he appointed a pharmacist to make potions, creams, and powders. Patients were given night clothes for winter and summer. Poor patients were given money when they left and were admitted to the hospital as equals to the rich. After the Friday prayer [Ya'qub al-Mansur] visited the hospital and spoke to the patients.[84]

In addition to epidemics, urban populations also experienced chronic diseases such as leprosy. Although it has been argued that Muslims had a less emotive response to leprosy than medieval Christians, many were, nonetheless, fearful of contagion and saw leprosy as divine retribution for 'crimes' against the community such as hoarding grain. When the disease had progressed to a certain point, lepers were segregated but charity towards them was encouraged.[85] In the Maghrib and al-Andalus, this often took the form of endowed institutions supported by one or more benefactors, or even entire suburbs, located outside city walls to separate the lepers from the rest of the population but still provide for them. One such leper colony resided outside Bab Khukha in Fes until a flood forced the removal of their dwellings to a new site outside Bab al-Shari'a. When the new location met with vociferous public complaints because it resulted in the lepers using the river water before the inhabitants of the city, leading to fears of contagion via the 'dirty' water, the settlement was moved again.[86]

For the majority of other illnesses and afflictions that people suffered, they resorted to a selection of herbal remedies bought in the market place. However, as in most medieval societies, healing was not considered purely medical but also a spiritual or religious matter, and when disease or injury struck many sought healing through items associated with religious figures which were believed to possess a beneficent power, popularly called *baraka*. We have already mentioned the talismanic papers given by Ibn Tumart to people as gifts and one use of sacred writing was to dissolve it in water which a sick person would then drink. Even more explicit is a reference in Ibn 'Idhari's *al-Bayan* to people travelling to two pilgrim centres (*rābiṭa*) that had been set up near the cave at Igiliz in the Sus where Ibn Tumart was recognised as the *mahdī* in order 'to collect the earth from them seeking *baraka* and give it to the sick'.[87] Meanwhile, the women of Fes sought to ease their labour pains through the *baraka* of local scholars.

84 al-Marrakushi, *Mu'jib*, pp. 364–5.
85 Dols, 'The leper', pp. 897–900.
86 Ferhat, 'Marinid Fez', p. 252.
87 Ibn 'Idhari, *al-Bayan*, vol. 4, p. 221.

Al-Jazna'i writes that the Fasi jurist 'Abd Allah al-Quda'i (d. 1218), who served as Almohad *khaṭīb* of Fes for a time, was known for sending the boys from his Qur'an school to women in labour to ease their pains.[88] The editor of the text explains that when a woman was undergoing a difficult labour it was customary for the jurists teaching in Qur'an schools to send their pupils to parade through the streets holding a cloak by its edges shouting for God to relieve her pains. Shopkeepers and passers by would throw figs, dates, coins and eggs in the cloak. The pupils would visit the tombs of the most venerated mystics in the city and submerge the cloak in their fountains. They would continue until one or more of the eggs broke, believing that the breaking egg(s) indicated that the woman had given birth or her pain had ceased. Then the pupils returned to the Qur'an school and gave the jurist the money and food, a practice that endured into the twentieth century.[89] In a similar fashion, the biography of the founder of the Marinid dynasty, 'Abd al-Haqq b. Mahyu al-Marini (d. 1217), whose descendants wished to stress his saintly credentials, includes references to the use of caps and trousers that he had worn to ease women's labour pains.[90]

The Lives of Women

Such references to women and childbirth bring us to the subject of female experiences from the eleventh to thirteenth centuries. Both al-Andalus and the Maghrib are areas where women have been seen as enjoying higher status than in other parts of the Islamic world, albeit for quite different reasons. In the case of al-Andalus, the implicit assumption that Andalusi Muslims were 'European' and therefore more liberal than their 'Oriental' counterparts contributes to the belief that women had a higher status there than further east.[91] In the Maghrib, the status of women is seen as being higher due to Berber tribal norms that supposedly accorded women more freedom than in Islamic societies elsewhere. In fact, both these positions are hard to prove and one can find similar patterns in the Islamic east, where Seljuk Turkish women were renowned for their assertiveness, or indeed in early Islamic Arabia. The fact that the sources that we have were often written by men for men and that the sparse information we have about women relates primarily to those from the elite means that many aspects of female life remain frustratingly shadowy and broad conclusions are often based on very slim evidence. Nonetheless, legal opinions and manuals, folklore and passing references give us some glimpses

[88] al-Jazna'i, *Zahrat al-As*, p. 59.
[89] Ibid., p. 59, n. 124.
[90] *al-Dhakhira al-Saniyya*, p. 30.
[91] See Mourtada-Sabbah and Gully, 'On the political role of women in al-Andalus'.

into the lives of women during this period, as the above description of popular remedies for easing labour pains shows.

The dominant social conceptualisation of gender understood women primarily in terms of their relationships with male blood relatives, or the patrilineal family, most importantly their fathers, sons and brothers, and their husbands, who took over the legal paternal responsibility of guardianship through marriage. Since the most important social unit was the family rather than the individual, marriages were viewed as an important way of making alliances and consolidating relationships between families, and the majority were not love matches but legal contracts agreed between a man and the male guardian (*wakīl*) of the woman, her father, or if he were deceased, a brother or uncle. Of course, mothers played a role in the selection of husbands for their daughters and interactions between the women of two families provided the backdrop to many marriages, but the ultimate decision rested with a woman's guardian unless she was a widow of independent means, in which case she might have more agency. In the absence of monasticism, Muslim women who were single did not have the option of entering a convent, although a handful of women adopted a celibate, mystical path as Sufism became more widespread.

Most marriages were between individuals of the same faith as the Shari'a prohibits the marriage of Muslim women with non-Muslim men and, although Muslim men are permitted to marry Christian or Jewish women, such marriages were infrequent due to the concern of all parties about breaching the faith boundary.[92] Although considered highly socially desirable, the nature of Islamic marriage differed from its Christian equivalent. Polygamy and concubinage were both permitted by Islamic law and were widespread in the medieval Islamic world, so a wife often did not have the same degree of access to her husband as in monogamous societies such as Christian Iberia where the conjugal pair was relatively more important than the kin group as a whole. The difference should not be pushed too far, however, given the fact that wealthy Christian men might well also have mistresses or concubines (*amigas*)[93] and that across Muslim society as a whole monogamy was common since the seclusion of free women within the home and the expense of maintaining multiple wives and concubines was not economically viable for many families.

Although some women dominated their husbands or secured their affection for long periods due to their personal qualities, male-initiated divorce

[92] Safran, *Defining Boundaries in al-Andalus*, pp. 128–9.
[93] Barton, *Conquerors, Brides and Concubines*, pp. 123–7.

(*ṭalāq*) was a relatively easy process making a wife's legal position precarious and dependent upon the social and political importance of her male blood relatives. This meant that wives in tribal society and among the elite often had higher status vis-à-vis their husbands than their 'middle-class' urban counterparts due to the fact that marriage entailed the joining of two armed lineages and 'insults' to wives could easily escalate into armed conflict. Conversely, the breakdown in relations between lineages might well be signalled by such an 'affront'. When relations between Ibn Mardanish and his father-in-law, Ibn Hamushk, soured in 1169, Ibn Mardanish's repudiation of Ibn Hamushk's daughter played its part in the drama, as we have seen.[94]

In the upper echelons of society, concubinage was common and, in contrast to wives, concubines were generally non-Muslims from sub-Saharan Africa or the Christian areas of the Iberian peninsula, due to the prohibition on the enslavement of Muslims. Many were captives from raids and battles in the marches between Muslim and Christian territory given to members of the military elite as booty or sold in Muslim slave markets, a fate that also befell Muslim girls captured by Christians in their raids south. For both sides, the capture of women and their sexual exploitation was a statement of power, while the loss of women to the religious 'other' was a matter of deep shame.[95] Many such women converted to the faith of their master, adding to the gravity of the loss. For the women themselves, their position within a household, whether Muslim converts or not, depended totally on their ability to attract and charm their master and produce children. A girl who failed to do either was likely to spend her life as a domestic servant or be sold on.

Once a concubine gave birth to a son her legal status improved considerably as she became an *umm walad* (mother of a son) who was legally entitled to be kept within the household and manumitted, either at the death of her master or before. In contrast to the situation in Christian lands where illegitimacy carried a significant social stigma, Islamic law did not distinguish between the children of free women and concubines as long as they were recognised by their father, and such children had an equal claim on their father's inheritance. In fact, Islamic rulers often exhibited a preference for having children with concubines to avoid the social and political entanglements that could come from marriage and to keep the dynastic lineage separate from, and therefore above, other lineages in society. Concubines could, therefore, become extremely powerful and involved in court politics to promote the interests of their sons as heirs and rulers. One example of a powerful

[94] See p. 95, above

[95] See Barton, *Conquerors, Brides and Concubines*, pp. 39–42, 108–9 ff.

concubine was Qamar, the mother of Sir, one of 'Ali b. Yusuf's sons and his heir until his premature death, who strongly forwarded her son's interests and then tried unsuccessfully to block the appointment of Tashfin b. 'Ali as heir.

The Almoravid era is especially interesting in terms of the position of women due to the relatively high status and freedom accorded to Saharan Sanhaja women and the way in which this shaped the character of the ruling elite. Among the Sanhaja of the Sahara, divorce was common and does not seem to have had any stigma attached to it. When Ibn Yasin arrived among the desert tribes, he is said to have married as many beautiful women as he could and then divorced them, a pattern of behaviour that would have been intolerable if it tarnished the reputation of all the women involved.[96] Women played important, if informal, roles as advisers to male relatives, and the pattern of inheritance among the Sanhaja was often matrilineal rather than patrilineal.

Sanhaja Matrilineal Succession

A man might bequeath his estate to his sister's son since women did change sexual partners and this kind of matrilineal inheritance kept property within a blood line in a way that father to son inheritance might not: while one could not prove paternity in the eleventh-century Sahara, maternity was always obvious. We saw this pattern in evidence in Yahya b. 'Umar's assumption of the chieftaincy of the Lamtuna and Guddala via his mother, Safiyya, who was probably the sister of the deceased chief, Yahya b. Ibrahim.

The Zirid rulers of Ta'ifa Granada were also of Sanhaja ancestry, albeit from the central Maghrib rather than the Sahara, and the memoirs of 'Abd Allah b. Buluggin, the last Zirid ruler, provide insight into the importance of women among his Talkata Sanhaja kinsmen in the decades before the Almoravid arrival in al-Andalus. He repeatedly mentions the influence of the women in his grandfather Badis's household and describes his aunt, Umm al-'Uluww, as having virtually proposed her own marriage to her paternal cousin, Maksan, and then leading the wives of the Talkata amirs in a campaign against Maksan when he rejected the match at the instigation of one of his father's women.[97] On other occasions too, Sanhaja women appear as powerful influences upon their husbands and male kin. 'Abd Allah

[96] See Chapter 6, below, for the possible religious significance of Ibn Yasin's multiple marriages.
[97] Tibi, *The Tibyan*, p. 86.

himself was extremely deferential to his mother and when summoned to meet Yusuf b. Tashfin and hand Granada over to him, he left the city with her to avoid their being separated in case of his arrest by the Almoravids.[98]

The prominent social status of elite women grew further under the Almoravids and is dramatically confirmed by the fact that, unlike in most other Islamic societies where men were known as the son of their father, Ibn Muhammad, for example, several Sanhaja amirs were identified by their mother's name, for example, Muhammad b. 'A'isha, Sir b. Fatima, Yahya b. al-Sahrawiyya, and Muhammad and Yahya b. Ghaniya. Although this might seem a natural way to distinguish between the progeny of different mothers in polygynous societies, most Islamic dynasties practised polygamy and concubinage but they considered it an insult to refer to a prince as the son of his mother rather than his father, and, in other circumstances, a mother or female ancestor was named only if she was significantly more important than the father.[99] Only the Almoravids regularly identified elite men by reference to their mothers in a non-derogatory way. This practice was, however, limited to free-born mothers considered part of the Almoravid elite whose male relatives provided their children with a prestigious circle of maternal kin and it did not apply to slave mothers.

Given the unusual degree of official recognition and importance within Sanhaja genealogies granted to free-born Saharan women by identifying men by their mothers, it is not surprising that one of the criticisms against the Almoravids was precisely that they violated gender norms and accorded women far too much of a public role. We have seen this negative view in the disparaging Almohad references to Almoravid use of the *lithām* and Ibn Tumart's mocking description of 'Ali b. Yusuf and his entourage as men dressed like women, and it is developed by the early thirteenth-century Almohad historian al-Marrakushi, who commented that powerful women fatally compromised political stability during 'Ali b. Yusuf's reign.

> Women took charge of matters and public affairs were entrusted to them and every important Lamtuna or Masufa woman acted as the protector of rebels, evildoers, bandits, and tavern and brothel keepers.[100]

Sometimes the high status of elite women in Almoravid times is presented more positively as in the stories about Zaynab al-Nafzawiyya, mentioned in

[98] Tibi, *The Tibyan*, p. 156.

[99] A good example of this is the Andalusi historian Ibn al-Qutiyya, the 'Son of the Gothic Woman', whose illustrious female ancestor was Sara, daughter of the Visigothic king Witiza, who married into the Arab aristocracy after the conquest.

[100] al-Marrakushi, *Mu'jib*, p. 260.

Chapter 2. While Zaynab was not herself of Sanhaja origin, she was treated according to Sanhaja norms. Abu Bakr married her without concern about her previous marriage to the ruler of Aghmat, after he was killed in action against the Almoravids,[101] and after he divorced her, probably at her own request, Yusuf b. Tashfin married her with a similar lack of concern for her previous marriage to his cousin. Later writers such as Ibn ʿIdhari highlight Zaynab's role as Yusuf's chief adviser and suggest that she was, in fact, politically indispensable. Although Zaynab bore Yusuf b. Tashfin at least two sons, al-Muʿizz Bi'llah and al-Fadl, it is her political rather than her maternal role that the sources emphasise.

The public visibility of Saharan Sanhaja women and their training in 'male' pursuits is confirmed by other anecdotes. The first, recounted by Ibn Khaldun, describes Ibn Tumart physically attacking the sister of the amir ʿAli b. Yusuf for riding through the streets of Marrakesh unveiled.[102] The second is al-Baydhaq's assertion that the citadel of Marrakesh was defended from the Almohad onslaught by an Almoravid woman, Fannu bint ʿUmar, who fought to the death 'in the guise of a man' rather than surrender.[103] Sanhaja women also participated in cultural life. Hawwa' bint Tashfin, Yusuf b. Tashfin's niece, is described as a renowned poetess and literary figure who held salons in Seville where her husband, Sir b. Abi Bakr, was the governor,[104] a cultural role more commonly played by elite Muslim women than that of a warrior. Nonetheless, it adds to the impression that women within the Sanhaja aristocracy could exert considerable power and clearly had a voice in policy, state affairs and culture.

The role of elite women in the Almohad era is much more difficult to ascertain, although there are hints that in pre-Almohad times matrilinearity had its role to play in the Masmuda environment.[105]Al-Baydhaq's biography of Ibn Tumart makes incidental references to the activities of women, but their primary status was as child-bearers and any direct political influence they may have wielded has been elided from the historical record. One of the only women associated with the Almohad movement itself was Zaynab, the sister of Ibn Tumart, who seems to have been a member of his inner circle and a trusted adviser. No mention is made of Ibn Tumart himself marrying,

[101] See above, p. 33, n. 30.

[102] Ibn Khaldun, *Kitab al-ʿIbar*, vol. 8, p. 468; Ibn Khaldun, *Histoire des Berbères*, vol. 2, p. 167.

[103] al-Baydhaq, *Akhbar*, p. 117.

[104] Hawwa''s father, Tashfin, was the younger half-brother and cousin of Yusuf b. Tashfin whose mother had first married Tashfin then, on his death, married his brother ʿAli. Ibn ʿIdhari, *al-Bayan*, vol. 4, p. 49.

[105] Ghouirgate, *L'Ordre almohade*, p. 217.

possessing concubines or fathering children, a posture reminiscent of that of celibate mystics. His successor ʿAbd al-Muʾmin used marriage judiciously to form alliances with important allies and his wives included Masmuda women, a Sanhaja bride called Hasha, and the unnamed daughter of the lord of Melilla, Maksan b. al-Muʿizz, but none of his wives emerge from the extant texts as significant political players. Nonetheless, the accession of Abu Yaʿqub Yusuf supported by his full brother, Abu Hafs ʿUmar, when ʿAbd al-Muʾmin died may have been facilitated by the fact that their mother Zaynab was a Masmuda tribeswoman from Tinmall.[106]

Taking al-Baydhaq as our starting point, the most forceful women during the rise of the Almohad empire continue to be Almoravid women such as Tamakunt bint Yintan, who was captured by the Almohads and demanded that ʿAbd al-Muʾmin release her and her fellow female Sanhaja war captives on the grounds that her father, Yintan, had interceded with ʿAli b. Yusuf on behalf of Ibn Tumart in Marrakesh.[107] ʿAbd al-Muʾmin acceded to her request and an exchange of women took place. Another rare example of a woman mentioned in the chronicles in any capacity other than motherhood is Zaynab, sister of Yahya b. al-Sahrawiyya, granddaughter of Yusuf b. Tashfin and the wife of ʿAbd al-Muʾmin's chief secretary, Ahmad b. ʿAtiyya, whose story was recounted above. According to al-Marrakushi's report, Zaynab conveyed the message from her husband Ibn ʿAtiyya to her brother, the ex-Almoravid prince Yahya, warning him that ʿAbd al-Muʾmin intended to punish him for the unguarded comments he had made. Zaynab's small role in the fall from grace of both her brother and her husband, and their subsequent deaths, as recounted by al-Marrakushi, confirmed the Almohad stereotype of the parlous effect of women meddling in politics.

The lives of wealthy women from the urban notability were less charged with excitement than that of princesses. One Almohad era source that sheds a glimmer of light on the way in which wealthy urban women and concubines lived is a tale of courtly love called *Hadith Bayad wa-Riyad*, the story of Riyad, a beautiful slave girl, and Bayad, a young merchant from Damascus, set in an unnamed Andalusi town.[108] Riyad's mistress was the rich daughter of the *ḥājib*, the ruler's chief adviser, who spent her days with an entourage of female musicians and poets to entertain her in her home, which had a luxurious and verdant walled garden. One day the group were in the garden and the slave girl Riyad decided to climb a tree to have a look at the riverside promenade beyond the house walls. There she spied a handsome young man

106 See p. 93, above.
107 al-Baydhaq, *Akhbar*, pp. 90–1.
108 See Robinson, *Medieval Andalusian Courtly Culture in the Mediterranean.*

whom the women daringly invited in to entertain them. Courtly poetic recitations followed and Riyad and Bayad fell in love. This chaste but passionate relationship was tolerated by Riyad's mistress until she gave full vent to her feelings in a stormy poem, after which Bayad was banned from the garden and had to resort to sending messages to Riyad via an elderly woman, a Muslim version of the nurse in 'Romeo and Juliet'.

The manuscript of this tale is sadly incomplete so we cannot know of the denouement of the story of the two pining lovers, which, as it stands, is a timeless tale of social conventions barring the course of true love. In twelfth-century al-Andalus, those conventions included the sexual rights of masters over slaves and fathers over daughters, which both Riyad and her mistress challenged by allowing Bayad access to the garden. It is impossible to say whether the mistress of the house allowed Bayad to entertain them as a small gesture of rebellion or whether she simply wished to alleviate her boredom, or to pander to Riyad's desire when she, as a free-born woman, could do no such thing. However, Riyad was apparently popular with the master of the house as well as his daughter and when the strength of her feelings for Bayad threatened to disrupt the delicate equilibrium of the household, her mistress intervened on the side of convention rather than allowing the consummation of Riyad's desire.

The story also reveals the very separate lives rich men and women lived, socialising in parallel rather than together. The place of homosexuality in such homosocial environments is an area of debate. Although homosexuality is denounced in the Qur'an and the Shari'a, it is evident from a range of sources that it was practised with varying degrees of toleration. Arabic poetry is full of homoerotic tropes, particularly male desire for beautiful youths, the market inspector Ibn 'Abdun fulminated against male prostitutes, and several rulers of al-Andalus were widely reported to have been homosexual. The appeal of the concubine Subh to al-Hakam II was supposedly her boyishness and short haircut, which enabled him to surmount his lack of interest in women to conceive an heir. Female homosexuality is even less well-documented, but undoubtedly occurred too in the cloistered world of elite women.

For ordinary women life was different to that enjoyed – or endured – by princesses, rich urban women and slave girls in the palaces and great houses of Marrakesh, Seville and other cities. The public appearances of Sanhaja women aside, female seclusion was only a feature among the wealthier sectors of society. Although middle-ranking urban men probably aspired to seclude their women as much as possible to indicate their wealth and respectability, in the majority of less affluent urban families and in rural environments women often had to work and had greater access to public space and regular dealings with male counterparts, as did servants and slaves. The strictures of the *muḥtasib* Ibn 'Abdun provide a window onto the daily life of ordinary women in Seville who could be found selling their embroidery in the market, washing linen in the river or in irrigated gardens, attending public festivals, going to the judge with legal problems, and paying their respects at the tombs of their dead relatives.[109] Similarly, Ibn Tumart's biography frequently mentions with disapproval mixed crowds of men and women enjoying themselves together in public spaces, women drawing water 'alongside men performing their ablutions' or milking their animals 'adorned and beautified as if they are on their way to their bridegrooms'.[110]

An anecdote about the sagacity of the Banu Hammad prince, Hammad b. Manad, recounted by al-Bakri and reprised in the *Kitab al-Istibsar*, sheds a rueful light on gender and family relations in the eleventh-century central Maghrib (modern Algeria). An elderly man set out with his wife from his hometown to Qal'at Bani Hammad, the seat of the prince. They were accompanied on the trip by a handsome young man and, predictably, the young man and the wife fell in love. They therefore decided to pretend that they were married and abandon the old man when they reached Qal'at Bani Hammad. The jilted husband went to Hammad to complain and he summoned the two young people who insisted that they were married. The prince then asked the old man if anyone else had been with them on the journey and he replied, 'No, only my dog!' In response, the prince requested that each person in turn tie up and untie the dog. While the dog allowed the old man and the woman to do this, he did not let the young man near him so the prince ordered the execution of the latter and left the old man to deal with his errant wife.[111]

Whether this ever happened or not does not really matter, it still sheds light on social mores. First, it highlights the problems caused by older, wealthier men securing partners at the expense of younger men and, secondly, the fact that men and women could mix quite freely and get to know each other well enough to risk everything in certain contexts, travel in this case. However, freedom had its limits and the tale also demonstrates the popular view that women were possessions: when the young pair's deception was revealed, the young man was executed in effect for stealing another man's property, while the woman was 'returned' to her husband and master for chastisement, making her situation little different to that of Riyad, the Andalusi slave girl, despite her legally free status.

[109] Ibn 'Abdun, *Séville Musulmane*, pp. 25, 59, 70–1, 101, 105.

[110] al-Baydhaq, *Akhbar*, pp. 36, 47, 48.

[111] al-Bakri, *Description de l'Afrique*, Arabic text, p. 184; French text, pp. 343–4; *Kitab al-Istibsar*, pp. 168–9.

The next anecdote in al-Bakri's *Description de l'Afrique* is equally revealing and places stress on the notion that family honour resided in the chastity of its women and that female sexual intercourse outside marriage brought shame on the entire family, which could be erased only by killing the culprit, an attitude often analysed by anthropologists in terms of a Mediterranean honour–shame complex. In this second morality tale, a man married two women but was fondest of the second. His jealous first wife then came to him to say that the woman he loved so much had been unfaithful with a young man in his entourage. The wily husband gave no obvious sign of anger, but instead went out riding and faked a serious fall. He asked to be carried to his second wife's room where he pretended to fall asleep once they were alone. She immediately sneaked out to see her lover whom she reassured for her lateness by telling him that she loved him and that her husband was simply the father of her children. The husband crept after her and listened to their conversation through the door but then continued to feign sleep rather than reacting.

However, the next day he used the opportunity of a raid by an enemy tribe to send the young man into the fray of battle where he was killed. He returned to his home and his wife expressed her joy and relief that he was safe, but he replied that only the father of the children was safe and sound not the beloved. She realised that he had overheard her conversation and asked to visit her family. When she prolonged her absence, her husband went to her family to ask why she had not returned and they said that she refused to. The terms for a divorce were discussed and the husband insisted that he receive back the bride price he had paid and be released of all marital obligations. Once all was settled, he told the woman's family about her affair and they killed her for dishonouring them. al-Bakri admiringly adds that in this way the husband was avenged on both his wife and her lover without raising a finger himself or losing any money.[112]

Such stories show the extent to which women's lives were regulated by their male relatives as well as the lengths to which they might go to circumvent these narrow parameters. At the elite level, the role of women depended greatly upon customary practice among their kin group. Although Andalusi women are often seen as enjoying higher status than women in other parts of the Islamic world, in this era it is Almoravid Sanhaja women who emerge from the sources as the best placed to exercise soft power in the guise of patrons and political advisers to their husbands and male relatives. In the subsequent Almohad era, however, the extant sources suggest a retrenchment

112 al-Bakri, *Description de l'Afrique*, Arabic text, pp. 184–5; French text, pp. 344–6.

of such power and a reassertion of the domestic and child-bearing roles of women, perceived as normative by Ibn Tumart's circle. Nonetheless, maternal links continued to have some degree of influence on politics.

The dramatic political changes that took place at the top of society, however, probably had relatively little effect on the daily lives of the majority of women, although the impact of the loss of menfolk in battle or capture by the enemy could have devastating consequences for some women. Despite the religiously inflected efforts of men like Ibn 'Abdun and Ibn Tumart to circumscribe women's public presence, many worked and socialised outside the home. Whether women cherished the freedom and responsibility granted by economic necessity or preferred the more constrained but comfortable life of the wives and concubines of the affluent is impossible to say. Many probably simply saw their situation as part of the normal order of things as defined by family, custom and God's law.

Religious Minorities and their Place in Society

From the perspective of many medieval Muslim historians from Ibn Hayyan to al-Maqqari, the era of the Umayyad caliphate of Córdoba (929–1031) was a cultural high point in Andalusi history with which the Ta'ifa interlude and the era of the Berber empires could not compare. This perspective has been shared by many later western historians in Islamic and Jewish Studies, who connect the cultural flowering of the Umayyad caliphate with harmonious and fruitful social interactions between Muslims, Christians and Jews, a phenomenon known as *convivencia* (living together).[113] This picture has multifaceted appeal as a source of Spanish nationalist pride for those wishing to integrate the Muslim era into the national historical narrative, and as a counterpoint to the poor treatment of Jews in Latin Christendom and the Europe of nation-states that emerged in the nineteenth century. It can also provide a model for those wishing to juxtapose a 'moderate' European version of Islam against more 'extreme' African and Middle Eastern forms of the faith.

From these vantage points, the subsequent era of the Berber empires is viewed as a time of conflict, social dislocation and intolerance towards religious minorities, which began with the massacre of Jews in Zirid Granada in 1066. The situation of the religious minorities in Almoravid and Almohad al-Andalus, however, reflected the new geopolitics of the mid-eleventh to the mid-thirteenth centuries, which differed greatly from the situation pertaining in tenth-century Umayyad Córdoba, mentioned in the introductory background, or indeed ninth-century Baghdad, which is also regarded as a high

[113] See, for instance, Menocal, *Ornament of the World.*

point for inter-communal relations, while in Ifriqiya the faltering of the Zirid governorate and Arab tribal migrations from Egypt in the eleventh century also mark the period as one of change for minorities.

The *Dhimma*

The basic Muslim principle for the treatment of fellow Abrahamic monotheists, the peoples of the book (*ahl al-kitāb*), was that of the covenant (*dhimma*), an unwritten contract that evolved during the early and classical Islamic eras from previous Byzantine and Sasanian regulations. The basic specifications of this agreement were that non-Muslim monotheists were entitled to practice their religion discreetly and enjoy protection of life and property in return for obedience to Muslim political authority and payment of the *jizya* (poll tax). Additional specifications could include prohibitions on the building of churches and synagogues, the carrying of weapons or employment that gave them power over Muslims, and requirements for different faith groups to wear certain types of clothing or identifying marks. Many of these strictures were, however, more honoured in the breach than the application, and it is clear from archaeological and textual evidence, for instance, that many churches and monasteries were built in al-Andalus in the Muslim era.

The demographic distribution of minorities across North Africa and al-Andalus was uneven and naturally altered over time in response to many factors, ranging from the financial benefits of conversion to the vitality of local ecclesiastical structures in the case of Christians, a numerically larger group than Jews. By the rise of the Almoravids in the eleventh century, the long-established sedentary Christian population of Ifriqiya, which had produced St Augustine and the Donatist movement, had decreased in number, although there were still Christian communities in many towns, including Carthage, al-Mahdiyya, Gabes and Gafsa, and pockets of indigenous Christians living alongside Ibadi Kharijites in the southern Ifriqiyan mountains and oases.[114] These communities were supported by an attenuated Latin Christian episcopal structure, which was, however, in steep decline by the eleventh century. In 1053, Pope Leon IX lamented that there were only five bishops left in Ifriqiya, including the bishops of Carthage and al-Mahdiyya who were further undermining their community by arguing over who should be considered archbishop, and by

[114] Prevost, 'Les dernières communautés chrétiennes', p. 464. See also Valérian, 'La permanence du christianisme au Maghreb'.

1076 that number had declined to two, one in Carthage and one in Bijaya.[115] By this era, the Christian communities of Ifriqiya were largely Arabised, but al-Idrisi does mention that the 'Berberised' Christians of the Gafsa region were still speaking a Romance dialect (*al-lisān al-lāṭinī al-Ifrīqī*) in the late twelfth century.[116] On the other hand, what is now Morocco may not have had any indigenous Christian inhabitants at all by the eleventh and twelfth centuries, although northern towns such as Tangier, Ceuta and Tlemcen had harboured small indigenous Christian communities in earlier centuries.[117]

The area with the largest Christian population was al-Andalus where Christians could be found in both urban and rural settings. As mentioned in the Introduction, this group are usually known in secondary literature as Mozarabs, apparently from the Arabic term *mustaʿrab* (Arabised), but, perplexingly, this term is found in later Christian sources but not in contemporary Arabic sources where Christians are described not according to their language, but by their legal or religious status, that is, as *ahl al-dhimma* (people of the covenant), *muʿāhidūn* (contractual partners), *naṣārā* (Nazarenes, Christians).[118] There is, therefore, a growing preference for calling them Andalusi Christians rather than Mozarabs. Although a handful of these Christians in al-Andalus were migrants from the Islamic east or the Christian north, the vast majority were the descendants of the indigenous pre-conquest Christian population.

As in Ifriqiya, one of the challenges for the Christians of al-Andalus was the maintenance of an episcopal infrastructure to baptise infants and minister to the population. There were certainly bishops in several cities during the Umayyad era, but by the eleventh century that number seems to have decreased with clear allusions to bishops only in Málaga,[119] Seville, Medina Sidonia and Niebla,[120] and possibly Lisbon.[121] Similarly, while there were churches and monasteries in and outside Córdoba and dotted through the countryside of the south in the Umayyad era, references to such institutions are much more occasional by the eleventh century, implying that the Christian population had steadily reduced over the centuries to become a numerical as well as a symbolic minority.[122]

115 Prevost, 'Les dernières communautés chrétiennes', p. 472.
116 Ibid., pp. 472–3; al-Idrisi, *Opus Geographicum*, fasc. 1–4, p. 278.
117 Benhima, 'l'Islamisation du Maghrib al-Aqṣā', pp. 319–20.
118 de Epalza, 'Mozarabs', pp. 149–50.
119 Ibid., p. 156.
120 Molénat, 'Sur le rôle des Almohades', p. 396.
121 Ibid., p. 392.
122 See Aillet, 'Islamisation et évolution'.

In comparison with the Christians, the smaller Jewish population was more evenly spread across the entire region from Ifriqiya through the Maghrib and western Sahara to al-Andalus. It was also predominantly urban, with the exception of parts of the western Maghrib where some indigenous Jewish communities, known as Judaeo-Berbers, lived in villages. It is possible that the Barghawata tribes of the Atlantic littoral whom the Almoravids fought after crossing the High Atlas were of Judaeo-Berber background, although references to entire Berber tribes practising Judaism are late and unreliable.[123] The urban Jews of the Islamic west maintained close relations with co-religionists in northern Christian lands and Jewish communities across the Mediterranean and eastern Islamic lands, and their economic, social and cultural life flourished under Islamic rule. In speaking of the Jewish experience in al-Andalus, Scheindlin says:

> No other Jewish community produced as many Jews who achieved positions of status and even power in the non-Jewish world and no other Jewish community produced such an extensive literary culture reflecting the deep impact of an intellectual life shared with non-Jews.[124]

Relations between these minorities and political powers seem to have been mostly harmonious with occasional moments of discrimination, such as an abortive attempt by the Aghlabids in the ninth century to force Christians and Jews in Ifriqiya to wear small linen badges depicting either a pig or a monkey on their clothes.[125] Conversely, the preference many rulers showed for Christian or Jewish advisers, physicians, bodyguards and tax collectors, was often interpreted by Muslims as a breach of the *dhimma* regulation that non-Muslims should not hold positions of power over them and it could trigger popular hostility towards minorities and eruptions of violence. The most striking case of violence directed at minorities occurred in the Ta'ifa kingdom of Granada where Samuel b. Naghrila and his son, Joseph, served in turn as viziers to the Zirid amirs alongside other Jewish and converted Jewish courtiers until palace intrigue led to the assassination of Joseph in 1066, after which the mob 'turned their swords on every Jew in the city and seized vast quantities of their goods and chattels'.[126]

This marked a negative turn in the fortunes of the Jewish inhabitants of al-Andalus, but its roots lay in a struggle between factions composed of Sanhaja amirs, elite slaves – often of Christian origin – and the Jewish vizier

[123] Benhima, 'l'Islamisation du Maghrib al-Aqṣā', pp. 318–19.
[124] Scheindlin, 'The Jews in Muslim Spain', p. 188.
[125] Prevost, 'Les dernières communautés chrétiennes', p. 465, n. 11.
[126] Tibi, *The Tibyan*, p. 75.

for control of the Zirid polity, as well as in popular jealousy and resentment of the powerful economic and social position of the Naghrila family and other Jews in the government of Granada. Ibn Naghrila's religion provided an excuse to denounce him and enabled his opponents to tap into popular Andalusi Muslim prejudice against the Jews of the city which had been exacerbated by their role in imposing and collecting high taxation. It was obviously not, however, an example of 'Berber fanaticism' since it was the Sanhaja Berber Zirids who employed the Naghrilas and other Jewish officials and the incident occurred twenty years before the Almoravids arrived in the peninsula. In the period between 1066 and 1086, Muslim suspicion towards the Jews was compounded by the employment of Arabised Andalusi Jews by Christian kings as bilingual ambassadors. The hostility this aroused could provoke extreme reactions, as we saw in Chapter 2 when al-Mu'tamid of Seville became so incensed by the presumption of Ibn Shalib, Alfonso VI's Andalusi Jewish ambassador, that he had him executed.[127]

The Almoravids probably had minimal contact with religious minorities in their Saharan homeland, but there were Jewish trading communities in Saharan oases and towns and, as the Almoravids added towns such as Sijilmasa, Awdaghust and Aghmat to their domains, they became the rulers of these communities. References to the early response of the Almoravids to religious minorities in the Maghrib are limited to the report that Yusuf b. Tashfin imposed a harsh levy on the sizable mercantile Jewish population of Aghmat around 1071,[128] suggesting his intention to levy the canonical *jizya* and perhaps back-payments of it after a period when it had fallen into abeyance. Al-Idrisi's account of the Jewish presence in Aghmat and Marrakesh in Almoravid times also implies a preference for segregation, but whether that was inspired by the Almoravids' desire to make Marrakesh an aristocratic Sanhaja enclave or to exclude the *ahl al-dhimma* is not clear.

> Aghmat Iylan is a small town at the foot of the afore-mentioned Jabal Daran (High Atlas) to the east of Aghmat Warika, discussed previously. There are six miles between them and in this town live the Jews of the region. It is a pleasant town with plentiful produce and full prosperity. The Jews used not to live in Marrakesh by order of its amir 'Ali b. Yusuf and only entered by day, departing at nightfall . . . for business or work they specialised in.[129]

While Jewish communities constituted the main minority in the Maghrib, once the Almoravids crossed into al-Andalus, they encountered a society in

[127] al-Himyari, *Rawd al-Mi'tar*, p. 84; *al-Hulal al-Mawshiyya*, pp. 41–2. See also p. 42, above.
[128] *al-Hulal al-Mawshiyya*, p. 13.
[129] al-Idrisi, *Opus Geographicum*, fasc. 1–4, p. 235.

which Christians were much more visible and embedded in social, political and economic life. As they became masters of such religious minority populations, the Almoravids adopted an orthodox position towards them conditioned by Malikism in its Qayrawani and Córdoban forms.[130] Their personal reaction is difficult to gauge beyond references to their antipathy to the close relationships between some Christian and Muslim rulers and to leisure pursuits that implied Christian influence such as wine drinking, which actually had long Muslim antecedents but was, nonetheless, shocking to the first generation of Almoravids.

In this they were in harmony with many Andalusi Maliki jurists who were disgruntled with their Ta'ifa rulers and favoured the strict application of *dhimma* rules, which may have been the background to Yusuf b. Tashfin's order that a visually prominent church in Granada be demolished in 1099.[131] One source that indicates rising Andalusi intolerance towards religious minorities in the late eleventh century is the *ḥisba* manual of Ibn 'Abdun, which we have already referred to several times. Ibn 'Abdun reflects the sentiments of a section of the Andalusi *fuqahā'* who favoured strict application of the *dhimma* regulations, but his strictures about Muslim and non-Muslim mixing also reveals the imbrication of Muslims, Christians and Jews in the daily life of Seville.

He insists that Muslims should not serve Christians and Jews as bathhouse staff, latrine cleaners or grooms, and that any Muslim taking such a job should be punished, implying that Muslims were perfectly happy to take service with non-Muslim masters and that some Jews and Christians were prosperous enough to employ them. He places similar strictures on Muslims using Christian doctors.[132] He continues to denounce the sexual misdemeanours of supposedly celibate Christian priests, and to fulminate against Christian use of churches for social events and the entry of Muslim women to churches,[133] presumably to join in with such events, a fact that hints at the existence of extended families containing Muslims and Christians or friendships between women of the two faiths. He also reiterates the standard *dhimma* regulation that Christians and Jews should not be allowed to hold positions of power as tax farmers or policemen, nor dress and behave in the manner of Muslim notables, all of which indicate the varied roles of Christians and Jews in Seville and their integration into wider society.[134]

130 Molénat, 'Sur le rôle des Almohades', p. 391.
131 Aillet, 'Islamisation et évolution', pp. 177–8.
132 Ibn 'Abdun, *Séville Musulmane*, pp. 108, 114.
133 Ibid., pp. 108–9.
134 Ibid., p. 128.

This tendency towards strict boundary maintenance between communities cannot be disentangled from the political uncertainties of the eleventh and twelfth centuries and the dramatic transformation of the small, divided northern Christian principalities into aggressive and expansionist neighbours, which came as a great shock to the Muslims of the rich, sophisticated south and produced a surge in jihad rhetoric, the depiction of northern Christians as the 'enemy of God', and heightened concern about the political loyalties of Andalusi Christians. Such concerns came to a head in 1125–6 when Alfonso I El Batallador of Aragon launched a lengthy campaign through the Muslim south with the ultimate aim of capturing Granada at the instigation of the Christians of the region. The Aragonese king proceeded slowly south towards Valencia, Dénia and Murcia before turning west towards Guadix, then Granada which he besieged. The Andalusi Christians living in these towns welcomed the raiders, but the Aragonese failed to make any lasting gains and eventually returned towards Aragon by way of Seville and Córdoba where some local Christians again offered them support. When it became obvious that Alfonso I and his army were returning to Aragon, many Andalusi Christians migrated north with them rather than risk Almoravid reprisals, but many remained, leaving the Almoravid authorities pondering what to do with their Christian subjects.

From the juridical perspective, the Christians had broken the *dhimma* by collaborating with the Christian enemy, making their lives and property forfeit. From a pragmatic point of view, however, the main concern of the authorities was not to punish but to prevent them offering further support to northern Christian invaders. These two strands came together in Ibn Rushd al-Jadd's legal recommendation that such Christians should be deported to the Maghrib to distance them from the sensitive Andalusi frontier.[135] Christians from Seville were resettled around Meknes and Salé, and those of Granada were transported to Marrakesh, while their churches in al-Andalus were transformed into mosques and the endowments that had supported them were re-dedicated for Muslim use.[136] This series of events marked the start of a steep numerical decline in the number of Christians in al-Andalus, the growth of a Mozarabic Christian minority in the Latin north, and the introduction of a Christian population to parts of the Maghrib south of the old Roman *limes* where it had never existed before.

The sense of polarisation between Muslims and Christians in Almoravid times created by events in al-Andalus should not be pushed too far, however.

[135] Ibn 'Idhari, *Bayan*, vol. 4, p. 63; *al-Hulal al-Mawshiyya*, p. 97.

[136] Lagardère, *Le djihâd andalou*, pp. 98–114.

Once Christians were resettled in the Maghrib, they resumed their peacetime status as *dhimmis* with rights as well as duties. They were probably still administered by their priests from al-Andalus and practised their faith either in private homes or churches such as Santa Eulalia which they were allowed to build in Marrakesh. Many found gainful employment on Almoravid irrigation and building projects, and it is likely that ʿAli b. Yusuf's chief hydraulic engineer, ʿUbayd Allah b. Yunus, was an Andalusi Christian.[137] The Almoravids also recruited many Christians, captives and mercenaries from the north and Andalusis, into their army, a development that provided Ibn Khaldun with one of the permutations of his theme that recruiting slave troops extended the life of a dynasty.

While some Christians in Almoravid service retained their religious identity, others, especially captives, converted to Islam becoming 'renegades' (*ʿilj*, *ʿulūj*), although this term could also be used in a pejorative way for Christians in general, making it difficult to be certain whether an *ʿilj* was a convert or not.[138] In some cases, conversion may have been a tactical move to enhance an individual's status despite a secret attachment to Christianity as indicated by a *fatwā* concerning the correct approach towards a convert to Islam found with items apparently used to perform the mass in his house.[139] The legal decision not to prosecute the man for apostasy shows that the Almoravids and their jurists could be pragmatic and valued their Christian and convert troops. Despite the dubious loyalty of Andalusi Christians in the context of struggles between Muslim and Christian powers, Christian soldiers proved themselves to be devoted supporters of the Almoravids in intra-Muslim struggles. The Catalan Reverter, captured by the Almoravid sea captain ʿAli b. Maymun, became head of ʿAli b. Yusuf's Christian corps and he proved to be Tashfin b. ʿAli's staunchest supporter as the Almohad pincer closed around the Almoravids in the Tlemcen area in the 1140s, and the men around Tashfin at his last stand included the Christian convert Bashir.[140]

At the outset, the Almohads had a very different attitude to religious minorities. Many sources describe them as rejecting the *dhimma in toto* on the grounds that all monotheists, Muslim, Christian and Jewish, should accept Ibn Tumart as the *mahdī* and renewer of the pure monotheistic message, common to them all in its essentials.[141] This radical ideological stance led

[137] See p. 292, n. 38, below.

[138] Lapiedra Gutiérrez, *Cómo los Musulmanes Llamaban a los Cristianos Hispánicos*, pp. 190–2, 244.

[139] Lagardère, *Le djihâd andalou*, p. 111; Gómez-Rivas, *Islamization of Morocco*, pp. 79–83.

[140] See pp. 59–60, above.

[141] al-Marrakushi, *Muʿjib*, p. 435.

to bold proclamations by 'Abd al-Mu'min commanding the Jewish and Christian inhabitants of conquered regions to accept Almohad Islam, depart into exile or risk the death penalty. According to the eastern Islamic historian al-Nuwayri:

> There is no 'polytheist' (*mushrik*) in ['Abd al-Mu'min's] lands and no holy building (*kanīsa*) [meaning church or synagogue] in any district of them because when he took possession of a Muslim town, he prevailed on every *dhimmī* to convert. Those who converted were saved and he permitted those who requested it to go to Christians lands. Those who refused were killed and all the people of his empire are Muslims and others do not mix with them.[142]

As a result, the Almohads have frequently been depicted as violent fanatics and persecutors of religious minorities, and the Almohad era as a disaster, especially for Jewish populations. However, the Almohads wished to convert all monotheists, including the existing Muslim majority of Kharijite, Maliki Sunni or Shi'i persuasion, to their way of thinking, therefore, they did not necessarily single out the religious minorities for persecution and the realities of medieval conquest and government make it unlikely that the Almohads had the physical capacity to monitor the religious beliefs of all their subjects or to carry out their threats, except in isolated incidents designed to act as exemplary warnings.[143]

During the first phase of the Almohad conquest in the western Maghrib, religious minorities and Almoravids shared the dubious honour of being categorised as errant monotheists and they were mutual targets of the Almohad *da'wa*. During the conquest of towns seen as 'Almoravid' in their proclivities such as Tlemcen, Fes and Marrakesh, for instance, religious minorities were often targets of violent reprisals which hit the population as a whole for their 'collaboration' with the veiled Sanhaja. Violence could also be preceded by preaching and calls to convert. In Sijilmasa, the Jewish community was subjected to months of religious disputations designed to convince them to convert to Almohadism after which the majority converted. The remaining 150 Jews were killed.[144] This, however, bears comparison with the earlier massacre of Muslim tribesmen considered lukewarm in their adherence to Ibn Tumart in Tinmall, the so-called *tamyīz*, and al-Baydhaq's reference to the division of Aghmat's population into sparring factions for and against Almohadism.[145]

142 al-Nuwayri, *Nihayat al-Arab*, vol. 24, p. 176.
143 See Bennison, 'Almohad *tawḥīd*, pp. 195–216.
144 Bennison and Gallego, 'Jewish trading in Fes on the eve of the Almohad conquest', p. 40.
145 al-Baydhaq, *Akhbar*, p. 60.

Once the Almohads expanded beyond the frontiers of the Almoravid empire, other constituencies who resisted them fiercely, such as the inhabitants of Tunis, became the targets of violence. In fact, it is in the context of 'Abd al-Mu'min's 1159–60 campaign to recapture al-Mahdiyya from the Normans, during which he conquered Tunis, that his reported ultimatum to Christians and Jews to convert, go into exile or risk death appears. However, when he took Tunis, all the inhabitants suffered for their opposition by means of a general confiscation of wealth.[146] Conversely, when urban communities sent representatives to 'Abd al-Mu'min offering their submission, as the people of Sousse and Sfax did, there is no indication that Almohad troops then entered and attacked any sector of the population.[147] That being said, indigenous Christian communities in southern Ifriqiya caught up in the violence of the conquest seem to have fled from towns such as Gafsa to oasis villages only to face extinction when the Banu Ghaniya insurgents ravaged the region in the late twelfth to early thirteenth centuries, events which together marked the demise of an indigenous Christian minority in North Africa.[148]

As well as responding differently to urban communities that submitted or resisted, the treatment the Almohads meted out to Christians and Jews depended on whether they were considered 'indigenous' inhabitants of the House of Islam (*dār al-islām*) or 'foreigners' from the House of War (*dār al-ḥarb*). They allowed the Norman Christian garrison besieged in al-Mahdiyya to sail for Sicily once they had capitulated and they granted the Christian troops in Almoravid service in Marrakesh, who helped them to breach the walls, a safe conduct to Iberia. Moreover, the decline of the indigenous Christian community of the Maghrib was accompanied by the settlement of new communities of foreign Christian merchants in many North African coastal towns during the course of the Almohad century, and Almohad recruitment of Christian troops as a core component in their army, like the Almoravids before them. As we saw above, the number of these troops in Marrakesh may have numbered as many as 12,000 by the late Almohad era.

The arrival of the Almohads in al-Andalus triggered a steady northward flow of Andalusi Christians into Christian-ruled areas such as the Tagus valley controlled by the Portuguese or Toledo in the kingdom of Castile.[149] They were encouraged in this by Alfonso VII of León-Castile, who offering concessions to Andalusi Christians willing to repopulate the countryside in the southern Toledan stretches of his kingdom from around 1146, the year

[146] Bennison, 'Almohad *tawḥīd*', pp. 212–13.

[147] Ibid., pp. 210–11.

[148] Prevost, 'Les dernières communautés chrétiennes', pp. 482–3

[149] Molénat, 'Sur le rôle des Almohades', p. 396.

before the fall of Seville to the Almohads.[150] From the mid-twelfth century, references to Andalusi Christians virtually cease, leading Molénat to conclude that an Arabised Christian community no longer existed in al-Andalus due to the vicissitudes of the Almohad conquest and the choice such Christians were able to make to migrate north into Christian territory. As in Ifriqiya, those later references to Christians that do appear, especially in eastern al-Andalus, seem to refer to merchant communities from other places rather than the remnants of an indigenous Christian population.[151]

For the Andalusi Jewish community, migration meant swapping the life of a minority in one place for that of a minority in another, which might be equally hazardous, reducing their options in the face of the Almohad conquest. They were also predominantly urban and therefore more visible than Christians living in rural areas, and faced intense Almohad pressure to convert as in Maghribi towns like Sijilmasa and, like the Sijilmasan Jews, they often took that option rather than taking the difficult, if not impossible, decision of selling up and migrating out of the Almohad empire or risking the death penalty. A notable example is the family of the famous Jewish philosopher and jurist, Maimonides, from Córdoba who seem to have converted and migrated to Fes where they lived for many years before Maimonides decided to leave for Egypt and live openly as a Jew once more. Although many Jewish scholars are uncomfortable with the idea that such an important medieval Jewish scholar as Maimonides may have converted, his biography in Ibn al-Qifti's *Ta'rikh al-Hukama'* reports that after he moved to Egypt, a Muslim from al-Andalus publicly asserted that he had practised Islam in the Maghrib and was therefore an apostate, an accusation rebuffed by a Muslim judge in Egypt on the grounds that one cannot be an apostate if compelled to convert in the first place.[152] Both the position of the Andalusi accuser and the Egyptian *qāḍī*, however, assume that the family were converts for a time even if they differed on the accusation of apostasy.

As Christian Iberian powers found later when they forcibly converted their Jewish and Muslim subjects to Catholicism, conversion under duress created more problems than it solved. Two examples of such problems encountered by the Almohads spring to mind. As we saw in Chapter 3, the Islamised Jews of Granada – whom Ibn Sahib al-Salat specifically states had been compelled to convert (*aslamū 'alā kurh*^{in}), probably around 1155 when the Almoravids in the city finally capitulated to the Almohads – entered into a conspiracy with those most fervent Andalusi opponents of the Almohads,

150 Molénat, 'Sur le rôle des Almohades', p. 402.

151 Ibid.

152 Ibn al-Qifti, *Ta'rikh al-Hukama'*, pp. 317–18.

Ibn Hamushk and Ibn Mardanish, in 1162 and the leader of the converted Jews, Ibn Dahri, let Ibn Hamushk and his men into the city in the hope that they would expel the Almohads.[153] The alliance was unsuccessful and the Almohads fiercely punished the collaborators, but the incident clearly showed the resentment created by forced conversion.

Thirty years later, when the dust of the conquest had settled and Almohad rule had become embedded, the long-term consequences of such conversion created concerns of a different nature, related to the sincerity of converts and their social interaction with other Muslims. The converted Jew Ibn ʿAqnin talks of impediments placed in the path of 'new' Muslims of Jewish origin, such as prohibitions on owning slaves and marrying 'old' Muslim women,[154] and towards the end of his reign, Yaʿqub al-Mansur issued a decree commanding that Islamised Jews wear distinctive clothing and be prevented from mixing and marrying with other Muslims. He gave as grounds for this discrimination his view that 'the Jews among us make a show of being Muslim, they pray in the mosques, teach their children to recite the Qur'an, and carry themselves according to our religion and custom but God only knows what their hearts conceal or their homes contain'.[155]

The underlying reasons behind these strictures towards Jewish converts to Islam are opaque. As in early modern Spain, accusations of religious deviance or insincerity could indicate socio-economic competition between new converts and old adherents to the faith,[156] although ideological concerns and issues of loyalty to the regime might have been equally pressing. At around the same time that Yaʿqub al-Mansur issued his decree, the philosopher Ibn Rushd was temporarily exiled to Lucena, a town with a large (converted?) Jewish population, after other jurists accused him of pagan beliefs, an accusation that may have been underpinned by allusions to his supposed Jewish ancestry and thus 'tainted' Islamic beliefs.[157] It is possible that the Almohad caliph felt that converted Jews, like philosophers, could be sacrificed in order to rally the rest of the Muslim population behind the Almohads to better face military threats from the north.

In contrast to the Christian case, the demise of the Almohad empire in the middle decades of the thirteenth century saw the rapid reappearance of

153 Ibn Sahib al-Salat, *al-Mann bi'l-Imama*, pp. 123–4. He describes Ibn Dahri as related by marriage to Ibn Zayd, the previous *mushrif* of Granada, implying that the Jews had been involved in financial administration under the Almoravids as well as the Zirids.

154 Fierro, 'Conversion, ancestry and universal religion', p. 161.

155 al-Marrakushi, *Muʿjib*, p. 435.

156 Fierro, 'Conversion, ancestry and universal religion', p. 165.

157 Serrano Ruano, 'Explicit cruelty, implicit compassion', p. 226.

an Arabised Jewish minority in North Africa despite the undoubted pressure placed on Jews within the Almohad empire and the forced conversion of Jewish communities in major cities. This suggests that many converts had indeed continued to practise their faith in private and that they reverted to Judaism once the political and ideological situation changed in their favour and more orthodox ideas about the *dhimma* reasserted themselves. In more isolated locations, conversion had probably never been enforced. The Jewish communities of the Maghrib grew further as the situation of Jews in Iberian Christian territories deteriorated and many decided to migrate south across the Straits of Gibraltar and settle in towns such as Tetuan and Fes, creating a resurgence of the western Maghribi Jewish community. As the hard-line ranting of the fifteenth-century Tlemcen-born jurist al-Maghili about the wealth and privilege of Jews in the oasis of Tuwat (southern Algeria) shows, Jews were as important in commercial and governmental circles in the Almohad successor states as they had been before the Almohad interlude, confirming its transient, albeit harsh, character.

5

Economy and Trade Within and Beyond Imperial Frontiers, 1050–1250

All empires and states depend on control of resources, human and material, to survive and flourish. However, the ways in which empires acquire resources differ and depend on the underlying nature of the economy, modes of production, and a cluster of legal, political and social factors. A term often used for government in the Maghrib is *makhzan*, meaning a storehouse, a term that encapsulates the importance of accumulating resources to government and its tribute-gathering character. From the perspective of rulers of the western Maghrib, land was viewed as either 'lands of government' (*bilād al-makhzan*), where taxes could be levied, or 'lands of dissidence' (*bilād al-sība*), where it was often impossible to do this, terms that were echoed in the French colonial designations of the fertile, exploitable and controllable Atlantic plains as *le Maroc utile* and the mountain ranges whose tribal populations resisted conquest until they were subjected to aerial bombardment in the 1930s as *le Maroc inutile*. While the terms *bilād al-makhzan* and *bilād al-sība* were not commonly used in the Almoravid and Almohad centuries and apply particularly to Morocco, the idea of the state as a storehouse (*makhzan*) as well as the locus of power (*sulṭān*) had emerged, and the ability to control men, grain and commerce was more crucial to these empires' success or failure than their much-vaunted jihad victories or, conversely, defeats.[1]

In order to get an insight into economic life between the eleventh and thirteenth centuries in North Africa and Iberia, we turn again to geographical works composed during this era, the most important being Abu 'Ubayd al-Bakri's (d. 1094) *al-Masalik wa'l-Mamalik* written in the 1060s or later, from which much of our knowledge about the early Almoravids has been drawn; the fragments of his teacher Ahmad b. 'Umar al-'Udhri's (d. 1085) work; al-Sharif al-Idrisi's *Kitab Nuzhat al-Mushtaq* or *Opus Geographicum*, dated to 1154; and the anonymous and entertaining *Kitab al-Istibsar* written by a

[1] For instance, the *Kitab al-Ansab* and other sources mention slave soldiers called the *'abīd al-makhzan*. Hopkins, 'The Almohade Hierarchy', p. 94.

native of Marrakesh in 1191, which extensively plagiarises al-Bakri and other famous writers including al-Mas'udi (d. 956) and his younger contemporary, Ibn Hawqal.[2]

Most of these geographies were composed in the form of 'road books' with information about each town and travelling distances between them.[3] They are partial to the extent that their educated, urban authors perceived the Maghrib and al-Andalus, like other parts of the Islamic world, as a network of towns and the land between them primarily as a 'route' (*maslak*) from one town to the next. Geographers, therefore, comment on the countryside primarily from the point of view of mercantile travellers, but, nonetheless, they offer scattered information about local produce, products and prices as well as other observations. Another problem with them is the repetition of material from one generation to the next, giving it a generic rather than a specific quality that sometimes makes it challenging to pin down changes over time. On the other hand, each generation of geographers needed to verify information and update it where possible for such books to have any value at all.

We can supplement our information with pilgrimage accounts (*raḥalāt*), such as Ibn Jubayr's famous description of his 1182–5 pilgrimage to Mecca; letters between merchants from the Genizah collection in Cairo; *ḥisba* manuals about good market practice; and judicial opinions (*fatāwā*) that mention trade or other economic matters. Historical chronicles also sometimes allude to inflation, droughts, crop failures, as well as material contributions made by monarchs to economic life. Another valuable source of evidence is surviving Almoravid and Almohad coinage, which appears across the Mediterranean and demonstrates the strength of these empires' currency and their economic vitality.

Although it is the hardest aspect of economic life to chart in the absence of detailed statistics, censuses or surviving tax registers, the backbone of the economy during these centuries was rural production, including the cultivation of cereals, fruits and vegetables, and the herding of livestock for milk, meat and hides. Many people simply consumed what they grew or raised, bartering or selling the surplus to acquire other necessary items in village markets and regional market towns. The government's tax collectors, whether local tribal chiefs, officials dispatched from major towns or land-grant holders, creamed off a proportion in cash or kind when they could. The regime also imposed upon rural communities the obligation to provide food and supplies

[2] Ducène attributes the *Kitab al-Istibsar* to Muhammad b. 'Abd Rabbihi. Ducène, 'al-Bakrī, Abu 'Ubayd 'Abd Allāh'.

[3] Lévi-Provençal, 'al-Bakrī, Abu 'Ubayd 'Abd Allāh'; Ducène, 'al-Bakrī, Abu 'Ubayd 'Abd Allāh'.

for troops who passed through their area. This form of extraction affected some communities disproportionately, especially those living on the Atlantic plains of the western Maghrib or the route from Algeciras to Seville, which were regularly traversed by Almohad contingents from the 1160s onwards. Conversely, tribes living in inaccessible mountain regions or herding their flocks over long distances in arid zones were much more difficult to tax or exploit and their way of life, off the beaten tracks followed by merchants and soldiers, is rarely described.

The urban economy was naturally more diverse and encompassed artisanal production of all kinds from humble wooden, metal and leather items for daily use to luxurious garments, jewellery and perfumes which manufacturers sold to local customers or mercantile agents. Towns were also the site of service industries and the literate professions connected to religion, law and the arts. Commerce – local, inter-regional and long distance – was very much at the heart of urban life in the western reaches of the medieval Islamic world, just as it was in the Middle East and Central Asia. It was trade in and across the Sahara as much as religion that tempted the Sanhaja Almoravids out of the desert and encouraged them to conquer the string of trading cities that stretched from Awdaghust and Sijilmasa in the Sahara all the way north to Seville and Córdoba. The subsequent conquests of the Almohads gave them control over the land caravan routes across the Maghrib to Ifriqiya and on to Egypt, as well as a massive rural hinterland. In contrast to the situation on land, however, neither empire developed Mediterranean commercial, as opposed to war, fleets, leaving the Italian city states, Genoa especially, to develop a monopoly over commercial maritime carriage, something that proved to be a serious liability in the long run.

While the creation of large, centralising empires created economic and commercial opportunities in the form of new markets, access to greater resources and vast imperial trading areas, the repeated phases of warfare and unrest that occurred between the eleventh and thirteenth centuries were a destabilising factor in several regions. It seems that Andalusi frontier communities found it harder and harder to recover from the depredations of armies, Christian and Muslim, during this period. In Ifriqiya and the central Maghrib, the effects of the Banu Hilal migrations westwards from Egypt, the Norman occupation, and the persistent raiding and pillaging of the Banu Ghaniya combined with Almohad reprisals had a deleterious effect from which the region did not really recover until after the demise of the Almohad empire. However, the western Maghrib seems to have had sufficient demographic and economic reserves to recover from the great struggle between the Almoravids and the Almohads, as well as repeated tribal rebellions. In other words, the economic as well as the political centre of gravity during these centuries was located in modern Morocco, a region that had been something of a backwater prior to the tenth century but now sustained two centuries of Berber empire, while previous economic centres in Ifriqiya and al-Andalus had a more chequered trajectory.

The Rural Economy

As we saw in the previous chapter, the countryside of the Maghrib was primarily inhabited by communities organised into tribes, while in al-Andalus rural social organisation revolved instead around village communities with considerable continuity from Visigothic into Muslim times. These communities sustained a variety of relationships to the land upon which they lived. According to Islamic law, a large proportion of land belonged to the ruler who granted it to others to use, sometimes for temporary periods and sometimes over many generations. Other legally recognised categories of land tenure were privately owned land (*milk*), land held as a religious endowment (*ḥabs, waqf*), communal land held by villages (*mushāraka*) or tribes (*'arsh*), and also marginal or 'dead' land (*mawāt*) to which individuals could earn rights by its cultivation. One important point to note is that neither al-Andalus nor the Maghrib hosted feudal societies like those of medieval Latin Christendom in which lords possessed the land and the serfs or villeins upon it, although different types of state land grants, reviewed below, did exist. The exact character of land tenure in any area, however, was also conditioned by custom (*'urf*) and traditions that could reach back many centuries into pre-Islamic times. While political change could occur very quickly, life in the countryside tended to be less prone to dramatic ruptures as successive regimes wished to maintain and consolidate rural production rather than to disrupt it.

The actual modes of production and subsistence in North Africa and Iberia, however, were determined not by the absence or presence of tribes or types of land tenure, but by climate, ecology and topography. At the risk of over-simplification, the more arid the climate and the more mountainous the terrain, the more likely it was for people to supplement the cultivation of crops with livestock herding and move with their flocks to find pastures and water. This pattern culminated in the Sahara where the primary mode of subsistence was nomadic herding, the lifestyle of the Sanhaja Almoravids before they expanded northwards into more fertile areas to secure the grain and other foodstuffs they needed. Conversely, the Masmuda supporters of the Almohad movement were mountain villagers who farmed on irrigated terraces, kept fruit trees and moved their flocks to the high pastures in summer, as the inhabitants of the High Atlas still do today.

Although we do not possess statistics or detailed accounts of rural life, it is possible to get a basic idea about the way in which country people survived.

Despite the fact that the geographers organised their works around routes and towns, they also discuss the agricultural hinterland of each town, called its *bādiya* (countryside) by Ibn Hawqal and a *naẓr* in the *Kitab al-Istibsar*, a word that denotes an Almohad province or administrative unit as well as an agricultural zone. These sometimes hyperbolic descriptions of the fine and plentiful produce of numerous parts of Ifriqiya, the Maghrib and al-Andalus should be taken with a pinch of salt, but, nonetheless, they do convey the normal range of agricultural activities found on the fertile coastal strip running across North Africa from Tripoli in modern Libya to Tlemcen and then expanding beyond the Middle Atlas into the rolling Atlantic plains of the western Maghrib and across the Straits into southern Iberia.

The agricultural activities that transformed 'dead' or unproductive land into 'living' (*'āmir*) or productive soil fell into three main categories. First, the cultivation (*zar'*) of cereals where there was sufficient annual rainfall or riverine water supplies; secondly, the maintenance of irrigated gardens, groves and orchards (*jannāt wa-basātīn*) in the immediate vicinity of towns and villages to produce fruit and vegetables; and, thirdly, the keeping of animals (*ḍar'* lit. an udder) for farm work, dairy products, meat, hides and wool. The rural population cultivated cereal staples across Iberia and North Africa using ploughing techniques of a common Mediterranean type which had their origins in Antiquity. The most important staples were wheat, barley and millet, followed by rice which Muslims had introduced from India and cultivated in many areas of al-Andalus, most notably Valencia, Murcia, Seville and Mallorca.[4] Such cereals were vitally important to the survival of humans and animals: rice and bread were human staples, while barley and millet were also used to feed animals during the winter.

Land fertility varied greatly as did levels of precipitation, and while it was possible to rely on rainfall to cultivate cereals in some areas, in many others irrigation was essential. Al-Idrisi claims that some of the land between Lisbon and Santarem could produce 100 measures of grain from one measure of seed, an observation that puts the struggle between the Portuguese and Almohads for control over the area into a new light.[5] Conversely, in the Ziz valley where Sijilmasa was located, the inhabitants struggled to produce sufficient grain in the fierce heat. The author of the *Kitab al-Istibsar* claims that they sowed their seed only one year in every three or four. In the intervening years, so much grain fell out of the desiccated crop into the dry cracked soil as it was harvested that when the farmers watered the land from the river

[4] See Lagardère, 'Le riziculture en al-Andalus (VIIIe–XVe siècles)'.

[5] al-Idrisi, *Opus Geographicum*, fasc. 5–8, pp. 549–50.

in spring they simply ploughed without adding more seed. The frequent drought conditions meant that they also consumed all their grain even if it had sprouted as they could not afford to waste it.[6]

Some grain was given to tax collectors, sold or stored as it was, but a large proportion needed to be milled to make various grades of flour. Although windmills and handmills were sometimes used, for the most part wheat was milled using watermills located wherever water flowed strongly and many rivers are described as having numerous mills dotted along their banks. Al-Idrisi remarks that on the Rio Seguro at Murcia, there was a bridge made of boats with mills on board, a feature also found on the River Ebro in the vicinity of Saragossa, where the mill boats were carefully manoeuvred to maximise their use of the river current and brought under the shelter of the walls if an enemy threatened the city.[7]

In Latin Christian societies, mills generally belonged to the feudal lord who was able to monopolise access to them and demand heavy fees for their use. This was not the case in Muslim lands where mills were constructed by wealthy individuals, small investors working in partnership or village communities, and could be owned publicly or privately, and rented out.[8] As a result, mills were numerous, easily accessible facilities with fees charged in coin or as a proportion of the flour, the running of which was regulated by the urban-based market inspector (*muḥtasib*) whose role is described in more detail below. The complicated shenanigans recorded in the manual of the Malagan *muḥtasib* Muhammad b. Abi Muhammad al-Saqati show that this was not necessarily an easy job and that customers bringing loads of grain for milling were well advised to monitor the process closely to ensure that the miller returned the correct amount of flour for the grain supplied, of the composition and grade paid for.[9]

The second widespread usage of land was the cultivation of fruit-bearing trees, plants and vegetables for human consumption and industrial purposes. The most important of these 'orchard' crops were olives, figs and grapes along the Mediterranean littoral and in Iberia, with dates gaining importance in the arid regions of the Maghrib closest to the Sahara. Olive cultivation, in particular, was ubiquitous and many places, of which Seville was the most famous, produced olive oil for export as well as the local market. The Mediterranean appetite for olive oil appears to have been more or less insatiable due to its versatility as a foodstuff, fuel for lamps and as an ingredient for

[6] *Kitab al-Istibsar*, p. 201.
[7] al-Idrisi, *Opus Geographicum*, fasc. 5–8, p. 559.
[8] Lagardère, *Campagnes*, pp. 340–57.
[9] al-Sakati, *Hisba*, pp. 21–6.

soap. Oil could also be used in building as a mixing agent in place of water to produce stronger and more durable structures. Smaller orchards and gardens produced fruit such as quinces, apples, pistachios, almonds and occasionally bananas. Expanding on al-Bakri's earlier description, the author of the *Kitab al-Istibsar* comments on the particularly good and varied fruits produced around Gafsa in Ifriqiya:

> Gafsa is surrounded by a forest 10 miles in diameter in which there are 18 villages. It is enclosed by a wall with gates and inhabited towers called *durūb*. The forest has many date palms and olive trees and other superior fruits such as apples with a fine aroma, pomegranates, citron medicus (*utruj*), bananas, dates including a type called *al-kasbā* which is unlike dates elsewhere . . . They put [the dates] in water jars with pointed bottoms and when they take them out a substance sweeter than bees' honey is left in the bottom which they use in cooking and for making desserts. Gafsa has more pistachios than anywhere else which are conveyed all over Ifriqiya, the Maghrib, al-Andalus and Egypt. The Syrian pistachio nut is small but the Gafsi nut is almost as large as a walnut.[10]

This description is more detailed than some, but not unique or anomalous for towns across al-Andalus and the coastal areas of North Africa. Ceuta was surrounded by gardens and orchards, while figs and almonds grew in abundance near Sefrou in the Middle Atlas. The agricultural hinterlands of Seville, Almería and Granada were similarly blessed. According to al-Idrisi, Jabal al-Sharaf outside Seville stretched for forty miles, all of which one could 'traverse in the shade of olive and fig trees' interspersed with 8,000 villages full of dovecotes and attractive cottages.[11] Even in the more arid Ziz valley where the great caravan city of Sijilmasa was located, the inhabitants cultivated dates and grapes from which they produced both shade and sun-dried varieties of raisins, alongside struggling to produce grain. The oasis around Biskra in the central Maghrib was also famed for dates of all kinds.[12]

One important plant the Muslims introduced across their Mediterranean conquests was sugar cane (*qaṣab*), which is first attested in al-Andalus in 756 and in the Maghrib by 895.[13] Sugar cane flourished in the same warm, well-watered conditions as bananas, and could be found in al-Andalus in the lower

[10] *Kitab al-Istibsar*, pp. 153–4; al-Bakri, *Description de l'Afrique*, Arabic text, p. 47; French text, pp. 100–1; al-Idrisi adds henna to the list, *Opus Geographicum*, fasc. 1–4, p. 278.

[11] al-Idrisi, *Opus Geographicum*, fasc. 5–8, p. 541.

[12] al-Bakri, *Description de l'Afrique*, Arabic text, p. 52; French text, p. 111.

[13] For a detailed account of sugar production in al-Andalus and the Maghrib, see Lagardère, *Campagnes*, pp. 361–90.

Guadalquivir valley and the area between Málaga and Almería, and in Ifriqiya around Gabes.[14] By the end of the tenth century, it was also being cultivated in the Maghrib around Ceuta and in the Sus valley. Most of the geographers of the Almoravid and Almohad eras from al-Bakri to al-Idrisi comment on the high quality sugar produced by the villages of the Sus dotted along the valley of the Massa River near Igli using servile or slave labour.[15] In addition to fruits for consumption, people also cultivated odiferous and flowering plants to produce flavourings, perfumes and medicines. These included saffron, for which Baeza near Jaén was famous,[16] violets, roses and aloeswood.

In some areas farmers produced silk, flax and cotton for the vibrant textile industry. Silk worms had been introduced to al-Andalus by Muslims from Syria and sericulture flourished in the mountains of the south around Jaén and Granada where mulberry trees were plentiful.[17] Although al-Andalus was especially renowned for its silk, which was said to rival that of Transoxiana, according to al-Bakri, it was also produced in other places such as the land around Gabes in Ifriqiya.[18] Flax (*kattān*), introduced to Iberia in Roman times, grew in many parts of al-Andalus and in the Maghrib around Basra, south of Tangier, which was called Basrat al-Kattan as a result,[19] and cotton (*quṭn*) was one of the products of the Sijilmasa area.[20]

Irrigation was essential to many of these types of cultivation and, as a result, hydraulic engineering and the social organisation of the dispersal of water played a large part in the management of the rural economy. Well before the eleventh century, Muslims had developed sophisticated methods of irrigation, which sometimes used the remnants of the Roman infrastructure in Ifriqiya and al-Andalus but also greatly expanded it, deploying technologies such as the underground water channels (*qanāt*), also found in Persia. Extensive networks of canals, smaller channels and aqueducts diverted water from rivers or springs to fields, gardens and storage facilities, including stone basins, cisterns and reservoirs. Where necessary, water was raised by wooden wheels powered by a river current, mules and donkeys, or people.

Using examples from eastern al-Andalus, Glick has identified three main levels of irrigation. At one end of the scale there were macro-systems that

[14] al-Bakri, *Description de l'Afrique*, Arabic text, p. 17; French text, p. 42.

[15] al-Bakri, *Description de l'Afrique*, Arabic text, p. 161; French text, pp. 306–7; *Kitab al-Istibsar*, p. 212; al-Idrisi, *Opus Geographicum*, fasc. 1–4, p. 227.

[16] al-Idrisi, *Opus Geographicum*, fasc. 5–8, p. 569.

[17] Lagardère, *Campagnes*, p. 391.

[18] al-Bakri, *Description de l'Afrique*, Arabic text, p. 17; French text, p. 41.

[19] al-Bakri, *Description de l'Afrique*, Arabic text, 110; p. French text, p. 216; *Kitab al-Istibsar*, p. 189.

[20] al-Idrisi, *Opus Geographicum*, fasc. 1–4, p. 226.

watered large areas of the alluvial *huerta* of Valencia using underground channels and large water wheels (*nāʿūra, dūlāb*). Next there were medium-sized village irrigation systems that channelled the water from local springs or rivers to cisterns from which it was dispersed to terraced fields and gardens, usually weekly in time slots determined by water clocks. In these systems water was raised using smaller water wheels (*sāniya*) worked by animals or simple lifting mechanisms similar to the eastern *shādūf*. At the other end of the scale, there were micro-supply systems consisting of cisterns, wells and small water wheels powered by animals that raised water for a single farm or family.[21] Many of these methods were used in the gardens of the Maghrib and Ifriqiya too. In Sijilmasa, the groves of dates and grape vines were watered in rotation, and it is still possible to see the remains of the vertical wells that drew water from *qanāt*s in the landscape west of the Ziz valley where Sijilmasa was located.

The vital importance of access to water ensured that its distribution was minutely managed and regulated by a mixture of customary practice and Islamic law. According to the latter, the first call on water was for drinking and ablutions, following by farming, and then industrial procedures like milling and tanning. In the countryside, villages upstream generally had prior rights to water for their fields and gardens than those lower down the river course, although the creation of new irrigation channels upstream might be a cause of conflict with users downstream. In addition to looking at need and custom, the allocation of water within communities also considered the contribution made by individuals to constructing, maintaining and repairing wells, water channels and storage facilities.[22] The author of the *Kitab al-Istibsar* reports that in Gafsa (Ifriqiya) people paid large sums for a share of the water available. As a result, the teams of irrigation workers who managed the supply system and the fair distribution of water to the extensive area of gardens and orchards on an hourly basis had developed a superb ability to tell the time to within ten minutes of accuracy using the sun.

> The workers in these gardens and orchards are the most knowledgeable people in the times of the day. If you ask one of these men, when he has not been paying attention to the passing of the hours of the day, he stands and looks at the sun, then measures his shadow with his feet, and then says to you, 'So many hours have passed and so many sixths of an hour have passed'.[23]

The placing of mills and latrines whose effluent entered rivers and streams also had to be carefully managed. When a water dispute involving

[21] See Glick, 'Hydraulic technology in al-Andalus'.

[22] See Lagardère, *Campagnes*, pp. 253–86.

[23] *Kitab al-Istibsar*, p. 153.

some gardens at Balyunish, around three miles from Ceuta, came before the famous Qadi 'Iyad, he consulted with the most eminent Andalusi and Maghribi jurists of the Almoravid age to resolve it. The matter revolved around whether it was acceptable to divert the water of a stream across a road to irrigate nearby orchards, despite a previous ruling that it was not. The situation was complicated by the installation downstream of a mill that also needed to use the river waters. This legal wrangle went on for many years.[24] Quite apart from its role as a marker of Sunni sectarian identity, the Maliki legal system promoted by the Almoravids provided a framework for dealing with these types of interaction and disputes in a coherent manner. For many people, Maliki *fatwā*s and rulings of this kind were much more relevant to their lives than theological or doctrinal issues, and use of the Maliki school of law expanded through the countryside in subsequent centuries, in spite of Almohad ambivalence to other aspects of Malikism.[25]

The third common rural activity was the herding of animals and stock-rearing. Most people kept a few chickens for eggs, a handful of sheep, goats or cattle for milk and meat, and working animals such as bullocks and mules, which were pastured on fallow and harvested fields and common land. Sheep and goats could be pastured on a variety of terrains, while well-watered parts of al-Andalus such as the water meadows of the Guadalquivir and Guadiana valleys supported large herds of dairy cattle, and the land around Niebla and in the Balearics was well suited to horses and mules.[26] In the Maghrib, tribal communities often had extensive flocks of sheep and goats as well as some cultivated fields and gardens. The Ghumara Berbers of the Rif mountains, for instance, are described as living in one of the most fertile areas of the Maghrib and cultivating its valleys to produce grapes, other fruits, and honey as well as keeping large flocks of animals.[27]

In arid and mountainous areas, pastoralism was the dominant economic pursuit due to the nature of the terrain and the profits to be made from stock-rearing. Dairy foods were an important component of the diet, as was meat in more affluent circles, creating demand for such foodstuffs from urban populations,[28] while rams were needed in large quantities annually for slaughter at the feast of the sacrifice (*'īd al-aḍḥā*). Sheep, mules and horses were in constant demand by the army as food for fighters on campaign, beasts of

[24] Gómez-Rivas, *Islamization of Morocco*, pp. 121–48.

[25] See Powers, *Law, Society and Culture*, pp. 95–140.

[26] Lagardère, *Campagnes*, pp. 441–2, 467–8.

[27] *Kitab al-Istibsar*, pp. 190–1.

[28] The preferred meat was lamb rather than beef, therefore cattle were primarily used as farm animals and to supply milk. Lagardère, *Campagnes*, p. 443.

burden and as cavalry mounts. Meanwhile, camels had a vital role to play in the transport of commodities across the Sahara desert and the nourishment of the nomads who herded them and operated the trans-Saharan caravan trade. As we saw in Chapter 2, al-Bakri famously described the Sanhaja of the Sahara as living solely on strips of dried meat and milk from their animals and as enjoying bread only when they obtained some flour from passing merchants.

In addition to providing food, animal hides and skins were an important source of leather for the manufacture of saddles, bags, shoes and other items, and there was constant demand for wool from the textile industry and felt for tents. As a result, many Maghribi tribes made a living by selling their animals, their hides, or their wool in the case of sheep. The Zanata tribes of the central Maghrib, for instance, were transhumant stock herders who moved large flocks of sheep between their summer and winter pastures. The Banu Marin, who eventually ousted the Almohads from power in the western Maghrib, began their career as shepherds, driving their flocks annually from the northern fringe of the Sahara to Agarsif in the Muluwiya valley between modern Morocco and Algeria. The wool of their sheep was sought after in both Muslim and Christian areas and it is thought that 'Merino' wool is named after the original Banu Marin owners of the breed.[29]

One of the features of rural life in eleventh- to twelfth-century North Africa was a rise in pastoralism at the expense of agriculture. The incursion of nomadic pastoralists into 'sown' areas and the subsequent reversion of agricultural land to pasture is not unique to North Africa, but the particular reasons for this example of the phenomenon are hotly debated in the historiography of these centuries. Increased pastoralism seems to have coincided with the movement of the nomadic Banu Hilal and Banu Sulaym tribes from Fatimid Egypt into Ifriqiya, and many medieval authors writing in Arabic refer to these nomads in a derogatory way as destroyers of cities and their hinterlands – mostly notably Qayrawan, the ancient capital of Ifriqiya – and as 'locusts' ravaging the region to an epic degree. French historians during the colonial era picked up on this interpretative thread, expressed most vigorously by Ibn Khaldun, and dubbed the movement west of these tribes as an invasion or even a 'catastrophe'.

However, this assessment of the Banu Hilal migration west was queried by Poncet many decades ago as a rather uncritical reading of the Arabic sources.[30] Since then, Brett has analysed the mythic and fictive elements in

[29] Shatzmiller, 'Islam and the "Great Divergence"', pp. 39–40.

[30] See Poncet, 'La mythe de la "catastrophe" hilalienne'.

the chroniclers' accounts of the Banu Hilal's supposed irruption into Ifriqiya and repeatedly referred to the lack of evidence for the widespread dislocation they supposedly caused to the economy and trade, proposing instead that they drifted westwards rather more gradually.[31] A similar case has been made for the limited impact of the arrival of these Arab tribes in what is now Libya slightly earlier.[32] The summary of these arguments is that the Banu Hilal migrations were a symptom rather than the cause of the decline in cultivation in Ifriqiya, which was triggered instead by struggles between the rival Zirid lineages of Qayrawan and Qal'at Bani Hammad, the weakening control of the former over Ifriqiya, and the Norman occupation of coastal towns, which together created a political vacuum only partially rectified by 'Abd al-Mu'min's incorporation of the region into the Almohad empire.

There were certainly a complex range of political and demographic factors at play during this era, including the demise of the Zirids, the arrival of the Arab tribes, and the formation of the Almoravid and Almohad empires in turn, all of which could impact on agricultural production. One of the most economically damaging factors in Ifriqiya, however, was the persistent raiding of the Almoravid Banu Ghaniya and their allies from the 1180s onwards, which had a significant impact on cultivation and trade in some areas at least.[33] That is not to say, however, that Arab tribes were necessarily more disruptive to agriculture than indigenous Berber tribes or, indeed, the armies of the Almohads themselves. The Banu Ghaniya had Berber as well as Arab allies and although the Almohad transfer of Arab tribes to the western Maghrib as military auxiliaries put a degree of pressure on the existing rural economy, it is Zanata Berbers who are described as 'locusts' ravaging the lands near Fes and Meknes in the early thirteenth century, not the Arab newcomers.[34] As we shall see below, persistent Christian raiding into Muslim-inhabited areas of al-Andalus similarly depressed the rural economy in that region without the existence of a nomadic element to blame.

One semi-rural industrial activity that was clearly of importance during the eleventh to thirteenth centuries, as in earlier times, was the mining or quarrying of metal ores, stone and minerals. Metals such as gold, silver, lead and iron were important for the production of coinage, weapons, farming implements and jewellery. The ores most commonly found in al-Andalus and the Maghrib were silver, copper and iron. In a short section on mines

31 See Brett, 'Ifriqiya as a market for Saharan trade'; Brett, 'The way of the nomad'.

32 Thiry, 'Sahara libyen', pp. 78–9. See also Baadj, *Saladin, the Almohads and the Banū Ghāniya*, pp. 24–9.

33 Thiry, 'Sahara libyen', pp. 79–80.

34 *al-Dhakhira al-Saniyya*, pp. 26–7.

in al-Andalus, al-Bakri says that there were numerous silver mines many of which could be found in the southeast of the peninsula.[35] Other writers also mention the silver mines in this area.[36] Across the Straits of Gibraltar there was another silver mine at Warkannas, three days' travel from Meknes, but the main concentration of Maghribi mines was below the High Atlas in the mountains fringing the Sus and Dar'a valleys. Although they name different mines, al-Bakri and al-Marrakushi speak of numerous silver- and copper-mining communities in these regions, including Tamdult, Tarudant, Kust, Nul Lamta and Zagundar, which al-Marrakushi describes as inhabited almost exclusively by the miners who extracted the ore from the silver mine.[37] He adds that copper from local mines was transported to Igli, where it was prepared into ingots for export to sub-Saharan Africa, and to a place called Tutiya, where it was smelted into brass.[38]

Iron was also mined at several locations in al-Andalus and the Maghrib. Al-Idrisi mentions a number of Andalusi iron mines, including one near Lorca,[39] while al-Marrakushi lists iron mines at Karish near Almería, Awriba between Dénia and Játiva, Timsaman in the Rif mountains, and an isolated mine a day's journey inland from the Atlantic coast between Salé and Marrakesh, where only those wishing to transport iron went.[40] In contrast, there were relatively few gold mines and gold became plentiful only in the Almoravid era as a result of their ability to import it across the Sahara from the West African gold fields at Bambuk and Buré, a source that was less accessible in Almohad times. Stone quarries provided materials for building, decoration and utensils. Marble, quarried at several Iberian locations, was extensively used in mosques and palaces for columns, basins and decorative features, and also for tomb stele. Medieval geographers also mention an Ifriqiyan quarry at Majana or Marmajanna between Gafsa and Tebessa famous for the production of millstones.[41]

Minerals of various kinds were also sourced in Almoravid and Almohad territories and traded within them and further afield. One of the most important minerals mined in these centuries was rock salt, which was extracted at several semi-legendary sites in the Sanhaja's desert domains – Taghaza, Awlil

[35] al-Bakri, *Jughrafiyat al-Andalus*, p. 129.
[36] al-'Udhri, *Nusus 'an al-Andalus*, p. 2.
[37] al-Marrakushi, *Mu'jib*, p. 509.
[38] Ibid., p. 510; see also *Kitab al-Istibsar*, p. 212.
[39] Al-Idrisi also mentions mines near Lorca, *Opus Geographicum*, fasc. 5–8, p. 561.
[40] al-Marrakushi, *Mu'jib*, pp. 509–11.
[41] Ibn Hawqal, *Kitab Surat al-Ard*, p. 84; *Kitab al-Istibsar*, p. 161. Al-Bakri does not mention millstones, but says there were silver mines in the area. al-Bakri, *Description de l'Afrique*, Arabic text, p. 145; French text, p. 278.

and Tatintal – all of which were the supposed location of a town built exclusively of rock-salt blocks where slaves toiled endlessly cutting salt.[42] As we shall see in the section below on trade, salt played a vital role in the Saharan economy and by extension the rise of the Almoravids. Another important mineral was alum, which was widely used as a mordant for dyes, while there was a mercury mine at Shalun north of Córdoba whence the mineral was exported all over the Maghrib,[43] an antimony mine near Nedroma in the central Maghrib,[44] and sulphur mines in al-Andalus and modern Libya between Barqa and Tripoli.[45] Geographers also refer to the locations where precious and semi-precious stones of many kinds were to be found.[46] The state had a keen interest in the produce of mines of all kinds for strategic and fiscal reasons, and was entitled to receive a share that was set at one-fifth (*khums*) in Islamic law. This was not a right the Almohads were prepared to relinquish, as we saw in Chapter 3 when the caliph Abu Yaʿqub Yusuf postponed travelling to al-Andalus in June 1182 to march against a mining community in the Sus because they were not paying the ruler's share.[47]

Another rural commodity that people exploited was timber. Woodland was an important source of firewood for villages and tribes and it was usually held collectively, but there were also some forested regions where logging on a larger scale was possible. In fact, al-Andalus and the western Maghrib had greater forests in the Algarve, eastern al-Andalus and the Middle Atlas mountains than any other part of the southern Mediterranean. Al-Idrisi comments that the best wood for the shipbuilding industry came from the Tortosa region due to the length and soundness of the planks.[48] Wood gathered in these forests was transported to towns for use in construction, craftwork and shipbuilding. Transport of timber could be a difficult job so loggers used rivers where they could. Pine trees felled in the vicinity of Cuenca, for instance, were cast into the river to be floated down to supply the shipyards of Dénia

[42] al-Bakri, *Description de l'Afrique*, Arabic text, p. 171; French text, p. 322, and the *Kitab al-Istibsar*, p. 213, describe a mine they call Tatintal in this way. Hunwick identifies this location as possibly the same site as al-Qazwini's Taghaza, the name also later given to the salt mines by Ibn Battuta (Hunwick, 'Taghāza'). Awlil mentioned by Ibn Hawqal (*Surat al-Ard*, p. 92) and al-Bakri (*Description de l'Afrique*, Arabic text, p. 171; French text, p. 322) was almost certainly closer to the Atlantic coast. McDougall, 'The Sahara reconsidered', pp. 276–7.

[43] al-Marrakushi, *Muʿjib*, p. 510.

[44] al-Bakri, *Description de l'Afrique*, Arabic text, p. 80; French text, p. 162.

[45] al-Bakri, *al-Andalus*, p. 129; al-Marrakushi, *Muʿjib*, p. 510.

[46] See, for example, al-Bakri, *al-Andalus*, pp. 127–8.

[47] Ibn ʿIdhari, *al-Bayan*, vol. 4, p. 220. See, p. 000, above.

[48] al-Idrisi, *Opus Geographicum*, fasc. 5–8, p. 555.

and Valencia.[49] The Middle Atlas mountains, meanwhile, produced pine and cedar, which was highly prized for making beams, carved lintels and doors.

Whilst much rural produce was consumed locally, the examples of olive oil, sugar cane, metal ores, minerals and timber, which needed to be transported elsewhere for processing or usage, remind us of the connections between town and countryside and the complementarity of the two economic spheres. It is, therefore, to the urban economy that we shall now turn to explore the manufacturing and commercial dimensions of economic life under the Almoravids and Almohads, before looking at the ways in which the two Berber regimes tapped into the wealth of their domains and nurtured it, and also the factors liable to undermine the economy.

The Urban Economy

As in most medieval Islamic societies, the urban economy in Almoravid and Almohad times was very diverse and commercially oriented. In the centuries following the Islamic conquest, the urban networks of al-Andalus and North Africa expanded as Muslims took over many ancient urban sites continuously inhabited from Roman or Carthaginian times (e.g., Córdoba, Seville, Saragossa, Ceuta), rebuilt others that had experienced a period of disuse (e.g., Tahart), and founded their own garrison towns (e.g., Qayrawan) and palatine cities (e.g., Fes, al-Mahdiyya). As new areas were drawn into the Islamic orbit, other new towns developed on the sites of occasional tribal markets (e.g., Sijilmasa). Good natural harbours and anchorage also encouraged the development of towns, as did the existence of mines. This process continued with the Almoravids and Almohads who founded and invested heavily in cities, especially in what is now Morocco. The rise of new western Maghribi urban centres, however, went along with the gradual loss of cities to the northern Christian powers in al-Andalus and political upheavals in Ifriqiya. Nonetheless, the functions of towns and cities remained stable, as did the main contours of urban economic life.

Access to water was naturally crucial for all towns and the majority, therefore, stood on or near rivers or springs that provided drinking water for the population and irrigation for their gardens. Where water supply was a challenge, townsfolk dug wells and their rulers constructed complicated hydraulic systems to transport and preserve water, such as the great Aghlabid cisterns (*mawājil*) outside Qayrawan and the irrigation system constructed by the Almoravids outside Marrakesh, to be discussed in Chapter 7.[50] Where

[49] al-Idrisi, *Opus Geographicum.*, fasc. 5–8, p. 560.

[50] al-Bakri, *Description de l'Afrique*, Arabic text, p. 26; French text, pp. 59–60.

possible, they also renovated and used Roman structures such as the aqueduct at Toledo described by al-Idrisi:

> [At Toledo] there is an aqueduct of wondrous workmanship [consisting of] a single arc and the river flows beneath this arc with great force and at the end of the bridge there is a water wheel 90 feet high which raises the water to the height of the aqueduct then flows along it into the city.[51]

On occasion, rivers facilitated the transport of commodities in and out of town. For instance, Córdoba and Seville are both located on the Guadalquivir River which empties into the Atlantic at Cádiz and was navigable by sea-faring vessels as far as Seville in Almohad times. Similarly, the Wad Sebou was used to convey items up towards Fes which would then be carried overland for the last leg of the journey. A later fourteenth-century reference describes this process: when the Marinid sultan Abu'l-Hasan ordered a marble basin from Almería in 1325, it was transported by sea to the Atlantic coast, then up the Wad Sebou on a barge, after which it was moved to Fes on wooden rollers or wheels.[52]

Towns of all sizes were surrounded by the extensive enclosed gardens (*jannāt*) and orchards (*basātīn*) mentioned in the previous section in which local people produced a rich variety of fruits and vegetables. There was, therefore, no sharp divide between rural and urban economies, but a gradual intensification of inhabitation and cultivation culminating in a dense ring of urban gardens as one approached town. As we saw in the last chapter, the features that distinguished so-called towns or cities (*madīna*) from fortified settlements (*ḥiṣn*, *qal'a*) and large villages (*qarya*) were physical, socio-political and economic, but also quite subjective. Al-Idrisi remarks that 'the village of 'Adhra is a small town'.[53] Settlements existed on a continuum along which size, population density, fortifications and the range of religious, governmental and economic services provided all contributed to the popular perception of whether a place was a *madīna* or not. While scholars have sometimes assumed that the mention of the trio of great mosque, markets and baths provides us with the quintessential characteristics of an imagined 'Islamic city', one could equally well argue that geographers, in fact, mentioned these facilities because not all towns had them.

As we have seen above, towns lacked the independent legal status enshrined in charters and privileges granted to the community by monarchs

[51] al-Idrisi, *Opus Geographicum*, fasc. 5–8, p. 551.
[52] al-Jazna'i, *Zahrat al-As*, p. 37.
[53] al-Idrisi, *Opus Geographicum*, fasc. 5–8, p. 564.

that Latin Christian cities of the same era often possessed.[54] The relevance of this statutory discrepancy is much debated in medieval urban studies, but, from the economic point of view, what is important is reference to markets since the term *sūq* (market) or its plural *aswāq* not only reveals the presence of buying and selling, it also implies the presence of a range of industrial and artisanal undertakings from the processing of agricultural produce to high-end manufacturing of jewellery and luxury textiles, and economic diversity. Market is, of course, itself a very elastic term ranging in meaning from a weekly tribal market with temporary stalls to a substantial sector of a city with permanent shops, ateliers and warehouses.

Some settlements are described as small and in possession of a basic market(s) that served only the local population. Al-Idrisi calls Badis on the Mediterranean coast of the western Maghrib 'a somewhat cultured town with a few markets and workshops which the Ghumara tribes visit for necessities'.[55] The majority of the towns of the Islamic west doubtless fell into this category of market towns serving neighbouring tribes and communities, too small and humble to merit more than a passing and slightly disparaging reference, despite their indispensability to the local economy. There were also numerous respectable provincial towns of medium size such as Baza near Guadix in al-Andalus, which al-Idrisi describes rather more approvingly as 'a pleasantly located, well-populated, medium-sized town with fortified walls, a clean market, and finely appointed houses which has commerce of many kinds and labourers in all types of craft'.[56]

At the other end of the scale, there were larger urban centres, provincial or monarchical capitals and major ports with a more complex and varied economic life and an array of markets and industries. The presence of a ruler or a governor and his court, either permanently or temporarily, naturally provided a great stimulus to manufacturers and traders of all kinds of items from pots and pans to fine textiles. It is in this sense, as well as to signal its scholarship, that Gafsa, where they manufactured cloaks (*ardiya*), shawls (*ṭayālis*) and turbans from the best wool, very fine white pottery dishes known as *rīḥiyya*, good glassware and gilded dishes, is called a place of culture or civilisation (*ḥaḍāra*).[57] A fourteenth-century passage about Fes, said to have been taken from a late twelfth-century financial administrator's records, provides further insight into the myriad professions, as well as other facilities, that one could

[54] See p. 146, above.
[55] al-Idrisi, *Opus Geographicum*, fasc. 5–8, p. 532.
[56] Ibid., fasc. 5–8, p. 568.
[57] *Kitab al-Istibsar*, p. 154. Al-Bakri locates the production of *rīḥiyya* pottery in Tunis. Al-Bakri, *Description de l'Afrique*, Arabic text, p. 40; French text, p. 88.

find in a provincial capital, as well as the positive impact of the Almoravids and Almohads on urban economic life:

> In the days of the Almoravids and Almohads, Fes enjoyed more development, luxury, security and prosperity than any other city in the Maghrib especially in the days of [Ya'qub] al-Mansur and his son Muhammad al-Nasir [1184–1213]. There were 782 mosques, 42 ablution buildings, 80 water fountains, 93 baths, 472 water mills, 89,236 residential homes, 17,041 apartments, 469 *funduq*s, 9,280 shops, two state-controlled covered markets – one on each bank – two mints – one on each bank – 3,094 textile workshops, 47 soap-making workshops, 86 tanneries, 116 dyers, 12 iron and copper smelting workshops, 11 glass-making workshops, 135 lime kilns, 1,170 bread ovens, and 400 stones for making paper, all in the city. There were 188 potteries outside the city . . . There were also on the bank of the great river from its entry into the city until its exit, dyers' ateliers and shops, tanneries, soap factories, fishmongers, butchers and doughnut-makers, places prepared for the boiling of yarn and beans and other things requiring water. Above all that were ateliers for weaving.[58]

This description of the burgeoning economic life in Fes could be applied to many Andalusi and Maghribi cities. It is of particular importance, however, because it highlights a significant shift in the locus of manufacturing that took place, or at least commenced, during the Almoravid and Almohad centuries. In the mid-eleventh century when the Almoravids emerged from the desert, most Maghribi towns were market towns or entrepôts along the trade routes moving commodities between sub-Saharan Africa, al-Andalus, Ifriqiya and the Islamic east with limited manufacturing complexes, and Marrakesh did not yet exist. The cities of al-Andalus, in contrast, had been thriving centres of manufacture for centuries, producing high-quality swords, armour and other weapons, fine leather goods, embroidered silk textiles, woollen cloth and rugs, books, paper, wooden utensils, and processed agricultural commodities, especially olive oil, honey and raw silk. Al-Andalus also had a shipbuilding industry centred in the eastern port cities of Dénia and Valencia, the destinations of some of the timber mentioned in the previous section.

With the rise of dynasties of Maghribi provenance and the transformation of al-Andalus into a province rather than an imperial metropole, some

[58] al-Jazna'i, *Zahrat al-As*, pp. 43–5. Al-Jazna'i states that his information came from the financial administrator (*mushrif*), 'Ali b. 'Umar al-Awsi, who found it in the documents of al-Gharighar, who was *mushrif* in 585 (1189–90). Ibn Abi Zar' gives a similar list, and I have preferred his number of potteries rather than the 888 in the printed edition of al-Jazna'i; *Rawd al-Qirtas*, p. 58.

of this manufacturing dynamism moved south across the Straits of Gibraltar to new centres such as Fes, Ribat al-Fath-Salé and Marrakesh, all of which expanded greatly at this time. It was in Andalusi cities that the Almoravids and Almohads recruited master craftsmen for their building projects, indicating the existence of substantial professional corps of master builders, carpenters, engravers and marble carvers among others. The movement south of these artisans then stimulated the development of these skills in the Maghrib and encouraged the formation of cohorts of skilled craftsmen in Marrakesh, Fes and other western Maghribi locations. The forced transportation of skilled Andalusi Christians to the Maghrib bolstered this process. Towns and their immediate hinterlands also supplied unskilled labour for the numerous construction projects undertaken by the Almoravids and Almohads in Seville, Marrakesh and Ribat al-Fath among other places, which must have greatly stimulated local economies by providing paid employment to large numbers of people, sometimes for years at a time.

Meanwhile, as Portugal, León-Castile and Aragon pushed on the northern reaches of Muslim power, taking Toledo, Lisbon and Saragossa and raiding into the hinterland of Córdoba, the centre of Muslim economic power in al-Andalus shifted south to Seville, Granada and the southern ports of Málaga and Almería. The latter city, above all, flourished between the eleventh and thirteenth centuries as the foremost industrial centre in al-Andalus, famed for its silk textiles of myriad kinds from shimmering diaphanous veils to brocades and taffetas.[59] In addition to silks, Almería was an important centre for the production of copper utensils and marble objects, including luxurious basins and tombstones, a handful of which found their way to Gao-Sané in West Africa.[60] It was therefore a great economic loss as well as a political embarrassment when Almería was captured in 1147 by Alfonso VII of León-Castile and held for a decade.

Although the sources are rarely explicit about the organisation of labour or who exactly participated in it, workers in each trade or craft were generally gathered into more or less formal associations or guilds, and it was normal for skills to be transmitted down the generations through apprenticeships within the family or with trusted friends and colleagues. Each profession had its masters (*ʿurafaʾ*, *shuyukh*) from whom a head would be chosen to deal with issues of quality control, production and taxation. Reputable master craftsmen might also be called upon to work with the market inspector (*muḥtasib*) as an *amīn* to ensure good practice in their trade or craft. The hierarchy of

[59] al-Idrisi, *Opus Geographicum*, fasc. 5–8, p. 562.
[60] See p. 38, above.

professions was headed by literate and religious employments, followed by prestigious and highly skilled crafts, moving down through the ranks to the 'dirty' trades such as the tanners, potters and lime makers, whose premises were located on the urban fringe to avoid pollution. The urban labour force also worked in service industries as policemen and prison guards, legal witnesses, domestic servants, bath-house attendants and masseurs, water carriers, grave diggers and much else besides.

Although men dominated most urban professions, women and children were an essential part of the workforce as occasional references to their activities in manufacturing, agriculture and the marketplace show. In the case of agriculture and cottage industries, whole families were involved in production: the labour-intensive Andalusi silk industry is a case in point. From as early as the tenth century, women are depicted carrying silk worm eggs in small pouches in their armpits or close to their stomachs to keep the incubating eggs warm, while children were used to unravel the fine silk fibres from the cocoons after they had been loosened by a dousing in hot water.[61] When it came to dealing with people, there were often parallel female professions to serve women such as female bath attendants, servants, hairdressers, secretaries, prison officers and even collectors of taxes on prostitutes. There were also some professions exclusive to women such as midwifery and wet-nursing.[62]

Other industries where women are often mentioned are textile and food production, although the consensus is that they generally worked within the home rather than in more public workshops. Their presence in public areas whether as producers or sellers could generate antagonism and, as we saw above, Ibn 'Abdun criticised the presence in the marketplace of female brocade makers, whom he rated as little better than prostitutes, in his *ḥisba* manual from Almoravid Seville.[63] This points to the tension between economic and social realities and religio-legal paradigms of appropriate male–female inhabitation of public urban space. It is interesting, however, that this complaint should arise in the Almoravid century when the relaxed attitude of the Sanhaja towards women participating in public life may have offered economic opportunities to Andalusi women, resisted and resented by their male counterparts.

[61] Shatzmiller, 'Aspects of women's participation', p. 39; Lagardère, *Campagnes*, p. 394; Constable, *Trade and Traders in Muslim Spain*, p. 174.

[62] Shatzmiller, 'Aspects of women's participation', pp. 41–5.

[63] Ibn 'Abdun, *Séville Musulmane*, p. 105; Shatzmiller, 'Aspects of women's participation', p. 48.

Traders, Trade Routes and Commodities

In one sense almost everyone was a trader, selling local agricultural produce or their own manufactures, but the larger-scale acquisition and circulation of urban manufactures and agricultural surpluses was in the hands of the mercantile profession, described as given to trickery in order to make a profit by Ibn Khaldun, but nonetheless vital to economic wellbeing.[64] The commercial sector encompassed a vast range of individuals from peddlers to brokers, agents, wholesalers and merchants working in regional commerce and the more well-known and glamorous long-distance trade that linked the Islamic west to the Islamic east, sub-Saharan Africa and Latin Christendom. Even pilgrims heading to Mecca for the *ḥajj* joined in, funding their journey, which could take years, by buying and selling along the way.

Due to the frequent emphasis in the sources on luxury trades, it is easy to underestimate the importance of local and regional exchanges of bulky, cheap commodities such as grain, but this was the real bread and butter of trade rather than gold, slaves, spices and perfumes. Even in the case of the Almoravids who benefited greatly from their access to West African gold, the initial impetus to control the trans-Saharan trade reflected their need for grain and West African demand for salt rather than a lust for gold *per se*.[65] Moreover, most high-value commodities were traded alongside more humble items, creating mixed cargoes in which some items were conveyed for relatively short distances and others the length of the Mediterranean or the breadth of the great Saharan sea of sand.

The lands controlled by the Almoravids and the Almohads in al-Andalus and the Maghrib stood at the intersection of the European, Middle Eastern and African commercial zones. Although some merchants plied their trade across the Muslim–Christian frontier regions in Iberia, the two dominant trade systems that linked these zones were the maritime Mediterranean system, which included Andalusi and Maghribi Atlantic ports beyond the Straits of Gibraltar, and the trans-Saharan and North African caravan trails, which connected with Mediterranean sea routes at certain points such as Ceuta on the Straits. Both these systems considerably pre-dated the foundation of the Almoravid and Almohad empires, but experienced various alterations during this period in terms of the ports and routes used, the traders to be found along them and the commodities exchanged.[66] This reflected the same dynamics that affected the urban economy as a whole: the inexorable

[64] Ibn Khaldun, *Muqaddimah*, p. 300.
[65] McDougall, 'The Sahara reconsidered', p. 266.
[66] This section draws extensively on Constable, *Trade and Traders in Muslim Spain*.

pull factor represented by the new concentration of wealth in the western Maghrib and the push exerted by the Christian advance south in the Iberian peninsula. Internal political changes also played their role, as did factors such as the rise of new trading centres outside Islamic lands and fluctuating demand for various goods.

To begin with the Mediterranean maritime system, trade in this period followed well-established routes. Ships setting out from al-Andalus or the western Maghrib occasionally made a direct voyage to Alexandria, but a more normal pattern was either to island-hop via the Balearics and Sicily or to travel eastwards towards Ifriqiya and Egypt as close to the African coast as possible. Other smaller ships and boats simply sailed from southern al-Andalus to 'facing' Maghribi ports such as Arshgul, which served Tlemcen, or Oran, founded in 902–3 by Andalusi traders according to al-Bakri.[67] By way of example, when the Almohad official Ibn Jubayr set off to perform the pilgrimage in February 1182, he first sailed from Tarifa to Qasr Masmuda, then made the short land journey to the great port of Ceuta to take passage on a Genoese ship that sailed up the eastern seaboard of al-Andalus before striking out to Ibiza, Mallorca, Menorca, Sardinia, Sicily and Crete to reach Alexandria.[68]

The sea routes were quicker and less arduous than the land routes, but they were also seasonal, particularly in the case of longer journeys, since high winds and storms could prove lethal during the winter. There are many references to ships being wrecked, cargoes being lost and passengers being drowned. Ships carrying soldiers sometimes met the same fate with potentially dire consequences for campaigns. Ibn 'Idhari reports for 507 AH (1113–14) that:

> This year 500 vessels set out for the Christian lands of Europe, carrying 100,000 fighters including 1,500 horsemen and 50,000 militiamen. God sent a violent icy gale against them, drowning them all. The *ḥajj* ships and all the supply boats were also destroyed by that [storm].[69]

Ibn Jubayr experienced several storms at sea during his voyages to the east and back, and he was shipwrecked off Messina in Sicily on his way home. He gives a graphic account of the first storm he encountered:

> Early on the night of Wednesday [16 March 1182], the wind blew with violence upon us, throwing the sea into a turmoil and bringing rain and driving it with such force that it was like a shower of arrows . . . waves like mountains came upon us from every side.[70]

67 al-Bakri, *Description de l'Afrique*, Arabic text, p. 70; French text, p. 144.

68 Ibn Jubayr, *Travels*, pp. 25–7.

69 Ibn 'Idhari, *al-Bayan*, vol. 4, p. 51.

70 Ibn Jubayr, *Travels*, p. 27.

As the storm continued it tore down the sails and broke the ship's mast, leaving the crew and passengers praying desperately for salvation. With the advantage of hindsight, Ibn Jubayr observed that spring and autumn provided the best balance of winds and fair weather,[71] and that 'there should not be a reckless venturing forth in the months of winter as we did'.[72]

The formation of the Almoravid and Almohad empires did not dramatically alter the routes across the Mediterranean, but it may have modified them. Constable suggests that the higher levels of political centralisation under these dynasties impacted upon the number of ports involved in trade. Although it is difficult to be sure due to the sometimes patchy nature of our information, both the Almoravids and the Almohads seem to have preferred to channel trade through a limited number of larger ports in order to tax it more easily, in contrast to the more diffuse pattern evident during the Ta'ifa period when rival Ta'ifa rulers and their Maghribi counterparts competed for a slice of the Mediterranean trade.[73] Secondly, there was a shift of commerce towards southeastern Andalusi ports, such as Dénia and Almería, and ports on the Straits of Gibraltar that connected the 'two shores' of the Almoravid and Almohad empires, such as Algeciras and Tarifa, which both regimes used to disembark Maghribi troops.

On the southern Maghribi side of the Straits, Ceuta rose to its greatest prominence at this time, a factor that later made it a target for the commercially minded Portuguese who captured it in 1415. Tangier prospered as a subsidiary commercial port to Ceuta, while troops crossing the Straits were generally transported through Qasr al-Majaz, also known as Qasr Masmuda (modern Ksar el-Seghir), Ibn Jubayr's landing point. These Straits ports were connected in a westerly direction to a small line of Atlantic ports, including Asila and, most importantly, the new Almohad coastal base of Ribat al-Fath/al-Mahdiyya adjacent to Salé on the estuary of the Bu Regreg River, which was temporarily captured for its strategic and commercial value by the Castilians in 1260 as the Almohad empire contracted. To the east, Ceuta and Tangier were connected to the long string of Mediterranean harbours and ports that stretched along the Maghribi coast towards Ifriqiya, including Arshgul, Oran, Algiers and Bijaya.

This latter port gained considerable importance in the eleventh century as a result of its re-foundation by the Zirid Banu Hammad who left their inland capital, Qal'at Bani Hammad, to settle there in 1090. Although outside Almoravid territory, Bijaya was a valuable trading partner and a frequent

[71] Ibn Jubayr, *Travels*, p. 326.
[72] Ibid., p. 332.
[73] Constable, *Trade and Traders in Muslim Spain*, p. 32.

destination for traders from the empire. During 'Abd al-Mu'min's 1153 campaign eastwards, it was incorporated into the Almohad empire and it became the governorial seat of a *sayyid* in 1160 in recognition of its commercial and political status. Bijaya's burgeoning commercial role is shown by the fact that it was the chosen landing point of Ibn Ghaniya when he crossed from Mallorca with his Almoravid army in 1184, and its unwary inhabitants seem to have been surprised to find that the new arrivals were warriors (*ghuzāt*) rather than Mallorcan merchants.[74] In the heartland of Ifriqiya, there were also changes triggered by the demise of Qayrawan and al-Mahdiyya as commercial centres. In their place, Tunis, adjacent to ancient Carthage, emerged as the paramount city and port of Ifriqiya, a status it retained under the Hafsid successors of the Almohads who made it their capital and thereby laid the foundations for the transformation of Ifriqiya into Tunisia.

While the establishment of the Berber empires did not radically change the east–west routes from al-Andalus to Egypt and the Levant, the eleventh and twelfth centuries did witness momentous developments in the maritime commercial sphere as a result of the rise of the northern Italian city-states. Prior to the eleventh century, the Mediterranean had been a Muslim-dominated sea, but the Crusades (1096–1292) marked the beginning of a phase in which the Italian city-states and the Catalans gradually became more prominent in Mediterranean trade. During the second half of the twelfth century, the Genoese, Pisans and Catalans virtually replaced Muslim and Jewish shippers throughout the western Mediterranean and established important trading colonies in several Muslim ports, linking them to the north in new ways.[75]

The other great commercial system straddling the territories of the Almoravids and Almohads was the trans-Saharan and Maghribi caravan network, which intersected with the routes of pilgrim caravans to Mecca and provided an alternative to sea voyages when travelling in winter. Geographers often organised their descriptions of North Africa according to the coastal (*sāḥiliyya*) routes and the more southerly desertic (*ṣaḥrāwiyya*) routes. Like the maritime Mediterranean network, the trans-Saharan trade had been in operation for centuries before the emergence of the Almoravids from the Sahara, facilitated by the introduction of the camel to North Africa in late Roman times. From the outset, it had been a Berber enterprise in which the Sufri Kharijites of Sijilmasa and the extensive Ibadi Kharijite trading network of the central Maghrib and southern Ifriqiya played a major role. Many of the Kharijites were Zanata Berbers with whom the Sanhaja of the western

[74] Ibn 'Idhari, *al-Bayan*, vol. 4, p. 247.
[75] Constable, *Trade and Traders in Muslim Spain*, pp. 42–4, 108–11.

Figure 5.1 The ruins of Sijilmasa

Sahara competed for resources, and this economic incentive played its part in motivating the Lamtuna to follow Ibn Yasin and extend their control over the desert.

There were a handful of routes across the Sahara whose existence was determined by the siting of wells and oases. A western set of routes led from the western Sudan up to Azuggi, the Almoravids' Saharan base, then on to Aghmat and Marrakesh, or from Awdaghust to Sijilmasa, after which caravans travelled north towards Fes and the Straits of Gibraltar or northeast up the other side of the Middle Atlas to Tlemcen. Several inland towns and cities, including Rustamid Tahart and the Zirid centres of Ashir and Qalʿat Bani Hammad, then serviced the caravan trade during its passage on towards Qayrawan in Ifriqiya. A more central route linked Tadmakka to Wargla, the Jarid (southern Tunisia) and Ifriqiya, and an eastern route connected Kuwar to Zawila in the Fezzan (southern Libya), which then branched back west to Tripoli or east to Egypt.[76] Saharan pilgrims such as Yahya b. Ibrahim followed these same routes on their long journey to Mecca.

Over the centuries, the weight of traffic on different trans-Saharan routes varied with climatic and political fluctuations in the desert and beyond. Water

[76] Brett, 'Ifriqiya as a market for Saharan trade', p. 350.

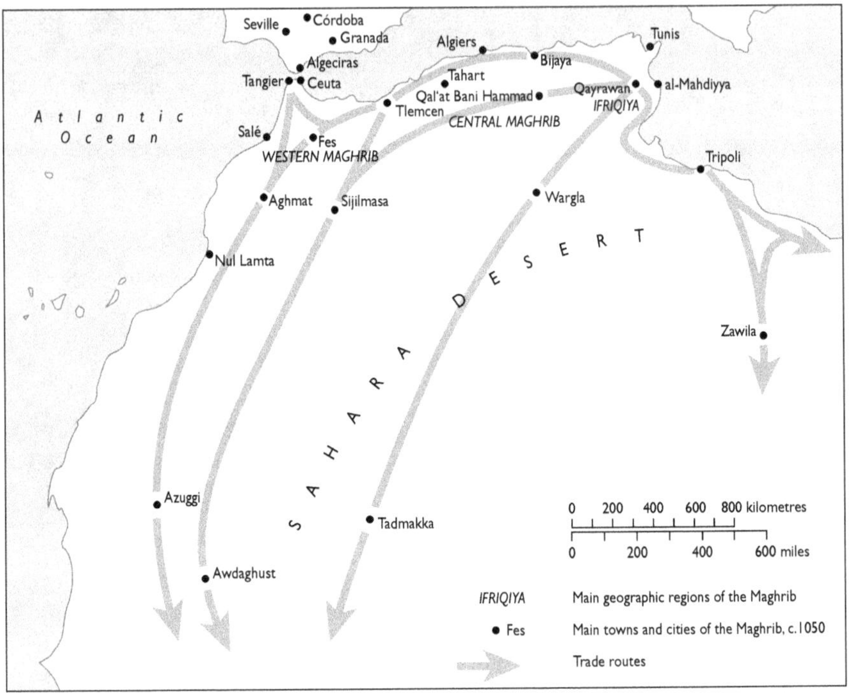

Figure 5.2 The Maghribi and trans-Saharan trade routes, *c.* 1050

was always the most vital factor, but the security of persons and property also figured heavily in the calculations of the trans-Saharan caravaneers. As we have already seen, the desire of the Lamtuna to control the desert had a commercial dimension and, as the Almoravid empire grew, the western Saharan routes that the Lamtuna and their Masufa and Lamta allies controlled and protected rose in significance. A symbiotic relationship existed between the flourishing western trans-Saharan trade, the urbanisation undertaken by the Almoravids and perpetuated by the Almohads, and the shift in regional economic and demographic weight to the western Maghrib. As Sijilmasa, Marrakesh and Fes became major cities, they developed from entrepôts for the onward conveyance of products to and from west Africa into consumers of a wide range of goods and, by the end of the Almohad era, manufacturers and exporters too, as the 3,000-odd textile workshops and 469 *funduqs* in the list of Fasi establishments quoted above implies.

Ifriqiya, at the eastern end of the Almohad empire, remained another destination for trans-Saharan caravans and the connection point between the western Maghrib and the Middle East, despite the decline of Qayrawan and the disruption caused in the eleventh to twelfth centuries by Arab tribal migrations, the collapse of the Zirid polity, and the Norman conquest of the Ifriqiyan coast. As in the agricultural sector of the economy, however, debates have raged as to the impact of the migrations of the Banu Hilal and Banu Sulaym on the trans-Saharan trade to Ifriqiya. At one stage the assumption was that they had disrupted and destroyed it, but the consensus has shifted towards seeing trade as moving away from Qayrawan towards a variety of other Ifriqiyan destinations with a period of intense disruption in the late twelfth to early thirteenth centuries occasioned by the activities of the Banu Ghaniya in alliance with Arab and Berber tribes, rather than by the eleventh-century Hilali migrants alone.[77]

Although it was of lesser importance to the Maghrib-centred Berber empires than to their Andalusi predecessors, it is important to note the continued existence of trade across the Christian–Muslim marches in al-Andalus. Tariff lists (*portazgos*) and charters (*fueros*) from many Christian towns allude to goods from the sophisticated, highly developed Muslim south.[78] This land trade had flourished during the tenth century when the many manufactures of al-Andalus travelled north in exchange for furs and slaves, but the levels of land trade suffered during the eleventh century as the frontier became more dangerous and raiding intensified. Moreover, as the Christian kingdoms conquered sizable tracts of Muslim land, they acquired populations of skilled Muslim subjects, the Mudéjars, able to produce commodities for the internal domestic market. Finally, the establishment of Genoese and Catalan merchants in Andalusi and Maghribi ports meant that commodities and manufactures from Muslim areas could be imported to Iberia by sea, reducing the need for exchange across the militarised marches.

The merchants who plied these maritime and land routes counted Muslims, Jews and Christians among their number, although it was Muslim and Jewish merchants who dominated the Andalusi and Maghribi trades at the beginning of the Almoravid era. They maintained connections with fellow merchants across the Mediterranean and the Islamic world, usually, although not always, working in partnership with their own co-religionists.[79] The Jews, in particular, formed a dynamic and extensive trading community with family members in a number of ports and widespread connections from the Saharan fringe to the Iberian marches, Egypt and even India. The Jewish mercantile community included itinerant pedlars, travelling commercial agents and wealthy sedentary merchants, with young men often starting their

77 Brett, 'Ifriqiya as a market for Saharan trade', p. 360; Thiry, 'Sahara libyen', pp. 78–80.
78 Constable, *Trade and Traders in Muslim Spain*, pp. 44–7.
79 Ibid., pp. 57–9.

careers on the road before becoming less peripatetic, established merchants as they grew older.

The Genizah correspondence shows the vitality and enormous scope of this community as well as giving many personal insights into the day-to-day worries of eleventh- and twelfth-century merchants, from the late arrival of ships to the problems caused by political changes. One famous letter that encapsulates several of these dimensions is a letter from a Jewish merchant in Fes to his partner in Almería, written in 1140, that gives instructions about orders and purchases of scales, silk garments, gold, lac, brazilwood and alum. It also expresses the writer's worry about the trustworthiness of a local Jewish agent called Yishaq b. Barukh, his deep sadness about the recent death of a rabbi, as well as referring to the temporary slowing of trade caused by the rise of the Almohads in the Sus valley to the south.[80] Letters such as these depict a close-knit mercantile community, handling an array of commodities, and communicating regularly over long distances about business and more personal matters.

Although we have less information about them, Andalusi and Maghribi Muslims were also extensively involved with regional and long-distance trade. Despite some disdain for commerce, it was quite honourable to be a merchant, a career undertaken after all by the Prophet Muhammad himself, and some religious scholars listed in biographical dictionaries made a livelihood by trade to supplement the sometimes meagre rewards for scholarship. The number of Andalusi merchant-scholars recorded in biographical works fell in the Almoravid era, but this may reflect a reduction in scholarly travel east as other sources show that many types of Muslim merchant, including easterners coming west, remained active in trade.[81] Numerous Maghribi ports were frequented or even colonised by Andalusi Muslim merchants and, as mentioned above, the trans-Saharan trade was dominated by Zanata Berber communities, often of a Kharijite religious persuasion, who formed an extensive trading network located between the fertile coastal strip and the Sahara. Although one of the results of the political disruption in Ifriqiya seems to have been the contraction of this previously vibrant sectarian network, other Muslim and Jewish traders stepped into the breach.

One group that appears not to have participated in local or long-distance trade to any notable extent is the indigenous Arabised Christian minority to be found in al-Andalus and Ifriqiya, a situation that can perhaps be attributed

[80] Goitein, *Letters of Medieval Jewish Traders*, pp. 264–8; Bennison and Gallego, 'Jewish trading in Fes', pp. 41, 47–9.

[81] Constable, *Trade and Traders in Muslim Spain*, pp. 83–5.

to the low social status of the merchant profession in some Christian circles.[82] However, this is not a wholly satisfactory explanation: although merchants were considered of low status in Castile, the situation in Aragon, which included Barcelona with its active Catalan merchant community, was rather different. Indeed, the main change in the composition of the mercantile cohort in the eleventh to twelfth centuries was the steady growth of a foreign Christian mercantile presence in al-Andalus and North Africa as the Catalans and the inhabitants of the Italian city-states, most notably Genoa, captured a growing proportion of the Andalusi and Maghribi trades.

This change was fostered by the Almohads who were willing, if not eager, to make trade treaties with Genoa from at least 1161. Consequently, foreign Christian mercantile enclaves called *funduq*s were established in many coastal ports, including Bijaya, Tunis and al-Mahdiyya. Although the term *funduq* usually means a hostelry or warehouse, Genoese, Catalan and Pisan *funduq*s quickly became entire urban quarters with chapels and breweries as well as storage units and accommodation for merchants.[83] The importance of this trade to the Genoese is shown by the fact that in 1182, 37 per cent of the city's trade was with Almohad territories in North Africa.[84] Inland trade, however, remained the preserve of indigenous Muslim and Jewish merchants who sold on commodities to the Genoese and other foreign merchants in the coastal ports where their *funduq*s were located.

The commodities traded by these groups of merchants were very varied in nature and value as the famous list of the items that the Almoravid amir Yusuf b. Tashfin reputedly gifted to his cousin Abu Bakr in the early 1070s shows:

> The bulk of [the gift] was: 25,000 *dīnār*s in gold coin (*dhahab al-'ayn*), 70 horses of which 25 had gold-decorated bridles, 70 swords of which 20 were decorated with gold and 50 undecorated, 20 sets of spurs embellished with gold, 150 excellent male and female mules, 100 bleached (*maqṣūra*) turbans, 400 [made] from Susi material, 100 cloaks, 200 hooded outer robes (*burnūs*) including black, white and red ones, 1,000 lengths [of cloth] the colour of pomegranate seeds, 100 lengths of Huéscan (Ushkari) [cloth], 700 white and dyed robes (*kisā'*), 200 linen shawls of different colours and types, 252 tailored gowns (*jubba*) from fine woollen cloth, 70 hooded capes of fine woollen cloth, 7 large flags including one embroidered banner, 20 virgin slave girls, 151 eunuchs/servants, 10 *raṭl*s of green

[82] Constable, *Trade and Traders in Muslim Spain*, pp. 62–3.
[83] See Abulafia, 'Christian merchants in the Almohad cities'.
[84] Ibid., p. 253.

> aloeswood (*'ūd*), a *raṭl* of precious *ghālī* perfume, 5 packages (*nawāfij*) of fine musk, 2 *raṭls* of good ambergris, 15 *raṭls* of *nadd* perfume, and too much cattle, livestock, wheat and barley to mention.[85]

The amounts in this list may have become exaggerated over time and its items amended, but it provides a very good sense of the range of luxury goods that elites wished to acquire from major manufacturing centres across the Islamic world, in addition to large amounts of meat, milk and grain from the countryside. Many of these items could only be procured in a few places and demand for them fuelled the long-distance trade that functioned in tandem with the local transfer of more basic items and staples.

At the top of the list is gold, an integral item in the trans-Saharan trade, which was acquired in West Africa from the Bambuk and Buré gold fields in exchange for rock salt mined at the various salt mines in the Sanhaja's desert domains.[86] West African gold had an international reputation in the medieval Islamic world for being both plentiful and relatively pure in its unrefined state, and it was therefore sought after for coinage as well as to decorate metal items and make jewellery.[87] Gold could be transported as dust, bullion, coin or jewellery, and legal opinions (*fatwās*) from Almoravid Marrakesh indicate the need to establish firm guidelines for the exchange of gold in different currencies and forms to ensure fairness and avoid illicit usurious profit-making.[88]

The next set of items on the list are the accoutrements of a warrior, fine horses and mules, and weapons, some intricately inlaid and decorated with gold, which were probably the product of Andalusi ateliers at this time. Although not mentioned in Yusuf's gift, another valuable Andalusi product was Córdoban leather, used for harnesses, saddles, shoes and other items, which was well known and prized in both Muslim and Christian areas. Twelfth-century geographers also mention Ghadamsi leather, sourced in Ghadames in modern Libya. Many fine metalwork and leather items were in high demand at courts where they formed an integral element in gifts granted

[85] This list is taken from *al-Hulal al-Mawshiyya*, pp. 27–8. A similar list appears in Ibn 'Idhari's *al-Bayan* (vol. 4, p. 22), and both are probably derived from a lost chronicle written by an Almoravid official called al-Sayrafi.

[86] See the classic 1950s work by Edward Bovill, *The Golden Trade of the Moors*.

[87] Messier points out that although West African gold was quite pure in its unrefined state (around 92 per cent), refined gold coinage from other areas was usually around 97 per cent pure, meaning that Almoravid *dīnārs* actually had a lower gold content than some other contemporary currencies despite their reputation for soundness. Messier, 'West African gold', pp. 36–7.

[88] Gómez-Rivas, *Islamization of Morocco*, pp. 59–65.

by rulers to favoured members of the elite, who might then circulate them to their own followers or sell them if circumstances required.

Textiles, which abound in the list, also featured in the normal patterns of gift-giving in medieval al-Andalus and North Africa, as well as having a huge range of other practical and decorative functions. They were by far the most heavily traded article throughout this period, with each region specialising in the weaving of different types of silk, cotton, linen and woollen fabric or garments, many dyed in rich colours using mineral or plant dyes. The Andalusis also excelled at imitating eastern fabrics such as Isfahani and Jurjani cloth from Iran. Although it is not possible to be sure of the origins of all the items in this gift, it certainly included fabric and garments from the Maghrib (turbans of Susi fabric and the typical Maghribi hooded outer robe, the *burnūs*) and al-Andalus (cloth from Huésca), with the possibility that some of the fine wool cloth (*milif*) mentioned may have come from further afield, given the possible derivation of the material's name from Amalfi.[89]

The most valuable textiles, represented by the embroidered banner, were Andalusi silks and brocades, which were not only exported to the Maghrib but also to Latin Christendom and the Islamic east. In addition to the brocades worked by women in Seville and other places that were available on the open market, rulers maintained their own textile ateliers to produce the richly embroidered calligraphic bands (*ṭirāz*) that formed another essential component of state gifts, as well as monarchical banners for ceremonial and military purposes.[90] The Andalusi silk textile trade reached its peak during the Almoravid and Almohad periods, but subsequently contracted as trading patterns changed: in post-Almohad Granada, Genoese buyers preferred to export raw silk to supply Italian workshops than purchase Muslim textiles.

Yusuf's gift also contained male and female slaves who were acquired from the caravans of slave traders or through war, raiding and capture on the frontiers between Muslim and non-Muslim lands, as mentioned in the previous chapter. The ethnic origin of slaves in any particular Islamic society reflected proximity to these frontiers and the perceived virtues, and thus monetary value, of different groups. The Malagan market inspector al-Saqati summarises Andalusi attitudes in the late eleventh to early twelfth centuries:

> They say that the Berber slave girl is for pleasure, the Christian is for preserving wealth, the Turk is for begetting children, the African is for wet-nursing, the Meccan is for singing, the Iraqi and the Circassian are for playing music. As for men, the Nubian is for guarding people and wealth,

[89] *al-Hulal al-Mawshiyya*, p. 27, n. 41.

[90] Bennison, 'Drums, banners and *baraka*', pp. 209–13.

> the African and the Armenian are for hard labour and service, the Turk and the Slav are for war and valour.[91]

The two main sources of slaves in al-Andalus and North Africa were the northern Christian territories and sub-Saharan Africa. In tenth-century al-Andalus, large numbers of Slavs (*ṣaqāliba*) were imported to serve as soldiers in the army of the Umayyad caliph ʿAbd al-Rahman III (r. 912–61). During the Ta'ifa era, however, the use of Slavic slave soldiers petered out and under the Maghribi dynasties Iberian Christian mercenaries, slaves and renegades, and sub-Saharan African slaves took their place. Male slaves also served in the capacity of household servants. A proportion of the boys enslaved were brutally castrated before crossing the Sahara to create eunuchs (*khiṣyān*) who were a permanent feature of royal Islamic households, including those of the Almoravids and Almohads, where they served as major-domos or chamberlains, as we saw in the last chapter.

In the case of women, many Christian girls from Navarre and the Basque country entered the Umayyad harem as war captives or through diplomatic exchanges. In Almoravid and Almohad times, warfare and raiding continued to generate a southward flow of northern Christian captives into the slave markets of al-Andalus, while slaves from Saharan and sub-Saharan Africa, many of whom were exported on to the Middle East, were brought north after raids in the Sahel. Al-Bakri remarks that one could purchase excellent black cooks and patissières in Awdaghust and voluptuous lighter-skinned girls as concubines, and his comments were quoted afresh in the *Kitab al-Istibsar* over a century later.[92] Muslims were not alone in raiding and enslaving captives, and Ibn Jubayr comments with indignation on the wretched sight of eighty Muslim men and women, who had been captured by Christian raiders, for sale in the slave market at Cape St Mark in Sardinia.[93]

The last set of commodities in Yusuf's gift are expensive perfumes, some of which were produced in al-Andalus, while others came from eastern Islamic lands. Among those listed, green aloeswood and ambergris, an oily scented substance secreted by sperm whales, were both local products, while *ghālī* or *ghāliya*, a perfume of musk and ambergris, came from the east and the best *nadd*, an incense made of aloeswood, ambergris, musk and frankincense, came from India. In addition to these expensive perfumes and aromatics, many plants produced essential oils or waters that were used for fragrancing the home

[91] al-Sakati, *Hisba*, pp. 49–50.
[92] al-Bakri, *Description de l'Afrique*, Arabic text, pp. 158–9; French text, pp. 300–1; *Kitab al-Istibsar*, pp. 215–16.
[93] Ibn Jubayr, *Travels*, p. 27.

and in cooking. Although not specifically mentioned in this gift list, spices were another valuable commodity. While saffron and cumin were produced in the region, as we have seen, cinnamon, pepper and cloves were imported from lands further east. Dyes such as Andalusi kermes (*qirmiz*) and Indian lac, red dyes produced from scale insects, and indigo were also much-traded items.

The more mundane items at the end of the list – grain and livestock – were traded according to demand and, in the case of grain, the vagaries of weather and the harvest. The grain trade was particularly fluid with al-Andalus, North Africa and Sicily exporting grain in times of surplus and importing it in periods of drought and crop failure. The vital role of grain and meat in feeding the population and the army meant that regimes kept a closer eye on the export of these staples than many other commodities to avert famine, distress and rebellion. As we shall see in the section below, modulating the grain market and avoiding swindles and sharp practice in the sale of grain, flour and bread was a major concern of the market inspector due to the critical importance of maintaining urban and military food supplies. Jurists also deliberated on the religious acceptability of exporting such essential items to the Christian 'enemy' as Christian raids intensified and more territory was lost to them, making such trades much more ideologically charged than the commerce in flamboyant luxuries.

The State's Role in the Economy

The Almoravid and Almohad governmental structures were small in comparison with those of the modern state, and they offered a more reduced range of services than we expect today. They did not need to fund universal healthcare or education, for example, but they were expected to provide security and a safe environment in which their subjects could live a prosperous (and pious) life, which required the maintenance of a substantial military machine, oversight of the market by means of market inspectors (*muḥtasib*s), and the appropriate adjudication of commercial disputes by judges. Rulers were also expected to offer gifts and charity regularly to certain groups in society, such as the *ʿulamāʾ* and the poor, as well as to circulate the benefits of power among the ruling elite, which was generally tax-exempt as in other Muslim societies.

In order to fulfil these roles, the state functioned as an extractive machine with a bureaucratic apparatus geared towards gathering revenues, storing them and disbursing a proportion of them, hence the use of the word *makhzan* (storehouse) for government in the western Maghrib and Weber's identification of this (non-European) type as a tributary state. The state's primary role in the economy were therefore tax or tribute collection, whether direct or by means of land grants. However, rulers were also involved in a range of other economic activities, such as the production of coinage and oversight of the market, direct participation in trade and agricultural development.

Islamic Taxation

Muslim rulers, the Almoravids and Almohads included, were entitled to collect the range of annual taxes sanctioned by the Shari'a from the subject population. Licit taxes included the alms tax (*ṣadaqa*, *zakāt*), the tithe (*'ushr*) on cereals and produce payable in kind, which varied between 10 per cent for crops watered naturally and 5 per cent for artificially irrigated crops, the tithe on livestock, called either *'ushr* or *zakāt*, a tithe on commercial products, imports and the minting of coins, the *kharāj* tax on land originally conquered and held by non-Muslims and the poll tax (*jizya*) on non-Muslim subjects. The ruler was also entitled to one-fifth (*khums*) of war booty and the produce of mines. He could also raise a tax called the *ma'ūna* to support a war effort, a levy that was meant to be extraordinary, but often became a regular imposition.

The Shari'a-approved tax regime presented Islamic rulers with a number of challenges: first, there were differing views on whether the state was entitled to collect and use alms, or whether they should be distributed directly to the poor and needy; secondly, it was a major task to assess land and produce and to enforce the collection of even canonical taxes across an empire, encouraging rulers to use indirect modes of taxation such as land grants; and, thirdly, the amount of canonical taxation collected rarely covered government expenses. As a result, these licit taxes were supplemented by a whole range of more controversial levies, commonly called *mukūs*, *maghārim* or *rusūm*, which covered tolls, gate taxes, sales duties and similar impositions.

Although he is speaking of Ayyubid Alexandria rather than the Almohad empire he had just left, Ibn Jubayr gives insight into the activities of customs officials in the late twelfth-century Muslim Mediterranean:

> All the Muslims [on the ship] were brought forward one by one, and their names and descriptions, together with the names of their countries recorded. Each was questioned as to what merchandise or money he had, that he might pay *zakāt*, without any enquiry as to what portion of it had been in their possession for a complete year and what had not . . . The Muslims were then ordered to take their belongings, and what remained of their provisions, to the shore, where there were attendants responsible for them and for carrying to the Customs all that they had brought ashore. There they were called one by one, and the possessions of each were produced. The Customs was packed to choking. All their goods, great and small, were searched and confusedly thrown together, while

> hands were thrust into their waistbands in search of what might be within.[94]

Ibn Jubayr goes on to say that many people lost their possessions in the chaos. His disapproving report points to a number of things: the legitimisation of duties as *zakāt*; the illicit extension of the tithe to all items, regardless of whether the tax had been paid before, that is, on items owned for a complete year, or whether they were provisions for the journey rather than merchandise; and the rapacity of officials and their humiliating treatment of the new arrivals.

Agricultural producers were also keenly aware which taxes were religiously licit and which were not, and the excessive non-Qur'anic taxation levied by the Ta'ifa kings, including a poll tax on Muslims, had been a factor in Andalusi appeals to the Almoravids, who had proclaimed their intention to only levy canonical taxes. Although this seems to have been their policy for many decades, in the long run the amir was forced to reintroduce other taxes to fund his perpetual campaigns against the Almohads and defence of the Andalusi frontier. This enabled the Almohads to make similar assertions about their commitment to levying only canonical taxes, although they had slightly greater scope to define what was canonical due to the fact that they had theoretically dispensed with Maliki law in favour of the legal interpretations of the *mahdī* and his Mu'minid caliphs.[95] However, like their predecessors, they ultimately found it impossible to fund their activities solely by canonical taxation and therefore levied other taxes as well.

After the Christian conquest of eastern al-Andalus in the thirteenth century, the Muslim population tried again to limit taxes to those endorsed by the Shari'a and insisted to their new Christian masters that the customary tithe was the only tax they should have to pay.[96] Farmers in this region also attempted to use the new circumstances pertaining after the Christian conquest to end 'abuses' of various kinds, such as the assessment of tax liability before the harvest of a particular crop and its collection in cash rather than kind, which often obligated farmers to take out loans against an uncertain future crop. Such appeals strongly suggest that many taxes had previously been gathered in cash and that mixed economies operated in both the Andalusi and Maghribi provinces of the Almoravid and Almohad empires. Tribute gathered in kind filled *makhzan* storehouses, while revenues collected in coin were used to pay those soldiers and officials who received salaries.

Although some tribes might have functioned as more or less self-sufficient

94 Ibn Jubayr, *Travels*, pp. 31–2.

95 Buresi and El Aallaoui, *Governing the Empire*, pp. 176–9.

96 Benhsain-Mesmoudi, Guichard and Domenech, 'Biens sultaniens', p. 601.

economic entities, the economic relationship between the state and rural producers, including tribesmen, was often much closer and, in parts of the Maghrib, became more intrusive during this era. As the first regime to directly rule over large territories on both sides of the Straits, the Almoravids had the capacity to form an over-arching governmental system operating from Córdoba to Sijilmasa. Like the bureaucracy as a whole, the Almoravid fiscal administration relied heavily on the recruitment of Andalusi officials, who were instrumental to the incorporation of the western Maghrib into a more homogeneous tax system predicated on Maliki norms rather than on the decisions of individual chiefs and leaders. Although each major city had an Almoravid Sanhaja governor who had overall responsibility for fiscal as well as political and military matters, direct oversight for financial affairs seems to have been in the hands of an official called a *mushrif* (overseer) who was often of civilian Andalusi background.

An unknown proportion of Almoravid tax collection was, however, devolved down to Sanhaja amirs by means of land grants that entitled the holder to a share of the usufruct of the territories named in the grant, an institution frequently used in Islamic lands.

Land Grants

Although a system of land grants (*iqṭāʿ*, *iqṭāʿāt*), sometimes compared with feudalism, did become prevalent in the Seljuk empire in the Islamic east during this era, Islamic land grants were qualitatively different to feudalism because they denoted a temporary right to the usufruct of the granted territory not an heritable estate and the grant-holder generally resided in town and dispatched tax collectors rather than becoming personally involved in the running of his estate. The majority of *iqṭāʿāt* were granted to military men who were obliged to bring a certain number of men to war in return, but members of the ruling family, including women, and senior civil servants could also receive land grants. They were, in effect, a form of devolved administration and taxation by which the ruler remunerated his army and servants, but avoided the cost and labour of having to collect taxes from every district. This could work well, but there were dangers in the form of grantees over-exploiting their holdings and rulers being left with insufficient directly levied revenue in their coffers. Many types of state land grant existed in the Islamic west over time with a plethora of names – *muqaṭṭaʿa*, *iqṭāʿ*, *inzāl*, *sihām* – although it is often unclear exactly what such terms meant to grantees and to those tilling the land. The relationship between such non-heritable grants and private aristocratic estates is just as vague.

In the Maghrib, it is likely that private estates and land grants were not that common because tribal land rights pertained across much of the region and the organisation and distribution of resources tended to be more egalitarian where this was the case. That being said, there are vague indications that the Almoravids and their predecessors did exercise some control over land and its usufruct, and made allocations to their military commanders in the Maghrib. The *Hulal al-Mawshiyya* describes Yusuf b. Tashfin augmenting his army with Saharan tribes around 1077 to whom he 'granted provinces (*a'māl*)', presumably in the newly conquered environs of Tlemcen and Fes, while paying their leaders with assignments of revenue (*mahammāt al-ashghāl*) from which 'they gained great wealth'.[97] Later on, the Ta'ifa kings of Seville and Granada exiled to Aghmat may have been allocated estates rather than monetary pensions to support themselves.[98]

In al-Andalus, the holding of aristocratic estates had a long tradition, such estates are often called *ḍiya'* (sing. *ḍay'a*) to distinguish them from villages of free proprietors (*qarya, qurā*), while the personal estates or villas of the Umayyads around Córdoba were known as *munyāt*, and estates to bring marginal land into cultivation in eastern al-Andalus were termed *raḥalāt.*[99] Sometimes land was acquired in a coldly calculating way: in Valencia such heavy taxes were imposed upon peasants that they abandoned their land enabling the rapacious Ta'ifa amirs Mubarak and Muzaffar to appropriate it. The destitute peasants then returned to work on it as sharecroppers on the amir's terms.[100] In the century prior to the imposition of Almoravid rule, land concessions began to be made by the 'Amirid ministers of the last Umayyad caliphs and then by Ta'ifa rulers. In Granada, the Sanhaja and Zanata amirs recruited by the Zirids competed for good land grants (*inzālāt*) and their bitter squabbles over their allocation formed the backdrop to the assassination of Joseph b. Naghrila in 1066.[101]

Many exploited their grants mercilessly, levying much more than the canonical 10 per cent (*'ushr*) owed as tax, and their rapacity was one of the causes of popular disgruntlement against the Zirids expressed in complaints to Yusuf b. Tashfin about Zirid 'tyranny'.[102] Nonetheless, the Almoravids confirmed many such land concessions when they entered the peninsula in the 1080s, and part of Yusuf b. Tashfin's appeal to Zirid courtiers apparently

97 *al-Hulal al-Mawshiyya*, p. 33.
98 Lagardère, *Campagnes*, p. 39.
99 Ibid., pp. 19–20.
100 Ibid., pp. 32–3.
101 Tibi, *The Tibyan*, p. 75.
102 Kennedy, *Muslim Spain and Portugal*, p. 167.

lay in his promises to them of 'rich estates (*inzālāt*), large sums of money (*mathāqīl*) and high positions'.[103] As the Almoravids consolidated their rule in al-Andalus by ousting one Ta'ifa ruler after another from the 1090s onwards, they sold off some land for the benefit of the public treasury and reallocated land grants to their own amirs.[104] The *Hulal al-Mawshiyya* states that:

> [The Almoravids] did not give a cavalryman more than 5 *dīnār*s a month along with expenses and fodder for his mount [but] they rewarded those who showed their nobility and courage with control of land whose revenues they profited from.[105]

Such vague and brief comments, however, leave a large margin for interpretation and could denote governorships rather than land grants.[106] 'Ali b. Yusuf's subsequent re-appropriation of land grants has been taken to indicate that many had been made by his father,[107] but it is not clear whether Ibn 'Idhari is actually referring to land grants (*iqṭā'*), as opposed to salaries (*a'ṭā'*), in the passage concerned.[108]

When the Almohads supplanted the Almoravids, they centralised the administration of their empire more thoroughly and frequently circulated governorships and other administrative positions to reduce provincial autonomy, a key feature of which was non-remittance of revenues to the centre. In order to regularise and increase tax receipts, 'Abd al-Mu'min ordered a census of his North African territories, a vast area stretching from modern Morocco to Libya, whose inhabitants were henceforth required to pay *kharāj* on the two-thirds of land deemed to be productive.[109] Like their predecessors, Almohad governors (*wālī*, *'āmil*) had a range of responsibilities that could well have included tax collection and salary payments. Below the governor, teams of officials also called *'ummāl* administered the Almohad tax system. It is not clear whether these teams were headed by a *mushrif* in keeping with previous Almoravid practice or not. The term does appear in chronicles, but it is non-existent in extant thirteenth-century appointment documents.[110]

103 Tibi, *The Tibyan*, p. 153.
104 Lagardère, *Campagnes*, pp. 39–40.
105 *al-Hulal al-Mawshiyya*, p. 82.
106 Lagardère, *Campagnes*, p. 47.
107 Ibid.
108 Ibn 'Idhari, *al-Bayan*, vol. 4, p. 88.
109 Huici Miranda, *Historia política*, pp. 193, 215–16; Buresi and El Aallaoui, *Governing the Empire*, p. 178.
110 Buresi and El Aallaoui, *Governing the Empire*, pp. 174–5. The authors point out that we should be wary of seeing Almohad government in terms of precise offices with set titles since some of the titles used in the appointment documents (*taqādīm*) they reviewed were interchangeable.

However denominated, financial officials were responsible for maintaining the registers of taxes due and revenues received and were, on occasion, summoned to meet with the caliph in Marrakesh or in other regional centres with their accounts. Unfortunately, the Almohad registers are not extant, but it is obvious from the pages of Ibn 'Idhari's chronicle that audits did occur and could lead to great consternation among provincial financial administrators who had perhaps syphoned off a proportion of the revenues for their personal benefit or imposed illicit taxes in their areas. Conversely, the caliph's concern to ensure financial probity could be exploited by courtiers or ill-wishers to attack their rivals by making accusations of theft from the public purse.

An incident of this kind befell the historian Yusuf b. 'Umar, who had served as the secretary of the Almohad caliph Ya'qub al-Mansur and become manager of some *makhzan* revenues and royal land grants in the Seville area under his son, Muhammad al-Nasir. When the governorship of Seville was transferred to a new individual, Ibn 'Umar was accused of financial misdemeanours, probably as part of a wider attempt to discredit the previous governor. He was summoned and imprisoned, but exonerated of any wrongdoing by the caliph after an investigation. Ibn 'Idhari quotes Ibn 'Umar's own account of the frightening situation he found himself in as he travelled towards Marrakesh:

> When I reached the encampment, one of the amir's trusted servants met me with a unit of cavalry and foot soldiers who surrounded me and my companions. He took possession of all the loads that had arrived for the ruler and he sequestered my things hoping that there would be proof of my wrongdoing in them . . . he took everything from me and appropriated my personal effects and all the containers, records, specie, and other things my dependants were riding with. I arrived under guard with all of that at the financial office (*dār al-ishrāf*) and there I remained imprisoned for three days.[111]

Luckily an investigation proved Ibn 'Umar innocent and he was released by order of the caliph, along with all his effects. However, their appropriation, albeit temporary, reminds us that the disgrace and dispossession of wealthy courtiers and military commanders could also be a lucrative pursuit for the monarch.

The Almohads also used land grants, called *sihām* or *iqṭā'*, to support the royal Mu'minid clan and military commanders, and remunerate courtiers.

[111] Ibn 'Idhari, *al-Bayan*, vol. 4, p. 323.

However, the more highly centralised character of Almohad government meant that the state kept a close eye on such grants through its officials, enabling them to be reallocated or returned to central government use as desired. The most famous and frequently quoted mention of Almohad land grants occurs in the context of Almohad recruitment of the so-called Ghuzz from the Middle East, who were offered both land grants (*iqṭāʿāt*) and salaries paid monthly, in contrast to the usual quarterly payment of military salaries, on the grounds that the Almohads already had access to substantial landed wealth as natives of the region. This was a lucrative privilege: the Andalusi villages in a grant made to one such military adventurer, Shaʿban al-Misri, were said to have yielded 9,000 gold *dīnār*s per annum.[112]

Another major aspect of the state's role in the economy was its monopoly over the minting of coinage (*sikka*). The amount of currency in circulation and its type was thus controlled by the state, which also levied duties on gold, silver and copper brought to the mints for striking. Many historians have noted that the Almoravid and Almohad empires benefited from their access to sub-Saharan gold. This was particularly true for the Almoravids, who began to mint gold coins in Sijilmasa shortly after their conquest of that city and Awdaghust in the southern Sahara in the mid-1050s. The production of gold coinage in the Maghrib took off under Yusuf b. Tashfin, who authorised the striking of Almoravid *dīnār*s in Aghmat, then later in Marrakesh, Fes, Tlemcen and Nul Lamta. As Messier notes, this proliferation of mints was a stark contrast to previous Umayyad and Fatimid practices,[113] although it did hark back to the practice of the Idrisids two centuries before.

The Almoravids began to strike gold coins in al-Andalus in 1096 in their regional capital Seville, and in the first decade of ʿAli b. Yusuf's reign, the minting of Andalusi Almoravid *dīnār*s peaked, greatly outstripping production in the Maghrib, a fact that Messier attributes to the extensive range of imports and exports in Andalusi commerce in contrast to the transit-oriented character of trade in North Africa.[114] In total, the number of Almoravid mints is estimated to have been twenty-eight, thirteen of which were in the Maghrib and fifteen in al-Andalus. Almoravid gold *dīnār*s percolated throughout the Mediterranean world and, for a time, they were the most widely used and copied gold currency in Muslim and Christian areas due to their abundance and stability. These high-value coins were supplemented by silver *qirāṭ*s and *dirhams* as well as smaller copper coins for everyday use.

112 al-Marrakushi, *Muʿjib*, pp. 414–15; Lagardère, *Campagnes*, pp. 48–9.
113 Messier, 'Quantitative analysis', pp. 108–10.
114 Ibid., pp. 115–17.

The Almohads also minted gold coins, but in much lower quantities than the Almoravids. In the early Almoravid era, the average amount of gold minted per annum was 1,422 kg rising to a massive 2,000 kg in the reign of Tashfin b. ʿAli, while it fell to 629 kg per annum under ʿAbd al-Mu'min (r. 1130–63) before descending precipitously to 63 kg per annum during the reign of Yusuf al-Mustansir (r. 1213–23).[115] Consequently, although there are references to Almohad gold *dīnārs*, they are not that abundant in coin hordes and some scholars suggest that the Almohad *dīnār* may have been as much a measurement as a coin and that soldiers' salaries, assessed in *dīnārs* in historical chronicles, may actually have been paid in silver *dirhams* as well as, or instead of, gold *dīnārs*.[116]

The prevalence of silver rather than gold coinage during the Almohad era suggests that they did not have as easy access to Sudanese gold as their predecessors. Frequent Sanhaja opposition to them on the southern fringes of their empire may have played a part in reducing the amount of gold in circulation and encouraging the use of silver coin in its place. However, the apocryphal warning given by ʿAli b. Yusuf's chief jurist, Malik b. Wuhayb, that Ibn Tumart was 'the lord of the square *dirham*' destined to overthrow the Almoravids, also points to coinage as a means of propaganda and differentiation:[117] the shift from round gold coins to square silver ones indubitably had a polemical edge to it.

Figure 5.3 An Almoravid gold *dīnār* minted in Córdoba (Fitzwilliam Museum, Cambridge, Accession No. CM.PG.7805-2006 © Fitzwilliam Museum)

115 Benhsain Mesmoudi et al., 'Biens sultaniens', pp. 608–9.
116 Ibid., p. 605, n. 44.
117 al-Baydhaq, *Akhbar*, p. 58.

Figure 5.4 An Almohad square silver *dirham* minted in Málaga (Fitzwilliam Museum, Cambridge, Accession No. CM.IS.279-R © Fitzwilliam Museum)

In addition to the right to raise taxes and mint coins, Islamic regimes had the responsibility of ensuring that markets functioned in a fair and honest way, a task that also benefited them by stimulating commerce and thus tax revenues. A key institution in this respect was that of *ḥisba*, a term denoting public morality and order. Although originally a religious office that encompassed religious lapses, criminal acts and good market practices, these aspects of *ḥisba* became differentiated over time and the ruler or his governors became directly involved in appointing *muḥtasib*s responsible for overseeing the market and public areas in each town. The *muḥtasib* led a team ideally recruited from among the most trustworthy and eminent practitioners of each trade and craft to keep an eye on these sectors, check for frauds and swindles, and punish offenders. In order to do his job effectively, he also worked closely with the local police and the judge. The Malagan *muḥtasib* al-Saqati summarises the process for dealing with commercial infringements in his short manual on the topic of *ḥisba*:

> The treatment of the perpetrator should be chastisement and a reprimand for a first offence, imprisonment and an admonition for a second offence, and for the third a beating and public humiliation. If he continues with his transgression and malpractice he should be repeatedly punished and [the *muḥtasib*'s] most important task should be monitoring him so that he loses the trust [of his customers] and either repents or leaves the market of the Muslims.[118]

[118] al-Sakati, *Hisba*, p. 9.

The range of possible frauds that al-Saqati lists and the spheres in which he considered them most harmful offer insight into the management of the commercial sector. Checking weights and measures, particularly of critical foodstuffs like wheat and flour, is the foremost of al-Saqati's concerns, followed by monitoring the quality of flour and bread, which was often adulterated by adding cheaper types of flour or even stones and soil then sold as a higher-quality product.[119] He also lists similar problems to watch for in butchers and those who sell cooked meats and pretend that they are using better cuts than they are. In a section that moves on to what we would consider health and safety, he recommends that meat should only be cooked in the morning, with all aspects of its preparation in full view, in whitewashed premises that can be cleaned easily.[120] He also reviews the tricks of apothecaries, perfumers, slave dealers and craftsmen of many kinds, showing the concern of the *muḥtasib*, and by extension the ruler, to ensure that a reasonable level of trust and confidence prevailed in the manufacturing and commercial sectors.

Another area in which the ruler played an economic role was in what we might today call agricultural research and development. In al-Andalus there was a long tradition of monarchical interest in agriculture and patronage of agronomists that had been concentrated in Córdoba in Umayyad times, but spread across the Muslim parts of the peninsula with the rise of the Ta'ifa kings who established gardens and estates outside their capitals. These included the gardens of al-Ma'mun outside Toledo, the Sumadihiyya gardens outside Almería, and the Jabal al-Sharaf or Aljarafe estates outside Seville. Numerous agronomists, such as Ibn Wafid in Toledo, Ibn Bassal in Toledo and Seville, and al-Tighnari in Granada, worked to improve soil, create better strains of fruit tree, strengthen seed stock, and develop grafting techniques on the gardens and estates of the Ta'ifa kings.

This phase of experimentation and development spurred a veritable 'agricultural revolution' that continued through the Almoravid and Almohad eras with individuals such as Ibn al-Hajjaj and Ibn al-'Awwam who worked in the hinterland of Seville, which was located at the centre of this revolution.[121] Similar estates also began to flourish in the Maghrib, starting with 'Ali b. Yusuf's irrigation and garden projects outside Marrakesh. The Almohads, in particular, invested significantly in a new set of vast irrigated suburban estates called *baḥā'ir* (sing. *buḥayra*). Although the word *buḥayra* usually means a pool or lake, it is clearly used in the Almohad context to

[119] al-Sakati, *Hisba*, pp. 20–2.
[120] Ibid., p. 34.
[121] Lagardère, *Campagnes*, pp. 481–6.

Figure 5.5 The Menara gardens, originally an Almohad *buḥayra*, Marrakesh (the pavilion dates to the nineteenth century)

denote not only the artificial reservoirs they constructed, but also the entire irrigated orchard zone around them where olives and other fruit trees were cultivated. One or more such estates were established outside almost every major Almohad city, including Marrakesh, Fes, Meknes and Seville, with a peak of activity during the reigns of Abu Ya'qub Yusuf and his son Ya'qub al-Mansur, stretching from 1163 to 1199.

Seville, the city where most Almohad armies gathered for Andalusi campaigns, was endowed with at least three such estates, Buhayrat al-Wadi, Buhayrat Bab Jahwar and Buhayrat Hisn al-Faraj, while one of the Almohads' Marrakesh estates, the Menara, still exists today along with its vast pool situated amongst endless olive and citrus groves. These estates fulfilled multiple functions for the Almohad government: they provided produce that could be used to supply the army; they contained luxurious residences where the caliph, the *sayyids* and other important personages could relax; and, when the army was mobilised, they provided space for arriving soldiers to camp and water for their animals. From the economic and agricultural point of view, however, their importance lay in their role as flagship projects for agricultural experimentation and innovation which could then spread to other areas.

The Impact of Warfare and other Disasters on the Economy

As we have seen, the impact of the Almoravid and Almohad states on the economy oscillated between more or less harmful exactions and the nurturing of commerce and agriculture. In times of war, however, the balance tipped dangerously towards harm. The constant stream of military campaigns against political and ideological rivals, rebels and foreign Christian threats recorded in the sources may give excessive weight to military activities as an indicator of a ruler's commitment to jihad, but warfare and its consequences played a major, if sporadic, role in the lives of many inhabitants of al-Andalus, the Maghrib and Ifriqiya. The impact of warfare fell into a number of different categories from predictable stresses related to recruitment and provisioning to the more random impact of enemy raiding and livestock rustling, scorched-earth policies, and the destruction of towns or their outlying suburbs.

In the first place, any campaign required the mobilisation of large numbers of men from the countryside. Although both the Almoravid and Almohad armies included what we might call professional soldiers who were paid salaries and resided in large cities, their tribal contingents spent a proportion of their time cultivating their land or herding their flocks and their absence on campaign could have negative consequences for the economy, particularly if the campaign ran for years at a time. Immediately before an engagement, the Almoravids and Almohads also mobilised local contingents and encouraged jihad 'volunteers' to join the army with similar consequences for local agriculture if the campaign ran beyond the normal summer season and interfered with sowing or harvest times.

As armies moved through the countryside, they required provisioning with food, water, animal fodder and firewood. One of 'Abd al-Mu'min's preparations for the al-Mahdiyya campaign, for instance, was to command the digging of wells along the army's route to Ifriqiya.[122] Provisioning was something that Almohad officials were suppose to arrange, but it could have an inflationary effect on the local economy and sometimes denude a region of foodstuffs completely, as occurred during the ill-fated Almohad campaign to Murcia in 1172 during which men and animals died of thirst and starvation. Sometimes officials failed to fulfil their orders due to incompetence or their syphoning off of supplies for personal profit. In Chapter 3, we saw the Almohad caliph al-Nasir become furious as he moved his army from Fes to the Straits of Gibraltar in 1211 only to find that provisions for the army had not been arranged, behaviour that led to the controversial execution of two Almohad governors in 1212 shortly before the Battle of Las Navas de Tolosa.

In addition to the predictable burden on the economy caused by military mobilisations and troop movements, warfare had more direct and random effects on people's lives. During the eleventh, twelfth and thirteenth

[122] See p. 87, above.

centuries, pitched field battles were actually a fairly unusual occurrence, and it was more normal for conflict to entail raids designed to cause economic havoc in enemy territory. In al-Andalus, frontier raiding across the marches was a centuries-old practice but, in this era, Christian raiding parties began to push further and further south undermining cultivation by killing men, seizing women and children, rustling livestock and destroying crops. Muslim raiders responded in kind, but there is general agreement that whilst the societies of Portugal, León-Castile and Aragon became more and more geared towards warfare in this era, Andalusi Muslim communities seem to have relinquished the military initiative to the Almoravids and Almohads, the bulk of whose forces were often in the Maghrib leaving Andalusi villagers exposed and vulnerable to attack.

For towns and cities, the main threats presented by warfare were the devastation of their agricultural hinterlands, sieges and violent conquest. During the second Almoravid siege of Fes in the late 1060s or early 1070s, the economic situation within the city became critical. Ibn Abi Zar' reports that food shortages and soaring inflation took hold as the ruling Maghrawa Berbers lost control of their agricultural hinterland. In response, they resorted to plundering the homes of their subjects to take any food they had. If anyone objected, they killed him. To try to avoid their depredations, people built underground rooms in their homes to store and grind flour and to cook. They also constructed upper rooms without staircases that could be reached only by a ladder which was pulled up once the family retired each night.[123] In these circumstances, the subsequent Almoravid conquest of Fes may well have been a welcome resolution of the siege, regardless of the population's feelings towards them as conquerors.

Sometimes departing armies wreaked as much damage as they could to undermine the value of a city for the incoming victors. After the long struggle for Valencia between Rodrigo Díaz de Vivar El Cid and the Almoravids, Rodrigo's widow Chimene finally departed from the city in 1102 at the behest of Alfonso VII, but the Christians torched the great mosque and set many other buildings alight as they left.[124] When 'Abd al-Mu'min's Almohad armies advanced into Ifriqiya during his 1159–60 al-Mahdiyya campaign, the inhabitants of many cities sent delegations to offer their submission in order to avoid sieges and violent assaults. As we have seen, Tunis, controlled by the Banu Khurasan, was not one of those cities, however, and its population paid the price after 'Abd al-Mu'min conquered it and allowed his army to pillage and

[123] Ibn Abi Zar', *Rawd al-Qirtas*, p. 144.

[124] See pp. 46–7, above.

extort booty from them in retaliation for their resistance. In 1182, Alfonso VIII of Castile led an army south to besiege Córdoba and raid other Muslim territories, which caused the price of food in the city to escalate rapidly.[125] The impact of the Banu Ghaniya invasion of the Bijaya region and Ifriqiya a few years later was equally negative. Ibn ʿIdhari sums it up in the following passage:

> When civil war broke out in Bijaya and its districts, its settlement and cultivation dwindled, its agriculture and cereals were plundered, its resources declined, its amenities and food supplies were no more, and injustice injured its population who were scattered by flight and the sword, those who survived sought refuge in rugged mountain fastnesses and those who were weak sought protection from the Arabs. Bijaya's gardens turned to wasteland, its produce was scarce and prices soared.[126]

In a similar vein, he says that when Yaʿqub al-Mansur's army launched its final assault on Gafsa, one of the strongholds of the Banu Ghaniya coalition, in 1187, 'in two days it returned to scattered dust as fires were lit in all the catapults and war machines. The people departed and [Gafsa] became black as the darkest night, its homes like those of ʿAd after the devastating wind, when previously it was a flowering garden.'[127] The author of the *Kitab al-Istibsar* gives a very effusive description of Gafsa a few years later, however, suggesting not only a degree of literary exaggeration on the part of Ibn ʿIdhari but also the resilience of towns after such attacks, or perhaps the *Istibsar*'s out-dated information.

Price rises, food shortages and wanton destruction of land and property were only one aspect of the impact of war. Further long-term economic and demographic damage was caused by the killing of combatants and male civilians and the capture of women and children. Most famously, the number of deaths at the Battle of Las Navas de Tolosa is described in the anonymous *al-Dhakhira al-Saniyya* as completely depopulating the plains around Fes and Meknes, where the land remained uncultivated henceforth.[128] The predatory activities of the Arab and Berber tribes in alliance with the Almoravid rebel, Ibn Ghaniya, are said to have led to a similar decline in cultivation in parts of Ifriqiya, as mentioned above. However, the capture of prisoners could also present economic opportunities as we see in the development of ransoming,

125 Ibn ʿIdhari, *al-Bayan*, vol. 4, p. 218.

126 Ibid., vol. 4, p. 252.

127 Ibid., vol. 4, p. 266. The reference to ʿAd refers to the Qur'anic mention of this legendary ancient people whom God destroyed with a mighty storm for their overweening pride: Qur'an 69: 6–8.

128 *al-Dhakhira al-Saniyya*, p. 26.

which burgeoned into a veritable 'trade' during this era with both Muslims and Christians collecting money to ransom their co-religionists.[129] As an example, when the Muslim outpost of Setefilla in the southwest fell to the Castilians, 700 men and women were supposedly captured and ransomed by the people of Seville for 2,775 gold *dīnārs*, of which the jurist Ibn Zuhr personally contributed a hefty 100 *dīnārs*.[130]

In addition to the danger and destruction wreaked by warfare, both rural and urban populations had to face floods, droughts and crop failure, as well as the epidemic diseases mentioned in the previous chapter. In 1137–8, for instance, a 'great flood in Tangier carried away houses and walls and a great number of people and animals died',[131] while in 1201 the Guadalquivir flooded and broke its banks from Córdoba to Cádiz. When the flood reached Seville it was said to have swept away 6,000 homes and claimed around 7,000 victims, some of whose corpses were discovered by merchants arriving in the port, strewn upon the river banks in a gruesome display.[132]

Although it was impossible to predict when rivers might rise to the point that they breached flood defences, the threat of drought and famine was ever-present. It was therefore normal during good years to preserve surpluses of grain in communal and state granaries, and it was considered the mark of a good ruler to open the granaries when drought and famine struck. The troubled circumstances in the Bijaya region in the 1180s, however, meant that there were no such supplies on which to draw:

> Famine intensified and disease spread to epidemic proportions until the vulture and the eagle grew reckless in seizing their livelihood and the pillaged and despoiled [population] confined themselves to the town in countless numbers . . . The townsfolk were unable to shroud the dead or find space for the living and they entered a state of devastation with piles of dead men and women lying in the streets of the city.[133]

In contrast, when a major famine occurred in the Maghrib in 1219 and prices rose to unaffordable levels, the caliph Yusuf al-Mustansir 'commanded that the storehouses used to keep foodstuffs should be opened, so they were opened to the public and the food shared among them. It is said that the wealthier paid but there was no charge for the poor.'[134]

[129] See Gómez-Rivas, 'The ransom industry'.
[130] Ibn 'Idhari, *al-Bayan*, vol. 4, p. 219.
[131] Ibid., vol. 4, p. 83.
[132] Ibid., vol. 4, p. 310.
[133] Ibid., vol. 4, p. 252.
[134] Ibid., vol. 4, p. 339.

Towns also faced the danger of fires, which could destroy homes, shops and large quantities of merchandise and food, particularly in hot weather when the timbers of buildings were dry and fire spread rapidly. One such fire raged in Marrakesh in the vicinity of the *qayṣariyya*, the royal market, one hot summer night in 1210 when everyone had gone to bed:

> The fire gained hold on the dry timbers and flimsy fabrics and spread like a meteor through the arcades of the market. Those closest to it did not wake up and the roar did not arouse them from their sleep until the flames were blazing across the sky, the tumult had engulfed the city, and the common people had rushed out of their alleyways undressed, clutching their possessions. The clamour reached [the caliph] al-Nasir li-Din Allah who rushed out of his palace and climbed the minaret of the mosque next to it to witness an event for which there was no response or strategy except surrender to God Most Great and High. The lowest rabble and all kinds of strangers plunged into the fire and pillaged what they discovered from among the goods saved from the fire and slipped away with it in every direction.[135]

In the aftermath of this disaster to the Marrakesh market district and its commerce, al-Nasir sent out investigators to catch anyone said to have the possessions of a merchant in his hands and those few who were caught were executed. Nonetheless, both resident and visiting merchants lost an inestimable amount of wealth in the fire and 'a community accustomed to ease was impoverished and reduced to begging in a state of confusion across the land'.[136]

The eleventh to thirteenth centuries thus witnessed both stability and change in economic life. The basic vectors of the economy – agriculture, pastoralism, manufacturing and trade – remained constant, but different sectors experienced a combination of positive stimuli and vicissitudes during the Almoravid and Almohad eras. These were not solely the responsibility of rulers, whose control over land, climate and natural disasters was obviously limited, but fiscal policies, elite investment and war played their parts in shaping economic life. The fact of empire encouraged the development of large trading zones straddling the Straits of Gibraltar and the rise of new urban centres (Marrakesh) and the renewal and expansion of older ones (Almería, Fes, Bijaya), creating a vigorous urban network across the entire Islamic west. Both manufacturing and trade flourished in these cities and supported the cultural flowering we shall review in the next two chapters. The Almoravids and Almohads also regularised and increased taxation upon the rural sector,

135 Ibn 'Idhari, *al-Bayan*, vol. 4, p. 329.

136 Ibid., vol. 4, p. 330.

especially in the Maghrib, and this may have lain at the root of some of the many rural tribal rebellions they faced. However, repeated cycles of war and rebellion, especially across the Andalusi marches, which crept ever southward between the eleventh and thirteenth centuries, and in Ifriqiya due to the (disputed) impact of the Banu Hilal migrations and the Banu Ghaniya insurrection, impoverished some communities and encouraged a rise in pastoralism at the expense of agriculture.

6

Malikism, Mahdism and Mysticism: Religion and Learning, 1050–1250

The spread of Islam, the propagation of different Islamic sects and approaches, and the blending of indigenous and Islamic beliefs, in sum the long and uneven process of Islamisation, thread through many of the preceding chapters. Now we shall turn to look at this process more closely by exploring the evolution of Islamic religious culture in al-Andalus and the Maghrib as the religion (*dīn*) practised by a steadily increasing proportion of the population and as a form of specialist learning (*'ilm*), which was the matrix around which other forms of learning coalesced, including Arabic literacy, *belles lettres* and the sciences, due to a primary education system that taught Muslim children to read and write Arabic by means of the Qur'an, even if they became poets, secretaries, physicians or philosophers later.

The modalities for the spread of Islam in its many varieties and the formation of scholarly and literary elites were shared with other parts of the Islamic world. During the conquest era, the faith was carried forward in embryonic form by the army and took root in the towns founded or occupied by Muslim fighters, who were soon joined by scholars. In the centuries after the conquest, Islam became embedded in towns and religious learning emanating from the east was carried westwards along the routes of trade and pilgrimage. As in the Islamic east, the locus for higher learning was the great mosque where the religious scholars in each town gathered and engaged with aspiring students of every bent who had travelled from their natal regions to meet them. Although mosques were supplemented by colleges (*madrasas*) for the teaching of law and then other religious subjects in the Islamic east from the mid-eleventh century, the *madrasa* was not part of the western Islamic education system until after the demise of the Almohads in the thirteenth century.[1]

Such higher-level Islamic knowledge was, however, the preserve of a

[1] The first *madrasa* in Ifriqiya was founded in Tunis by the Hafsids in 1238 and the first *madrasa* in the western Maghrib was founded in Fes in 1271 by the Marinids.

minority, and was quite inaccessible to those who did not speak Arabic or have access to urban-based cliques of scholars. Understanding the religious stance of this silent Romance- and Berber-speaking majority presents numerous challenges related to our very patchy knowledge of the processes of both Islamisation and Arabisation outside major cities. Scholars are increasingly aware that the religious practices of the rural population across the region, both before and after the Islamic conquest, are virtually unknown and that the details of the early spread of Islam are equally hazy. Mosques, for instance, were urban institutions and there is little evidence for their construction in smaller settlements where Islamisation was often mediated through institutions such as the *ribāṭ* which played such a crucial role in the genesis of the Almoravid movement. Our understanding of religious learning and culture is therefore heavily conditioned by the snippets of information that we have from towns such as Córdoba and Qayrawan, and also by how Andalusi and Maghribi geographers and historians viewed the spread of Islam in preceding centuries.[2]

The general impression given by our sources, patchy as they are, is that the era of the Berber empires was a crucial phase both in the long process of Islamisation and in the development of higher Islamic learning in the western reaches of the Dar al-Islam. In al-Andalus, the period after the fall of the Umayyads saw various adjustments and changes in emphasis to modes of learning, occasioned by alternating phases of centralisation and decentralisation and the moral and ideological challenges presented by the Almoravids and Almohads respectively, and also the psychological crisis triggered by the reversal of power relations in the Iberian peninsula in favour of the northern Christian kingdoms.[3] Ifriqiya remained a portal for the westwards dissemination of eastern Islamic learning and, in particular, the consolidation of Sunnism across the west through the medium of Maliki *fiqh*, in its later rather than archaic form, which had integrated legal methodologies from other schools of law and also Ash'ari theology. The greatest change, however, took place in the western Maghrib, an area that witnessed the exponential growth of a scholarly class as a consequence of the selection of Marrakesh as the capital of both the Almoravid and Almohad empires and the increasing urbanisation of the region. This was accompanied by the spread of Arab-Islamic knowledge and culture in areas previously only lightly touched by it, and the assimilation of much of the countryside into the Islamic sphere by means of the Almoravid and Almohad *da'wa*s, and the even more efficacious spread of Sufism in their wake.

2 Pichard, 'Islamisation et arabisation', p. 38.

3 For a full analysis of Andalusi intellectual life at this time, see Urvoy, *Penseurs d'al-Andalus*.

Religious Learning Prior to the Almoravid Era

In its early stages, Islamic religious knowledge was legalistic and praxis-oriented, as one would expect during the conquest phase when large numbers of people converted to Islam and needed to understand the basic daily ritual requirements and regulations of their faith. In the eight and ninth centuries, various legal 'schools' (*madhāhib*) developed in the Islamic east, each named after an eponymous scholar whose intellectual production was codified and built upon by successive generations of followers. The differences between the schools lay primarily in their approaches to deriving the law or Shari'a. While the followers of Abu Hanifa (d. 767) in Kufa put greater stress on learned rational opinion (*ra'y*) and reasoning (*ijtihād*) to formulate analogies (*qiyās*), the school of Malik b. Anas (d. 796) preferred to use the practice (*'amal*) of Medina, site of the earliest Muslim community, as the benchmark for approving legal positions. Ja'far al-Sadiq (d. 765), the sixth Shi'i imam and the prime legal authority for later Imami Shi'a, included the 'Alid imams and their sayings (*akhbār*) as sources of law.

A few generations later, al-Shafi'i (d. 820), a student of Malik, tried to reconcile different approaches to the formulation of law by putting forward a method for it by which a jurist should look first at the Qur'an for an answer, then the Hadith, then the consensus of the Muslim community (*ijmā'*) and then, finally, use his mental acuity to form an analogy (*qiyās*) with an existing situation if no other option was available. Al-Shafi'i's incorporation of Hadith, the sayings or traditions attributed to the Prophet and passed down orally through generations of Muslims, coincided with strenuous efforts by Traditionists (*muḥaddithūn*) to compile and verify written collections of Hadith which began to replace the *'amal* of Medina as the primary reference material for early Muslim praxis.

The Malikis deeply resented this and, according to some sources, al-Shafi'i was murdered by an outraged Maliki in Fustat in Egypt. However, the turn towards Hadith also paved the way for the formation of the *madhhab* of Ahmad b. Hanbal (d. 855) in Baghdad, which put heavy emphasis on the primacy of Hadith. Although the Maliki, Hanafi, Shafi'i and Hanbali schools eventually became recognised as the orthodox schools of Sunni law, prior to the twelfth century they shared the field with many other schools and their adherents could be deeply antagonistic to each other, a fact that helps to explain the resistance of some western Malikis towards the ideas of al-Ghazali, who was a Shafi'i jurist.

As Muslims came into contact with the theological and philosophical traditions of their Christian and Jewish subjects and urban scholarly communities (*'ulamā'*) coalesced, some scholars moved from codifying religious praxis using the Qur'an and Hadith to engaging with metaphysical questions about the nature of God, man's relationship to the divine, and free will from the Muslim perspective. Translations into Arabic of classical Greek texts on rhetoric, dialectic and philosophy helped provide Muslims with the intellectual tools to produce their own scholastic theology, known as *kalām* or *uṣūl al-dīn*, and Islamic philosophy (*falsafa*). As in the case of jurisprudence, there were rival theological approaches whose adherents were sometimes virulently opposed to each other, as well as fault lines between those jurists who favoured a strongly exoteric approach to Islam rooted in the careful preservation of the views of earlier authorities and those who wished to incorporate more esoteric theological and philosophical approaches and think about the principles underlying law rather than simply its concrete manifestations.

In addition to conflicts among scholars over the correct approaches to religious knowledge, tensions also arose vis-à-vis the relative religious status of the 'Abbasid caliphs and the *'ulamā'*. Was the caliph the ultimate religious authority? Or were the *'ulamā'*, in their self-appointed role as custodians of the Qur'an and Hadith, in such a position? The stance taken by a series of ninth-century 'Abbasid caliphs during disputes between the Mu'tazila theologians and the Traditionists sheds light on the evolving role of the caliph in religious affairs. In the last months of his reign, the caliph al-Ma'mun (r. 813–33) asserted that the Mu'tazili view that the Qur'an was created was doctrinally correct rather than the Traditionist belief that it was uncreated and co-eternal with God. He then instituted a *miḥna*, usually translated as an inquisition, in which *'ulamā'* were required to publicly agree with the premise that the Qur'an was created.[4]

Whilst the majority of *'ulamā'* acknowledged that the caliph knew best, a few resisted making this acknowledgement and were imprisoned, punished and, in a few cases, killed. The *miḥna* continued very sporadically through the reigns of al-Mu'tasim and al-Wathiq and petered out under al-Mutawakkil, who appears to have reached a compromise with the *'ulamā'* who slowly consolidated their role as the guardians of Islamic doctrine. As we shall see below, the religious status of an Islamic ruler in relation to the scholarly class evolved along its own trajectory in the Islamic west with the assertion of the ruler's religious authority coming to the fore under the Fatimids and Umayyads in the tenth century and surging to a peak in the twelfth century with the Almohads.

A third approach to Islam that gained ground in the Islamic east from the ninth century onwards was that of pietistic asceticism, which absorbed many

[4] See Cooperson, *al-Ma'mūn*, pp. 115–28; Turner, *Inquisition in Early Islam*, pp. 118–50.

pre-Islamic mystical and gnostic elements from the Christian and Zoroastrian environments to produce the Islamic mystical tradition known as Sufism which focused on the individual soul's search for God rather than orthopraxis or rational dialectical arguments to define orthodoxy. Early Sufism had many manifestations ranging from ecstatic mystical practices rooted in much older ideas of the individual becoming inhabited by the divine, to sober self-abnegation combined with maintenance of the usual external Muslim religious practices. Some mystics were highly intellectual and attracted by neo-Platonism, which had begun to circulate in Arabic translations of Greek neo-Platonic writers such as Plotinus, while others were uneducated charismatics. However, whatever combination of traits they exhibited, legal scholars and political authorities shared deep suspicions about the orthodoxy of Sufism, which was exacerbated by the ability of some mystics to drum up massive support among the subject population that could easily become a discourse of opposition towards religious and political establishments, viewed as being less just, pious or moral than they should be.

Between the Islamic conquest and the rise of the Almoravids, North Africa and al-Andalus were exposed to these numerous different religious trends by means of the intellectual and commercial networks forged by practices of travel to the Middle East and performance of the pilgrimage. The impact of this, however, varied widely. The growing urban elites of al-Andalus, and Córdoba in particular, eagerly set off for Qayrawan or Alexandria from whence students travelled on to Fustat (Cairo), the holy cities in the Hijaz, and the great centres of Syria and Iraq where they encountered the range of religious ideas and other forms of knowledge generated by the Greek to Arabic translation movement, and the Arabic literary output of the 'Abbasid world, ranging from music to mathematics, medical science and philosophy. This led to the consolidation of an elite urban Arabic-Islamic culture in al-Andalus calqued on that to be found in Baghdad, Basra or Kufa, which was considered 'provincial' from the eastern Islamic perspective, but 'metropolitan' in the Islamic west itself.

The connections between the vast rural expanses of the Maghrib and the Islamic east naturally manifested themselves differently. Several easterners travelled westwards as refugees and missionaries in the hope that the Maghrib would prove more fertile ground for their teachings than their eastern homelands. While Qur'an reciters and Muslims versed in the early Islamic tradition from the Hijaz and Syria settled in Qayrawan and Córdoba, and circles of Arab *literati* gathered around the governors and amirs based in these cities, the understanding of Islam among the rank and file of the army, which was predominantly Berber across the west, was extended and deepened by contact with Kharijite missionaries, the *ḥamalat al-'ilm* or 'bearers of knowledge' from Iraq who carried the religio-political message that Islam was a universal faith and that the head of the community should be selected according to religious merit rather than aristocratic Qurashi Arab ancestry. This was an appealing message to converts, drawn to the Islamic paradigm of a Prophet, a revealed book and certain quotidian ritual requirements, but resentful of the privileged status of Arabs within the Muslim hierarchy and, as mentioned in the Introduction, many Berber converts joined the Kharijite rebellion that erupted in 739 in the North African garrison towns and spread to al-Andalus.

Although the Kharijite rebellion was quelled in al-Andalus and Ifriqiya, these political setbacks had important consequences for the Islamisation of the Berber interior, to which the Kharijites retreated. Subsequently, two types of moderate Kharijism were implanted in rural North Africa: Sufri Kharijism in Salé, Tlemcen and Sijilmasa; and Ibadi Kharijism in the central Maghrib and in southern Ifriqiya after ʿAbd al-Rahman b. Rustam, a Kharijite missionary of Persian origin, whom several tribes recognised as imam, was driven out of Qayrawan and founded the town of Tahart. Under the leadership of the Rustamid imams, the Ibadis had a significant role in spreading Islam among the Berber tribes of the North African interior and the desert fringe who had been untouched by the earlier Islamic conquest. Ibn Rustam himself composed one of the earliest known works of Qur'anic exegesis, the *Tafsir Kitab Allah*, while continued links with the Kharijites of southern Iraq fostered the development of an indigenous North African Kharijite scholarly tradition, which has been maintained by the Ibadi Kharijites of the Mzab in modern Algeria to the present.

Kharijism and Religious 'Others'

In theory, the Kharijites considered all other Muslims to be unbelievers, but in its moderate North African form, Kharijism acted as a sectarian Islamic identification that differentiated Berber tribes or confederations from one another but did not demand constant warfare against Muslims of other sects. The Maghribi Kharijites also maintained a tolerant attitude towards the *ahl al-dhimma*, which contributed to the intermingling of Christian and Ibadi communities mentioned in Chapter 4, and the presence of important Christian and Jewish merchant colonies in Kharijite centres.

After the demise of the Rustamid imamate in 909, Ibadi Kharijism developed its characteristic austere, grass-roots organisation based on councils (*ḥalaqāt*) of celibate elders known as *ʿazzāba* that were headed by a shaykh and oversaw the affairs of the local Ibadi laity. The regulations for one such council in the eleventh-century Jarid (southern Ifriqiya) include the stipulations that the *'azzāba* must have shaven heads and wear simple white robes to indicate their ascetic, religious status.[5] This appearance, highly reminiscent of a priesthood, points to the Christian origins of many Ibadis in Ifriqiya and the generally good relations between the two communities.

It was not only Kharijite missionaries who travelled west: 'Abbasid opposition to the 'Alids also encouraged them to seek refuge and support in the Maghrib. The most notable such figure was Idris b. 'Abd Allah, one of al-Hasan b. 'Ali's grandsons, who fled Egypt after an abortive 'Alid uprising against the 'Abbasids in 756, gained the support of the Awraba Berbers of the Sais plain, where modern Meknes is located, and founded Fes. We know relatively little about the religious programme of the Idrisids, but coinage suggests that Idris I conceived of himself as the religious leader (imam) of the Awraba Berbers by virtue of his descent from the Prophet. The legal or theological consequences of this proto-Shi'i or 'Alid position for his followers are unknown, but they probably entailed reliance on the Idrisid imam as the fount of religious knowledge, a person-based rather than a text-based approach to religion that had repeated success in the Maghribi countryside over the centuries. Idrisid influence extended over the High Atlas mountains to the Sus valley, where al-Bakri describes an 'Alid sect with an Idrisid imam, called the Bajaliyya after its Ifriqiyan founder Muhammad b. Warsand al-Bajali.[6] 'Alid sentiment could also be found in rural al-Andalus, often among Berbers. The eighth-century rebel Shaqya b. 'Abd al-Wahid al-Miknasi, for instance, claimed to be a descendant of the prophet's grandson Husayn, giving an 'Alid colour to the rebellion he launched in 768 in the mountainous province of Santaver, northeast of modern Madrid.[7]

The notion of a charismatic imam deriving his authority from his prophetic descent leading a select group of true Muslims amidst the misguided Muslim masses proved to have enduring appeal in the Islamic west. Such figures often took the title of *mahdī*, the 'recipient of God's guidance', a messianic title denoting a religio-political leader of the Prophet's house who would renew religion and institute true justice. Although the idea of the *mahdī* became most fully articulated within Shi'i circles, belief in the coming of a *mahdī* to renew Islam was widespread among Muslims of all colours. In 850–1, an inhabitant of eastern al-Andalus claimed to be a prophet and gave his followers new ritual instructions and a new interpretation of the Qur'an.

5 Lewicki, 'Ḥalka'.

6 al-Bakri, *Description de l'Afrique*, Arabic text, p. 161; French text, pp. 304–5.

7 See Aguadé, 'Sectarian movements in al-Andalus'.

Fifty years later, Ibn al-Qitt, a member of the extended Umayyad family, claimed to be the *mahdī* in alliance with one Abu ʿAli al-Sarraj, who played the role of propagandist (*dāʿī*) or 'announcer' for him. These constructs resurged in the twelfth century, as we shall see below.

The encounter between Muslim missionaries and the pagan and Judaeo-Berber tribes of the western Maghrib also produced a variety of hybrid heterodox cults that subsisted alongside the Kharijite and ʿAlid sects of the interior. In this, the Berber west was rather like the eastern Perso-Turkish provinces of Khurasan and Transoxiana, where the slow process of Islamisation similarly advanced through the medium of local cults that blended pre-Islamic and Islamic ideas. The best known examples of Maghribi heterodoxy are those described by al-Bakri that we have come across already, the Barghawata and the cult of Ha-mim. The Barghawata tribes of the Atlantic plains identified one of their own chiefs, Salih, as their prophet and conveyor of a Qur'an for the Berbers in place of Muhammad and the Arabic Qur'an, a position similar to that taken by the Ghumara prophet Ha-mim, whose followers also acknowledged his father, aunt and sister as holders of supernatural powers.[8] Barghawata practices included distinct prayer cycles, food taboos and fasts that may well have blended Judaeo-Berber and Islamic prescriptions.[9] Denounced as unbelievers by the Idrisids of Fes, the Barghawata subsequently became a target of the Almoravids in their bid to spread Maliki Sunni orthodoxy across the western Maghrib, after which they disappeared into the majoritarian Muslim community.

While Kharijite, pro-ʿAlid, and pseudo-Islamic cults had a powerful appeal in the Berber countryside, a plethora of scholars promoting the nascent eastern schools of law settled in Qayrawan and Córdoba and local juridical and scholarly elites began to coalesce in Ifriqiyan and Andalusi towns. For a time, the teachings of the Syrian jurist al-Awzaʿi, whose school identified the living practice (*sunna*) of the Muslim community rather than Hadith as the source of guidance,[10] predominated in al-Andalus, but over the long term it was the Maliki school of law, derived by the followers of Malik b. Anas from his collection of Hadith called the *Muwatta'*, that had the most long-term success in the Islamic west. Several famous early Maliki jurists lived and worked in Qayrawan, the hub for the transmission of Maliki jurisprudence westwards across the Maghrib to Córdoba, which became a second centre of the Maliki school in the ninth century.

The person credited with the promotion of Maliki law in the Islamic west

[8] See p. 143, above.
[9] See le Tourneau, 'Barghawāṭa'.
[10] Urvoy, *Penseurs d'al-Andalus*, pp. 80–1.

is the jurist Abu Sa'id 'Abd al-Salam b. Sa'id al-Tanukhi, known as Sahnun (d. 855), who studied with the Hanafis and Malikis of Qayrawan before travelling to the east and reworking the book of a fellow Qayrawani jurist, Asad b. al-Furat, the *Asadiyya*, into his own *Mudawwana*, which became the most widely used compendium of Maliki *fiqh* in the Islamic west. The Maliki method in Ifriqiya and al-Andalus focused very strongly on Malik's *Muwatta'* and these commentary texts, whose study was known as the science of derivative works (*'ilm al-furū'*, lit. science of the branches), rather than on the study of the sources of law (*'ilm al-uṣūl*), and Maliki practitioners could prove very resistant to other religio-legal approaches. The stiff opposition and accusations of 'heresy' (*zandaqa*) faced by the famous jurist Baqi b. Makhlad when he tried to introduce al-Shafi'i's legal methodology and use of Hadith to tenth-century Córdoba is a case in point.[11]

Although Maliki law ultimately triumphed across North Africa and Islamic Iberia, in Sahnun's own lifetime, Kharijites and Hanafis were as prominent in Qayrawan as Malikis. Then in the tenth century a new, powerful wave of 'Alid influence washed over the Maghrib in the form of the Isma'ili Shi'i *da'wa*, which made significant headway in Ifriqiya thanks to the activities of the missionary (*dā'ī*) Abu 'Abd Allah al-Shi'i among the Kutama Berbers.[12] The decision of the Fatimid *mahdī*, 'Abd Allah, to seek refuge in Sijilmasa to avoid attack by the 'Abbasids or rival Isma'ilis confirmed the importance of this movement, which reinforced existing 'Alid and mahdistic sentiments in the Maghrib and filtered into al-Andalus too, where the inveterate rebel Ibn Hafsun exchanged letters and ambassadors with the Fatimids.[13]

A central tenet of Isma'ili Shi'ism was belief in a line of imams, descended from 'Ali and Fatima via Isma'il b. Ja'far al-Sadiq, who acted as living infallible guides of the Muslim elect who recognised them. Isma'ilis believed that phases when the imams existed in otherworldly concealment (*sutūr*) alternated with phases of their open active engagement in the world (*ẓuhūr*) characterised by probity and justice: the proclamation of 'Abd Allah signalled the start of one such phase of *ẓuhūr*. The Isma'ili belief system also included a complex cosmology inspired by neo-Platonism with connections to Mu'tazilism. From the perspective of the Kutama Berbers of the Maghrib, the appeal of Isma'ilism probably lay in the idea of a divinely inspired imam and the inauguration of a revolutionary era of justice that would empower them against their enemies, while its sophisticated theology

11 Fierro, 'Accusations of "zandaqa" in al-Andalus', pp. 251–8.
12 See Brett, *Rise of the Fatimids*.
13 See Martínez Enamorado, 'Fatimid ambassadors in Bobastro'.

and cosmology appealed to that section of the *'ulamā'* in Qayrawan that already harboured Shi'i sympathies as well as some followers of the Hanafi school.[14]

After the return of 'Abd Allah to Ifriqiya in triumph as the Fatimid caliph-imam in 909, Isma'ili Shi'ism became the 'state religion', forcing the Kharijites and the Malikis onto the defensive. Nonetheless, the Maliki juridical substratum remained popular with the subject population and a cluster of scholars emerged to join Sahnun as the great authorities of western Maliki law. The most important of these figures was Ibn Abi Zayd al-Qayrawani (d. 996), who produced a famous *Risala* designed to promote Malikism and counteract Isma'ili Shi'i didactic materials, a new compendium to supplement Sahnun's *Mudawwana* called the *Kitab al-Nawadir*, as well as a summary of the *Mudawwana*. His pupil and cousin, al-Qabisi (d. 1012), succeeded him as the foremost Maliki scholar in Qayrawan.

This generation played an important role in the reform of the traditional corpus of Maliki law by engaging with Shafi'i legal methods and the theological trend named Ash'arism after Abu'l-Hasan 'Ali al-Ash'ari (d. 936), who began his career as a Mu'tazili before converting to the views of the Hadith specialists on several key points, including the eternal rather than created nature of the Qur'an. However, al-Ash'ari continued to use the intellectual tools of Mu'tazilism, including rational dialectic and logic, to defend his new position which was taken forward by a cluster of eastern scholars, including Abu 'Abd Allah b. Mujahid (d. 980–1), al-Baqillani (d. 1013) and Ibn Furak (d. 1015) whose works gradually percolated west. The use of a wider range of Hadith collections and Ash'ari theology invigorated the Maliki school in Ifriqiya and definitively reduced the Isma'ili Shi'i sphere to the point that the Zirids, autonomous Fatimid governors of Ifriqiya since 972, officially abandoned Isma'ili Shi'ism in favour of Maliki Sunnism.

Among the chief exponents of this new trend was Abu 'Imran al-Fasi, who encountered the Sanhaja delegation whose arrival in Qayrawan around 1036 set in train the Almoravid adventure. Abu 'Imran was a native of Fes, educated in Qayrawan, Córdoba and Baghdad where he had studied with al-Baqillani. When he returned to Qayrawan, he joined those scholars championing Maliki *fiqh* and Ash'ari *kalām* at the expense of Fatimid Shi'ism.[15] He was also instrumental in the westwards dissemination of the works of al-Baqillani and his colleagues through his instruction of an important cohort of Andalusi pupils in Ash'ari theology, including al-Ghassani, one of the

[14] Madelung and Walker, *The Advent of the Fatimids*, pp. 30–1.

[15] Lagardère, *Le djihâd andalou*, pp. 190–1.

teachers of the famous Córdoban jurist, Ibn Rushd al-Jadd.[16] In addition to Andalusis, there were also Maghribi Berbers among Abu ʿImran's students, including a handful of scholars who settled in the Atlas town of Aghmat, and Waggag b. Zalwi, who probably modelled his *ribāṭ* in the Sus on those of Ifriqiya.[17]

The reception of Ashʿari ideas among western Malikis during the eleventh century was not completely smooth. In the sophisticated urban centres of al-Andalus it provoked opposition from some sectors of the long-established Maliki *fuqahā'*, who saw in source-based dialectics a slippery slope towards the questioning of the fundamentals of the faith and the introduction of doubt into ordinary religious practices that should be rooted in faith and obedience to canonical Maliki authorities, rather than subjected to an ongoing debate about their underlying meaning and significance. However, these issues were not so pressing on the Saharan frontier in the deep south where Waggag's *ribāṭ* was dedicated to propagating basic Maliki law as the vehicle of Sunni orthodoxy among communities of Kharijite, ʿAlid and pre-Islamic persuasion.

Ifriqiya and al-Andalus also had their share of ascetics and mystics, who blended local Christian monastic and eremitic traditions with pietistic, theosophical and Sufi ideas from the Islamic east. As in the case of jurisprudence and theology, travel to the great centres of the Islamic east enabled westerners to meet and engage with early Sufi masters and then transmit their ideas to their home regions. A famous early example was Ibn Masarra (d. 931), a Córdoban ascetic and mystic, possibly of Christian origin, who drew inspiration for his mystical programme from Muʿtazili theology, neo-Platonism, and the Sufism of early exemplars such as Dhu'l-Nun al-Misri (d. 861) and al-Junayd (d. 910). Like many other ascetically inclined Muslims, Ibn Masarra retreated from the city with all its temptations, Córdoba in his case, to the hills to live as a recluse with a small number of devotees, but his reputation for sanctity encouraged many others to seek him out, indicating the popular appeal of self-denial versus the aristocratic and worldly profile of many scholars.

Although not a Sufi in the later sense of the word, Ibn Masarra is often seen as a founding figure in the emergence of an Andalusi Sufi tradition that escaped from the constraints of a narrow legalistic interpretation of Islam by means of spiritually focused contemplation which the masses found much more attractive than dry debates among jurists. Men and women of this ilk

[16] Lagardère, *Le djihâd andalou*, pp. 192–4.
[17] See Amri, '*Ribāṭ* et idéal de sainteté à Kairouan'.

were often called the 'righteous ones' (*al-ṣāliḥūn* or *al-ṣulaḥā'*), who stood in juxtaposition to the *fuqahā'*, the Maliki juridical cliques whose receipt of state patronage and exercise of religious power over others in the form of the Shari'a often seemed self-serving rather than righteous. Asceticism and Sufism therefore had the ability to provide not only a spiritual path for the chosen few, but also an idiom of piety for the masses, which was not sectarian in the same way as Kharijism or Shi'ism, or legalistic like Malikism. Sufism spread massively in al-Andalus and the western Maghrib during the eleventh and twelfth centuries, overlapping with mahdism on several occasions and, ultimately, transforming the outlook of the religious elite as well as the religious life of the population as a whole.

Religion under the Almoravids

The preceding discussion reveals that religious life in the Maghrib and al-Andalus was a rich tapestry of competing beliefs and approaches to Islam when the Guddala chief Yahya b. Ibrahim and his companions set out to perform the pilgrimage to Mecca in the mid-eleventh century. While erudite scholars, many of whom specialised in Maliki law, clustered in towns, knowledge of Islam was limited, sectarian and frequently mixed with pre-Islamic beliefs in the Saharan borderlands inhabited by the Sanhaja tribes. In Chapter 2 we recounted the rise of the Almoravids from the political perspective, but if we shift to a religious-scholarly perspective, the key seems to be the growing confidence and missionary thrust of the Sunni Malikis of Qayrawan, born out of their encounter with Fatimid Shi'ism, and their eagerness to inculcate nominally Islamised populations with a knowledge of the orthodox religious requirements of the faith. Abu 'Imran's student, Waggag, was in the vanguard of this Sunni missionary movement and passed the torch on to 'Abd Allah b. Yasin, whom he sent to educate the Sanhaja Guddala in the tenets of their religion in response to Abu 'Imran's request that he do so.

Ibn Yasin, therefore, presented Maliki *fiqh*, on the one hand, as the orthodox Sunni alternative to Kharijism and Isma'ili Shi'ism, both of which were also conveniently associated with tribal peoples other than the Sanhaja, and, on the other hand, as a system to more fully Islamise daily life. According to al-Bakri, the heart of Ibn Yasin's teachings was to promote true religion (*al-ḥaqq*), put an end to injustice and to abolish illicit taxation, none of which are specifically Maliki tenets. True religion, however, took the form of Ibn Yasin's firm insistence that his Guddala and then Lamtuna followers obey his, sometimes quite idiosyncratic, versions of Maliki rules relating to prayer, marriage, inheritance and war booty. If tribesmen failed to adhere closely to Ibn Yasin's interpretation of Malikism, they could be subjected to harsh beatings. A man arriving late to pray received five lashes, while anyone who forgot one of their prostrations received twenty lashes. The very process of entry into Almoravid ranks took the form of an intense initiation ritual during which tribesmen were lashed for their previous misdemeanours (100 lashes for fornication, eighty lashes for false speech, eighty lashes for consuming alcohol). Following a similar logic, Ibn Yasin required his adherents to perform each prayer four extra times in order to make up for the numerous times they had undoubtedly failed to perform their prayers before his arrival among them.[18]

As these rigorous punishments imply, Ibn Yasin did not operate in the guise of an orthodox Maliki *faqīh*, leading Bosch Vilá to consider him a poorly educated and 'fanatical' ascetic.[19] However, he was acting as a charismatic holy man similar to numerous other Berber prophets, *mahdī*s and mystics. He maintained an aura of personal sanctity and difference from other men through food taboos, eating only game from the desert rather than the meat or milk of the Almoravid herds, and also through taking the most beautiful women as his brides then divorcing them soon afterwards, a mode of behaviour indicating not simply his passion for women but also a certain charismatic *droit de seigneur*.[20] In the Sanhaja context where divorce was common, Ibn Yasin's ex-wives had no difficulty in finding new husbands, and men may have enhanced their status through marrying women who transferred the charisma of the saint to them.[21] Although al-Bakri's information was not first-hand and may be flawed in its details, it has a certain consistency in its stress upon performance of a set of defined rituals as an initiation to a sect on the path to salvation and on the physical and psychological conditioning of the Almoravids, by extreme and repeated lashings, to wage war on those who did not conform to Ibn Yasin's interpretation of Islam.

Ibn Yasin's militancy brings us to the religious idea with which the Almoravids are most closely associated, that of jihad, which figures in the titles of both Lagardère's and Messier's books on the Almoravids and overlaps with the concept of *ribāṭ* and interpretations of the Almoravids' Arabic name, men of (the) *ribāṭ* (*al-murābiṭūn*). In the Almoravid case, their jihad was Ibn Yasin's mission in its entirety, encompassing not simply fighting deviant non-Maliki Muslims and non-Muslims but also abolishing injustice and illicit taxation.

18 al-Bakri, *Description de l'Afrique*, Arabic text, pp. 169–70; French text, pp. 319–20.

19 Bosch Vilá, *Los Almorávides*, p. 53.

20 al-Bakri, *Description de l'Afrique*, Arabic text, pp. 165, 169; French text, pp. 313, 318.

21 One of the disciples of the twelfth-century Sufi saint, Abu Madyan Shu'ayb willingly married the latter's concubine when he decided to follow a celibate life as a service to his master. Cornell, *Abu Madyan*, p. 14.

Jihad

The Islamic theory of jihad is a vast area that covers military combat, spiritual endeavour and religious reform. Derived from an Arabic root denoting 'effort', it is usually understood to be part of a construct phrase, 'striving in the way of God' (*jihād fī sabīl Allāh*), which was understood over time to encapsulate both internal spiritual jihad to perfect the soul and external jihad to defend Islam against its opponents by the sword, pen or tongue. For early Muslims and those resident on frontiers such as southern Anatolia, northern al-Andalus or the southern Maghrib, military jihad tended to take precedence, although it was often those keen to test their spiritual mettle who devoted themselves to the pursuit of fighting in God's path on the frontiers of the Islamic world. Conversely, the proximity of non-Muslim enemies encouraged political powers to label all kinds of politico-military action 'jihad', formulations that could be contested by rivals, as the Almoravids were to find. Despite this military stress, jihad was, in essence, an abstract principle of religious activism, not a holy war or a crusade with which it is often compared.

The other term closely associated with the Almoravid mission was *ribāṭ* from an Arabic root 'to tie', which we have already encountered in the form of Waggag's *ribāṭ* in the Sus. In the early Islamic era, *ribāṭ* denoted the practical gathering and tethering of horses for a military campaign and, by extension, the act of fighting for the faith, making it a near synonym for jihad. Later it came to mean a scholarly, ascetic or militant frontier community dedicated to spreading the faith and defending Muslim lands – or the building housing them – giving it didactic and spiritual as well as military dimensions. In the absence of detailed contemporary accounts of Ibn Yasin's doctrine, the degree to which the early Almoravids understood their activities as jihad and whether their interpretation of *ribāṭ* entailed spiritual adherence to Ibn Yasin, residence in a special community founded by him or associated with the *ribāṭ* of Waggag, or warfare against non-Muslims and non-Malikis may never be known.

Later writers such as Ibn 'Idhari and Ibn Khaldun certainly considered jihad to be an important frame for Almoravid action, but Ibn 'Idhari, in particular, perceived the entire history of al-Andalus and the Maghrib from that perspective due to his fears about the thirteenth-century advances of the Christian kingdoms in Iberia. Nonetheless, the Maliki juridical nexus in Qayrawan that had begun to draw the western Maghrib into its sphere of influence could have produced genuinely Almoravid ideas of jihad and *ribāṭ*. In his assessment of the Almoravid jihad, Lagardère interprets it as rooted in the Maliki–Ash'ari position on jihad explicated in Qayrawan by Ibn Abi Zayd in his *Risala* and conveyed to the desert edge by Abu Bakr Muhammad b. al-Hasan al-Muradi, a native of Qayrawan educated in Córdoba, who entered the service of the Almoravid Abu Bakr b. 'Umar and became judge of the Almoravids' Saharan capital, Azuggi.[22] This is important as it helps us to see the Almoravid interpretation of Islam not simply as an unimaginative puritanical Saharan Berber form of the faith, but as a dynamic religious system deeply influenced by Qayrawan and contemporary Andalusi centres of learning, even though opponents of the Almoravids later elided those dimensions in favour of using the trope of the ignorant Sanhaja to delegitimise the system as a whole.

For their supporters, the Almoravids' adoption of rigorous, pietistic Maliki praxis entitled and obligated them to expand the sphere of true Islam by a jihad of the sword that followed the basic rules of engagement set out in the jihad section of Maliki *fiqh* manuals. These rules, based on Prophetic precedent, stated that warfare should be the last resort after requests to the enemy to convert to Islam or submit and pay the *jizya* had failed, the procedure followed by the Almoravids against their non-Muslim and sectarian opponents in the Sahara and the Maghrib. This jihad dynamic had to be modified in more urbanised al-Andalus where Maliki law was already dominant and where the elites saw themselves as much better educated Muslims than their new masters. The religious programme of the Almoravids in al-Andalus therefore shifted to moral renewal and reform, encapsulated in the contrast between the pious Almoravids and the Andalusi Maliki *fuqahā'* who supported them on one side, and the 'immoral' Ta'ifa kings and their allies on the other.

This produced a new jihad conceptualised by a group of Andalusi Maliki jurists who saw in the Almoravids military and socio-economic reformers who would right the debauched, exploitative behaviour of many Ta'ifa rulers and end the collection of illicit taxes to pay tribute to Christians. The Almoravid jihad thus became a comprehensive programme of reform to unite the Muslims of al-Andalus as a necessary precondition for jihad against the Christian 'unbelievers' to the north. This modified jihad attracted many important and influential members of the juridical class in al-Andalus and the northwestern Maghrib. Foremost among those jurists were Ibn Rushd al-Jadd of Córdoba, Qadi 'Iyad of Ceuta and Abu Bakr b. al-'Arabi of Seville, who represented the Maliki–Ash'ari synthesis that valued the authoritative literature of the Maliki school, but also accepted the merit of Hadith study and *kalām* methods of argumentation.

Under the aegis of such scholars, Maliki law spread across the Almoravid

[22] Lagardère, *Le djihâd andalou*, pp. 164–6.

empire binding Seville, Ceuta, Marrakesh and Fes into a single religious system in place of the bewildering array of competing heterodox, Kharijite, 'Alid and Isma'ili strands. That is not to say that these religious ideas disappeared, but the slow process by which the western Maghrib joined Ifriqiya and al-Andalus as a zone of Maliki dominance had begun. These positive aspects of the Almoravid jihad, however, went hand in hand with a certain rigidity that had the potential to become oppressive and to stifle alternative approaches to Islam, especially if their exponents seemed to present a political challenge to the Almoravid Maliki legal system so recently put in place.

The most notorious examples of this tendency occurred in the reign of 'Ali b. Yusuf when a groundswell of opposition arose towards the controversial synthesis of Islamic orthodoxy proposed by the eastern Shafi'i scholar Abu Hamid Muhammad al-Ghazali (d. 1111) in his *Ihya' 'Ulum al-Din* (*Revivification of the Religious Sciences*). This seminal summation of Muslim belief and practice had four sections divided into ten books each, dealing with ritual and worship (*'ibādāt*), social customs (*'ādāt*), vices leading to perdition (*muhlikāt*) and virtuous practices leading to salvation (*munjiyāt*), and it came to represent what we now call Sunnism, but it was not uniformly accepted at the outset due to its incorporation of Sufism alongside Ash'ari theology and law, its advocacy of individual social and moral activism (*ḥisba*), and its criticism of the *'ulamā'*, whom al-Ghazali characterised as worldly, power-hungry and self-seeking due to the lack of a Sufi dimension to their faith.

Al-Ghazali's work was introduced to al-Andalus in the late 1090s by Abu Bakr b. al-'Arabi, who had studied with the great master during his period of travel and study in the Islamic east and returned not only with the *Ihya'* but with a legal opinion (*fatwā*) from al-Ghazali expressing support for the Almoravids as legitimate defenders of the Sunni faith in the west. Ibn al-'Arabi's promotion of al-Ghazali's work immediately gained him the hostility of many Maliki *fuqahā'* who felt that al-Ghazali's critique of jurists, obsessed with worldly power and position and lacking moral and spiritual depth was directed at themselves, and saw in his call for the integration of orthodox Sufism, theology and law, and his emphasis on engaged *ḥisba* (the active promotion of good and denunciation of wrong) a dangerous and revolutionary programme liable to lead ordinary Muslims astray.

This hostility was ameliorated in the short term when Ibn al-'Arabi gained the support and patronage of Yusuf b. Tashfin, but the *Ihya' 'Ulum al-Din* came under scrutiny again soon after the accession of 'Ali b. Yusuf to power in 1106 when 'the *fuqahā'* of Córdoba discussed it and rejected some things in it'.[23]

[23] *al-Hulal al-Mawshiyya*, p. 104.

According to Ibn al-Qattan, cited in the *Hulal al-Mawshiyya*, the book's main opponent was the *qāḍī* of Córdoba, Muhammad b. ʻAli b. Hamdin:

> His rejection reached the point that he accused all who read it or acted upon it of unbelief and he incited the sultan [ʻAli b. Yusuf] against it. He summoned the *fuqahā'* to testify and they reached a consensus that it should be burnt. ʻAli b. Yusuf acted on their legal opinion and ordered its burning and so it was burnt in Córdoba. He wrote to the rest of his lands with the command to burn it and its destruction occurred according to his decree across the Maghrib at that time.[24]

This purging of the books of al-Ghazali was repeated in 1143. Although not common, book burning was not unknown in al-Andalus nor was it a purely doctrinal matter, even when the 'false' doctrines contained in works provided the ostensible reason for their destruction.[25] The Umayyad ʻAbd al-Rahman III had ordered the burning of the works of Ibn Masarra in 961 as a trenchant statement about the caliph's right to define doctrine, and the ʻAbbadid ruler of Seville, al-Muʻtadid had ordered the burning of Ibn Hazm's works in the early 1060s at the incitement of the Zahiri scholar's enemies who pointed to a passage in which he had mocked the ʻAbbadid elevation of a fake Umayyad caliph.[26] The fate of the *Ihya' ʻUlum al-Din* in the Almoravid empire was no exception. Its burning in 1109 at the instigation of the judge Ibn Hamdin was not a simple case of Almoravid narrow-mindedness, but part of a larger struggle between different juridical factions. On the one hand, stood the Banu Rushd, who dominated the Córdoban legal establishment and whose chief scion, Ibn Rushd al-Jadd, frequently served as the Almoravid amir's foremost religio-legal adviser, and, on the other hand, the ambitious Banu Hamdin. Muhammad b. Hamdin sought to accrue support among the Maliki *fuqahā'* for his candidacy as premier jurist in Córdoba by allying closely with ʻAli b. Yusuf and pitting himself against the proponents of Ashʻarism, Shafiʻi *fiqh* and al-Ghazali's work in particular.[27]

The second book-burning decree issued in 1143 occurred in the context of the rising religio-political threat posed to the Almoravids in the Maghrib by Ibn Tumart's Almohads and the spread of mahdism and Ghazalian Sufism across the empire. From this perspective, it was al-Ghazali's syncretism and support for Sufism that appeared threatening.[28] In fact, ʻAli b. Yusuf's Maliki

[24] Lagardère, *Le djihâd andalou*, p. 104. See also Ibn ʻIdhari, *al-Bayan*, vol. 4, p. 52.

[25] See Safran, 'Politics of book burning'.

[26] Kaddouri, 'Dissimulation des opinions politiques', p. 143; Safran, 'Politics of book burning', pp. 154–5.

[27] Safran, 'Politics of book burning', pp. 157–60.

[28] Urvoy, *Penseurs d'al-Andalus*, pp. 91–3.

advisers had warned him against the potential dangers presented by the growing popularity of Sufis only a few years before in 1141. Although these Sufi figures suddenly emerge onto the political stage in the 1140s, the maturity of their work shows that Sufism had been developing in southern al-Andalus and the northwest Maghrib for some time, with groups of mystics clustered in Almería, Fes and Tlemcen. Their mystical stance was Ghazalian in the sense that most of them advocated firm adherence to normal ritual practices, and were trained in Hadith studies, theology and the readings of the Qur'an (*qirā'āt*), which they combined with asceticism and spiritual contemplation to draw closer to God.

The most prominent member of this group was Ibn Barrajan of Seville (d. 1141), suggestively known by the epithet, 'al-Ghazali of al-Andalus', who taught Ibn al-'Arif al-Sanhaji (d. 1141) and thus inspired the Almería school of Sufism headed by the latter.[29] Similar figures could be found on the southern side of the Straits of Gibraltar, such as 'Ali b. Hirzihim (d. 1164)[30] of Fes and al-Daqqaq,[31] a native of Sijilmasa who moved between his home town and Fes. Although many Almerían jurists and ascetics had denounced the 1109 decree to burn al-Ghazali's works, the degree to which mystics actually posed a political threat to the establishment is debatable. In the case of Ibn Barrajan, a reclusive individual, this seems to be a misplaced interpretation derived from much later sources.[32]

Nonetheless, in 1141 the Maliki judge of Almería, Ibn al-Aswad, persuaded the Almoravid amir that mystics posed a serious doctrinal and political threat and 'Ali b. Yusuf summoned Ibn Barrajan, Ibn al-'Arif and Abu Bakr al-Mayurqi, a Granadan mystic, to Marrakesh. Al-Mayurqi escaped and travelled east, stopping in Bijaya *en route*, while Ibn Barrajan and Ibn al-'Arif were taken to the Almoravid capital in chains. The course of events that took place in Marrakesh is debated, but the elderly Ibn Barrajan probably died of the rigours of the journey and his imprisonment. Then, due to a disparaging comment he had made, 'Ali b. Yusuf ordered that his body be thrown on a dung heap. When the population heard from the Fasi mystic, 'Ali b. Hirzihim, that the great Andalusi Sufi's corpse had been denied a proper burial, they retrieved it, washed it and performed the funerary prayer.[33] It appears from this anecdote that the idea of the *ṣāliḥīn*, the pious and spiritual adepts worthy of popular admiration and respect, was already widespread in Marrakesh too. Although we do not know how or why, Ibn al-'Arif

[29] Ibn al-Zayyat, Biography 18, *Tashawwuf*, pp. 96–101.
[30] Ibid., Biography 51, pp. 147–53.
[31] Ibid., Biography 41, pp. 135–7.
[32] See Bellver, 'Ibn Barrajān'.
[33] Ibn al-Zayyat, *Tashawwuf*, p. 149; Bellver, 'Ibn Barrajān', pp. 674–7.

was restored to the amir's good graces, but he also died soon afterwards with some claiming he was poisoned by Ibn al-Aswad, the Maliki judge of Almería who had denounced him in the first place.

Almoravid concerns about the spread of Sufism and the influence of al-Ghazali's *Ihya' 'Ulum al-Din* cannot be disentangled from the rise of a series of mahdistic movements that overlapped in significant ways with Sufism and the persistent 'Alid undercurrent in the Islamic west. While mystics did not necessarily see themselves as charismatic religio-political leaders, the charisma (*baraka*) that the population believed inhered in them encouraged mass veneration and action, as the example of the people collecting Ibn Barrajan's body for burial shows. This endowed those who wished to use it with the ability to mobilise large numbers of followers and to take their mystical programme one stage further into the realm of mahdism in which the Sufi exemplar (*quṭb*) became the ultimate Rightly-Guided one, the *mahdī*.[34] The idea of the *mahdī* who would restore justice and religion when Islam reached its nadir was prevalent in both Shi'i and Sunni circles in the early twelfth century, stimulated by the passing of the year 500 (1106) and the psychological shock waves generated by the Crusades and the Christian advance in Iberia. The times seemed strange, threatening and 'out of joint' to many, who sought reassurance and solace in mystical and mahdistic leadership.[35]

In western al-Andalus, today's Algarve, the Sufi Ibn Qasi launched a mahdistic movement in 1142 that recruited numerous followers, his *murīdīn* (disciples, aspirants), including several local notables.[36] Ibn Qasi founded a *ribāṭ* or *rābiṭa* and, with his allies, gained control of Silves, Evora, Beja and Mertola before the movement faltered and Ibn Qasi was forced to seek an alliance with 'Abd al-Mu'min, as we saw in Chapter 3.[37] The ultimate failure of Ibn Qasi's movement led to its denunciation in later Arabic sources as Shi'i extremism (*ghuluww*), or trickery, and Ibn Qasi's *murīdīn* as a rabble of men of dubious morals. However, Ibn Qasi was a correspondent of the mystic Ibn al-'Arif and he was familiar with al-Ghazali's thought as shown by the title of his book, the *Kitab Khal' al-Na'layn* (*The Casting Off of the Two Sandals*), a reference to Moses' removing his sandals at God's command, an incident whose symbolism al Ghazali had analysed.[38] In Ibn Qasi's movement, ascetic Sufism and mahdism fused to forge a resistance movement against the Almoravids and their Maliki *fuqahā'*. However, by far the most successful

[34] García-Arenal, *Messianism and Puritanical Reform*, p. 121.
[35] See Fierro, 'Spiritual alienation and political activism'.
[36] García- Arenal, *Messianism and Puritanical Reform*, pp. 136–9.
[37] See pp. 74–5, above.
[38] Lagardère, *Le djihâd andalou*, pp. 236–8.

movement of this kind was the Almohad mission (*da'wa*) to replace previous approaches to Islam with a renewed, pure monotheism, which had begun in the mountains and valleys south of Marrakesh in the 1120s.

The Almohad Mission and its Theology

Ibn Tumart's mission developed out of the fusion of the religious ideas circulating in al-Andalus, Ifriqiya and the Mashriq. In contrast to the preference for Maliki juridical culture exhibited by the Almoravids, Ibn Tumart professed a sophisticated hybrid form of Islam that wove together strands from Hadith science, Zahiri and Shafi'i *fiqh*, Ghazalian social action (*ḥisba*), and spiritual engagement with Shi'i notions of the imam and *mahdī* to create what he considered to be much more than the sum of its parts, the ultimate revived monotheistic message – *tawḥīd* – giving his followers the name 'the advocates of *tawḥīd*' or 'the true monotheists' (*al-muwaḥḥidūn*). Almohadism has intrigued many scholars including Goldziher, who prepared an introduction to the compilation of Ibn Tumart's teaching called the *A'azz ma yutlab* (*The Greatest Object of Desire*) or the *Book of Ibn Tumart*, and Montgomery Watt, who saw in it not only an Islamic reform movement, but, in aspiration, a new dispensation related to Islam in the same way that Islam was related to its own monotheistic precursors, Christianity and Judaism.[39] For some, Almohadism emerges as a radical synthesis of the many trends within eleventh–twelfth-century Islam, for others it was merely a pastiche of elements that, ultimately, did not fuse into a satisfactory, integrated religious system.[40] Whether rated as a success or failure, however, Almohadism was revolutionary in its time and marked a significant religious rupture with the past that lasted for nearly a century, as well as a new phase in the Islamisation of the western Maghrib.[41]

According to most accounts, Ibn Tumart's education commenced in his natal village in the Sus, an area with known 'Alid proclivities prior to the Almoravid conquest, which he left, probably around 1106, for Córdoba, a city characterised in the late Almoravid era by fissures between Maliki *fuqahā'* sympathetic to Ash'ari theology and the ideas expressed by al-Ghazali in his *Ihya' 'Ulum al-Din* and those who were vehemently opposed to altering the established Maliki religio-legal system. He then travelled eastwards across North Africa, encountering the eminent Maliki *fiqh* and Hadith specialist Abu

[39] Goldziher, *Mohammed Ibn Toumert*; Montgomery Watt, 'The decline of the Almohads'.

[40] Huici Miranda, for instance, describes the *A'azz ma yutlab* as incoherent and lacking in unity; *Historia Política*, vol. 1, p. 96.

[41] For a comprehensive account of Almohad religiosity, see Fierro's collected articles in *The Almohad Revolution*.

Bakr Muhammad al-Turtushi (d. 1126) in Alexandria before apparently heading east to Baghdad. As we saw in Chapter 3, his 'search for knowledge' (*ṭalab al-'ilm*) was reputed to have included an encounter with al-Ghazali himself in Baghdad during which he received from him the mission to overthrow the Almoravids in revenge for their burning of his works. Although the veracity of this legend has been widely dismissed, Ibn Tumart's symbolic contact with Ghazalian Islam with its Shafi'i, Ash'ari and Sufi elements marked his stance as diametrically opposed to that of many of the Almoravid Maliki *fuqahā'*.

From the snippets of information that we have in al-Baydhaq's biography and the core ideas expressed in the *A'azz ma yutlab*, compiled later from 'Abd al-Mu'min's 'lecture notes', we can gain an insight into Ibn Tumart's religious beliefs. In this book, the Islamic message is presented as nothing more nor less than pure Semitic monotheism (*tawḥīd*) or belief in God and His eternal Oneness, a position expressed in two creeds (*'aqīda*), one probably composed later by Ibn Rushd al-Hafid and noted for its rational, philosophical tone.[42] According to the *A'azz ma yutlab*, *tawḥīd* lay at the core of the messages brought by all the prophets and messengers, which were thus one and the same. No true monotheist could understand *tawḥīd* without proper knowledge of the Qur'an and Hadith, and understanding of the sciences related to their study, especially the *'ilm al-ḥadīth* methodology that enabled one to assess each saying of the Prophet appropriately and to dispel doubt (*shakk*) and avoid speculative propositions (*ẓann*). Reason or logic thus joined the Qur'an and Hadith as sources of law in preference to the accumulated wisdom of secondary Maliki commentators, and jurists in general, which contained unacceptable levels of diversity, contradiction and arbitrariness.[43] Opinion (*ra'y*) and interpretation (*ta'wīl*) had their places, but only in the hands of the imam-*mahdī* and his successors.

Al-Baydhaq's description of Ibn Tumart's long journey from Tunis to Marrakesh provides insight into the practical application of his doctrines in relation to both the scholarly class and the mass of the Maghribi population, through teaching, disputation and a radical application of a form of *ḥisba* similar to that advocated by al-Ghazali, although a direct connection cannot be adduced.[44] We have previously met the concept of *ḥisba* in its more limited meaning of proper business practice and public probity imposed on communities by *muḥtasib*s like Ibn 'Abdun of Seville or al-Saqati of Málaga. For al-Ghazali, however, the commanding of good and prohibiting of wrong

[42] Constable, *Medieval Iberia*, pp. 190–7.

[43] Bennison, 'Almohad *tawḥīd*', pp. 199–202; Urvoy, *Penseurs d'al-Andalus*, p. 84; Brunschvig, 'Sur le doctrine du Mahdī Ibn Tūmart'.

[44] Cook, *Commanding Right and Forbidding Wrong*, pp. 427–59.

(*al-amr bi'l-ma'rūf wa'l-nahy 'an al-munkar*) was a broader moral duty incumbent upon individual Muslims to promote ethical behaviour consonant with Islamic law and denounce behaviour contrary to Islamic law. Ibn Tumart took a similar but more radical view, which Cornell describes as 'a theology of moral and political imperatives', in which understanding of one's religion should be manifested not simply through advocacy of what was right but also action against infringements of the Shari'a.[45]

For Ibn Tumart this began by addressing 'mistakes' on the part of Maliki *fuqahā'* and tackling social and religious behaviours that he deemed inappropriate to deepen Islamic knowledge and understanding among the population of the Islamic west as a whole. On several occasions, Ibn Tumart reacted to 'incorrect' or abusive juridical decisions that illustrated the ignorance of Maghribi Maliki *fuqahā'* and their subjection to the whims of political authorities, and reminded or informed them of their duty to 'command good and forbid wrong' and uphold legal positions derived from the Qur'an and Sunna rather than local customs or juridical opinions.

At Sa' (modern Tawrirt), on the route between Tlemcen and Fes, Ibn Tumart saw a group of women adorned and dressed in finery and said to the local *faqīh* who was with him:

> How can you leave women adorned and beautified as if they are on their way to their grooms (*bu'ūl*), do you not fear God and change what is wrong (*taghyīr al-munkar*). There is no way [to God] in what they are doing, for their actions are those of the first *jāhiliyya*. Moreover they are in opposition to God in their actions. Consider His words: They should only show of their adornment what [normally] appears [Qur'an 24: 30].[46]

This short comment both directed the *faqīh* towards the primary source of law, the Qur'an, and his responsibility to command or prohibit behaviour in accordance with it. Frequently Ibn Tumart himself went further than admonition and committed acts of violence towards moral infractions by smashing wine containers, breaking musical instruments, and dispersing men and women mixing in public with indiscriminate beatings. He was forced to leave Bijaya, for instance, after an incident at the end of Ramadan when men and women gathered to celebrate *'īd al-fiṭr* in a market place outside the town. According to al-Baydhaq:

> The imam entered among them with his staff [striking] right and left until he dispersed them. When [his disciple] Ibn al-'Aziz saw him do this he said,

[45] Cornell, 'Understanding is the mother of ability', p. 73.

[46] al-Baydhaq, *Akhbar*, p. 48.

> 'Oh *faqīh*, do not command the market people to do the right thing when they do not know what it is (*lā ya'rifūnahu*) for I am afraid that they will take against you and destroy you.[47]

Similarly, when he reached Tlemcen, his first action was to attack and dismantle a bridal cortege:

> When the Infallible One entered Tlemcen, he found a bride going in a procession to her husband, mounted on a saddle with entertainment and [other] wrong-doing in front of her. He broke the tambourines and other [instruments] of merriment and halted the wrong-doing, and made the bride dismount.[48]

Ibn Tumart increasingly expected his disciples to also 'command good and prohibit wrong'. Al-Baydhaq gives the first indication that Ibn Tumart had begun to delegate the role of zealot to his seven core disciples when they reached the small settlement of Qalal on the road to Fes, stating that he and another disciple called al-Dukkali were sent to 'command the good' when the Almohad party were disturbed by the sound of music and dancing. They failed to convince the villagers who retorted, 'You have your accepted practice (*ma'rūf*) and we have ours. Go or we shall make an example of you and your *faqīh*!'[49] One gets the impression that these young 'trainees', the nucleus of the later *ṭalaba*, did not have quite the aura of Ibn Tumart. The situation was different in Fes soon afterwards:

> One day [Ibn Tumart] came to his disciples and said, 'Where are the young men?' We answered 'We're here!' He said, 'Is anyone absent?' We said, 'All of us are here' and the Infallible One said, 'Go and cut branches from the fig tree which does not bear fruit at the bottom of the valley.' The seven of us went out and collected seven branches from the fig tree. [Ibn Tumart] said, 'Hide your sticks' and we went with him without knowing where we were going until we reached the alleys of the riff-raff where he said, 'Spread out among the shops.' The shops were full of tambourines, rattles, flutes, lutes, rababs, zithers, and other musical instruments. The Infallible One said, 'Break all the instruments you find.' The shopkeepers made a clamour and went to their *qaḍı*, Ibn Ma'isha, to complain. He said to them, 'He [Ibn Tumart] would not have broken and rent them apart if it was not for what he saw (*ra'ā*) in the Sunna. Go, for you are in opposition to the Truth.'[50]

[47] al-Baydhaq, *Akhbar*, p. 36.
[48] Ibid., p. 46.
[49] Ibid., p. 50.
[50] Ibid., p. 52.

These incidents together point to the deeper Islamisation of the countryside envisaged by Ibn Tumart and his desire to replace local 'accepted practice' (*ma'rūf*) with a more universal understanding of the Shari'a and its sources, the Qur'an and Sunna, given integrity and coherence by his *ra'y* (opinion of the sources' meaning). His righteous violence was balanced by a commitment to improving the Islamic infrastructure of the Maghrib and creating an environment in which men and women could live as good Muslims. As the party crossed the central Maghrib, al-Baydhaq notes that they passed many settlements without mosques or with mosques that had fallen into a dire state of disrepair and tried to remedy this situation: they repaired ruined mosques at Akhmas and Gassas an U-Marmur and constructed a new mosque at Tinmalt for the Banu Iznasan.[51] Later, at Wajda, Ibn Tumart 'observed women drawing water alongside men performing their ablutions and said, "Is this not prohibited – the mixing of men and women?"' and then encouraged the community to build a water channel and cistern adjacent to the mosque for ablutions alone.[52]

Ibn Tumart's approach was rooted in his view that every person was responsible for their own soul and their own salvation, and that lack of knowledge or comprehension did not provide an excuse for the commission of sins. Comprehension, however, depended upon intellect and education, and in recognition of the limits of the former, Ibn Tumart's successors formulated two Almohad creeds, one in a traditional Qur'anic form for the masses and one in a rational, philosophical form for the intellectual elite.[53] Although the existence of these two creeds points to Almohad acceptance of a hierarchy of intellect, Ibn Tumart saw religious education of the masses as the duty of religious scholars and, above all, a Muslim ruler who had responsibility both for the temporal material and eternal spiritual welfare of his flock. As we have already noted, he composed his didactic works in both Berber and Arabic to ensure that the principles of *tawḥīd* were accessible to the layman as well as to the scholar.[54]

It was on these grounds that Ibn Tumart most fiercely attacked the Almoravids: his accusation that they were anthropomorphists who took literally Qur'anic verses that describe God as having human attributes, referred to their failure to instruct their Muslim flock that God's transcendence meant that His attributes could not be of the same nature as human ones.[55] From the Almohads' perspective, the Almoravids were, therefore, unqualified to

[51] al-Baydhaq, *Akhbar*, p. 44.
[52] Ibid., p. 47.
[53] Urvoy, *Penseurs d'al-Andalus*, p. 97.
[54] See p. 67, above.
[55] Serrano Ruano, 'Antropomorfistas', pp. 821–2.

lead other Muslims and their reliance on Maliki *fuqahā'*, who were themselves unwilling to engage with new modes of thinking, rendered the entire religio-political edifice bankrupt.

Al-Baydhaq conveys this partisan position in his account of Ibn Tumart's attempts to improve the level of religious learning (*'ilm*) among the *'ulamā'* which juxtaposes his learning and humility with the ignorance and/or hostility of the Maghrib's existing religious elite. Whenever Ibn Tumart and his party reached a town they made their way to a mosque. These mosques were generally not the great mosques of each settlement, but smaller more peripheral institutions where the travellers probably also slept during their sojourn in the town in the normal manner of pious wanderers. He then presided over study circles within each mosque, where he substituted his characteristic taciturnity for eloquence, a tactic that enhanced the impact of his speech. In a typical entry, al-Baydhaq describes the situation in Meknes:

> They received knowledge from him and they told him what knowledge and understanding they had, and the Infallible One made clear to them things they were ignorant of and informed them about things they had not mentioned to him.[56]

Al-Baydhaq conveys the process of dialectic and teaching that took place by using the phrase – *faḥḥamahum wa-fahhamahum* – a word play meaning that he confounded or silenced them and then made them understand.[57] The implication is that Ibn Tumart used the dialectical, logical methods of scholastic theology (*kalām*, *'ilm al-naẓar*) to convey to his audience what he considered to be the correct understanding of the Qur'an and Sunna, while Maliki *fuqahā'*, who relied upon memorisation of the works of early Maliki authorities (*'ilm al-furū'*) and whose knowledge of Hadith science and Ash'ari methods was either minimal or non-existent, were reduced to silence by his superior knowledge and his skills of argumentation. Such encounters varied from teaching sessions at which Ibn Tumart was the recognised master to more contentious situations where elite jurists argued against him, the prime example of which was his disputation with the jurists at the Almoravid court in Marrakesh. Al-Baydhaq describes him again as 'silencing' (*afḥamahum*) his opposition because of their lack of familiarity with scholastic theology, which in this case led to his denunciation by 'Ali b. Yusuf's chief *faqīh*, Malik b. Wuhayb.[58]

This stereotypical contrast between Maliki *fuqahā'* unaware of both the sources (*uṣūl*) of religion and dialectic theology (*kalām*) and Ibn Tumart's

[56] al-Baydhaq, *Akhbar*, p. 54.
[57] Ibid., p. 51.
[58] Ibid., pp. 57–8.

facility and deep knowledge of these sciences was, of course, Almohad propaganda. As we have seen, although there was resistance to Ash'arism among the *fuqahā'*, it had been percolating through Maliki ranks for around a century and had supporters, including Abu Bakr b. al-'Arabi and Ibn Rushd al-Jadd, as well as opponents. Despite Ibn Hamdin's very public denunciation of al-Ghazali's work and burning of the *Ihya 'Ulum al-Din* in 1109, the Almoravid position towards those who favoured new religious trends of eastern origin only conclusively hardened from the 1120s in response to the religio-political challenge posed by Ibn Tumart and the Almohads, the 'Ghazalian' Sufis, and the mahdistic movement of Ibn Qasi in the Algarve.

Ibn Tumart's identification with these religious trends was confirmed by his own adoption of the typical practices of the Sufi *ṣāliḥīn* – asceticism, celibacy and contemplation – and the demeanour of a reformist mystic. His incorporation of Sufi spirituality and personal contact with God alongside strict adherence to the Shari'a, again places Ibn Tumart in the company of al-Ghazali but also of the Andalusi mystics mentioned above, Ibn Barrajan, the 'al-Ghazali of al-Andalus', Ibn al-'Arif and, most of all, the mahdistic Sufi activist Ibn al-Qasi. Fierro has explored this link in terms of a religious trope of alienation in an irreligious world that rendered many pious individuals *ghurabā'* or strangers to the world they were forced to inhabit and its incipient reformers.[59] However, while the Sufis were a community of *ghurabā'* upholding the essence of Islam in a decadent and corrupt world, Ibn Tumart's recourse to the more activist and politically engaged model of the *mahdī* in the 1120s placed him above all other saintly 'strangers' and set him upon a political as well as a religious path.

This personal metamorphosis from a spiritual guide or 'imam' in the sense of teacher to that of the 'infallible imam and undisputed *mahdī*' took place in the context of the rebuffal of Ibn Tumart's message by the Maliki *fuqahā'* in Marrakesh which forced him to retreat to Aghmat and then to the Sus. His transition from inspired teacher to charismatic messianic leader took place during a period of retreat in a cave near his birthplace at Igli in the Sus, a calque on the cave of Hira' where the Prophet Muhammad first received revelations.[60] This transformed his rejection into a necessary stage on his religious path, consolidated his reputation for sanctity among his Berber followers, and enabled him to reconstitute the Masmuda tribes as Almohad fighters for the faith ready to wage a jihad against the Almoravids for their religious failings, and institute God's religion on earth.

[59] See Fierro, 'Spiritual alienation and political activism'.

[60] On the importance of Igli and its location, see Fromherz, 'The Almohad Mecca'.

Ibn Tumart's idea of the *mahdī* may have been inspired by Isma'ili Shi'ism in its later form or by the more general flow of Shi'i ideas into Sunnism that shaped Ghazalian and Sufi concepts of a divinely inspired guide. Urvoy summarises the role of the Almohad imam-*mahdī* as that of interpreter of the Qur'an, using allegorical readings (*ta'wīl*) in conformity with the Almohad creed where necessary, and as elaborator of the Shari'a, but not as an imam of a Shi'i type.[61] From the outside, however, the Almohad *mahdī*'s characteristics, particularly his infallibility (*'iṣma*) or sinlessness, seemed very 'Shi'i', and whether the Almohad understanding of the infallibility of the imam-*mahdī* constituted an inherent quality in the Shi'i sense or a reflection of God's perpetual guidance remains an object of discussion.[62] In either case, it entitled Ibn Tumart to unqualified obedience from his disciples and tribal followers, placing him in the long tradition of charismatic Berber prophets and, from his own perspective, the Semitic prophets of the Qur'an and the Judaeo-Christian scriptures whose missions culminated with his own project to restore primordial monotheism (*tawḥīd*) by overthrowing the Almoravids and converting the Muslims, Christians and Jews of the Islamic west to the true path.

Ibn Tumart's premature death around 1130 transferred responsibility for the Almohad mission to his disciples, headed by 'Abd al-Mu'min and his successors, the Mu'minid caliphs. Although the Mu'minids could not claim the same status as the *mahdī*, they inherited the position of imam from him and remained active heads of the religious, as well as political, community, unlike the Almoravid amirs who had not assumed such a direct role in religious life. The chronicles depict each major Almohad caliph as actively engaged in teaching and promoting Almohad Islam, determining the law and overseeing the moral lives of their subjects. Although 'Abd al-Mu'min is remembered as the warrior who founded the empire and imposed Almohad tenets by force, from the bloody retribution for small Muslim religious infractions criticised by al-Nuwayri to his edict that non-Muslims must convert, his didactic role appears at the beginning of the *A'azz ma yutlab*, where it is stated that the book was compiled by a scribe to whom he dictated his reminiscences of Ibn Tumart's teaching.[63]

'Abd al-Mu'min is also credited with the institutionalisation of the Almohad scholarly class, the *ṭalaba*, and the *ḥuffāẓ* cadres, described in Chapter 3. Members of the *ṭalaba* regularly attended the caliph's council

[61] Urvoy, *Penseurs d'al-Andalus*, p. 96.

[62] Huici Miranda, *Historia política*, vol. 1, pp. 92–3; Cornell, 'Understanding is the mother of ability', pp. 101–2.

[63] Ibn Tumart, *A'azz ma yutlab*, p. 32.

(*majlis*) at which a portion of time was said to have been devoted to religious instruction before affairs of state were dealt with. At the caliph's behest, groups of *ṭalaba* were also stationed in Almohad garrisons across the empire to minister to the troops, to educate them and to act as Almohad missionaries among the subject population. Where necessary, this teaching took place in the 'western tongue' to ensure that Berberophone tribesmen understood what was said to them.

'Abd al-Mu'min's son and successor, Abu Ya'qub Yusuf, emerges from the sources as a ruler and a religious leader of a very different temper whose primary interest was in elite Arabic intellectual culture. He was a skilled Arab grammarian interested in *belles lettres* (*adab*), philosophy (*falsafa*) and medicine, branches of learning that will be considered more fully below. He was also a bibliophile who collected books so avidly that he was compared with the tenth-century Umayyad caliph al-Hakam II, who was also famed for his huge library. In addition to his secular and literary interests, however, Abu Ya'qub Yusuf was also an expert in Qur'anic recitation and exegesis, Hadith science and *fiqh*, both the *'ilm al-uṣūl* and the *'ilm al-furū'*, which enabled him to elaborate law according to Almohad principles.[64] As caliph-imam he maintained the tradition of holding sessions at which the *ṭalaba* discussed theological matters, and he is credited with ordering the compilation of a book of Hadith related to jihad as a prelude to his 1184 Santarem campaign, maintaining the tradition of composition initiated by Ibn Tumart and 'Abd al-Mu'min. The personal role of the caliph in religious instruction and the veneration accorded to him is conveyed by al-Marrakushi's description of this event:

> When the Commander of the Faithful started to prepare to campaign against the Christians he commanded the *'ulamā'* to collect Hadith on jihad to dictate to the Almohads so that they could study them – this continues to be their custom until today. The *'ulamā'* gathered them and brought them to him and he used to dictate them to the people himself. Each of the Almohads and the Mu'minid princes used to come with a tablet upon which to take dictation. One day Hilal came without his tablet and when the people took out their tablets, the chief minister said to him, 'Where is your tablet, Abu Qamar?' When he became embarrassed and began to apologise, the Commander of the Faithful took a tablet from beneath his cloak and gave it to him, saying, 'This is his tablet.' The next day [Hilal] came with a different tablet to the one given to him by the Commander of the Faithful and when he glanced at him he asked, 'Where is your tablet from yesterday, Abu Qamar?' He said, 'I have hidden it and made a testament

[64] See p. 95, above.

> that it should be placed between my skin and my shroud if I die.' He then continued to weep until others in the gathering wept too. The Commander of the Faithful interjected, 'This is true devotion!' and bestowed horses, money and robes upon him and his family.[65]

In the event, the Santarem campaign proved fatal for Abu Ya'qub Yusuf himself. He was succeeded by his son, Ya'qub al-Mansur, whose reign has gone down in the annals as a phase during which Almohad religious principles were imposed more aggressively and the continued circulation and study of Maliki juridical commentaries was directly challenged by the Almohads. According to Ibn 'Idhari, Ya'qub al-Mansur showed great personal interest in the maintenance of Islamic legal prescriptions and the active 'commanding of good and forbidding of wrong'. When he reached Marrakesh for the first time after his accession, he was shocked and angered to find 'wantonness openly declared and [people] competing to satiate their passions and business flourishing in the slave market for female singers and entertainers'. In response,

> He commanded that intoxicating beverages be poured away and prohibited, and warned that their use would be punishable by death. He dispatched missives to that effect to all the provinces and cities and the amount poured away was worth a vast sum. The letters putting this into effect included sections on the spreading of justice and insisted that officials and governors must treat the subject flock well with the object of giving them satisfaction in the fulfilment of their rights, the staying of the hand of their oppressors, and permission to plaintiffs and the oppressed to cross the sea [to see the caliph].[66]

This righting of wrongs committed by those in power was both a religious and social responsibility of an Islamic ruler which Ya'qub al-Mansur further fulfilled by holding open sessions in one of the great mosques of Marrakesh to dispense justice to petitioners, although the popularity of these sessions led to their eventual restriction:

> His first session took place at the beginning of Rajab 580 (October 1184) in the great mosque adjacent to the Qasr al-Hajar from the morning prayer until nearly noon as he put the plaintiffs at ease by asking them about what wealth they had. The notables were terrified that his presence in such a place might lead to attacks [on them] and their humiliation with little room for discussion. The lower classes came among them and they were fined a lot of money. Everyone who made a claim based on suspicion or an allegation was

[65] al-Marrakushi, *Mu'jib*, p. 369.
[66] Ibn 'Idhari, *al-Bayan*, vol. 4, p. 244.

> persuaded to reach a settlement that satisfied him instead of going to trial. Yusuf b. ʿUmar said, 'I was present when market folk and merchants made claims against the *sayyid* Abu Zayd. One of them said, "I gave him a horse", another said, "A slave girl", and many other claims [were made too] and all received satisfaction. However, when the rabble started to crowd in and the benefits to plaintiffs declined, and people started to come with the smallest petition, sometimes just for a glimpse of the sultan rather than to secure their rights, the sessions were closed to the common people.'[67]

The caliph's status as the religious head of the community was also conveyed through elaborate public religious rituals which developed gradually from the reign of ʿAbd al-Mu'min onwards. When the caliph was in residence in Marrakesh, he orchestrated the Friday prayer in the Kutubiyya great mosque which he entered directly from the palace via an enclosed walkway with his entourage. In the Almohad capital at least, the *khaṭīb* gave two sermons, the second of which included prayers dedicated to Ibn Tumart and the Mu'minid caliphs. The caliph personally concluded the gathering with a prayer then left the mosque.[68] Almohad military progresses also had an intense ritual dimension that foregrounded the religious position of the caliph and the *ṭalaba*: before departing the caliph recited a prayer after which the *ṭalaba* in attendance recited a portion (*ḥizb*) of the Qur'an, followed by selected Hadith and Ibn Tumart's creed 'in their language [i.e., Berber] and Arabic'. The ceremony of departure ended with the caliph reciting further prayers.[69]

As mentioned in Chapter 3, the Almohads also included religious artefacts in their military progresses: the Qur'ans of ʿUthman b. ʿAffan and Ibn Tumart. From the perspective of legitimacy, the privileging of the Qur'an of ʿUthman over that of Ibn Tumart indicated an attempt on the part of the Mu'minid caliphs to connect themselves to the Córdoban Umayyad heritage, but from a religious perspective, the public honouring of two copies of the Qur'an also reminded the Almohad army and the population who massed to see the passing caliph of the primacy of the word of God in religious life and the caliph's role in preserving and transmitting that.

This role was particularly evident during the reign of Yaʿqub al-Mansur who made a point of leading efforts to enhance the range of accepted Almohad Hadith by ordering the *ṭalaba* to compile a manual on prayer drawn from those Hadith collections tolerated by the Almohads, which included the

67 Ibn ʿIdhari, *al-Bayan*, vol. 4, pp. 244–5.
68 al-Marrakushi, *Muʿjib*, pp. 485–8.
69 Ibid., p. 485.

canonical six collections (the *Sahihayn* of al-Bukhari and Muslim the *Sunans* of Abu Dawud, al-Nasa'i and Ibn Maja, the *Jami'* of al-Tirmidhi), the *Muwatta'* of Malik and a few other titles. Al-Marrakushi specifically compares the caliph's action with Ibn Tumart's gathering of Hadith on the topic of purification (*ṭahāra*).[70] It also calls to mind the example of his father who had ordered the compilation of a similar Hadith manual on jihad. Like his predecessors, Ya'qub al-Mansur is then depicted in an active didactic role 'dictating' the Hadith to the Almohads and expecting them to memorise them in a *majlis* setting, and also sending the new compilation to the provinces with instructions that those who memorised it should be rewarded handsomely.

In the case of Ya'qub al-Mansur, attention to Hadith collecting was part and parcel of a last strenuous effort to inculcate the Almohad source-based approach to law in place of the commentary-based Maliki *madhhab*. In addition to collecting Hadith and extending particular favour to experts in Hadith among the *ṭalaba*, Ya'qub al-Mansur also openly denounced Maliki *'ilm al-furū'* and overly speculative approaches to extrapolating legal positions, the *'ilm al-ra'y*, and ordered the first recorded action against Maliki commentary works (*furū'*), including the seminal *Mudawwana* of Sahnun, the *Kitab* of Ibn Yunus,[71] and Ibn Abi Zayd's *Nawadir* and *Risala*, which were collected up and publicly burnt across the empire.[72] These actions led al-Marrakushi to later describe him as determined to efface the *madhhab* of Malik, a task his father and grandfather had not dared to undertake.[73]

The Almohad position on formulating law has sometimes been seen as Zahiri in its preference for looking for evident (*ẓāhir*) guidelines in the Qur'an and Sunna, and this position is summed up in an anecdote from this period traced back to Abu Bakr b. al-Jadd who said that when he went to meet Ya'qub al-Mansur for the first time, he found him with the Maliki commentary work of Ibn Yunus in front of him and he said:

> 'Abu Bakr, I am looking into these disparate opinions which make mischief with God's religion. Abu Bakr, have you seen the cases with four, five or even more comments? Which one is the Truth? Indeed which one should a non-expert (*muqallid*) follow?' So I began to explain to him what he had found obscure but he cut me off, saying, 'Abu Bakr, there is nothing but

[70] al-Marrakushi, *Mu'jib*, p. 401.

[71] Abu Bakr Muhammad b. 'Abd Allah b. Yunus al-Tamimi (d. 1049) from Sicily who studied in Qayrawan with Abu 'Imran al-Fasi and wrote a book on the *Mudawwana*. Makhluf, *Tabaqat al-Malikiyya*, pp. 164–5.

[72] al-Marrakushi, *Mu'jib*, p. 400; Safran, 'Politics of book burning', pp. 162–4.

[73] al-Marrakushi, *Mu'jib*, p. 401.

this,' and he indicated the Qur'an, 'and this,' and he indicated the *Sunan* of Abi Dawud which was to his right, 'or the sword!'[74]

This story reveals a great deal about the challenge faced by the Almohads in trying to impose an Almohad legal system, which may be compared with the challenge faced centuries earlier by the Fatimids when they tried to impose Isma'ili Shi'ism in Ifriqiya. In both cases, the Maliki school proved to be too firmly embedded to be dislodged entirely. The jurist Abu Bakr b. al-Jadd was still thinking like a Maliki, despite having spent decades of his life in the circles around the Almohad caliph. Moreover, the greatest juridical compilation of the era, Ibn Rushd al-Hafid's *Bidayat al-Mujtahid wa-Nihayat al-Muqtasid fi'l-Fiqh*, which reviews the divergent opinions of the different law schools and presents Ibn Rushd's own assessment of the most rational solution in each case, is routinely described as Maliki rather than Almohad, despite the author's long service as an Almohad judge.

If the Almohad religious experiment began to falter after Ya'qub al-Mansur's final push, it received a much greater blow thirty years later when the caliph al-Ma'mun publicly denied that Ibn Tumart had been the *mahdī*. Although many Almohad shaykhs and *ṭalaba* resisted this dramatic reversal of position and the Hafsid governors declared their independence in the name of preserving Almohadism in Ifriqiya, the tide had turned towards a reassertion of Malikism as the dominant religio-legal school of the Maghrib and al-Andalus. Urvoy suggests that this was because only thinkers or intellectuals were seriously influenced by the Almohad system, which was often considered a school of thought (*madhhab al-fikr*) rather than law.[75] Ironically, then, Almohadism did not transform the lives of ordinary Muslims, but contributed instead to a dramatic flowering of philosophy, both Muslim and Jewish, and the stimulation of the more intellectual aspects of Sufism.

The Conundrum of Philosophy

Although we would not necessarily consider the study of philosophy to be a religious matter, in the pre-modern world the nature of philosophical questions about the origins of life and the world and what created them naturally impinged upon religion. During the 'Abbasid translation movement many classical Greek philosophical works were translated into Arabic, including Aristotle and Plato, and became accessible to the Muslim intellectual elite. Although the fact that the ancient Greeks were polytheists was problematic, the example of Christian Aristotelians who had managed to marry Greek

[74] al-Marrakushi, *Mu'jib*, pp. 401–2.
[75] Urvoy, *Penseurs d'al-Andalus*, p. 97.

philosophy and Semitic monotheism, provided the tools for Muslims to do the same, and an important Islamic philosophical tradition emerged in Iraq. Exponents of philosophy (*falsafa*) often enjoyed state patronage, but some religious scholars viewed philosophy as a dangerous pursuit liable to lead practitioners to atheism and their souls to perdition, and attitudes to philosophy varied greatly from one era and location to another.

In the Islamic east, the sciences of the Ancients (*'ulūm al-awā'il*), including philosophy, could be found in all the major libraries and were popular with private collectors too. During the Umayyad caliphal era, the inhabitants of the Islamic west also became interested in such elite intellectual pursuits and the impressive library collection of the Umayyad caliph al-Hakam II, which we have mentioned already, included many philosophical works composed in the east. An indigenous Andalusi philosophical tradition, of which Ibn Masarra has sometimes been seen as the first exemplar, also began to develop, coming to fruition not during the Umayyad era but in the Almohad age. Most of the great names in Andalusi philosophy worked for the Almoravids and Almohads and, in many cases, received direct patronage to compose their philosophical works. This has always been something of a conundrum, given the tropes about ignorant and fanatical Berber rulers. However, if we put such prejudices aside, it becomes clear that the Almoravids' patronage of Arabic letters in general allowed some latitude for philosophical pursuits, while the Almohad religious programme actually encompassed a rational and philosophical strand. Nonetheless, patronage and state support for philosophy tended to be conditional and when antagonistic religious scholars exerted sufficient pressure, the alliance broke down.

The golden age of western Islamic philosophy began with Ibn Bajja (Avempace), a native of Saragossa, who was a young man when the city fell to the Almoravids around 1110. He took service with the Almoravids as a *wazīr*, a role that involved advising the governor of Saragossa, Ibn Tifalwit, and providing the Arabic-Andalusi expertise that the Saharans lacked at this point. He then had a chequered career involving service to the Almoravids in various cities including Seville and periods of imprisonment for heresy. He died in 1139 in Fes. Like his contemporaries, Ibn Bajja was interested in a range of secular subjects, including poetry, astronomy and botany as well as philosophy. His philosophical position drew inspiration from neo-Platonic works such as the treatise of Alexander of Aphrodisias and from eastern Islamic philosophers like al-Farabi. Although not all his works are extant, those that remain consider the ascent of the soul to the Divine from an intellectual rather than a mystical perspective and ponder how the enlightened man or philosopher should react to the imperfection of society around him. His conclusion is that in the absence of the perfect city, *al-madīna al-fāḍila*, the philosopher should withdraw and keep to himself, a position rendered particularly pragmatic by his imprisonment for heresy.

The next philosopher of note to emerge was Ibn Tufayl (Abubacer) (d. 1185–6) who came from Guadix, a polymath with an interest in Sufism and the sciences who practised medicine in Granada as his profession. At some point he entered the service of the Almohads as a secretary and worked in Granada and Ceuta before joining the court of Abu Ya'qub Yusuf as his personal physician. He seems to have developed a close relationship with the caliph who was very interested in philosophy and discussed philosophical questions with him at length. He is primarily famous for his allegorical treatise, *Risalat Hayy b. Yaqzan* (*Alive Son of Awake*), which explores the issue of how a human apprehends God.[76]

Hayy is abandoned as a baby (or born) on an island and brought up by a gazelle, but nonetheless perceives the existence of a Creator by use of observation, experiment and his intellect. He passes through many stages of understanding as the doe nurtures him then dies, leaving him to look after himself and to ponder the natural order. Eventually, he retreats into a cave to commune with God in a mystical sense, gaining focus through whirling like a dervish but, ultimately, putting physical sensations aside to apprehend God in utter stillness. In the period after this epiphany, Hayy encounters Absal, an ascetic seeking retreat on the island, who teaches him to speak and compares his revealed religion, 'a "thinly veiled" generic counterpart to Islam', to Hayy's self-taught philosophy and mysticism.[77] The two men return to Absal's land, ruled by a devout and pious king called Salman, in the hope of showing its inhabitants the commonality of theological and philosophical truth, but they fail and Hayy b. Yaqzan returns to his island with Absal.

There is a varied literature on *Hayy b. Yaqzan* and its interpretation, but, put simply, Hayy represents an approach to God rooted in the intellect, a philosopher, albeit of a mystical bent; Absal stands for the pious theologian; while King Salman is the epitome of the masses who live by unquestioning faith.[78] The retreat of Hayy and Absal to their island signals the fact that while an intellectual elite can appreciate rational moral truths, 'the mass of mankind have neither the force of intellect to apprehend them clearly as ideas, or the force of character to follow them strictly as laws'.[79] In these circumstances, revealed religion is necessary to emotionally engage people and provide them

[76] Goodman, *Ibn Tufayl's Hayy b. Yaqzān.*

[77] Goodman, 'Ibn Ṭufayl', p. 321.

[78] See Conrad, *The World of Ibn Ṭufayl.*

[79] Goodman, 'Ibn Ṭufayl', p. 328.

with a symbolic explanation for the path that should be followed to ensure some measure of social and spiritual harmony. This story encapsulated the Almohad recognition of the role of reason, but also the limitations imposed by the disparities in human intellect. It also captured the imagination of Edward Pocock who published it with a Latin translation in 1671. That was followed by Simon Ockley's English translation in the eighteenth century, which may have been the inspiration for Defoe's *Robinson Crusoe.*

As a close confidant of the caliph Abu Ya'qub Yusuf, Ibn Tufayl was in a position to promote other philosophers and, according to al-Marrakushi, he was responsible for introducing the young Ibn Rushd al-Hafid (Averroes) to him. Ibn Rushd is the best known of the Almohad-era Muslim philosophers. As a scion of the important Córdoban Banu Rushd family and the grandson of Ibn Rushd al-Jadd, he was well educated in the religious sciences, medicine and astronomy, and he became a proficient jurist who had a glittering judicial as well as intellectual career. Like many other notable Andalusi lineages, the Banu Rushd offered their allegiance to the Almohads when they replaced the Almoravids and quickly became part of the Almohad establishment. Ibn Rushd held the judgeships of Seville and Córdoba during his career and wrote a jurisprudential manual, the *Bidayat al-Mujtahid* mentioned above, in addition to his philosophical work which centred on interpreting and commenting upon the Aristotelian corpus. He has also been credited with redacting the Almohad creed in its mature rationalist form. He was therefore the quintessential Almohad intellectual, able to move between the Maliki *fuqahā'*, the Almohad *ṭalaba* and the circle of thinkers around the caliph.

In al-Marrakushi's account, Ibn Rushd commenced his great Aristotelian project after the caliph expressed his lack of comprehension of Aristotle's works and asked Ibn Tufayl to explain them. Ibn Tufayl demurred on the grounds of his advanced age and passed the task to Ibn Rushd. However, it is likely that Ibn Rushd had begun his work on Aristotle prior to joining the caliph's intimate circle. Over the course of his life, he wrote a series of paraphrases, summaries and commentaries on Aristotle's corpus in its Arabic form, as well as other works such as the famous 'Refutation of the Refutation' (*Tahafut al-Tahafut*), which strongly critiqued al-Ghazali's much earlier 'Refutation of the Philosophers' (*Tahafut al-Falasifa*).

As a jurist and a philosopher, Ibn Rushd very much believed that these different approaches to knowledge were not antagonistic but, rather, different aspects of a single reality, making the Aristotelian creative principle and God parallel concepts. Many religious scholars did not agree and, despite Ya'qub al-Mansur's support for him, the elderly philosopher fell foul of the Maliki *fuqahā'* in the mid-1190s when they accused him of holding unorthodox beliefs derived from his excessive interest in classical pagan philosophy. The caliph somewhat ambiguously avoided taking direct measures against Ibn Rushd, but ordered the *ṭalaba* in attendance at his *majlis* to issue a statement of the caliph's right to determine doctrine and take action against deviance – a stance maintained by all his Almohad predecessors – which he probably hoped would put an end to the agitation of the *fuqahā'*. Instead of respecting the caliph's rights, however, Ibn Rushd's Córdoban enemies took this as an endorsement of their stand against 'deviance' and hounded the philosopher from the great mosque.

In 1196, Ya'qub al-Mansur bowed to the pressure and issued a decree prohibiting the study of philosophy and non-religious science in general, although applied sciences such as medicine, mathematics and astronomy were exempted from the purge, while Ibn Rushd was temporarily exiled to the small town of Lucena.[80] Ya'qub al-Mansur's treatment of Ibn Rushd did not necessarily reflect his personal feelings as he restored the philosopher to favour when he left al-Andalus for Marrakesh, instead it expressed his official role as guarantor of the religious welfare of his subjects and the importance of Muslim unity, rather than doctrinal disagreement, in the face of the ever-present Christian pressure on the Iberian frontier. It also confirmed the practical impossibility of dislodging the Maliki *fuqahā'* at the expense of Ibn Rushd and other intellectuals who had previously been well supported by the regime.

Although Ibn Rushd's philosophy marked an end rather than a beginning for Islamic philosophy in the west, it was more influential in Jewish and Latin Christian circles. Jewish philosophy and thought developed in tandem with Islamic philosophy during this period, and any discussion of the discipline in Almohad times must mention Musa b. Maymun or Maimonides (d. 1204), a towering figure in medieval Jewish philosophy, law and medicine who grew up in the Almohad empire and probably spent a period of time as a convert to Islam, that is, one of the *islamiyyūn*, before migrating to Egypt and reverting to the open practice of Judaism. Maimonides studied Muslim as well as Jewish thinkers, including al-Farabi, al-Ghazali and the Andalusi philosophers Ibn Bajja and Ibn Tufayl, who all contributed to the evolution of his philosophic thought which developed in parallel to that of his contemporary Ibn Rushd. After his migration to Egypt, he also read Ibn Rushd whose ideas thus made their way into Jewish philosophy.[81] Meanwhile translations of Ibn Rushd's work into Latin provided the material for Latin Averroism, promoted by Thomas Aquinas among others.

[80] Serrano Ruano, 'Explicit cruelty, implicit compassion', p. 223.
[81] Urvoy, *Penseurs d'al-Andalus*, pp. 190–2.

Other Forms of Knowledge and Learning

In addition to philosophy, there was a range of less contentious learned pursuits cultivated in the Almoravid and Almohad eras, although neither stand out in Arabic literary and scientific terms to the same extent as the Umayyad caliphal era, which is generally taken as the cultural benchmark for the rest of the Islamic west. This is valid for some areas of learning but less so for others, particularly philosophy as we have seen, and poets, writers and physicians clustered around the Almoravid and Almohad rulers, just as they had gathered around their Ta'ifa or Umayyad predecessors. Many of these men were *'ulamā'* in the wider sense of the word, who were trained in the religious sciences as well as their chosen intellectual, scientific or literary field, and many spent their careers between al-Andalus and North Africa. This transferred urban Andalusi literary and scientific expertise ever southwards, most notably to Marrakesh which, like any Islamic capital, came to host a courtly circle of Arabophone *literati* and scientists.

From the point of view of literary historians, the decline of the Umayyad caliphate had a parlous effect on courtly poetry, which Gruendler sums up in her comment that, 'Under the Ta'ifa kings and even more so under the Almoravids, literary patronage waned and the status of poets fell beneath that of other professions.'[82] The Saharan Sanhaja's poor command of Arabic certainly did not help the situation, but, given that second-generation Lamtuna princes and princesses were literate in the high Arabic tradition, this can be overstressed. The austere religious culture preferred by the Almoravids, which included disapproval of the drinking practices and sexual freedom, including homosexuality, rightly or wrongly associated with poetic gatherings, may also have impacted on their patronage of poets. Despite this, the unique strophic poetry forms of al-Andalus, the vernacular *zajal* and the more literary *muwashshaḥa*, remained extremely popular and cultivated by many. Moreover, the relative insecurity of patronage gave poets a certain freedom of opinion which made them as likely to criticise as to compliment the ruling elite, or to eulogise rival patrons. The Córdoban Ibn Quzman, renowned for his *zajal* poems that frequently mocked the public austerity of the Almoravid era with references to wine, adultery and prostitution, stands out in this respect.[83]

The Almohads certainly patronised poets, particularly the authors of the panegyrics (*madīḥ*) which the Mu'minids expected to hear on every occasion. Ibn Sahib al-Salat repeatedly mentions poets gathering in Marrakesh, Ribat

[82] Gruendler, 'The Qasida', p. 224.
[83] Buturovic, 'Ibn Quzmān'; see also Urvoy, *Penseurs d'al-Andalus*, pp. 126–7.

al-Fath, Jabal al-Fath (Gibraltar) and Seville, and peppers his text with selections of the poetry recited on these occasions and the generous rewards doled out by the caliphs and princes of the blood. These poems, often regarded as perfunctory or sycophantic rather than accomplished in a poetic sense, await a comprehensive study. Al-Marrakushi provides an anecdote on the authority of the son of a poet called Muhammad b. Habbus al-Fasi that contrasts the difficult circumstances of poets under the Almoravids with their return to prosperity under the Almohads:

> I entered Silves in al-Andalus, and on the day I entered the town I had not eaten for three days. I asked who would be an appropriate person to seek out and someone directed me to a man called Ibn al-Malh. I went to a paper seller and asked him for a sheet of paper and an inkwell. He gave them to me and I composed some verses praising [Ibn al-Malh] and set off for his house. He was in the vestibule so I greeted him and he welcomed me and returned my greetings in the nicest way. He said, 'I reckon you are a stranger!' 'Indeed,' I replied, and he asked me, 'From what class of person are you?' I informed him that I was a literary man, a poet, and then recited the verses I had composed. They made a fine impression on him and he admitted me to his home, brought me food and started to talk to me. I never experienced a better encounter than that and when the time for my departure came, he left and then returned with two slaves carrying a trunk which they set down before me. He opened it and took out 700 Almoravid *dīnār*s and gave them to me, saying, 'This is for you!' Then he gave me a bag with 40 *mithqāl*s in and said, 'This is from me!' I was astonished at his words which seemed very obscure to me, so I asked him, 'How does this come to me?' He replied, 'I will tell you: I made an endowment of some land which is part of my estate for poets and it has produced 100 *dīnār*s profit per annum but for seven years no one has come to me because of the civil strife that plagues the land. So I have gathered the money and now I am giving it to you! As for this, meaning the 40 *dīnār*s (sic), it is my own money. So I came to him hungry and poor and left satiated and rich![84]

Ibn Habbus went on to become the first poet to recite in front of 'Abd al-Mu'min in Gibraltar in 1160, and a member of the circle of poets at court. His name indicates his Maghribi Berber origin and thus the entry of North Africans into the court circle of poets, previously dominated by Andalusis. However, his poetry was reckoned to be derivative by al-Marrakushi, who adds that Ibn Habbus' poetry was of the school of Muhammad b. Hani', a tenth-century Andalusi poet educated in Seville, but that the latter's poetry was naturally

[84] al-Marrakushi, *Mu'jib*, pp. 311–12.

superior to that of his Maghribi imitator.[85] Another poet present in Gibraltar was Abu 'Abd Allah Muhammad b. Ghalib of Valencia, known as al-Rusafi, who presented panegyric *qaṣīda*s to the Almohad caliph, but preferred to spend most of his time away from court making a living mending clothes in order to retain his independence from power.[86]

Although Ibn Quzman and al-Rusafi held aloof from power, other poets joined the ranks of Almoravid and Almohad secretaries (*kuttāb*) who often had to compose poetry as part of their official role. Among the best known of these were 'Abd al-Mu'min's chief secretary and then minister, Ibn 'Atiyya, whose story was recounted above, and also the late Almohad poet, the Sevillan Abu'l-Hasan 'Ali al-Ru'ayni, who worked as a secretary in various Andalusi and Maghribi towns.[87] Another important late Almohad literary figure was Abu 'Abd Allah Muhammad b. al-Abbar of Valencia, who served as an Almohad secretary during the decades before Valencia fell to the Aragonese, then left for Ifriqiya where he entered Hafsid service. A religious scholar, a poet and a writer of literary prose, Ibn al-Abbar is best known for his extension to the biographical dictionary written by Ibn Bashkuwal.

In addition to supporting poetry and epistolary writing (*inshā'*), the Almoravid and Almohad courts also encouraged the composition of dynastic chronicles, even if historical production in general did not flourish as it had previously. Although many of the chronicles of this era are lost, it is obvious that the works of the Almoravid historian al-Sayrafi, or the Almohad historians Ibn Sahib al-Salat and al-Marrakushi, provided much of the material upon which the famous Maghribi and Andalusi historians of the next centuries, namely, Ibn 'Idhari, Ibn Khaldun and Ibn al-Khatib, relied. While the predecessors of these historians, such as Ibn Hayyan, lived and worked in al-Andalus, the Almoravid and Almohad historians all worked in Marrakesh at some point, underlining the importance of the era for the development of Arabic literary culture in the western Maghrib and its contribution to the later emergence of schools of history writing in Marrakesh and Fes.

In the scientific sphere, the established range of subjects continued to be taught and practised, including medicine, mathematics and astronomy in which many of the philosophers we have mentioned, including Ibn Tufayl and Ibn Rushd, specialised alongside philosophy, and which did not face

85 Ibn Hani' al-Andalusi's father was a Fatimid missionary sent to Seville where Ibn Hani' received his education. He fled across the Straits of Gibraltar and joined the Fatimids when his Isma'ili sympathies made life in al-Andalus under the Umayyad caliph 'Abd al-Rahman III untenable. Dachraoui, 'Ibn Hāni''.

86 Garulo, 'al-Ruṣāfī'.

87 Fierro, 'al-Ru'aynī'.

the same disapproval as the latter. In the first field, medicine, one family dominated over several generation, the Banu Zuhr who hailed from Játiva and produced a succession of *'ulamā'*, government officials and physicians from the Ta'ifa era until the last decades of the Almohad empire.[88] They excelled in both the theory and practice of medicine and were renowned for their clinical skills. The run of eminent physicians in the family began with Abu'l-'Ala' Zuhr b. 'Abd al-Malik (d. 1130), who was born in Seville during the 'Abbadid era. Although patronised by al-Mu'tamid b. 'Abbad, he subsequently transferred his allegiance to the Almoravids and gained a high position in the government of Yusuf b. Tashfin. In keeping with custom, he studied the religious sciences and Arabic literature as well as learning medicine, which became his primary interest, with his father. He both practised medicine and entered into dialectics with many of the established canons of eastern medicine, including work by Hunayn b. Ishaq, al-Razi, Ibn Ridwan and Ibn Sina (Avicenna). He also composed books based on his own medical observations and on drugs.

His son Abu Marwan 'Abd al-Malik b. Zuhr (d. 1161) had a similar well-rounded education that included *fiqh* and other religious sciences, literature and medicine. He entered Almoravid service and travelled to North Africa, joining the many scientists, scholars and literati working for the Almoravids in Marrakesh. In 1121, he completed a summary of medicine, *Kitab al-Iqtisad fi Islah al-Anfus wa'l-Ajsad*, that he dedicated to the Almoravid prince, Ibrahim b. Yusuf b. Tashfin, but he fell foul of the amir 'Ali b. Yusuf for unknown reasons and spent some time in prison. When the Almoravids were swept away by the Almohads nearly three decades later, Ibn Zuhr entered the service of 'Abd al-Mu'min as a physician. The profile of his son, Abu Bakr Muhammad b. 'Abd al-Malik b. Zuhr al-Hafid (d. 1198–9), was similar. Growing up in Almoravid times, he studied Maliki *fiqh*, including the *Mudawwana* of Sahnun and the *Musnad* of Ibn Abi Shayba, and also Arabic literature, becoming an accomplished *muwashshaḥa* poet, as well as following the family tradition of studying medicine with his father. He also held the post of physician to the third Almohad caliph, Ya'qub al-Mansur, who is said to have put him in charge of purging works of philosophy in the 1190s while permitting him to keep his own books.

In the interconnected realms of mathematics and astronomy, also practised by Ibn Tufayl and Ibn Rushd, experts continued to work and build on earlier Andalusi and eastern knowledge. A particular feature of the era was the so-called 'astronomical revolution' in which Andalusi astronomers called into question some of the assumptions in Ptolemy's *Almagest* about the

[88] See Arnaldez, 'Ibn Zuhr'; Urvoy, *Penseurs d'al-Andalus*, pp. 151–3.

movements of the sun and the planets, thereby prefiguring the later findings of Galileo.[89] The most famous mathematician and astronomer of the period was Jabir b. Aflah, who lived in Seville and composed not only a correction to the Ptolemy's *Almagest* (*Islah al-Majisti* or *Kitab al-Hay'a*), but also a treatise on trigonometry that was quickly translated into Latin.

Popular Religiosity and the Rise of Sufism

One of the most significant religious developments during the eleventh and twelfth centuries was the adoption of Sufism by many individuals, which invigorated the older Andalusi esoteric tradition represented by Ibn Masarra and encouraged the spread of Sufism across southern al-Andalus and the Maghrib, and its infiltration of other religious and intellectual pursuits such as the philosophy of Ibn Tufayl. As we saw above, Sufism emerged into the historical light at the end of the Almoravid era with Andalusi figures such as Ibn Barrajan, Ibn al-'Arif al-Sanhaji and Ibn Qasi, who combined Sufism with orthodox religious praxis in the spirit of al-Ghazali and were identified as part of the same oppositional bloc as Ibn Tumart. The biographies in Ibn al-Zayyat's dictionary of Sufis, *al-Tashawwuf ila Rijal al-Tasawwuf*, indicate, however, that there were many Maghribi mystics too, with a cluster in Fes and individual Sufis dotted through the countryside and in smaller towns.

As the number of Sufis rose, it had a massive impact on the religiosity of the ordinary population and challenged the religious establishment in a number of ways. Eminent jurists often came from notable urban families with generations of privilege and wealth behind them, and they cultivated followings of students, often of similarly privileged background, who aspired to become religious scholars themselves. Mystics, on the contrary, were frequently of humble or Berberophone origin and devoted themselves to asceticism and spiritual exercises to draw closer to God, attracting both disciples who wished to follow the Sufi way and large numbers of followers who saw them as men and women with a special connection to God who ministered to their socio-religious needs in a way that bookish urban scholars from aristocratic juridical families in service to the state could or did not. The importance of Sufism was thus twofold: on the one hand, a series of great Andalusi and Maghribi mystics, including Abu Madyan Shu'ayb, al-Shadhili and Ibn 'Arabi of Murcia, contributed greatly to the evolution of the Islamic Sufi tradition as a whole, and, on the other hand, veneration of mystics became a significant and powerful stream of popular piety that has shaped mass religious culture in parts of the Maghrib until today. While the Maliki *fuqahā'*

[89] Urvoy, *Penseurs d'al-Andalus*, pp. 140–51.

and the Almohad *ṭalaba* struggled for hegemony, a quiet religious revolution took place beneath them, impinging on the official religio-political narrative only when Sufis were identified as a political threat.

The Sufi Path

Most of these Sufis partook of the sober Sufi tradition represented in the east by al-Junayd which stressed the importance for Muslims to follow the external ritual practices of their religion decreed by the Shariʿa in combination with adopting simple types of dress and nourishment, fasting, praying or reciting the Qur'an through the night, and undergoing periods of retreat and silence. The aim of such practices was to achieve *fanāʾ* or the dissolution of the self in God, a form of death before death, after which Sufis lived in a state known as *baqāʾ*, transformed by their experience but returned to the world. The path to *fanāʾ* took the aspirant through a number of different stages (*maqāmāt*), during which they experienced emotional and psychological states (*aḥwāl*) bestowed upon them by God. The rare theophanic glimpses of divine reality (*ḥaqīqa*) that Sufis might be vouchsafed were known as 'unveiling' (*kashf, mukāshafāt*). Sufi knowledge (*maʿrifa*) was very different to the learning of jurists and scholars (*ʿilm*) because it was not seen as the outcome of a didactic process, but as a gift from God that Sufis could prepare themselves to receive but could not acquire through studying. Although many Sufis were extremely erudite scholars, there were also illiterate Sufis 'illuminated' by knowledge directly bestowed by God.

Sufi masters of all kinds helped their disciples advance along the mystical path, often stressing a particular attitude of mind, such as 'thankfulness' (*shukr*) or trust in God (*tawakkul*), and their approaches gradually became codified for the benefit of subsequent generations into the different Sufi ways (*ṭarīqa, ṭuruq*) or communities (*ṭāʾifa, ṭawāʾif*) named after their eponymous founders in the same way as the legal schools. It thus became possible for an aspiring Sufi to enter an institution called a *khānqāh* in the Islamic east and a *zāwiya* in the west where a particular way would be taught. As these *ṭuruq* became more widespread they also acquired what has sometimes been called a 'lay' membership, whose participation was social as well as religious and for whom Sufism represented a form of piety rather than the path to *fanāʾ* desired by Sufi adepts. In addition, the potent connection that people believed existed between eminent 'saints' or 'friends [of God]' (*awliyāʾ*) and the divine continued after their deaths and their burial places became shrines, often managed by their lineal descendants, that attracted pilgrims and devotees.

The intellectual development of Sufism and its institutionalisation commenced in the Islamic west during the Almoravid and Almohad centuries. It was very much a two-way, cross-Straits phenomenon, giving it what Cornell calls a bi-directional character.[90] While Ibn al-ʻArif al-Sanhaji was the son of a Berber nightwatchman from Tangier who moved to al-Andalus, Abu Madyan (d. 1197), whom we shall consider now, was an uneducated Andalusi orphan from the village of Cantillana near Seville who travelled to the Maghrib in search of religious knowledge which he eventually found in Fes. Abu Madyan has been described as 'the most influential figure of the developmental period of North African Sufism' and his biography provides a vivid panorama of the twelfth-century world of the mystics.[91]

After the premature death of his father, Abu Madyan ran away to escape life as a shepherd (or weaver's apprentice) and travelled in search of a teacher who could instruct him in the Qur'an and the basics of religion. From Seville he proceeded south to the Straits of Gibraltar, crossing from Algeciras to Tangier and journeying to nearby Ceuta, where he earned money working as a fisherman. He then travelled south to Marrakesh and spent a period in the Andalusi corps of the Almoravid army before heading to Fes where he finally found the teacher he was looking for in the shape of Abu'l-Hasan ʻAli b. Hirzihim, whom we have already encountered in Marrakesh saving Ibn Barrajan's corpse from the ignominy of being dumped and ensuring his proper burial in 1141.

It is noteworthy that Abu Madyan's biography states that he retained nothing of the teaching of most of the scholars in the Qarawiyyin mosque in Fes and it was only Ibn Hirzihim's words that he remembered, a fact that the Sufi explained by saying that, unlike the other teachers, he sought only God with his words so 'they come from the heart and enter the heart'.[92] Abu Madyan became part of ʻAli b. Hirzihim's following and studied the works of the Baghdad ascetic and traditionist al-Muhasibi (d. 857) and al-Ghazali's *Ihya' ʻUlum al-Din* with him, thereby joining the group of orthodox 'Ghazalian' Sufis who combined their spiritual pursuits with careful maintenance of Muslim ritual and social behaviour and, indeed, believed that their asceticism, piety and humility prevented the performance of the prayers, for instance, being mere outward lip-service to convention as it was for many. Abu Madyan also studied with the mystic Abu ʻAbd Allah al-Daqqaq, a native of Sijilmasa about whom little is known, and Abu Yaʻza

90 Cornell, 'Ḥayy in the land of Absāl', p. 143.
91 Cornell, *Abu Madyan*, p. 2; Biography 162, Ibn al-Zayyat, *Tashawwuf*, pp. 316–25.
92 Cornell, *Abu Madyan*, p. 4.

Yalannur al-Dukkali (d. 1177), a Berber charismatic who lived in the Middle Atlas mountains.[93]

Although later accounts of his biography report that Abu Madyan performed the pilgrimage and met the eastern Sufi master, ʿAbd al-Qadir al-Jilani in Mecca before settling in Bijaya in Ifriqiya, this is not mentioned in his early biographies. It is therefore more likely that when he left the western Maghrib, he travelled straight to Bijaya where he established a *zāwiya* in which he taught and practised a Sufi programme that combined personal abnegation, humility and trust in God with socio-moral engagement, thereby confirming the underlying character of Maghribi Sufism. His social activism included outspoken criticism of scholars and rulers whom he perceived as arrogant and lacking in integrity, and his formation of a large group of devotees committed to implementing his way, comparable to the chivalric *futuwwa* orders of Iraq and Khurasan but also to Ibn Tumart's band of zealots fifty years earlier.

Abu Madyan's residence in Bijaya coincided with the period in which this flourishing port became an Almohad provincial capital and then, in the mid-1180s, the seat of the invading Banu Ghaniya from Mallorca. Although the Almohads eventually reasserted their control over Bijaya, they remained suspicious of the political and religious sympathies of its scholars and Sufis, of whom Abu Madyan was one of the most popular. Soon after the indictment of Ibn Rushd in al-Andalus and around the same time that the order was given for Jewish converts to Islam to wear distinguishing clothes, Yaʿqub al-Mansur summoned the elderly Abu Madyan from Bijaya to Marrakesh. He died at Tlemcen in 1197 or 1198 during his journey and was buried at al-ʿUbbad, a cemetery area already popular with ascetics and mystics, where his tomb is still an important pilgrimage site today.

The death of Abu Madyan in no way halted the spread of orthodox Sufism across the Almohad empire and his mantle was taken up in subsequent generations by the Maghribi masters, ʿAbd al-Salam b. Mashish (d. 1228) and his much more famous disciple, Abu'l-Hasan ʿAli al-Shadhili (d. 1258). Ibn Mashish is a mysterious figure who came from an Idrisi sharifian lineage of the Banu ʿArus tribe resident in the Jabal ʿAlam below Tetuan. He is reported to have travelled east, performed the pilgrimage, and then spent time in Bijaya studying with Abu Madyan on his return, although Abu Madyan does not appear in his list of teachers. He then established his own *zāwiya* in his natal region, where he enjoyed considerable local popularity as a mystic and a

93 Cornell, *Abu Madyan*, pp. 8–10.

purported descendant of the Prophet until he was murdered around 1228 by Abu Tawajin al-Kutami, a rival who claimed to be a prophet.[94]

In keeping with other Andalusi and Maghribi mystics of this era, Ibn Mashish favoured a moderate approach in which maintenance of the Shari'a had to precede spiritual exercises in search of enlightenment. As he instructed one follower:

> The most obligatory of duties is the observance of the essential commandments and abstention from decreed sins; continue your obligatory deeds and refrain from those prohibited and secure your heart from worldly inclinations, lusts and ambitions, accepting with contentment whatever has been allotted to you by God.[95]

Although Ibn Mashish was later recognised as one of the foremost mystics of his generation, a Sufi pole (*quṭb*), his main importance lies in his role as al-Shadhili's teacher and thus the link between Abu Madyan and al-Shadhili, who was too young to have met the latter, having been born either in 1187 or 1197, the year of Abu Madyan's death. Al-Shadhili hailed from the Ghumara region on the edge of the Rif mountain range near Jabal 'Alam where the prophet Ha-mim had once held sway. Like Ibn Mashish, he claimed to be a descendant of the Prophet via Hasan, a genealogical status now associated with sanctity as the idea that the *shurafā'*, as well as mystics, possessed a special connection to God became widespread among the population. Al-Shadhili is said to have begun his religious studies in Fes with 'Abd Allah b. Harazim before departing for the east and meeting Abu'l-Fath al-Wasiti of the Rifa'iyya order in Iraq around 1218. He then returned west to his homeland and settled with Ibn Mashish, probably until the latter's murder *c.* 1228, after which he travelled east again to the village of Shadhila between Tunis and Qayrawan, from which he took his name 'al-Shadhili', at the time that the Hafsid governors broke with the Almohad caliph al-Ma'mun for his denial that Ibn Tumart was the *mahdī*.

Al-Shadhili was regarded by many as the supreme Sufi pole of his age, the *quṭb al-zamān*, who represented the divine on earth, and his growing popularity, the attribution of miracles to him, and his claim to both mystical and sharifian status provoked the *'ulamā'* of Qayrawan to denounce him as a 'Fatimid', meaning that they suspected he might lead a mahdistic religio-political movement against them or the Almohad Hafsids as many earlier 'Fatimid' claimants had done.[96] In order to avoid their hostility, al-Shadhili

[94] le Tourneau, 'Ibn Mashīsh'; Mackeen, 'al-Shādhilī', pp. 479–81.

[95] Mackeen, 'al-Shādhilī', p. 480.

[96] 'Fatimid' in this sense did not mean a scion of the defunct Fatimid dynasty, but any descendant of 'Ali and Fatima, that is, a *sharīf*, from the lines of Hasan or Husayn.

departed to perform the pilgrimage, which he completed several times, before settling in Alexandria for the last phase of his life. In Shadhila and Alexandria, al-Shadhili pursued and further developed the orthodox and moderate Sufi paths of his predecessors, creating in the process one of the most influential Sufi brotherhoods in the Islamic world, the Shadhiliyya, which after his death spread not only across the Maghrib but also across the Mashriq into Arabia, Iraq, Iran and the Indian subcontinent.

Like Abu Madyan, al-Shadhili put considerable stress on teaching and assisting his numerous followers to live a more pious and religiously-informed life. He continued to emphasise the application of the Shari'a as the essential prerequisite for spiritual cognisance (*kashf*). Although he believed that Muslims should struggle against their carnal appetites and passions and show their trust in God by accepting whatever life threw at them with resignation, he did not advocate extreme asceticism or celibacy, and the gatherings of Shadhili initiates to remember God (*dhikr*) focused upon the calm recitation of litanies and prayers, rather than the music to induce trances found in some Sufi orders. This was the natural culmination of the strand of Andalusi–Maghribi Sufism that was rooted in the Shari'a and adopted a didactic approach, offering its adherents practical exercises and advice in the form of litanies and aphorisms.

However, Andalusi and Maghribi Sufism also possessed an illuminationist (*ishrāqī*) strand and theosophical elements in the tradition of Ibn Masarra. We have already mentioned Abu Ya'za Yalannur al-Dukkali, a teacher of Abu Madyan, who was one of a number of Maghribi mystics who claimed to have received direct spiritual illumination from God without needing the intermediary contribution of teachers. The most famous and controversial Sufi figure of the Almohad age, however, was the Murcian mystic Muhyi al-Din b. al-'Arabi, often known simply as Ibn 'Arabi to distinguish him from the Almoravid-era jurist Abu Bakr b. al-'Arabi. Born in Murcia in 1165, Muhyi al-Din moved to Seville with his family after the Banu Mardanish capitulated to the Almohads in 1172 and his father gained employment with the new masters of al-Andalus. He received a thorough education in the religious sciences and literature and was living the 'carefree life typical of a wealthy young man of noble Arab stock' when he fell ill and received a frightening vision that he interpreted as a direct instruction from God to give up his frivolous life.[97]

He then abandoned his worldly pursuits in favour of ascetic exercises and the study of Sufi texts, and he began to seek out Sufis, a group

[97] Knysh, 'Ibn 'Arabī', p. 331.

disparaged by his peers as 'worthless beggars, bumpkins and tricksters', in southern al-Andalus and the Maghrib.[98] After a period in the Maghrib and Ifriqiya, he returned to al-Andalus where he attended the funeral of Ibn Rushd in Córdoba in 1199. By this time, he was already a prolific author with as many as sixty works to his name and he had exhausted the spiritual resources that the Islamic west had to offer. Therefore, in 1201, he left the Maghrib for good, travelling to Tunis and then on to Cairo, Jerusalem and Mecca. From Mecca he travelled north to Baghdad, then northern Iraq and Anatolia, where he spent some time in Konya before moving to Damascus, the city where he died in 1240. Ibn 'Arabi did not choose the celibate path taken by some Sufis and he married several times and had children, including at least two sons. Although he had a devoted group of disciples, a huge popular following and enjoyed the patronage of many rulers of his era, including the Seljuks of Konya and the Ayyubids, he was a great mystical thinker and writer rather than the founder of a Sufi *ṭarīqa*.

He composed his most famous works during his long decades in the east. They include the *Tarjuman al-Ashwaq*, a series of love poems dedicated to 'Ayn al-Shams Nizam, the daughter of one of his teachers whom he met in Mecca in 1202, which Ibn 'Arabi insisted were metaphors for the soul's love of God, his magisterial religious compendium, the *Futuhat al-Makkiyya*, and the notoriously elliptical *Fusus al-Hikam*. His total production, however, may have been as many as 250–300 works.[99] Ibn 'Arabi was a very different character to the pragmatic and moderate Sufis of humble background whom we have already met. He was a highly-educated urbanite, fully conversant with the Qur'an and Hadith as well as philosophy and Sufism, whose work is brilliant, complex, multilayered and highly influenced by theosophical neo-Platonic ideas. Although he revealed his most controversial ideas only to his closest disciples, many *'ulamā'* caught a whiff of heterodoxy, if not heresy, in his teachings and protested about him both during his lifetime and for centuries afterwards. Even today, he remains *al-shaykh al-akbar* (the greatest master) for some and a heretic for others.

One controversial aspect of his doctrine was the concept of *waḥdat al-wujūd*, the unity of creation, a view that could be taken to breach the Islamic position that the Creator and the created are completely separate and encourage pantheism, the idea of God being in everything and everything being God. The idea of God's immanence rather than his transcendence

[98] Knysh, 'Ibn 'Arabī', pp. 331–2.

[99] Ibid., pp. 333–4.

and the nature of the individual soul's relationship to God were issues with which religion, philosophy and Sufism had grappled for some time, but for many *'ulamā'* Ibn 'Arabi's notion of *waḥdat al-wujūd* went too far and compromised the essential Islamic notion of God. Ibn 'Arabi's doctrines also contained a messianic dimension that grew out of the earlier Sufi mahdism of Ibn Qasi and, although this is rarely mentioned, the Almohad mahdism of Ibn Tumart.[100] For Ibn 'Arabi, the bridge between the animal and divine spheres, between the change and corruption inherent to creation and the changeless purity of the creator, was the perfect human (*al-insān al-kāmil*), a semi-divine individual who appeared incarnate in the form of the supreme Sufi *quṭb* or pole, a role indistinguishable from that of the *mahdī*. In his writings and poetry, Ibn 'Arabi admitted that he considered himself this figure, the seal of Muhammadan sainthood (*khatam al-wilāya al-Muḥammadiyya*).

It is easy to see why the Almohad establishment saw such Sufi ideas as dangerous, and Ibn 'Arabi's departure for the east a few years after the caliph's peremptory summoning of Abu Madyan to Marrakesh may have been driven in part by the rivalry between the Almohads, who desired to limit the bridging role of the *mahdī* to Ibn Tumart, and Sufis who placed the *quṭb* in an equivalent position. Despite these tensions, Sufism became an acknowledged aspect of religious life in the last decades of the Almohad empire, and during the twelfth century several important communities of mystics and ascetics coalesced, often in suburban burial areas such as Shalla (Chellah) outside Rabat and al-'Ubbad outside Tlemcen. The prominence of Shari'a-based Sufism enabled many to combine juridical and mystical pursuits, an example being Ibn 'Abbad, a native of Ronda in al-Andalus who resided with the famous mystic Ibn 'Ashir in Shalla before taking up the post of *khaṭīb* at the Qarawiyyin Mosque in Fes.[101] Nonetheless, the political and religious establishments continued to view mystics with trepidation, due to the esteem in which the population held them and their consequent ability to voice and mobilise popular dissent. In many parts of North Africa, older forms of religiosity were finally Islamised through the agency of Sufis and Sufi lineages who functioned as rural holy men, mediating tribal disputes, interceding with God for tribesmen and women, and providing shelter for travellers in their lodges. This was a slow, evolving process, but if one compares the rural religious landscape of the mid-eleventh century when the Almoravid movement began and the decades of the Almohad decline in the mid-thirteenth century,

100 Ibn Qasi's son gave Ibn 'Arabi a copy of his father's work, the *Khal' al-Na'layn*, in 1194 and Ibn 'Arabi subsequently wrote a commentary on it. Knysh, 'Ibn 'Arabī', p. 338.

101 See Nwyia, *Un mystique prédicateur à la Qarawīyīn de Fès: Ibn 'Abbād de Ronda 1332–1390.*

the change is dramatic: under the aegis of the Almoravid and Almohad missions and, most importantly, the spread of popular Sufism, the contours of Maghribi Islam with its combination of Maliki Sunnism and the cult of holy men had emerged.

7

'The most wondrous artifice': The Art and Architecture of the Berber Empires

In the course of this volume, many aspects of Almoravid and Almohad cultural production have been noted from dynastic chronicles composed to laud their political and military achievements, to botanical manuals produced as a stimulus to agriculture, works of jurisprudence and *ḥisba*, and the impressive philosophical œuvre of Ibn Tufayl and Ibn Rushd. Mention has also been made of the thriving world of artisanal production in the context of manufacturing, commerce and economic life. This chapter returns to material culture to explore it from the perspective of architectural and artistic developments rather than commerce and profit. As in the case of philosophy and intellectual production, rulers and the ruling elite played a disproportionate role in the architectural and artistic spheres by virtue of their financial ability to commission buildings and art works, and their status as trendsetters to be emulated. In order to show their power and host guests appropriately, rulers strove to build the most splendid palaces and gardens, while their responsibilities as custodians of their subjects' wellbeing obliged them to construct walls and fortresses for defence, and to restore and enhance mosques, through which they might also project messages about their religious position and legitimacy. Moreover, it was the presence of a court that stimulated demand for luxurious robes and textiles, expensive ceramic platters, gold and silverware, ivory caskets and jewellery.

As in many other areas of life, the artistic achievement of the Almoravids and Almohads lies to some extent in their integration of several areas into a single political unit and the resultant development of a widespread Andalusi–Maghribi style greater than the sum of its parts, and the emergence of the western Maghrib as a centre of culture alongside the older centres of al-Andalus and Ifriqiya. However, questions of agency remain: the Maghribi Berber dynasties have tended to be seen as dependent on the superior artistic heritage of al-Andalus and as passive borrowers rather than as active innovators in the architectural and artistic fields, an attitude related to the colonial and Eurocentric prejudices about the supposed ignorance and barbarism of the North Africans discussed previously, which rendered architecture in Morocco, for instance, as no more than 'l'art andalou' transposed.[1]

Certainly, both dynasties emerged from rural areas with vernacular rather than monumental building traditions and they employed Andalusi craftsmen and builders in the Maghrib, but as patrons they also had an important role in determining building designs that would convey the image they desired to project, selecting the materials used and choosing skilled labour. Although the participation of Islamic rulers in founding cities was a widespread literary trope that took the Prophet's foundations in Medina as a starting point, it also expressed the idea that such rulers did have direct involvement in the projects they sponsored.[2] Numerous Almoravid and Almohad rulers are depicted doing just that, and their creations were not solely imitations of what already existed in al-Andalus, even when the prestige of al-Andalus encouraged, and still encourages, indigenous observers also to see the architecture of much of the Maghrib as 'Andalusi'.

From the broader perspective of Islamic art history writ large, the Islamic west as a whole sometimes fares rather badly due to its definition as a provincial periphery when viewed by historians of the Islamic east whose perspective then impacts on even sympathetic art historians. Hillenbrand's general estimation of the art and architecture of al-Andalus is that it was archaic, limited and trapped by 'a well-nigh crippling mental dependence' on Umayyad Syria, meaning that 'tradition exerted a vice-like grip on the visual arts which, despite their distinctive character and some significant innovations, favoured the imitation of earlier modes', in comparison to the varied, dynamic and evolving art and architecture of the Islamic east.[3] Hillenbrand sees the Maghrib, meanwhile, as provincial even in comparison with al-Andalus and the contributions of the Almoravids and Almohads as sparse, possibly as a result of their 'puritanical fervour' and the ephemeral character of their empires.[4] However, these observations seem to reflect broader historical prejudices about the Islamic west and they are belied by his actual descriptions of Andalusi and Maghribi art and architecture that reveal his appreciation of its treasures, many of which rank highly within the canon of Islamic art and architecture.[5]

This chapter will provide an introduction to the architecture and art of

[1] Rosser-Owen, 'Andalusi *spolia* in Morocco', pp. 152–4. See also Navarro Palazón and Jimenez Castillo, 'La yesería en época almohade', pp. 253–4.
[2] See O'Meara, 'The foundation legend of Fez'.
[3] Hillenbrand, *Islamic Art*, p. 170.
[4] Ibid., p. 184.
[5] Hillenbrand, 'Medieval Córdoba'.

the Islamic west, especially its cultural poles, Qayrawan and Córdoba, to contextualise the later contributions of the Berber empires, whose founders came from the very edges of the Islamic world of their day. It will then explore Almoravid and Almohad material culture from the perspectives of urban planning and architecture, both of which showed the impact of the new imperial orders, and the visual arts where they were perhaps not so evident, and consider their contribution to the long-term development of material culture in the Islamic west.

Sources of Almoravid and Almohad Inspiration: Córdoba and Qayrawan

At the dawn of the Almoravid movement in the mid-eleventh century, the two main nuclei of artistic production in the west were, first, Ifriqiya, site of Qayrawan, the historic Islamic capital of the region and more recent Fatimid royal foundations, and, secondly, al-Andalus, where Córdoba's domination through the Umayyad era had given way to the rich multicentred cultural world of the Ta'ifa kingdoms. Although there were many similarities between al-Andalus and Ifriqiya produced by their common Roman heritage, which enabled Islamic rulers to employ vast amounts of Antique *spolia* in their buildings, they were distinct in their courtly cultural and artistic repertoires as a result of their different relationships to the powers of the Islamic east.

Ifriqiya had marked the westernmost point of the 'Abbasid empire from around 760 until 909, and its hereditary 'Abbasid governors, the Aghlabids, thus looked eastwards, creating an architectural style that existed on a continuum with contemporary 'Abbasid building in Baghdad and Samarra, whilst also responding to the Antique heritage of Ifriqiya itself. This blend can be seen clearly in the great mosque of Qayrawan, founded by 'Uqba b. Nafi', legendary conqueror of the Maghrib, but reconstructed by the Aghlabids in 836. Like contemporaneous 'Abbasid mosques, it was a large, high-walled rectangular enclosure, longer than it was wide, with a tall, striking minaret centrally located behind the back wall in what was called the *ziyāda* or outer enclosure.[6] The unusual tapered shape of the tower, on the other hand, may have been inspired by the ancient lighthouse at Alexandria.[7]

The enclosure was divided into a spacious courtyard surrounded by a colonnade and a hypostyle prayer hall, meaning that its roof was supported by rows of pillars, a traditional design derived from the Prophet's mosque where the roof had been supported by rows of palm trunks. The *miḥrāb* niche

[6] Bloom, *Minaret*, p. 66.

[7] Stierlin, *Early Architecture from Baghdad to Córdoba*, pp. 169–70.

Figure 7.1 Aghlabid minaret, Great Mosque of Qayrawan

was decorated with lustre tiles from Baghdad, again flagging up the ʿAbbasid links to the Aghlabids. In contrast to the eastern Islamic elements of the building, however, the majority of the pillars in the great mosque were reused Roman or Byzantine marble *spolia*. A wide, elevated central nave with ribbed domes at either end, reminiscent of Byzantine churches, led to the *miḥrāb*. The bay running along the *qibla* wall was also wider and higher, creating an arrangement known as a T-plan because of the 'T' created by the raised nave and *qibla* bay perpendicular to it.

The arrival of the Fatimids, easterners themselves, in the early tenth century did not rupture this orientation, but it did introduce a new dynamic to religious architecture which the Fatimids used to differentiate themselves from the 'Abbasids and Umayyads and to express their Isma'ili Shi'i identity. This took the form of denouncing minarets as an illicit 'Abbasid innovation (*bid'a*) and substituting them for corner turrets and massive mosque portals, which evoked the pre-Islamic Persian *pishtāq*, thereby returning the place where the call to prayer was given to the doorway, its original location.[8] This polemical Fatimid Shi'i attitude towards minarets made them into an accessible visual marker of identity for non-Shi'i regimes and, as Bloom has convincingly shown, for the next several centuries minarets or their absence played an important role in expressing a dynasty's sectarian position in the Islamic west.[9]

Ifriqiya was also the site of various urban planning experiments in the shape of the palatine cities of Aghlabid Raqqada (876), Fatimid al-Mahdiyya (921) and al-Mansuriyya (945), which included numerous palaces and large pools or reservoirs, as well as mosques and markets that pilgrims, merchants and, later, armies from further west had the opportunity to observe. Finally, we have frequently mentioned the *ribāṭ* as a Maliki institution from Ifriqiya which was exported to the western Maghrib. However, the *ribāṭ* was also a built form, a coastal fort or watchtower, and the striking *ribāṭ*s of Sousse and Monastir can still be seen today. These forts, manned by the pious who studied and prayed while they watched the horizon for sightings of Byzantine ships, may have provided material as well as ideological inspiration for the *ribāṭ*s of the western Maghrib, from Waggag's *ribāṭ* in the Sus and the mysterious *ribāṭ* of Ibn Yasin, to the great fortress city of Ribat al-Fath on the Atlantic coast alongside Salé, and Ribat Taza between Fes and Tlemcen founded by the Almohads.

Al-Andalus, at the western extremity of the Islamic world, developed its own architectural and artistic traditions that made multiple references to the Umayyad heritage in Syria and to local Romano-Visigothic precedents, whilst also engaging with the material modes of expressing Islamic royal power developed by the 'Abbasids and Fatimids in Iraq, Egypt and Ifriqiya. In and around Córdoba, the Umayyad capital, and the nearby caliphal city of Madinat al-Zahra' founded by 'Abd al-Rahman III in the 930s, great

8 Bloom, *Minaret*, p. 102.

9 Ibid., pp. 99–124.

mosques, palaces, rural villas and gardens expressed the aesthetic of the peninsula. Tenth-century Córdoba's buildings and culture acted as a reference point for the rest of al-Andalus, and they made a huge impression on Berber embassies visiting from North Africa who were accommodated in villas and taken on long processions through Córdoba to Madinat al-Zahra' to meet the caliph.[10] Some stayed for many months and gained an intimate knowledge of these two cities and their monuments which they took back with them to North Africa.

The importance of Córdoba to the Maghribi imagination of the city justifies us dwelling a little on its features. Situated on the northern bank of the Guadalquivir River, Córdoba was already old when it was conquered by the Muslims. The core of the Roman and Visigothic cities became the walled *madīna* and, as the status of Córdoba grew during Umayyad times, as many as twenty-one suburbs (*rabaḍ*, *arbāḍ*) sprung up around it, some considered towns in and of themselves, creating what Hillenbrand terms a 'megapolis'.[11] The religio-political heart of the city, located alongside the river, consisted of the great mosque and the Umayyad palace, which were linked by a covered walkway (*sābāṭ*) enabling the ruler to enter the great mosque for Friday prayers directly from the palace. The main gate to the palace, the Bab al-Sudda (Threshold Gate), pierced the walls on the river side and opened on to an esplanade, the *raṣīf*, which functioned as a important space for parades and ceremonies.

Nearby Madinat al-Zahra' did not need to adapt to an existing cityscape and, therefore, had a more regular rectangular plan arranged in tiers that cascaded down the hillside on which it was situated. The palace and its gardens stood on the top tier with the best views across the plain, while subaltern areas, such as the barracks, were situated lower down the slope. The city had a perimeter wall punctuated by towers and its main gate was called Bab al-Sudda, like the main gate of the palace in Córdoba, and decorated with a statue, probably a Roman Venus, that the Almohad caliph Ya'qub al-Mansur later removed from the ruins.[12] Here ceremonies and audiences took place in the great reception halls of the palace, which visitors entered on foot after coming slowly up from the gate below through numerous colonnades and courts.

The elements of these two cities that had the most impact on contemporaries and subsequent generations were the iconic great mosque of Córdoba and the reception halls of Madinat al-Zahra'. The great mosque, founded

[10] See Bennison, 'Power and the city'; Safran, 'Ceremony and submission'.
[11] Hillenbrand, 'Medieval Córdoba', p. 118.
[12] See pp. 106–7, above.

Figure 7.2 Reception hall, Madinat al-Zahra'

by 'Abd al-Rahman I in 784, was a flagship building that generations of Umayyad rulers extended and remodelled to present an image of their rule to their subjects. The original mosque consisted of a rectangular hypostyle prayer hall and a colonnaded courtyard that were roughly equal in size, unlike the great mosque of Qayrawan in which the courtyard was larger than the prayer hall. Extensions to the mosque gradually increased the size of the prayer hall in relation to the courtyard, reducing the latter to around one-third of the mosque's area. This gave it a very different feel to Mashriqi great mosques, and prefigured the even greater diminution in courtyard size that occurred under the Almoravids and Almohads.

Within the prayer hall, the Umayyads acknowledged the past by reusing Roman and Visigothic marble columns and capitals which they surmounted with distinctive horseshoe arches, probably copied from Visigothic churches, that had alternating red brick and sandstone voussoirs. An additional upper row of smaller arches compensated for the relative shortness of the reused columns and gave the prayer hall extra height and light, an arrangement possibly inspired by the design of the Roman aqueduct at Mérida. The endless rows of columns have also been likened to a forest in stone that reminded worshippers of the garden of paradise, a theme apparent also in the tree-planted courtyard.[13] Over time, the Umayyads made the area preceding the *miḥrāb* niche more elaborate, enhancing it with cupolas and scalloped, interlaced arches that defined the royal enclosure (*maqṣūra*) where the amir and his entourage prayed.

When 'Abd al-Rahman III claimed the status of caliphs for the Córdoban Umayyads in 928, this important political and religious change naturally found expression in the fabric of the great mosque. In a counter-statement to the Fatimids' polemical rejection of minarets, he added a square tower minaret with an entwined double-staircase to the back wall of the mosque courtyard in 952, proclaiming his Sunni Maliki position.[14] His son, al-Hakam II (r. 961–76), further extended the great mosque and commissioned an extraordinary new *miḥrāb* in the form of a polygonal chamber surmounted by a scallop shell cupola with a mosaic-encrusted façade, preceded by an elaborate royal enclosure (*maqṣūra*) with multifoil interlaced arches and a ribbed dome decorated with gold and blue mosaics imported from Byzantium, along with craftsmen to mount them. This bolstered the Córdoban Umayyads' reclamation of the caliphal title by creating an analogy with their ancestors, the Syrian Umayyad caliphs, who had built the great mosque of Damascus using

[13] Hillenbrand, 'Medieval Córdoba', pp. 133–4.

[14] Bloom, *Minaret*, p. 106.

Byzantine mosaic and mosaicists.[15] On each side of the *miḥrāb* there were chambers that held the mosques' treasures, the Qur'an of 'Uthman and a moveable pulpit (*minbar*).

Despite the demise of the Umayyad caliphate and the concomitant decline of Córdoba's political status, its great mosque remained one of the most thoroughly described and lauded Islamic buildings for centuries to come. Al-Idrisi, writing in the Almohad era, devoted almost his entire entry on Córdoba, several pages in all, to describing the great mosque, giving almost forensic detail about its constituent parts.[16] The key elements in this respect were its marble columns, its polygonal *miḥrāb* chamber, its Qur'an and its *minbar*, all of which went on to have long histories in the Maghrib, appropriated and adapted by the Almoravids and the Almohads in turn.

The great halls of Madinat al-Zahra' also stimulated the imagination of subsequent generations as examples of the luxurious materials, *objets d'art*, aesthetic virtuosity and architectural wonders one might expect from a caliphal palace. The eleventh-century Andalusi chronicler, Ibn Hayyan, writing in the shadow of the Umayyad caliphate's collapse, wrote about Madinat al-Zahra' in glowing terms, which passed down the generations to be quoted afresh by the seventeenth-century Maghribi historian al-Maqqari in his *Nafḥ al-Tib*, written to introduce an Ottoman audience in Syria and Egypt to the glories of al-Andalus. It is striking that the memory of Madinat al-Zahra' was so clear for a North African writing in Egypt seven centuries after its demise. There were two aspects of Ibn Hayyan's account that al-Maqqari focused on, the first of which was the material investment, including the cost of the project and the importation of luxury objects from across the Mediterranean, the medieval equivalent of good economic statistics:

> Ibn Hayyan said ['Abd al-Rahman III] al-Nasir began the construction of al-Zahra' on the first day of Muharram 325 (November 936) . . . He said he spent 10 *dīnārs* on every piece of marble, large and small, not counting the amount required for cutting them, transporting them, and the equipment for carrying them. He brought white marble from Almería, streaked marble from Rayya, rose and green marble from Sfax and Carthage in Ifriqiya, and a carved, gilded basin on which there were engravings and figures of the human form from Syria, or it is sometimes said from Constantinople. It was of incalculable value.[17]

[15] Bloom, 'Early Islamic architecture', p. 37.
[16] al-Idrisi, *Opus Geographicum*, fasc. 5–8, pp. 575–8.
[17] al-Maqqari, *Nafḥ al-Tib*, vol. 1, pt 2, ch. 4, p. 67.

The second aspect of interest to al-Maqqari was the regal combination of both rich materials and ingenious devices, a feature of Islamic courts from the 'Abbasid era onwards that confirmed the caliphal status of the Umayyads:

> In the palace, he built the hall called the Palace of the Caliphate (*qaṣr al-khilāfa*) whose ceiling was of gold and thick marble of pure colours of all kinds. The walls of this hall were the same and in the middle was the 'Incomparable Pearl' (*yatīma*) which the Byzantine Emperor Leo had given as a gift to al-Nasir. The tiles of this palace were gold and silver. In the middle of this hall was a great pool filled with mercury. There were eight archways on each side of this hall connected to arches of ebony and ivory inlaid with gold and jewels resting upon pillars of multi-coloured marble and clear crystal. The sun used to enter through these archways and cast its rays into the heart of the hall and onto its walls dazzling the sight with its light. If al-Nasir wished to intimidate one of the people in his *majlis*, he would signal to one of his Slavic troops (*ṣaqāliba*) to disturb the mercury causing lightening-like flashes of light to appear in the hall until it appeared to all in the *majlis*, their hearts captivated, that the place was revolving around them as long as the mercury continued to move. It is said that this hall used to revolve to face the sun, or that it was fixed on the ledge of this pool. The building of this hall was not surpassed by anyone in the Jahiliyya or Islam.[18]

This kind of eulogistic description of the precious and expensive materials used in the Umayyad palaces and references to clever mechanical devices inspired and galvanised the Umayyads' successors in al-Andalus, the Ta'ifa kings, who proved extremely eager to employ the skills of artists and craftsmen trained in Córdoba and to cultivate the emergence of new talent in their own cities. This was the pool that the Almoravids and Almohads were later able to draw upon and cultivate themselves from the early twelfth to mid-thirteenth centuries. The Dhu'l-Nunids of Toledo, the Hudids of Saragossa, the 'Abbadids of Seville and Ibn Sumadih in Almería are all famous for their fabulous palaces and gardens, and the luxury of their courts as they strove to out do each other in emulating the memory of Umayyad Córdoba.

The political and military dangers of the time encouraged rulers to enclose their palaces with sound walls and towers and they were much smaller than Umayyad palaces, but their interiors were characterised by an opulent baroque style still evident in the interlocking multifoil arches decorated by

18 al-Maqqari, *Nafh al-Tib*, vol. 1, pt 2, ch. 4, pp. 67–8. The reference to mercury is a common trope that also appears in descriptions of Ibn Tulun's palace in al-Qata'i'. In reality, a pool would have required an impossibly large amount of mercury and probably poisoned its users!

lacy carved stucco that flank the halls and courts of the Ja'fariyya (Aljafería) palace in Saragossa, and in al-Maqqari's fulsome descriptions of lost Ta'ifa palaces. His description of the spectacular, if rather gimmicky, water feature in the palace of al-Ma'mun of Toledo gives the flavour of the period:

> He spent a huge amount of money on [his palace]. He constructed a pool (*buḥayra*) at its heart and at the centre of the pool he constructed a pavilion of coloured glass, etched with gold. Water was drawn to the top of the pavilion by a mechanism set up by the engineers so that it would cascade from the top of the pavilion down its sides, enveloping it entirely. The glass pavilion was encased in a diaphanous cloak of [water] whose flow never faltered while al-Ma'mun sat inside untouched by it. Candles were lit inside and it was a wondrous and splendid sight.[19]

While the larger towns and cities of al-Andalus and Ifriqiya displayed an array of monuments by the eleventh century, the largely rural character of the vast swathes of the Maghrib between them limited the development of monumental architecture prior to the rise of the Almoravids. The towns that existed were fairly small and their public buildings were probably functional rather than ornamental and many settlements had no great mosque of any stature.[20] The foremost urban centres were Sijilmasa, Ceuta on the Straits of Gibraltar, Fes, Tlemcen and further east Tahart and the later Zirid foundations of Ashir and Qal'at Bani Hammad. Of these, Sijilmasa did have a substantial great mosque whose ruins can still be seen today, described by al-Bakri rather laconically as 'solid and well-maintained', as well as many 'beautiful houses and magnificent buildings'.[21] Fes, which consisted of two small townships, and Tlemcen (Agadir) had early great mosques founded by the Idrisids, but the monumentality of these buildings is a moot point.

In the case of Fes, fourteenth-century histories of the city imply that the Idrisid great mosques – the Mosque of the Shurafa' in al-'Aliya next to the Idrisid royal residence and the Mosque of the Shaykhs in Madinat Fas – were simple diminutive structures which ceased to be used as great mosques in the tenth century as a result of the Fatimid–Umayyad struggle for control of the western Maghrib. The Mosque of the Shaykhs was replaced by the Andalus mosque in Madinat Fas, known by this time as the Andalus quarter, and the Mosque of the Shurafa' in al-'Aliya, henceforth the Qarawiyyin quarter, was abandoned for the Qarawiyyin Mosque.[22] Although elided by the

[19] al-Maqqari, *Nafh al-Tib*, vol. 1, pt 2, ch. 4, p. 69.

[20] See Bennison, 'Mosques in the Maghrib'.

[21] al-Bakri, *Description de l'Afrique*, Arabic text, p. 148; French text, pp. 282–3.

[22] Bennison, 'Sectarianism in the landscape', p. 24.

Figure 7.3 Umayyad-style minaret, Qarawiyyin Mosque, Fes

later prominence of the Qarawiyyin as the foremost great mosque of Fes, it seems that the Andalus quarter was the larger and more important of the two settlements at this time.[23] The Umayyads, however, lavished their patronage on the Qarawiyyin Mosque, which was extended and endowed with a new tower minaret similar to the one being constructed for the great mosque of Córdoba by ʿAbd al-Rahman III, stressing Sunni Maliki power in the city.[24]

[23] On the early history of Fes, see García-Arenal and Manzano Moreno, 'Idrīssisme et villes idrīssides'.

[24] The Umayyad governor also added a smaller tower minaret to the al-Andalus mosque, Bloom, *Minaret*, p. 109.

The slow retrenchment of Umayyad power in the western Maghrib during the early eleventh century facilitated the emergence of smaller principalities whose rulers, like the Ta'ifa kings, indulged in the construction of palaces, mosques and fortifications. Moving from west to east, the Banu 'Ashara, who claimed Umayyad ancestry, established Salé where they built a lavish palace later requisitioned by the Almohads, and in 1018 the Hammudids endowed Ceuta with a new great mosque with five aisles articulated using 180 marble columns, a design choice that Greenhalgh attributes to Córdoba,[25] while their lieutenant and successor, Saqqut al-Barghawati, made further palatial additions to the city. Meanwhile, in the central Maghrib the ebbing of Fatimid power allowed their erstwhile deputies, the Zirids, to chart their own course and in 1007–8 the Zirid prince Hammad founded Qal'at Bani Hammad in the mountains at the edge of the Hodna plain. This striking site is described by al-Bakri as a 'centre of commerce attracting caravans from Iraq, the Hijaz, Egypt, Syria and all parts of the Maghrib'.[26] The Hammadids shared in the city's wealth and invested in splendid palaces and a great mosque befitting an Islamic capital, thereby transferring the architectural language of power further into the Berber interior.

Art historians see the ruins of Qal'at Bani Hammad as an enigmatic combination of elements from the Fatimid, Umayyad and 'Abbasid spheres. The city had a fortress and palaces, including one with the now *de rigueur* large pool, but the site's most spectacular feature is the looming tower (*manār*) of the great mosque that still dominates the abandoned town. Bloom associates the tower's construction after the rest of the mosque and its placing in the 'Abbasid position along the back wall with the Zirids' rejection of Fatimid suzerainty. In form, however, the square tower was closer to Umayyad minarets further west. Its decoration was similarly eclectic, with blind panels or niches featuring incipient *muqarnas* (honeycomb or stalactite vaulting) associated with the 'Abbasid east and polychrome tile mosaics, probably of western Islamic derivation.[27] The end result was quite unique and this innovative tower in the central Maghrib built for Sanhaja Berber Zirid patrons, prefigures the developments of the Almoravid and Almohad centuries during which the architecture of the urbanised north and east filtered south and west to be transformed in the hands of Berber regimes.

25 Greenhalgh, *Marble Past, Monumental Present*, p. 308.

26 al-Bakri, *Description de l'Afrique*, Arabic text, p. 49; French text, p. 105.

27 Bloom, *Minaret*, p. 115. See also Golvin, 'Ḳal'at Banī Ḥammād'. Tabbaa disagrees that the minaret of Qal'at Bani Hammad has fully developed *muqarnas* elements; Tabbaa, 'Muqarnas dome', pp. 61–2.

Almoravid Art and Architecture

The Almoravid Sanhaja did not have a well-developed architectural style of their own when they emerged from their Saharan homelands, but they soon developed an approach to urbanism and architecture that responded to their political and social needs. Their first inspiration probably came from the local Sahelian and pre-Saharan tradition of building in *pisé* or rammed earth (*ṭūb*, *ṭābiya*) that was prevalent in Sijilmasa and the small towns of the Sus and still exists in the kasbahs (*qaṣaba*s) and ksars (*qaṣr*s) of southern Morocco today. The Almoravids also had experience of Saharan cities such as Azuggi and Awdaghust, described as very impressive by al-Bakri, and Aghmat, north of the High Atlas, with its settlers from Qayrawan in Ifriqiya. A handful of Sanhaja pilgrims had travelled across North Africa to Egypt and on to Arabia to perform the *ḥajj*, perhaps stopping at Qal'at Bani Hammad and admiring its mosque *en route*, and Ibn Yasin had studied in Córdoba, giving the Saharans some awareness of architecture further afield.

However, when Abu Bakr b. 'Umar decided to found a town north of the Atlas, the indications are that local vernacular architecture took precedence. The sources describe those working with him as the Sanhaja, their local Masmuda allies and labourers, presumably from the nearby Aghmat area, whose knowledge and skills would have informed the building techniques used.[28] Moreover, the sources describe Marrakesh as being built of *pisé* with only one stone building at the start, the aptly if rather unimaginatively named Qasr al-Hajar, 'Palace of Stone', which Abu Bakr founded as a residence, treasury and storage facility. Only the southeastern angle of the fortress wall remains to show that it was strongly constructed of an inner and outer stone wall infilled with rammed red clay, a design that may have been original or of sub-Saharan inspiration.[29] Individual Almoravid amirs constructed residences of mud-brick or *pisé* dotted on the plain for their families and retainers to reside it.

When Yusuf b. Tashfin became Abu Bakr's deputy in the Maghrib shortly after Marrakesh was founded, he continued with the works, including a great mosque with simple rammed earth walls, located between the Qasr al-Hajar and the Wad Issil where the facilities to prepare bricks and other building materials were situated.[30] Marrakesh was probably very like

[28] Ibn 'Idhari, *al-Bayan*, vol. 4, pp. 17–18.

[29] Triki, 'Marrakech', p. 94.

[30] Ibid., p. 95. Although Yusuf's mosque has been identified with the 'Mosque of the *pisé* tower' (*masjid ṣawma'at al-ṭūb*) mentioned by al-Baydhaq, this attribution is uncertain and problematic.

early Islamic Kufa or Basra, a dispersed, unwalled garrison town with wide thoroughfares and a dusty central area where men gathered to pray in a simple mosque building. This simplicity may have had its own ideological implications: the second caliph 'Umar b. al-Khattab famously warned against compromising the hardy and egalitarian ethos of the Arab tribes by allowing them to build permanent houses of more than three rooms or of unequal height in Kufa, a tale echoed in al-Bakri's comment that all the buildings in Ibn Yasin's mythic town of Aratnanna were the same height.[31]

The new city was distinguished by its duo-centric plan with the Qasr al-Hajar anchoring its southwestern end and the great mosque situated to the northeast.[32] This was in contrast to the earlier Syrian and Córdoban Umayyad arrangement of an adjacent great mosque and ruler's residence (*dār al-imāra*) and to other palatine cities where the mosque and palace were also in close proximity. Fatimid cities, for instance, tended to be centred on the caliph's palace to underline his pivotal religious role. The juxtaposition of a centrally located great mosque and a peripheral palace or citadel was more commonly a solution when a new foreign regime took over a long-established urban centre and chose to locate themselves in a secure location on its edge as in Ayyubid Aleppo or Cairo.

Given that Marrakesh was an Almoravid royal foundation, one might logically have expected the palace and mosque to be built close to each other at its heart since there was no pre-existing sacred centre or 'subject' population likely to be aggravated by the presence of warriors in their midst. Two possibilities for the Almoravid planning of Marrakesh spring to mind. On the one hand, Abu Bakr b. 'Umar and Yusuf b. Tashfin had very little experience of cities other than Awdaghust and Sijilmasa and may have taken a practical rather than ideological stance towards urban planning. The positioning of the great mosque towards the area where labourers and then traders would have congregated made it accessible to the mass of the population, while it made sense for a warrior chief such as Yusuf b. Tashfin to locate his residence close to open space where his fighters could mobilise. On the other hand, the name 'Marrakesh', which is derived from two Berber terms, *amūr* and *yākush* meaning lands of God,[33] suggests that the Almoravids did see their city as the realisation of God's plan on earth and sited the palace and great

[31] Bennison, *The Great Caliphs*, pp. 60–1; al-Bakri, *Description de l'Afrique*, Arabic text, p. 165; French text, p. 313.

[32] Ghouirgate, *L'Ordre almohade*, pp. 96–7; Tabbaa, 'Andalusian roots', pp. 134–5.

[33] al-Tawfiq, 'Ḥawla ma'nā ism Marrākush', pp. 15–19, quoted in Benhima, 'l'Islamisation du Maghrib al-Aqṣā', p. 329.

mosque deliberately apart.[34] It may have been a mark of humility on the part of the Almoravid amir that he should ride across the city to the great mosque, rather than enter it via a passage from his palace, and a sign of social parity among the Almoravids, who viewed their amir as first among equals and not a hidden potentate, or simply an opportunity for people to see their amir.

As more cities were added to the Almoravid empire, Yusuf b. Tashfin ordered urban improvements, the construction of Almoravid citadels and several new great mosques. In 1081, he founded the Almoravid palatine city or citadel of Tagrart alongside old Tlemcen (Agadir), and once he had conquered Ceuta he ordered the building of walls for the lower harbour supervised by the *qāḍī* Ibrahim b. Ahmad. Some years later, in 1098, he 'commanded the *qāḍī* Muhammad b. 'Isa to start work on the great mosque of Ceuta and extend it until it overlooked the sea',[35] thereby increasing the great mosque's size by two-thirds, to the disgruntlement of nearby shopkeepers who were forced to move.[36] He also ordered the construction of great mosques in Algiers and the small town of Nedroma, both of which were simple multi-naved structures with a relatively small courtyard, encircled by a colonnade in keeping with the Córdoban Umayyad paradigm. Somewhat puzzlingly, these Almoravid mosques did not have tower minarets, suggesting that the Almoravids were not aware of their polemical significance and saw them as unnecessary for the performance of the call to prayer.[37]

Almoravid art and architecture came into its own during the reign of 'Ali b. Yusuf (r. 1106–45) when Marrakesh gained a new monumentality and splendour and became a capital in form as well as function, and Almoravid mosques across the empire were enlarged and given more luxurious decoration. As the child of an Iberian Christian concubine brought up in Ceuta, 'Ali was familiar with the Andalusi artistic heritage and may well have turned to Andalusi master craftsmen, both Christian and Muslim, to make Marrakesh fit for a king and embellish the mosques of his empire, and it is, therefore, in relation to these building projects that the balance of Andalusi, Maghribi and eastern Islamic elements becomes a subject of debate.

In the 1110s and 1120s, before 'Ali b. Yusuf was overwhelmed by the problems of Andalusi regional separatism, Christian raids into Muslim territory and the Almohad rebellion in the High Atlas, he focused considerable

[34] Ghouirgate, *L'Ordre almohade*, p. 98.

[35] Ibn 'Idhari, *al-Bayan*, vol. 4, p. 51. The author of the *Hulal al-Mawshiyya* says that Yusuf added the great courtyard or bay (*al-balāṭ al-a'ẓam*) of the great mosque of Ceuta; *al-Hulal al-Mawshiyya*, p. 73.

[36] Cherif, *Ceuta aux époques almohade et mérinide*, p. 81.

[37] Bloom, *Minaret*, pp. 116–17.

attention on Marrakesh. His first and most pressing challenge was to improve and secure the water supply, which he did through developing a system of underground channels, known locally as *gattaras*, to irrigate the land around Marrakesh, supply the Qasr al-Hajar and provision the rest of the city. This water system was designed for the amir by the engineer 'Ubayd Allah b. Yunus, who was probably an Andalusi Christian.[38] The estates laid out around Marrakesh included a large pool or reservoir (*buḥayra*) which functioned as a prototype for Almohad suburban garden estates and in whose vicinity the Battle of the Buhayra between the Almoravids and Almohads took place in 1130. This eminently practical project also symbolically transformed the dry 'dead' land upon which Marrakesh was founded into a living paradisal garden and showed the Almoravid amir fulfilling one of the most ancient duties of Near Eastern and Islamic kings, the provision of water and fertility.[39]

Once the water supply was resolved, 'Ali b. Yusuf followed the Umayyad and Ta'ifa lead by adding at least two garden courts to the Qasr al-Hajar, transforming it from a fortress into a royal palace. The excavated remains of these courts show that they were similar to Andalusi walled gardens (*rawḍa*, *riyāḍ*), with a fountain in one and a cruciform patio with four planted quadrants in the other, and were probably made, or the works directed, by craftsmen from al-Andalus.[40] The Andalusi connection was enhanced by the importation of Umayyad marble capitals, probably spoliated from Madinat al-Zahra'. However, fragments of wall decoration from these courts reveal painted designs of interlocking geometric lines, an indigenous decorative technique called Tadelakt, showing that Almoravid decoration was not simply a copy of what was done in al-Andalus but a creative and selective engagement with it.[41]

From the palace, 'Ali b. Yusuf's water system carried the precious liquid northwards across town in terracotta pipes towards his father's simple great mosque, which he rebuilt in the 1120s in a more permanent and monumental form. Fragmentary ruins, in the same bluish-grey local Gueliz stone used for the Qasr al-Hajar, suggest that this mosque did have a square tower minaret made with two entwined staircases in the style of the minaret of the Umayyad

[38] al-Idrisi gives the engineer's name but not his religion (*Opus Geographicum*, fasc. 1–4, pp. 233–4), while Lagardère describes him as Andalusi and links him to the Christians forced to migrate from Granada, *Le djihâd andalou*, p. 133.

[39] Ghouirgate, *L'Ordre almohade*, pp. 88–9.

[40] al-Idrisi specifically mentions 'Ali b. Yusuf's recruitment of Andalusi craftsmen and experts to build a bridge over the Wad Tansift, showing that they were present in Marrakesh; *Opus Geographicum*, fasc. 1–4, p. 235.

[41] Triki, 'Marrakech', p. 96.

Figure 7.4 The Almoravid Qubbat al-Ba'diyyin, Marrakesh

great mosque of Córdoba.[42] Fairly close to this location, 'Ali b. Yusuf built a small stone and brick pavilion containing a marble basin or fountain, the

[42] Triki, 'Marrakech', p. 97. Bloom, however, does not think the remains indicate an Almoravid tower minaret; *Minaret*, p. 116.

Qubbat al-Ba'diyyin or Barudiyyin, that still stands as a tantalising glimpse of the rich Almoravid fabric of Marrakesh and their 'vividly ingenious and stridently original' style.[43] Due to the partial defacement of its foundation inscription, art historians disagree over whether this pavilion was built in 1117, 1125 or even 1146.[44] The majority opt for the 1125 date and believe that it was part of the ablutions complex of 'Ali b. Yusuf's great mosque which was called the Fountain Mosque (*jāmi' al-siqāya*) suggesting that it did have a noteworthy fountain or water basin. Tabbaa, however, opts for the 1117 foundation date and then argues that because the pavilion was built over a decade before the great mosque and located at a short distance from it, rather than in its immediate vicinity, it was a building to celebrate 'Ali's massive project to supply Marrakesh with running water and create a paradise in the desert.[45]

Whether a commemorative pavilion or part of the great mosque's ablutions complex, the Qubbat al-Ba'diyyin is now an important testament to 'Ali b. Yusuf's urban beautification project. In form, it is a small, domed rectangular building with open arched doorways on each side at ground level surmounted by a gallery of smaller windows – three on the short sides and five on the long sides – with horseshoe, scalloped or pointed trilobe arches. Above them rises an ovoid dome boxed in by stepped merlons that run along the roof line. The dome's exterior is decorated by a band of interlocking horseshoe arches surmounted by a row of chevrons with a seven-pointed star at the apex, a design without precedent in the Islamic west but with possible forerunners in Baghdad and Mecca.[46] The unusual and eclectic decorative schema continues inside the pavilion, where the zone of transition between the rectangular walls and the small eight-lobed inner dome is decorated by eight triangular panels of delicately carved stucco ornament with large scallop shells nestling in deep-carved lacy vegetation that still surprises and delights viewers today.

What is intriguing about the pavilion is the way its creator appears to have blended architectural elements and ideas from al-Andalus with those emanating from further east and possibly even 'Abbasid Baghdad. While the stucco inner dome is visually evocative of the dome of the great mosque of Córdoba, in actual structure and material it bears some resemblance to eastern *muqarnas* (stalactite) domes. Yasser Tabbaa has speculated that when it was first used, the *muqarnas* dome was a peculiarly Sunni decorative choice

[43] Tabbaa, 'Andalusian roots', p. 143.
[44] Rosser-Owen, 'Andalusi *spolia* in Morocco', p. 170.
[45] Tabbaa, 'Andalusian roots', pp. 143–4.
[46] Ibid., p. 142.

Figure 7.5 Interior ceiling, Qubbat al-Ba'diyyin, Marrakesh

that symbolised belief in the atomistic nature of the heavens and their infinite variety held in place by God's will, and was therefore favoured by the 'Abbasids.[47] Although his theory is not accepted by everyone, he suggests that the Almoravids' choice of architectural and decorative elements in the *qubba* showed their religious and ideological affiliations with the 'Abbasid present as well as the Córdoban Umayyad past, and that its inner dome was 'a synthesis of the ribbed domes of Córdoba and the *muqarnas* domes of Baghdad, a cultural duality that parallel[ed] its patron's links with al-Andalus and the 'Abbasid caliphate'.[48]

From this perspective, the Almoravid adoption of *muqarnas* was not simply because it was aesthetically pleasing, but also because it expressed the Sunni–Ash'ari view of the universe in opposition to Fatimid Shi'ism. As we have seen, however, many Almoravid *fuqahā'* had an ambiguous relationship with eastern Sunni theology and it is not clear whether *muqarnas* decoration entered the Maghrib directly from the east or via al-Andalus.[49] More importantly, perhaps, the Qubbat al-Ba'diyyin testifies to the innovativeness of 'Ali b. Yusuf as a patron and his investment in an architecture that was neither Andalusi nor 'Abbasid, but rather a stage in the articulation of a specifically Maghribi architectural idiom that drew on a wide range of motifs. As Bloom sagely notes, buildings cannot influence each other, design is all about human responses to what they have seen and their decisions to compile elements in particular ways, and that was what the Almoravids did.[50]

Although the Almoravid great mosque of Marrakesh is no longer extant and available for analysis, 'Ali b. Yusuf was responsible for the remodelling and decoration of several other great mosques in the Maghrib at Ceuta, Fes, Tlemcen, Nedroma and Algiers, and these buildings reveal the general style of Almoravid great mosques. A typical Almoravid mosque followed the well-established hypostyle T-plan with a wider and higher central aisle and transversal bay along the *qibla* wall, but, in place of the rows of spoliated or freshly cut marble columns that supported the roof in the great mosques of Córdoba and Qayrawan, the Almoravids used bulky brick piers to support massive round horseshoe arches. It is hard to say whether Almoravid use of brick piers was a nod to the 'Abbasid tradition, which also employed brick, or simply a reflection of local building norms and expertise that paralleled

47 Tabbaa, 'Muqarnas dome', pp. 68–72.

48 Tabbaa, 'Andalusian roots', p. 138.

49 For opposing views, see Rosser-Owen, 'Andalusi *spolia* in Morocco', pp. 153–4; Bloom, 'Minbar', pp. 24–5.

50 Bloom, 'Early Islamic architecture', pp. 36–7.

Figure 7.6 Brick piers, Almoravid great mosque, Algiers

those of Iraq.[51] The horseshoe shape of the arches, however, was of Andalusi Umayyad derivation, as were the polygonal *miḥrāb* chambers favoured by the

[51] Rosser-Owen, 'Andalusi *spolia* in Morocco', p. 168.

Almoravids. The multi-lobed arches that often lightened the bulk of the piers near the *miḥrāb* were also based on Andalusi examples.

While the Umayyads themselves had reused Roman and Byzantine columns and capitals as well as carving their own, the Berber dynasties showed a strong predilection for Umayyad-carved items from Madinat al-Zahra', the site most representative of the Umayyad caliphal era. The reference to the great mosque of Córdoba inherent in the polygonal chamber design of the new Almoravid *miḥrāb* of the Qarawiyyin Mosque in Fes was underlined by the use of four marble columns and capitals from Madinat al-Zahra' to flank its entrance. The discovery of similar imported column capitals in the vicinity of the Qubbat al-Ba'diyyin as well as the Qasr al-Hajar confirms the importance to the Almoravids of this visual link with the Umayyads, as does the presence of a beautifully carved rectangular marble basin dated to 1004–7, which Rosser-Owen suggests was part of a shipment of Umayyad *spolia* that 'Ali b. Yusuf imported to the Maghrib to reuse in his buildings.[52]

As Rosser-Owen shows in her discussion of Maghribi use of Andalusi *spolia*, the view that Almoravid (and Almohad) reuse of Andalusi marble columns and capitals reflected the natural superiority of Andalusi architecture, the artistic poverty of the Maghrib or the absence of a skilled workforce able to carve marble does not really stand up to scrutiny, given the very high cost and logistical challenges of transporting heavy marble items from al-Andalus and the evidence for very skilled artisans in Córdoba, Almería and other places who could have been seconded to the Maghrib to do the work. The use of such columns and capitals was, rather, a deliberate choice made by the Berber dynasties to connect themselves with the Umayyad tradition and legitimise themselves as heirs to it.[53] 'Ali b. Yusuf's builders, however, also endowed Almoravid mosques with elements not drawn from the Umayyad canon, namely, *muqarnas* domes before and above their *miḥrāb*s. Such a dome was added to the Qarawiyyin Mosque in Fes when it was extended by 'Ali b. Yusuf in 1135. The form reached fresh heights in the great mosque of Tagrart, the new Almoravid section of Tlemcen, which 'Ali b. Yusuf enhanced in 1136, where the deeply cut *muqarnas* pierced the *miḥrāb* dome to create a tracery of miniature windows that allowed light to flood in and illuminate the space.

A millennium on, we cannot know the full significance of these forms to the Almoravids or the messages they hoped to convey, but the references inherent in Umayyad items could be expected to have been widely

[52] Rosser-Owen, 'Andalusi *spolia* in Morocco', p. 182.

[53] Ibid., p. 178.

understood by viewers as a result of the constant traffic between al-Andalus and the Maghrib. In contrast, visual cues to the 'Abbasid world could only have been picked up by the educated minority who had had the opportunity to travel to the east. For many of their Maghribi subjects, however, the main impact of Almoravid mosques must have lain simply in their size, richness and beauty, all of which marked the coming of a new era in which the great mosque and the Islamic rituals of the Maliki rite performed within it took centre stage and the wonders of the palaces of Ifriqiya and al-Andalus suddenly found analogues on the dusty plains of Marrakesh.

Respect for the existing Umayyad and Maliki religious infrastructure of al-Andalus precluded any similar project of Almoravid mosque construction in the Iberian peninsula, although some Almoravid mosque enhancement probably did take place where repairs were necessary such as Valencia, whose great mosque was damaged and burnt when the Christians abandoned it in 1102. The main Almoravid contribution in al-Andalus seems to have been the construction of walls and fortresses to protect cities such as Córdoba, Seville, Granada, Jaén and Almería from Christian attacks and provide residential space on the urban periphery for Almoravid garrisons. It is, however, unclear to what degree these were state initiatives or local contributions. In Seville, for instance, the Ta'ifa king al-Mu'tamid began work on the walls in 1091, which was reprised by the Almoravids around 1126 and probably funded by taxes collected in the province. In Córdoba, however, each local mosque congregation seems to have been responsible for repairing and maintaining the section of wall in their district rather than the Almoravids taking the initiative.[54]

The Almoravids also built numerous fortresses in the Maghrib, especially during the decades of war with the Almohads when 'Ali b. Yusuf fortified the High Atlas with a line of strongholds in the vain hope of keeping the Almohad tribes at bay, a task entrusted to al-Fallaki, an erstwhile military adventurer from al-Andalus.[55] The two most famous Almoravid fortresses are Amargu overlooking the Wargha valley northeast of Fes, which some archaeologists believe was built earlier, and Tasghimut, located between the Warika and Issil river valleys in the northern foothills of the High Atlas, which was intended to guard the southern approach to Marrakesh and monitor the Almohad tribes in the mountains. Tasghimut is built of *pisé* upon a stone base, rather than ashlar (cut stone) masonry, materials that reflect the Almoravid need to erect defences quickly against the rising Almohad tide,

[54] Lagardère, *Le djihâd andalou*, pp. 135–6.
[55] Ibid., pp. 125–32.

but some have also seen in its design elements derived from Qalʿat Bani Hammad or from Andalusi fortresses, showing again the eclectic character of Almoravid building.[56]

Almoravid patronage did not encompass architecture alone, Almoravid rulers were also keen to commission portable *objets d'art* and textiles, predominantly from the numerous ateliers of the Iberian peninsula. There are several categories of extant objects that we shall discuss here, first, the incredibly fine Almoravid *minbars* (pulpits) produced in Córdoba, secondly, marble basins and tombstones fashioned in Almería, and, thirdly, rich textiles manufactured predominantly in Almería, Málaga and Seville. Textiles, of course, were not only commissioned or used by the court, and the same is also true of luxury ceramics which were another highly-sought after item. Together these artefacts provide a slice of the tastes of the rich at the time and the high level of skill in the Andalusi luxury manufacturing sector, skill that started to also develop in Maghribi towns as a result of the foundation of the Berber empires.

Although it would be wrong to attribute all artistic production directly to the Almoravids, rather than to those craftsmen and artists living under their rule, they were intimately involved in the commissioning of *minbars* (pulpits), which was a royal prerogative and the natural accompaniment to the foundation or remodelling of a great mosque. Derived from a small set of portable steps made for the Prophet, the *minbar* evolved into a high set of eight steps with a seat at the top during the Syrian Umayyad caliphate when it shared the functions of throne and pulpit. Subsequently, the *minbar* became simply the pulpit from which the *khaṭīb* (sermon giver) would pronounce the Friday sermon standing mid-way up the stairs. However, the fact that the sermon had to be dedicated to an Islamic ruler ensured that the *minbar* retained huge political as well as religious significance. It was an essential accoutrement of any great mosque and some geographers describe an area as having a certain number of *minbars* rather than great mosques.

In the Maghrib, *minbars* were often moveable and stored in a small chamber located to the right of the *miḥrāb*, a characteristic that Schacht attributed to their importance as symbols of monarchy as well as to the Maliki fondness for Medinese precedent.[57] Sfax, Tunis and possibly Qayrawan in Ifriqiya all had such moveable *minbars*. Fierro suggests that in al-Andalus moveable *minbars* were an Umayyad caliphal innovation made to strengthen associations between Córdoba and Medina, the home of the Maliki law school's

[56] Lagardère, *Le djihâd andalou*, p. 126.

[57] Schacht, 'An unknown type of minbar', p. 149.

founder, during the sectarian struggle between the Fatimids and Umayyads for the hearts and minds of Andalusi and Maghribi Muslims. The Umayyad caliph al-Hakam II crowned his extension of the great mosque of Córdoba by having a new portable *minbar* made for it, completed in 975–6 to serve as a platform for his public naming of his young son, Hisham, as the heir apparent. A few years later, the pro-Fatimid Zirids provided a new moveable *minbar* for the Andalus Mosque in Fes during their brief rule over the city from which Hisham II's minister, Ibn Abi 'Amir, the *de facto* ruler of the Umayyad caliphate, carefully erased all Fatimid references when his forces re-imposed Umayyad control over the city in 984.[58] By the early eleventh century moveable *minbars* existed in the great mosques of Almería and Qal'at Bani Hammad as well.[59]

It was therefore natural for 'Ali b. Yusuf to adopt the moveable *minbar* form, which had the double advantage of evoking Maliki practice in Ifriqiya and the all-important imperial Umayyad heritage in al-Andalus, when he commissioned a *minbar* to complete the great mosque of Marrakesh. To underline the Umayyad association and to ensure the artistic virtuosity of his *minbar*, 'Ali b. Yusuf gave the job to Córdoban craftsmen. The result was a spectacular and finely wrought piece of work, widely recognised as an outstanding piece of medieval Islamic art, which can still be viewed today in the Badi' Palace Museum in Marrakesh.[60] The *minbar* frame was made of cedarwood and lavishly decorated with polychrome bone and wood marquetry and wood carving. The design on its flanks is a repeating pattern of eight-sided stars, 'Y'-shaped panels and hexagonal lozenges surrounded by interlocking marquetry straps rendered in bone and different coloured woods, boxwood, jujube and African black wood, which most chroniclers mistook for ebony.[61] In contrast to the geometric tenor of the decoration on the flanks, the stair risers are decorated by rows of horseshoe arches filled with floral arabesques picked out in marquetry, while more sinuous curvilinear marquetry designs grace the back and sides of the 'seat' at the top of the *minbar*.

The inscriptions on the back of the *minbar* seat, which name 'Ali b. Yusuf as the patron, and the Qur'anic verses along the edges of the flanks are rendered in a combination of carved wood and marquetry.[62] Their content,

58 Fierro, 'The mobile *minbar*', pp. 111–12.

59 Ibid., p. 159.

60 For a full account of the *minbar*'s history, composition and restoration, see *The Minbar from the Kutubiyya Mosque*.

61 Bloom, 'The minbar from the Kutubiyya mosque', p. 7.

62 Qur'an 7: 54–61, 2: 255–7, 112: 1–4, 113: 1–5. Bloom, 'Appendix: Arabic text of the inscriptions on the minbar from the Kutubiyya mosque', p. 104.

carefully chosen as all such Qur'anic inscriptions were, includes references to God's 'throne' (*'arsh*), (Qur'an 7: 54 and the so-called 'Throne verse' Qur'an 2: 255) and evokes God's majesty and beneficence, but also the obedience owed to him and the need to follow the correct path.[63] It is intriguing to note that while verses referring to God's throne seem particularly apt for a piece of furniture somewhat like a throne, these verses also formed part of the polemic between the Almoravids and the Almohads, with the latter accusing the former of interpreting such verses literally and thereby falling into the trap of viewing God in an anthropomorphic manner. Surat al-Ikhlas, a popular epigraphic assertion of the Oneness of God against Christian Trinitarianism, and Surat al-Falak also figure on the *minbar*.[64]

Work on the *minbar* began in 1137 and, based on al-Idrisi's estimate that it took six craftsmen and their apprentices seven years to make al-Hakam II's *minbar*, Bloom suggests that it must have required 'at least a dozen workers' labouring 'over some five years' to complete it.[65] After it had been painstakingly made in sections in Córdoba, the *minbar* was transported to Marrakesh where it was reassembled and glued together. As in the case of marble columns and capitals, the transport of the *minbar* was no mean feat, involving as it did land or riverine conveyance to an Iberian port on the Straits, followed by a sea crossing to Ceuta or another Maghribi port, and then the long land journey down to Marrakesh. A similar *minbar*, most likely made in Córdoba too, was commissioned for the Qarawiyyin Mosque in Fes.

In combination with the great mosques themselves, Almoravid *minbar*s were highly public statements of royal patronage, wealth and the Almoravids' inheritance of the Umayyad imperial role, but also their extension of that role deep into the Maghrib and the Sahara, a reach that the Umayyads had never achieved. This reach is confirmed by the appearance of worked marble in the Sahel at Gao-Sané in the form of royal tombstones which are believed to have come from Almería.[66] This important find suggests that in addition to reusing Umayyad marble basins, columns and capitals, the Almoravids and other wealthy patrons also commissioned new marble objects, showing that this skill, like the crafts required for the execution of *minbar*s, flourished into Almoravid times and found support from Maghribi rulers as they had from their Andalusi predecessors.

Other luxury products such as gleaming, iridescent lustreware ceramics and rich textiles had wider circulation. As we have already seen in Chapter 5,

63 Bloom, 'Minbar', pp. 18–20.
64 Ibid., p. 20.
65 Ibid., p. 21.
66 Moraes Farias, *Arabic Medieval Inscriptions*, pp. cxxvi, 3–9.

the production of silk brocades continued to flourish in the Almoravid era in Seville, which was joined by new southern centres including Málaga and, above all, Almería which became the foremost producer of a wide range of fabrics in the twelfth century. Although the initial Almoravid reaction against the sumptuous lifestyle of the Ta'ifa kings may have put a temporary break on demand for such textiles, Ibn Tumart's criticism of 'Ali b. Yusuf for sitting on a luxurious silken cloak in the great mosque of Marrakesh, suggests that demand quickly rose again. In addition to private textile workshops, the Almoravids had royal workshops to manufacture *ṭirāz*, bands or garments embroidered with the ruler's moniker, often in gold, which were given out as state gifts. As in the case of wood carving and marquetry, there is no strong indication that standards dropped under the Berber empires even if the changed political environment impacted on individual centres. The Malagan *muḥtasib* al-Saqati talked about the importance of monitoring dyers to make sure that they used the best dyes rather than cheaper alternatives to ensure that colours lasted, and textile fragments show high levels of skill in weaving and embroidering silk and other fabrics.[67]

A large proportion of the fabrics that we have from this era have been preserved through their reuse as Christian vestments and burial outfits which required re-cutting and alterations. Many, therefore, are small fragments from larger pieces and it is difficult to say what they were used for in Almoravid times, although many were probably cushion covers, curtains or wall hangings. Some notable eleventh- to twelfth-century examples include the cloth found lining the reliquary of San Isidore, a chasuble from San Sernin in Toulouse and a fragment from the Church of Thuir in the French Pyrenees. From these pieces it is possible to make some broad observations about the 'tastes' of the time. While textiles used for clothing were plain or featured repeating abstract and geometric patterns with more ornate borders, larger decorative pieces included figures of animals often enclosed in large roundels on a ground decorated with curved, scrolled and entwined vegetal motifs, known collectively as arabesque. Some had borders that included both calligraphy and rows of smaller roundels, with or without figures inside them, and many were worked in gold and silk, a technique that seems to have been an Andalusi speciality.[68]

The figures selected were not innovative but drew on a long-established Islamic iconographic tradition that had absorbed many pre-Islamic motifs, including the tree of life, and royal animals and mythical creatures such as

[67] al-Sakati, *Hisba*, p. 63.

[68] Shepherd, 'Treasure', p. 128.

lions, eagles, peacocks, gazelles, griffins and harpies. As in other areas of art and architecture, motifs favoured during the Umayyad caliphate continued to be used in Almoravid contexts, reflecting the expertise of the workforce as well as the taste of patrons, while the market for Baghdad imitations, some with false 'made in Baghdad' inscriptions,[69] may also have been encouraged by the Almoravids' self-presentation as lieutenants of the 'Abbasids. Large pairs of beasts either face to face (affronted) or back to back (addorsed) seem to have been popular: the Saint Sernin chasuble fragment, for instance, depicts two affronted peacocks with the tree of life between them. It also includes calligraphic elements in the form of bands containing the phrase 'perfect (or complete) blessing' (*al-baraka al-kāmila*). Contrary to what one might assume, then, figurative designs did not disappear as a consequence of the Almoravids' strict interpretation of Islamic law. As in many Islamic societies, the prohibition on figural representation ended at the mosque door and it was accepted, if not actively desired, as ornamentation of domestic and secular spaces.

Like textiles, ceramics also ranged from cheap ware for daily use to luxury objects that only the rich could afford. They were also another category of object that Christians found attractive and sought to acquire through trade and sometimes as plunder. The disruption caused by the Almoravid conquest of the Ta'ifa kingdoms and, perhaps, their distaste for unnecessary display seems to have put a temporary break on luxury ceramics production, but during the twelfth century it picked up again. Unlikely as it may seem, one of the largest collections of Andalusi and Maghribi pottery is in Pisa, where approximately 2,000 glazed ceramic basins or bowls (*bacini*) were used to decorate churches from the early eleventh to fifteenth centuries.[70] These bowls include smooth monochrome examples, dishes with designs stamped in the clay prior to glazing and firing, *cuerda seca* (dry cord) ware, brown and green 'caliphal ware', and the most luxurious type of all, lustreware items given an iridescent sheen by means of a metallic glaze applied prior to a second firing, a technique that spread from Iraq and flourished in Fatimid Egypt while also disseminating across North Africa to al-Andalus.

Mathews sees this use of basins of Islamic provenance as a way of publicly celebrating Pisa's growing trade with the Muslim Mediterranean. From our perspective here, however, it also shows the sustained production of glazed ceramics in the Almoravid and Almohad eras with a similar range of designs – geometric, figural and calligraphic – to those evident upon textiles.[71]

[69] Partearroyo, 'Almoravid and Almohad textiles', p. 106.
[70] Mathews, 'Plunder of war', p. 246.
[71] Ibid., p. 252.

One new use of ceramics, the decoration of buildings with mosaic tiles (*zillīj*), which became ubiquitous in the Maghrib under the Almohads and later dynasties, may well have commenced in Almoravid Córdoba and Seville.[72]

In summary, the Almoravid era was largely one of artistic and architectural continuity in the Iberian peninsula after the short hiatus created by the disappearance of the Ta'ifa rulers. It also witnessed the widespread fortification of the landscape in response to the turbulence of the times. In the Maghrib, it was a period of change and innovation that witnessed the widescale development of a monumental architectural tradition characterised by large T-plan hypostyle great mosques whose sanctuaries were embellished with fine stucco-carved *muqarnas* domes and beautifully fashioned *minbars*. It is likely that work in the Maghrib was carried out by some master craftsmen or migrant workers from al-Andalus as well as growing numbers of local labourers and craftsmen, giving it local vernacular elements and encouraging the emergence of a skilled indigenous Maghribi workforce over time. Almoravid palaces, at least in Marrakesh, were finely crafted and decorated not only with stucco and marble, but also with wall-hangings of gold and silk brocade that introduced a new southern audience to Andalusi, and possibly 'Abbasid, styles of building and décor.

Urbanism, Architecture and Art under the Almohads

Once we reach the Almohad era, we are on somewhat firmer ground due to the survival of many more of their buildings and the detailed descriptions of some of their construction projects by Ibn Sahib al-Salat which convey the scale of such projects, the craftsmen involved and contemporary perceptions of them. Like the Sanhaja, the Masmuda were not heirs to a monumental building tradition and, as they advanced and captured Almoravid fortresses and cities, they had to decide whether to destroy or appropriate the monuments they found. In the event, they made a variety of choices and then went on to develop a triumphal and militant architecture to express their own revolutionary politico-religious stance as true monotheists and defenders of that faith. As Ewert notes, however, the changes in architectural style between the Almoravid and Almohad eras, unlike those in ideology, tended to be evolutionary rather than revolutionary due to an unavoidable reliance on the existing workforce with their particular skills and experience.[73]

The first Almohad town was Tinmall, perched in the High Atlas and

[72] Bloom, 'Minbar', p. 26.
[73] Ewert, 'El registro ornamental', p. 225.

accessible only by a single causeway. The Almohads fortified the site with walls and Ibn Tumart's house and the great mosque formed the new town's core.[74] They were probably simple functional structures that formed a single complex like the Prophet's house in Medina which also served as a mosque. Almohad architecture began to gain a monumental form during the reign of 'Abd al-Mu'min (r. 1130–63), who combined his martial and political activities with keen attention to the elaboration of a material language of power in Tinmall, Taza, Marrakesh, Gibraltar, renamed 'Mountain of Victory' (Jabal al-Fath), and al-Mahdiyya or Ribat al-Fath (modern Rabat). This was part and parcel of the radical Almohad programme to herald in God's true kingdom by reshaping all aspects of life. They expressed their position in bold militant forms, simple and sometimes stark decoration in their mosques, and a sharp rise in the use of calligraphic motifs that expressed the tenets of Almohadism.

The tone was set shortly after the death of Ibn Tumart when 'Abd al-Mu'min had the gateway at Tinmall embellished with wooden gates taken from the Almoravid fortress of Tasghimut after it was conquered in 1132, a transfer reminiscent of the conveyance of the gates of Umayyad Wasit to 'Abbasid Baghdad in the 750s. The following year, 'Abd al-Mu'min captured Taza, a small town strategically located 60 miles northeast of Fes on the narrow corridor leading between the Rif and Middle Atlas mountains to Tlemcen. Here he built a fortified citadel, evocatively called Ribat Taza, which was entirely orientated in the direction of prayer (*al-qibla*), a plan facilitated by the concurrence of the *qibla* direction with the slope of the land.[75] Despite this grand religiously inflected plan, the great mosque itself, probably dating to 1141–2, was small and followed the Almoravid mosque form: a hypostyle T-plan realised with brick piers rather than columns and a *miḥrāb* preceded by a dome. The original *miḥrāb* area, lost during the extension of the mosque in the 1290s, may have announced the arrival of the new regime by swapping rich Almoravid decoration for simpler ornamentation. The tower, however, is probably a later addition.

Almohad architectural self-expression began to come into its own with the capture of Marrakesh from the Almoravids in 1147. As the city closest to the Masmuda homelands, it was the natural Almohad capital but its strong association with the Almoravids, who had not only used it as their imperial capital but actually founded it, was problematic. On the one hand, it made sense for the Almohads to exploit the powerful evocation of Marrakesh as

[74] Ferhat, 'Tinmal'.
[75] Bonine, 'The sacred direction and city structure', pp. 67–8, 69.

a paradisal 'domain of God', but they also needed to reshape that domain in a new Almohad image. Al-Baydhaq's account of the fall of Marrakesh suggests that 'Abd al-Mu'min achieved this not only through his three-day purge of the Almoravid population, but also by his symbolic refusal to enter Marrakesh on the grounds of its misaligned mosques and, therefore, its defective sacred geography. As al-Baydhaq puts it, 'the *qiblas* of the mosques were too far east, a practice not for Muslims but for the Jews'. The Almohad reshaping of the city thus took the very physical form of destroying mosques 'for their incorrect *qiblas*, including part of the mosque of 'Ali b. Yusuf', and then rebuilding them to make it 'licit' for the Almohads to live (and pray) in Marrakesh.[76]

Whether this was a polemical exchange or a rigorously implemented policy is not clear since some references suggest that 'Ali b. Yusuf's mosque was left derelict rather than destroyed.[77] In any case, the incident was not really about mathematical accuracy, as there was a great deal of variety in medieval estimations of the *qibla* direction, but a sign that the Almoravids had been religious deviants, a flaw symbolically corrected by the construction of mosques with a slightly different orientation which transformed the city into the utopian Almohad 'city of perfection' (*al-madīna al-fāḍila*). The Almohads showed a particular concern for this with the majority of their mosques oriented around 150 degrees, close to the orientation of the great mosque of Córdoba,[78] an alignment that correlated with the desire of 'Abd al-Mu'min and his descendants to create a link with the Umayyads of Córdoba as well as Tinmall, the burial place of Ibn Tumart and the Almohads' new Medina.[79]

'Abd al-Mu'min also supposedly destroyed the Almoravid Qasr al-Hajar palace and built a new great mosque there,[80] later known as the Kutubiyya, with a T-plan, seventeen naves formed of brick piers and a comparatively small courtyard integrated into the prayer hall rather than adjacent to it, a further stage in the steady reduction of the size of mosque courtyards in comparison with prayer halls in the Maghrib. The Almohad citadel and palace were built next to the new mosque and connected to it by a passageway called

76 al-Baydhaq, *Akhbar*, pp. 119–20; *al-Hulal al-Mawshiyya*, p. 144.

77 al-Idrisi, *Opus Geographicum*, fasc. 1–4, p. 234; Bennison, 'Power and the city', p. 84.

78 Bonine, 'The sacred direction and city structure', p. 52; King, 'The orientation of medieval Islamic religious architecture and cities', p. 267.

79 Ghouirgate, *L'Ordre almohade*, p. 91.

80 *al-Hulal al-Mawshiyya*, p. 144. The accounts of what was or was not destroyed are neither coherent nor detailed and the name Qasr al-Hajar continued to be used for an Almohad palace in the area.

a *sābāṭ*, like the walkway that connected the great mosque of Córdoba and the Umayyad palace.[81] This pattern of a great mosque and royal residence constructed alongside the existing urban centre with an open plaza (*raḥba* or *sharī'a*) where rulers and ruled could interact became a feature of Almohad urbanism in other towns too.[82] It also gave the city a different orientation to its original Almoravid one by combining religion and power in the south-western quadrant, where it was to stay for centuries, and introducing a bifurcation between the civilian and politico-military halves of the city.

Outside Marrakesh, 'Abd al-Mu'min followed 'Ali b. Yusuf's lead and established a large estate irrigated by water from Aghmat where fruits of all kinds were grown.[83] He appointed the exiled lord of Guadix, Ahmad b. Milhan, a keen agronomist, as head of the project.[84] According to Ibn al-Yasa', the profit from selling the estate's fruit and olives was a massive 30,000 Mu'minid *dīnārs* in 1148, despite the low price of fruit at the time.[85] The estate included a large pool (*buḥayra*) and it may well have been the site of the pavilion from which 'Abd al-Mu'min supposedly told his minister and companion, Ibn 'Atiyya, that he much preferred to review troops than admire rows of flowers![86] The construction of such suburban 'lake' estates, the *baḥā'ir* mentioned in Chapter 5, would become common Almohad practice and the modern olive and citrus planted Menara gardens arranged around a vast pool outside Marrakesh started as one such estate. As modern visitors to Marrakesh will know, the Menara pool is now popularly associated with the caliph al-Rashid's estate where he drowned or caught a fatal chill in 1242. For the Almohads, as for the Almoravids, these estates had practical functions but also symbolic associations as earthly evocations of paradise and demonstrations of royal bounty through the provision of water.

During the late 1140s, 'Abd al-Mu'min turned his attention to recently conquered al-Andalus and ordered the construction of an Almohad citadel (*qaṣaba*) in Seville to house the garrison in response to bitter complaints from the population about the Almohad troops who had spilled out of the old 'Abbadid and Almoravid *qaṣaba* and taken over the Jabbana quarter. Ibn 'Idhari gives a fairly negative description of this process which is in contrast to

[81] The most recent edition of the *Hulal* uses the term *nafaqayn*, 'two passages', which the editor says is the word used by the manuscript version while the older edition used *sābāṭ*. *al-Hulal al-Mawshiyya*, p. 144, n. 69.

[82] Bennison, 'Power and the city', p. 86.

[83] He may have simply repaired and renovated the Almoravid *buḥayra*.

[84] Huici Miranda, *Historia política*, vol. 1, p. 180.

[85] *al-Hulal al-Mawshiyya*, pp. 145–6.

[86] Bennison, 'The salutary tale of Ibn 'Aṭiyya', pp. 260–1.

Ibn Sahib al-Salat's often eulogistic description of Almohad urban development. He says:

> They took possession of the place that [the citadel] now occupies and evicted people from their homes and compensated them by giving them in exchange houses owned by the *makhzan* in the city which did not satisfy them. This was harder for people than being killed and it greatly increased their cares and woe. [The Almohads] destroyed the walls of Ibn 'Abbad and built the *qaṣaba* using their stones. The people did not stop complaining about this exchange [of houses] through the reigns of the first, second and third caliphs.[87]

'Abd al-Mu'min also commenced work on al-Mahdiyya or Ribat al-Fath (modern Rabat), constructed across the Bu Regreg River estuary from the older coastal town of Salé. This mid-way point between Marrakesh and the northern ports of the Straits of Gibraltar served as a mustering point for armies from the south, a naval embarkation station and a commercial port. Ibn Sahib al-Salat describes the land across the river from Salé as open farmland belonging to the state (*makhzan*), the townsfolk of Salé and one Ibn Wajjad, who may have been the scion of an aristocratic family from Seville.[88] The only significant building was a small tower (*burj*), reputedly built by the penultimate Almoravid amir, Tashfin b 'Ali.[89] Around the time of his reception of Andalusi notables in 1150–1 at the palace of the Banu 'Ashara in newly conquered Salé, 'Abd al-Mu'min decided to enhance this strategic site by ordering 'the construction of a well-fortified fortress (*qaṣaba*) in that place at the mouth of the river leading to Salé', known today as the Qasaba of the Udaya.

He then commanded the Almohad contingents, labourers and engineers to build an underground water channel from the Ghabula spring to the new *qaṣaba* where it emerged into an open channel from which people and animals could drink and the surrounding land could be irrigated.[90] The project took two months during which time 'Abd al-Mu'min remained encamped in the vicinity while his soldiers laboured away. This formed the prelude to the further development and urbanisation of the area. Ibn Sahib al-Salat adds that after the water supply was secured, 'Abd al-Mu'min and later caliphs established lakeside estates (*baḥā'ir*) and cultivated gardens around the new settlement and then ordered people to take up residence there and build

[87] Ibn 'Idhari, *al-Bayan*, vol. 4, p. 117.
[88] Ibn Sahib al-Salat, *al-Mann bi'l-Imama*, p. 357.
[89] Ibn 'Idhari, *al-Bayan*, vol. 4, p. 103.
[90] Ibn Sahib al-Salat, *al-Mann bi'l-Imama*, p. 358.

Figure 7.7 Great mosque, Tinmall (photograph Mariam Rosser-Owen)

houses and markets.[91] As we shall see below, this process culminated thirty years later with Ya'qub al-Mansur's spectacular additions to Ribat al-Fath.

Soon after founding Ribat al-Fath, 'Abd al-Mu'min set in train the creation of a splendid new great mosque at Tinmall to form part of a shrine complex centred on the tomb of Ibn Tumart, to enhance the role of Tinmall as the Almohad Medina to Marrakesh, their Mecca, retrieved from the 'pagan' Almoravids. Although we do not know how large Tinmall was in the Almohad era, it is hard to underestimate the eccentricity of building a substantial mosque in such an isolated mountain location which was clearly difficult to reach throughout the Almohad era. It was, however, crucial to the sacred landscape of the Almohads as the burial place of the *mahdī* and the cradle of the Almohad movement, an identification that 'Abd al-Mu'min and his successors enhanced and perpetuated by patronage, pilgrimages to Tinmall and, ultimately, their own burials there.

'Abd al-Mu'min's Tinmall mosque was constructed around 1153, probably by a team of craftsmen from Marrakesh.[92] It was similar to the

91 Ibn Sahib al-Salat, *al-Mann bi'l-Imama*, pp. 358–9, 479–82; Ibn 'Idhari, *al-Bayan*, vol. 4, p. 122.
92 Ewert, 'El registro ornamental', p. 225.

Figure 7.8 *Miḥrāb*, great mosque, Tinmall (photograph Mariam Rosser-Owen)

Kutubiyya, albeit smaller since it was designed for the inhabitants of Tinmall and pilgrims not the population of a capital city, but it also had experimental aspects that hinted at the full-blown imperial Almohad style to come. Like its predecessors, it perpetuated the hypostyle T-plan but with variations such as wider lateral aisles and more slender piers supporting ogival horseshoe arches. Decorative multifoil arches graced the transversal bay along the *qibla* wall, with the most intricately decorated one in front of the *miḥrāb*. The latter was built in the polygonal chamber style of Córdoba and preceded by a *muqarnas* dome as in Almoravid mosques, but the façade of the *miḥrāb* was decorated with geometric patterns in place of the floral and vegetal decoration popular with the Almoravids. This move to rigorous geometric designs and décor is seen as a distinguishing characteristic of the Almohad era, viewed in contrasting ways, either as proof of a puritanical dislike for rich decoration or as a demonstration of admirable geometric control and the architectural manifestation of their rationalist theology. In the latter camp, Barrucand and Bednorz write, 'It is the harmony between ground plan, typological concept, geometric foundations and ornamentation that make these mosques into remarkable masterpieces.'[93]

Externally, the mosque was distinctive for its strong resemblance to a fortress, another hallmark of Almohad mosque architecture, and its introduction of a 'hesitant and experimental' minaret, which looked more like wall tower and was placed on the *qibla* wall encasing the *miḥrāb* rather than the back wall.[94] This experiment was not widely repeated, although it may have been tried in the great mosques of Algiers and Salé too.[95] Instead, the Almohads left their hesitation behind and began to build much taller, massive square minaret towers bearing a resemblance to Umayyad minarets and the tower at Qal'at Bani Hammad, located either on the wall opposite the *qibla* or along one of the lateral walls of the mosque.[96] The first tower minaret of this type appeared when 'Abd al-Mu'min built the second Kutubiyya mosque in Marrakesh around 1158, either to correct the *qibla* orientation of the first Kutubiyya or, more likely, as the *Kitab al-Istibsar* asserts, to double its size to make it more imposing.[97] Ghouirgate suggests that the argument that the *qibla* needed reorientation might have served as an excuse to leave the old *qibla* wall intact and create, in effect, two mosques connected to each other, one for the ruling class and one for the population of Marrakesh, rather than follow the usual mode of mosque extension by demolishing the old *qibla* wall and extending the prayer hall.[98]

The minaret tower was located on the left-hand wall of the mosque at the intersection between its old and new sections. It soared 77 metres in the air

93 Barrucand and Bednorz, *Moorish Architecture*, p. 154.
94 Bloom, *Minaret*, p. 118.
95 Hillenbrand, *Islamic Art*, p. 186.
96 Golvin, 'Ḳal'at Banī Ḥammād'.
97 Ghouirgate, *L'Ordre almohade*, p. 361.
98 Ibid., p. 361.

Figure 7.9 Kutubiyya minaret, Marrakesh

and each façade was enlivened with horseshoe arched windows in arrangements of one, two, three or four set into panels decorated with carved scalloped trellis designs, reminiscent of multilobed Ta'ifa and Almoravid arches, with a band of geometric coloured tiles surmounted by stepped merlons at the top. The minaret was crowned by a miniature second tower with a ribbed dome. Inside, the tower's builders swapped the entwined double staircases of Umayyad and Almoravid minarets with a wide ramp which was said to have allowed the muezzin to ride to the top on a mule. Small chambers used for religious retreat and contemplation came off the ramp making the tower not just an elevated place for the call to prayer, but also a space for the promotion of Almohad Islam. In its difference of scale and design to preceding towers, this tower and others like it became physical beacons of Almohadism that dominated the landscape.

The new mosque section followed the established Almohad T-plan, while pursuing the trend towards reducing the size of the courtyard by making it half the width of the mosque and integrating it further within the prayer hall. The three naves leading to the polygonal *miḥrāb* chamber were accentuated by means of transversal as well as lateral arches, which also defined the caliph's royal enclosure (*maqṣūra*). Engaged columns with marble capitals from Córdoba or Madinat al-Zahra' on the piers closest to the *miḥrāb* maintained the Córdoban Umayyad connection.[99] The effect of the building itself was enhanced by complex mechanisms constructed by a Malagan engineer, probably al-Hajj Ya'ish, that enabled the beautiful Almoravid *minbar* transferred from 'Ali b. Yusuf's mosque to silently emerge from its chamber next to the *miḥrāb* and the finely carved wooden *maqṣūra* screens to rise smoothly from the floor at the approach of the *khaṭīb* and caliph, respectively.[100] Just as the great mosque of Córdoba was a 'copy' of the great mosque of Damascus in the medieval sense of possessing similar elements,[101] so the Kutubiyya in its mature form seemed to 'copy' the great mosque of Córdoba in its polygonal *miḥrāb* with flanking chambers, Córdoban *minbar* and *sābāṭ*. However, it also had peculiarly Almohad features, such as the eccentric placing of two differently oriented sections alongside each other, its massive laterally placed minaret and the transposition of mechanical wonders, which had long been found in palaces, to the mosque.

In 1160, on the eve of his return from the recapture of al-Mahdiyya from the Normans, 'Abd al-Mu'min ordered the building of another grand new city on the rock of Gibraltar as a seat of Almohad government at the gateway

99 Ewert, 'El registro ornamental', p. 228.
100 *al-Hulal al-Mawshiyya*, pp. 144–5.
101 Bloom, 'Early Islamic architecture', p. 40.

to al-Andalus, a status held by Algeciras during the Almoravid era. While the project was the responsibility of his sons who were serving as governors in al-Andalus at the time, among the engineers, architects and master craftsmen involved were al-Hajj Ya'ish of Málaga and Ahmad b. Basuh of Seville, along with a veritable army of builders, carpenters and plasterers from across the Almohads' Andalusi territories.[102] Although a detailed plan of Almohad Gibraltar does not survive, it was said to have included well-built palaces and houses built on the lower slopes of the rock on platforms made of stone and lime, walls, and an imposing entrance gateway called Bab al-Futuh on the tongue of land leading to the mainland. According to Ibn Sahib al-Salat, figs, grapes, apples, pears, quinces, apricots, citrons and bananas were grown on the limited arable land available, and the engineer al-Hajj Ya'ish erected a windmill on the rock summit which, unfortunately, was allowed to fall into disrepair when he left Gibraltar for Marrakesh.[103]

Two years later, in 1162, the two princely governors in al-Andalus, Abu Ya'qub Yusuf and Abu Sa'id, followed their father's command to transfer the Almohad seat from Seville to Córdoba, in recognition of its status as the historic Umayyad capital of al-Andalus, and initiated a programme of building work there directed by Ahmad b. Basuh to repair the immense damage caused during the preceding war-torn decades and encourage the population which had fled to return. As Ibn Sahib al-Salat poetically puts it:

> They brought in builders, master craftsmen, and labourers to re-build the ruined palaces and houses and restore [the city's] domes to their previous height and transform its state from old age to youth.[104]

Interestingly, the chronicler does not mention the erection of an Almohad *qaṣaba* in Córdoba which, for all its historic and symbolic centrality, was actually on the northern fringe of the empire and only used as the Almohad capital for eight months. It was at this time, shortly before 'Abd al-Mu'min's death, that the precious Qur'an of 'Uthman was dispatched from Córdoba to Marrakesh to be housed, we assume, in the new Kutubiyya and to deepen the connection the Mu'minids wished to make with the Umayyad past.

During the reigns of Abu Ya'qub Yusuf (r. 1163–84) and his son, Ya'qub al-Mansur (r. 1184–99), the Almohads continued to expand cities and develop new settlements that expressed their militant and imperial ethos. The main recipients of attention were the Almohad capitals of Marrakesh, Ribat al-Fath and Seville, which were endowed with large fortified palatine enclaves, great

[102] Ibn Sahib al-Salat, *al-Mann bi'l-Imama*, pp. 130–1.
[103] Ibid., pp. 84–9.
[104] Ibid., p. 140.

mosques, monumental gateways and new ramparts. In Marrakesh and Seville at least, the Almohads also constructed a lockable royal market (*qayṣariyya*) close to their palatine quarter, thereby creating new commercial areas and stimulating the economy. Numerous other citadels and fortresses were built across the empire. Each caliph built on the foundations laid by his successor, giving Almohad imperial architecture a cumulative, layered character with 'Abd al-Mu'min's vision at its heart.

In al-Andalus, the Almohads focused their energies on Seville, which was less exposed to Christian attack than Córdoba and became their *de facto* capital in the peninsula. During the course of the Almohad age, Seville's Umayyad great mosque was replaced and it gained a new palatine quarter, extensive ramparts, riverine defences and a series of suburban estates centred on artificial lakes, the so-called *baḥā'ir*.[105] We are lucky to have quite a detailed account of building in Seville from the pen of Ibn Sahib al-Salat, whose Sevillan origin made him attentive to the changes made in his home town. As we have already seen, 'Abd al-Mu'min had ordered the construction of a new *qaṣaba* in Seville in the late 1140s to house the Almohad governor and garrison. When Abu Ya'qub Yusuf, who had served as governor of Seville during his father's reign, returned to the city as caliph in the late 1160s he initiated a series of more ambitious interrelated projects.

These involved the construction and repair of walls and the addition of gate fortifications, the extension of the *qaṣaba* down to the river, the addition of run-off channels or gutters for flood water to gateways on the riverside, the building of bridges to facilitate the passing of commercial and military traffic in and out of the city, and the construction of palaces outside Bab Jahwar which became part of Seville's first *buḥayra* estate.[106] The irrigation works, built to supply the Buhayrat Bab Jahwar by 'the engineer Ya'ish', carried the water on into Seville itself 'for the noble and common man to drink', a project highly reminiscent of 'Ali b. Yusuf and 'Abd al-Mu'min's hydraulic works in Marrakesh.[107]

In 1171, Abu Ya'qub Yusuf commenced another major project to replace the existing Umayyad mosque of 'Addabas, which had purportedly become too small for its congregation, with a grand new Almohad great mosque. In keeping with the plan already evident in Mu'minid Marrakesh, the new great mosque was placed adjacent to the Almohad *qaṣaba* on the urban periphery rather than in the locale of the existing great mosque, thereby creating a new

[105] For a full resumé of the works in Seville, see Valor Piechotta and Tabales Rodríguez, 'Urbanismo y arquitectura almohades en Sevilla'.

[106] Ibn Sahib al-Salat, *al-Mann bi'l-Imama*, pp. 165–6.

[107] Ibid., p. 377.

Figure 7.10 Giralda minaret, Seville

religio-political nexus for the city. As with earlier urban projects, craftsmen were mobilised from all over al-Andalus but, for the first time, Ibn Sahib al-Salat adds that master builders also came from,

> The capital, Marrakesh, and the city of Fes and the Maghrib in general (*al-'udwa*). [Huge] numbers of them, and representatives of all types of carpenter, sawyer and practitioners of all forms of construction, the most outstanding of the skilled craftsmen in every art, came together in Seville.[108]

They were headed by the Sevillan architect Ahmad b. Basuh who had previously worked for the Almohads in Gibraltar. As well as the construction of the building itself, the project required complicated engineering works to divert the old city sewer that ran under the ground allocated for the mosque to a new wider channel. The initial works took nearly four years, during which time the caliph was said to have personally visited the site on a daily basis when he could. By the time Abu Ya'qub Yusuf returned to Marrakesh in early 1176, the mosque itself was more or less complete but, according to Ibn Sahib al-Salat, the Friday prayer was not held there until 1182 and the building of its tower minaret only started in 1184 when the caliph was back in Seville for his ill-fated Santarem campaign.[109] After his death during the campaign, the tower was completed by order of his son, Ya'qub al-Mansur, although he halted expenditure and work on other projects such as the *qaṣaba* walls.[110]

Much of the mosque was destroyed in the centuries after the Christian conquest of Seville to make way for the cathedral, but its courtyard, the Patio de los Naranjos, and its tall laterally placed tower minaret, the Giralda, provide indications as to its original size, which was close to that of the great mosque of Córdoba, and its monumental form akin to that of the Kutubiyya in Marrakesh. Ibn Sahib al-Salat talks about its lofty appearance and its beauty, while making more specific mention of the stucco-carved dome over the *miḥrāb*, the arched passageway (*sābāṭ*) to its left that led to the caliph's palace and the matching doorway to the right, leading to the chamber where the *minbar* was kept when not in use, and the wood-carved *maqṣūra* screens,[111] all features shared by the Kutubiyya mosque that contributed to the 'sacralisation du caliphe' by conjoining the palace and mosque and separating the Almohad ruler from the masses, in contrast to previous Almoravid practice.[112]

108 Ibn Sahib al-Salat, *al-Mann bi'l-Imama*, pp. 383–4.
109 Ibid., pp. 389, 390.
110 Ibid., p. 391.
111 Ibid., p. 387.
112 Ghouirgate, *L'Ordre almohade*, p. 368.

The *minbar* itself was finely worked in the Córdoban style and probably made in the ateliers of Córdoba, like the earlier *minbar* of 'Ali b. Yusuf and the one Ya'qub al-Mansur commissioned for the *qaṣaba* mosque in Marrakesh:

> This *minbar* was made using the most marvellous techniques possible (*gharābat al-ṣan'a*). It made use of the most noble wood intricately carved, embellished to perfection, with all types of arts and craft of the rarest workmanship (*gharīb al-'amal*), wondrous of form (*'ajīb al-shakl*), ornamented with sandalwood, variegated with ivory and ebony which gleamed like coals in a torch and with discs of gold and silver. The shapes of the pure gold work radiated such light that an observer on a dark night would reckon them full moons.[113]

The tower, commissioned by Abu Ya'qub Yusuf and completed by Ya'qub al-Mansur, was the great mosque's crowning glory and the ultimate symbol of the triumph of Almohad Islam in al-Andalus, just as the Kutubiyya minaret announced their success in the Maghrib:

> This minaret, the description of which surpasses speech and whose mention comes first for every historian, has no equal in any of the mosques of al-Andalus in its lofty elevation, its firm foundations, its solid workmanship, brick construction, rare craftsmanship (*gharābat al-ṣan'a*), and splendid appearance. It soared into the air and towered in the sky and could be seen by the naked eye a day's journey (*marḥala*) from Seville.[114]

Again, the work was not constant and after a first burst of activity in 1184, it lapsed until 1188 when an order arrived from the caliph in Marrakesh for it to recommence. The interior design of the tower followed that of the Kutubiyya tower and featured a ramp to the top that was wide enough for 'beasts of burden, people and the custodians',[115] and chambers for religious retreat giving the regime a physical beacon of Almohadism in al-Andalus as well as the Maghrib. The architect Ahmad b. Basuh led the team building the tower, which reused stone from the palace of the 'Abbadids of Seville, but Ibn Sahib al-Salat also mentions one 'Ali al-Ghumari, a Maghribi Berber, who was responsible for the brick decoration that faced the stone and various repairs to the mosque:

> 'Ali al-Ghumari began the work in brick that faced the forementioned work in stone and he repaired the damage to the three arcades (*balāṭāt*) of the

[113] Ibn Sahib al-Salat, *al-Mann bi'l-Imama*, pp. 387–8.
[114] Ibid., p. 390.
[115] Ibid., p. 391.

mosque on the eastern, western and north sides. He improved the mosque with staircases on the west side and surfaced the [ground] around it with *kadān* stone.[116] He made windows of glass inside the roofed section and surfaced it with baked brick.[117]

As with the earlier reference to the mobilisation of craftsmen from both al-Andalus and the Maghrib to build the mosque, this mention of a master craftsman from the Berber Ghumara tribe of the western Rif indicates that by the Almohad period a true cultural synthesis was occurring with both Andalusi and Maghribi craftsmen working together to create monuments in a new imperial style, neither 'Andalusi' nor 'Maghribi' in a chauvinistic sense, but rather a fortuitous blend of the two. The final flourish was added to the tower in 1198, shortly before the caliph left Seville for the last time, when a set of golden globes mounted on an iron pole were ceremoniously fixed onto its summit in the presence of the caliph.[118] In the meantime, assessors had valued the homes, shops and inns of the nearby 'Nail Market', purchased them from the owners and demolished them to make way for a series of enlarged plazas around the great mosque and a new royal market (*qayṣariyya*), located opposite the north gate of the great mosque, which subsequently housed high-value perfumes, textiles and tailors.[119]

In the Maghrib, Marrakesh continued to be the prime site for investment and expansion as the Almohad capital and permanent seat of the caliph. The Almohads concentrated on developing new areas to the south of the Almoravid Qasr al-Hajar area, where the Almohad great mosque and Qasr al-Khilafa were situated, into a veritable palatine city, known variously in the sources as the *qaṣaba*, Tamurakusht and al-Saliha.[120] Although Marrakesh flourished in the early 1170s, the devastating plague epidemic of 1175–6 decimated the population, prompting Abu Ya'qub Yusuf, who had returned from Seville just prior to the epidemic, to order tribesmen to resettle the city.[121] This appears to have been very successful and by 1183 over-population and a lack of housing for migrants had become serious issues. Ibn 'Idhari says that Abu Ya'qub Yusuf ordered the extension of Marrakesh, including the replacement of its ramparts because after the conquest of the Maghrib, Ifriqiya and al-Andalus, migrants had flooded in from all directions and the existing city

[116] Archaeological work has shown that *kadān* or *kadhān* stone refers to reused ashlar paving slabs. Valor and Tabales, 'Urbanismo y arquitectura almohades en Sevilla', p. 206, n. 48.

[117] Ibn Sahib al-Salat, *al-Mann bi'l-Imama*, p. 392.

[118] Ibid., pp. 393–4.

[119] Ibid., pp. 396–7.

[120] Bennison, 'Power and the city', p. 85; Ghouirgate, *L'Ordre almohade*, pp. 357–9.

[121] Triki, 'Marrakech', p. 100.

had become too small, with the effect that the population 'found no plot to build on and no place to live'.[122] The situation reached crisis point when the caliph ordered Haskura and Sanhaja tribes to migrate to the city and they found nowhere to settle:

> They complained to him, so he sent his son, al-Sayyid [Ya'qub] al-Mansur, with the Almohad shaykhs and building experts to explore, with his oversight, where this extension should be. They agreed upon the addition of an adjacent city (*madīna muttaṣila*) to the south [of Marrakesh]. The *'abīd* and infantry were ordered to demolish the walls in the [current] Bab al-Shari'a area and build new walls and the Bab al-Shari'a. They did this in 40 days![123]

This reference to Ya'qub al-Mansur reveals that the future caliph was already interested in urbanism and architecture and perhaps more involved with the project than his father, certainly the bulk of it was carried out after Abu Ya'qub Yusuf's precipitous death outside Santarem in 1184. The new urban enclave boasted wide streets, a parade ground, a great mosque, a *qayṣariyya* and a series of palaces said to have numbered twelve by the end of the Almohad era.[124] Ya'qub al-Mansur also developed the old Almoravid city by providing it with a long canal to supply additional water for its growing population and he augmented the suburban lake estates on its perimeter. A final architectural addition to Marrakesh, which may have been located in al-Saliha or the old city, was a hospital, a form of philanthropy already well established in the Middle East and popular with the new politico-military rulers of the twelfth century, the Zangids and the Ayyubids.

It may have the simmering rivalry between the Almohads and the Ayyubid Salah al-Din, founder of an impressive hospital in Cairo in 1182, that encouraged Ya'qub al-Mansur to found his own in Marrakesh shortly afterwards.[125] Certainly, Salah al-Din's hospital was warmly described as 'a palace, goodly for its beauty and spaciousness' by the Almohad official Ibn Jubayr who returned from his pilgrimage to the Maghrib in 1185.[126] The hospital building is now lost, but it is described by al-Marrakushi very much in terms of palatial architecture as a series of courts graced with running water and pools as well as pleasant halls for its patients:

[122] Ibn 'Idhari, *al-Bayan*, vol. 4, p. 225. In the extant part of his work, Ibn Sahib al-Salat simply says that Abu Ya'qub Yusuf was the one 'who built a second city adjacent to Marrakesh'; *al-Mann bi'l-Imama*, p. 168.

[123] Ibn 'Idhari, *al-Bayan*, vol. 4, pp. 225–6.

[124] Triki, 'Marrakech', p. 102; Bennison, 'Power and the city', pp. 85–6.

[125] See pp. 152–3, above.

[126] Ibn Jubayr, *Travels*, p. 43.

> [Ya'qub al-Mansur] chose the best spot and ordered the builders to do their finest work including carving and decoration. He ordered perfumed and fruitbearing trees to be planted within and installed flowing water to all the rooms in addition to four pools in the centre, one made of white marble. He then ordered rich furnishings of wool, cotton, silk, and skins.[127]

Ya'qub al-Mansur also turned his indefatigable attention to Ribat al-Fath, perched on the Atlantic coast across the Bu Regreg from Salé. Like the expansion of Marrakesh, the transformation of Ribat al-Fath from a citadel into a much larger imperial city seems to have been a project initiated by Abu Ya'qub Yusuf, who had added a cistern to improve the water supply, repaired 'Abd al-Mu'min's bridge and built another one to provide access to Salé and the route north, and commenced work on the northern and western ramparts.[128] However, the project was brought to completion by Ya'qub al-Mansur, who presided over the foundation of its crowning glory, its great mosque, which the caliph hoped would be the largest sanctuary in the Islamic west, if not the Islamic world, and certainly a rival to, or calque on, the vast Umayyad great mosque of Córdoba.

The mosque was carefully located at the top of the steeply rising south bank of the Bu Regreg River estuary in a position visible for miles around from both land and sea to further enhance its impact. This was a suburban location at the time so there was no large resident urban population to fill the great mosque, and historians have thus speculated that it was designed as much to serve the army when it mustered in the area for campaigns as for the permanent inhabitants of Ribat al-Fath, and was perhaps used as a fortress as well as a mosque. It was unusual in other ways too. Ya'qub al-Mansur swapped the now typical Almohad brick piers for huge round stone columns, probably to evoke the Umayyad great mosque of Córdoba, and substituted the usual single integrated courtyard for a set of three small courtyards, one in the usual position towards the back of the mosque parallel to the *qibla wall* and another two positioned perpendicular to the *qibla* wall, one on each side of the prayer hall. The mosque was never completed and it suffered extensive damage in the 1755 Lisbon earthquake so it is difficult to imagine what it originally looked like, but the courtyards must have acted rather like glades in a forest, allowing light and air to diffuse through the endless columned arcades.

The great mosque naturally also had a massive tower minaret, now known as the Tour Hassan, positioned directly opposite the *qibla* as at the

[127] al-Marrakushi, *Mu'jib*, pp. 364–5.
[128] Ibn Sahib al-Salat, *al-Mann bi'l-Imama*, pp. 359–60.

Figure 7.11 Tour Hassan minaret, Rabat

great mosques of Qayrawan and Córdoba rather than on a lateral wall like the Almohad minarets in Marrakesh and Seville. This position was not only redolent of tradition and pleasing from the point of view of symmetry, the siting of the tower on the seaward side of the mosque above the river estuary ensured that it would dominate the landscape even more thoroughly than its sister minarets in Marrakesh and Seville and announce the Almohad presence from the sea as well as on land. The tower was designed following the same plan as its sibling towers with an internal ramp leading to the summit and chambers coming off it on each floor. Its façades were similarly decorated with small horseshoe arched windows set into panels of carved trelliswork that allowed light into the chambers. It was to have been the tallest of all the Almohad minarets, rising 80 metres in the air, but it was left incomplete at the death of Ya'qub al-Mansur and his successors lacked the resources or the fervour for construction to continue with the work.

Alongside their fortresses of the faith, the Almohads build extensive fortifications, including miles of high urban ramparts, monumental gateways and towers. Like the Almoravids, the Almohads built city walls using a combination of rubble masonry and *pisé* to which they often added crushed stone to increase its strength. Their urban gateways, however, tended to be built of finely carved ashlar masonry and are among their most important contributions to Islamic architecture in the Maghrib due to their innovativeness and their deep impact on the design of subsequent gateways. The best-known Almohad gateways are to be found in modern Morocco in Rabat – Almohad

Ribat al-Fath – and Marrakesh. Almohad gateways, like their other buildings, evolved over time and many of their early gateways show continuity from the Almoravid era, but the overall trend was towards large quadrangular gateways with inner chambers for guards and bent entrance passages to make it difficult for an enemy force to storm through it.

However, the complex interior plans of many Almohad gateways went beyond the requirements of defence as did their profusely decorated façades, both of which point to their symbolic importance to the Almohads as ideological markers and ceremonial sites.[129] The most ornate of these gateways – Bab Agnaw (1188) in Marrakesh, Bab Qasabat al-Udaya (1194) and Bab al-Ruwah in Rabat – were constructed for Ya'qub al-Mansur, and taken together their inscriptions and decoration form a compelling presentation of Almohadism that acted as a complement to their tower minarets and a stage for the theatrical religio-political ceremonial of which the Almohads were so fond. The decorative elements of these gateways include scallop shells superimposed upon a floral, arabesque ground in the spandrels of the entry arch, embraced colonnettes, and bands of decorative carving around their arches featuring stone renderings of the polychrome mosaic stripes of the *miḥrāb* arch in the great mosque of Córdoba. Although several of these motifs were clearly drawn from the great mosque of Córdoba, the 'eruption of ornamentation upon these monuments previously not touched by it constitute[d] a major innovation'.[130] It also showed that the Almohad aesthetic was not always austerely geometric, but could be as exuberant and rich as in earlier eras.

An additional innovative touch on these gateways was the use of potent epigraphic borders, citing Qur'anic verses that touched directly upon the religious ideology of the Almohads. The Umayyads and Almoravids did not use lengthy inscriptions but the Fatimids further east had done so, and the Almohads introduced this mode of self-promotion and religio-political propaganda to the western Maghrib.[131] The verses on Bab Agnaw in Marrakesh, which led into the caliphal section of the city, refer to the entry of the faithful into paradise (Qur'an 15: 46–8), creating an implicit analogy between the faithful Almohads entering the caliphal palace and the believers entering paradise. On the gateway of the Qasaba of the Udaya in Ribat al-Fath, the muster point for armies heading to al-Andalus, the Qur'anic quotation (Qur'an 61: 11–13) also talks about admission to paradise but links it to striving in the path of God, a cognate of jihad. On Bab al-Ruwah, the citation (Qur'an 3: 110–11) praises the believers for commanding the right and prohibiting wrong, in other

[129] For a full analysis of Almohad gateways, see Cressier, 'Les portes monumentales'.

[130] Ibid., p. 171.

[131] See Bierman, *Writing Signs*.

Figure 7.12 Detail, Almohad gateway, Qasaba of the Udaya, Rabat

words the performance of *ḥisba* enjoined by Ibn Tumart, a key Almohad tenet that overlapped with the caliph's role as a dispenser of justice.[132]

These Almohad gates and other simpler versions were set within the extensive *pisé* ramparts that encircled their cities and sometimes much larger tracts of land in an expression of grand urban aspirations, which were often not fulfilled until modern times. Almohad defensive systems also included external 'albarrane' military towers that were sometimes connected to urban ramparts by wall extensions or located slightly further away to guard important facilities such as bridges. One of the most famous of these towers is the Torre del Oro (*burj al-dhahab*) in Seville, an early thirteenth-century tower on the bank of the Guadalquivir River which formed part of the city's riverine defences. The twelve-sided polygonal tower made of ashlar and mortar was originally faced in a gleaming limewash which may have given it its name, the Tower of Gold. The tower held a chain that could be drawn across the river

[132] Cressier, 'Les portes ornamentales', pp. 168–70. See also the numerous works of M. A. Martínez Núñez on Almohad epigraphy, e.g., 'El proyecto almohade a través de la documentación epigráfica' and 'Ḥisba y ŷihād en época almohade: el testimonio epigráfico'.

Figure 7.13 Torre del Oro, Seville

to another now destroyed tower on the opposite bank to block the entrance to the port and protect it from attack and, possibly, ensure that vessels paid customs on their cargoes. The quadrangular Calahorra tower (*qal'at al-ḥurra*) across the Guadalquivir River from the great mosque in Córdoba is also probably an Almohad structure designed to protect the bridge into the city.

In the realm of the visual arts that were not so closely connected to the dynasty, such as carpentry, marquetry, weaving and pottery, stylistic evolution was the order of the day rather than a decisive break between the Almoravid and Almohad periods. The main development, which had a lasting impact on decorative schemas, was the turn towards calligraphic ornamentation, which not only affected architecture but also textiles and ceramics. In the case of textiles, the early Almohad era may have seen a reduction in the manufacture of silk and gold brocades and *ṭirāz* in response to strict Almohad adherence to Islamic injunctions on men wearing silks and gold, but such sumptuary regulations appear not to have lasted.[133] Rich fragments from the later Almohad era exhibit a variety of geometric, floral or vegetal, and figurative designs including people, animals and mythical creatures, as well as calligraphy, both cursive and Kufic in design.[134]

As with Almoravid textiles, the majority of the surviving pieces were preserved by their use in Christian burials, particularly the Castilian royal burials at Las Huelgas in Burgos and the burials of prelates. The famous Rodrigo Ximénes de Rada, archbishop of Toledo, for instance, was buried in vestments made from Islamic textiles.[135] Important textile fragments from this era include the scattered pieces salvaged from the tomb of Bishop Gurb of Barcelona (d. 1284), which seems to have been a large wall hanging with a series of roundels containing figures involved in princely pursuits set upon a plain background. Each roundel has a calligraphic border repeating the phrase 'There is no god but God' (*lā ilāha illā Allāh*), and the hanging is bordered with bands incorporating the phrase 'perfect blessing' (*al-baraka al-kāmila*).[136] While it is dangerous to make assumptions from one textile, the use of the first part of the Muslim profession of faith, 'There is no god but God', does have a particular Almohad resonance as the tenet that underlay their claim that all monotheism was one and that the Muslims, Jews and Christians of their empire should subscribe to the same message. Another major item often discussed in analyses of Almohad textiles is the so-called Las Navas de Tolosa banner, which may have been captured by the Christians as a trophy during the Battle of Las Navas de Tolosa in 1212, or may actually be a Marinid banner from the later thirteenth or fourteenth centuries.[137] This sumptuous banner or wall hanging of red silk and gold tapestry features an eight-pointed star inside a large roundel with border bands of black cursive calligraphy and it confirms the strong presence of calligraphy and geometry in Almohad design that henceforth characterised the regional aesthetic.

[133] Partearroyo, 'Los tejidos', p. 305.

[134] Ibid., p. 312.

[135] Ibid., p. 322.

[136] See Shepherd, 'Treasure'.

[137] See Ali-de-Unzaga, 'Quranic inscriptions on the so-called "Pennon of Las Navas de Tolosa"'.

The potteries of al-Andalus and the Maghrib also continued to produce a range of wares ranging from the quotidian to luxury *cuerda seca* and lustreware. The most popular means of decorating pottery seem to have been *sgraffito* (incised to reveal a contrasting ground) and *estampillado* (stamped) designs, including floral, vegetal, geometric, calligraphic and figural elements which 'reached their greatest refinement' in Almohad times. Based on archaeological ceramic finds, pottery production flourished in southwestern al-Andalus in Mértola and Seville, while geographers talk of the fine pottery and glass of Málaga, Murcia and Almería.[138] Some of the most distinctive Almohad-era wares are the famous *estampillado* jars produced in Seville, large green-glazed conical jars nearly a metre tall that may have been used in the homes of the wealthy as decorative vessels to hold purified water for ablutions.[139] The jars were decorated with designs stamped into the clay prior to firing in repeating bands including calligraphic elements such as *al-mulk* (kingship, power), *yumn* (prosperity, happiness) and *baraka* (blessing). Their patterning confirms the importance of decorative calligraphy as a key component in Andalusi and Maghribi design and the gradual demise of figural representation. The use of ceramic mosaic tiles to form geometric patterns (*zilīj*) also became more important in the decoration of walls and façades, flowering fully in post-Almohad times.

The Almohad century thus set the tone for the art and architecture of both al-Andalus and the western Maghrib for centuries afterwards. Their imperial architecture, especially, had a major impact on subsequent dynastic building in the Maghrib. Their looming square tower minarets have defined the style of Maghribi minarets for nearly a millennium, finding their most recent evocation in the Hassan II Mosque in Casablanca, built between 1986 and 1993 with a square tower minaret in the Almohad style rising an astonishing 210 metres in the air. Almohad gateways, meanwhile, provided the inspiration for the gateways built by their immediate successors, the Marinids, and also later Moroccan sultans such as Mawlay Isma'il, founder of Meknes, who gave his new royal city a massive portal that evoked both the triumphal arch of Caracalla at Volubilis and the great Almohad gateways of Rabat and Marrakesh. In decoration more generally, geometry and calligraphy gained the place that they have held until the present in the schema routinely called 'Andalusi', but more properly a legacy of the cross-Straits culture of the Berber imperial age.

[138] Rosselló Bordoy, 'The ceramics of al-Andalus', pp. 100–1.

[139] D. Lallone, 'Almohad stamped jars of Seville', presented at the 'Best Practice in Heritage Conservation Management from the World to Pompeii' conference, Capri, June 2014.

8

Conclusion

What factors underlay the demise of the Berber empires? Like so many aspects of their story, this question is also tangled and twisted by the assumptions of its tellers. From Ibn Khaldun's cyclical interpretation of the rise and fall of tribal empires to European colonial stereotypes about the failed pre-modern states of North Africa, and modern nationalistic Spanish or Moroccan history writing, the Almoravids and Almohads have been fitted into narratives not of their own making. For Medieval Muslim historians, their passing was triggered by military defeats and corrupt, weak or divided leadership, and these elements figure in later historiographical narratives that see the end of each empire in terms of failure: military failure against the Christian advance in Iberia; ideological failure to convince and unify the Muslim populations under their rule, especially those of al-Andalus; and the failure to create a stable, self-perpetuating ruling group.

There is also a tendency to consider both empires as ephemeral, a position rooted in the chronologies of their time in al-Andalus, which was considerably shorter than their duration in North Africa where they had much more lasting effect. In fact, many other Islamic dynasties survived for similar lengths of time, the Umayyads of Damascus or the contemporary Zangids and Ayyubids spring to mind. On the other hand, neither empire could boast the longevity of the 'Abbasids, the Umayyads of Córdoba or the Fatimids. Duration is not, of course, a necessary measure of achievement. From Ibn Khaldun's perspective, each dynasty had a natural lifespan and its replacement was therefore inevitable, even if it could be postponed. The question is thus, perhaps, what remains when a dynasty passes and how has it contributed to longer-term developments?

From this perspective, the era of the Berber empires stands out as a formative two centuries in the Islamic west, which transformed its politics, society and religious culture, and enabled the Berbers to stand tall as one of the great peoples of medieval Islam. All the more impressively, these changes were directed by tribal dynasties with little experience of state-building, who emerged as unexpectedly as the Arabs themselves from isolated areas on the periphery of the Islamic world. As the Spanish Arabist Bosch Vilá noted in the 1950s, echoing the French historian of the Maghrib, Henri Terrasse, the rise of the Almoravids figures as one of the great surprises of history.[1] If we consider the formation of the Maghribi Berber empires as an unexpected development and look at the circumstances of Islamic polities contemporary with them, then their achievements as well as failures come into focus.

The Almoravid warriors emerged from the desert inspired by religion and created an empire, apparently out of nothing. As late as the 1060s, al-Bakri saw the Saharan Sanhaja movement as little more than a frontier phenomenon and an example of the many strange cults of the Maghrib. Thirty years later, those same veiled warriors ruled the cities in which he lived and worked, and another Andalusi, Abu Bakr b. al-ʿArabi, was able to tell the ʿAbbasid caliph in Baghdad that the Almoravid amir Yusuf b. Tashfin controlled the vast area from ancient Ghana to the lands of the Franks. This was a massive political achievement and, as we have seen, the Almoravid conquest state continued to grow in Iberia during the first decades of the twelfth century and eventually incorporated the Balearics as well.

If the tenth century was the 'Shiʿi century' in the Islamic world, the eleventh century was the Sunni 'Sanhaja' century in the Islamic west, during which the western Sanhaja triumphed over their Zanata rivals of Kharijite and Shiʿi persuasion, thereby prompting a consolidation of Sunnism that complemented the Sunni 'revival' in the Seljuk east. We have referred several times to Ibn ʿIdhari's understanding of the Almoravid mission as the unification of the Maghrib under a single Islamic ruler and a single system of law, developments he saw as not only positive but as necessary for the security and prosperity of the Muslim community. The Sanhaja Almoravids achieved this under the banner of a simple, ascetic form of Malikism that has led some to perceive in their movement the triumph of Córdoba over Qayrawan. However, Qayrawan's Maliki tradition was as strong, if not stronger, than its Fatimid Shiʿi adherence and it was Maliki missionaries from Qayrawan, with their particular emphasis on combining Maliki *fiqh* with the pious, ascetic practices of the denizens of Ifriqiya's *ribāṭ*s, who inspired the Almoravid movement, not the well-to-do urban Maliki *fuqahā'* from al-Andalus who entered Almoravid service later.

Moreover, for the Malikis of Qayrawan, the head of the Sunni community was the ʿAbbasid caliph, a religio-political stance taken up by the Almoravids who presented themselves as heirs to the Umayyad caliphs of Córdoba, but who also acknowledged the symbolic sovereignty of the ʿAbbasid caliph. They

[1] Bosch Vilá, *Los Almorávides*, pp. 23, 44.

thereby placed both al-Andalus and the Maghrib firmly within the wider Islamic world where significant realignments of power were taking place in the eleventh and twelfth centuries due to rise of Muslim Turkish military regimes such as the Ghaznavids and the Seljuks, and the consolidation of Sunnism after the phase of Shiʿi political dominance.

Although the Seljuks ruled over the ʿAbbasid heartlands and controlled the person of the ʿAbbasid caliph to a greater or lesser degree and the Almoravids did not, they form an important pair which shaped the history of large sections of the eleventh-century Dar al-Islam. Their rise signalled the integration of nominally Muslim tribal peoples, the Ghuzz Turks and the Saharan Sanhaja Berbers, into the Dar al-Islam and the development of non-caliphal political systems, the Seljuk sultanate and the analogous Almoravid amirate, which prefigured the federated Islamic world that emerged fully after 1258. The administration of both regimes depended upon alliances with the established urban Arabic- or Persian-speaking bureaucratic and religious classes and the legitimation of their military rule through engagement (jihad) on 'hot' frontiers, Anatolia and Syria in the Seljuk case and Iberia and West Africa for the Almoravids. Both regimes also devolved the government of sedentary areas through land grants, Seljuk *iqṭāʿāt* and Almoravid *inzālāt*, to their followers.

The challenges they faced were also similar: both the Seljuks and the Almoravids struggled to reconcile monarchical and clan norms in the appointment of heirs and found the dynastic structure undermined by rivalry between competing princes which tended towards the division of their empires into autonomous provinces. This was more pronounced in the Seljuk sultanate, but it was also apparent in the division between the Almoravids' Saharan and Maghribi domains. The allocation of land grants and hereditary appanages, and the management of their pastoral tribal contingents in settled areas such as Iraq and al-Andalus were other shared concerns. Both regimes also faced rising Christian aggression against Muslim areas characterised by political disaggregation. Just as the political fragmentation characterising the Taʾifa era in al-Andalus enabled Alfonso VI to acquire Toledo in 1085, political divisions in Seljuk Syria greatly aided the Crusaders' advance to Jerusalem little more than a decade later. The inability of the Great Seljuk sultan to unite his Syrian *atabeys* to resist the unexpected Crusader onslaught, sheds a favourable light upon the Almoravid intervention in al-Andalus and absorption of the Taʾifa kingdoms in order to prevent a Christian advance beyond Toledo.

Despite its relative military success, the Almoravid empire did not stabilise when it reached its greatest territorial extent between 1110 and 1120, but, instead, began to lose control of its territories to northern Christians, local Muslim lords in al-Andalus and the Masmuda tribes of the High Atlas and Sus. In al-Andalus, this reverse is often attributed to the alien character of the Almoravids, their re-imposition of uncanonical taxation and the over-extension of their military resources, but no real Andalusi rival for power emerged. The real challenge to their rule was Maghribi and can be seen as a result of their success in inculcating the notion of a centralised Muslim Berber polity in the region that is now southern Morocco. The Masmuda, galvanised by the Sanhaja example, were transformed from the perpetually feuding agglomeration of tribes whom Ibn Yasin despaired of ever uniting, into a new Berber religio-political movement determined to overthrow their erstwhile allies and found a second indigenous Berber empire. It is not incidental that Ibn Tumart's primary objective, according to the myth of his encounter with al-Ghazali, was to overthrow the Almoravids and inherit their empire in the Maghrib and al-Andalus, and, despite being highly critical of the religion and culture of the Almoravids, the Almohad movement depended heavily upon the conceptual and structural foundations laid by them, from the notion of regional political unity to the establishment of Marrakesh as an imperial capital.

The Almohad project, however, aimed to do more than simply replace the Almoravids. On the politico-military plane, 'Abd al-Mu'min sought to create an empire that encompassed the entire Islamic west and took the jihad not only north to the Andalusi marches but also east to the Ifriqiyan coast and perhaps beyond. From the ideological and religious perspective, the Almohad *da'wa* stood out as a moment of supreme Berber cultural and religious confidence. The Almoravid mission was home-grown in the sense that Ibn Yasin was a native of the western Sahara, but he subscribed to a universal school of Islamic law and the Almoravids did not question the dominance of Arabic or the primacy of the 'Abbasids. In contrast, Ibn Tumart acquired his education outside his homeland, but then claimed to be the sole guide (*mahdī*) to Islam's truth and gave the Masmuda Berbers the role of a new chosen people not subservient to any eastern Islamic caliphate, but superior to them and destined to reunite the Dar al-Islam.

In contrast to the bifurcation of religious authority and political power apparent in the Almoravid and Seljuk systems, the Almohad movement was both archaic and revolutionary. On the one hand, it rejected the implicitly federal solution of sultans and amirs owing nominal allegiance to the 'Abbasids in favour of the traditional paradigm of a universal caliphate. However, the character of that caliphate was radical and unique in that it was initially constituted as the succession not to Muhammad but to the *mahdī* Ibn Tumart. Although the Mu'minids worked hard to present themselves as heirs to the Sunni Umayyad caliphate of Córdoba, the source of their legitimacy in Almohad circles remained their inheritance of the mantle of the *mahdī* for which there was no contemporary analogue in the Islamic east. Instead, the rise of the Zangids and Ayyubids, Kurdish warlords who nominally served the Seljuks, in Syria led to the demise of the Fatimid caliphate in 1171 and a shift in effective Seljuk power towards Iran and Anatolia, leaving the 'Abbasid caliphs with a small area of control in Iraq.

In these circumstances, the Almohad empire emerges unexpectedly as one of the largest Islamic polities of the time and the most convincing holder of a caliphal title. For a brief moment, the periphery became the centre, at least in the Almohads' own estimation, and no embassies were sent east for recognition, rather Ayyubid proxies sought to push back the Almohads in Ifriqiya, fearing perhaps their further advance towards Egypt, and eventually Salah al-Din's ambassadors came west to make peace. The new inscription of western Islamic empires within the tableau of the Islamic world found expression in the inclusion of the Almoravids and the Almohads in the universal histories of the era, such as Ibn al-Athir's *al-Kamil fi'l-Ta'rikh* and al-Nuwayri's *Nihayat al-Arab*, as well as Ibn Khaldun's own Maghrib-centric universal history.

The Almohad empire was more centralised than its Almoravid predecessor, its bureaucracy drew on both the existing Arabised urban elite and new Maghribi recruits, and its army was backed up by the demographic strength of the western Maghrib and new resources drawn from the Arab Banu Hilal and Sulaym from Ifriqiya. Nonetheless, it too went into decline after a century. Again, clan and tribal rivalries played their role as factions coalesced around different Mu'minid princes, depriving a succession of caliphs of the full support of the ruling group. The very size of the empire encouraged provincial autonomy, with regional Almohad powers emerging in Tunis, Bijaya, Tlemcen and Granada among other places. Moreover, the eccentricity of the Almohad caliphate put a significant limit on the religious support that the Almohads could accrue in their own domains. The loyalties of the Arab tribal auxiliaries were often suspect, the vast majority of Maliki *fuqahā'* continued to quietly adhere to their *madhhab*, and the Maliki Almoravid Banu Ghaniya found ready support across Ifriqiya. Even the Almohad elite became divided between those who supported and those who dismissed its central tenet, acknowledgement of Ibn Tumart as the *mahdī*.

The collapse of the Almohad empire between the 1220s and the 1260s, nonetheless revealed a profoundly changed Islamic west. The most obvious geopolitical change was the reduction of Muslim political control in al-Andalus by the mid-thirteenth century to the small sultanate of Granada. It is likely that the Berber empires prevented these losses occurring sooner, but the Almohad failure to coordinate an effective defence of Córdoba, Seville and

Valencia against the advance of Castile and Aragon in the 1230s and 1240s was a massive humiliation. In the Maghrib and Ifriqiya, however, their rule laid the administrative and political contours for their successor states – the Hafsids, Zayyanids and Marinids – and witnessed the maturing of Islamic state structures. The most notable development in the geopolitics and society of the era was the surge in significance of the western Maghrib and its transformation from an often lawless (Islamic) frontier into the metropole of empire.

The foundation of Marrakesh and Rabat, the expansion of Fes and the consolidation of the status of Ceuta and Sijilmasa, replaced an older network of small towns and villages with an urban hierarchy comparable with that found in other parts of the Islamic world from Seville to Samarkand. The new cities of the Maghrib were then peopled by migrants from across the Almoravid and Almohad empires, including skilled migrants from Andalusi cities who contributed to the enlargement of an indigenous pool of literate and skilled individuals. While many of the great religious scholars, *literati* and thinkers of this period claimed Andalusi connections, a large number spent part of their career in Marrakesh and by Almohad times many were born in the Maghrib. This urban growth was accompanied by the Almohad transferral of the Arab tribes who had settled in Ifriqiya to the Maghrib, initiating the linguistic Arabisation of the previously Berberophone countryside with major consequences for the later history of the Maghrib and, ultimately, its twentieth-century pan-Arab recognition as one of the 'wings' of an Arab nation, conceived as a bird with its heart in Egypt and wings to the east and west.

In the realm of religion, the Almoravids' implantation of Maliki *fiqh* in the western Maghrib and Sahara as the Sunni alternative to Kharijism, Fatimid Shiʿism and local Berber cults was a pivotal phase within the long process of Islamisation. The diverse, local cults of the rural Maghrib disappeared and the pious, mystically inflected Malikism connected to international scholarly networks that became mainstream in later centuries began to spread. Although Almohadism did not survive as a distinct doctrine, its proponents also aspired to endow the Islamic west with a common Islamic identity and worked to give tribesmen with little or no religious education a grounding in their faith. This deepening of the previous Islamic veneer facilitated the penetration of Sufism across the region, which then, in turn, perpetuated the further, slow integration of the countryside into the universal Islamic sphere.

The religious policies of the Almoravids and Almohads had a more negative effect on the Christian and Jewish minorities of the region, although their reactions to religious minorities cannot be disentangled from the political and military situation in the Islamic west as a whole. For Arabised Christians, the rise in hostilities with the Christian north in al-Andalus made Muslim authorities suspicious of them and encouraged them to collaborate with their Latin co-religionists with disastrous effects, while the Ifriqiyan Christian community seems to have been scattered and decimated by war. For Jewish communities, the greatest challenge was 'Abd al-Mu'min's conversion policy which forced Jewish communities in major towns to convert to Almohad Islam or leave the empire on pain of death. Forcible conversion generated the same official concerns about Jewish converts' religious sincerity as those later generated by the Spanish forced conversions of Jews then Muslims to Catholicism. The Jewish community did not, however, permanently disappear. The only partial enforcement of Almohad doctrines, the reversion of forced converts to Judaism and the migration of Jews from Christian Iberia to Muslim lands ensured that Jews remained a vitally important component of Maghribi society until the twentieth century, with the Almohad century considered an aberration rather than the norm.

In the spheres of elite learning, culture and the arts, the Almoravids and, above all, the Almohads proffered patronage in the same manner as Islamic rulers elsewhere. While their support for Arabic literature, and poetry in particular, was perhaps perfunctory and overly weighted towards eulogistic content rather than literary talent, their patronage of the applied and theoretical sciences and philosophy led to a flowering of botany, clinical medicine, astronomy and mathematics, and the emergence of the great masters of western Islamic philosophy. However, the consolidation of an orthodox scholarly class with a taste for al-Ghazali and Sufism but suspicious of pure philosophy, meant that Ibn Tufayl and Ibn Rushd stood on the intellectual margins of their society and found a readier audience in Latin Christendom than in the Islamic west. Their truest disciples were the western Islamic Sufis, some of whom adopted highly theosophical approaches and became leading lights within Islamic Sufism as a whole.

Finally, the material contribution of the Berber dynasties was also striking and enduring. Sadly, the Almoravid mark on the landscape has been largely erased, although, as in other areas, it is abundantly clear that the Almohads entered into a dialectic with them and that Almohad building owed much to Almoravid antecedents. The Almohad heritage, in contrast, has endured for nearly a millennium in the distinctive style of Maghribi mosques and minarets from the Zaytuna in Tunis to the Kutubiyya in Marrakesh and the Giralda in Seville, and in the ramparts and gateways that still dominate Rabat today. While the origins of the Berber dynasties, the peculiarities of their religious doctrines, their role in rural Islamisation and Arabisation may not be widely known, their monuments stand as living testimony to their impact on the medieval Islamic west.

Chronological Outline

Date	Western Maghrib and Sahara	Ifriqiya	al-Andalus
c. 1036	Pilgrimage of Yahya b. Ibrahim (and/or Jawhar b. Saqqum) of the Saharan Sanhaja Guddala tribe to Mecca.	Legendary meeting of Yahya b. Ibrahim with Abu 'Imran al-Fasi in Qayrawan.	
c. 1038	Arrival of 'Abd Allah b. Yasin to teach the Guddala the precepts of Islam.		Accession of Badis as ruler of Zirid Granada.
1040s	The rejection of 'Abd Allah b. Yasin by the Guddala and his transfer to the Lamtuna tribe.		Accession of al-Mu'tadid as ruler of 'Abbadid Seville.
c. 1050	Emergence of the Almoravid leadership: Ibn Yasin and the Lamtuna amirs, Yahya b. 'Umar and his brother Abu Bakr b. 'Umar.		
1050s	Start of the Almoravid jihad and consolidation of Lamtuna power over the Saharan tribes.		
1054–5	Almoravid conquest of the Dar'a valley and capture of Sijilmasa. Almoravid capture of Awdaghust.		
1055–6	Almoravid conquest of the Sus valley. Death of Yahya b. 'Umar in battle.		

Date	Western Maghrib and Sahara	Ifriqiya	al-Andalus
1058	Almoravid crossing of the High Atlas and conquest of Aghmat. Death of 'Abd Allah b. Yasin in battle.		
1060s			The geographer al-Bakri writes his account of the Almoravid movement.
1066			Massacre of Jews in Granada.
1069			Accession of al-Mu'tamid b. 'Abbad as ruler of Ta'ifa Seville.
c. 1070	Abu Bakr b. 'Umar founds Marrakesh (*c.* 1060 in some sources).		
1071	Abu Bakr b. 'Umar returns to the Sahara and Yusuf b. Tashfin becomes amir of the Almoravids north of the High Atlas.		
1072	Abu Bakr relinquishes control of the north to Yusuf b. Tashfin.		
1073			'Abd Allah b. Buluggin becomes ruler of Zirid Granada.
1073–4	The Almoravids conquer Salé and Meknes.		
1074–5	The Almoravids conquer Fes and begin to advance through the Rif mountains to Ceuta and Tangier on the Straits of Gibraltar.		
1075–6	The Almoravids conquer Tlemcen and begin to advance towards Oran and Algiers.		
1076–7	The 'conquest' of Ghana by the southern Almoravids led by Abu Bakr b. 'Umar.		
1077–8	Almoravid conquest of Tangier.		

Date	Western Maghrib and Sahara	Ifriqiya	al-Andalus
1083–4	Almoravid conquest of Ceuta with the assistance of al-Mu'tamid b. 'Abbad of Seville.		
1085			Alfonso VI of Léon-Castile captures Toledo.
1086			Crossing of the Almoravids to al-Andalus and defeat of the Christians in the Battle of Sagrajas (Zallaqa).
c. 1087	Death of Abu Bakr b. 'Umar.		
1088			Yusuf b. Tashfin's second crossing to al-Andalus.
1090			Yusuf b. Tashfin's third crossing to al-Andalus. Almoravid conquest of the Zirid kingdom of Granada. Exile of 'Abd Allah b. Buluggin to Aghmat.
1091			Almoravid conquest of the Ta'ifa kingdom of Seville and exile of al-Mu'tamid to Aghmat.
1092			Beginning of the struggle between the Almoravids and El Cid for Valencia.
1094			Almoravid conquest of the Ta'ifa kingdom of Badajoz.
1095	Death of al-Mu'tamid b. 'Abbad in Aghmat.		
1097			Yusuf b. Tashfin's fourth crossing to al-Andalus.
1099			Death of El Cid.

Date	Western Maghrib and Sahara	Ifriqiya	al-Andalus
1102	ʿAli b. Yusuf becomes the heir apparent of Yusuf b. Tashfin.		Christian surrender of Valencia to the Almoravids.
1106	Death of Yusuf b. Tashfin. ʿAli b. Yusuf becomes Almoravid amir.		Ibn Tumart arrives in Cordoba to study.
1108			Almoravid acquisition of Saragossa. ʿAli b. Yusuf's first crossing to al-Andalus.
1109			Ibn Hamdin persuades ʿAli b. Yusuf to order the burning of al-Ghazali's *Ihya' ʿUlum al-Din*.
1110			Almoravid conquest of the Ta'ifa kingdom of Saragossa.
1110s	Development of the Almoravid Buhayra outside Marrakesh.		
1115			Almoravid conquest of the Balearics.
1117			ʿAli b. Yusuf's second crossing to al-Andalus.
1118			Loss of Saragossa to the Aragonese.
1120	Return of Ibn Tumart to the western Maghrib and the start of his mission against the Almoravids in Marrakesh.		
1121	Ibn Tumart is recognised by his disciples and the Masmuda tribes as the *mahdī*.		Rebellion of Cordoba against the Almoravids and ʿAli b. Yusuf's third crossing to al-Andalus.
c. 1124	Almohad occupation of Tinmall in the High Atlas.		
1125	Probable date for the construction of the Almoravid *qubba* in Marrakesh.		Alfonso I El Batallador of Aragon's attempt to capture Granada.

Date	Western Maghrib and Sahara	Ifriqiya	al-Andalus
1126	Forced migration of Andalusi Christians to the Maghrib. Construction of the walls of Marrakesh.		Fortification of Andalusi towns.
1130	The Almoravids defeat the Almohads at the Battle of the Buhayra. Death of Ibn Tumart (concealed for up to three years).		
1132	Transfer of the Almoravid gates of Tasghimut to Tinmall.		
c. 1133	ʿAbd al-Muʾmin consolidates his position as the Almohad leader and caliph of Ibn Tumart and leads the Almohad conquest of the Atlas mountains.		
1135	Almoravid extension of the Qarawiyyin Mosque in Fes.		
1136	Almoravid embellishment of the new great mosque of Tlemcen.		
c. 1137			In Cordoba, work commences on the Almoravid *minbar*.
1138	Recall of Tashfin b. ʿAli to the Maghrib to lead the Almoravid offensive against the Almohads.		
1141	ʿAli b. Yusuf summons the mystics Ibn Barrajan and Ibn al-ʿArif to Marrakesh and imprisons them. Both die soon afterwards.		
1142	Foundation of Almohad Ribat Taza and its great mosque.		Appearance of Ibn Qasi in the Algarve claiming to the the *mahdī*.
1143	Death of ʿAli b. Yusuf. Tashfin b. ʿAli becomes Almoravid amir.		

Date	Western Maghrib and Sahara	Ifriqiya	al-Andalus
1144			Decline of Almoravid power in al-Andalus. Ibn Qasi and his Muridin establish a principality in the Algarve.
1145	Death of Tashfin b. 'Ali at Oran in action against the Almohads. Ibrahim b. Tashfin becomes Almoravid amir, but is quickly ousted by his uncle Ishaq b. 'Ali.		
1146	Almohad siege and conquest of Tlemcen and Fes.		Ibn Hud declares his independence in Murcia and Valencia, only to be ousted by Ibn Mardanish. Almohad entry into al-Andalus.
1147	Almohad conquest of Marrakesh. Death of the last Almoravid amir.		Castilian occupation of Almería. Portuguese capture of Santarem and Lisbon. Almohad siege of Seville.
1148	Insurrection of al-Massi and Yahya b. al-Sahrawiyya against the Almohads. Construction of Kutubiyya Mosque I in Marrakesh and the first Almohad *buḥayra* estate.	Norman capture of al-Mahdiyya and other coastal towns in Ifriqiya.	Construction of an Almohad citadel (*qaṣaba*) in Seville.
1150	Foundation of Ribat al-Fath opposite Salé.		
1151			Formal submission of southwestern al-Andalus to the Almohads.
1153	Construction of the great mosque of Tinmall.	Almohad advance east across the Maghrib to Bijaya. Almohads defeat the Arab Banu *[cont.*	

Date	Western Maghrib and Sahara	Ifriqiya	al-Andalus
1153		Hilal and Sulaym tribes at the Battle of Setif.	
1154–5	'Abd al-Mu'min names his son Muhammad as his heir. Rebellion of the brothers of Ibn Tumart.		
1155	Surrender of the Almoravid rebel Yahya b. al-Sahrawiyya.		Imposition of direct Almohad rule in Granada. Retreat of the remaining Almoravids to the Balearics under the leadership of the Banu Ghaniya.
1158	Fall of the chief minister Ibn 'Atiyya. Construction of Kutubiyya Mosque II in Marrakesh.		
1159		Commencement of the Mahdiyya campaign.	
1160		'Abd al-Mu'min recaptures al-Mahdiyya from the Normans and adds Ifriqiya to the Almohad empire. Issue of the decree that Jews and Christians must convert to Almohad Islam, leave the empire or risk execution.	Foundation of Jabal al-Fath at Gibraltar.
1162			Rebellion of the Islamised Jews of Granada against the Almohads.

Date	Western Maghrib and Sahara	Ifriqiya	al-Andalus
1163	Removal of Muhammad from the succession. Death of 'Abd al-Mu'min. Accession of Abu Ya'qub Yusuf supported by his brother Abu Hafs 'Umar.		
1171			Abu Ya'qub Yusuf crosses to al-Andalus. Construction of the Almohad great mosque of Seville begins.
1172	Construction of the Almohad great mosque of Salé.		Death of Ibn Mardanish of Murcia. Submission of the Banu Mardanish to the Almohads. Portuguese capture of Beja.
1176	Plague epidemic in Marrakesh.		
1179	Death of the caliph's brother Abu Hafs 'Umar.		
1180		Abu Ya'qub Yusuf goes on campaign to Ifriqiya.	
1182	Almohads demand that the Almoravid Banu Ghaniya in the Balearics acknowledge them as overlords.		
1183	Foundation of a new Almohad palatine city (Tamurakusht/al-Saliha) at Marrakesh begins.		
1184		Capture of Bijaya by the Almoravid Ibn Ghaniya.	Abu Ya'qub Yusuf crosses to al-Andalus. Work commences on the minaret tower of the Almohad great mosque of Seville. Death of Abu Ya'qub Yusuf during the Santarem campaign. Accession of Ya'qub al-Mansur.

Date	Western Maghrib and Sahara	Ifriqiya	al-Andalus
1187		Almohads defeated by the Banu Ghaniya and their allies at the Battle of 'Umra. Ya'qub al-Mansur then defeats the Banu Ghaniya at the Battle of Hamma.	
1190	Salah al-Din sends Ibn Munqidh on an embassy to the Almohads.		Ya'qub al-Mansur crosses to al-Andalus. Continued construction in Seville, including the Hisn al-Faraj and its *buḥayra*.
1191	Construction of the great mosque of Ribat al-Fath begins.	Rebellion of al-Ashall in the Zab in the central Maghrib.	Almohad recapture of Silves from the Portuguese.
1195			Almohad victory against a Christian coalition at the Battle of al-Arak (Alarcos).
1197	Construction of the *qaṣaba* mosque in Marrakesh.		Almohad–Castilian truce. The exile of Ibn Rushd to Lucena.
1198	Ya'qub al-Mansur returns to the Maghrib with Ibn Rushd.		Completion of the tower minaret of the great mosque of Seville and mounting of its gold orbs.
1199	Death of Ya'qub al-Mansur. Accession of Muhammad al-Nasir.		
1203	Work begins on the extension of the Qarawiyyin Mosque in Fes.		Almohad conquest of Mallorca from the Banu Ghaniya.
1205		al-Nasir leads a campaign to Ifriqiya to dislodge the Banu Ghaniya.	

Date	Western Maghrib and Sahara	Ifriqiya	al-Andalus
1206		Restoration of Almohad control over al-Mahdiyya.	
1207		Appointment of 'Abd al-Wahid b. Abi Hafs as governor of Ifriqiya.	
1211			al-Nasir crosses to al-Andalus. Almohad recapture of the fortress of Salvatierra.
1212			Almohads defeated by a Christian coalition at the Battle of Las Navas de Tolosa (al-'Uqab).
1213	Death of al-Nasir. Accession of Yusuf al-Mustansir, a minor. Infiltration of the Zanata Banu Marin into the western Maghrib.		
1221			Construction of the Torre del Oro, Seville.
1224	Death of Yusuf al-Mustansir. Struggle among Almohad princes for the caliphate.		
1226	Accession of al-Ma'mun.		
1228			Muhammad b. Hud declares his independence from the Almohads in Murcia.
1229	Rejection of Almohad mahdism by al-Ma'mun.	Secession of Hafsid Ifriqiya from the empire.	
1236			Ferdinand III of Castile captures Cordoba.
1246	The Banu Marin capture Meknes.		
1248	The Banu Marin capture Fes.		Ferdinand III of Castile captures Seville. Jaime I of Aragon advances into Valencia.

Date	Western Maghrib and Sahara	Ifriqiya	al-Andalus
c. 1250			Muhammad b. Nasr b. al-Ahmar becomes ruler of Granada.
1269	The Banu Marin capture Marrakesh. Death of Abu Dabbus the last Almohad caliph.		

Place Names with Latin and Arabic Designations

al-Andalus (Iberian Peninsula)

Alarcos (al-Arak)
Algarve (al-Gharb)
Algeciras (al-Jazīra al-Khaḍrā')
Aljarafe (Jabal al-Sharaf)
Almería (al-Māriya)
Badajoz (Baṭalyūs)
Baeza (Bayāsa)
Baza (Basṭa)
Beja (Bāja)
Cádiz (Qādis)
Carmona (Qarmūna)
Catalayud (Qal'at Ayyūb)
Córdoba (Qurṭuba)
Cuenca (Quwanka)
Dénia (Dāniya)
Rio Ebro (Wād Ibruh)
Fraga (Afrāgha)
Gibraltar (Jabal Ṭāriq, Jabal al-Fatḥ)
Granada (Gharnāṭa)
Guadalquivir (al-Wād al-Kabīr)
Guadix (Wādī Āsh)
Huete (Ubdha/Wabdha)
Jaén (Jayyān)
Játiva (Shāṭiba)
Jerez (Sharīsh)
Lerida (Lārida)
Lisbon (Ushbūna)
Lucena (Lusāna)
Málaga (Mālaqa)

Mallorca (Mayūrqa)
Medina Sidonia (Shadhūna)
Mertola (Mīrtula)
Murcia (Mursiya)
Niebla (Labla)
Sagrajas (Zallāqa)
Salvatierra (Shalbaṭira)
Santarem (Shantarīm)
Saragossa (Saraqusṭa)
Rio Seguro (al-Nahr al-Abyaḍ)
Setefilla (Shantafila)
Seville (Ishbīliyya)
Almadén (Shalūn?)
Silves (Shilb)
Tarifa (Ṭarīf)
Tavira (Ṭabīra)
Toledo (Ṭulayṭula)
Tortosa (Ṭurṭūsha)
Valencia (Balansiya)

The Maghrib and Ifriqiya (North Africa)

Aghmat (Aghmāt)
Arzila (Aṣīla)
Barqa (Barqa)
Bougie (Bijāya)
Ceuta (Sabta)
Chellah (Shālla)
Fes (Fās)
Gabes (Qābis)
Gafsa (Qāfiṣa)
Ghadames (Ghadāmis)
Guercif (Agārsīf)
Kairouan (Qayrawān)
Ksar es-Seghir (Qaṣr al-Majāz, Qaṣr al-Maṣmūda)
al-Mahdiyya, Morocco (see Rabat)
al-Mahdiyya, Tunisia
Marrakesh (Marrākush)
Meknes (Miknās)
Monastir (Munastīr)
Mzab (Zāb)
Nedroma (Nadrūma)

Nūl Lamṭa
Oran (Wahrān)
Qal'at Banī Ḥammād
Rabat (Ribāṭ, Ribāṭ al-Fatḥ, al-Mahdiyya)
Salé (Salā)
Sfax (Ṣafāqis)
Sijilmasa (Sijilmāsa)
Souss valley (Sūs)
Sousse (Sūsa)
Tangier (Ṭanja)
Taza (Tāza, Ribāṭ Tāza)
Tebessa (Tibasā)
Temsaman (Timsāmān)
Tinmel (Tīnmall, Tīnmalal)
Tlemcen (Tilimsān)
Tripoli (Ṭarābulus)
Tunis (Tūnis)
Wad Sebou (Wād Sābū)

Glossary of Arabic Terms

'abīd	slaves, usually black, military slaves
Afāriqa	Latinate inhabitants of Ifriqiya
agraw	Berber equivalent of *jamā'a*, tribal council
ahl	people, the inhabitants of a town, a lineage
ahl al-dār	Ibn Tumart's immediate circle and household
ahl al-dhimma	'peoples of the covenant', i.e., Christians and Jews
ahl khamsīn	descendant of the Almohad Council of Fifty
ahl al-kitāb	'peoples of the book', i.e., Christians and Jews
ait	Berber equivalent of *banū*, sons of
'ālim, 'ulamā'	religious scholars
'amal	custom, the custom of Medina which provided Islamic legal precedents
amān	safe conduct
amghār	Berber equivalent of shaykh, a tribal chief or elder
'āmil, 'ummāl	governor, official
amīr	military commander, prince
amīr al-muslimīn	'Commander of the Muslims', the title used by the Almoravids
amīr al-mu'minīn	'Commander of the Faithful', a caliphal title used by the Almohads
'āmma	the general population, the masses, see also *ra'āyā*
al-Andalus	the Iberian peninsula, especially the Muslim-ruled areas
'aqīda	creed
'aṣabiyya	group feeling, tribal solidarity
awlād	see *banū*
bāb	urban gateway, door
bādiya	countryside, steppe
badw	nomads, Bedouin
banū/banī	sons of, a common part of the name of a tribe or lineage

baraka	charisma, blessing, the beneficent power of holy men and women
al-Barānis	one of the branches of the Berber peoples in medieval Arabic taxonomies
bay'a	oath of allegiance
buḥayra, baḥā'ir	lit. lake, a garden estate with a lake or pool
burnūs or *burnus*	a hooded cloak or outer robe
bustān, basātīn	orchard
al-Butr	one of the branches of the Berber peoples in medieval Arabic taxonomies
dār al-ḥarb	the 'house of war', the non-Islamic world
dār al-imāra	ruler's residence
dār al-Islām	the 'house of Islam', the Islamic world
da'wa	mission, message
dawla	dynasty, dynastic state, empire
ḍay'a, diyā'	private estate
dhimma	the pact of protection offered by Muslims to their non-Muslim subjects in return for submission
dīwān, dawāwīn	administrative offices, a collection (of literary materials)
dīwān al-inshā'	chancery, office of official correspondence
dīwān al-jund	military register
falsafa	philosophy
faqīh, fuqahā'	jurists
fatwā, fatāwā	legal opinion
fiqh	jurisprudence
funduq	inn, hostelry, warehouse
futuwwa	chivalric orders with a religio-moral ethos
ghayba	a Shī'ī term denoting the occultation from ordinary time of the last imam, also used for the period when Ibn Tumart's death was kept secret
ghāzī, ghuzāt	a holy warrior, synonym for *mujāhidīn*
ghifāra	a luxurious, silken cloak
Ghuzz, Aghzāz	military adventurers of varied ethnicity from the Islamic east
Guddāla	one of the desert Sanhaja tribes
ḥabs, ḥubūs	see *waqf*
ḥaḍar	sedentarists, townsmen and peasants
ḥaḍāra	culture, civilisation
Ḥadīth	Sayings of the Prophet
ḥaḍra	a centre of culture, capital city, the caliph's 'presence'

ḥājib	chamberlain, the amir or caliph's major domo
ḥajj	the pilgrimage to Mecca performed in the month of Dhū'l-Ḥijja
ḥasham	bodyguard
hijra	migration, Muhammad's migration from Mecca to Medina
ḥisba	maintenance of public order and morals, following the religious injunction to command right and prohibit wrong
ḥiṣn	fortress, fortified town
ḥuffāẓ, sing. *ḥāfiẓ*	Almohad cadres, lit. a memoriser
'īd al-aḍḥā	festival of the sacrifice
'īd al-fiṭr	festival of fast-breaking at the end of Ramaḍān
Ifrīqiya	Tunisia, eastern Algeria and western Libya
ijmā'	legal consensus
ijtihād	use of reasoning in the formulation of law
'ilj, *'ulūj*	'renegades', Christians, Christian converts to Islam
'ilm	learning, especially religious learning
'ilm al-furū'	science of the 'branches', i.e., the secondary literature of religion/law
'ilm al-uṣūl	science of the foundations (of religion or jurisprudence)
imam	prayer leader, head of the Muslim community
inzāl, inzālāt	Almoravid land grants
iqṭā', *iqṭā'āt*	land grants
'iṣma	infallibility
jamā'a	tribal council (Maghrib); village community (al-Andalus)
janna, jannāt	garden
jizya	poll tax on non-Muslim subjects
kāhina	priestess, soothsayer
kalām	lit. speech; scholastic theology
kalām al-Barbar	the Berber tongue
kātib, kuttāb	secretary, scribe
khalīfa, khulafā'	caliph
kharāj	a tax on land conquered by Muslims
Khārijite	an early Islamic sect with many adherents in North Africa
khāṣṣa	social elite
khaṭīb	the giver of the Friday sermon
kūra, kuwar	province

laff	see *ṣaff*
Lamtūna	one of the desert Sanhaja tribes
lisān	tongue, language
al-lisān al-gharbī	the 'western tongue', i.e., Masmuda Berber
lithām	veil and specifically the male face veil worn by desert Sanhaja
madhhab, *madhāhib*	school of Islamic law
madīna	town, city
madrasa	college for the teaching of Islamic law or religious sciences
Maghrib	North Africa excluding Egypt
mahdī	the Muslim equivalent of a messiah
majlis	gathering, council, salon
makhzan	lit. storehouse, used in the Maghrib for government or the state
maqṣūra	royal enclosure in a great mosque
ma'rifa	mystical knowledge
masjid	neighbourhood mosque
masjid jāmi'	great mosque, often just called a *jāmi'*
Masūfa	one of the desert Sanhaja tribes
miḥrāb	niche in the centre of the back wall of a mosque indicating the *qibla*
minbar	pulpit in a great mosque
miṣr	garrison town
mizwār	Berber term for a tribal chief or mediator, a repository of tribal knowledge, head of a rural religious lodge
mu'āhidūn	contractual partners; see *ahl al-dhimma*
muḥtasib	market inspector, one who commands right and prohibits wrong
mujāhidūn	fighters of jihad
al-mulaththamūn	veiled ones, a synonym for the Almoravids
muqarnas	plasterwork decoration in the form of 'stalactites' used for ceilings, domes, arches
al-murābiṭūn	the men of the *ribāṭ*, i.e., the Almoravids
murīdūn	disciples of a Sufi master
muṣḥaf, *maṣāḥif*	copy of the Qur'an
mushrif	official, financial overseer
al-muwaḥḥidūn	adherents of *tawḥīd*, i.e., the Almohads
al-muwalladūn	a term used for Christian converts to Islam in al-Andalus

naṣārā	Christians
qabīla, qabā'il	tribe
qāḍī, quḍāt	judge
qal'a, qilā'	citadel
qānūn	customary law; see also *'urf*
qarya, qurā	village
qaṣaba, qaṣabāt	citadel, fortress
qaṣr, quṣūr	palace, fortress, fortified clan dwelling
qibla	the direction of prayer
qiyās	legal analogy
quṭb	Sufi pole
ra'āyā	lit. flocks, the subject population
rābiṭa	holy person's shrine
ra'y	opinion, the use of rational opinion to formulate law
ribāṭ	a fortified frontier settlement used to propagate Islam or defend Islamic territory
ridda	apostasy
riḥla, raḥalāt	journey, a form of travel literature
sābāṭ	a covered passageway
ṣaff	lit. a row, a tribal alliance group
ṣaḥāba	companions (of the Prophet), used also for Ibn Tumart's companions
al-ṣāliḥūn	the 'pious', used for mystics
ṣaqāliba	'Slavs', northern slave troops recruited by the Umayyads
sayyid	noble, used in the Almohad empire for Mu'minid princes of the blood
Sharī'a(1)	Islamic law
sharī'a (2)	a plaza, open space
sharīf, shurafā'	descendant of the Prophet
shaykh, shuyūkh	tribal chief, elder, mystic
shūrā	consultation; an urban council of jurists
sihām, ashām	Almohad land grants
sikka	currency mint
Sufism	Islamic mysticism
sulṭān	lit. power and its holder, sultan
sunna	custom, practice; the practice of the Prophet
ṭā'ifa	a group, sect or party
Ṭā'ifa kings	the eleventh-century Muslim rulers in al-Andalus
ṭālib, ṭalaba	an Almohad scholar, used elsewhere for a student

tamyīz	sorting, troop reviews, the Almohad purge of Tinmall
ṭarīqa, ṭuruq	Sufi brotherhood
tawḥīd	oneness, especially the oneness of God, monotheism
thaghr, thughūr	a frontier settlement, the marches in al-Andalus
ṭirāz	richly embroidered textile bands given by rulers as gifts
umm walad	'mother of a son'; a concubine who has given her master a male child
'umrān	urban prosperity, civilisation
'urf	customary or tribal law
waḥḥada	to accept (Almohad) *tawḥīd*
wālī	governor
waqf, awqāf	pious endowment
wazīr, wuzarā'	government minister
yākūt	gemstone usually corundum (ruby, sapphire) or spinel (balas ruby)
zakāt	tithe, alms tax
zāwiya, zawāyā	Sufi lodge

Bibliography

Primary Sources

anon, *al-Dhakhīra al-Saniyya fī Ta'rīkh al-Dawla al-Marīniyya (al-'Abd al-Ḥaqqiyya)*, ed. Abdelwahab Benmansour (Rabat: Dār al-Manṣūr, 1972).

anon, *Kitāb al-Ansāb*, in E. Lévi-Provençal (ed. and trans.), *Documents inédits d'histoire almohade* (Paris: Geuthner, 1928), pp. 18–49.

anon, *Kitāb al-Ḥulal al-Mawshiyya fī Dhikr al-Akhbār al-Marrākushiyya* (Tunis: Maṭba'at al-Taqaddum al-Islāmiyya, 1979), variously attributed to Ibn al-Khaṭīb or Ibn Simāk al-Mālaqī.

anon, *Kitāb al-Istibṣār fī 'Ajā'ib al-Amṣār*, ed. 'Abd al-Ḥamīd Sa'd Zaghlūl (Alexandria: University of Alexandria Press, 1958), recently attributed to Muḥammad b. 'Abd Rabbihi.

al-Bakrī, Abū 'Ubayd, *Description de l'Afrique septentrionale par el-Bekri*, ed. and trans. W. MacGuckin de Slane (Paris: Paul Geuthner, 1913).

al-Bakrī, Abū 'Ubayd, *Description de l'Afrique septentrionale par el-Bekri*, texte Arabe, ed. W. MacGuckin de Slane ([Algiers: Imprimerie du Gouvernement, 1857] Paris: Maisonneuve, 1965).

al-Bakrī, Abū 'Ubayd, *Jughrāfiyat al-Andalus wa-Urūba*, ed. 'Abd al-Raḥmān 'Alī al-Ḥajjī, (Beirut: Dār al-Irshād, 1968).

al-Baydhaq, 'Alī al-Ṣanhājī, *Kitāb Akhbār al-Mahdī Ibn Tūmart*, ed. 'Abd al-Ḥamīd Hajiyāt (Algiers: al-Sharika al-Waṭaniyya li'l-Nashr wa'l-Tawzī', 1975).

al-Ghazālī, Abū Ḥāmid Muḥammad, *al-Wasīṭ fī'l-Madhhab*, ed. Aḥmad Maḥmūd Ibrāhīm (Cairo: Dār al-Salām, 1997).

al-Ḥimyarī, Abū 'Abd Allāh Muḥammad, *Ṣifat Jazīrat al-Andalus muntakhaba min Kitāb al-Rawḍ al-Mi'ṭār fī Khabr al-Aqṭār*, ed. E. Lévi-Provençal (Cairo: Maṭba'at Lajnat al-Ta'līf wa'l-Tarjama wa'l-Nashr, 1937).

Ibn al-Abbār, Abū 'Abd Allāh Muḥammad, *Kitāb al-Ḥulla al-Siyarā'*, ed. Ḥusayn Mu'nis (Cairo: al-Sharika al-'Arabiyya li'l-Ṭibā'a wa'l-Nashr, 1963).

Ibn 'Abdūn, *Séville Musulmane au début du XIIe siècle: le traité d' Ibn 'Abdun sur la vie urbaine et les corps de métiers*, ed. and trans. E. Lévi-Provençal (Paris: Maisonneuve, 1947).

Ibn Abī Zar', 'Alī, *al-Anīs al-Muṭrib bi-Rawḍ al-Qirṭās fī Akhbār Mulūk al-Maghrib wa-Ta'rīkh Madīnat Fās*, ed. Abdelwahab Benmansour (Rabat: Imprimerie Royale, 1999).

Ibn al-Athīr, *al-Kāmil fī'l-Ta'rīkh*, ed. C. J. Tornberg, 13 vols (Beirut: Dar Sader/Dar Beyrouth, 1965–7).

Ibn Ḥanbal, Aḥmad, *al-Musnad*, ed. Aḥmad Muḥammad Shākir (Cairo: Dār al-Hadith, 1995).
Ibn Ḥawqal, *Kitāb Ṣūrat al-Arḍ*, ed. J. H. Kramers (Leiden: Brill, [1938–9], 2014).
Ibn ʿIdhārī, *al-Bayān al-Mughrib fī Akhbār al-Andalus wa'l-Maghrib*, ed. ʿAbd Allāh Muḥammad ʿAlī, based on the edition of E. Lévi-Provençal and G. S. Colin, 4 vols (Beirut: Dār al-Kutub al-ʿIlmiyya, 2009).
Ibn Jubayr, *The Travels of Ibn Jubayr*, trans. R. Broadhurst (Delhi: Goodword Books, 2003).
Ibn Khaldūn, ʿAbd al-Raḥmān, *Histoire des Berbères*, trans. W. MacGuckin de Slane, 4 vols (Paris: Geuthner, 1925–6).
Ibn Khaldūn, ʿAbd al-Raḥmān, *Kitāb al-ʿIbar wa-Dīwān al-Mubtada' wa'l-Khabar fī Ayyām al-ʿArab wa'l-ʿAjam wa'l-Barbar*, 10 vols (Beirut: Dār al-Kitāb al-Lubnānī, 1956–).
Ibn Khaldūn, ʿAbd al-Raḥmān, *The Muqaddimah*, trans. Franz Rosenthal, abridged N. J. Dawood, with an introduction by Bruce Lawrence (Princeton, NJ: Princeton University Press, 2005 edn).
Ibn al-Qaṭṭān, *Naẓm al-Jumān li-Tartīb mā Salafa min Akhbār al-Zamān*, ed. Maḥmūd ʿAlī al-Makkī (Beirut: Dār al-Gharb al-Islāmī, 1990).
Ibn al-Qifṭī, *Ta'rīkh al-Ḥukamā'*, ed. Julius Lippert (Leipzig: Dietrichische Verlagsbuchhandlung, 1903).
Ibn al-Qūṭiyya, *Ta'rīkh Iftitāḥ al-Andalus*, ed. Ibrāhīm al-Abyārī (Cairo and Beirut: Dār al-Kutub al-Islāmiyya and Dār al-Kitāb al-Lubnānī, 1982).
Ibn al-Qūṭiyya, *Early Islamic Spain: The history of Ibn al-Qūṭīyah*, ed. and trans. David James, (Leiden: Brill, 2009).
Ibn Ṣāḥib al-Ṣalāt, *al-Mann bi'l-Imāma*, ed. ʿAbd al-Hādī al-Tāzī (Beirut: Dār al-Gharb al-Islāmī, 1987 edn).
Ibn Tūmart, Muḥammad, *Aʿazz mā yuṭlab*, ed. ʿAbd al-Ghānī Abū'l-ʿAzm (Rabat: Mu'assasat al-Ghānī li'l-Nashr, 1997).
Ibn al-Zayyāt, Yūsuf b. Yaḥyā al-Tādilī, *al-Tashawwuf ilā Rijāl al-Taṣawwuf* (Rabat: Maṭbūʿāt Ifrīqiya al-Shamāliyya al-Faniyya, 1958).
al-Idrīsī, *Opus Geographicum (Nuzhat al-Mushtāq fī Ikhtirāq al-Āfāq)*, ed. E. Cerulli et al. (Naples: Instituto Universitario orientale di Napoli, Instituto Italiano per il Medio ed Estremo Oriente, 1970–), fasc. 1–4 and fasc. 5–8.
al-Jaznā'ī, ʿAlī, *Janā Zahrat al-Ās fī Binā' Madīnat Fās*, ed. Abdelwahab Benmansour (Rabat: al-Maṭbaʿa al-Malakiyya, 2008 edn).
al-Maqqarī, Aḥmad b. Muḥammad, *Nafḥ al-Ṭīb min Ghuṣn al-Andalus al-Raṭīb*, ed. Muḥammad Muḥyī al-Dīn ʿAbd al-Ḥamīd, 10 vols in 5 (Cairo: Maṭbaʿat al-Saʿāda, 1949).
al-Marrākushī, ʿAbd al-Wāḥid, *al-Muʿjib fī Talkhīṣ Akhbār al-Maghrib*, ed. Mamdūḥ Ḥaqqī (Casablanca: Dār al-Kitāb, 1978 edn).
al-Nuwayrī, Shihāb al-Dīn Aḥmad *Nihāyat al-Arab fī Funūn al-Adab*, vol. 24, ed. ʿAbd al-Majīd Tarḥīnī (Beirut: Dār al-Kutub al-ʿIlmiyya, 2004).
al-Sakaṭī, Abū ʿAbd Allāh Muḥammad, *Un manuel hispanique de Ḥisba: le traité d'Abī ʿAbd Allāh Muḥammad b. Abī Muḥammad as-Sakaṭī de Malaga*, ed. and trans. G. S. Colin and E. Lévi-Provençal, vol. 1, Texte Arabe, *Publications de l'institut des hautes études marocaines* 21, (Paris: Leroux, 1931).
Tibi, Amin (ed. and trans.), *The Tibyān: Memoirs of ʿAbd Allāh b. Buluggīn, last Zīrid Amīr of Granada* (Leiden: Brill, 1986).

al-ʻUdhrī, Aḥmad b. ʻUmar b. Anas (Ibn al-Dalāʼī), *Nuṣūṣ ʻan al-Andalus min Kitāb Tarṣīʻ al-Akhbār wa-Tanwīʻ al-Āthār wa'l-Bustān fī Gharāʼib al-Buldān wa'l-Masālik ilā jāmiʻ al-Mamālik*, ed. ʻAbd al-ʻAzīz al-Ahwānī (Madrid: Instituto de Estudios Islámicos, 1965).

Secondary Sources

Abulafia, David, 'Christian merchants in the Almohad cities', *Journal of Medieval Iberian Studies*, 2(2) (2010): 251–8.
Aguadé, J., 'Some remarks about sectarian movements in al-Andalus', *Studia Islamica*, 64 (1986): 53–77.
Aillet, Cyrille, 'Islamisation et évolution du peuplement chrétien en al-Andalus (VIIIe–XIIe siècle)', in Dominique Valérian (ed.), *Islamisation et arabisation de l'Occident musulman médiéval (VIIe–XIIe siècle)* (Paris: Publications de la Sorbonne, 2011), pp. 151–92.
Ali-de-Unzaga, Miriam, 'Quranic inscriptions on the so-called "Pennon of Las Navas de Tolosa" and three Marînid banners', in Fahmida Suleman (ed.), *Word of God, Art of Man: The Quran and its Creative Expressions* (Oxford: Oxford University Press and the Institute for Ismaili Studies, 2007), pp. 239–70.
Allaoua Amara, 'L'Islamisation du Maghreb centrale', in Dominique Valérian (ed.), *Islamisation et arabisation de l'Occident musulman médiéval (VIIe–XIIe siècle)* (Paris: Publications de la Sorbonne, 2011), pp. 103–30.
Amri, Nelly, '*Ribāṭ* et idéal de sainteté à Kairouan et sur le littoral ifrīqiyen du IIe/VIIIe siècle d'après le *Riyāḍ al-nufūs* d'al-Maliki', in Dominique Valérian (ed.), *Islamisation et arabisation de l'Occident musulman médiéval (VIIe–XIIe siècle)* (Paris: Publications de la Sorbonne, 2011), pp. 331–68.
Arnaldez, R., 'Ibn Zuhr', *EI2*.
Al-Azmeh, Aziz, *Ibn Khaldun, An Essay in Reinterpretation* (London: Frank Cass, 1982).
Baadj, Amar, *Saladin, the Almohads and the Banū Ghāniya: the Contest for North Africa (12th and 13th Centuries)* (Leiden: Brill, 2015).
Barrucand, Marianne and Achim Bednorz, *Moorish Architecture in Andalusia* (Cologne: Taschen, 1992).
Barton, Simon, *Conquerors, Brides and Concubines: Interfaith Relations and Social Power in Medieval Iberia* (Philadelphia, PA: University of Pennsylvania Press, 2015).
Barton, Simon, and Richard Fletcher, *The World of El Cid: Chronicles of the Spanish Reconquest* (Manchester: Manchester University Press, 2000).
Bellver, J., '"al-Ghazālī of al-Andalus": Ibn Barrajān, Mahdism and the emergence of learned Sufism on the Iberian peninsula', *Journal of the American Oriental Society*, 133(4) (2013): 659–81.
Benhima, Yassir, 'Quelques remarques sur les conditions de l'Islamisation du Maghrib al-Aqṣā: aspects religieux et linguistiques', in Dominique Valérian (ed.), *Islamisation et arabisation de l'Occident musulman médiéval (VIIe–XIIe siècle)* (Paris: Publications de la Sorbonne, 2011), pp. 315–30.
Benhsain, R. and J. Devisse, 'Les almoravides et l'Afrique occidentale XIe–XIIe siècle', *Arabica*, 47(1) (2000): 1–36.
Benhsain-Mesmoudi, R., P. Guichard and C. Domenech, 'Biens sultaniens, fiscalité et monnaie à l'époque almohade', in P. Cressier, M. Fierro and L. Molina (eds),

Los Almohades: problemas y perspectivas, 2 vols (Madrid: Consejo Superior de Investigaciones Científicas, 2005), vol. 2, pp. 585–615.

Bennison, Amira K., 'Power and the city in the Islamic west from the Umayyads to the Almohads', in Amira K. Bennison and Alison L. Gascoigne (eds), *Cities in the Premodern Islamic World: The Urban Impact of Religion, State and Society* (London: RoutledgeCurzon, 2007), pp. 65–95.

Bennison, Amira K., 'The Almohads and the Qur'ān of 'Uthmān: the legacy of the Umayyads of Córdoba in the twelfth-century Maghrib', *Al-Masaq*, 19(2) (2007): 131–54.

Bennison, Amira K., 'The necklace of al-Shifā': 'Abbasid borrowings in the Islamic west', *Oriens*, 38 (2010): 249–73.

Bennison, Amira K., 'Almohad *tawḥīd* and its implications for religious difference', *Journal of Medieval Iberian Studies*, 2(2) (2010): 195–216.

Bennison, Amira K., 'Tribal identities and the formation of the Almohad élite: the salutary tale of Ibn 'Aṭiyya', in Mohamed Meouak (ed.), *Biografías magrebíes. Identidades y grupos religiosos, sociales y políticos en el Magreb medieval* (Madrid: Consejo Superior de Investigaciones Científicas, 2012), pp. 245–72.

Bennison, Amira K. (ed.), *The Articulation of Power in Medieval Iberia and the Maghrib* (Oxford: Oxford University Press, 2014).

Bennison, Amira K., 'Drums, banners and *baraka*: symbols of authority during the first century of Marīnid rule', 1250–1350, in Amira K. Bennison (ed.), *The Articulation of Power in Medieval Iberia and the Maghrib* (Oxford: Oxford University Press, 2014), pp. 195–216.

Bennison, Amira K., 'Sectarianism in the landscape: the transfer of the *khuṭba* of Fes from the Mosque of the Shurafā' to the Qarawiyyīn Mosque in 933 (321 AH)', *Maghreb Review*, 40(1) (2015): 12–27.

Bennison, Amira K., 'Mosques in the Maghrib', *Cambridge World History of Religious Architecture*, forthcoming.

Bennison, Amira K. and María Angeles Gallego, 'Jewish trading in Fes on the eve of the Almohad conquest', *Miscelánea de Estudios Árabes y Hebraicos: Sección de Hebreo*, 57 (2008): 33–51.

Bennison, Amira K., *The Great Caliphs: The Golden Age of the 'Abbasid Empire* (London: I. B. Tauris, 2009).

Bennison, Amira K. and María Angeles Gallego (eds), *Religious Minorities under the Almohads*, special issue, *Journal of Medieval Iberian Studies*, 2(2) (2010).

Bierman, Irene, *Writing Signs: The Fatimid Public Text* (Berkeley, CA: University of California Press, 1998).

Bloom, Jonathan, 'The revival of early Islamic architecture by the Umayyads of Spain', in M. J. Chiat and K. L. Reyerson (eds), *The Medieval Mediterranean. Cross Cultural Contacts, Medieval Studies at Minnesota 3* (St Cloud, MN: North Star Press, 1988), pp. 35–41.

Bloom, Jonathan, *Minaret: Symbol of Islam* (Oxford: Oxford University Press, 1989).

Bloom, Jonathan, 'The minbar from the Kutubiyya Mosque', in *The Minbar from the Kutubiyya Mosque* (New York, Madrid and Rabat: Metropolitan Museum of Art, Ediciones El Viso and Ministry of Cultural Affairs, 1998).

Boloix Gallardo, Barbara, *De la Taifa de Arjona al Reino Nazarí de Granada (1232–1246)* (Jaén: Instituto de Estudios Giennenses, 2005).

Bonine, Michael, 'The sacred direction and city structure: a preliminary analysis of the Islamic cities of Morocco', *Muqarnas*, 7 (1990): 50–72.

Bosch Vilá, Jacinto, *Los Almorávides* (Tetuan: Editora Marroquí, 1956), republished with a new foreword by Emilio Molina López (Granada: Universidad de Granada, 1998).

Bovill, Edward W., *The Golden Trade of the Moors* (Princeton, NJ: Marcus Wiener, 1999 edn).

Brett, Michael, 'Ifriqiya as a market for Saharan trade from the tenth to the twelfth century AD', *Journal of African History*, 10(3) (1969): 347–64.

Brett, Michael, 'The Islamisation of Morocco from the Arabs to the Almoravids', *Morocco: The Journal of the Society for Moroccan Studies*, 2 (1992): 57–71; reprinted as ch. VI in idem, *Ibn Khaldun and the Medieval Maghrib.*

Brett, Michael, 'The way of the nomad', *Bulletin of the School of Oriental and African Studies*, 58(2) (1995): 251–69.

Brett, Michael, *Ibn Khaldun and the Medieval Maghrib* (Aldershot: Ashgate Variorum, 1999).

Brett, Michael, *The Rise of the Fatimids: The World of the Mediterranean and the Middle East in the Fourth Century of the Hijra, Tenth Century CE* (Leiden: Brill, 2001).

Brett, Michael, "Abbasids, Fatimids and Seljuks', in David Luscombe and Jonathan Riley-Smith (eds), *The New Cambridge Medieval History*, vol. 4 (Cambridge: Cambridge University Press, 2004), pp. 675–720.

Brett, Michael and Elizabeth Fentress, *The Berbers* (Oxford: Blackwell, 1996).

Brunschvig, Robert, 'Sur le doctrine du Mahdī Ibn Tumart', *Arabica*, 2(2) (1955): 137–49.

Buresi, Pascal, 'Une relique almohade: l'utilisation du coran de la Grande mosquée de Cordoue (attribué à 'Utmān b. 'Affan (644–656))', in *Lieux de cultes: aires votives, temples, églises, mosquées* (Paris: CNRS Editions, 2008), pp. 273–80.

Buresi, Pascal and Hicham El Aallaoui, *Governing the Empire: Provincial Administration in the Almohad Caliphate (1224–1269)* (Leiden: Brill, 2013).

Burkhalter, Sheryl, 'Listening for silences in Almoravid history: another reading of the "Conquest that never was"', *History in Africa*, 19 (1992): 103–31.

Buturovic, Amila, 'Ibn Quzmān', in M. R. Menocal, R. P. Scheindlin and M. Sells (eds), *The Literature of al-Andalus* (Cambridge: Cambridge University Press, 2000), pp. 292–305.

Cheddadi, Abdesselam, *Ibn Khaldûn: l'homme et le théoreticien de la civilisation* (Paris: Gallimand, 2006).

Cherif, Mohamed, *Ceuta aux époques almohade et mérinide* (Paris: L'Harmattan, 1996).

Clarke, Nicola, *The Muslim Conquest of Iberia: Medieval Arabic Narratives* (London and New York: Routledge, 2012).

Collins, Roger, *Visigothic Spain, 409–711* (Oxford: Blackwell, 2004).

Conrad, David and Humphrey Fisher, 'The conquest that never was: Ghana and the Almoravids 1076. I. The external Arabic sources', *History in Africa*, 9 (1982): 21–59.

Conrad, Lawrence (ed.), *The World of Ibn Tufayl: Interdisciplinary Perspectives on Ḥayy b. Yaqẓān* (Leiden: Brill, 1996).

Constable, Olivia R., *Trade and Traders in Muslim Spain* (Cambridge: Cambridge University Press, 1996 edn).

Constable, Olivia R. (ed.), *Medieval Iberia* (Philadelphia, PA: University of Pennsylvania Press, 1997).
Constable, Olivia R., *Housing the Stranger in the Mediterranean World: Lodging, Trade and Travel in Late Antiquity and the Middle Ages* (Cambridge: Cambridge University Press, 2003).
Cook, Michael, *Commanding Right and Forbidding Wrong in Islamic Thought* (Cambridge: Cambridge University Press, 2000).
Coope, Jessica, *The Martyrs of Córdoba: Community and Family Conflict in an Age of Mass Conversion* (Lincoln, NE: University of Nebraska Press, 1995).
Cooperson, Michael, *al-Ma'mūn* (Oxford: One World, 2005).
Cornell, Vincent, 'Understanding is the mother of ability: responsibility and action in the doctrine of Ibn Tumart', *Studia Islamica*, 66 (1987): 71–103.
Cornell, Vincent, 'Ḥayy in the land of Absāl: Ibn Ṭufayl and Sufism in the western Maghrib during the Muwaḥḥid era', in Lawrence Conrad (ed.), *The World of Ibn Ṭufayl: Interdisciplinary Perspectives on Ḥayy b. Yaqẓān* (Leiden: Brill, 1996), pp. 133–64.
Cornell, Vincent, *The Way of Abu Madyan* (Cambridge: Islamic Texts Society, 1996).
Corriente, Federico, *A Dictionary of Andalusi Arabic* (Leiden: Brill, 1997).
Cressier, Patrice, 'Les portes monumentales urbaines almohades', in P. Cressier, M. Fierro and L. Molina (eds), *Los Almohades: problemas y perspectivas*, 2 vols (Madrid: Consejo Superior de Investigaciones Científicas, 2005), vol. 1, pp. 149–87.
Dachraoui, F., 'Ibn Hāni'', *EI2*.
Dodds, Jerrilyn D. (ed.), *al-Andalus. Art of Islamic Spain* (New York: Metropolitan Museum of Art, 1992).
Dols, Michael, 'The leper in medieval Islamic society', *Speculum*, 58(4) (1983): 891–916.
Dozy, Reinhart, *Dictionnaire détaillé des noms des vêtements chez les Arabes* (Amsterdam: Jean Müller, 1845).
Ducène, J.-C., 'al-Bakrī, Abu 'Ubayd 'Abd Allāh', *EI3*.
El Hour, Rachid, 'Córdoba frente a los almorávides: familias de cadíes y poder local en al-Andalus', *Revista del Instituto Egipcio de Estudios Islámicos*, 29 (1997): 182–210.
El Hour, Rachid, 'Sevilla en época almorávide: sede de una importante administracíon judicial', *Revista del Instituto Egipcio de Estudios Islámicos*, 31 (1999): 33–50.
El Hour, Rachid, 'Almería almorávide: sede de una oposición política y de un importante poder judicial', *Revista del Instituto Egipcio de Estudios Islámicos*, 32 (2000): 99–118.
El Hour, Rachid, 'El Levante de al-Andalus en época almorávide: jueces ye élites locales', *Al-Andalus-Maghreb*, 10 (2003): 53–89.
El Hour, Rachid, 'El Cadiazgo en Granada bajo los Almorávides: enfrentamiento y negociacíon', *Al-Qanṭara*, 27(1) (2006): 5–23.
Epalza, Mikel de, 'Mozarabs: an emblematic Christian minority in Islamic al-Andalus', in Salma K. Jayyusi (ed.), *The Legacy of Muslim Spain*, 2 vols (Leiden: Brill, 1994), vol. 1, pp. 149–70.
Ewert, Christian, 'El registro ornamental almohade y su relevencia', in P. Cressier, M. Fierro and L. Molina (eds), *Los Almohades: problemas y perspectivas*, 2 vols

(Madrid: Consejo Superior de Investigaciones Científicas, 2005), vol. 1, pp. 223–47.
Fancy, Hussein, 'Theologies of violence: the recruitment of Muslim soldiers by the crown of Aragon', *Past and Present*, 221 (2013): 39–73.
Fancy, Hussein, 'The last Almohads: universal sovereignty between North Africa and the crown of Aragon', *Medieval Encounters*, 19 (2013): 102–36.
Ferhat, Halima, 'Marinid Fez: zenith and signs of decline', in Salma K. Jayyusi et al. (eds), *The City in the Islamic World*, 2 vols (Leiden: Brill, 2008), vol. 1, pp. 247–67.
Ferhat, Halima, 'Tinmal', *EI2*.
Fierro, Maribel, 'Accusations of "zandaqa" in al-Andalus', *Quaderni di Studi Arabi*, 5/6 (1987–8): 251–8.
Fierro, Maribel, 'Spiritual alienation and political activism: the *ġurabā'* in al-Andalus during the sixth-twelfth century', *Arabica*, 47(2) (2000): 230–60.
Fierro, Maribel, 'Las genealogías de 'Abd al-Mu'min, primer califa almohade', *Al-Qantara*, 24 (2003): 77–108.
Fierro, Maribel, 'The mobile *minbar* in Córdoba: how the Umayyads of al-Andalus claimed the inheritance of the Prophet', *Jerusalem Studies in Arabic and Islam*, 33 (2007): 149–68.
Fierro, Maribel, 'Conversion, ancestry and universal religion: the case of the Almohads in the Islamic West (six/twelfth to seventh/thirteenth centuries), *Journal of Medieval Iberian Studies*, 2(2) (2010): 155–74.
Fierro, Maribel, *The Almohad Revolution: Politics and Religion in the Islamic West during the Twelfth–Thirteenth Centuries* (Aldershot: Ashgate Variorum, 2012).
Fierro, Maribel, 'al-Ru'aynī', *EI2*.
Fischel, Walter, *Ibn Khaldun in Egypt* (Berkeley, CA: University of California Press, 1967).
Fletcher, Madeleine, 'Almohad Tawḥīd: theology which relies on logic', *Numen*, 38(1) (1991): 110–27.
Fletcher, Madeleine, 'Ibn Tumart's teachers: the relationship with al-Ghazali', *Al-Qantara*, 18(2) (1997): 305–30.
Fletcher, Madeleine, 'The doctrine of divine unity: the Almohad creed (1183)', in O. R. Constable (ed.), *Medieval Iberia* (Philadelphia, PA: University of Pennsylvania Press, 1997), pp. 190–7.
Fricaud, Émile, 'La place des *ṭalaba* dans la société almohade mu'minide', in P. Cressier, M. Fierro and L. Molina (eds), *Los Almohades: problemas y perspectivas*, 2 vols (Madrid: Consejo Superior de Investigaciones Científicas, 2005), vol. 2, pp. 525–45.
Fricaud, Émile, 'Les *ṭalaba* dans le société almohade (le temps d'Averroès), *al-Qanṭara*, 18(2) (1997): 331–88.
Fromherz, Allen, 'The Almohad Mecca: locating Igli and the cave of Ibn Tumart', *al-Qanṭara*, 26(1) (2005): 175–90.
Fromherz, Allen, 'North Africa and the twelfth-century renaissance: Christian Europe and the Almohad Islamic empire', *Islam and Christian–Muslim Relations*, 20(1) (2009): 43–59.
Fromherz, Allen, *Ibn Khaldun, Life and Times* (Edinburgh, Edinburgh University Press, 2010).

Fromherz, Allen, *The Almohads: The Rise of an Islamic Empire* (London: I. B. Tauris, 2010).
García-Arenal, Mercedes, *Messianism and Puritanical Reform: Mahdis of the Muslim West* (Leiden: Brill, 2006).
García-Arenal, Mercedes and Eduardo Manzano Moreno, 'Idrīssisme et villes idrīssides', *Studia Islamica*, 82 (1995): 5–33.
García Fitz, Francisco, *Las Navas de Tolosa* (Barcelona: Ariel, 2005).
García Fitz, Francisco, 'Was Las Navas a decisive battle?', *Journal of Medieval Iberian Studies*, 4(1) (2012): 5–9.
Gallego, María Angeles, 'The languages of medieval Iberia and their religious dimension', *Medieval Encounters*, 9(1) (2003): 107–39.
Garulo, Teresa, 'al-Ruṣāfī', *EI2*.
Gellner, Ernest, *Muslim Society* (Cambridge: Cambridge University Press, 1981).
Gellner, Ernest, 'Tribalism and the state in the Middle East', in P. Khoury and J. Kostiner (eds), *Tribes and State Formation in the Middle East* (Berkeley, CA: University of California Press, 1990), pp. 109–26.
Ghouirgate, Mehdi, *L'Ordre almohade (1120–1269): une nouvelle lecture anthropologique* (Toulouse: Presses Universitaires du Mirail, 2014).
Glick, Thomas, 'Hydraulic technology in al-Andalus', in Salma K. Jayyusi (ed.), *The Legacy of Muslim Spain* (Leiden: Brill, 1994), vol. 2, pp. 974–86.
Goldziher, Ignaz, *Mohammed Ibn Toumert et le théologie de l'Islam dans le nord de l'Afrique au XIe siècle* (Algiers: Fontana, 1903).
Golvin, Lucien, 'Ḳal'at Banī Ḥammād', *EI2*.
Gómez-Rivas, Camilo, *Law and the Islamization of Morocco under the Almoravids* (Leiden: Brill, 2014).
Gómez-Rivas, Camilo, 'The ransom industry and the expectation of refuge on the western Mediterranean Muslim–Christian frontier, 1085–1350', in Amira K. Bennison (ed.), *The Articulation of Power in Medieval Iberia and the Maghrib* (Oxford: Oxford University Press, 2014), pp. 217–32.
Goodman, Lenn E., *Ibn Tufayl's Hayy b. Yaqzān* (New York: Twayne, 1972).
Goodman, Lenn E., 'Ibn Ṭufayl', in M. R. Menocal, R. P. Scheindlin and M. Sells, *The Literature of al-Andalus* (Cambridge: Cambridge University Press, 2000), pp. 318–30.
Goitein, Shelomo, *Letters of Medieval Jewish Traders* (Princeton, NJ: Princeton University Press, 1973).
Greenhalgh, Michael, *Marble Past, Monumental Present: Building with Antiquities in the Medieval Mediterranean* (Leiden: Brill, 2009).
Gruendler, Beatrice, 'The Qasida', in M. R. Menocal, R. P. Scheindlin and M. Sells (eds), *The Literature of al-Andalus* (Cambridge: Cambridge University Press, 2000), pp. 211–31.
Griffel, Frank, 'Ibn Tumart's rational proof for God's existence and his unity and his connection to the Niẓāmiyya Madrasa in Baghdad', in P. Cressier, M. Fierro and L. Molina (eds), *Los Almohades: problemas y perspectivas*, 2 vols (Madrid: Consejo Superior de Investigaciones Científicas, 2005), vol. 2, pp. 753–813.
Guichard, Pierre, *Structures sociales 'orientales' et 'occidentales' dans l'Espagne musulmane* (Paris: Mouton, 1977).
Guichard, Pierre, *Les musulmans de Valence et la reconquête (XIe–XIIIe siècles)*, 2 vols (Damascus: Institut français de Damas, 1990).

Hammoudi, Abdellah, 'Segmentarity, social stratification, political power and sainthood. Reflections on Gellner's theses', *Economy and Society*, 9(3) (1980): 279–303.
Harvey, L. P., *Islamic Spain, 1250–1500* (Chicago: University of Chicago Press, 1990).
Hillenbrand, Robert, 'The ornament of the world: medieval Córdoba as a cultural centre', in Salma K. Jayyusi (ed.), *The Legacy of Muslim Spain*, 2 vols (Leiden: Brill, 1994), vol. 1, pp. 112–35.
Hillenbrand, Robert, *Islamic Art and Architecture* (London: Thames & Hudson, 1999).
Hitchcock, Richard, *Muslim Spain Reconsidered from 711 to 1502* (Edinburgh: Edinburgh University Press, 2014).
Hopkins, J. F. P., 'The Almohade hierarchy', *Bulletin of the School of Oriental and African Studies*, 16(1) (1954): 93–112.
Hopley, Russell, 'Nomadic populations and the challenge to legitimacy: three cases from the medieval Islamic west', in Amira K. Bennison (ed.), *The Articulation of Power in Medieval Iberia and the Maghrib* (Oxford: Oxford University Press, 2014), pp. 233–50.
Huici Miranda, Ambrosio, *Historia política del imperio almohade*, 2 vols (Tetuan: Editora Marroquí, 1956–7).
Huici Miranda, Ambrosio, *Las grandes batallas de la reconquista durante las invasiones africanas* (Madrid: Instituto de Estudios Africanos, CSIC, 1956).
Hunwick, John, 'Gao and the Almoravids: a hypothesis', in B. Swartz and R. Dumett (eds), *West African Culture Dynamics* (The Hague: Mouton, 1980), pp. 413–30.
Hunwick, John, 'Taghāza', *EI2*.
Jayyusi, Salma Khadra (ed.), *The Legacy of Muslim Spain*, 2 vols (Leiden: Brill, 1994).
al-Jazīrī, 'Abd al-Raḥmān, *al-Fiqh 'alā al-Madhāhib al-Arba'a* (Beirut: al-Maktab al-Aṣriyya, 2003).
Kably, Mohamed, *Société, pouvoir et religion au Maroc à la fin du Moyen Age (XIVe–XVe siècle)* (Paris: Maisonneuve et Larose, 1986).
Kaddouri, Samir, 'Dissimulation des opinions politiques sous contrôle: le cas d'Ibn Ḥazm à Séville', *al-Qanṭara*, 35(1) (2014): 135–50.
Kennedy, Hugh, *Muslim Spain and Portugal: A Political History of al-Andalus* (London: Longman, 1996).
Khoury, Philip and Joseph Kostiner (eds), *Tribes and State Formation in the Middle East* (Berkeley, CA: University of California Press, 1990).
Knysh, Alexander, 'Ibn 'Arabī', in M. R. Menocal, R. P. Scheindlin and M. Sells (eds), *The Literature of al-Andalus* (Cambridge: Cambridge University Press, 2000), pp. 331–44.
King, David, 'The orientation of medieval Islamic religious architecture and cities', *Journal for the History of Astronomy*, 26 (1995): 253–74.
Krasner-Balbale, Abigail, 'Jihād as a means of political legitimation in thirteenth-century Sharq al-Andalus', in Amira K. Bennison (ed.), *The Articulation of Power in Medieval Iberia and the Maghrib* (Oxford: Oxford University Press, 2014), pp. 87–105.
Lacoste, Yves, *Ibn Khaldun: The Birth of History and the Past of the Third World* (London: Verso, 1984).
Lagardère, Vincent, *Les Almoravides I* (Paris: L'Harmattan, 1989).

Lagardère, Vincent, *Le vendredi de Zallaqa, 23 octobre 1086* (Paris: L'Harmattan, 1989).
Lagardère, Vincent, *Campagnes et paysans d'Al-Andalus VIIIe–XVe siècles* (Paris: Maisonneuve et Larose, 1993).
Lagardère, Vincent, 'Le riziculture en al-Andalus (VIIIe–XVe siècles)', *Studia Islamica*, 83 (1996): 71–87.
Lagardère, Vincent, *Les Almoravides: le djihâd andalou* (Paris: L'Harmattan, 1998).
Lange, Dierk, 'Les rois de Gao-Sané et les Almoravides, *Journal of African History*, 32(2) (1991): 251–75.
Lantschner, Patrick, 'Fragmented cities in the later Middle Ages: Italy and the Near East Compared', *English Historical Review*, 130(544) (2015): 546–82.
Lapidus, Ira, 'Tribes and state formation in Islamic history', in P. Khoury and J. Kostiner (eds), *Tribes and State Formation in the Middle East* (Berkeley, CA: University of California Press, 1990), pp. 25–47.
Lapiedra Gutiérrez, Eva, *Cómo los Musulmanes Llamaban a los Cristianos Hispánicos* (Valencia: Instituto de Cultura, 1997).
Lévi-Provençal, Evariste, 'Le titre souverain des Almoravides et sa légitimation par le califat 'abbāside', *Arabica*, 2(3) (1955): 265–80.
Lévi-Provençal, Evariste, 'al-Bakrī, Abu 'Ubayd 'Abd Allāh', *EI2*.
Lewicki, Tadeusz, 'Les origines de l'Islam dans les tribus berbères du Sahara occidental: Mūsā ibn Nuṣayr et 'Ubayd Allāh b. al-Ḥabḥāb, *Studia Islamica*, 32 (1970): 203–14.
Lewicki, Tadeusz, 'Ḥalka', *EI2*.
Mackeen, A. M. Mohamed, 'The rise of al-Shādhilī (d. 656/1258)', *Journal of the American Oriental Society*, 91(4) (1971): 477–86.
Madelung Wilferd and Paul Walker, *The Advent of the Fatimids: A Contemporary Shī'ī Witness* (London: I. B. Tauris, 2000).
Mahdi, Muhsin, *Ibn Khaldun's Philosophy of History* (London: George Allen & Unwin, 1957).
Makhlūf, Muḥammad b. Muḥammad b. 'Umar b. Qāsim, *Shajarat al-Nūr al-Zakiyya fī Ṭabaqāt al-Mālikiyya* (Beirut: Dār al-Kutub al-'Ilmiyya, 2002).
Manzano Moreno, Eduardo, 'Quelques considérations sur les toponymes en Banû – comme reflet des structures sociales d'al-Andalus', in Dominique Valérian (ed.), *Islamisation et arabisation de l'Occident musulman médiéval (VIIe–XIIe siècle)* (Paris: Publications de la Sorbonne, 2011), pp. 247–63.
Marçais, Georges, 'Banū Ghāniya', *EI2*.
Marlow, Louise, *Hierarchy and Egalitarianism in Islamic Thought* (Cambridge: Cambridge University Press, 1997).
Martínez Enamorado, Virgilio, 'Fatimid ambassadors in Bobastro: changing religious and political allegiances in the Islamic west', *Journal of the Economic and Social History of the Orient*, 52 (2009): 267–300.
Martínez Núñez, Maria Antonia, 'El proyecto almohade a través de la documentación epigráfica: innovación y ruptura', in Patrice Cressier and Vicente Salvatierra (eds), *Las Navas de Tolosa (1212–2012) Miradas Cruzadas* (Jaén: Universidad de Jaén, 2014), pp. 139–57.
Martínez Núñez, Maria Antonia, '*Ḥisba* y *ŷihād* en época almohade: el testimonio epigráfico', in Carlos de Ayala Martínez and Isabel Cristina F. Fernandes (eds), *Cristãos contra muçulmanos na idade média peninsular/Christianos contra mesul-*

manes en la edad media peninsular (Lisbon: Ediçoes Colibri and Universidad Autónoma de Madrid, 2015), pp. 115–38.

Martinez-Gros, Gabriel, *Ibn Khaldoun et les sept vies de l'Islam* (Arles: Actes Sud, 2006).

Masonen, Pekka and Humphrey Fisher, 'Not quite Venus from the waves: the Almoravid conquest of Ghana in the modern historiography of western Africa', *History in Africa*, 23 (1996): 197–232.

Mathews, Karen R., 'Plunder of war or objects of trade? The reuse and reception of Andalusi objects in medieval Pisa', *Journal of Medieval Iberian Studies*, 4(2) (2012): 233–58.

McDougall, E. Ann, 'The Sahara reconsidered: pastoralism, politics and salt from the ninth through the twelfth centuries', *African Economic History*, 12 (1983): 263–86.

Melchert, Christopher, 'The destruction of books by Traditionists', *al-Qanṭara*, 35(1) (2014): 213–31.

Menocal, María Rosa, *The Ornament of the World: How Muslims, Jews and Christians Created a Culture of Tolerance in Medieval Spain* (New York: Little, Brown, 2002).

Messier, Ronald, 'The Almoravids, west African gold and the gold currency of the Mediterranean', *Journal of the Economic and Social History of the Orient*, 17(1) (1974): 31–47.

Messier, Ronald, 'Quantitative analysis of Almoravid dinars', *Journal of the Economic and Social History of the Orient*, 23(1/2) (1980): 102–18.

Messier, Ronald, 'Rethinking the Almoravids, re-thinking Ibn Khaldun', in Julia Clancy-Smith (ed.), *North Africa, Islam and the Mediterranean World* (London: Frank Cass, 2001), pp. 59–80.

Messier, Ronald, *The Almoravids and the Meanings of Jihad* (Santa Barbara, CA: Praegar, 2010).

Molénat, Jean-Pierre, 'Sur le role des Almohades dans la fin du christianisme local au Maghreb et en al-Andalus', *Al-Qanṭara*, 18 (1997): 389–413.

Montagne, Robert, *Les Berbères et le Makhzen dans le sud du Maroc* (Paris: Félix Alcan, 1930).

Montgomery Watt, W., 'The decline of the Almohads: reflections on the viability of religious movements', *History of Religions*, 4(1) (1964): 23–9.

Moraes Farias, P. F. de, *Arabic Medieval Inscriptions from the Republic of Mali: Epigraphy, Chronicles and Songhay–Tuāreg History* (Oxford: Oxford University Press, 2003).

Mourtada-Sabbah, Nada and Adrian Gully, 'I am, by God fit for high positions': on the political role of women in al-Andalus', *British Journal of Middle Eastern Studies*, 30(2) (2003): 183–209.

Navarro Palazón, Julio and Pedro Jimenez Castillo, 'La yesería en época almohade', in P. Cressier, M. Fierro and L. Molina (eds), *Los Almohades: problemas y perspectivas*, 2 vols (Madrid: Consejo Superior de Investigaciones Científicas, 2005), vol. 1, pp. 249–303.

Norris, Harry T., 'Yemenis in the western Sahara', *Journal of African History*, 3(2) (1962): 317–22.

Norris, Harry T., 'New evidence on the life of 'Abd Allāh b. Yāsīn and the origins of the Almoravid movement', *Journal of African History*, 12 (1971): 255–68.

Norris, Harry T., *The Berbers in Arabic Literature* (London and New York: Longman, 1982).

Norris, Harry T., 'al-Murābiṭūn', *EI2.*

Nwyia, Paul, *Un mystique prédicateur à la Qarawīyīn de Fès: Ibn 'Abbād de Ronda 1332–1390* (Beyrouth: Imprimerie Catholique, 1961).

O'Meara, Simon, 'The foundation legend of Fez and other Islamic cities in light of the life of the Prophet', Amira K. Bennison and Alison L. Gascoigne (eds), *Cities in the Premodern Islamic World: The Urban Impact of Religion, State and Society* (London: RoutledgeCurzon, 2007), pp. 27–41.

O'Shea, Stephen, *Sea of Faith: Christianity and Islam in the Medieval Mediterranean World* (Vancouver, BC: Douglas & McIntyre, 2006).

Partearroyo, Cristina, 'Almoravid and Almohad textiles', in Jerrilyn D. Dodds (ed.), *Al-Andalus: The Art of Islamic Spain* (New York: Metropolitan Museum of Art, 1992), pp. 105–14.

Partearroyo, Cristina, 'Los tejidos del periodo almohade', in P. Cressier, M. Fierro and L. Molina (eds), *Los Almohades: problemas y perspectivas*, 2 vols (Madrid: Consejo Superior de Investigaciones Científicas, 2005), vol. 1, pp. 305–52.

Pellat, Ch. 'Nafzāwa', *EI2.*

Pichard, Christophe, 'Islamisation et arabisation de l'occident musulman médiéval (VIIe–XIIe siècle): le contexte documentaire', in Dominique Valérian (ed.), *Islamisation et arabisation de l'Occident musulman médiéval (VIIe–XIIe siècle)* (Paris: Publications de la Sorbonne, 2011), pp. 35–61.

Poncet, Jean, 'La mythe de la "catastrophe" hilalienne', *Annales, Histoire, Sciences Sociales*, 22(5) (1967): 1099–120.

Powers, David, *Law, Society and Culture in the Maghrib, 1300–1500* (Cambridge: Cambridge University Press, 2002).

Prevost, Virginie, 'Les dernières communautés chrétiennes autochtones d'Afrique du Nord', *Revue de l'Histoire des Religions*, 224(4) (2007): 461–83.

Ramírez-del-Río, J., '*Al-Dajīra al-Saniyya*: una fuente relevante para el siglo XIII en la Península Ibérica', *al-Qanṭara*, 33(1) (2012): 7–44.

Robinson, Cynthia, *Medieval Andalusian Courtly Culture in the Mediterranean: Hadith Riyāḍ wa Bayāḍ* (London: Routledge, 2007).

Rosselló Bordoy, Guillermo, 'The ceramics of al-Andalus', in Jerrilyn D. Dodds (ed.), *Al-Andalus: The Art of Islamic Spain* (New York: Metropolitan Museum of Art, 1992), pp. 97–104.

Rosser-Owen, Mariam, 'Andalusi *spolia* in Morocco: architectural politics, political architecture', *Medieval Encounters*, 20 (2014): 152–98.

Ruggles Fairchild, Dede, 'Mothers of a hybrid dynasty: race, genealogy and acculturation in al-Andalus', *Journal of Medieval and Early Modern Studies*, 34 (2004): 65–94.

Safran, Janina, 'Ceremony and submission: the symbolic representation and recognition of legitimacy in tenth century al-Andalus', *Journal of Near Eastern Studies*, 58 (1999): 191–201.

Safran, Janina, *Defining Boundaries in al-Andalus, Muslims, Christians and Jews in Islamic Iberia* (Ithaca, NY: Cornell University Press, 2013).

Safran, Janina, 'The politics of book burning in al-Andalus', *Journal of Medieval Iberian Studies*, 6(2) (2014): 148–68.

Sánchez, Ignacio, 'Ethnic disaffection and dynastic legitimacy in the early Almohad

period: Ibn Tumart's *translatio studii et imperii*', *Journal of Medieval Iberian Studies*, 2(2) (2010): 175–93.
Schacht, Joseph, 'An unknown type of minbar and its historical significance', *Ars Orientalis*, 2 (1957): 149–73.
Scheindlin, Raymond P., 'The Jews in Muslim Spain', in Salma K. Jayyusi (ed.), *The Legacy of Muslim Spain* (Leiden: Brill, 1994), vol. 1, pp. 201–34.
Sermonin, Paul, 'The Almoravid movement in the western Sudan: a review of the evidence', *Transactions of the Historical Society of Ghana*, 7 (1964): 42–59.
Serrano Ruano, Delfina, 'Los Banū 'Iyāḍ, de la caída del Imperio Almorávid a la instauracíon de la dinastía nazarí', in M. Fierro and M. L. Ávila (eds), *Estudios Onomástico-Biográficos de al-Andalus 9* (Madrid: Consejo Superior de Investigaciones Científicas, 1999), vol. 1, pp. 352–406.
Serrano Ruano, Delfina, 'Ibn al-Sīd al-Baṭalyawsī: de los Reinos de Taifas a la época Almorávide a través de la biografía de un ulema polifacético', *al-Qanṭara*, 23(1) (2002): 53–92.
Serrano Ruano, Delfina, 'Por qué llamaron los almohades antropomorfistas a los almorávides?', in P. Cressier, M. Fierro and L. Molina (eds), *Los Almohades: problemas y perspectivas*, 2 vols (Madrid: Consejo Superior de Investigaciones Científicas, 2005), vol. 2, pp. 815–52.
Serrano Ruano, Delfina, 'Explicit cruelty, implicit compassion: Judaism, forced conversion and the genealogy of the Banū Rushd', *Journal of Medieval Iberian Studies*, 2(2) (2010): 217–34.
Shatzmiller, Maya, 'Aspects of women's participation in the economic life of later medieval Islam: occupations and mentalities', *Arabica*, 35(1) (1988): 36–58.
Shatzmiller, Maya, *The Berbers and the Islamic State: The Marīnid Experience in Pre-Protectorate Morocco* (Princeton, NJ: Marcus Weiner, 2000).
Shatzmiller, Maya, 'The fall of the Khaṭīb Abu'l-Faḍl al-Mazdaghī', in idem, *The Berbers and the Islamic State*, pp. 71–81.
Shatzmiller, Maya, 'Islam and the "Great Divergence": the case of the Moroccan Marīnid empire, 1269–1465 CE', in Amira K. Bennison (ed.), *The Articulation of Power in Medieval Iberia and the Maghrib* (Oxford: Oxford University Press, 2014), pp. 25–46.
Shatzmiller, Maya, 'al-Muwaḥḥidūn', *EI2*.
Shepherd, Dorothy, 'A treasure from a thirteenth-century Spanish tomb', *Bulletin of the Cleveland Museum of Art*, 65(4) (1978): 111–34.
Smith, Richard L., 'What happened to the ancient Libyans? Chasing sources across the Sahara from Herodotus to Ibn Khaldun', *Journal of World History*, 14(4) (2003): 459–500.
Stierlin, Henri, *Islam, vol. 1: Early Architecture from Baghdad to Córdoba* (Cologne: Taschen, 1996).
Tabbaa, Yasser, 'The Muqarnas dome: its origin and meaning', *Muqarnas*, 3 (1985): 61–74.
Tabbaa, Yasser, 'Andalusian roots and Abbasid homage in the Qubbat al-Barudiyyin in Marrakesh', *Muqarnas*, 25 (2008): 133–46.
al-Tawfīq, Aḥmad, 'Ḥawla maʿnā ism Marrākush', in *Marrākush: min al-taʾsīs ilā ākhir al-ʿaṣr al-muwaḥḥidī* (Marrakesh, 1988), pp. 15–19.
Thiry, Jacques, 'Le Sahara libyen médiévale', *Civilisations*, 38(1) (1988): 74–81.
Tourneau, R. le, 'Ibn Mashīsh', *EI2*.

Triki, Hamid, 'Marrakech: retrato histórico de una metrópolis medieval. Siglos XI–XII', in Rafael López Guzmán (ed.), *La Arquitectura del Islam Occidental* (Granada: Legado Andalusí, 1995), pp. 93–106.

Turner, John P., *Inquisition in Early Islam* (London: I. B. Tauris, 2013).

Urvoy, Dominique, *Penseurs d'al-Andalus: la vie intellectuelle à Cordoue et Seville au temps des empires berbères* (Toulouse: Editions du CNRS, 1990).

Valérian, Dominique, 'La permanence du christianisme au Maghreb: l'apport problématique des sources latines', in idem (ed.), *Islamisation et arabisation de l'Occident musulman médiéval (VIIe–XIIe siècle)* (Paris: Publications de la Sorbonne, 2011), pp. 131–49.

Valor Piechotta, Magdalena and Miguel Angel Tabales Rodríguez, 'Urbanismo y arquitectura almohades en Sevilla. Caracteres y especifidad', in P. Cressier, M. Fierro and L. Molina (eds), *Los Almohades: problemas y perspectivas*, 2 vols (Madrid: Consejo Superior de Investigaciones Científicas, 2005), vol. 1, pp. 189–222.

Viguera Molins, María Jesús (ed.), *Historia de España, vol. 8: El retroceso territorial de Al-Andalus: Almoravides y Almohades siglos XI al XIII* (Madrid: Espasa-Calpe, 1997).

Wasserstein, David, *The Rise and Fall of the Party Kings: Politics and Society in Islamic Spain 1002–1086* (Princeton, NJ: Princeton University Press, 1985).

Wasserstein, David, 'The language situation in al-Andalus', in A. Jones and R. Hitchcock (eds), *Studies on the Muwashshah and the Kharja* (Oxford: Oxford University Press, 1991), pp. 1–15.

Zadeh, Travis, 'From drops of blood: charisma and political legitimacy in the *translatio* of the 'Uthmanic codex of al-Andalus, *Journal of Arabic Literature*, 39 (2008): 321–46.

Index

Note: page numbers in *italics* indicate illustrations

Abū Madyan Shuʿayb, 239, 267, 269–70
Abū Marwān ʿAbd al-Malik b. Zuhr *see* Banū Zuhr
Abū Muḥammad ʿAbd Allāh b. ʿAbd al-Muʾmin, 93
Abūʾl-Rabīʿ Sulaymān b. ʿAbd al-Muʾmin, 83, 106, 109
Abū Saʿīd ʿUthmān b. ʿAbd al-Muʾmin, 83, 88, 89, 90, 93, *110*
Abū Yaʿza Yalannūr al-Dukkālī, 270, 272
Abū Yaḥyā b. Abī Yaʿqūb, 100
Abū Yūsuf Yaʿqūb b. Yūsuf *see* Yaʿqūb al-Manṣūr
Abū Yaʿqūb Yūsuf b. ʿAbd al-Muʾmin, Almohad caliph, 78, 83, 88, 89–90, 91–103, *110*, 134, 136, 137, 152, 190, 260, 261
accession of, 92–3, 160, 343
  building projects of, 98–9, 220, 315–18, 319, 320–1, 322, 343
  character of, 94–5
  death of, 102–3, 321, 343
  religious beliefs of, 254–2
Abū Zayd ʿAbd al-Raḥmān b. Abī Ḥafṣ ʿUmar 103, 105
Abū Zayd b. al-Lamṭiyya, 83
Abū Zayd b. Yujjān, 111
Abū Zayd al-Ḥarḍānī b. Abī Yaʿqūb, 100
afāriqa, 10, 350
Agādīr *see* Tlemcen
Agārṣīf, 187, 348
Aghmāt, *xiv*, *25*, 31, 35, 36, 47, *48*, 66, 67, 141, 159, 172, 201, *202*, 213, 216, 237, 252, 289, 308, 337, 338, 348
  Aghmāt-Īlān (Haylāna), 32
  Aghmāt-Warīka, 32, 33, 34
  Almoravid conquest of, 32–4
  Jewish population of, 168
agriculture, 2, 8, 21, 142, 180–8, 196, 219, 221, 223, 225, 226, 276
agronomy, 219–20, 308
ahl, 140
  al-dār, 68
  al-dhimma, 119, 165, 168, 232
  khamsīn, 80, 131
Aḥmad b. Bāsuh, architect, 315, 318, 319
Aḥmad b. Ḥanbal, 229
Aḥmad b. Milḥān of Guadix, 308
ʿAjam, 9
ʿAjīsa tribe, *13*, 14
Alfonso I El Batallador of Aragon, 55, 56, 57, 129, 170, 339
Alfonso VI of León-Castile, 20, 41, 42, 43, 44, 45, 46, 47, 55, 56, 168
  capture of Toledo, 43, 331, 338
Alfonso VII of León-Castile, 74, 77, 173, 195, 222
Alfonso VIII of Castile, 97, 99, 106, 108, 223
ʿAlī b. ʿĪsā b. Maymūn, 60, 65, 171
ʿAlī b. Isḥāq b. Ghāniya, 104, 105, 108, 112
ʿAlī b. Ḥirzihim, 244, 269
Almería, *xiv*, 45, 47, *48*, 61, 63, 119, 127, 183, 184, 189, 192, 199, 204, 225, 284, 298, 299, 300, 303, 328
  Castilian capture of, 75, 78, 195, 341
  great mosque of, 301
  marble tombstones from, 38, 195, 300, 302
  religious culture in, 244–5
  Ṣumādiḥiyya gardens, 219, 285
Alvar Fañez, 46
Amargū, fortress of, 299
Amazigh, 9
ʿĀmir b. Muhīb of Tavira, 77
Arabs, 4, 10–12, 14, 32, 52, 68, 79, 80, 102, 108, 112, 123, 128, 133, 141, 223, 232, 329
  and Ibn Khaldūn, 6–8
  in al-Andalus, 15–18, 145–6
Arabisation, 2, 11, 16–18, 80, 132–3, 228, 334, 335
Aragon, 2, 4, 41, 46, 55, 75, 98, 117, 129, 170, 195, 205, 222, 334
Arshgūl, 198, 199
Artabas, 15
ʿaṣabīyya, 7–9, 29–30, 125, 130, 131, 139, 140
Asad b. al-Furāt, 235
al-Ashʿarī, Abūʾl-Ḥasan ʿAlī, 236
Ashʿarī theology, 228, 236–7, 242, 246, 296
Ashīr, 201
Aṣīla, *xiv*, 199
astronomy, 266–7
Averroes *see* Ibn Rushd al-Hafīd
Awlīl, 189, 190

Awraba, *13*, 14, 233
Ayyūbids, 1, 3, 104, 105, 107, 137, 152, 210, 273, 290, 321, 329, 333
Azdāja tribe, *13*, 14
Azuggī, *25*, 37, 38, *48*, 126, 201, *202*, 241, 289

bacini, 304
Badajoz, *xiv*, 43–4, 46, 47, *48*, 77, 98, 102, 148, 338
Bādīs, 193
badw, 7, 119, 121, 139, 350; *see also* tribes
Bajaliyya sect, 31, 233
al-Bakrī, Abū ʿUbayd ʿAbd Allāh, 26–8, 47, 162–3, 177, 187–8, 330, 337
Banū Amghār, 83–4
Banū ʿAshara of Salé, 77, 288, 309
Banū Ghāniya, 61, 91, 270, 333, 342, 343, 344
  insurrection in North Africa, 104–5, 111–12, 137, 152, 173, 179, 188, 203, 223, 226
Banū Ḥammād, 79, 82, 162, 199
Banū Hilāl (and Sulaym), 11, 79–80, 81, 90, 132–3, 141, 179, 187
  ʻinvasion' of North Africa, 187–8, 203, 226, 333
Banū Ifrān, 32, 39
Banū Khurāsān of Tūnis, 88, 222
Banū Mardanīsh, 74, 78, 136–7, 272, 343
Banū Marīn, 114, 116, 133, 142, 187, 345, 346
Banū Sulaym *see* Banū Hilāl
Banū Targūt/Tūrgūt, *51*, 52, 60, 125, 129
Banū Zuhr, 266
Bāqī b. Makhlad, 235
al-Bāqillānī, 236
baraka, 153, 245
Barānis, 12, 14
Barcelona, 55, 59, 113, 133, 205, 327
Barghawāṭa, 27, 32, 38, 40, 73, 167, 234
Barrāz b. Isḥāq al-Masūfī *see* Abū Isḥāq Barrāz al-Masūfī
Bashīr al-Rūmī, 59–60
Baṣra (Iraq), 231, 290
Baṣra (Morocco), 184
al-Baydhaq, Abū Bakr ʿAlī al-Ṣanhājī, 62, 68
Berber languages, 9, 11, 67, 130–1, 134
Berbers, 9–12, 24, 32, 38, 79, 80, 88, 126, 130, 186, 188, 200, 222, 329, 331, 332
  and Ibn Khaldūn, 7–8
  European historiography of, 6, 118, 123
  genealogies of, 12–14, 25–6, 123–4, 128
  Islamisation of 233, 234, 235, 237
  Judaeo-, 167
  settlement in al-Andalus, 16, 18, 141, 145–6
Bijāya, *xiv*, *25*, 64, 78, 79–80, 82, 83, 88, 93, 99, 108, 111, 134, 150, 152, 199–200, *202*, 205, 223, 224, 225, 244, 248, 270, 333, 341, 343, 348
  bishopric of 166
  capture by the Banū Ghāniya 104
bishops, 121, 165–6, 327
al-Biṭrūjī, Yūsuf b. Muḥammad of Niebla, 74, 76, 77
Buḥayra, battle of the, 69, 70, 292, 340
buḥayra estates, 97, 100, 102, 219–20, 292, 308, 309, 316

Castile, 2, 4, 20, 55–6, 74, 97, 98, 99, 106, 108, 115, 117, 173, 195, 205, 222, 223, 334, 338, 345
  and the Ta'ifa kingdoms, 41–7
ceramics, 300, 304–5, 327, 328
Ceuta, *xiv*, 10, 15, 27, 43, *48*, 54, 83, 93, 102, 112, 114, 119, 127, 166, 183, 184, 186, 191, *202*, 242, 260, 269, 286, 302, 334, 337, 338, 348
  Almoravid conquest of, 40, 42
  Balyūnish, 186
  commercial role of, 197, 198, 199
  great mosque of, 288, 291, 296
  rebellion against the Almohads, 73, 77
  urban governance of, 147–8, 149
Christianity, 86–7, 171
  Arian, 14
  Catholic, 14, 46, 174, 335
  conversion to, 115, 117
  in Iberia, 14–15, 16–18, 41
  in North Africa, 10
Christians, 16, 20
  Andalusi, 17, 129, 166, 170–1, 173–4, 195, 292, 340
  mercenaries, 21, 35, 47, 52, 57, 59, 60

merchants, 21
Northern Iberian, 19, 20, 23, 24, 29, 41, 44–5, 47, 55, 57, 58
cloth *see* textiles
concubines, 18, 41, 92, 127, 139, 145, 155–7, 160, 164, 208
Constantine, 14
Córdoba, *xiv*, 2, 3, 12, 14, 15, 16, 17, 22, *25*, 27, 31, 32, 41, 45, *48*, 55, 56, 58, 63, 74, 86, *91*, 93, 96, 97, 100, 101, 106, 116, 126, 134, 135, 139, 147, 164, 179, 191, 192, *202*, 212, *217*, 219, 223, 224, 228, 235, 236, 237, 273, 278, 299, 300, 305, 314, 315, 316, 330, 333, 339
Almohad capture of, 77
architecture of, 280–1, 290
ateliers of, 301–2, 319
Bāb al-Sudda, 281
Calahorra tower (Qalʿat al-Ḥurra), 326
Castilian capture of, 117, 345
great mosque of, 42, 281–4, 287, 288, 291–2, 294, 296, 298, 301, 307, 308, 312, 314, 318, 322, 324
hinterland of, 144–5, 195, 213
Madīnat al-Zahrāʾ, 42, 106, 280–5, 292, 298, 314
rebellion against the Almoravids, 57, 58, 127, 339
religious culture of, 241–3, 246, 262
religious minorities in, 164, 166, 170, 174
urban elites of, 231, 234
convivencia, 3, 119–20, 164
cotton, 184, 207, 322
Council of Fifty, 68, 130, 131
Council of Seventy, 68, 130
Council of Ten, 68, 130
Crusades, 1, 3, 19, 44, 79, 87, 107, 200, 245, 331

al-Daqqāq, Abū ʿAbd Allāh, 244, 269
Dār al-Islām, 5, 44, 79, 86, 173, 228, 331, 332
date production, 182, 183, 185
dhimma, 119–20, 165, 166, 167, 169, 170, 171, 176, 232
Dhū'l-Nūn al-Miṣrī, 237
Dhū'l-Nūnids, 41, 46, 285
Ḍiyāʾ al-Dawla al-Barghawāṭī, 40
Dukkāla tribes, 73

Egypt, 1, 9, 10, 11, 12, 26, 79, 96, 104, 105, 132, 165, 174, 179, 183, 187, 198, 200, 201, 229, 233, 262, 280, 284, 288, 289, 304, 333, 334
El Cid *see* Rodrigo Díaz de Vivar
Elvira *see* Granada
Eulogius, 17
Eunuchs, 138, 205, 208

al-Fallākī, 299
famine, 152, 209, 224–5
Fannū bint ʿUmar, 61, 159
al-Fārābī, 259, 262
Fāṭima, daughter of the Prophet, 235, 271
Fāṭimids, 1, 5, 49, 258, 265, 280, 329
opposition to minarets, 283
rivalry with the Umayyads, 230, 235, 280, 301
use of public text, 324
Fes, *xiv*, 2, 22, *25*, 32, 35, *48*, 54, 55, 75, 83, 84, 85, 101, 102, 103, 105, 112, 113, 114, 116, 126, 129, 133, 147, 153, 174, 176, 188, 191, 192, 201, *202*, 202, 204, 213, 221, 223, 225, 234, 242, 244, 248, 249, 259, 265, 267, 280, 286, 299, 306, 334, 345
Almohad conquest of, 60, 71–2, 74, 133, 172, 341
Almoravid conquest of, 39–40, 222, 337
Andalus Mosque, 286, 301
foundation of, 12, 233
leper colony of, 153
mint of, 216
mosques of, 150, 286, 296
professions in, 193–4, 195, 318
Qarawiyyīn Mosque, 147, 286–7, 298, 302, 340, 344
religious elite of, 131, 134, 135, 148, 154, 236, 269, 271, 274
suburban estates of, 220
fiqh, 21, 147, 228, 235, 236, 238, 241, 243, 246, 254, 258, 266, 330, 334
al-Fishtālī, ʿAbd Allāh b. Mūsā, 148
flax, 184

fruit production, 178, 180, 181, 183, 186, 192, 219, 220, 308, 322
fuqahā', 24, 47, 53, 65, 121, 169, 237, 238, 241, 242–3, 245, 246, 247, 248–9, 251–2, 261–2, 267, 296, 330, 333
  and urban governance, 147–9
Fusṭāṭ, 229, 231

García Jiménez, 44–5
Gazūla (Jazūla) tribe, *13*, 25, 27
Genizah, 178, 204
Ghana, medieval kingdom of, 27, 31, 37–8, 48, 106, 330, 337
al-Ghazālī, Abū Ḥāmid Muḥammad, 27, 47, 50, 229, 242–4, 245, 262, 267, 335
  and Ibn Tūmart, 63–4, 246–8, 252, 332
Ghumāra tribe, *13*, *25*, 40, 143, 186, 193, 234, 271, 320
Gibraltar
  Jabal al-Fatḥ, 88–9, 93, 102, 264–5, 306, 314–5, 318, 342
  Straits of, *xiv*, 2, 4, 10, 11, 16, 32, 40, 41, 42, 43, 55, 57, 58, 73, 75, 77, 96, 102, 106, 113, 114, 118, 119, 174, 189, 195, 197, 199, 201, 221, 225, 244, 269, 286, 309, 337
gold, 21, 30, 38, 55, 61, 188–9, 197, 204, 205, 206, 224, 276
  coinage, 216–17
  decoration, 283, 285, 286, 319, 320
  embroidery
  see also ṭirāz 303, 305, 327
grain, 30, 147, 153, 177, 180, 181–2, 183, 197, 206, 209, 224
Granada, *xiv*, 18, *25*, 43, 44, 45, 47, *48*, 54, 55, 57, 61, 74, 77, 78, 83, 84, 88, 100, 117, 118, 129, 138, 141, 148, 157, 158, 169, *202*, 213, 260, 299, 333, 336, 337, 338, 339, 342, 346
  Christians in, 170
  economy of, 183, 184, 195, 207, 219
  massacre of Jews in, 164, 167–8
  rebellion against the Almohads, 89–90, 92, 174

ḥaḍar, 7, 119, 121, 139, 140, 141, 144–54
Ḥadīth, 66, 95, 229–30, 234, 235, 236, 241, 244, 246, 247, 251, 254, 256–7, 273
Ḥadīth Riyāḍ wa-Bayāḍ, 160–1
Ḥafṣids, 113, 116, 200, 227, 258, 265, 271, 245, 334, 345
al-Ḥājj Ya'īsh, 314, 315
al-Ḥakam II, Umayyad caliph, 161, 254, 259, 283, 302
Ḥā-mīm, 143, 234, 271
Ḥamma, Battle of, 105, 137, 344
Ḥammād b. Manād, 162
Hargha tribe, 62, 130
al-Ḥasan b. 'Alī b. Abī Ṭālib, 233
Haskūra tribe, 34, 73, 321
Ḥawwā' bint Tāshfīn, 128, 159
Hawwāra tribe, *13*, 14, 33
Haylāna tribe, 32, 33, 34, 73
Hazmīra tribe, 34
Ḥimyar, *13*, 25, 123–4, 128
Hintāta tribe, 70
ḥisba, 64, 169, 178, 196, 218–9, 242, 246, 247, 276, 325; *see also muḥtasib*
Hishām II, Umayyad caliph 301
homosexuality, 161, 263
ḥuffāẓ, 80, 81, 130, 131, 253
Ḥunayn b. Isḥāq, 266
Ḥusayn b. 'Alī b. Abī Ṭālib, 233

Ibāḍism *see* Khārijism
Ibn 'Abbād, Abū 'Abd Allāh of Ronda, 274
Ibn al-Abbār, Abū 'Abd Allāh Muḥammad, 265
Ibn 'Abdūn, *muḥtasib* of Seville, 120, 126, 150–2, 161–2, 164, 169, 196, 247
Ibn Abī Zar', 'Alī, 34, 39, 69
Ibn Abī Zayd al-Qayrawanī, 236, 241, 247
Ibn 'Aqnīn, 175
Ibn al-'Arabī, Abū Bakr, 50, 75, 76, 128, 241, 242, 252, 272, 330
Ibn (al)- 'Arabī, Muḥyī al-Dīn, 267, 272–4
Ibn al-'Arīf al-Ṣanhājī, 244–5, 252, 267, 269, 340
Ibn 'Āshir, Abū'l-'Abbās Aḥmad, 274
Ibn 'Aṭiyya, Abū Ja'far Aḥmad, 54, 77, 84–5, 127, 133–4, 160, 265, 308
Ibn al-'Awwām, Abū Zakarīyā Yaḥyā, 219
Ibn 'Azzūn of Jerez, 77

Ibn Bājja (Avempace), 259–60, 262
Ibn Barrajān, Abū'l-Ḥakam 'Abd al-Salām, 244–5, 252, 267, 269, 340
Ibn Bashkuwāl, Abū'l-Qāsim Khalaf, 265
Ibn Baṣṣāl, Muḥammad, 219
Ibn Fūrak, Abū Bakr Muḥammad, 236
Ibn Ḥafṣūn, 235
Ibn al-Ḥajjāj, Abū 'Umar Aḥmad, 219
Ibn Ḥamdīn, Muḥammad b. 'Alī, 63, 74, 147, 149
 and the burning of al-Ghazālī's *Iḥyā'*, 243, 252, 339
Ibn Hamushk, 89–90, 92, 95, 136, 156, 175
Ibn Hāni', Muḥammad, 265
Ibn Ḥarāzim, 'Abd Allāh, 271
Ibn Ḥawqal, Abū'l-Qāsim, 178
Ibn Ḥayyān, Abū Marwān, 265, 284
Ibn Ḥazm, Abū Muḥammad 'Alī, 243
Ibn Ḥirzihim, Abū'l-Ḥasan 'Alī, 244, 269
Ibn Hūd, Abū Ja'far Aḥmad, 74
Ibn Hūd, Muḥammad b. Yūsuf, 116–17
Ibn Jaḥḥāf, Abū Aḥmad Ja'far, 46, 147
Ibn Jubayr, Abū'l-Ḥusayn Muḥammad, 178, 198–9, 208, 210–11, 321
Ibn Khaldūn, 'Abd al-Raḥmān, 4–9, *13*, 29, 33, 62, 70, 107, 116, 119, 121, 125, 139, 141, 159, 171, 187, 197, 240, 265, 329, 333
 The *Muqaddimah*, 6–7
Ibn Maḥshuwwa, Abū'l-Faḍl Ja'far b. Aḥmad, 134
Ibn Masarra, Muḥammad b. 'Abd Allāh, 237, 243, 259, 267, 272
Ibn Mashīsh, 'Abd al-Salām, 270–1
Ibn Mujāhid, Abū 'Abd Allāh, 236
Ibn Munqidh, 107, 344
Ibn Qasī, Abū'l-Qāsim Aḥmad, 74, 75, 245, 252, 267, 274, 340, 341
Ibn al-Qaṭṭān, Ḥasan b. 'Alī, 62, 130
Ibn al-Qiṭṭ, Aḥmad b. Mu'āwiya, 234
Ibn al-Qūṭiyya, Abū Bakr b. 'Umar, 15, 158
Ibn Quzmān, Abū Bakr Muḥammad, 263
Ibn Rushd al-Ḥafīd (Averroes), 92, 101, 108–9, 133, 135, 175, 247, 258, 261–2, 265, 266, 270, 273, 276, 335, 344
Ibn Rushd al-Jadd, 101, 126, 128, 129, 170, 237, 241, 243, 252, 261
Ibn Ṣāḥib al-Ṣalāt, 76, 77, 94, 96, 102, 132, 133, 135, 265, 316
Ibn Shalīb, 42, 168
Ibn Sīnā (Avicenna), 266
Ibn Ṣumādiḥ, al-Mu'taṣim of Almería, 45, 285
Ibn Ṭufayl (Abubacer), 92, 95, 260–1, 262, 265, 266, 267, 276, 335
Ibn Tūmart, Muḥammad, 20, 50, 58, 62–70, 72, 73, 75, 76, 78, 81, 83–4, 85, 86, 104, 107, *110*, 116, 130, 135, 142, 143, 150, 158, 159, 172, 217, 243, 254, 256, 257, 258, 267, 270, 271, 274, 306, 332, 333, 339, 340, 342
 and religious minorities, 171
 attitude to women, 162–4
 baraka of, 153
 composition in Berber, 67–8, 131
 confrontation with, 'Alī b. Yūsuf 64–6, 129, 160, 303
 death of, 69–70, 253
 early years, 62–3
 meeting with al-Ghazālī, 27, 63–4, 247
 organisation of the Almohads, 68–9, 80, 130–1
 Qur'ān of, 96, 101, 256
 recognition as the *mahdī*, 66–7, 252–3
 shrine of, 85, 90, 100, 103, 109, 307, 310
 theology of, 246–53, 325
Ibn Wāfid, Abū'l-Muṭarrif, 219
Ibn Yāsīn, 'Abd Allāh, 48, 67, 143, 157, 201, 289, 290, 332, 336, 337
 mission to the Ṣanhaja, 27–32
 religious position, 27–8, 238–40
 ribāṭ of, 27–8, 280
Ibn Yūnus, Abū Bakr Muḥammad b. 'Abd Allāh al-Tamīmī, 257
Ibrāhīm b. Tāshfīn, Almoravid amir, 341, *51*, 55, 60, 72, 133
Idrīs b. 'Abd Allāh, 12, 233
al-Idrīsī, al-Sharīf, 177
Idrīsids, 12, 216, 233, 234, 286

Ifrīqiya, 1, 5, 9, 10, 11–12, *13*, 20, *25*, 26, 27, 32, 61, 91, 101, 116, 118, 123, 134, 139, 143, 146, 152, 180, 191, 194, 221, 222, 223, 226, 227, 228, 232, 233, 265, 270, 273, 276, 301, 333, 334
  Almohad campaigns to, 78–80, 87–9, 99, 105, 112–13
  and the Banū Ḥilāl, 132–3, 179, 187–8
  artistic culture of, 278–80, 284, 286, 289, 299
  Banū Ghāniya invasion of, 104–5, 108, 112
  rebellion of al-Ashall in, 107–8
  religious culture of, 235–7, 242, 246, 258
  religious minorities in, 165–7, 173
  rural economy of, 181, 183–5
  trade routes, 179, 198, 199, 200, 201, *202*, 203, 204
Īglī, 182, 189, 252
imazighen, 141
inzālāt see land grants
iqṭā'āt see land grants
irrigation, 56, 171, 181, 184–6, 191–2, 219, 316
Isḥāq b. 'Alī, Almoravid amir, *51*, 55, 60, 72, 341
Ismā'īlīs, 3, 26, 235–6, 238, 242, 253, 258, 280

Jabal al-Fatḥ *see* Gibraltar
Jābir b. Aflaḥ, 267
Jaén, *xiv*, 16, 77, 114, 184, 299
Ja'far al-Ṣādiq, 229, 235
al-Jāmi' of al-Tirmidhī, 257
Jarāwa tribe, 143
al-Jayyānī, 'Abd Allāh b. Khiyār, *mushrif* of Fes, 54, 72, 85, 133
al-Jaznā'ī, 'Alī, 131
Jews, 3, 12, 15, 17, 18, 20, 32, 67, 118, 119–20, 150, 155, 167–9, 229, 262, 307, 327, 334–5
  forced conversion of, 86, 88, 89, 171–6, 253, 270, 342
  Granadan massacre of, 164, 168, 337
  Merchants, 200, 203–4, 205, 232
Jihad, 19–20, 24, 28–30, 41, 42, 44, 45, 47, 53, 55, 57, 62, 69, 72, 78–9, 86–7, 89, 95, 98, 99, 102, 104, 106, 107, 111, 113, 170, 177, 221, 239–42, 252, 254, 257, 324, 331, 332, 336; *see also ribāṭ*
al-Jīlānī, 'Abd al-Qādir, 270
jizya, 16, 165, 168, 210, 241
Judaism, 167, 176, 246, 262, 335; *see also* Jews
al-Junayd, Abū'l-Qāsim, 237, 268

Khadīja, wife of the Prophet, 35
Khārijism, 30, 33, 165, 172, 204, 231–3, 234, 235, 236, 237, 238, 334
  Ibāḍī, 33, 165, 200, 232–3
  Ṣufrī, 200, 232
Khayr b. Khazar, 39
Khulṭ tribe, 80
Khumārawayh b. Aḥmad b. Ṭūlūn, 96
Kinship, 7, 8, 41, 52, 71, 125
  in tribal society, 7, 8, 140
  see also 'aṣabiyya
Kūmiya tribe, 64, 70, 83, 131–2
Kutāma tribes, 5, *13*, 14, 143, 235
Kuwār, 201

Lamṭa, *13*, 28, 84, 123, 126, 202
Lamtūna tribe, *13*, 25, 28–30, 32, 36, 38, 39, 49, 52, 54, 59, 60, 69, 77, 84, 123–6, 127–8, 129, 135, 142, 157–8, 201, 202, 238, 263, 336
land grants, 18, 52, 180, 209, 210, 212–14, 215–16, 331
Laqqūṭ b. Yusuf, 32, 33
Lisbon, *xiv*, 56, 58, 75, 98, 166, 181, 195, 322, 341

madhhab, 22, 229, 257, 258, 333
Madīnat al-Zahrā' *see* Córdoba
Maghrāwa tribe, 30, 31, 33, 39, 222
Mahdism, 3, 66–7, 68, 72, 73, 74, 76, 78–9, 85, 86, 96, 104, 116, 130, 135, 136, 171, 233–4, 238, 243, 245–6, 252–3
al-Mahdiyya, Ifrīqiya, *xiv*, *25*, 78, 79, 87, 88, 112–3, 132, 165, 173, 191, 200, *202*, 205, 221, 222, 280, 314, 341, 342, 345

al-Mahdiyya, Morocco *see* Ribāṭ al-Fatḥ
Maimonides (Mūsā b. Maymūn), 174, 262
Málaga, *xiv*, 45, 166, 184, 195, 218, 247, 300, 303, 315, 328
Mālik b. Anas, 229, 234, 257
Mālik b. Wuhayb, 66, 129, 217, 251
Mālikism, 186, 211, 212, 228, 234–5, 236–7, 238, 240–2
  Almohad criticism of, 246–52
al-Ma'mūn, 'Abbāsid caliph, 230
al-Ma'mūn, Abū'l-'Alā Idrīs, Almohad caliph, 116, 137, 258, 271
al-Ma'mūn b. Dhī'l-Nūn of Toledo, 219, 286
al-Manṣūr b. Abī 'Āmir, 141, 301
al-Manṣūriyya, 280
al-Maqqarī, 164, 284–5
maqṣūra, 283, 314, 318
Marīnids, 115, 137, 148, 154, 192
Marrakesh, *xiv*, 22, 36, 39, 40, 47, *48*, 50, 54, 60, 80, 84, 85, 86, *91*, 103, 105–6, 109, 116, 125, 133, 152, 159, 194, 228, 242, 244, 255, 256, 269, 270, 274, 299, 302, 305, 310, 315–16, 332, 334, 339, 340
  Almohad conquest of, 2, 60–1, 72, 74, 87, 306–7, 341
  Almoravid great mosque of (Fountain Mosque, Jāmi' al-Siqāya), 64, 294, 301, 303
  and Almohad government, 82, 83, 93, 95, 112, 113, 115, 215
  and Almoravid government, 50, 53, 128
  Andalusī delegations to, 75–6, 100
  Bāb Agnaw, 324
  Bāb al-Sharī'a, 321
  buḥayra of, 100, 219–20, 292, 308, 339, 341
  Christians in, 137, 170–1, 173
  craftsmen from, 310
  cultural life in, 263, 265, 266
  economy of, 2, 55, 195, 201, 202, 206, 216, 225
  foundation of, 19, 22, 33–4, 61, 125–6, 289–91, 337
  hospital in, 152, 321–2
  Ibn Tūmart in, 64–7, 129, 160, 251–2
  Jews in, 168
  judges of, 134
  Kutubiyya Mosque, 92, 307–8, 312–14, 335, 341, 342
  Menara gardens, 220
  Qaṣr al-Ḥajar, 104, 289, 290, 292, 307
  Qaṣr al-Khilāfa, 320
  qayṣariyya of, 225, 316
  Qubbat al-Ba'diyyīn or Barūdiyyīn, 294–6, 339
  Tāmurākusht (al-Ṣāliḥa), 100, 104, 320–1, 343
  water supply to, 56, 191, 219, 292
Maṣmūda tribes, 1, 5, 7, *13*, 14, 20, *25*, 31–2, 33, 38, 57, 62, 82, 119, 130, 132, 135, 136, 141, 143, 180, 289, 305, 306, 332
  attitude to 'Abd al-Mu'min, 70–1, 84, 85
  attitude to women, 159–60
  place in the Almohad hierarchy, 68–9, 76, 80–1, 83, 90, 93, 130
  support for Ibn Tūmart, 66–8, 130–1, 252, 339
al-Māssī, Muḥammad b. 'Abd Allāh, 72–3, 76, 77, 133, 341
Mas'ūd b. Wānūdīn, 30
al-Mas'ūdī, 178
Masūfa tribe, *13*, 14, 28, 38, 60, 71, 123, 124, 125, 129, 158, 202
mathematics, 231, 262, 265–6, 335
al-Mayurqī, Abū Bakr, 244
Mazdalī b. Tilānkān, 36, 39, 40, 47, *51*, 55, 56, 125
medicine, 184, 254, 260, 261, 262, 265, 266, 335
Medina, 34, 67, 229, 277, 300, 306, 307, 310
Medina Sidonia, 15, 166
Mecca, 12, 23, 26, 27, 64, 67, 69, 178, 197, 200, 201, 238, 270, 273, 294, 310
merchants, 21, 55, 119, 150, 173, 178, 179, 187, 197–205, 224, 225, 256, 280
mercury, 190, 285
Mérida, 14, 283
Midrārids, 12
miḥrāb, 278–9, 283–4, 297–8, 306, 312, 314, 318, 324
Miknāsa tribe, 12, *13*

minbar, 284, 300–1
  the Almoravid 301–2
mines, 188–90, 191, 206, 210
mizwār, 142
mosques, 18, 22, 23, 26, 43, 50, 63, 64, 87, 88, 92, 97, 99, 104, 108, 114, 126, 129, 145, 150–1, 152, 170, 175, 192, 194, 222, 255, 256, 262, 274
  and education, 227, 228, 250, 251, 269
  architecture of, 189, 276, 278–80, 281–4, 286–91, 292, 294, 296–9, 306–8, 310–14, 316–20, 321, 322–3, 324, 328, 335
Mozarabs, 17, 145, 166, 170; *see also* Christians, Andalusi
Muḥammad, the Prophet, 17, 32, 35, 67, 70, 73, 82, 135, 204, 234, 252, 332
Muḥammad al-Nāṣir, Almohad caliph *see* al-Nāṣir, Abū ʿAbd Allāh Muḥammad
Muḥammad b. ʿAbd al-Mu'min, Abū ʿAbd Allāh, 82, 83, 92, 342, 343
Muḥammad b. ʿĀ'isha, 46, *51*, 158
Muḥammad b. Ḥabbūs al-Fāsī, 264
Muḥammad b. al-Ḥajjām of Badajoz, 77
Muḥammad b. Naṣr b. al-Aḥmar, 117, 346
Muḥammad b. Saʿd b. Mardanīsh, 136
Muḥammad b. Tūmart *see* Ibn Tūmart
Muḥammad b. Yūsuf b. Wānūdīn, 132
al-Muḥāsibī, Abū ʿAbd Allāh al-Ḥārith, 269
muḥtasib, 126, 169, 247; *see also ḥisba*
Mujāhid of Denia, 18
muqarnas, 288, 294–6, 298, 305, 312
al-Murādī, Abū Bakr Muḥammad b. al-Ḥasan, 37, 241
Murcia, *xiv*, 16, 45, 46, 74, 90, 95, 97, 101, 105, 106, 116, 136, 170, 181, 182, 221, 267, 272, 328, 341, 343, 345
al-Murtaḍā, Almohad caliph, 116
Mūsā b. Nuṣayr, 11
Mūsā b. Ḥammād, 128
al-Mustaẓhir, ʿAbbāsid caliph, 50
al-Muʿtaḍid b. ʿAbbād of Seville, 148, 243, 336, 337
al-Muʿtamid b. ʿAbbād of Seville, 42, 45, 128, 266, 309
al-Muʿtaṣim, ʿAbbāsid caliph, 230
al-Mutawakkil, ʿAbbāsid caliph, 230
al-Mutawakkil b. al-Afṭas of Badajoz, 46, 47
Muʿtazila, 230
Muwalladūn, 17–18, 145
Muwaṭṭa' of Mālik, 234, 235, 257

Nafūsa tribes, 12, *13*
Nafzāwa tribes, 12, *13*, 33
al-Nāṣir, Abū ʿAbd Allāh Muḥammad, Almohad caliph, 107, 109–15, 116, 134, 135, 138, 194, 215, 221, 225, 344, 345
  and Las Navas de Tolosa, 111, 114
Las Navas de Tolosa (al-ʿUqāb), Battle of, 111–12, 114, 117, 221, 223, 327, 345
  banner of, 327
Niẓām al-Mulk, 129
Niẓāmiyya Madrasa, Baghdad, 63
Nūl Lamṭa, *25*, 31, *48*, 189, *202*, 216

olive production, 182–3, 191, 194, 220, 308

pastoralism, 9–10, 123, 132, 144, 178, 179, 180, 186–8, 221, 225, 226
Persians, 4, 53, 129, 331
philosophy, 6, 22, 230, 231, 254, 258–62
  Almohad edict against, 109, 261–2
poetry, 89, 92, 93, 128, 133, 134, 159, 160, 161, 227, 259, 263–5
Portugal, 1, 2, 4, 55, 75, 98, 117, 195, 222
portazgos, 203
ports, 40, 73, 79, 127, 193, 195, 197–200, 203, 204, 205, 309

al-Qābisī, Abū'l-Ḥasan ʿAlī, 236
al-Qāḍī ʿIyāḍ b. Mūsā of Ceuta, 27, 73, 77, 128, 148, 149, 186, 241
al-Qādir b. Dhī'l-Nūn of Toledo and Valencia, 46, 47, 147
al-Qālamī, Abū'l-Qāsim ʿAbd al-Raḥmān, 134
Qalʿat Banī Ḥammād, *xiv*, *25*, 162, 188, 199, 201, *202*, 286, 288, 289, 300, 301, 312
Qamar, mother of Sīr b. ʿAlī, 156–7
qānūn, 22, 53
Qarāqūsh, Sharaf al-Dīn, 137

Qaṣr al-Majāz (Qaṣr Maṣmūda), *xiv*, 96, 106, 198, 199
Qayrawān, *xiv*, 12, *25*, 188, 191, 228, 232, 271, 289, 336
and Malikism, 22, 143, 169, 234–6, 238, 240–1
cisterns of, 199
economy of, 187, 200, 202–3
foundation of, 11–12
great mosque of, 278–9, 283, 296, 300, 323
trade routes, 32, 201, *202*
visit of Yaḥyā b. Ibrāhīm to, 26–7
'ulamā' of, 37, 231, 234–7, 238, 240, 271, 330–1
qibla, 296, 306–7

rabbis, 121, 204
Raqqāda, 280
reconquista, 19, 98, 114
repartimientos, 140
ribāṭ, 29–30, 123, 228, 239–40, 280
of Ibn Qasi, 245
of Ibn Tumart, 66
of Ibn Yasin, 27–8, 29, 280
of Massa, 73
of Tlemcen, 64
of Waggag, 27, 237, 280
Taza, 280, 306
Ribāṭ al-Fatḥ (al-Mahdiyya), *xiv*, 84, 87, 89, 90, 96, 101, 103, 104, 106, 112, 113, 133, 199, 280, 306, 315
Bāb Qaṣabat al-Udāya, 324
Bāb al-Ruwāḥ, 324–5
baḥā'ir of, 309
economy of, 195
foundation of, 77, 309–10, 322, 341
great mosque of, 322–3, 344
Qaṣabat al-Udāya, 309
Tour Hassan minaret, 322–3
water supply, 309, 322
rice, 181
Risālat Ḥayy b. Yaqẓān, 260–1
Riyāḥ tribe, 80, 107
Roderic, king of the Visigoths, 15
Rodrigo Díaz de Vivar 'El Cid', 44, 46–7, 58, 98, 147, 222, 338
Roman empire, 10, 14
al-Ru'aynī, Abū'l-Ḥasan 'Alī, 265
al-Ruṣāfī, Abū 'Abd Allāh Muḥammad b. Ghālib al-Balansī, 265

Sahara desert, 1, 2, 5, 9, 10, 19, 20, 21, 24, 25, 26, 27, 30, 34, 35, 45, 48, 52, 106, 112, 116, 118, 123, 124, 157, 167, 180, 187, 208, 241, 289, 332, 334
Almoravid control of, 30, 31, 34–5, 37–8, 40, 125, 216, 302
Islamisation of, 61
trade across *see* trade routes, trans-Saharan
Ṣafiyya, mother of Yaḥyā b. 'Umar, 28, 157
saffron, 184, 209
Ṣāhir, mother of Ya'qūb al-Manṣūr, 103
Saḥnūn, Abū Sa'īd 'Abd al-Salām b. Sa'īd al-Tanūkhī, 235, 236, 257, 266
Salāḥ al-Dīn al-Ayyūbī, 105, 152, 321, 344
Salé, *xiv*, *25*, 32, 35, 39, *48*, 72, 73, 77; *see also* Ribāṭ al-Fatḥ
salt, 21, 30, 38, 197, 206
Saharan mines, 189–90, 206
Ṣanhāja tribes, 1, 5, 7, *13*, 14, 18, 19, 24–5, 35, 36, 37, 43, 47, 57, 62, 68, 71, 79, 99, 118, 119, 122–4, 128, 129, 130, 141, 143, 167, 168, 172, 179, 187, 202, 212, 213, 217, 238, 241, 288, 289, 321, 330–1
Almoravid movement among, 26–31, 37–8, 48, 52, 54, 68
and cattle rustling, 127
Arab origin myth of, 25–6, 123–4, 128
attitude to women, 20, 157–60, 161, 163, 196, 239
fighting tactics, 57–8
veiling practices of, 25–6, 64, 123–4, 126, 129–30, 136
Santarem, *xiv*, 56, 58, 75, 98, 102–3, 181, 254, 255, 318, 321, 341
ṣaqāliba, 18, 208
al-Saqaṭī, Muḥammad b. Abī Muḥammad, 182, 218–19, 247
Saqqūt al-Barghawāṭi of Ceuta, 40, 288
Saragossa, 44, 47, *48*, 55, 56–7, 74, 75, 182, 191, 195, 259, 285–6, 339
segmentarity, 8
Seljuks, 1, 3, 49, 50, 53, 129, 273, 331, 333

Seville, *xiv*, 15, 16, 23, *25*, 42, *48*, 56, 74, 83, 88, 96, 97, 100, 102, 103, 106, 107, 108, 114, 159, 179, 191, 215, 224, 242, 243, 259, 261, 264, 266, 267, 269, 272, 299, 333, 334, 336, 341
  Almohad conquest of, 75–7, 136, 174
  Almohad *qaṣaba*, 308–9
  Almohad urbanism in, 92, 98–9, 104, 195, 308–9, 315–20
  Almoravid conquest of, 45–6
  Bāb Jahwar, 220, 316
  baḥā'ir of, 219–20, 316
  bishopric of, 166
  Castilian capture of, 117, 345
  economy of, 179, 181, 182, 183, 192, 195, 196, 207, 216, 300, 303, 305, 328
  great mosque of, 92, 316–20, 343, 344
  Jabal al-Sharaf (Aljarafe), 183, 219
  Mosque of 'Addabas, 316
  religious minorities in, 169–70
  society in, 126–7, 151–2, 161–2
  Torre del Oro, 325–6, 345
Sha'bān al-Miṣrī, 216
al-Shādhilī, Abū'l-Ḥasan 'Alī, 267, 270–2
al-Shāfi'ī, 229, 235
Shaqya b. 'Abd al-Wāḥid al-Miknāsī, 233
Shi'ism, 30, 101, 172, 229, 233, 235–6, 296, 334, 238, 258
  influence on Almohadism, 70, 245, 246, 253
  see also Ismā'īlīs
Sidrāy b. Wazīr of Beja, 74, 75, 77
sihām see land grants
Sijilmāsa, *xiv*, 12, 21, 22, *25*, 32, 33, 36, 38, *48*, 73, 116, 179, 191, 212, 232, 235, 244, 269, 286, 289, 290, 334, 336
  Almoravid conquest of, 30–1, 168
  cultivation around, 181–2, 183, 184, 185
  Jews of, 172, 174
  mint in, 216
  role in trade, 200–1, *202*, 202
silk, 64, 65, 96, 184, 194, 195, 196, 204, 207, 303, 305, 322, 327
Sīr b. Abī Bakr, 45, 46, *51*, 56, 159
Sīr b. Isḥāq b. Ghāniya, 113
slaves, 7, 18, 21, 30, 35, 36, 45, 52, 57, 60, 69, 82, 127, 137–8, 152, 161, 167, 175, 190, 197, 203, 207–8, 264
Ṣubḥ, mother of Hishām, II 161
Sufism, 237–8, 242, 243–6, 252, 253, 267–75
sugar cane, 183–4, 191
Sulaymān b. 'Addū, 32
Sunan of Abū Dāwūd, 258
Sūs valley, 1, 20, 27, 31, 58, 62, 66, 71, 73, 83, 98, 100, 130, 133, 153, 184, 189, 190, 204, 233, 237, 240, 247, 252, 280, 289, 332, 336

Taghāza, 189, 190
Tāgrārt *see* Tlemcen
Tāhart, *xiv*, 12, *25*, 191, 201, *202*, 232, 286
Ṭā'ifa kingdoms, 18, 19, 20, 40, 41–7, 50, 57, 74, 76, 141, 147, 164, 169, 199, 208, 211, 213–14, 219, 241, 263, 266, 278, 285–6, 288, 292, 303, 304, 305, 314, 331, 338, 339
ṭalaba, 80–1, 94, 130, 131, 135, 249, 253–4, 256–8, 261, 262, 268
Talkāta (Ṣanhāja), 157
Tāmākūnt bint Yīntān, 160
tamyīz, the, 67
Ṭāriq b. Ziyād, 11, 15
Tarragona, 14
Tārūdānt, 189
Tāsghīmūt, fortress of, 299–300, 306, 340
Tāshfīn b. 'Alī, Almoravid amir, 59–60, 71, 72, 104, 133, 138, 157, 171, 217, 340, 341
Tātintāl, 190
tawḥīd, 67, 81, 131, 246–7, 250, 253
taxation, 5, 18, 21, 31, 52, 57, 82, 108, 122, 168, 195, 210–12, 225, 238, 239, 332
textiles, 36, 193, 194, 195, 205, 207, 276, 300, 302–4, 320, 327
Theodemir of Murcia, 16
thughūr, 19, 144
Tifinagh, 9
al-Tighnārī, Muḥammad b. Mālik, 219
ṭirāz, 207, 303, 327

Tlemcen, *xiv*, *25*, 32, *48*, 55, 56, 64, 79, 83, 88, 99, 105, 106, 113, 116, 126, 134, 147, 176, 181, 232, 244, 280, 286, 306, 333
  Agādīr, 40, 286, 291
  Almohad conquest of, 59, 60, 71, 74, 79, 171, 172, 341
  Almoravid conquest of, 40, 213, 337
  Christians in, 166
  great mosque of, 296, 340
  Ibn Tūmart in, 248–9
  mint of, 216
  ribāṭ of, 64
  Tāgrārt, 40, 298
  trade routes, 198, 201, *202*
  al-'Ubbād, 270, 274
Toledo, *xiv*, 14, 15, 19, 44, 46, 56, 173, 285, 327
  aqueduct, 192
  fall to Castile, 20, 43, 195, 331, 338
  gardens of al-Ma'mūn, 219
  palace of al-Ma'mūn, 286
trade routes, 34, 40, 194, 197, *202*
  coastal, 200
  maritime, 197–200
  trans-Saharan, 34, 37, 38, 187, 189–90, 197, 200–2, 204, 206
tribes 10–11, 121–2, 140–4, 179, 180, 187, 190, 211–12
  Ibn Khaldūn's theory of, 6–9, 29, 116, 119
  see also Arabs, Berbers, and individual tribes
Tudmīr *see* Murcia
Tunis, *xiv*, 2, *25*, 63, 64, 88, *91*, 99, 105, 112, 113, 118, 173, 200, *202*, 205, 222, 247, 271, 273, 300, 333
Tunisia, 1, 2, 10, 20, 26, 105, 200, 201; *see also* Ifrīqiya
al-Ṭurṭūshī, Abū Bakr Muḥammad, 247

'Ubayd Allāh b. Yūnus, 171, 292
al-'Udhrī, Aḥmad b. 'Umar, 177
'Umar b. al-Khaṭṭāb, 290
Umayyads
  of Córdoba 2, 3, 41, 49, 86, 213, 228, 230, 280–5, 287, 298, 301, 302, 307, 324, 329
  of Damascus 50, 280, 329
'Umra, Battle of, 105, 344
'Uqba b. Nāfi', 278
'Uthmān b. 'Affān, 86
  Qur'ān of, 86, 96, 101, 106, 256, 284, 315

Valencia, *xiv*, 46–7, 58, 74, 97, 113, 115, 117, 127, 133, 136, 144, 147, 170, 181, 185, 191, 194, 213, 222, 265, 299, 334, 338, 339, 341, 345
Visigoths, 14–16

Waggāg (Wajjāj) b. Zalwī, 27, 29, 32, 237, 238, 240
Wāraqlān, 38
Warīka tribe, 33, 34
al-Wāthiq, 'Abbasid caliph, 230
Witiza, king of the Visigoths, 15, 158
women, 20, 64, 65, 66, 72, 88, 106, 108, 118, 119, 124, 126, 127, 137, 141, 143, 148, 151, 152, 154–64, 169, 175, 208, 212, 237, 267, 274
  and war 222, 223, 224
  experience under the Almohads, 159–64, 248–50
  experience under the Almoravids, 123, 154–9, 239
  in the workplace, 196, 207

Yaḥyā b. Ghāniya, 58, 73, 74, 75, 77, 104, 158
Yaḥyā b. Ibrāhīm al-Guddālī, 26–7, 28, 157, 201, 238, 336
Yaḥyā b. Isḥāq al-Ingimār, 60, 129
Yaḥyā b. Mazdalī, 40
Yaḥyā b. al-Ṣaḥrāwiyya, 54, 60, 61, 71–2, 73, 77, 84–5, 133, 136, 158, 160, 341, 342
Yaḥya b. 'Umar, Almoravid amir, 28, 31, 48, *51*, 157, 336
Ya'qūb al-Manṣūr, Abū Yūsuf, Almohad caliph, 91, 104–9, 137, 152–3, 194, 215, 220, 266, 270, 281, 343, 344
  and Ibn Rushd, 108–9, 262
  building projects of, 315, 318, 319–24
  religious beliefs of, 255–8
  treatment of religious minorities, 175
Yīntān b. 'Umar, 66, 160

Yūsuf b. Tāshfīn, Almoravid amir, 19, 32, 34, 54, 55, 56, 71, 78, 84, 101, 108, 111, 125, 127, 128, 133, 137, 138, 141, 148, 158, 160, 216, 242, 266, 330, 337
  and Abū Bakr, 35–7, 125, 205
  conquest of al-Andalus, 40–7, 158, 213, 338
  conquest of the Maghrib, 38–40
  death of, 54, 339
  development of Marrakesh, 290–1
  marriage to Zaynab, 34–5, 159
  organisation of the Almoravid state, 35, 50–2, 213
  title of *amīr al-muslimīn*, 39, 49–50, 74
  treatment of religious minorities, 168–9
Yūsuf al-Mustanṣir, Almohad caliph, 115, 217, 224, 345

Ẓāhirī *madhhab*, 243, 246, 257
Zahr, mother of al-Nāṣir, 109
Zallāqa (Sagrajas), battle of, 43–4, 57, 108, 338, 348
Zanāta tribes, 2, *13*, *25*, 27, 38, 68, 70, 71, 113, 116, 141, 187, 188, 200, 204, 213, 345
  conflict with the Almoravids, 30–2, 38–40, 330
  in Almohad service, 79, 80, 83, 90, 130, 131–2
Zawīla, 201
Zaynab, sister of Ibn Tūmart, 70, 159
Zaynab bint Isḥāq al-Hawwarī or al-Nafzāwī, 33, 34–5, 36, 158–9
Zaynab bint Mūsā al-Ḍarīr, mother of Abū Ya'qūb Yūsuf, 93, 160
Zaynab bint al-Ṣaḥrāwiyya, 54, 84, 133, 160
Zayyānids, 116, 334
Zughba tribe, 80

EU representative:
Easy Access System Europe
Mustamäe tee 50, 10621 Tallinn, Estonia
Gpsr.requests@easproject.com

www.ingramcontent.com/pod-product-compliance
Lightning Source LLC
Chambersburg PA
CBHW070806300426
44111CB00014B/2435
9780748646807